MODERN PRICE THEORY

MODERN PRICE THEORY

Roy J. Ruffin
University of Houston

Scott, Foresman/Little, Brown College Division

Scott, Foresman and Company
Glenview, Illinois   **Boston**   **London**

To my Father

Library of Congress Cataloging-in-Publication Data

Ruffin, Roy, 1938–
   Modern price theory.

   Includes index.
   1. Microeconomics.   I. Title.
HB172.R746   1988   338.5   87–37617
ISBN 0-673-15985-X

Copyright © 1988 Scott, Foresman and Company.
All Rights Reserved.
Printed in the United States of America.

123456 KPF 939291908988

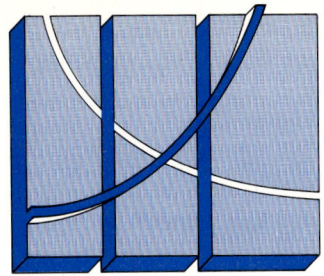

PREFACE

This book is intended for a course in intermediate or MBA microeconomics, or price theory. *Modern Price Theory* brings modern topics—such as the economics of information, Nash equilibrium, and even a simple treatment of Shepherd's lemma—into its discussions of traditional areas of study. No knowledge of calculus is assumed, but some footnotes explain concepts with the use of elementary calculus. The student is expected to be able to solve problems in algebra.

Economics is both rigorous and practical. This book attempts to steer a course between a completely formal treatment that suggests that economics is abstract and sterile and a completely informal, intuitive approach that suggests that economics is not a rigorous, logical subject. As John Maynard Keynes commented,

> The study of economics does not seem to require any specialized gifts of an unusually high order. Is it not, intellectually regarded, a very easy subject compared with the higher branches of philosophy and pure science? Yet good, or even competent, economists are the rarest of birds. An easy subject, at which very few excel! The paradox finds its explanation, perhaps, in that the master-economist must possess a rare *combination* of gifts. . . . He must be mathematician, historian, statesman, philosopher—in some degree. He must understand symbols and speak in words. He must contemplate the particular in terms of the general, and touch abstract and concrete in the same flight of thought. He must study the present in the light of the past for the purposes of the future. No part of man's nature or his institutions must lie entirely outside his regard. He must be purposeful and disinterested in a simultaneous mood; as aloof and incorruptible as an artist, yet sometimes as near the earth as a politician.

Consistent with my goal of presenting economics as a blend of the rigorous and the practical, each chapter attempts to set down the most logical treatment of any given theory or model. To demonstrate the applicability of the theory, each chapter includes illustrations in the text as well as boxed examples. In some cases, the examples illustrate the *usefulness* of the theory in the real world; in other cases, the examples show the *limits* of the theory in practice. Every chapter works out "Practice Exercises" to demonstrate how the theory is applied to a real problem. Each chapter concludes with a "Summary," a set of "Questions and Problems" to test the student's understanding of the chapter, and a list of "Suggested Readings" for further study. The answers to the even-numbered "Questions and Problems" are found at the end of the book; the answers to the odd-numbered "Questions and Problems" appear in the *Instructor's Manual*.

Because a precise understanding of the vocabulary of economics is critical to an understanding of economic theories, every important term appears in boldface type at its first use in text and is accompanied by a formal definition in the margin. A glossary of all important terms can be found at the end of the book, with the definitions referenced by chapter. Key ideas appear in color following the paragraphs of text they summarize.

It was a pleasure to work with Professor Henry Thompson of Auburn University, who wrote the excellent *Workbook* that accompanies this textbook and made many valuable suggestions for improving the text.

For those students who would find problem-solving software helpful in mastering the subject, KOHLER-1 is a set of three IBM disks that is available at low cost.

The following people gave me the benefit of their wise counsel and saved me from making errors of judgment or substance: Oded Palmon, Louis Stern, Paul Gregory, Tom Mayor, Ronald Jones, Farhad Rassekh, John Antel, and Joel Sailors. This book also benefited from the helpful suggestions of the following people, who reviewed it in the manuscript stage:

Jack E. Adams
University of Arkansas, Little Rock

Lanny Arvan
University of Illinois, Urbana-Champaign

Kerry Back
Northwestern University

John L. Fizel
Pennsylvania State University, Behrend College

Michael J. Greenwood
University of Colorado, Boulder

PREFACE

Hyman Joseph
University of Iowa

Ernest Koenigsberg
University of California, Berkeley

Jay Marchand
Radford College

Steven A. Matthews
Northwestern University

Richard P. McLean
Rutger's University

Yoshimasa Nomura
Ohio State University

Henry Thompson
Auburn University

Joseph Tracy
Yale University

I am indebted to George Lobell, economics editor at Scott, Foresman and Company, for his constant advice, encouragement, and assistance. Mary LaMont's skillful editing has no doubt eased the reader's task. My biggest debt is to my wife, Patti, for providing me with the perfect environment for the writing of this book.

Roy J. Ruffin

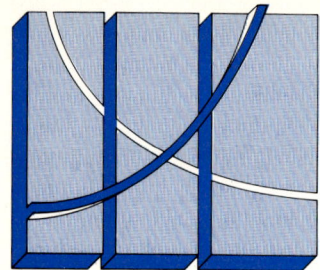

CONTENTS

CHAPTER 1   INTRODUCTION   1

The Law of Scarcity   2
Rational Economic Agents   4
Positive Versus Normative Economics   4
The Nature of Economic Theory   4
A Preview   6

CHAPTER 2   THE ESSENTIALS OF PRICING   9

The Economy   9
Stocks and Flows   11
   Present Values
   The Circular Flow—The Wheel of Wealth
The Laws of Supply and Demand   15
   Equilibrium of Supply and Demand
   Comparative Statics
   The Algebra of Supply and Demand
Equilibrium-Price Stability   23
Applications   25
   The Effects of Excise Taxes
   Joint Products
   Price Ceilings and Floors
   Example 2-1 Organized Commodity Exchanges   10
   Example 2-2 The Demand for Beef   21

CONTENTS

CHAPTER 3 MODERN UTILITY THEORY 35

The Rational Consumer 35
Consumer Behavior in the Case of Certainty 37
   Commodity and Service Flows
   Preferences
   The Axioms of Consumer Behavior in the Case of Certainty
The Utility Function 44
   Ordinal Utility Versus Cardinal Utility
   Why Discuss Utility?
   The Link Between Marginal Utility and the Marginal Rate of Substitution
   Indifference Curves When Some Commodities Are "Bads"
   Lexicographic Rankings
   The Properties of Indifference Curves
Consumer Behavior in the Case of Uncertainty 53
   Probability
   Conflicting Views About the Nature of Probabilities
   Expected Values
   The St. Petersburg Paradox
   The Axioms of Consumer Behavior in the Case of Uncertainty
The Expected-Utility Hypothesis 61
   Example 3-1 Are Consumer Tastes Stable? 36
   Example 3-2 Judging Quality by Price 46
   Example 3-3 Preference Reversals 63
   Example 3-4 Flood Insurance, Flight Insurance, and Lotteries 66

CHAPTER 4 THE THEORY OF CONSUMER DEMAND 70

The Budget Constraint 70
Consumer Equilibrium 73
Changes in Income 77
   Inferior and Normal Goods
   The Income/Consumption Curve
   Income Elasticity
   Engel Curves
   Inferior Goods and the Income/Consumption Curve
   The Absence of Money Illusion
Changes in Price 84
   The Price/Consumption Curve
   Substitution and Income Effects
   Giffen Goods
   The Compensated-Demand Curve
   Price Elasticity of Demand
Applications 93
   The Costs of Subsidies
   Price Indices and Revealed Preferences
Market Demand 101
Consumer Surplus 101
   Example 4-1 How to Give Away Food Stamps 79
   Example 4-2 Studying Money Illusion 86
   Example 4-3 Evidence for the Law of Demand 94

CHAPTER 5 THE CHARACTERISTICS OF MARKET DEMAND 106

The Market-Demand Function 106
Price Elasticity of Demand 108
    Arc Elasticity
    Point Elasticity
    Constant Slope Versus Constant Elasticity
Other Elasticities of Demand 114
    The Income Elasticity of Demand
    The Cross-Price Elasticity of Demand
    The Aggregation of Elasticities
Compensated Price Elasticity of Demand 117
    Slutsky's Equation
    Substitutes and Complements
Price Elasticity and Total Revenue 120
    Price, Marginal Revenue, and Elasticity
    The Average/Marginal Rule
Empirical Demand Analysis 128
    Regression Analysis
    Estimation Problems in Economics
    Elasticity Estimates
    Example 5-1   Cross-Price Elasticities for Coal and Oil   116
    Example 5-2   The Measurement of Substitution
                    and Income Effects   130

APPENDIX 5A STATISTICS 139

Basic Concepts 139
Linear Regression 140
The Least-Squares Property 141

CHAPTER 6 SPECIALIZATION AND EXCHANGE 144

The Theory of Exchange 144
    The Edgeworth Box
    Voluntary Exchange
Efficiency or Pareto Optimality 148
Competitive Equilibrium 151
    The Core
    Competitive Stability
The Law of Comparative Advantage 157
    The Ricardian Model of Comparative Advantage
    Absolute Advantage Is Irrelevant
    Example 6-1   Indian Giving and Silent Exchange
                    as Exchange Mechanisms   150
    Example 6-2   The Comparative Advantage of Fishers   160

CONTENTS xi

CHAPTER 7   THE TECHNOLOGY OF PRODUCTION   164

The Production Function   166
    Marginal and Average Products
    The Short Run and the Long Run
    The Law of Diminishing Returns
The Long-Run Production Function   168
    Returns to Scale
    Homothetic Production Functions
The Short-Run Production Function   176
    The Total-Product Curve
    The Three Stages of Production
    The Economic Region of Production
The Elasticity of Substitution   184
    Example 7-1   An Isoquant for Oil Pipelines   177
    Example 7-2   A Production Function for Eggs   179
    Example 7-3   The Substitutability of Capital and Labor   187

CHAPTER 8   THE COSTS OF PRODUCTION   190

Opportunity Costs   190
    Explicit and Implicit Costs
    Accounting Profit Versus Economic Profit
Long-Run Costs   192
    Isocost Curves
    The Optimal Combination of Inputs
    The Output Expansion Path
    Long-Run Cost Curves
Short-Run Costs of Production   204
    What is the Short Run?
    Short-Run Costs and the Production Function
    Fixed Cost and Variable Cost
    Average Fixed Cost, Average Variable Cost, Marginal Cost
    The Economics Behind Short-Run Cost Curves
Long-Run and Short-Run Cost Curves   211
    Constant Returns to Scale
    Increasing and Decreasing Returns to Scale
Changes in Factor Prices   215
    The Effect of Changes in Factor Prices on the Expansion Path
    Shepherd's Lemma
    The Role of the Expansion Path
    Changing Factor Prices and the Optimal Output Level
    Example 8-1   Opportunity Cost   191
    Example 8-2   Long-Run Cost Curves and Minimum Efficient Scale   207

APPENDIX 8A   LINEAR PROGRAMMING   222

Choosing the Least-Cost Diet   222
Determining the Least-Cost Method of Production   223
    Defining the Dual Problem
    Solving the Dual Problem

CHAPTER 9   THE THEORY OF PERFECT COMPETITION   228

The Meaning of Perfect Competition   228
Pricing in the Market Period   229
Pricing in the Short Run   230
   Price, Marginal Revenue, and Costs
   Profit Maximization
   The Firm's Supply Curve
   Short-Run Market Equilibrium
   The Price Elasticity of Supply
Pricing in the Long Run   244
   Long-Run Competitive Equilibrium
   The Behavior of the Firm in the Long Run
   The Freedom-of-Entry Case
   The Absence-of-Entry Case
   Ricardian Differential-Rent Theory
The Benefits of a Market: The Case for Free Trade   256
   Example 9-1   Auction Markets   231
   Example 9-2   Freedom of Entry   245
   Example 9-3   Price Controls   253

CHAPTER 10   THE THEORY OF MONOPOLY   261

The Definition of Monopoly   261
   Entry Barriers
   Monopoly Price and Marginal Revenue
   Marginal Revenue and Elasticity
Monopoly Pricing and Output in the Short Run   269
   Short-Run Profit Maximization
   The Second-Order Condition
   Monopoly Supply
Monopoly Pricing and Output in the Long Run   275
   Long-Run Profit Maximization
   Multiplant Monopolies
Characteristics of Monopoly Equilibrium   276
Monopoly and Perfect Competition Compared   278
   Sources of Inefficiency
   The Measurement of Monopoly Power
Multiple-Pricing Schemes   285
   The Conditions for Price Discrimination
   Why Price Discrimination?
   Perfect Price Discrimination
   Two-Part Pricing
   The Importance of Information Costs
   Example 10-1   How Important Is Monopoly?   282
   Example 10-2   Do Simple Profit Rates Capture Monopoly Profits?   284
   Example 10-3   Price Discrimination by Electric Utilities   290

CONTENTS xiii

CHAPTER 11   THE ECONOMICS OF INFORMATION   294

Information Costs   295
The Economics of Search   296
   Transaction Costs
   Centralized and Decentralized Markets
   The Optimal-Search Rule
Speculation   303
   Profitable Speculation
   Unprofitable Speculation
   The Pattern of Prices Over Time
   The Futures Market
   Hedging
   The Effects of Futures Trading
The Moral-Hazard Problem   310
   The Case of Disability Insurance
   Strategies for the Moral-Hazard Problem
The Adverse-Selection Problem   318
   Detecting Lemons
   The Case of Disability Insurance
   Separating Risk Groups
   Pooling Risk Groups
   Product Information
   Example 11-1   The Optimal-Shopping Rule for Hamburgers   299
   Example 11-2   The Effects of Disability Payments on Labor-Force Participation   319
   Example 11-3   Golden Parachutes and Hostile Tender Offers   320

CHAPTER 12   MONOPOLISTIC COMPETITION AND OLIGOPOLY   329

Measuring Concentration   330
   Measurement Problems
   Herfindahl Index
   Has Concentration Increased?
   The Equalization of Profit Rates
Monopolistic Competition   335
   Long-Run Equilibrium Under Monopolistic Competition
   The Welfare Aspects of Monopolistic Competition
Cooperative Oligopoly: Cartel Theory   340
   Joint Profit Maximization
   Antitrust Laws
Noncooperative Oligopoly   344
   Cournot Oligopoly
   N-Firm Cournot Oligopoly
   Mergers and Cournot Oligopoly
The Kinked-Demand-Curve Model   351
Potential Entrants   354
   Limit Pricing
   Contestable Markets

xiv CONTENTS

Game Theory   357
    Nash Equilibrium
    The Zero-Sum Game
    The Nonzero-Sum Game
    Example 12-1   The Persistence of Oligopoly Profits   338
    Example 12-2   The Organization of Petroleum-Exporting Countries (OPEC) Cartel   341

CHAPTER 13 COMPETITIVE RESOURCE MARKETS   365

The Laws of Derived Demand   366
Profit Maximization on the Input Side   367
The One-Input Case   369
The Two-Input Case   373
    The Elasticity of Substitution
    Relative Factor Shares
    The Long-Run Demand for Labor
Industry Demand for an Input   378
Characteristics of Input Supply   379
    The Supply of Labor Services
    The Supply of Land Resources
The Marginal-Productivity Theory of Distribution   389
    Example 13-1   Empirical Wage Elasticities of Demand   377
    Example 13-2   Overtime Pay   386
    Example 13-3   Immigration Winners and Losers   391

APPENDIX 13A THE LAWS OF DERIVED DEMAND   395

CHAPTER 14 IMPERFECTLY COMPETITIVE RESOURCE MARKETS   397

Monopoly on the Product Side of the Market   397
    Profit Maximization
    The Social Costs of Monopoly
    Market Equilibrium
Monopsony in the Resource Market   401
    Marginal Factor Cost
    Monopsonistic Equilibrium
Minimum-Wage Laws and Unions   404
    The Competitive Case
    The Monopsony Case
    Unions
Screening   410
    The No-Signaling Case
    Screening Devices
    Example 14-1   The Two Faces of Unionism   407

CONTENTS xv

CHAPTER 15   CAPITAL AND INTEREST   415

Interest Rates: Nominal and Real   416
Intertemporal Consumption and Saving   417
    The Budget Constraint
    Intertemporal Consumption
    Optimal Consumption Plans
    Wealth and Substitution Effects
Intertemporal Production and Investment   426
    The Present-Value Rule
    Investment and the Rate of Return
Market Equilibrium   431
Do Deficits Affect Real Interest Rates?   432
    Example 15–1   Real and Nominal Interest Rates   417
    Example 15–2   Short-Term and Long-Term Interest Rates   430

CHAPTER 16   GENERAL EQUILIBRIUM   435

The Nature of General Equilibrium   435
The Pure-Exchange Model   437
    Walras's Law
    The Edgeworth Box
    Pareto Optimality
    The Two Basic Theorems of Welfare Economics
The Two-Sector Production Model   448
    Constant-Returns-to-Scale Production
    The Production-Possibilities Frontier
    Factor Prices and Costs
    The Stolper-Samuelson Theorem
    Pareto Optimality
    The Grand Utility-Possibilities Curve
    Example 16–1   The Decline of Manufacturing   454

CHAPTER 17   EXTERNALITIES, PUBLIC GOODS, AND PUBLIC CHOICE   463

What Are Externalities?   463
Internalizing Externalities   466
    Voluntary Agreements
    Government Taxes and Subsidies
Allocating a Common-Property Resource   470
    Redefinition of Property Rights
    Government Taxes or Subsidies and Government Permits
Government Regulation of Pollution   473
Public Choice   475
    Unanimity: The Benefit Theory of Taxation
    Voting Mechanisms
    Example 17–1   The Depletion of the Ozone Layer   473

ANSWERS TO EVEN-NUMBERED QUESTIONS
AND PROBLEMS   485

GLOSSARY   501

NAME INDEX   515

SUBJECT INDEX   517

CHAPTER 1

INTRODUCTION

The central problem of economics is scarcity. People have unlimited wants, but society has limited resources. No matter how vast are a country's resources, they are meager compared to the number of ways its population wishes to use those resources. As long as there is scarcity, scarce goods must be rationed in some way among individuals competing for them. In such a world, three questions are paramount: (1) *What* goods will be produced? (2) *How* should the goods be produced? (3) *For whom* will scarce goods be produced?

An economic system is a set of customs, institutions, and rules for answering the questions of *what*, *how*, and *for whom*. A market economy is one in which resources are allocated by private individuals in a setting where the state defends and defines property rights. The right to use a scarce good or service is conveyed by the institution of markets, where prices are freely established among competing individuals. This right could be distributed by many other mechanisms: on a first-come, first-served basis; to the strongest; to the most attractive; to the fastest; by rationing. All of these mechanisms are used to some extent in the world in which we live. For example, in the Soviet Union, a modest price system plus the first-come, first-served system is used to allocate the most desirable commodities. In wartime, ration tickets or coupons may be issued by a government to control distribution of scarce goods.

Microeconomics, or *price theory*, is the study of the economic decision making of firms, individuals, and governmental units in a market setting.

Microeconomics, or *price theory*, studies the mechanism of resource allocation in a market economy. Because scarcity is the central problem of all economic systems, price theory can even be applied to socialist economies. We will devote nearly all of our attention to market economies, however, leaving the study of socialist economies to books on comparative economic systems.

THE LAW OF SCARCITY

Free goods are goods or services for which supply exceeds demand even at a zero price.

Scarce goods are goods or services for which demand exceeds supply at a zero price.

For **free goods**, such as air, supply exceeds demand even at a price of zero. Commodities or services are said to be **scarce goods** if the quantity people demand at a zero price exceeds the supply at that price. According to the law of scarcity, there will always be scarce goods in the economy. As long as human imaginations can soar, people will want the unattainable. How many times have we heard of very wealthy individuals owning as many as 85 Rolls Royces, several Boeing 747s, or 3,000 pairs of shoes? The rest of us can only imagine having a Mediterranean villa staffed with servants, all the cars and clothes we want, or all the caviar we can consume. At a zero price, we would try to make our dreams become reality. But with few exceptions (the so-called free goods), most of the interesting goods we could contemplate would turn out to be quite scarce.

Economics, as traditionally defined, is the study of how society allocates scarce resources among competing ends. What makes the economic problem (wants greater than resources) serious is that allocating resources requires sacrifice. Because of scarcity, we must make hard choices, and some people end up with more than others. Microeconomics can also be called the science of choice. Because of scarcity, people must economize and choose among the alternatives confronting them.

What makes the economic problem difficult is that information about the alternative uses of resources is costly to obtain. Indeed, it can be argued that the most important scarce commodity in society is *information*. If people had perfect information about everything, every resource could be immediately directed to its highest and best use. No consumer would ever be persuaded to pay too much for a product. No firm would ever commit resources to producing a product that did not sell. No skyscraper would ever stand empty (as in Houston, Texas, after the price of oil fell). No family would receive charity without being deserving. No unqualified employee would be promoted over one who was more qualified. Nobody would be unemployed because of not knowing about the best available job.

Figure 1-1 gives a picture of the economic problem. An economy consists of resources (land, labor, and capital) for producing goods and services. To simplify, imagine that those resources are used to produce only two goods: butter and guns. If all resources are devoted to butter production, the economy can produce at point *t* in Figure 1-1, where gun production is zero and butter production is maximized. If all resources are devoted to gun production, the economy can produce at *r*, where butter production is zero and gun production is maximized. This **production-possibilities frontier** (*PPF*) shows the maximum production of one good given the production of the rest of the goods in the economy for given resources and knowledge. The *PPF* curve shows all of the production possibilities as resources are shifted from butter production to gun production.

The **production-possibilities frontier** (*PPF*) shows the combinations of goods that can be produced when the factors of production are utilized to their full potential.

THE LAW OF SCARCITY

FIGURE 1-1   Production-Possibilities Frontier: Guns versus Butter

The production-possibilities frontier is downward-sloping and concave to the origin. Its slope, ΔButter/ΔGuns, reflects the opportunity cost of guns—the quantity of butter that must be given up to obtain one more gun.

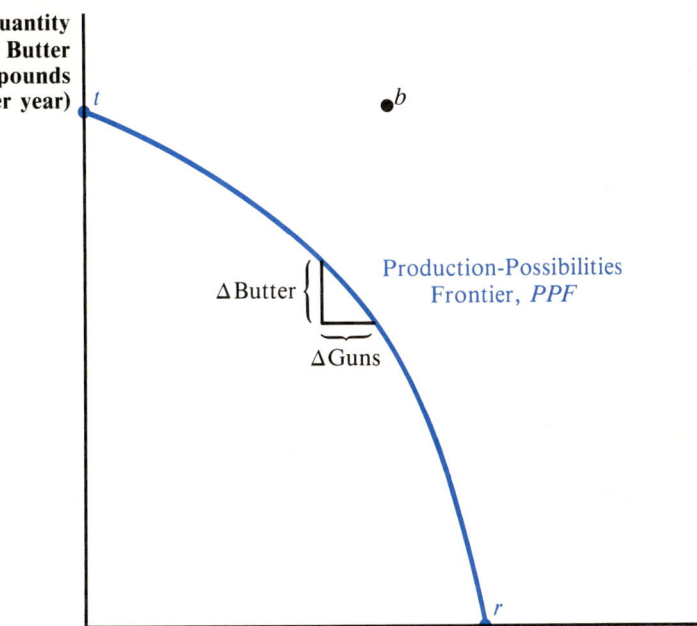

The **opportunity cost** of any activity is the best opportunity that must be sacrificed in order to expand the activity by one unit.

A key feature illustrated by the production-possibilities frontier is that to produce more guns, some butter production must be sacrificed (and vice versa). Indeed, the amount of butter production that is sacrificed for additional gun production is the **opportunity cost** to society of gun production. The slope—the change in the quantity of butter divided by the change in the quantity of guns—is a measure of that opportunity cost.

Notice that if the production-possibilities frontier is concave to the origin (as it is in Figure 1-1), the absolute slope increases as gun production expands. In other words, the opportunity cost of producing guns increases as output expands. This law of increasing opportunity cost owes its origin to the famous law of diminishing returns (see Chapter 7).

Scarcity exists simply because the population would prefer to consume butter/gun combinations that are impossible to achieve rather than those that are possible. For example, in Figure 1-1, point *b* would likely be preferred to any of the points on or inside the *PPF* curve.

The fact that something of value must be given up to acquire more of a scarce good is one of the key ideas of economics: "There is no such thing as a free lunch."

RATIONAL ECONOMIC AGENTS

A principal assumption of economic analysis is that economic agents are rational—that is, that economic actions follow some benefit/cost comparison. An economic agent buys another quart of milk because the extra, or *marginal*, benefits exceed the extra, or *marginal*, cost. A firm produces another widget if the marginal benefit of the additional widget exceeds the marginal cost. The calculation of marginal benefits or costs may involve psychological benefits or costs—in other words, economic agents are human.

The assumption of rationality is useful because it allows us to develop a coherent theory about the workings of an economy. This book will explain theories of consumer and producer behavior as well as theories of how different kinds of markets work.

POSITIVE VERSUS NORMATIVE ECONOMICS

Positive economics is the analysis of existing economic conditions and policies and their effects in the real world.

Normative economics involves making judgments as to the worth of existing economic policies and proposing changes in conditions and policies designed to improve existing situations.

The study of economics involves two distinctly different modes of analysis. **Positive economics** is the study of *what is*. How does the market for steel work? Why did the price of wheat rise? What causes inflation? What causes wages to rise? What is the impact of international trade on average real incomes?

Normative economics is the study of *what ought to be*. Is the distribution of income fair? Is the economy producing enough medical care? Should tariffs be lowered? Should a merger be allowed between IBM and Xerox?

The distinction between positive and normative economics helps explain why economists have a reputation for being often in disagreement. For example, two economists may make the same positive analysis of some economic problem, but their public statements about policy may differ because they reflect different views on what the state of the world ought to be. One economist may think that the distribution of income is fine; the other may think that it is unfair. These judgments will color their views on an income-tax policy even though their analyses of the impact of income taxes on work effort and income distribution are identical. Unfortunately, it may take another professional economist to determine that their positive analyses are identical; the public sees only the bottom line—their normative recommendations.

THE NATURE OF ECONOMIC THEORY

This book is about economic theory. Why do we use theories?

An economic **theory** consists of a set of careful assumptions and definitions about some aspect of the economy. From this set of assumptions and

THE NATURE OF ECONOMIC THEORY

A theory is a set of careful assumptions offered to explain a certain phenomenon.

definitions, certain conclusions or propositions follow. For example, the law of diminishing returns implies that a higher price is necessary to secure a larger quantity of coal, or steel, or oil. When the OPEC cartel collapsed in the mid-1980s and the price of oil dropped from $30 a barrel to $15 a barrel, many oil wells were shut down throughout the United States.

A theory is a simplified description of economic phenomena. The world is so complicated that our finite minds can comprehend only a simplified description. Although a theory can become so complicated that only computers can carry out the necessary calculations, the theory imposes certain limits on the subject we are studying. When economists study demand, they do not examine the innermost psychological desires of human beings or use psychological profiles and lie-detector tests. We do not say that economists should not study psychology, but only that there are many things we must leave out of the theory of demand. Why does Michael Jackson wear a white glove? Such a question is outside the scope of economic analysis.

Because theories are simplified descriptions of the real world, some methodologists argue that it is improper to test theories by looking at their assumptions. The best-known proponent of this viewpoint is Nobel-prize-winning economist Milton Friedman. According to Friedman, we should test a theory by examining its implications for the phenomena the theory was designed to explain. If the implications of the theory are incorrect, then the theory should be modified or discarded. If the theory has no other uses, it should be discarded. If it is useful in other applications, it should be modified.

The purpose of most assumptions is not just to make the calculations clean and simple. Assumptions make a theory more specific or precise. For example, in the theory of demand, economists used to make the assumption that the benefits of each good were independent. This assumption simplified the theory of demand, but at too high a cost. The assumption made it impossible to explain the rich tapestry of interrelationships between the demand for one good and the price of another, or the relationship between income and demand. Except in elementary expositions, economists no longer make this assumption. In this case, both the assumption and some of its predictions are wrong.

In some cases, it may be impossible to test the predictions of a theory. We cannot always test economic theories in a laboratory. If the implications of a theory cannot be directly tested, it may be very useful to test the assumptions directly. For example, the theory of perfect competition (explained in detail in this book) states that the economy will be efficiently organized under certain conditions, but the efficiency of an entire economy can be measured only by examining the impact of changes on the welfare positions of every individual in the economy. Thus, evaluations of the theory of perfect competition are based on the assumptions of the theory as well as its predictions.

The grain of truth in the Friedman position is that the assumptions of any theory are deliberate simplifications. Strictly speaking, they are false. A physicist's calculations may assume a nonexistent perfect vacuum; a chemist's deductions may assume pure water when, in applications, water will usually be impure. The issue is whether the predictions are approximately correct. Few would disagree with this position. For example, in the theory of oligopoly, economists often make apparently unrealistic assumptions because otherwise the computations become too difficult. The world is a complex place. The genius of the economic theorist is to pick that assumption which allows us to better comprehend the world in which we live. If the assumption works, why not use it?

What is a good theory? A theory is good if it works—if it explains real phenomena. In this regard, a theory may work for some things but not others. The usual practice is to use the simplest theory suitable for some particular task. In economics, the theory of perfect competition is suitable for explaining the consequences of price controls (see Chapter 9) but cannot explain price discrimination. The theory of monopoly must be used to explain price discrimination (see Chapter 10). In physics, Newtonian mechanics is adequate for designing rocket ships but breaks down in explaining objects traveling near the speed of light. The Bohr model of the atom (which pictures the atom as a miniature planetary system) is sufficient for describing the properties of a laser (a beam of concentrated light) but is considered inappropriate in most applications of atomic physics.

This book is concerned with *modern price theory*, or microeconomics. Microeconomics studies mechanisms of resource allocation and the role of consumers, producers, and markets. To the microeconomist, no detail is too small. The grand result of these individual considerations is a theory of how the economy as a whole fits together.

In macroeconomics, the analysis concentrates on certain big-picture questions, such as unemployment, inflation, economic growth, the business cycle, and the nature of money—but the study of macroeconomics is based on a thorough understanding of microeconomic theory. Thus, microeconomics is a foundation for all economics.

A PREVIEW

This book defines terms, makes assumptions, and uses economic reasoning to derive propositions about how the economy works. In most cases, the economic theories are illustrated by real-world examples.

Economic theory describes how economic agents (consumers and producers) interact through markets and prices. Chapter 2 begins the story by describing the basic law of supply and demand, which explains how prices emerge in markets. We go deeper into the law of demand by examining in detail the theory of consumer demand (Chapters 3, 4, and 5). Chapter 6 describes how specialization and exchange emerge, drawing on the theory of consumer behavior and making the simplest possible assumptions about production technology. Chapters 7 and 8 explain the theory of production and costs for any business firm. Chapter 9 applies the theory of production and costs to competitive markets, and Chapter 10 develops the theory of monopoly. The next two chapters add considerable realism to the story of how markets work: Chapter 11 is concerned with the problem of economic information, and Chapter 12 deals with oligopoly and monopolistic competition and completes our study of product markets. Chapters 13, 14, and 15 study the resource markets. Chapter 16 brings together all of our previous understandings of consumers, producers, and perfect competition to show how an entire economy fits together in a more advanced version of Chapter 6. Finally, Chapter 17 examines some major problems of resource allocation: externalities, public goods, and public choice.

SUMMARY

1. Scarcity is the central problem of all economic systems. Scarce goods are those for which demand exceeds supply at a zero price; free goods are those for which supply exceeds demand at any price, even a zero price. The production-possibilities frontier depicts the choices facing an economy; its absolute slope indicates the opportunity cost of production. The curve is downward-sloping and usually concave when viewed from the origin.

2. The assumption that rational economic agents follow benefit/cost comparisons to maximize their own net gains allows us to develop a useful theory of economic activity.

3. Positive economics is the study of *what is*, while normative economics studies *what ought to be*. One important school of methodology holds that positive economic theories can best be tested by their predictive power; however, it is sometimes necessary to evaluate theories by examining their assumptions.

4. Microeconomics is the foundation of all economics because it examines mechanisms of resource allocation and the role of rational economic agents.

QUESTIONS AND PROBLEMS

1. Define a scarce good. Give examples.

2. Define a free good. Give examples.

3. In Great Britain, medical care is free. Why is medical care not a "free good" as economists define that term?

4. What is the production-possibilities frontier? What is its shape?

5. Suppose an economy produces only goods x and y. Draw the production-possibilities frontier if $x + y = 100$ units. How would you criticize this *PPF* example?

6. Evaluate Friedman's view about testing a theory by examining its assumptions.

SUGGESTED READINGS

Friedman, Milton. "The Methodology of Positive Economics." In *Essays in Positive Economics*. Chicago: University of Chicago Press, 1953, pp. 1–43.

Gribbin, J. *In Search of Schrodinger's Cat*. New York: Bantam Books, 1984.

Koopmans, T. J. *Three Essays on the State of Economic Science*. New York: McGraw-Hill, 1957, pp. 129–50.

Mundell, R. A. *Man and Economics*. New York: McGraw-Hill, 1968, chap. 1.

CHAPTER 2

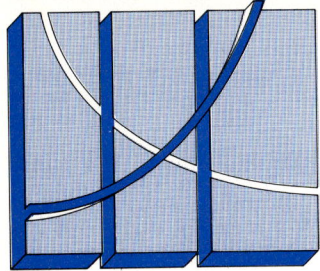

THE ESSENTIALS OF PRICING

We begin our study of price theory with an overview of the way markets work using the mechanism of pricing goods and services according to the laws of supply and demand. This chapter examines the essentials of pricing: scarce goods versus free goods, stocks versus flows, present values, the coordination of economic activity by price, and the general workings of the laws of supply and demand. Subsequent chapters will show how the incentives for consumers and producers to maximize their well-being lead to the laws of supply and demand. As the book nears its end, we will come back to this overview, but at a much more sophisticated level of analysis. We must always keep in mind the central question: How does an economy work?

THE ECONOMY

The supply of goods in the economy consists of free goods and scarce goods. Free goods are those for which demand falls short of supply even at a zero price. Examples are air, sand in the Sahara, tumbleweeds, and wildflowers. Scarce goods, on the other hand, are those for which demand exceeds supply at a zero price. It is necessary to ration scarce goods among all the competing claimants.

Ownership of a good or commodity is more than just possession of the physical good, such as wheat, shoes, or clothing. Ownership also involves the legal right to use the physical good. How much would you pay, for example, for stolen goods compared to legally acquired goods? Because stolen property can be claimed by the legal owner at any point in the future (unlike stolen money), stolen goods have less value than legally acquired goods. Anyone who paid full price for stolen goods would feel cheated, and

CHAPTER 2 THE ESSENTIALS OF PRICING

> ### EXAMPLE 2–1 Organized Commodity Exchanges
>
>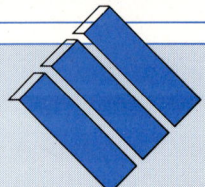
>
> A futures contract is a contract that requires delivery of some commodity at some stated date in the future. Each contract is standardized in terms of quantity and quality. The oldest commodity exchange is the Chicago Board of Trade, where trading takes place in wheat, corn, soybeans, rye, oats, soybean meal, and soybean oil.
>
> On the exchange floor, trading takes place in "pits." The pits are raised octagonal platforms with three small steps. The brokers and traders face each other around the platform, making animated, and noisy, bids and offers. Each broker shouts out his or her bid or offer together with an appropriate hand signal (the palm turned in means a bid to buy; the palm turned out means an offer to sell). Each transaction is reported to employees of the exchange, who record the prices and quantities on a long blackboard. The transaction immediately appears on all the tickers and terminals connected to the exchange. If the price is the same as in the preceding transaction, the ticker does not change. Transactions at higher or lower prices are immediately displayed as upward or downward "ticks" on television monitors all over the country. The market is chaotic, but efficient. It abides by certain well-known rules of the game, which spell out the duties and rights of buyers, sellers, and brokers.
>
> How big are the commodity futures markets? On June 20, 1986, the dollar volume of corn contracts in these markets was $219 million. As a comparison, on the same day, $209 million in General Motors common stock was traded on the New York Stock Exchange—another organized market institution.

rightly so. Similarly, a stolen car is not as valuable to the thief as a legally owned one is to its buyer—the thief must always keep an eye out for the police, and that fact severely reduces the economic value of the car.

A **market** is an institution through which people regularly exchange scarce goods and services. One type of market is described in Example 2-1. The exchange of goods or services is governed by property rights, which specify the way in which things can be bought, sold, or used. A primitive but most fundamental role of government in the economy is to defend and define these property rights. Societies have found that it is in the interests of all to have a cooperative solution to the acquisition and use of scarce resources. The government or sovereign creates property rights "by keeping other people off, by preventing robbery, trespass, stealing secrets, or preventing

<small>A **market** is an established arrangement that buyers and sellers use to regularly exchange goods and services.</small>

'infringement' upon one's opportunities to buy, sell, or compete."[1] In a free-for-all world, we would all lose. Why produce anything if your neighbor can steal it? When we buy, produce, or invent something, we expect to be able to use it in certain prescribed ways. Preservation of property rights allows us to expect such stable and predictable behavior on the part of others.

Capitalism is a type of economic system in which access to markets (as a buyer or seller) and the pricing of goods are more or less free of extensive government interference. The government states the rules by which we play the game. The butcher cannot weigh his or her thumb; the milk you buy at the supermarket must not be sour; you must pay for the things you take from the store or face the judge. The difference between capitalism and socialism is not in the presence or absence of property rights but in the nature of those rights. Socialism is a type of economic system in which access by sellers is generally reserved for state-operated enterprises and the pricing of goods and services is subject to rules set down by governmental authority.

Economic systems are badly damaged by unclear property rights. One of the disadvantages of socialistic systems is that the public—unless cowed by a police state, as in the Soviet Union—may not fully recognize the right of the state to set prices. For example, in Tunisia in the winter of 1983–84, riots were touched off by government-imposed food-price increases of more than 100 percent. Previously, the government had so heavily subsidized bread, for example, that it was being used as animal feed. (We shall see that such subsidies are inefficient.) Even though the price hikes could be justified, the economy became so paralyzed by the deadly riots that the government eventually backed off. Implicit in much of this book is the assumption that property rights are clear and rigidly enforced. This assumption is easier to justify in the case of a capitalist society because property rights are diffused rather than concentrated.

STOCKS AND FLOWS

A **stock variable** is a quantity of a good or commodity existing at a given point in time.

A **flow variable** is a movement in quantity or value over a period of time.

Without measurement there can be no science. Economics is no exception. Two economic measurements of interest to most individuals are (1) the amount of money he or she has in the bank and (2) the amount of income he or she earns per year. Notice that money in the bank is a **stock variable** at a moment in time; income is a **flow variable** over a period of time.

At any moment in time, the economy includes stocks of various kinds of people, land, and goods. A stock variable is a physical quantity of something existing at a particular moment in time; it is not measured over a period of time. Some examples are: the number of electrical engineers in the United States on a certain date, the number of tons of corn or wheat in silos on July

---

1. John R. Commons, *The Economics of Collective Action*, (New York: Macmillan, 1951), p. 81.

1, the number of acres of forestland on December 31, or the total inventory of all types of goods in various degrees of completion on January 1. These stocks give rise to flows—for example, labor services, food services, machine services—over the near or indefinite future. A flow variable represents a quantity measured per unit of time, such as worker hours per week, truck hours per month, warehouse hours per year, or the production or consumption of some good during a week or month. The flow of a good produced over a particular period equals the change in the stock of the good between two moments in time (ignoring depreciation).

The stocks and flows of an economy correspond to the wealth and income of the economy. As one learns in elementary economics, the income of an economy is the value of final goods and services produced over a particular time period.

Present Values

The prices for stocks and the prices for flows have different time dimensions. A price paid for a stock is simply an amount paid in dollars (or any other medium of exchange) per unit of the good. A price paid for a flow is a price per unit of time per unit of the good or service. For example, an automobile worker earns so many dollars per hour of labor, or a building rents for so many dollars per square foot per month.

The link between the price of a stock and its rental value is provided by the concept of **present value**. To determine the present value of an asset, we need to know the appropriate interest rate and the income flow generated by the asset. For example, if an asset yields $100 per year in perpetuity and the annual interest rate is 20 percent, the present value of the asset is $500 because investing $500 at 20 percent yields $100 per year. No one would pay more than $500 for the asset when those funds could earn more than $100 if invested elsewhere. Using a formula, if i is the interest rate per year, expressed as a decimal, the present value (PV) of the perpetual income flow y per year is

$$PV = y/i. \qquad (1)$$

*The **present value** of a future sum of money is the amount that must be invested at today's interest rates to generate that future sum of money.*

In other words, the earnings of an amount equal to PV invested at the interest rate i is $i(PV)$.

A perpetuity is paid forever. What about the present value of a sum of money, y_n, to be paid in year n? Investing $1 at interest rate i at compound interest (the dollar is reinvested each year) earns $(1 + i)^n$ in n years. At the end of the first year, the investor has $(1 + i)$ dollars, at the end of the second $(1 + i)^2$, and so on. Hence, the present value of y_n is

$$PV_n = \frac{y_n}{(1 + i)^n}. \qquad (2)$$

For example, the present value of $121 in two years when $i = 0.10$ (10

STOCKS AND FLOWS

percent) is $\$121/(1.1)^2 = \$100$. The present value of a stream of future payments $y_1, y_2, \ldots, y_N$ is simply the sum of the present values of each payment:

$$PV = \frac{y_1}{(1 + i)} + \cdots \frac{y_n}{(1 + i)^n} = \Sigma \frac{y_n}{(1 + i)^n} \qquad (3)$$

Formula (3) simplifies to formula (1) if $n =$ infinity and all ys are the same.[2]

Prices of certain kinds of things should be compared on the same basis. It would be senseless to compare the price of a car—a durable good—to the price of whiskey—a perishable good. Suppose a Toyota costs $5,000 for its stream of future services. A consumer who bought $100 worth of whiskey per month at a monthly interest rate of 1 percent would, in present-value terms, value the stream of future whiskey consumption at $10,000—twice as much as the value of future Toyota services! Another example: a watch lasting one year and costing $10 is more expensive than a watch lasting a lifetime costing $50 at any interest rate below 20 percent per year. If the interest rate is 20 percent, the $50 watch requires a sacrifice of exactly $10 per year; if the interest rate is, say, 10 percent, the $50 watch requires a sacrifice of only $5 per year. In general, one reason poor people buy "cheaper" (but actually more expensive) products than rich people is that the former face higher interest rates. High interest rates increase the costs of durable goods.

Present values also alert us to the fact that comparing economic values at different times requires interest discounting. Many car buyers compare the cash price of a car to the deferred payment price (a practice actually required by law). The "savings" of paying cash versus paying over time are then determined by deducting the cash price from the total of deferred payments. This procedure is nonsense. When a car is purchased (or a home, or anything that is financed), the amount that is financed is the present value of the stream of monthly payments.

---

2. The simplification is: Let $\lambda = 1/(1 + i)$ and $y = y_n$ for all n. Then PV formula (3) becomes

$$PV = y(\lambda + \lambda^2 + \ldots + \lambda^N).$$

Multiply both sides by λ.

$$\lambda PV = y[\lambda^2 + \ldots + \lambda^N + \lambda^{(N+1)}].$$

Subtract λPV from PV.

$$PV - \lambda PV = y[\lambda - \lambda^{(N+1)}].$$

Letting $N \to \infty$ implies $\lambda^{(N+1)} = 0$, since λ is less than unity. Thus, in the limit, $PV - \lambda PV = y\lambda$. It follows that

$$PV = \frac{y\lambda}{1 - \lambda}.$$

But

$$\frac{\lambda}{1 - \lambda} = \frac{1/(1 + i)}{1 - 1/(1 + i)} = \frac{1/(1 + i)}{i/(1 + i)} = \frac{1}{i}.$$

Accordingly, the value of a perpetuity y is $PV = y/i$, formula (1).

FIGURE 2-1 The Circular Flow of Economic Activity

The inner circle shows the flows of money expenditures from goods and services to productive factors; the outer circle shows the physical flows in the opposite direction. Households and firms are the key actors.

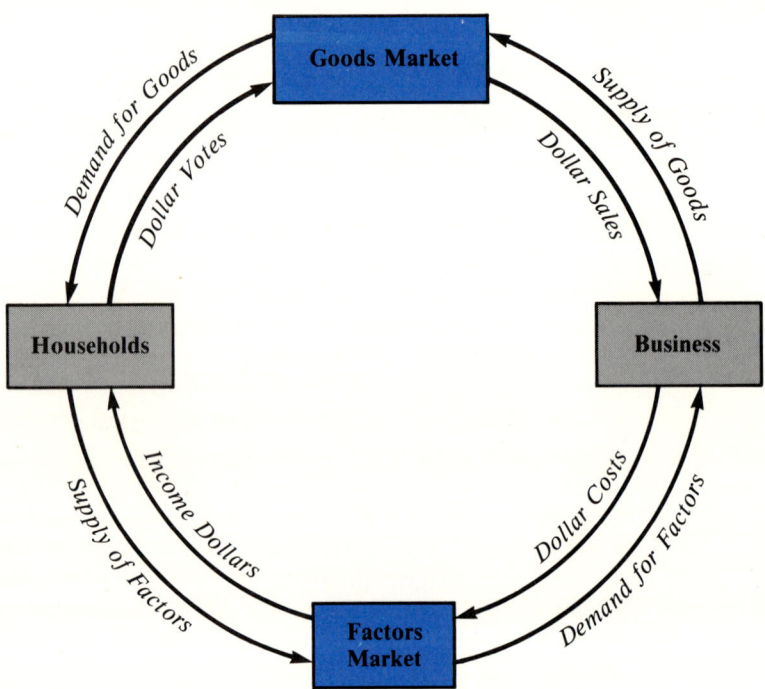

As an illustration, a $10,000 car purchased over 48 months at a 12 percent annual rate requires a monthly payment of $263.34. The present value of all the monthly payments is exactly $10,000. The undiscounted total of all the monthly payments is $12,640.24. But the buyer does not "save" $2,640 by paying cash for the car. The $10,000 today is equivalent to $263.34 paid over 48 months. Invest $10,000 today for 48 months at 12 percent interest (compounded monthly) and the money will grow to $16,122. Invest $263.34 at 12 percent every month for 48 months and at the end of the period you will have the same amount of money, $16,122. The only time something can be saved by paying cash is when the interest rate paid on the loan exceeds the interest that can be earned if those funds are used elsewhere.

The Circular Flow—The Wheel of Wealth

Economic activity is circular. Consumers buy goods with the incomes they earn by furnishing land, labor, and capital to the business firms that produce the goods they buy. The dollars that households spend come back to them in the form of income from selling productive factors.

Figure 2-1 illustrates the circular flow. The flows from households to firms and from firms to households are regulated by two markets: the market for goods and services and the market for the service flows from the factors of production. The circular flow consists of two circles. The outer circle shows the physical flows of goods and services and of productive factors. The inner circle shows the flows of money expenditures on goods and services and on productive factors. The physical flows and the money flows move in opposite directions. When households buy goods and services, physical goods flow to the households, but the sales receipts flow to the business sector. When workers supply labor to business firms, productive factors flow to the business sector, but the wage income flows to the household sector.

There are two fundamental pairs of supply and demand transactions in the circular flow: (1) supply and demand for consumer goods are mediated in the various markets for consumer goods; (2) supply and demand for factors of production are mediated by the various markets for resources—land, labor, and capital. Ignored in the Figure 2-1 simple circular flow are the transactions among business firms. These are of enormous magnitude. A more accurate wheel of wealth would include two wheels: the one in Figure 2-1 and a larger one within the business sector itself.

The circular-flow diagram helps us see how output and input decisions involving millions of consumers, hundreds of thousands of producers, and millions of owners of resources fit together. What coordinates the supplies and demands of all these economic agents is the price system. Each good, service, or resource has a price. Shortages of goods or of factors cause prices to rise; surpluses cause prices to fall. The predictable responses of consumers and producers to price changes are the laws of supply and demand.

How can we be sure that there is a price that will coordinate the supply and demand for a particular good? A more difficult question is: How can we be sure that there is a system of prices that will coordinate the supplies and demands for everything together? The first question is answered in *partial-equilibrium* economics, where each market is studied in isolation. The second question is answered in *general-equilibrium* economics, where the reaction of one market to another is taken into consideration. We will answer the first question in this chapter. A tentative answer to the second question will be given later in this book, but a complete analysis is the subject matter of advanced price theory.

THE LAWS OF SUPPLY AND DEMAND

Equilibrium of Supply and Demand

Demand and supply can be thought of in terms of stocks or flows. In monetary economics, economists typically use the demand for and supply of money as a stock. In price theory, because it deals with production and consumption, economists typically consider the demand for or supply of goods and services per unit of time. Unless otherwise specified, therefore, we shall refer to demand and supply as flow variables.

FIGURE 2-2 Quantity Demanded as a Function of Price

The demand curve $D(p)$ shows that quantity demanded increases at a lower price, *ceteris paribus*. The supply curve $S(p)$ shows that quantity supplied increases at a higher price, *ceteris paribus*. The equilibrium is determined where $D(p) = S(p)$. There is excess supply if the price exceeds the equilibrium price; there is excess demand if the price falls short of the equilibrium price.

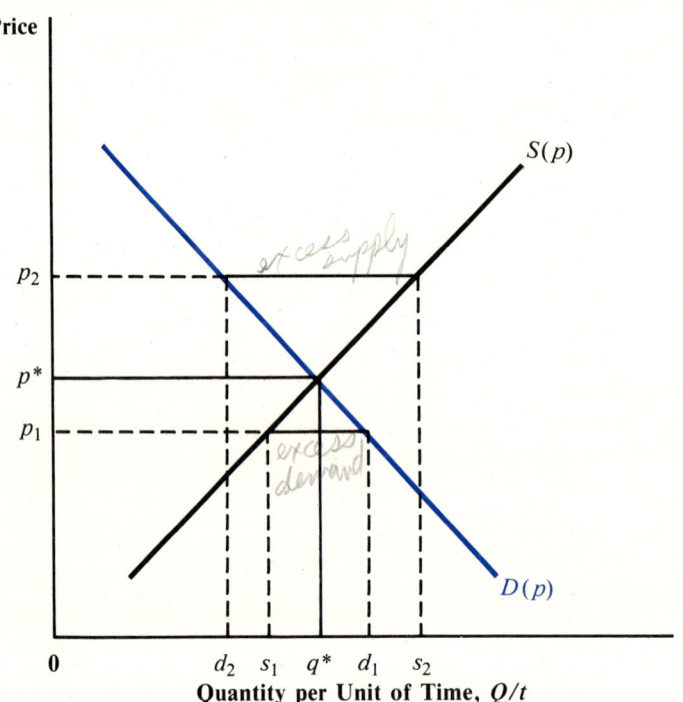

A **price taker** is a buyer whose purchases are not large enough to affect the price or a seller who is unable to control the price of the goods sold.

In this chapter, we make the assumption of perfect competition, which means that each buyer or seller is a **price taker**. Buyers and sellers will tend to be price takers when there are many competing buyers and sellers of a homogeneous product. The more competition any buyer (or seller) faces, the less control he or she has over the price paid or charged.

The Conditions of Demand

The **demand curve** for a product or service shows how quantity demanded varies with the price of the product, holding other factors constant.

Figure 2–2 shows the **demand curve** $D(p)$ for some product per unit of time as a function of the price (p) of the product itself. When the price falls, the quantity demanded of the good rises *holding the conditions affecting the demand curve constant*. The term *ceteris paribus* means "holding all other factors constant." These *ceteris-paribus* conditions (described in detail later) are the prices of other goods, income, tastes, and the size of the underlying population. The *law of demand* states that the demand curve $D(p)$ is downward-sloping. For the moment, we can regard the law of demand as simply an empirical generalization. Examples of its workings are: bumper crops causing food prices to fall, droughts causing food prices to rise, producers who desire increased sales lowering prices, and using bread as animal feed (representing part of the increase in quantity demanded) in Tunisia under heavy government subsidies.

According to the *law of demand*, a drop in the price of a good will tend to raise its quantity demanded when all other demand-affecting factors are held constant.

The Conditions of Supply

> The **supply curve** for a product or service shows how quantity supplied varies with the price of the product, holding other factors constant.

Figure 2–2 also shows the **supply curve** $S(p)$ for the product per unit of time as a function of the product's price. When the price rises, the quantity supplied rises *holding the conditions affecting the supply curve constant*. These *ceteris-paribus* conditions are other prices, technology, and the number of producers. Generally speaking, there is a law of supply such that the supply curve $S(p)$ is upward-sloping. Higher corn prices induce farmers to plant more corn; higher oil prices induce drilling for oil in smaller and smaller fields. A possible exception to this law of supply is the supply of labor. If wages were high enough, an increase in wages could bring about a reduction in quantity supplied (see Chapter 13 for an explanation).

An increase in the price of a good tends (with important exceptions) to increase its quantity supplied when all other supply-affecting factors are held constant.

The vertical axis in Figure 2–2 measures price in dollars per unit of the good. The horizontal axis measures the quantity of the good as a flow per unit of time (Q/t). The time period may be a day, a week, a month, or any time unit. In similar figures, we will nearly always be dealing with flows and will simply label the horizontal axis "Quantity" without indicating that it is a flow variable.

> An **equilibrium price** is achieved at the point where quantity demanded equals quantity supplied in a free, competitive market.

In a competitive market, the **equilibrium price** is determined at the point where the demand curve intersects the supply curve, or when price is p^*. At this point, quantity demanded is the equilibrium quantity, q^*. If the price exceeds the equilibrium price, the quantity supplied exceeds the quantity demanded, forcing the price down. For example, if the price is p_2, there is an excess supply equal to $s_2 - d_2$. The price is forced down by the combined actions of unsatisfied sellers, some of whom are experiencing unwanted inventories. If the price is below the equilibrium price, the quantity demanded exceeds the quantity supplied, forcing the price up. For example, if the price is p_1, there is an excess demand equal to $d_1 - s_1$. The price is pushed up by the combined actions of frustrated buyers. Only the equilibrium price/quantity combination can persist indefinitely.

Comparative Statics

> **Statics** is the study of the relations of forces that produce equilibrium.

Because the equilibrium price persists, the foregoing analysis is called **statics**. The study of changes in the equilibrium price or quantity, brought about by shifts in the demand or supply curve, is an example of **comparative statics**. The use of comparative statics in economics (and other sciences) is widespread.

PRACTICE EXERCISE 2-1

Q. Illustrate supply and demand curves for a free good and for a nonexistent good.

A. A free good is one for which quantity demanded falls short of supply at a zero price. Figure A shows this situation.

A nonexistent good is one for which, at the equilibrium price, quantity is zero. The curve is drawn by starting the demand curve below the supply curve, as shown in Figure B.

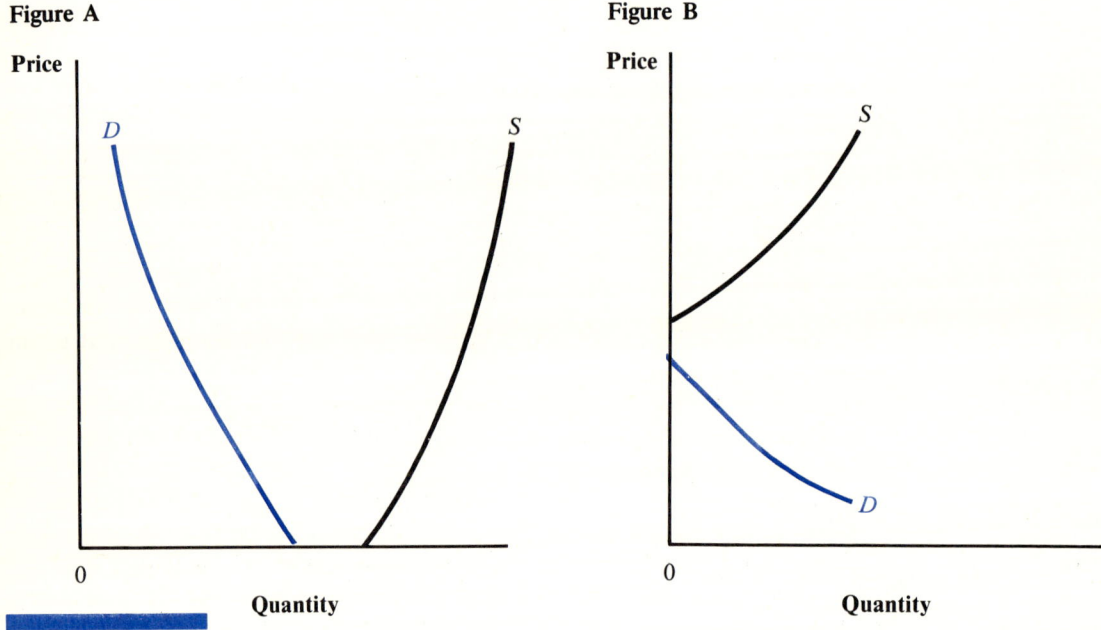

Figure A

Figure B

Comparative statics is the study of changes in equilibrium.

Economists distinguish between the phrases "changes in demand" and "changes in quantity demanded" and between the phrases "changes in supply" and "changes in quantity supplied." The phrases are defined differently in order to distinguish between situations in which quantity changes because of changes in the price of the good and situations in which changes are caused by other factors. The distinction is important because it allows us to discriminate between empirical cases in which price and quantity move together and cases in which price and quantity move in opposite directions.

Price and quantity move in the same direction when there is a change in demand. Panel A of Figure 2-3 illustrates an increase in demand, where the demand curve shifts to the right, from D to D'. We know there has been an increase in demand because at each price, quantity is larger along D' than

FIGURE 2-3   Changes in Supply and Demand

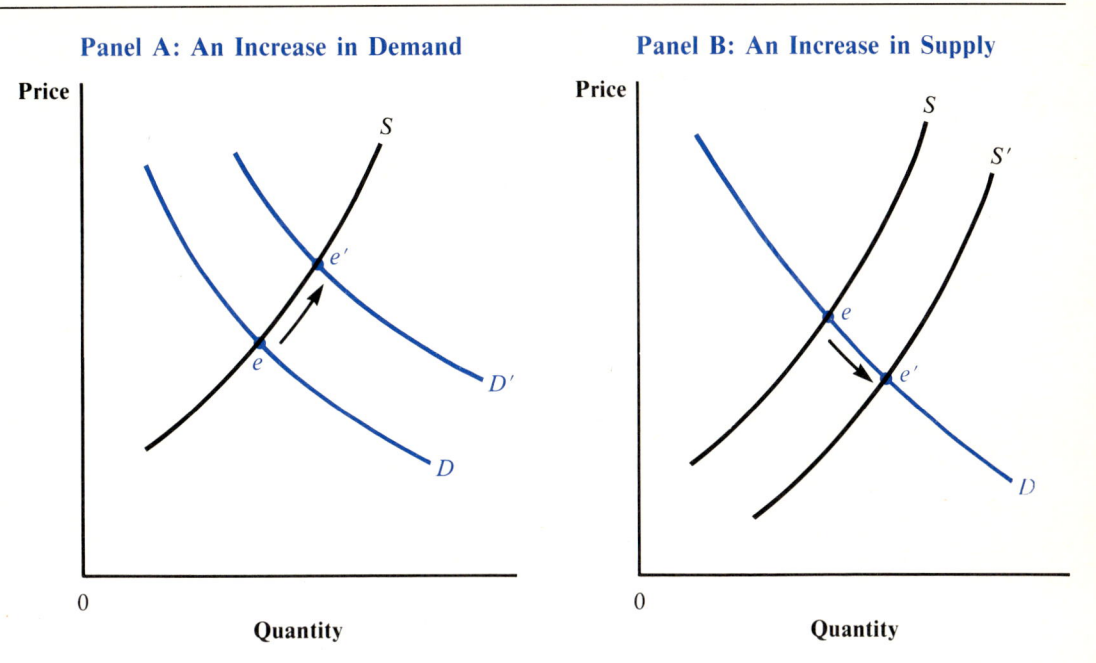

Panel A: An Increase in Demand

Panel B: An Increase in Supply

Panel A shows that an increase in demand causes an increase in price and an increase in quantity supplied. Panel B shows that an increase in supply decreases price and increases quantity demanded.

along D. The equilibrium shifts from point e to e'—moving up the supply curve. There has been an increase in quantity supplied (but no increase in supply). The situation is correctly described by saying that the increase in quantity supplied was brought about by the increase in price caused by the increase in demand.

Price and quantity move in opposite directions when there is a change in supply. Panel B of Figure 2-3 illustrates an increase in supply, where the supply curve shifts to the right, from S to S'. We know there has been an increase in supply because supply is greater at each price along S' than along S. The equilibrium point shifts down the demand curve from e to e'. There has been an increase in quantity demanded (but not an increase in demand). The situation is correctly described by saying that the increase in quantity demanded was brought about by the lower price caused by increase in supply.

If the distinction between shifts in curves and movements along curves is not heeded, only confusion can result. A famous example of such a fallacy is: "An increase in supply may not cause a price to fall because the reduction in price will cause demand to increase." What is wrong with this statement is that a reduction in price resulting from an increase in supply does not cause a price-raising increase in demand.

PRACTICE EXERCISE 2-2

Q. Suppose you observed that the price of a good fell but its quantity remained the same. How would you explain that situation?

A. There are three possible answers. The most likely case is shown in Figure C. The quantity will not change and the price will fall if there is a simultaneous decrease in demand (to D') and an increase in supply (to S') of equal but offsetting amounts. A less likely case occurs if the supply curve is perfectly vertical but the demand curve shifts to the left (a decrease in demand). The least likely case occurs when the demand curve is perfectly vertical but the supply curve shifts to the right (an increase in supply).

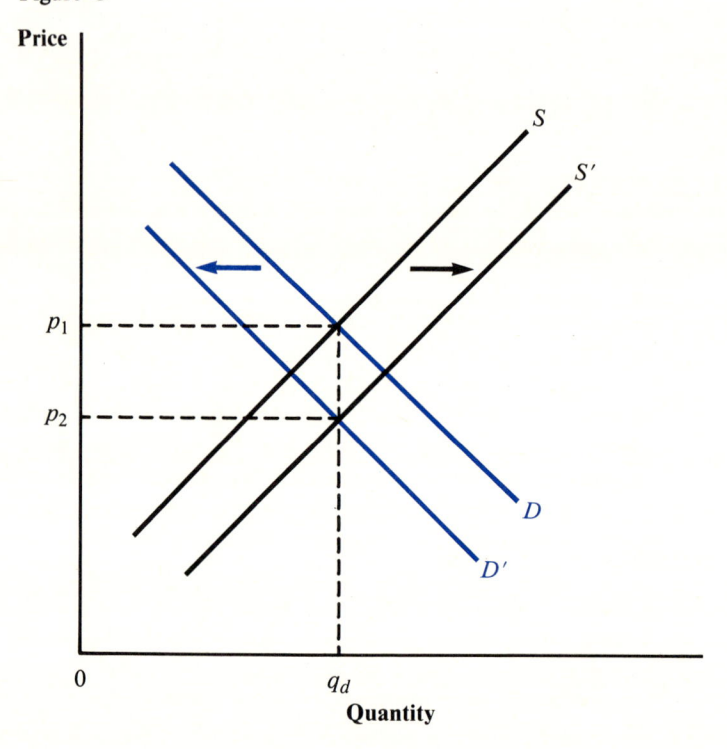

Figure C

There are numerous examples of the effects of changes in demand and changes in supply. Examples of changes in supply include the effects of bumper crops on prices (lowering prices), the lower prices of perishable vegetables at harvest times, the higher price of orange juice when a freeze hits the Florida orange crop, and higher oil prices caused by the political/economic revolution in Iran. Examples of changes in demand include seasonal pricing of clothing, post-Christmas department-store sales, a reduction

EXAMPLE 2–2   The Demand for Beef

A good example of the effects of a decrease in the demand for a product is what happened to beef between 1975 and 1984. When some researchers claimed that chicken and fish were healthier protein sources than beef, the popularity of beef suffered greatly. The allegation that beef is unhealthy was unproven, but what mattered was that people believed it.

When the demand for a commodity drops, the price should fall. From 1975 to 1984, the price of beef (on the farm) fell from $0.62 per pound to $0.57 per pound (in 1984 dollars). Over the same period, per-capita beef consumption declined from 119 pounds to 106 pounds per year. This example vividly illustrates how the price and quantity of a product can move in the same direction when demand changes. When the demand for beef fell, the price of beef also fell.

Source: *Statistical Abstract of the United States, 1986*, 106th ed., pp. 121, 477, 667.

---

in the demand for beef because of allegations that chicken and fish are healthier (see Example 2–2), and higher housing prices in areas of dense population (such as Los Angeles) than in areas of scattered population. (Suggestion: to test your understanding of these distinctions, try graphing all the above cases of changes in demand and changes in supply.)

The Algebra of Supply and Demand

Graphs are not the only way to study economics. Indeed, in complicated problems, mathematical equations are often not only necessary but far more illuminating. The basic method of solving for an equilibrium price and quantity is shown in the following example:

$$D(p) = 100 - 2p. \tag{4}$$

$$S(p) = 40 + p. \tag{5}$$

$$100 - 2p = 40 + p. \tag{6}$$

Equation (4) is the demand curve for some good. It shows that every $1 increase in the price of some good lowers quantity demanded by 2 units. Equation (5), for the supply curve, shows that every $1 increase in the price of this good raises quantity supplied by 1 unit. Equation (6) is the equilibrium condition that $D(p) = S(p)$ and determines the only price for which this is true. Solving Equation (6) yields the equilibrium price of $p^* = \$20$. If you

FIGURE 2-4 Deriving the Excess-Demand Curve

Panel A: Standard Demand and Supply Curves

Panel B: The Excess-Demand Curve

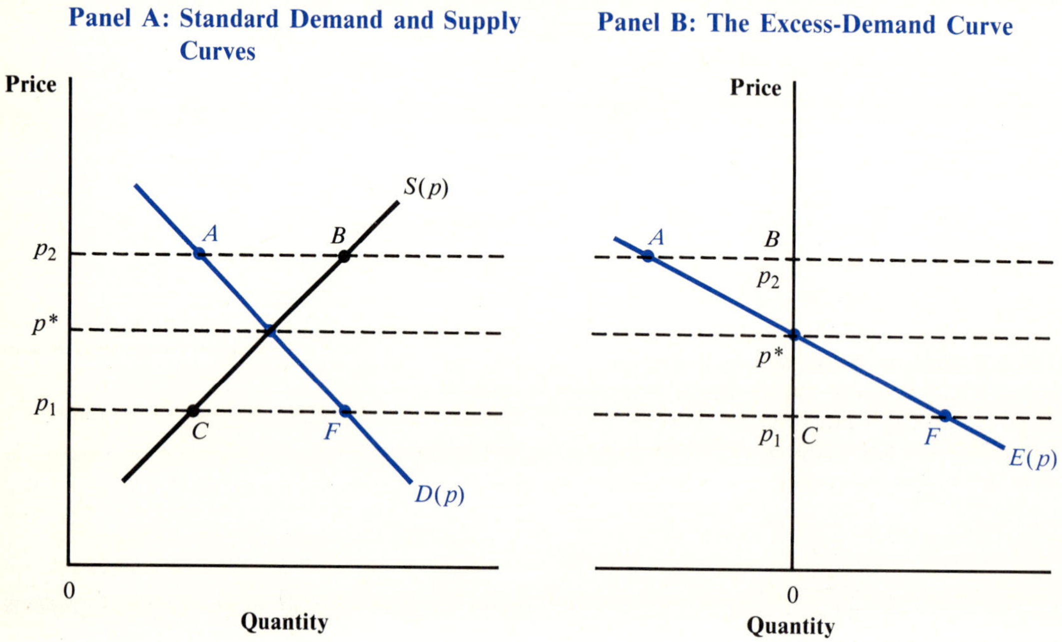

Panel A shows standard demand and supply curves. Panel B measures the algebraic difference $E(p) = D(p) - S(p)$, called the *excess-demand curve*. A key feature of stability is that $E(p)$ is negatively sloped through the equilibrium price p^*.

substitute $20 for p in Equation (4) or (5), you obtain the equilibrium quantity, q^*:

$$q^* = D(p^*) = 100 - 2(20) = 60.$$
$$q^* = S(p^*) = 40 + 20 = 60. \tag{7}$$

This example suggests a general method for solving linear demand and supply curves. Now we can represent the demand and supply curves as:

$$D(p) = A - Bp. \tag{8}$$
$$S(p) = G + Hp. \tag{9}$$

The letters A, B, G, and H, are given positive constants. The equilibrium price and quantity are solved by

$$A - Bp^* = G + Hp^*. \tag{10}$$
$$q^* = D(p^*) = S(p^*). \tag{11}$$

Solving yields

$$p^* = \frac{A - G}{B + H} \quad (12)$$

Substituting Equation (12) into (8) or (9) yields

$$q^* = \frac{AH + BG}{B + H} \quad (13)$$

Parallel shifts in the demand and supply curves occur when the parameters A and G change. A simple increase in demand would be represented by an increase in A. From Equations (12) and (13), an increase in A must increase p^* and q^*. A simple increase in supply is represented by an increase in the parameter G. The equations show that an increase in G must lower p^* [note that G has a negative coefficient in (12)] and raise q^* [note that BG in the numerator of (13) would increase]. The conclusions of the algebra and the geometry in Figure 2-3 coincide.

The alert reader will have noticed that we have written q as the dependent variable and p as the independent variable in our algebraic equations. This makes economic sense under the assumption that buyers and sellers are price takers. Generally speaking, in mathematics, dependent variables are put on the vertical axis of a graph, and independent variables on the horizontal axis. The same should be done in economics. However, in economics we do the opposite in the case of supply and demand curves, the reason being historical precedent. Alfred Marshall, who forged many of the tools used in partial-equilibrium economics, put quantity on the horizontal axis and price on the vertical axis.

EQUILIBRIUM-PRICE STABILITY

The equilibrium price coordinates disparate supply and demand decisions. An equilibrium price is said to be stable if any perturbation away from that price is restored by market forces. In Figure 2-2, the equilibrium price was stable because when price was above or below p^*, excess supplies or demands pushed the price back to the equilibrium. Because stability is so important to the workability of a competitive market, it is important to ask: What is the condition for stability?

Let us begin with the **excess-demand curve**. Panel A of Figure 2-4 shows standard supply and demand curves. Panel B illustrates the derivation of an excess-demand curve. When the price is above the equilibrium price, p^*, quantities on the excess-demand curve $E(p)$ are negative, meaning that there is absolute excess supply. When the price is less than p^*, quantities along $E(p)$ are positive, meaning that there is absolute excess demand. The critical feature for stability is that the excess-demand curve is negatively sloped through the equilibrium price. For example, when price is p_1, price rises

The **excess-demand curve** shows the algebraic difference between quantity demanded and quantity supplied at each price; it is $E(p) = D(p) - S(p)$.

FIGURE 2-5 An Example of Instability

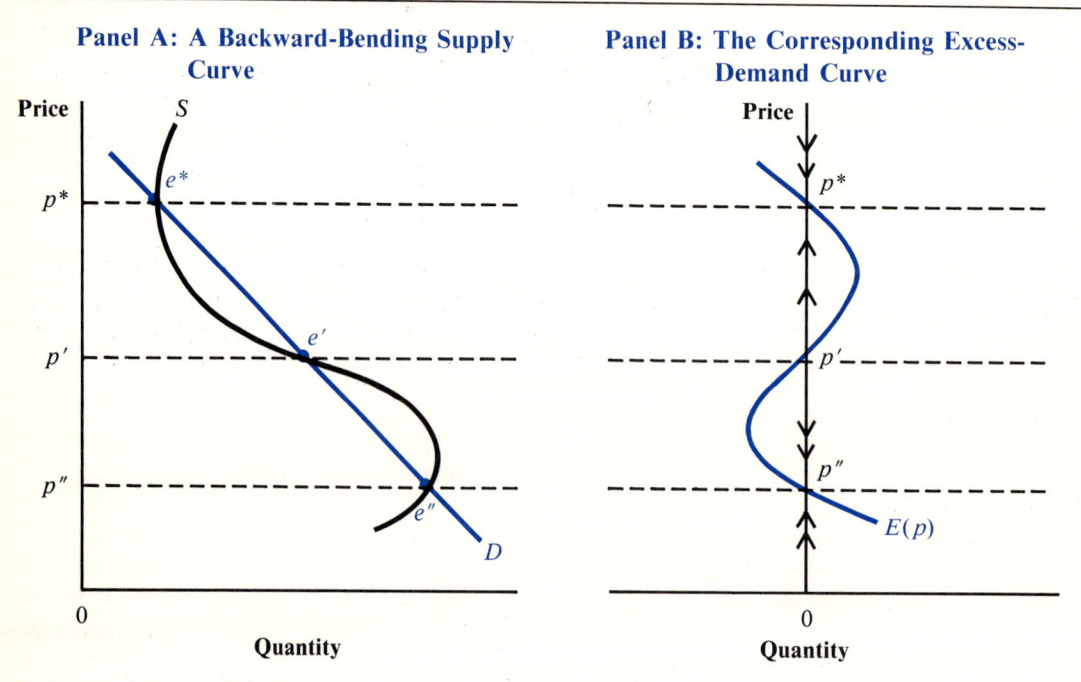

Panel A: A Backward-Bending Supply Curve

Panel B: The Corresponding Excess-Demand Curve

If the supply curve is backward-bending, as in Panel A, there can be several equilibrium prices. Panel B shows the corresponding excess-demand curve. The excess-demand curve $E(p)$ is upward-sloping through the equilibrium price p' and downward-sloping through the other equilibrium prices p'' and p^*. Only the equilibrium price p' is unstable.

toward p^* because $E(p)$ is greater than zero; when price is p_2, price falls toward p^* because $E(p)$ is less than zero.

An example of instability is shown in Figure 2–5. In Panel A, the supply curve, S, is backward-bending. It first rises and then falls as the price of the good increases. As mentioned earlier, there might be a backward-bending supply curve for labor (studied in detail later in this book). We have made the supply curve S-shaped. The demand curve, D, intersects the supply curve in three places, so that there are three equilibrium points, e^*, e', and e''. Panel B shows the corresponding excess-demand curve. The equilibrium prices p^* and p'' are stable, because $E(p)$ is negatively sloped through those prices, but the equilibrium price p' is unstable because at that point $E(p)$ is positively sloped. When the price is slightly above p', $E(p)$ is positive, so the price rises towards p^*; when the price is slightly below p', $E(p)$ is negative, so the price falls towards p''. If the $E(p)$ curve is positively sloped, an increase in price raises excess demand; thus, when excess demand is positive, an increase in price makes excess demand even larger.

An equilibrium price is stable if at that price the excess-demand curve is negatively sloped; an equilibrium price is unstable if at that point the excess-demand curve is positively sloped.

FIGURE 2-6 Effects of an Excise Tax

A per-unit tax of t dollars imposed on the seller shifts the supply curve facing consumers up from S to S' so that sellers may recoup their tax payments to the government. The price paid by consumers increases from p^* to p_c; the price received by producers falls from p^* to p_b.

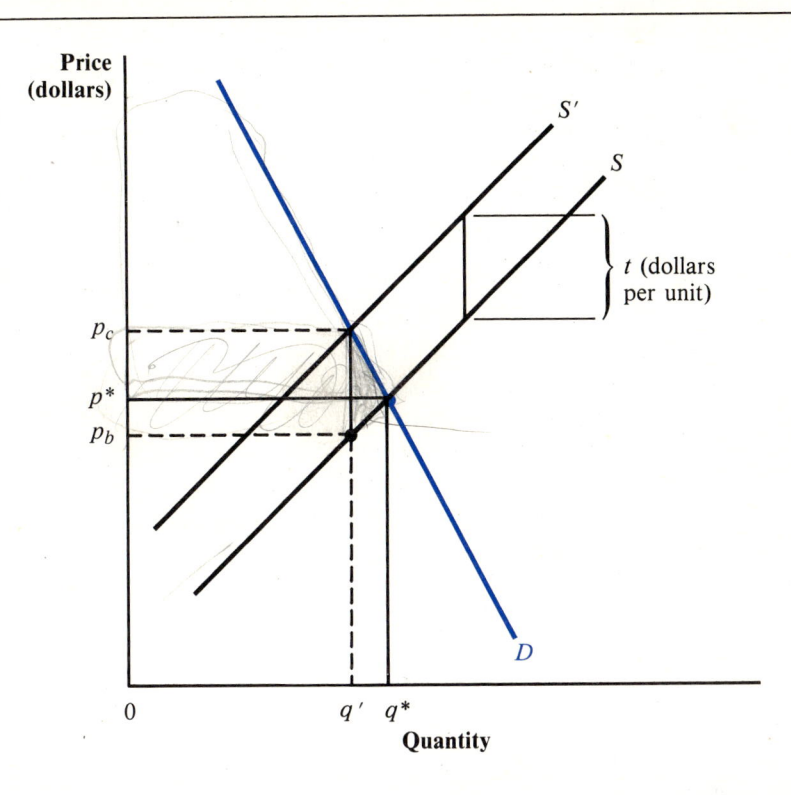

APPLICATIONS

The Effects of Excise Taxes

Excise taxes are taxes on specific goods and services. Local, state, and federal governments impose excise taxes on a variety of goods and services, including tobacco, alcohol, gasoline, and some foreign imports. Supply-and-demand analysis can be used to determine how such a tax affects consumers and producers.

Figure 2–6 shows the supply curve, S, and the demand curve, D, before the tax is imposed. The equilibrium price and quantity are p^* and q^*. Suppose sellers are now required to pay t dollars in tax per unit sold. What is the effect? The supply curve S can be interpreted as showing what prices sellers require in order to supply different quantities. Because the tax does not affect the conditions of supply postulated in the supply curve, S, sellers must still be paid the price along that supply curve after the tax of t dollars per unit has been paid. The supply curve for producers is still the same, but the supply curve facing consumers must shift up by exactly t dollars in order for sellers to remain on their original supply curve after paying the tax. Thus

PRACTICE EXERCISE 2-3

Q. Demand and supply curves show quantity as a function of price. It is often more convenient to work with inverse demand or supply curves, which show price as a function of quantity. The inverse supply and demand curves show the demand and supply prices for any particular quantity. Given the demand and supply curves $D(p) = 100 - 2p$ and $S(p) = 40 + p$, what are the inverse demand and supply curves?

A. The inverse demand curve is $p = 50 - 0.5q_d$. The inverse supply curve is $p = q_s + 40$. The inverse curves are obtained by solving $D(p) = q_d$ and $S(p) = q_s$ for p.

---

the supply curve facing consumers is S'. The conditions affecting the demand curve for the product are not changed by the tax, so the demand curve remains at D. As long as buyers are charged the same price (including the tax), the quantity demanded will remain the same. The equilibrium price paid by consumers will increase from p^* to p_c and the equilibrium price received by producers will fall to p_b.

The difference between the original price, p^*, and the prices paid by the consumers or received by the producer indicates the tax burden. The burden of the tax on consumers is $p_c - p^*$. The burden of the tax on producers is $p^* - p_b$. The graph suggests that the consumer pays a larger fraction of the tax. The reason is that we have assumed that the demand curve is steeper in the downward direction than the supply curve is in the upward direction. In other words, quantity supplied is more responsive to price than quantity demanded. Because consumers are less sensitive to price changes in this particular instance, they will end up paying a higher share of the tax than producers. On the other hand, if producers were less responsive to price than consumers, the opposite conclusion would follow. When there is a tax, a wedge is driven between the price consumers pay and the price producers receive. Under these circumstances, and in the study of topics such as joint products, it is useful to distinguish between the **demand price** and the **supply price**. For example, in Figure 2-6, at the quantity q', the demand price is p_c and the supply price is p_b.

The **demand price**—sometimes called the *demand reservation price*—is the maximum price buyers are willing to pay for an extra unit of the good.

The **supply price**—sometimes called the *supply reservation price*—is the minimum price sellers are willing to accept for an extra unit of the good.

Joint Products*

So far we have considered a simple market in which demand and supply are nonjoint. But there are both joint demands and joint supplies. An example of joint demand would be a knife that consists of two parts, a blade and a handle, in fixed proportions. The demand price for the knife must cover the

---

* This section is optional.

APPLICATIONS

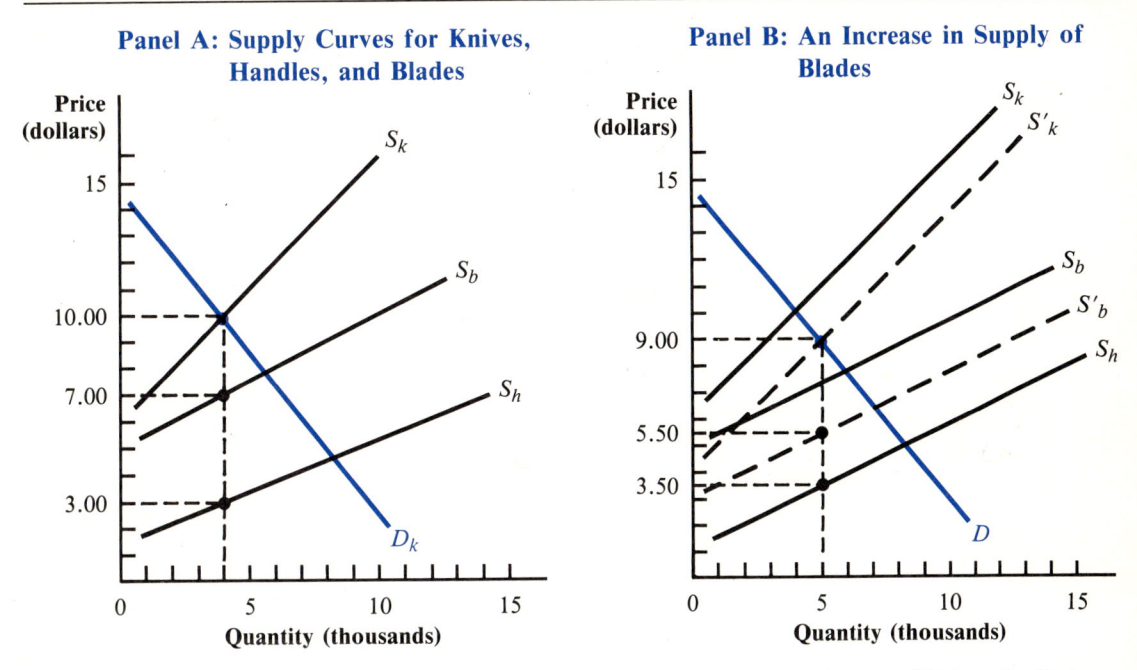

FIGURE 2-7 Joint Demand for Two-Part Knives

Panel A: Supply Curves for Knives, Handles, and Blades

Panel B: An Increase in Supply of Blades

Panel A shows that the separate supply curves for blades, S_b, and handles, S_h, are added vertically to obtain the supply curve for knives, S_k. Where the demand curve for knives, D_k, intersects the supply curve determines the equilibrium prices for knives, blades, and handles. The dotted lines in Panel B show that an increase in the supply of blades decreases the prices of blades and knives from $7 to $5.50 but increases the price of handles from $3 to $3.50.

separate supply prices of blades and handles. An example of joint supply would be mutton and wool, both derived from sheep. The supply price for sheep must be broken down into the separate demand prices for each of the products.

Joint Demand

Figure 2-7 shows how the prices of handles and blades are derived from the demand for knives. Panel A shows equilibrium in the market for knives. It assumes that one knife, k, equals one blade, b, plus one handle, h, that the cost of assembling blades and handles is negligible or zero and that blades and handles are used only in the production of knives. It should be clear that

$$p_k = p_b + p_h. \tag{14}$$

There are separate supply curves for blades and handles. The supply curves S_b and S_h are added vertically because the supply price of knives is the sum of the supply prices of blades and handles. The point at which the supply curve S_k intersects the demand curve D_k determines the equilibrium prices

FIGURE 2-8   Joint Supply of Sheep Products: Wool and Mutton

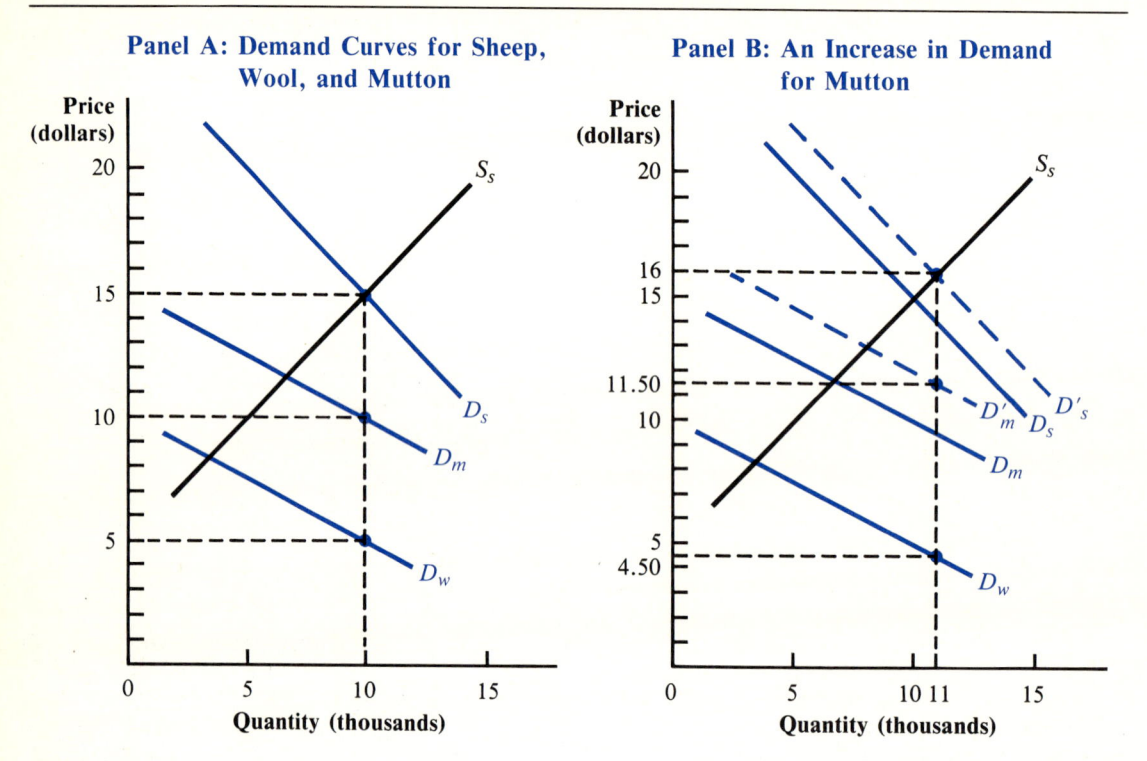

Panel A: Demand Curves for Sheep, Wool, and Mutton

Panel B: An Increase in Demand for Mutton

Panel A shows that the demand curves for wool, D_w, and mutton, D_m, are added vertically to obtain the demand curve for sheep, D_s. Panel B shows what happens if the demand curve for mutton increases to D'_m. The demand for sheep increases to D'_s; the price of wool falls from $5 to $4.50 and the price of mutton rises from $10 to $11.50.

of knives, blades, and handles—$10, $7, and $3, respectively. Panel B shows the effect of an increase in the supply of blades. The dashed lines S'_b and S'_k are the new supply curves for blades and knives. As the price of blades falls to $5.50, the price of knives falls to $9, and the price of handles rises to $3.50. The reason for the increase in the price of handles is that the supply conditions for handles have not changed, and a higher price is needed to coax out more handles to satisfy the increase in quantity demanded for knives.

Joint Supply

Now consider the case of wool and mutton—both products of sheep production. What is the effect of an increase in the price of beef on the price of wool? Supply-and-demand analysis allows us to generate an answer to this

APPLICATIONS

question. Panel A of Figure 2-8 shows the demand curves for sheep, s, mutton, m, and wool, w. It assumes that one sheep provides one unit of wool and one unit of mutton. The equilibrium price of one sheep, $15, equals the sum of the prices of wool, $5, and mutton, $10; that is,

$$p_s = p_w + p_m. \tag{15}$$

The demand prices for wool and mutton are added vertically to obtain the demand price for sheep. The equilibrium prices of sheep, wool, and mutton are determined where the supply curve for sheep, S_s, intersects the demand curve for sheep, D_s.

The effects of a change in the demand for mutton are shown by the dashed lines in Panel B. (For example, an increase in the price of beef might increase the demand for mutton.) The demand curve for mutton shifts to D'_m and the derived demand for sheep shifts to D'_s. As the price of a sheep rises to $16, the price of a unit of mutton rises to $11.50, and the price of a unit of wool falls to $4.50. With more sheep produced, to accommodate the increase in demand for mutton, the price of wool must fall because no increase in demand for wool has been registered—only an increase in quantity demanded.

Price Ceilings and Floors

Strong empirical support for the predictions of a competitive market is found in the effects of government price ceilings and floors. A *price ceiling* is an upper limit imposed on the price of a product, usually to contain inflation. A *price floor* is a lower limit imposed on the price of a product, usually to improve the incomes of sellers.

The supply curves for jointly demanded products are added vertically to obtain the supply curve for the complex product. The demand curves for jointly supplied products are added vertically to obtain the demand curve for the product generating the joint supply.

Figure 2-9 shows the results of an effective price ceiling. The ceiling price p_c is less than the equilibrium price p^*. This situation creates an excess demand for the good in the amount of $q_d - q_s$, or the distance ab. Because the price cannot increase, there is a shortage of ab units of the good per unit of time. Frustrated buyers and opportunistic sellers might (and often do) go to a black market, where the good is traded illegally. The incentive to engage in black marketing arises because the demand price, p_d, at point c, exceeds the supply price, p_c, at point a. Thus, there is either a shortage or a black market or both.

From the Edict of Diocletian in 301 A.D. to President Nixon's price-

FIGURE 2-9   Effects of a Price Ceiling

A price ceiling, p_c, causes a shortage of *ab* units per time period or a black market or both.

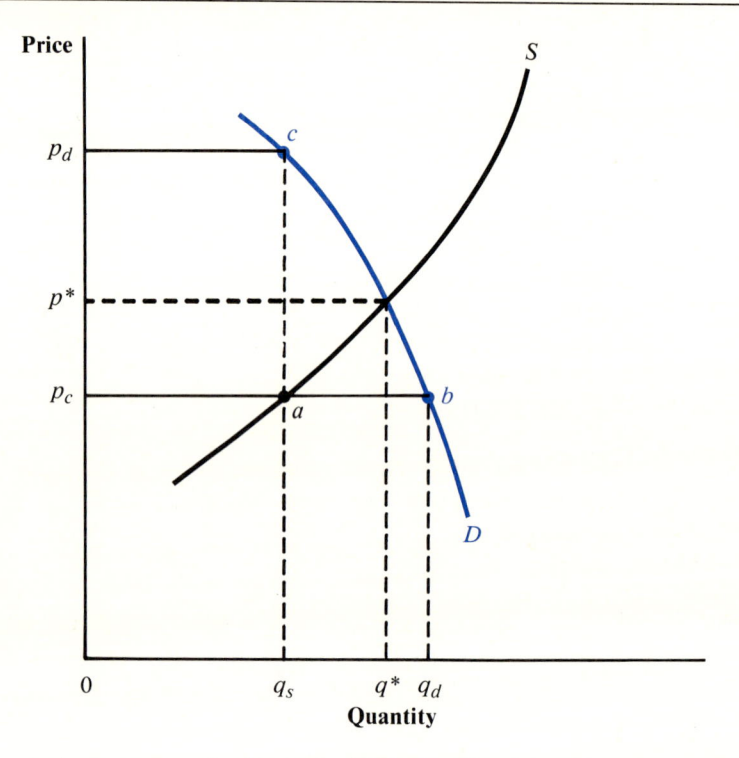

control program in the early 1970s (ending in 1974), the predicted effects of price controls are seen. Of the Edict of Diocletian, historian Will Durant remarked:[3]

> Its failure was rapid and complete. Tradesmen concealed their commodities, scarcities became more acute than before, Diocletian himself was accused of conniving at a rise in prices, riots occurred, and the Edict had to be relaxed to restore production and distribution.

The consequences of the Nixon price controls were not as dramatic, but shortages still occurred. Most Americans recall the gas lines of early 1974, produced by the combination of an Arab oil embargo and a price ceiling on gasoline. Without the price ceiling, there would have been no gas "shortage," as witnessed by the situation in Germany, where the price of gas was allowed to reach its equilibrium level. But shortages of many commodities—not just of gasoline—occurred. Charles Schultze, President Johnson's Chairman of the Council of Economic Advisers, has pointed out that there were also shortages of many types of industrial products—the small nuts and bolts that without price controls appeared to be in the right place at the right time.[4]

---

3. Will Durant, *Caesar and Christ*, (New York: Simon and Schuster, 1944), p. 643.
4. Charles Schultze, "Why Price Controls Don't Work," *Wall Street Journal*, February 27, 1980.

APPLICATIONS

FIGURE 2-10   **Effects of a Price Floor**

A price floor, p_f, produces a surplus of *ab* units per time period because quantity supplied exceeds quantity demanded at that price.

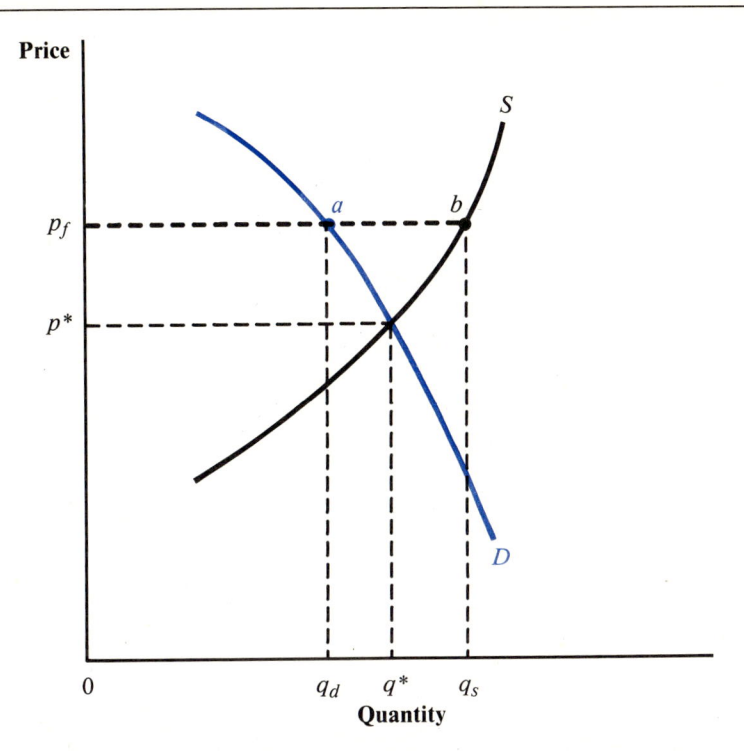

The evidence produced by price-ceiling analysis gives remarkable testimony to the coordinating function of equilibrium prices. The number of goods and services is vast. Until their prices are artificially manipulated, we often take for granted the degree of coordination required to run an economy smoothly. When you think of the myriad of products and services that go into the production of a pencil, a candy bar, or a jet airplane, it is no small matter to make sure that everything fits together in the right quantities, at the right times, and in the right places.

Figure 2–10 shows the effects of price floors. The two best examples of setting price floors are minimum-wage laws and government price supports of agricultural goods. The price floor, p_f, is above the equilibrium price p^* and produces an excess supply of $q_s - q_d$, or the distance *ab*. With agricultural price supports, the government stands ready to purchase the good at the official price floor. A surplus of *ab* units of a product is generated per unit of time. As evidenced by price supports of milk and cheese, the government over time accumulates stocks of the supported good.

With minimum-wage laws, the supply and demand curves are for some type of unskilled labor; the surplus *ab* is interpreted as being the excess number of people willing to work at the minimum wage (at point *a*) over the number of available jobs (at point *b*). Because younger workers tend to be more unskilled than older workers, some evidence for this effect is shown by the higher unemployment rates among teenagers than among adults.

SUMMARY

1. A market is an institution through which people regularly exchange goods and services with the protection of property rights by the state.

2. A stock variable is a quantity existing at a moment in time; a flow variable is a quantity defined over an interval of time. The present value of a future sum of money is what has to be invested at today's interest rates to generate that future sum of money; it is the most one would pay for an asset yielding future sums of money.

3. The demand curve shows how quantity demanded varies with the price of the product or service, holding other prices, income, and tastes constant; it is downward-sloping. The supply curve shows how quantity supplied varies with the price of the product or service, holding other prices and technology constant; the supply curve is usually upward-sloping. The equilibrium price is found where quantity demanded equals quantity supplied.

4. The equilibrium price is stable if the excess-demand curve is negatively sloped through that price; it is unstable if the excess-demand curve is positively sloped through that price.

5. The demand price is the highest price people will pay for a marginal unit of the good at the current quantity; the supply price is the lowest price firms will accept for a marginal unit of the good at the current quantity. The supply curves of jointly demanded products (such as knife blades and handles) are added vertically to obtain the supply curve for the joint product (knives). The demand curve for jointly supplied products (wool and mutton) are added vertically to obtain the demand curve for the product yielding the joint supply (sheep). Excise taxes on particular goods or services will raise the price to consumers and lower the price to producers, with the greatest burden falling on the party who is the least responsive to price.

PROBLEMS

1. Indicate the stocks and flows among the following:
   a. Today's milk consumption.
   b. The quantity of milk at your grocery store when it opened.
   c. The daily volume of sales on the New York Stock Exchange.
   d. American oil imports.
   e. The number of shares of General Motors common stock.
   f. Your income tax.

2. Assume the interest rate is 5 percent. Compute the present values of the following future values:
   a. $50 per year in perpetuity.
   b. $210 in one year and $110.25 in two years.

3. What happens to the present value of a future amount of money if the interest rate goes up? Why?

4. Many products, such as drugs, are illegal. What do you think would happen to the price of an illegal product if it were legalized?

5. Consider the following demand and supply curves:

$$D(p) = 150 - 3p; \ S(p) = 50 + 2p$$

   Answer the following questions:
   a. Calculate the excess-demand curve.
   b. What are the equilibrium price and quantity?
   c. Assume a price ceiling of $15. What is the shortage?
   d. Assume a price floor of $25. What is the surplus?

6. Consider the following demand and supply curves:

$$D(p) = 200 - 2p; \ S(p) = -40 + p$$

   Answer the following questions:
   a. Calculate the excess-demand curve.
   b. What are the equilibrium price and quantity?
   c. Assume a price ceiling of $60. What is the shortage?
   d. Assume a price floor of $100. What is the surplus?

7. Suppose the inverse supply curve for cattle is $p = 10 + q$. The inverse demand curves for beef and hides are both $p = 50 - q$. Assume that one animal provides one unit of beef and one unit of hides. (For inverse curves, see Practice Exercise 2-3.) Find:
   a. the equilibrium quantity of cattle.
   b. the equilibrium price of cattle.
   c. the equilibrium price of hides.
   d. the equilibrium price of beef.

8. Assume a restaurant meal equals one part food and one part service. The inverse demand curve for restaurant meals is $p = 100 - q$. The inverse supply curve of food to restaurants is $p_f = 10 + q$ and that for service is $p_s = 30 + q$. Find:
   a. the equilibrium quantity for restaurant meals.
   b. the equilibrium price of a meal.
   c. the price of restaurant food.
   d. the price of restaurant service.

CHAPTER 3

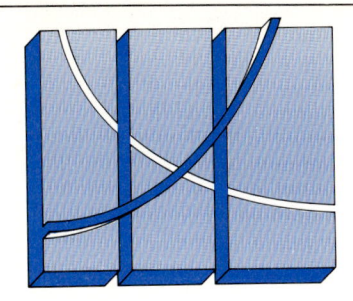

MODERN UTILITY THEORY

Scarcity arises from the mismatch between consumer wants and resources. In such a world, the consumer is a complex and bewildering creature. To begin a systematic study of economics, we must build a model of consumer behavior that can be used to (1) explain the law of demand, (2) serve as a framework for conducting empirical studies of the consumer, and (3) serve as a foundation for analyzing an economy subject to the law of scarcity. This chapter describes the preferences of a rational consumer in a world of scarcity; the next chapter imposes budgetary limitations on such a consumer. Consumer demand is the outcome of the confrontation between preferences and a consumer's budget.

THE RATIONAL CONSUMER

Does it make any sense to study rational consumer behavior? It is part of the conventional wisdom to think of the consumer as irrational—unpredictable, envious of others, easily manipulated by advertising, and driven by the desire to impress even strangers. In short, is it obvious before we start that we are about to embark on a frivolous exercise? Some people—upon learning that economists study rational consumers—assume that economics is based on an unrealistic postulate and hence is not to be taken seriously. After all, everyone knows that consumer tastes and preferences have irrational bases. Such a view represents a serious misunderstanding of what economists mean by rationality. It is true that consumer tastes often have their origins in petty jealousies, human insecurities, and even ignorance. When we say that consumer preferences are rational, we mean only that

> **EXAMPLE 3-1   Are Consumer Tastes Stable?**
>
> A crucial assumption in economics is that consumer tastes are stable. This view has been challenged by John Kenneth Galbraith, following in the footsteps of the iconoclastic Thorstein Veblen, author of *Theory of the Leisure Class*. Veblen argued that people consume in a conspicuous manner in order to make invidious comparisons with those around them. The Galbraith-Veblen argument is that the consumer is a capricious, irrational creature who is easily influenced by advertising, fads, and fancies—in marked contrast to the rather stable character posited in the axioms of utility theory. To Galbraith, consumer tastes are very much dependent on what is produced. Big companies produce goods and then, through massive advertising, persuade a rather gullible public to buy them.
>
> Most economists to not accept that argument. Why? First, because there are just too many examples of products produced by huge corporations that have failed to meet the market test. In the 1950s, Ford Motor Company produced the Edsel (named after Edsel Ford); a massive advertising campaign did not move the product. In the 1980s, Texas Instruments could not sell enough of its TI/99 personal computers even though it spent millions on advertising. While many of the computers were sold, the company miscalculated and produced too many. The TI/99 could not compete (in price) with other products in the market at that time, and the company stopped producing it.
>
> Second, other economists have an alternative theory to explain the appearance of unstable tastes. Kelvin Lancaster developed a theory of consumer behavior based on the characteristics of goods rather than the goods themselves. A car provides transportation, comfort, prestige, and performance. Different cars provide these characteristics in different proportions. As technology changes, the bundle of characteristics provided by a particular car can change dramatically. Thus, while consumers' preferences for particular characteristics may remain quite stable, their preferences for particular goods can change. Economists George Stigler and Gary Becker have argued that addiction, habitual behavior, advertising, and fashions can all be explained in terms similar to the Lancaster approach. For example, fashion trends occur because, to achieve social distinction, people must buy goods that have a certain style. Each style has a price and can be analyzed like any other commodity.
>
> ---
>
> Sources: Kelvin Lancaster, "A New Approach to Consumer Theory," *Journal of Political Economy* 74 (1966), pp. 132-57; George Stigler and Gary Becker, "De Gustibus Non Est Disputandum," *American Economic Review* 67 (1977), pp. 76-90; John K. Galbraith, *The Affluent Society* (Boston: Houghton Mifflin, 1958).

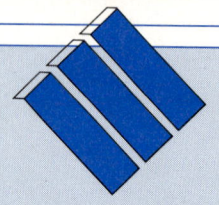

once those tastes are acquired, the consumer behaves according to certain simple axioms. This chapter describes those axioms.

We begin by describing the way consumers behave in a world of certainty and then turn to the case in which the consumer faces uncertainty.

CONSUMER BEHAVIOR IN THE CASE OF CERTAINTY

Economists regard consumers as being able to make consistent choices among the alternatives available to them. (See Example 3–1.) The precise meaning of this statement is a set of definitions and axioms from which certain empirical laws can be deduced about consumer demand. For example, the law of demand will be derived in Chapter 4.

Commodity and Service Flows

People consume goods and services over intervals of time. A person, for example, might drink 50 glasses of water per week, have the use of a Mercedes Benz for a week, live in a 20-room mansion, or consume three pounds of filet mignon per week. In what follows, we will think of commodities in terms of the services they yield per unit of time. The services of *nondurable* goods (for example, a glass of water) are identical with the good itself, so that the good perishes when it is consumed; the services of *durable* goods (for example, a TV set or a car) continue well into the future, until the good is no longer serviceable. Whatever the case, the convention of treating commodities in terms of service flows means that all goods are treated on the same basis. The price of a nondurable good in the market is the price that must be paid to consume the good for a week. The comparable price for a durable good is the equivalent rental on using the good for a week. For example, if you buy a car for $10,000, the weekly price would include interest on the $10,000, insurance, gas, oil, and depreciation for one week.

In this chapter, we will treat goods in terms of their service flows per unit of time; correspondingly, we will treat prices as the amounts people implicitly or explicitly pay per unit of time (that is, a week, a day, or a month) for the services yielded by the commodity over that unit of time.

Preferences

Think of consumers as choosing among different commodity bundles—that is, market baskets of the services of a variety of goods. As a highly simplified case, a consumer might choose between commodity bundle A—which consists of 10 glasses of milk per week, the use of a Cadillac for a week, and the use of a four-room apartment for the week—and commodity bundle B—which consists of 6 glasses of milk, use of a Rolls-Royce, use of a 50-room mansion, and 7 dinners at a French restaurant, each during one week. In real life, we choose between bundles on the basis of their costs as well as the enjoyment we get from them. Economists study choices in two ways: *modern utility theory* and *revealed-preference theory*. These theories are equivalent but are expressed in entirely different terms.

Modern utility theory considers preferences for commodities indepen-

PRACTICE EXERCISE 3-1

Q. Jones prefers bundle A to bundle B. Smith is smarter than Jones and prefers bundle B to bundle A. According to the axiom of comparison, whose preferences are correct?

A. The axiom says nothing about this situation. Both Smith and Jones are presumably correct in their rankings of the two bundles. As the saying goes, "There is no accounting for tastes." In economics, the tastes of the individual are considered basic data. The only requirement is that the consumer having a particular set of tastes pursues his or her satisfaction following the axioms of rational consumer behavior.

dently of their costs. The theory consists of assumptions about such preferences. *Revealed-preference theory* makes assumptions about the actual choices people make. Because it has been shown that the revealed-preference approach also leads to the concept of a utility function, we shall here develop modern utility theory and provide a briefer account of the revealed-preference approach in Chapter 4.

In modern utility theory, the consumer is said to *prefer* bundle A to bundle B if bundle A would be chosen independent of cost or budgetary considerations. The consumer is said to be *indifferent* between bundles A and B if the consumer literally does not care whether A or B is consumed.

The Axioms of Consumer Behavior in the Case of Certainty

Modern utility theory is based on five axioms, or assumptions, regarding the preferences of a prototype of the rational consumer.

The Axiom of Comparison

The theory of consumer behavior is not intended to address the problem of ignorance and learning. Thus, we wish to rule out the case where the consumer is confounded or confused about what to do when confronted with stating a preference between two bundles. The consumer must be decisive rather than confused.

The *axiom of comparison* is: When confronted by any two commodity bundles A and B, the consumer can always say whether he or she prefers A to B, prefers B to A, or is indifferent between A and B. The consumer cannot be indecisive.

The Axiom of Nonsatiation

In any given period of time (for example, a week) a person can be satiated with some particular commodity such as hot dogs or hamburgers. After eating 60 hot dogs in a week, one might prefer not to consume another hot dog, even if it were free. But while we may become satiated with some goods, we most certainly cannot become satiated in all goods. You might be perfectly content with having six different types of luxury cars and not want another, whatever its cost; but you might still want a jet airplane, a yacht, a villa overlooking the Mediterranean, or a certain designer's clothes. In other words, the human imagination is so great that people can always think of other things they would like to have even when a small range of desires have been satisfied. Perfect bliss is impossible for practical purposes. Oil-rich sheiks have been known to purchase one Boeing 747 for themselves and another just to carry their luggage! In the world of commodities, there is always another mountain to climb. When the consumer is not satiated with the goods under consideration, this assumption is often stated as "More is better."

The *axiom of nonsatiation* is: For any given commodity bundle A, there is always another bundle B that the consumer prefers to A.

The Axiom of Transitivity

There is no doubt that people are sometimes inconsistent. Human beings make errors. A person might say: "I prefer having $100 to owning a bicycle, and I prefer owning a bicycle to owning a stereo radio." A moment later, the person might indicate a preference for the radio over the $100! If you pointed out to this consumer that a moment earlier $100 was ranked first and the radio third, the consumer would alter either the original rankings or the later ones. Because we are interested in developing a theory that works over long rather than short periods and is incapable of dealing with learning situations, we will assume that consumers' preferences are transitive, or consistent, among any three commodity bundles. If you prefer $100 to a bicycle and a bicycle to a radio, you must prefer $100 to the radio. The assumption holds not only for simple commodity bundles consisting of only two or three goods, but also for extremely complicated bundles consisting of many goods. Of course, with extremely complicated commodity bundles it may be easy to trick a consumer into an inconsistent choice simply because it is difficult to distinguish between the bundles. But given understanding, the consumer must be consistent. Experimental studies show that consistency tends to improve with the age of the consumer.[1]

---

1. See Arnold A. Weinstein, "Transitivity of Preference: A Comparison Among Age Groups," *Journal of Political Economy,* March/April 1968, p. 310.

PRACTICE EXERCISE 3-2

Q. Draw your own indifference curve between quarters and half-dollars.

A. A representative indifference curve should be a straight line with a marginal rate of substitution of two quarters for one half-dollar. In terms of goods, one can purchase the same bundle with two quarters as with one half-dollar. A bundle of goods is indifferent to itself for every individual, so the indifference curve between quarters and half-dollars should be a straight line. The two goods are perfect substitutes.

The *axiom of transitivity* is: For any three commodity bundles A, B, and C, if the consumer prefers bundle A to bundle B and prefers bundle B to bundle C, the consumer must prefer bundle A to bundle C. Similarly, if the consumer is indifferent between bundles A and B as well as between bundles B and C, the consumer must also be indifferent between bundles A and C.

The Axiom of Substitution

What motivates consumers is not the goods they purchase but the characteristics those goods possess for satisfying a whole host of human wants such as hunger, thirst, shelter, transportation, comfort, and the desire to be envied. In any economy there is usually a vast variety of goods that will satisfy each of these types of wants.[2] In addition, people are often willing to substitute the satisfaction of part of one type of want (for example, shelter) for a quantity of some other type (for example, transportation). A consumer will, therefore, almost always be willing to substitute a little bit of one commodity for a sufficient amount of another. There is only one exception to this rule: the case in which the substitution pushes the consumer beyond the minimum quantity of a particular good that may be needed for survival purposes (for example, so much insulin, water, or food). If survival is not at stake, the consumer can decide how much of one good he or she is just willing to substitute for one unit of another good without experiencing a gain or loss in satisfaction, or well-being. This trade-off is called the **marginal rate of substitution** (*MRS*).

The **marginal rate of substitution** (MRS_{yx}) of good Y for good X is the amount of good Y that a consumer is just willing to substitute for another unit of good X, holding the level of satisfaction constant.

The marginal rate of substitution is just another name for a consumer's personal valuation of an additional unit of a good measured in terms of some other good or money. For example, if you were willing to pay $10 at most to go to a particular movie, your marginal rate of substitution of money for that

---

2. Kelvin A. Lancaster, "A New Approach to Consumer Theory," *Journal of Political Economy*, April 1966, pp. 132–57, develops the theory of consumer behavior from the characteristics of goods rather than the goods themselves.

FIGURE 3-1 An Indifference Curve

The consumer is indifferent between commodity bundles along an indifference curve; thus consumption bundles *a, b, c,* and *d* yield the same satisfaction to the consumer. The marginal rate of substitution is the absolute slope of the curve and shows—in this case—how much bread the consumer is willing to substitute for one more pint of ale.

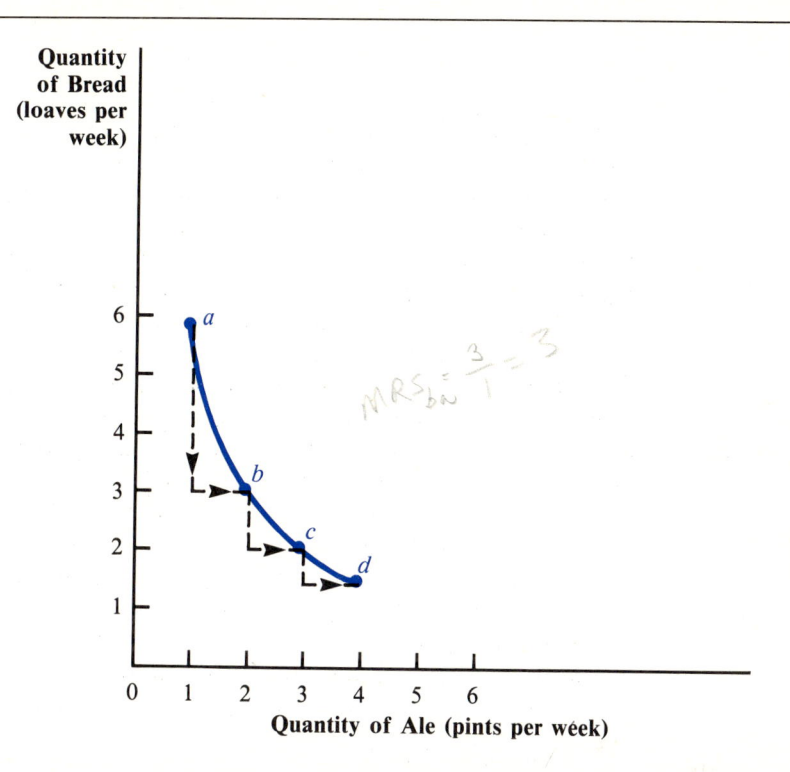

An **indifference curve** is a graph showing all the combinations or bundles of two commodities among which a particular consumer is indifferent.

movie would be $10. At any price less than $10, you would gain by going to the movie. (We will usually express the marginal rate of substitution in terms of goods other than money, but the concept is the same.)

Consider an individual who consumes only ale and bread. In Figure 3-1, the horizontal axis measures the quantity of ale consumed by the individual per week and the vertical axis measures the quantity of bread consumed per week. At point *a*, 6 loaves of bread and 1 pint of ale are consumed. Assume that at point *a*, the consumer is just willing to give up 3 loaves of bread for 1 more pint of ale. The marginal rate of substitution for bread over ale is $MRS_{ba} = 3$. This trade-off would move the consumer to point *b*, where 3 loaves of bread and 2 pints of ale are consumed. The consumer is indifferent between bundles represented by points *a* and *b*. At point *b*, the consumer can still substitute bread for ale without a loss or gain in satisfaction. The consumer may now be willing to give up only 1 loaf of bread to acquire 1 more pint of ale ($MRS_{ba} = 1$). This trade-off would put the consumer at point *c*, where 2 loaves of bread and 3 pints of ale are consumed per week. Finally, to acquire 1 more pint of ale, the consumer may be willing to give up only half a loaf of bread, moving the consumer to point *d*. The consumer in question is indifferent among bundles represented by points *a, b, c,* and *d*. A curve drawn through these points is, thus, called an **indifference curve**.

FIGURE 3–2   **The Indifference Map**

In the case of nonsatiation with both goods, more is better. Thus indifference curve U_3 represents a higher level of satisfaction than U_2; similarly, the consumer is better off on U_2 than on U_1.

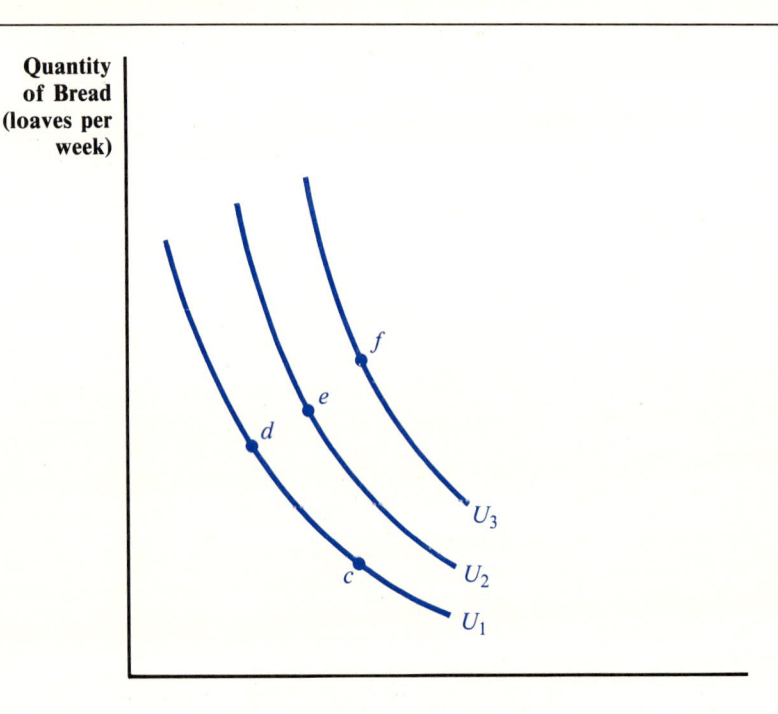

Quantity of Bread (loaves per week)

Quantity of Ale (pints per week)

The *axiom of substitution* is: For any given level of satisfaction, the consumer has an indifference curve that shows all the commodity bundles between which he or she is indifferent.

There is an infinity of indifference curves, one for each level of satisfaction. Figure 3–2 shows the same consumer at three different levels of satisfaction. If the consumer is not satiated with either commodity, "More is better." Bundle f contains more of both goods than bundle e, and e more of both goods than d. Thus, bundle f must be preferred to bundle e, and bundle e to bundle d. By the axiom of substitution, there are three distinct indifference curves going through points f, e, and d. Nonsatiation with both goods implies that higher indifference curves for any one consumer represent higher levels of satisfaction. Thus, the consumer prefers any point on U_3 to any point on U_2 or U_1. For example, bundle e on U_2 is preferred to bundle c on U_1, even though c contains more ale.

The Axiom of Convexity

The indifference curves shown in Figures 3–1 and 3–2 are convex when viewed from the origin. This convexity indicates that the consumer has a desire for variety. To understand this concept, consider Figure 3–3. Pick any

CONSUMER BEHAVIOR IN THE CASE OF CERTAINTY 43

FIGURE 3-3   **Convexity: The Desire for Variety**

Bundle *c* is a weighted average of bundles *a* and *b*. The desire for variety means that bundle *c* must be above the indifference curve passing through points *a* and *b*, so that the indifference curve is convex to the origin. Convexity also means that the tangent at point *b* is steeper than the tangent at point *a* or that the marginal rate of substitution of bread for ale is higher at point *b* than at point *a*.

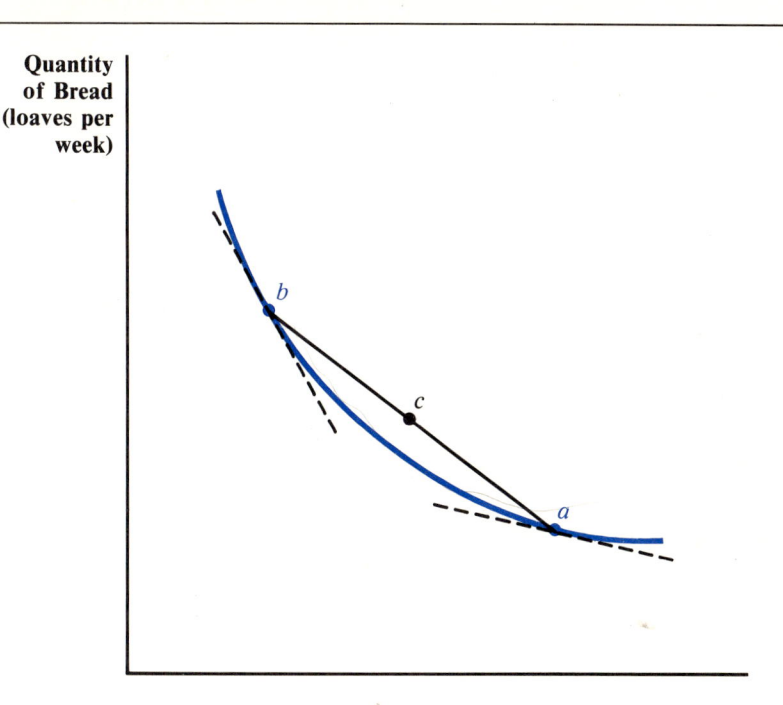

Quantity of Bread (loaves per week)

Quantity of Ale (pints per week)

two commodity bundles between which the consumer is indifferent—say, bundles *a* and *b*. Bundle *b* is more extreme in consuming bread than bundle *a* (which is more extreme in consuming ale). Now consider any intermediate bundle *c* drawn on a straight line connecting points *a* and *b*. If bundle *c* were halfway between points *a* and *b*, it would consist of half of bundle *a* plus half of bundle *b*. In general, any point *c* on the line segment from *a* to *b* is a weighted average of the two extreme points, where the weights add to unity. Thus $c = \lambda a + (1 - \lambda)b$, where λ is a positive fraction less than one. Clearly, such intermediate bundles are more balanced than the extreme bundles and hence represent more variety. The desire for variety means that any bundle such as *c* must be on a higher indifference curve. Thus, the indifference curve through points *a* and *b* must be convex towards the origin.

The *axiom of convexity* is: If the consumer is indifferent between commodity bundles a and b, then the consumer will prefer any weighted average of those two bundles $c = \lambda a + (1 - \lambda)b$ $(0 < \lambda < 1)$, to either bundle.

An equivalent formulation of this axiom may be stated in terms of the behavior of the marginal rate of substitution along a given indifference curve. The marginal rate of substitution of bread for ale can be measured by the absolute slope of the tangent to any point on the indifference curve; it indicates the instantaneous rate at which the consumer is willing to substitute bread for a unit of ale at that particular combination of bread and ale consumption. Convexity means that the tangent gets flatter as more ale is consumed. The convex curvature follows from the **law of diminishing marginal rate of substitution**: as more ale is consumed relative to bread for any given level of satisfaction, the consumer is willing to give up less and less bread in order to acquire an additional unit of ale. The flatter is the indifference curve, the lower is the relative valuation the consumer places on ale compared to bread.

The five axioms we have stated underlie a great deal of rational consumer behavior, but they are by no means the whole story. Example 3-2 discusses some additional factors that influence consumer choices.

> The **law of diminishing marginal rate of substitution** of good Y for good X is that MRS_{yx} declines as more X is consumed, holding the level of satisfaction constant.

THE UTILITY FUNCTION

Ordinal Utility Versus Cardinal Utility

> A **utility function** is a numerical representation of the way an individual agent ranks different bundles of goods and services. The utility of commodity bundle a is denoted by $u(a)$. If the agent prefers bundle a to bundle b, then $u(a) > u(b)$.

The axioms of consumer behavior lead to the concept of a **utility function**. This function is an arbitrary numerical value assigned to each commodity bundle to allow us to rank alternative bundles. For example, Figure 3-4 shows three indifference curves from some consumer's indifference map. By assigning higher numbers to higher indifference curves, we can compare specific bundles using those numbers. For instance, we have assigned the number 1,000 to indifference curve U_3, the number 10 to U_2, and the number 5 to U_1. Thus, the utility of commodity bundle c on U_3 is 1,000. In this way we see that $u(a) = 5$, $u(b) = 10$, and $u(c) = 1,000$ for the consumer in Figure 3-4. These numbers are measures of *ordinal utility* in the sense that they can only be used to rank bundles c, b, and a. Bundle c is in first place, bundle b is in second place, and bundle a is in third place among these three bundles. We cannot say that bundle c is more strongly preferred to bundle b than bundle b is to bundle a because $u(c) - u(b) = 990$ is larger than $u(b) - u(a) = 5$. The reason is that we could have used any other set of increasing numbers—for example, 3, 49, and 50—to describe the ordinal utility levels third, second, and first to the three indifference curves.[3]

Nineteenth-century economists such as William Stanley Jevons, Leon Walras, and Alfred Marshall treated utility as if cardinal numbers could be assigned to measure satisfaction. According to Jevons, "Now there can be

---

3. Let $u = u(x)$ be an ordinal utility function for a consumer where x is any commodity bundle—that is, a vector whose components indicate the consumption of each good in the bundle. Suppose we now transform the utility function by the monotonically increasing transformation $f(u)$, where the only necessary property of the function f is that $f' > 0$. The new utility function is now $u = f[u(x)]$. It is easy to show that the new utility function works the same as the old in terms of ranking bundles. Say $u(c) > u(b) > u(a)$. Because the transformation $f(u)$ is increasing in its argument u, it follows that $f[u(c)] > f[u(b)] > f[u(a)]$. Thus the function $f[u(x)]$ works exactly the same as $u(x)$. Example: if $u = x_1 x_2$, the transformation $f(u) = \ln u$ applied to $u(x)$ yields $f[u(x)] = \ln x_1 + \ln x_2$.

FIGURE 3–4 Utility Functions for Three Indifference Curves

Bundles *a*, *b*, and *c* lie on successively higher indifference curves. The arbitrary utility functions $U_1 = 5$, $U_2 = 10$, and $U_3 = 1,000$ have been assigned to rank the bundles. Any other increasing set of cardinal numbers—such as 1, 2, 3—would work equally well.

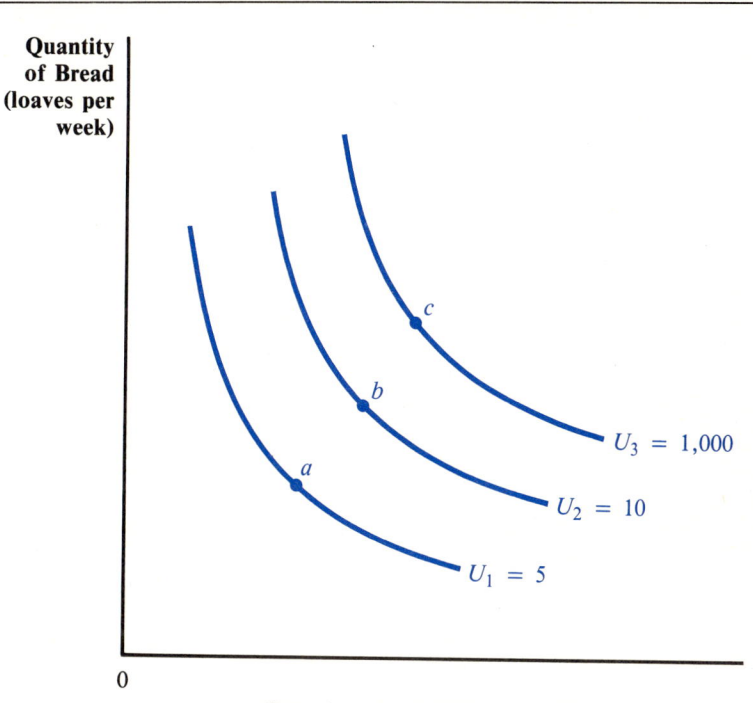

[Graph: Quantity of Bread (loaves per week) on vertical axis, Quantity of Ale (pints per week) on horizontal axis. Three indifference curves shown with points a, b, c on successive curves labeled $U_1 = 5$, $U_2 = 10$, $U_3 = 1,000$.]

no doubt that pleasure, pain, labor, utility, value, wealth, money, capital, etc., are all notions admitting of quantity."[4] A *cardinal-utility* measure goes beyond mere relative ranking of objects and assigns specific numeric values intended to measure the differences between goods. If Ms. A has $100, Mr. B has $50, and Mr. C has $45, then it is meaningful to say that A has significantly more money than B and B has only slightly more money than C. Jevons and others, thus, introduced the concept of **marginal utility** (*MU*).

If differences in utility level were considered significant, it was natural for early marginalist economists to believe—from introspection—that the first units of a commodity consumed had more marginal utility than later units. Surely the first unit of water consumed is more valuable to the thirsty consumer than the last unit. From such observation, it was concluded that there was a law of diminishing marginal utility—that is, the more of a good one consumes, the lower is its marginal utility.

While it is correct to say that the marginal rate of substitution of other goods for water will be much higher for the first unit than the last, the modern view is that nothing can be said about marginal utility because utility

> The **marginal utility** (*MU*) of a good is the increase in total utility brought about by increasing the consumption of that good by one unit, holding consumption of all other goods constant.

---

4. William Stanley Jevons, *The Theory of Political Economy*, ed. by R. D. Collison Black (New York: Penguin Books, 1970), p. 82.

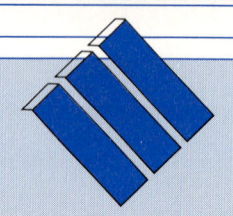

> **EXAMPLE 3–2**   Judging Quality by Price
>
> According to the axioms of consumer behavior, the *preferences* of each consumer with respect to different commodity bundles are independent of the costs of those bundles. In other words, the price of a good does not influence the way a consumer thinks about that good. This is not the same thing as saying that the consumer's *choices* are independent of prices. As we shall see later, choices are the outcome of the meeting between preferences (what the consumer wants) and the budget (what the consumer can afford).
>
> The theory of consumer behavior does not include the common practice of judging the quality of a commodity by its price or the size of its market. If a buyer had complete information, there would be no point in judging quality by price or market share. (Indeed, when the consumer is engaging in repeat purchases, it is often not necessary to judge quality except by satisfaction already achieved.) However, in the real world the consumer is often confronted with learning situations. The consumer does not know whether a product is worthwhile and acquiring information is costly. In such cases, rational behavior may require the consumer to judge a product on the basis of its market price. The consumer may reason as follows: Brand X is more expensive than brand Y; many people buy brand X; I want the highest quality product available; therefore, I will buy brand X. Or a consumer might say: I want the best buy, but I myself do not have the information to know what it is; the brand that is most successful is probably the best buy; so I will buy the brand with the largest market share. Thus we see that companies are anxious to advertise their products as "Number 1" to appeal to the mass market or as "the most expensive and darn well worth it" to appeal to the upper end of the market. If judging quality by market size is confirmed by actual experience, the assumption that preferences are independent of price works in the long run. Notice that the good is not really being judged on the basis of its market share; rather, the market is being used as a source of information. If that source proves unreliable, the practice may well be discontinued.
>
> Similarly, the practice of judging the quality of a product by its higher price will presumably work in the long run if, on the average, consumers are satisfied with their choices. But in a world of costly information, there will always be unscrupulous operators who will charge a high price just to take advantage of unwary consumers who follow this decision rule. Such fly-by-night operations are inevitable. An important question that arises is, how does the practice survive the presence of unscrupulous operators? The answer is that consumers use reputation as well as price in most instances (see Chapter 12).

is an ordinal measure. Given the axioms of consumer behavior under certainty, there need be no law of diminishing marginal utility simply because those axioms lead only to an ordinal measure of utility.

THE UTILITY FUNCTION   47

PRACTICE EXERCISE 3-3

Q. Does the utility function $u = 2X_1X_2$ obey the law of diminishing marginal rate of substitution?

A. Yes. The marginal utility of good 1 is $MU_1 = 2X_2$ and $MU_2 = 2X_1$. It follows that the rate at which the consumer is willing to substitute good 2 for good 1 is $MU_1/MU_2 = X_2/X_1$. Thus as X_2 falls and X_1 rises, the $MRS_{2,1}$ falls.

If, after this discussion, you still think that there should be a law of diminishing marginal utility, your intuition is serving you well. First, if the marginal utility of some good ever becomes negative, there must be a general tendency toward diminishing marginal utility for that good. Second, we shall see later that when the axioms are extended to uncertain situations, meaningful marginal-utility comparisons emerge.

Why Discuss Utility?

Utility functions are useful in the theory of consumer behavior for two reasons. First, because preferences can be represented by a utility function, the maximization of that function subject to constraint can be carried out using standard mathematical techniques. Thus, the whole apparatus of mathematical optimization theory can be used to analyze consumer behavior. Second, even though the concept of marginal utility is redundant, it aids our intuition in understanding the laws of consumer behavior. Thus, the marginalists' cost/benefit calculation is easy to understand in marginal utility terms.

The Link Between Marginal Utility and the Marginal Rate of Substitution

While marginal utility (MU) is not a unique measure, the concept can be used for pedagogical purposes. Suppose an individual consumes amounts equal to X_a of ale and X_b of bread. The total utility of consumption is shown by the utility function $u = u(X_a, X_b)$. Now change the X_a and X_b consumption by the amounts ΔX_a and ΔX_b. The change in total utility, Δu, is

$$\Delta u = MU_a \Delta X_a + MU_b \Delta X_b \tag{1}$$

The term $MU_a \Delta X_a$ represents the change in utility due to the change in ale consumption. Equation (1) holds for all small changes in ale and bread consumption. The link between the marginal utility and the marginal rate of substitution, MRS, can now be derived. The MRS between bread and ale is

$\Delta X_b/\Delta X_a$ when utility is constant. In other words, set Δu equal to zero. Equation (1) becomes:

$$0 = MU_a \Delta X_a + MU_b \Delta X_b \qquad (2)$$

Solving equation (2) for DX_b/BX_a:

$$-MU_b \Delta X_b = MU_a \Delta X_a$$

$$\frac{-\Delta X_b}{\Delta X_a} = \frac{MU_a}{MU_b} = MRS_{ba} \qquad (3)$$

For example, if the MU of ale is twice that of bread, it takes two units of bread to compensate the consumer for one unit of ale.

From Equation (3), we can see that there is no necessary link between the law of diminishing marginal rate of substitution and the law of diminishing marginal utility. Under the assumption that the marginal utility of ale is independent of bread consumption, and vice versa, diminishing marginal utility implies a diminishing marginal rate of substitution, because as ale is substituted for bread, MU_a falls and MU_b rises, so MRS_{ba} must fall. But in general this need not be the case. For example, assume $u = X_a X_b$. Then $MU_a = X_b$, because an extra unit of ale consumption increases utility in proportion to X_b, and $MU_b = X_a$ (for the corresponding reason). Clearly more ale consumption, holding bread constant, has no effect on MU_a. But $MRS_{ba} = X_b/X_a$ so that when ale consumption increases relative to bread consumption, the marginal rate of substitution of bread for ale falls.[5]

Indifference Curves When Some Commodities Are "Bads"

So far we have assumed that the marginal utility of both goods is positive: more of either commodity is better. But there are a vast number of commodities that yield negative MU—where more is worse, not better. Some examples are work (after a point, at least), garbage, and the 15th hot dog at a baseball game. When the marginal utility of a commodity is negative, the good is a "bad" rather than a "good."

---

5. Let $u = u(x_1, x_2)$ and define the marginal utility of good i as $u_i = \partial u/\partial x_i$. When good j increases, the marginal utility of i increases by $u_{ij} = \partial^2 u/\partial x_i \partial x_j$. By definition $MRS_{21} = u_1/u_2$. Thus, in general,

$$dMRS_{2,1}/dx_1 = (u_2 du_1/dx_1 - u_1 du_2/dx_1)/(u_2)^2$$
$$= [u_2(u_{11} + u_{1,2} dx_2/dx_1) - u_1(u_{21} + u_{22} dx_2/dx_1)]/(u_2)^2.$$

When $du = 0$ [for example, see Equation (2) in the text], $dx_2/dx_1 = -u_1/u_2$. Substituting this into the above equation yields (noting $u_{1,2} = u_{21}$):

$$dMRS_{21}/dx_1 = [(u_2)^2 u_{11} + (u_1)^2 u_{22} - 2 u_1 u_2 u_{12}]/(u_2)^3.$$

Since $u_i > 0$, the law of diminishing MRS holds if and only if

$$D = (u_2)^2 u_{11} + (u_1)^2 u_{22} - 2 u_1 u_2 u_{12} < 0.$$

We immediately see that if $u_{12} = 0$, the law of diminishing marginal utility ($u_{ii} < 0$) implies that $D < 0$. Notice that the law of diminishing MU need not hold at all if $u_{ii} > 0$, provided that $u_{12} > 0$. Example: if $u = (x_1 x_2)^2$, calculation shows that $D = -16(x_1 x_2)^4$ even though, for example, $u_{11} = 2(x_2)^2$.

THE UTILITY FUNCTION 49

FIGURE 3–5   Indifference Curves for Goods and Bads

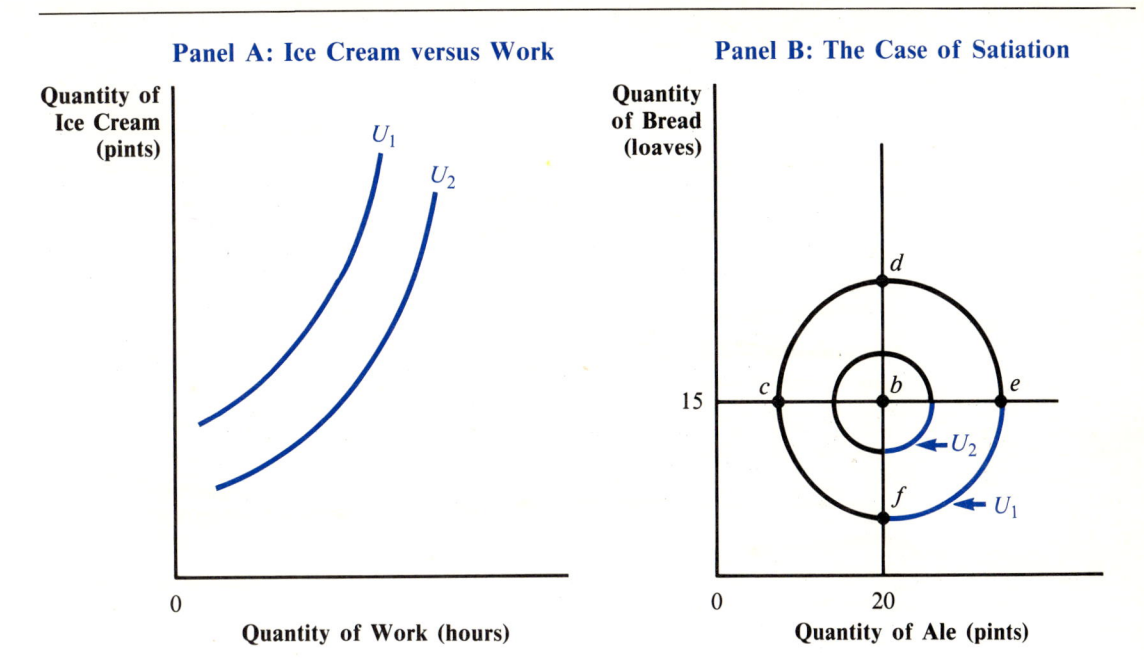

Panel A: Ice Cream versus Work

Panel B: The Case of Satiation

Panel A shows the indifference curves between work (a bad) and ice cream (a good); both are upward-sloping. Panel B shows the indifference curves for two commodities when excessive consumption of either leads to declining marginal utility. Beyond 20 pints of ale the marginal utility of ale is negative; beyond 15 loaves of bread, the marginal utility of bread is negative. Each indifference curve goes around in a circular fashion: downward-sloping when both goods are goods or bads; upward-sloping when one is a good and the other a bad. Each curve is convex to an inferior position. Point b represents absolute bliss.

The simplest example of a bad is work. Panel A of Figure 3–5 shows a consumer's indifference curves between eating ice cream and working. Each indifference curve is upward-sloping because more ice cream is necessary to just compensate the consumer for working an additional hour. With ice cream measured on the vertical axis, the indifference curves are convex to the horizontal axis. As the consumer works more, holding utility constant, larger and larger increases in ice cream consumption are necessary to compensate for having to work an additional hour.

Now consider the consumer whose indifference curves are depicted in Panel B of Figure 3–5. It is assumed that after 20 pints of ale per week MU_a is negative, and that after 15 loaves of bread MU_b is negative. (For simplicity, we will assume that the "badness" of either commodity does not depend on the consumption of the other commodity, although this assumption is unrealistic.) Along the indifference curve U_1, both bread and ale have positive MUs between points c and f. The curve is downward-sloping between c and f because additional ale is necessary to compensate the consumer for the loss of bread. But between f and e, where more than 20 units of ale are consumed and less than 15 units of bread, $MU_a < 0$ while $MU_b > 0$. Because ale is then a bad, more bread is necessary to compensate the consumer for drinking more ale! Thus between f and e, the indifference curve is upward-sloping. Similarly, between c and d the reverse is true: bread is a bad and ale a good, so that U_1 is again upward-sloping. Finally, between points d and e, both ale and bread have negative MUs. If more ale is consumed, which makes the individual worse off, less of other bads (in this case bread) must be consumed.

The inner indifference curve U_2 represents a higher level of satisfaction. As the consumer moves to higher and higher levels of satisfaction, the indifference curves make an ever-tightening circle around point b—the point at which the consumer is satiated with both goods. The indifference map in this case is analogous to a map showing the elevations of a mountain. On the map, each contour represents one elevation. In the figure, each indifference curve represents one level of utility. On a map, point b would represent the top of the hill.

Notice that the indifference curves in Figure 3–5 are convex to the region of lower satisfaction. Indifference curve U_2 is convex when viewed from indifference curve U_1. This reflects the axiom of convexity—any straight line connecting two points on an indifference curve must pass through higher indifference curves (superior commodity bundles).

Lexicographic Rankings

Lexicography is the practice or profession of compiling dictionaries. The words are listed in alphabetical order; so to look up a word in a dictionary, you look at the first letter in the word. If the first letters of two words are the same, the second letters determine which word comes first, and so on. An example of lexicographic behavior would be for a consumer to rank commodity bundles in the same way. Imagine, for example, a small child choosing between two commodity bundles, each containing bubble gum and $10 bills. A child who loves bubble gum is likely to choose bundles on the basis of which had the most bubble gum, regardless of how many dollars a bundle contains. Only if two bundles had the same amount of bubble gum would the child pick the one with the most $10 bills. Or imagine an adult dipsomaniac, for whom bundles containing the highest numbers of alcoholic drinks would be in first place. This kind of behavior is ruled out by the axiom of substitution. Dipsomaniacs and children may refuse to make any substitutions—no matter how valuable the other goods—but rational consumers will not.

Lexicographic preferences are illustrated in Figure 3–6. Assume that the consumer is a dipsomaniac who chooses bundles based on their ale content. Point c is a commodity bundle containing 10 pints of ale and 15 loaves of bread. Any bundle to the right of the vertical line through c will give the

THE UTILITY FUNCTION

FIGURE 3-6 Lexicographic Rankings

Here the consumer, a dipsomaniac, has lexicographic rankings because the bundle with the most ale is always preferred; the quantity of bread is decisive only if two bundles contain the same amount of ale. Any point to the right of bundle c is preferred to c; any point to the left is inferior to c. Any point above (below) c on the vertical line is preferred (inferior) to c.

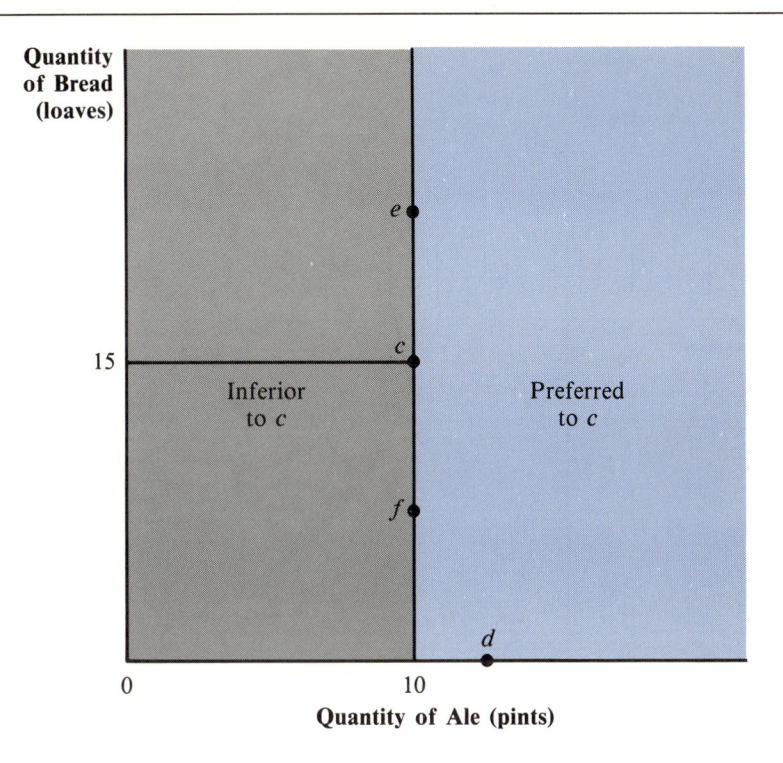

individual more satisfaction because it contains more ale. This includes, for example, bundle d, which contains no bread at all. Any point to the left of the vertical line through c is considered inferior to bundle c. Since more bread is better if the quantity of ale stays constant, commodity bundle e (on the vertical line) is preferred to bundle c, but commodity bundle f is considered inferior to bundle c. Thus, we can see that if preferences are lexicographic, indifference curves do not exist. It can in fact be proven that under these circumstances, a utility function cannot exist if the goods are perfectly divisible.[6]

The Properties of Indifference Curves

Indifference curves have five properties:

1. They are convex when viewed from inferior commodity bundles, which reflects the desire for variety or, equivalently, the law of diminishing

---

6. The proof, unfortunately, involves advanced mathematical methods. See Gerard Debreu, *Theory of Value: An Axiomatic Analysis of Economic Equilibrium* (New York: John Wiley, 1959).

FIGURE 3-7 An Impossible Intersection

Curve U_1 shows that the consumer is indifferent between bundles a and b, while curve U_2 shows indifference between b and c. By the axiom of transitivity, the consumer must be indifferent between a and c, but by the axiom of nonsatiation, a must be preferable to c. Intersection of the curves is, thus, contradictory and impossible under the axioms.

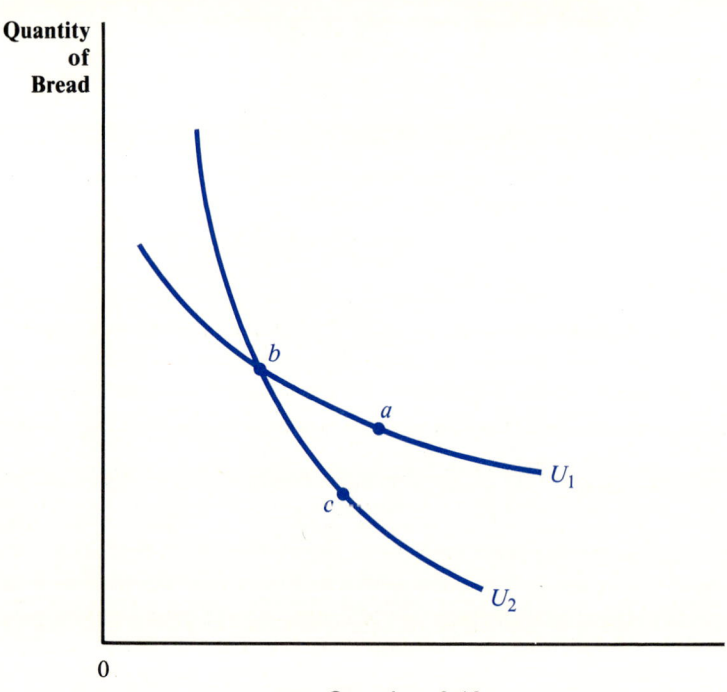

marginal rate of substitution. If the commodities are not bads (that is, if they yield positive marginal utility), indifference curves are convex to the origin.

2. Indifference curves that show preferences between two goods with positive marginal utility are downward-sloping; indifference curves between two goods with negative marginal utility are downward-sloping; and indifference curves between a "bad" and a "good" are upward-sloping.
3. Except for commodity bundles on which the consumer cannot survive, there is an indifference curve through every conceivable commodity bundle.
4. **Indifference curves cannot intersect.** Figure 3-7 illustrates why this is so. Nonsatiation holds, so both U_1 and U_2 are downward-sloping but intersect at point b. The consumer is indifferent between bundles a and b, and between bundles b and c. By the axiom of transitivity, the consumer must be indifferent between bundles a and c. But bundle a contains more of both ale and bread than bundle c; hence bundle a must be preferred to bundle c by the axiom of nonsatiation. Thus, assuming that the two indifference curves intersect leads to a contradiction: the individual cannot be indifferent between a and c if a is preferred to c. Notice that even

though indifference curves cannot intersect, they need not be parallel, since they are not straight lines.
5. Indifference curves are independent of prices and income.

CONSUMER BEHAVIOR IN THE CASE OF UNCERTAINTY

Thus far we have treated the individual as if he or she were choosing between options with certain consequences. Yet there are very few situations in which the individual knows with absolute certainty the consequences of any particular act. Buy a quart of milk and it might be spoiled; buy a car and it may turn out to be a lemon. Uncertainty, though present to some degree, is not the main element in purchasing things like a quart of milk, a loaf of bread, or a shirt. But uncertainty is paramount in buying such things as insurance, a used car, or a house, or in choosing a job, hiring an employee, or gambling.

Uncertainty is inherent in the economic system. Rainfall affects agricultural yields; it is too costly to test every product coming off the assembly line; imperfect human beings constantly make mistakes in servicing and producing products; as consumers we do not always know who is honest and who is dishonest in our business dealings. The economic system is too complex to predict what will happen tomorrow with perfect certainty.

Let us explore rational consumer behavior when the individual is making choices between uncertain commodity bundles. What matters in this case are probabilities and what people expect to occur on the average.

Probability

The **probability** of an event is the chance that the event will occur, expressed as a fraction of 1.

The **probability** of an event (for example, rainfall tomorrow) is a measurement of the likelihood of the event. Suppose an event can occur in N different, mutually exclusive, and equally likely ways. If n of these outcomes have attribute A, the probability of A is n/N. For example, if you flip a perfectly balanced coin, either heads or tails—but not both— will occur. Since only one of two things can happen, the probability of either heads or tails is 1/2. If you toss a perfect die, there is a 1/6 probability that two dots (or any other face of the cube) will appear. If you draw a card from an ordinary deck of playing cards, the probability of drawing a heart is 1/4 because there are 52 cards and 13 of them are hearts. These examples assume that all chances are equally likely, so that the flip, the toss, or the drawing is truly random.

Probabilities, of course, must lie between zero and one. If an event is impossible, its probability is zero. If an event is inevitable (like the setting sun), its probability is one.

If the different ways in which an event can occur are mutually exclusive, then their probabilities must add up to one. For example, when the weather forecaster states that the probability of rain tomorrow is 0.4, the probability that it will not rain is 0.6. When a die is tossed, the probabilities of the six outcomes add to unity.

How are probabilities combined? If events A and B cannot occur together, the probability of event A or B is simply the sum of the probabilities of original events. For example, the probability of tossing one or two dots with a perfect die is 2/6, the sum of 1/6 + 1/6. The probability of tossing an even number of dots is the sum of the probabilities of tossing two, four, and six dots: 1/6 + 1/6 + 1/6 = 1/2.

If events A and B can occur together and are independent of each other, the probability of events A and B both occurring is the product of the probabilities of A and B separately. For example, the probability of throwing two heads in two successive tosses of a coin is (1/2) × (1/2) = 1/4. To see this, consider the probability of throwing heads the second time. Because the second tossing is independent of the first, the probability of throwing heads the second time, even though heads occurred the first time, is still exactly 1/2. But the probability of being in that situation is only 1/2. Thus, the probability of tossing two heads in a row is 1/2 × 1/2 = 1/4. As a check, consider the possible combinations of heads (H) and tails (T) exhaustively. When two flips are made, the possible outcomes are HH, TT, TH, or HT. These mutually exclusive and equally likely outcomes each have a probability of 1/4. Another example: the probability of drawing two aces in succession from a deck of 52 well-shuffled cards is 4/52 × 3/51 = 1/221. In this case, 4/52 is the probability of drawing the first ace and 3/51 is the probability of drawing the second ace given that the first card was an ace. (After the first draw, the deck contains 51 cards, 3 of them aces.)

A more complicated problem would use both of the above rules. The probability of throwing a combined total of six with two dice can be calculated in the following way: a six can be obtained by any of the combinations (1, 5), (2, 4), and (3, 3). The probabilities of (1, 5) and (2, 4) are each $2 \times (1/6)^2 = 1/18$ because they can occur in two ways, while the probability of throwing a (3, 3) is 1/36. The probability of a 6 is then 5/36 = 1/18 + 1/18 + 1/36.

*A **random variable** is a variable that may take on different values, each with a definite probability, as the result of statistical experiments.*

When a variable can take on different values according to some specified probability, it is called a **random variable**. For example, let the random variable Y be the number of heads tossed in two flips. The only possibilities are TT (no heads), HT and TH (one heads each), and HH (two heads). Each possibility is equally likely, so that Y may equal 0, 1, or 2 with probability 1/4, 1/2, or 1/4, respectively.

Conflicting Views About the Nature of Probabilities

In the literature on probability theory, two concepts of probability have emerged. One view considers probability to be a measurable, *objective* characteristic of events. Probability experiments such as flipping a coin or drawing cards are simply carried out repeatedly, and the probability of the event is its relative frequency of occurrence. If, after the experiment is repeated many times, the relative frequency of the event converges to a particular number such as 1/2, that ratio is the objective probability. For example, flipping a fair coin 1,000 times is likely to lead to about 500 heads. The frequentist would then say that the probability of heads is 1/2.

The other view, which is shared by most economists as well as most probability theorists, considers probability to be a *subjective* concept. What we believe to be the probability of some event is considered the most defensible view of probability because subjective judgments cannot be avoided. As stated by economist William Fellner:

> A person may watch drawings of odd and even, or of red and black, to the end of his days, and yet he will not observe the theoretical value of any frequency in the sense in which he observes that a number is odd or a color is red . . . . insofar as a person makes a probability judgment about a physical process *of any kind*, he is making the subjective judgment . . . to apply a mathematically defined measure to that process.[7]

In practice, the subjective view often coincides with the objective because nearly everyone will treat the probability of, say, heads as 1/2 if the coin is perfectly balanced. In other words, if there is a strong objective basis for some subjective judgment, most people will make that judgment. People who tend to be gamblers often think that luck is on their side more than on that of others; hence, their behavior is governed by their subjective beliefs rather than by objective reality.

Expected Values

Suppose someone offers you the following deal: "I will flip this perfect coin. If heads appears, I will give you $2; and if tails appears, you give me $2." What is the expected gain or value of playing this game to you? If you weight the $2 gain with its probability and the $2 loss with its probability, the **expected value** is

The **expected value** of a set of probabilities is the sum of the values of a random variable, with each value multiplied by its probability of occurrence.

$$\frac{1}{2}(2) + \frac{1}{2}(-2) = 1 - 1 = 0.$$

If you played this game an indefinite number of times, you would expect to come out even on the average. To put this point a little more precisely, the probability of breaking even approaches one as the number of times the game is played approaches infinity.

Suppose a game pays y_1 with probability π and pays y_2 with probability

---

7. William Fellner, *Probability and Profit*, (Homewood, Ill.: Richard D. Irwin, 1965), p. 45. The subjective view of probability has been formalized in a system of axioms, which, if you believe them, imply subjective probability scales. The classic work is Leonard J. Savage, *The Foundation of Statistics* (New York: John Wiley, 1954).

$1 - \pi$, where y_i represents the positive or negative values of the random variable Y. The expected value of Y is

$$EY = \pi y_1 + (1 - \pi)y_2,$$

where E is the mathematical symbol for computing the mathematical expectations of a random variable. In general, if a game pays y_i with probability π_i, the expected value of the game is

$$Ey = \pi_1 y_1 + \pi_2 y_2 + \ldots + \pi_n y_n = \sum_{i=1}^{n} \pi_i y_i. \tag{4}$$

The sum of the π_is in Equation (4), of course, must be unity over the n mutually exclusive outcomes.

Expected values are extremely important. People furnish scarce capital to huge corporations such as General Motors on the expectation that, on the average, the stock will pay a positive return on their investment. Insurance companies and gambling casinos make a profit by offering their customers games with positive expected values to themselves and negative expected values to their customers. In Las Vegas, for example, the game of blackjack can be beaten by experienced customers who cooperate with one another; and any customers suspected of cooperating in this way are excluded from playing blackjack. The casino's position is no different from that of an insurance company which refuses to insure an unsafe driver.

The St. Petersburg Paradox

The expected value of a game does not indicate how much one is willing to pay to play the game. This fundamental point is vividly illustrated by a game proposed by the Swiss mathematician Nicholas Bernoulli in the late 1600s (perhaps after visiting the gambling casinos in St. Petersburg). Bernoulli imagined that someone offered to pay a player 2^n dollars if in a sequence of coin flips heads turned up only on the nth flip. For example, if heads turned up on the fourth flip, the sequence would be TTTH and the player would receive 2^4 dollars, or $16. The probability of getting heads only on the nth flip is $(1/2)^n$ because for the first flip the probability is $1/2$, for the second flip $(1/2)^2 = 1/4$, for the third flip $(1/2)^3 = 1/8$, and so on. Weighting the payoff for turning up heads on the nth flip with its probability $[(1/2)^n (2)^n]$ and summing all the possibilities gives the expected value of the game:

$$\sum_{i=1}^{i=\infty} \left(\frac{1}{2}\right)^n (2)^n = \frac{1}{2}(2) + \frac{1}{4}(4) + \frac{1}{8}(8) + \ldots \tag{5}$$
$$= 1 + 1 + 1 + \ldots = \infty$$

Because the rewards of the game increase in inverse proportion to the probability of their occurrence, the expected value of playing the game is, as shown in Equation (5), infinite! Yet no rational person would be willing to pay very much to play the game—perhaps not more than $10 or $20. To resolve the paradox, Bernoulli's younger cousin Daniel proposed that peo-

FIGURE 3-8 Expected Utility as the Square Root of Income

Graphing expected utility as the square root of income demonstrates diminishing marginal utility; the arrows show that diminishing increments of utility accompany equal increases in income.

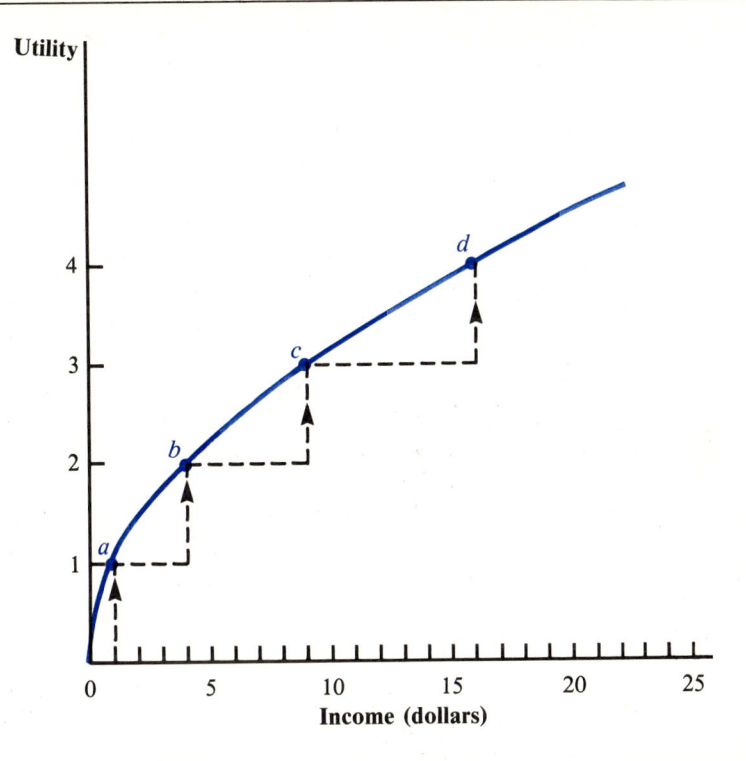

ple look at the subjective value of the reward, its *expected utility*. Daniel Bernoulli suggested a utility function in which utility increased in much smaller proportion than income. As an example, consider a Bernoulli-like function in which utility is the square root of income: $u(y) = y^{1/2}$. It follows that the expected utility from playing the game is

$$Eu = \sum_{i=1}^{i=\infty} (1/2)^n (2)^{n/2}. \tag{6}$$

It can be shown[8] that the expected utility of the game is only 2.414. Since this utility is the square root of the money payoff, the dollar value of the game would be $5.76 (2.414²).

The utility function used in Equation (6) is illustrated in Figure 3-8. Utility is measured on the vertical axis and income on the horizontal axis. The curve is concave to the horizontal axis because utility increases as the square root of the money payoff (income). The arrows show that with equal

---

8. Mathematical note: If $a < 1$, the sum is

$$S = \sum_{i=1}^{i=\infty} a^i = \frac{a}{1-a}.$$

This is true because $S - aS = a$. In Equation (6), because $(\frac{1}{2})^n (2)^{n/2}$ reduces to $(2^{1/2}/2)^n$, $a = 2^{1/2} \div 2$. Thus $Eu = 2.414$.

increments to income, increments to utility diminish. The graph appears to show that a law of diminishing marginal utility applies. How can this be? We saw earlier that according to the axioms of consumer behavior under perfect certainty, we are only permitted to discuss ordinal utility—that discussing diminishing marginal utility is meaningless.

The Axioms of Consumer Behavior in the Case of Uncertainty

A resolution of the apparent difficulty just discussed was developed by mathematician John von Neumann and economist Oskar Morgenstern. They developed a set of axioms that generate cardinal or measurable utility functions in which it is meaningful to discuss diminishing marginal utility. Indeed, diminishing marginal utility comes about because of a specific attitude on the part of consumers called *risk-averse behavior*. The reason people will only pay a finite sum to play a St. Petersburg game is that they are averse to taking risks under uncertainty.

What are the axioms of behavior under uncertainty? In uncertain situations, the objects of preference are not commodity bundles but rather a set of different mutually exclusive outcomes (which may involve commodity bundles), each with a specific probability. To simplify our presentation of the following axioms, imagine there are only two mutually exclusive outcomes. The objects of preference are x with probability π and y with probability $1 - \pi$. Instead of referring to commodity bundles, we shall refer to the foregoing as an **uncertain prospect** $(x, y; \pi)$. For example, a coin-flip game consisting of winning \$1 if heads appears and losing \$1 if tails appears would be described as the uncertain prospect (\$1, −\$1; 1/2). If tossing a die yielded \$100 when one dot appeared and \$10 when more than one dot appeared, the game would be described by (\$100, \$10; 1/6). Notice that the coin-flip game could also be described by (−\$1, \$1; 1/2); and the die-toss game could also be described by (\$10, \$100; 5/6).

An **uncertain prospect** $(x, y; \pi)$ is a situation in which x occurs with probability π and y occurs with probability $1 - \pi$.

The Axiom of Transitivity

Once again we must make the assumption that people behave consistently.

The *axiom of transitivity* in the case of uncertainty is: If uncertain prospect x is preferred to prospect y and prospect y is preferred to prospect z, then prospect x will be preferred to prospect z. The same applies to indifference.

The Axiom of Certainty Equivalents

Suppose there are three commodity bundles c, b, and a such that c is preferred to b and b preferred to a. The present axiom says that there exists an uncertain situation involving receiving a with probability π and c with probability $1 - \pi$ such that the consumer is indifferent between the uncertain prospect $(a, c; \pi)$ and the certain bundle b. Bundle b is the *certainty equivalent* of the uncertain prospect. For example, if the consumer is indifferent between zero dollars and the uncertain prospect ($1, -$1; 1/2) in a coin-flip game, then zero income is the certainty equivalent of that uncertain prospect. The axiom asserts the existence of certainty equivalents even if a happens to be something very bad (for example, being shot). Presumably, the probability of the worst occurrence can be made so low as to make the event nearly impossible (for example, the probability that when you try to boil water it will freeze—an infinitesimal number but not zero).

The *axiom of certainty equivalents* is: If a consumer prefers bundle c to b and b to a, then in every case there is a probability π that will make bundle b the certainty equivalent of the uncertain prospect $(a, c; \pi)$.

The Axiom of Independence

Suppose b is preferred to a by a consumer. Consider now an uncertain prospect involving a and c with some probability π, as well as a prospect involving b and the same c with the same probability. The axiom of independence asserts that the uncertain prospect containing the preferred bundle b is preferred to the one containing bundle a. One superficial objection to this axiom is that c may complement a but not b. This objection fails because the consumer receives either a or c but not both, and either b or c but not both.

The *axiom of independence* is: If b is preferred to a by a consumer, then for that consumer the uncertain prospect $(b, c; \pi)$ will be preferred to the uncertain prospect $(a, c; \pi)$ for any commodity bundle c, where π is any fraction.

The Axiom of the Irrelevance of the Probability Mechanism

The final axiom under uncertainty says that it makes no difference to the consumer how the probabilities are generated. See Example 3-3. If the process is changed but the probability of getting a or b remains the same, the consumer is indifferent to the change. This axiom means, for example, that people who derive no other utility from gambling would be indifferent between roulette, poker, and blackjack as long as the probabilities of winning or losing were the same.[9] More formally, consider the uncertain prospect $[(a, b; \pi_1), b; \pi_2]$. This means you can win the uncertain prospect $(a, b; \pi_1)$ with a probability of π_2. Thus, the probability of winning a is the compound probability $\pi_1\pi_2$.

---

9. Our discussion of the axioms is based upon Armen A. Alchian's "The Meaning of Utility Measurement," *American Economic Review*, March 1953, pp. 26–50. In addition to a clear discussion of the axioms, this article contains a lucid account of the difference between ordinal and cardinal utility.

PRACTICE EXERCISE 3-4

Q. Let uncertain prospect *a* be ($100, $10; 2/5). Now define uncertain prospect *b* as ($100, *a*; 1/2). What is the probability of winning $100 in prospect *b*? Of winning $10?

A. There is a 1/2 chance of winning $100 directly in *b*. But $100 can also be won by drawing *a* and winning $100 with a 2/5 chance. The probability of winning $100 in this indirect way is (1/2)(2/5) = 2/10. The chances of winning $100 in both ways is 1/2 + 2/10 = 7/10. Thus, *b* = ($100, $10; 7/10).

The *axiom of irrelevance of the probability mechanism* is: The consumer is indifferent between the uncertain prospect $(a, b; \pi_1\pi_2)$ and the more complicated prospect $[(a, b; \pi_1), b; \pi_2]$.

Implied in the set of axioms under uncertainty is a method for assigning cardinal utility to commodity bundles. The idea is simple. The scale of any kind of measurement is arbitrary in the sense that if we decide to measure height, we can choose feet, meters, or any unit of length as our scale. Such a measurement is cardinal; two different heights measured by the same scale can be added or subtracted. Suppose a consumer prefers commodity bundle *c* to bundle *b* and bundle *b* to bundle *a*. We may arbitrarily assign the utility numbers *u(c)* to *c* and *u(a)* to *a*, where by assumption *u(c)* is greater than *u(a)*. The axiom of certainty equivalents says that there is a probability π that will make that consumer indifferent between the uncertain prospect $(a, c; \pi)$ and the certain prospect *b*. In other words, we can say that the expected utility of the uncertain prospect equals the utility of prospect *b*:

$$u(b) = \pi u(a) + (1 - \pi)u(c). \qquad (7)$$

Once any two utilities are chosen, any third can be determined from Equation (7). Note that the π in Equation (7) comes from asking a particular individual. Thus, two different individuals, even if the same scale is chosen, may have different utility functions because their attitudes toward risky situations can differ.

Table 3-1 illustrates how a utility function for different levels of income can be constructed. Column (2) lists income levels from 0 to $40 in $10 increments. In column (3) we have arbitrarily chosen *u*(0) = 0 and *u*(40) = 10 as our scale for utility measurement. We now ask a hypothetical consumer what probability π will make him or her indifferent between the uncertain prospect (40, 0; π) and the income levels $10, $20, and $30. These probabilities are then entered in column (1). With probability 0, the consumer will certainly be indifferent between (0, 0; 0) and income of 0; and with probability 1 the consumer will certainly be indifferent between ($40,

$40; 1) and income of $40, as no gambles are involved. Assume now that our consumer would be indifferent between the certainty of $10 and the uncertain prospect ($40, 0; 0.6), that is, a 0.6 probability of $40 and a 0.4 probability of no income. Applying Equation (7), we see that $u(10) = 0.6u(40) + 0.4u(0) = 0.6(10) + 0.4(0) = 6$. Thus for $\pi = 0.6$ in column (1), we can enter $u = 6$ in column (3) of the table. By similar reckonings we can compute $u(20)$ and $u(30)$. Higher probabilities are needed to make the consumer indifferent between income levels higher than $10 and the uncertain prospect ($40, 0; π); thus, column (1) shows that a π equal to 0.8 is needed to make the consumer indifferent between $20 and the uncertain prospect. Column (3) shows diminishing marginal utilities because the utility increments become smaller as income rises.

Column (4) of Table 3-1 shows an alternative utility scale for the hypothetical consumer, where $u(0) = 10$ and $u(40) = 60$ have been assigned to set the scale. Notice that the relative increments in utility are the same in columns (3) and (4). In column (3), the increment in utility is three times as great between $0 and $10 as it is between $10 and $20 ($\Delta u = 6$ and $\Delta u = 2$); and the same is true in column (4): $\Delta u' = 30$ and $\Delta u' = 10$. Thus, the utility function in column (4) describes the same real behavior as the one in column (3).

THE EXPECTED-UTILITY HYPOTHESIS

Alfred Marshall pointed out long ago that risk aversion implied diminishing marginal utility. Consider the following gamble: flipping a coin with a 1/2 probability of winning a dollar and a 1/2 probability of losing a dollar. This is a fair gamble, because its expected value is zero. If the marginal utility of the dollar lost was 10 and the marginal utility of the dollar gained was only 8, the expected utility of the coin flip would be $1/2(-10) + 1/2(8) = -1$. Because the gamble has a negative expected utility, it will be refused. The one who refuses a fair gamble is a risk averter. Because Marshall believed in the law of diminishing marginal utility, he felt that it was irrational to gamble.

TABLE 3-1   **Cardinal Utility**

Certainty Equivalent π to (40, 0; π) (1)	Income Level (dollars) (2)	Utility Scale, u (3)	Alternative Utility Scale, u' (4)
0	0	0	10
0.6	10	6	40
0.8	20	8	50
0.9	30	9	55
1.0	40	10	60

FIGURE 3-9   Utility Function of a Risk Averter

When the utility function is concave, the individual is a risk averter. The curve shows the consumer's utility function for the uncertain prospect $(y_2, y_1; \pi)$. The coordinates of point *b* are the expected income, Ey, from the risky prospect, and the expected utility, Eu. The fact that $u(Ey) > Eu$ shows that the individual prefers the certainty of Ey to the uncertain prospect itself.

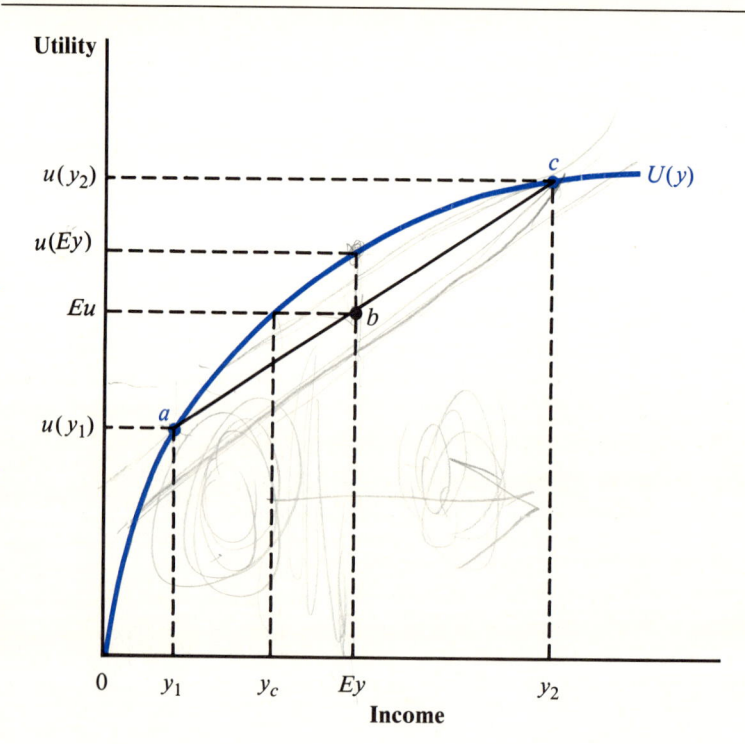

Increasing marginal utility of income implies risk-loving behavior. For example, for the coin-flip game in the preceding paragraph, assume that the marginal utility of the dollar lost was 10 while the marginal utility of the dollar gained was 12. The expected utility of the gamble would then be $1/2(-10) + 1/2(12) = 1$. The gamble would be worthwhile to the risk-loving consumer.

A risk averter has a utility function with a diminishing marginal utility of income; a risk lover has a utility function with an increasing marginal utility of income; and a risk-neutral person has a utility function with a constant marginal utility of income.

Figure 3-9 illustrates the following general proof that whenever the utility function is concave or the law of diminishing marginal utility holds, the individual will be risk-averse. To make matters concrete, imagine the uncertain prospect $(y_2, y_1; \pi)$, where y_2 is a person's income if his or her house does not burn down and y_1 is his or her income if the house does burn down. Points *a* and *c* in the figure represent the utility of y_1 and y_2 respectively, on this person's utility curve for y, the curve $U(y)$. Let π be the probability that the house will *not* burn down. Expected consumption is

EXAMPLE 3-3   Preference Reversals

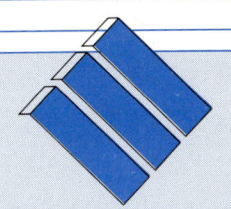

Experimental studies of preferences conducted by economists and psychologists have discovered an interesting phenomenon known as preference reversal. A subject will indicate that he prefers A to B and then turn around and assign a higher dollar value to B than to A! What is interesting is that when choices A and B are specified in a certain way, many subjects exhibit a preference reversal. An easy way to elicit reversals is to offer people a choice between a high probability of winning a small amount (a p bet) and a low probability of winning a relatively large amount (a $ bet). Experimenters have offered the following actual bets to subjects: (1) a p bet consisting of a 9 out of 12 probability of winning $1.20 and a 3 out of 12 probability of losing $0.10; and (2) a $ bet consisting of a 3/12 probability of winning $9.20 and a 9/12 probability of losing $2. The expected value of the p bet is $0.875 and that of the $ bet only $0.80; but people confronted with this choice often choose the p bet even though they assign a larger dollar value to the $ bet.

Experimenters have tried their best to make sure that such preference reversals are not simply the result of misunderstanding on the part of the subject—yet the phenomenon does not go away. One simple explanation is that the way people respond to inquiries depends on the way in which the inquiry is framed. Consider the following problems:

1. Suppose you have been given $200 and have been asked to choose between (a) a sure gain of $50 and (b) a 25 percent chance of winning $200 coupled with a 75 percent chance of winning nothing.

2. Suppose you have been given $400 and have been asked to choose between (c) a sure loss of $150 and (d) a 75 percent chance of losing $200 coupled with a 25 percent chance of losing nothing.

Clearly, a and c are the same because you will end up with $250 in either case. Moreover, b and d are the same because the 25 percent chance will yield $400 and the 75 percent chance will yield $200 in each case. But most people will choose a over b and then choose d over c!

Another explanation of preference reversals is that people simply cannot process probability events very efficiently (see Example 3-4).

The phenomenon of preference reversal can be regarded in two ways. First, it may simply reflect the fact that some people are smarter than others in specific skills required by the experiments. If this is the case, a learning phenomenon is involved and the theory does not apply. Second, the phenomenon can be regarded as a fundamental contradiction of the theory of utility (expected utility or otherwise), in which case it is necessary to revise utility theory in a dramatic way.

Note: For extended discussions of preference reversals, see Paul Slovic and Sarah Lichtenstein, "Preference Reversals: A Broader Perspective," *American Economic Review* 73 (1983), pp. 596–605; and David Grether and Charles Plott, "Economic Theory of Choice and the Preference Reversal Phenomenon," *American Economic Review* 69 (1979), pp. 623–38.

$$Ey = \pi y_2 + (1 - \pi) y_1 = \pi(y_2 - y_1) + y_1. \tag{8}$$

Similarly, expected utility is

$$Eu = \pi u(y_2) + (1 - \pi)u(y_1) = \pi[u(y_2) - u(y_1)] + u(y_1). \tag{9}$$

Solving Equations (8) and (9) for π yields the two ratios:

$$\pi = \frac{Ey - y_1}{y_2 - y_1} \text{ and } \pi = \frac{Eu - u(y_1)}{u(y_2) - u(y_1)}$$

Because the ratios are in proportion, the expected utility of the uncertain prospect $(y_2, y_1; \pi)$ is obtained by drawing a vertical line from the expected consumption level, Ey, to point b on chord ac. The height of that vertical line locates Eu on the vertical axis. The consumer with this utility curve is risk-averse. He is willing to pay an insurance company $y_2 - Ey$ to avoid the uncertain prospect of the loss $Ey - y_1$. He feels better off because $u(Ey)$ is greater than Eu. In other words, a risk averter will always prefer the certainty of the mean income of an uncertain prospect to the uncertain prospect itself, according to the **expected-utility hypothesis.**

The **expected-utility hypothesis** is that, in general, consumers rank uncertain prospects, such as $(a, b; \pi)$, on the basis of their expected utility, $Eu = \pi u(a) + (1 - \pi)u(b)$.

If an insurance company established premiums such that its income without fires was $y_2 - Ey$ (as in Figure 3-9) and its payout with a fire was $Ey - y_1$, the consumer would be guaranteed a consumption of Ey in any case. With this premium structure, the insurance company's expected profit would be zero. Why?

Expected profit

$$= \pi(y_2 - Ey) - (1 - \pi)(Ey - y_1)$$
$$= [\pi y_2 + (1 - \pi) y_1] - Ey$$
$$= Ey - Ey = 0.$$

Thus, if the company insured a large number of cases, it would make no profit. In order to make a profit, the insurance company would have to raise its premium. Since its customers are risk-averse, the company can add a risk premium. People will pay to avoid risky situations. Figure 3-9 locates the most they will pay by constructing a certainty-equivalent income for the uncertain prospect. The uncertain prospect has an expected utility of Eu. The certainty-equivalent income, y_c, would generate the same utility as the expected utility of the uncertain prospect; that is, $Eu = u(y_c)$. As long as the utility function is concave, y_c is less than Ey. The difference between Ey and y_c in Figure 3-9 can be regarded as the risk premium. Thus there is a "market" for insurance—sometimes an unpredictable market (see Example 3-4).

In reality, people both gamble and take out insurance. How can we account for such seemingly conflicting behavior? Milton Friedman and Leonard Savage have hypothesized that although a utility function may be concave overall, there may be sections of it that are convex. The Friedman-Savage utility function is shown in Figure 3-10. Around the level of income Ey marginal utility is increasing, so the individual will prefer gambles that

FIGURE 3–10   The Friedman-Savage Model

This model assumes a curve that is concave except within a small range around the consumer's current income level, Ey. The convex curve in this area means that within the range y_1 to y_2, the consumer's behavior may be risk averse and risk-loving simultaneously (for example, both buying insurance and gambling). The certainty-equivalent income, y_c for these risks exceeds Ey.

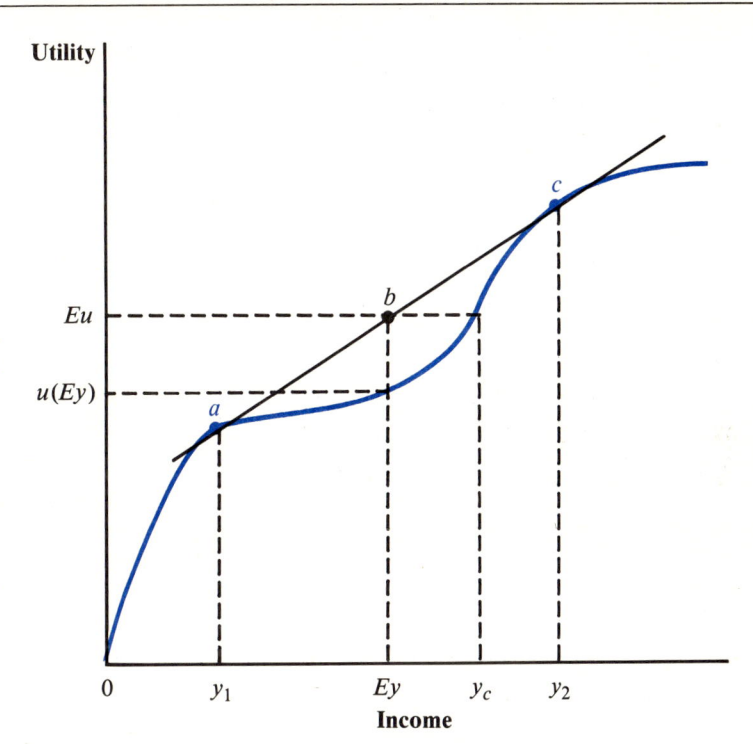

keep him or her in that range, with a certainty-equivalent income y_c that exceeds Ey. But the consumer's attitudes will differ in regard to gambles that are sufficiently outside the convex range.

Is it possible for the utility function to be everywhere convex? If the utility function were linear or convex, it would be possible to construct St. Petersburg games in which the expected utility is infinite. Since no one pays an infinite amount for such games (indeed, perhaps no more than $20 or $30), the utility function must generally display diminishing marginal utility. The Friedman-Savage utility function in Figure 3–10 satisfies this condition.

SUMMARY

1. A rational consumer is an economic agent who behaves according to the five axioms of consumer behavior under conditions of certainty: the axioms of comparison, nonsatiation, transitivity, substitution, and convexity.

2. Indifference curves show the various combinations of commodity bundles between which a consumer is indifferent. The marginal rate of

EXAMPLE 3-4 Flood Insurance, Flight Insurance, and Lotteries

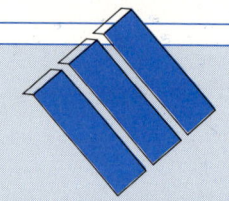

Kenneth Arrow, a Nobel laureate in economics, has offered a striking real-world counterexample to the expected-utility hypothesis. Since 1969 the U.S. government has subsidized flood insurance rates in certain areas of the country in which floods are particularly likely. These subsidized rates are so favorable that even risk-averse consumers should be willing to make a bet with the government. Nevertheless, many people in those areas do not take out such insurance.

In a field study by Kunreuther et al., 2,000 homeowners living in floodplains were interviewed. Many of these acted contrary to the hypothesis of expected-utility maximization. According to Arrow, the main factor determining whether people took out such insurance was whether their friends had taken it. These results seriously question the ability of ordinary people to process low-probability events with chances of large losses (or gains).

While flood insurance offers an example of people refusing a favorable bet, flight insurance and state lotteries offer examples of people accepting extremely unfavorable bets. Robert Strotz and Robert Eisner have argued that people purchase too much flight insurance when one compares the cost of such insurance to the safety records of the airlines. State lotteries pay out less than $0.50 on the dollar; yet there is considerable demand for lottery tickets.

Buying flight insurance may show extreme risk aversion, while buying state lottery tickets or refusing flood insurance may indicate extreme risk-seeking behavior. These examples cast some doubt on whether ordinary people follow the expected-utility hypothesis. Hence, economists are not entirely satisfied with the hypothesis. A new theory of choice—compatible with a richer menu of empirical possibilities—is clearly needed.

Sources: Kenneth Arrow, "Risk Perception in Psychology and Economics," *Economic Inquiry* 20 (1981), pp. 1–9; Howard Kunreuther, Ralph Ginsberg, Louis Miller, et al., *Disaster Insurance Protection: Public Policy Lessons* (New York: John Wiley, 1978); R. E. Brinner and C. T. Clotfeler, "An Economic Appraisal of State Lotteries," *National Tax Journal* 28 (1975).

---

substitution (MRS_{yx}) is the rate at which the consumer can substitute Y for X and still maintain the same utility. When an indifference curve is convex to the origin, the MRS_{yx} declines as more X is consumed.

3. Utility is a numerical representation of a consumer's preferences so that if bundle *a* is preferred to bundle *b*, $u(a) > u(b)$. Marginal utility is the rate of increase in utility per unit of increase in the consumption of a good, holding the consumption of other goods constant. The link between marginal utility and *MRS* is: $MRS_{yx} = MU_x/MU_y$. Indifference curves between two "goods" (commodities with positive marginal utilities) are

downward-sloping. Indifference curves between a good and a "bad" (a commodity with negative marginal utility) are upward-sloping. Indifference curves are always convex to the region of lower utility.

4. Probability is a measurement of the likelihood of some event occurring. If the outcomes are mutually exclusive, the sum of the probabilities of all the possible outcomes must be unity. If a and b are independent events, the probability of both events occurring together is the product of the two probabilities. A random variable is a variable that can take on different values according to some specified probability. The St. Petersburg Paradox is a game with an infinite expected value for which no individual would pay more than a finite sum, such as $30 or even $1 million. It is explained by the assumption that utility is a concave function of income.

5. The expected-utility hypothesis argues that people choose among uncertain situations by picking the one with the highest expected utility. The hypothesis follows from the axioms of behavior under uncertainty: the axioms of transitivity, certainty equivalents, independence, and irrelevance of the probability mechanism. For risk-averse behavior, the utility-of-income function is concave, indicating diminishing marginal utility of income. For risk-loving behavior, the utility-of-income function is convex, indicating increasing marginal utility of income. A risk-averse person will refuse a fair gamble (one with a zero expected value).

QUESTIONS AND PROBLEMS

1. A consumer buys a $6,000 Toyota rather than a $10,000 Chevrolet. Does the consumer prefer a Toyota to a Chevrolet?

2. For a given set of prices, draw a consumer's indifference curves between money and some highly desirable good. Compare these curves to ones depicting a consumer's preferences between money and a good that is a relatively undesirable good but still has positive marginal utility.

3. Using modern utility theory, can the utilities that different consumers derive from the same commodity bundle (or income) be compared? Why or why not?

4. Since indifference curves cannot intersect, must they be parallel? Explain your answer.

5. The following market baskets are on the same indifference curve: 1 unit of food, 10 units of clothing; 2 food, 9 clothing; 3 food, 7 clothing; 4 food, 4 clothing. Draw the indifference curve. How does MRS_{cf} vary as more food is consumed?

6. The following market baskets are on the same indifference curve: 1 unit

of eggs, 2 units of cereal; 2 eggs, 8 cereal; 3 eggs, 6 cereal; 4 eggs, 4 cereal; 5 eggs, 2 cereal. Draw the indifference curve. How does the *MRS* behave? What would you say about the substitutability of the two products?

7. Consider the commodity bundles of goods X and Y in Table A. Which of the indicated utility functions are compatible with the axioms of consumer behavior? In each case, which axioms (if any) are violated?

8. Draw a consumer's indifference curve between two bads, work and garbage.

9. A martini is made of gin and vermouth in various parts, depending on the tastes of the consumer. Goods used in combination to produce more complex goods are said to be complements. Draw the indifference curves for martini drinkers Alice and Cathy, whose tastes for gin *(g)* and vermouth *(v)* are as follows:
    a. Alice gets utility from one part gin and one part vermouth. More gin or vermouth adds or subtracts nothing from her utility. Thus, for Alice $u = \min(X_g, X_v)$.
    b. Cathy is not particular—she receives utility from more gin or more vermouth.

10. (Calculus required.) Calculate the marginal utilities for the following utility functions: $u = x_1 x_2$, $u = \ln(X_1) + \ln(X_2)$, and $u = x_1^2 x_2$.

11. How might you explain why some restaurants give free refills for tea but not for beer?

12. There are four aces in a deck of 52 cards. Suppose drawing an ace pays $26. What is the expected value of drawing an ace?

13. A consumer who has the utility function $u = m^{1/2}$ is offered a gamble paying $100 with probability 1/2 and paying 0 with probability 1/2. What is the certainty equivalent of this gamble?

14. A consumer's utility function is described by the following combinations of utility *(u)* and income *(m)*: $(u, m) = (10, 10), (18, 20), (24, 30), (28, 40),$

Table A

Bundle	Quantity of Good X	Quantity of Good Y	U_1	U_2	U_3	U_4
a	1	1	10	10	5	200
b	2	2	25	15	5	202
c	3	1	20	20	5	201
d	1	3	20	20	5	201

(30, 50). What is the expected utility of the following uncertain prospects?
a. (10, 50; 1/2)
b. (20, 30; 1/6)
c. (20, 40; 1/3).

15. A consumer is indifferent between $60 and the uncertain prospect ($100, $40; 1/2). She is also indifferent between $80 and the uncertain prospect ($100, $40; 3/4). According to the axioms of consumer behavior under uncertainty, how should she rank the uncertain prospects ($100, $60; 3/4) and ($100, $80; 1/2)?

SUGGESTED READINGS

Alchian, Armen A. "The Meaning of Utility Measurement." *American Economic Review*, March 1953, pp. 26–50.
Baumol, William J. *Economic Theory and Operations Analysis,* 2nd ed. Englewood Cliffs, N.J.: Prentice-Hall, 1965, pp. 180–88.
Dorfman, Robert. *The Price System*. Englewood Cliffs, N.J.: Prentice-Hall, 1964, chap. 3.
Friedman, Milton, and Leonard J. Savage, "The Utility Analysis of Choices Involving Risk." *Journal of Political Economy,* 1948, pp. 463–74.
Hayek, Frederich A. "The *Non Sequitur* of the 'Dependence Effect'." *Southern Economic Journal,* 1961.
Hicks, John R. *Value and Capital*. London: Oxford University Press, 1939, chap. 1.

CHAPTER 4

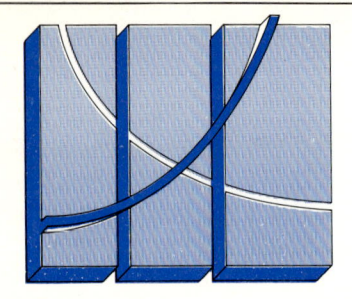

THE THEORY OF CONSUMER DEMAND

The last chapter described the way commodity bundles are ranked by a rational consumer. We assume that the economic agent is decisive, consistent, nonsatiated, willing to make substitutions, and variety-seeking. The preferences or tastes of the consumer are given independently of prices or income—his or her budget. In this chapter we will study the consumer's actual choices. The theory of consumer demand follows from the assumption that the consumer maximizes utility by selecting the most preferred commodity bundle from those that can be afforded. Demand is the outcome of the meeting between preferences and affordable commodity bundles.

THE BUDGET CONSTRAINT

What the consumer can afford is dictated by the budget constraint. Two considerations enter into the determination of the budget constraint: (1) the consumer's income, and (2) the prices of the goods to be bought. High incomes and low prices promote greater opportunities than low incomes and high prices.

Income is, of course, determined by such factors as the wage rate, hours worked, and earnings from the ownership of assets. Later on we will study the determination of individual income. For the moment we will make two assumptions.

Assumption 1. Consumer income is fixed or exogenous (received from the outside).

The next assumption describes the market faced by the consumer. Under many circumstances, the individual consumer has very little control over the

FIGURE 4-1 A Consumer's Budget Constraint for Two Goods, X and Y

The shaded area is the set of affordable commodity bundles; its boundary is the budget line. The slope of the budget line is p_x/p_y in absolute value.

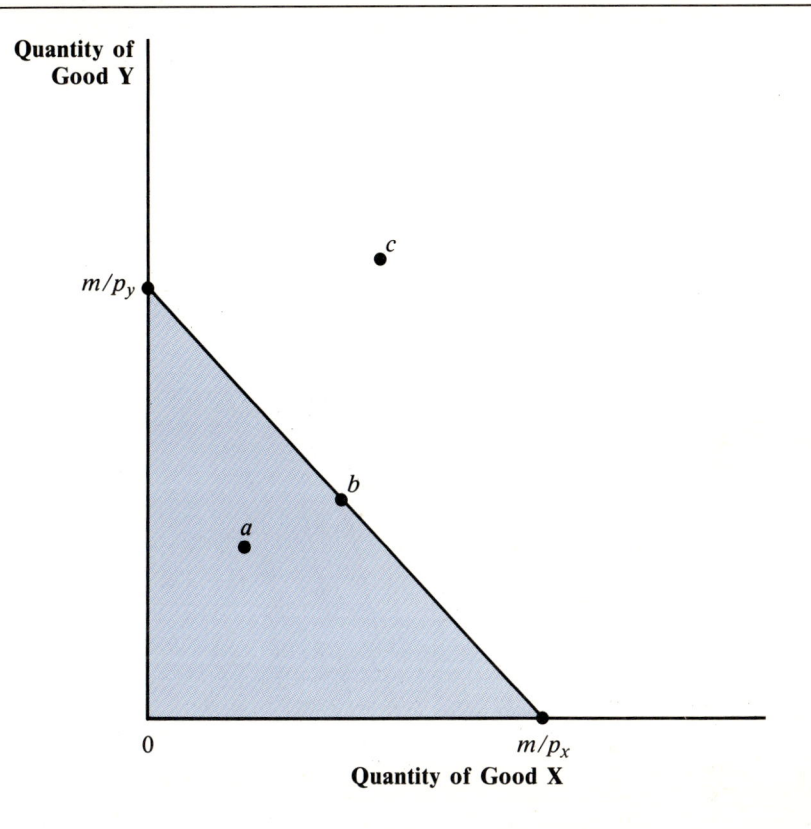

[Figure: Budget constraint diagram with Quantity of Good Y on vertical axis and Quantity of Good X on horizontal axis. Vertical intercept at m/p_y, horizontal intercept at m/p_x. Shaded triangular affordable region. Point a is inside the region, point b is on the budget line, point c is outside the region.]

prices of things to be bought. This is especially true for prices paid in everyday shopping for groceries, gasoline, clothing, and for prices paid for utilities like gas, electricity, and water. From time to time the consumer engages in bargaining (for example, when buying a new car), but the gains may be relatively limited. The consumer can also partly determine a price by shopping for the cheapest price (see Chapter 12 for a discussion of comparison shopping). In this chapter, we abstract from search and bargaining and focus on the central fact: when a commodity is traded on a market, the price the individual faces is more or less fixed.

Assumption 2. The consumer faces fixed prices for goods to be bought; that is, the consumer is a *price taker*. This assumption implies that the consumer, as a price taker, can buy all he or she wants at the posted prices.

Given these two assumptions, it is easy to see how much a consumer can afford under his or her budget constraint. For simplicity, imagine the consumer buys only two goods: goods X and Y. Figure 4-1 graphs quantities of good X (on the horizontal axis) and quantities of good Y (on the vertical axis) in service flows per unit of time. Let p_x be the price per unit of good X and p_y

FIGURE 4-2   **Consumer Equilibrium under Budget Constraint**

Consumer equilibrium is attained at point *e*, where $MRS_{yx} = p_x/p_y$. At point *e*, the highest possible indifference curve, in this case U_3, is tangent to the budget line.

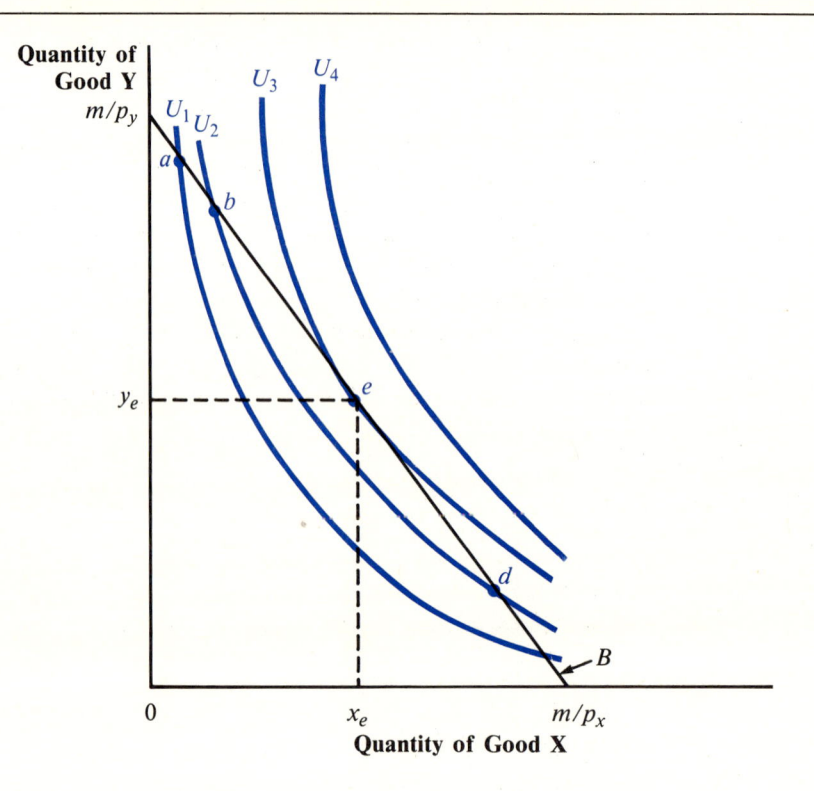

[Figure: Indifference curves U_1, U_2, U_3, U_4 with budget line from m/p_y on Y-axis to m/p_x on X-axis. Points a, b on budget line above equilibrium, point e at tangency with U_3 at (x_e, y_e), point d below equilibrium on budget line, point B beyond budget line.]

the price per unit of good Y, and let *m* be the consumer's income per unit of time. Assume also that the consumer can neither borrow nor lend. The assumptions that there are only two goods and that the consumer cannot borrow or lend are not restrictive. We assume two goods so that the theory can be presented graphically; later we will see that the theory can be extended to borrowing or lending situations by treating saving as a demand for future goods.

With our simplifications, the amount spent on goods X and Y is limited by the consumer's income, *m*. The quantity of good X is *x*; the quantity consumed of good Y is *y*. The amount the individual spends on good X is $p_x x$ and the amount spent on good Y is $p_y y$. Thus,

$$p_x x + p_y y \leq m \tag{1}$$

Figure 4-1 shows the budget constraint graphically. The most the consumer can spend on good X is m/p_x; the most the consumer can spend on good Y is m/p_y. The color shaded area is the set of affordable bundles, called the *consumption possibilities*, or *budget set*. A point such as *a*, inside the shaded triangle, is a bundle that costs less than *m*; a point such as *b*, on the boundary, costs exactly *m*. Any point outside the shaded region, such as *c*,

The **budget line** consists of all the commodity bundles that cost the same as the consumer's income, m. For two goods, X and Y, the slope is p_x/p_y in absolute value and is interpreted as the price of good X in terms of the good Y.

costs more than m. The outer boundary is called the **budget line**, or budget **constraint**.

The slope of the budget line in absolute value is the ratio of the y-intercept, m/p_y, to the x-intercept, m/p_x, or:

$$\frac{m}{p_y} \div \frac{m}{p_x} = \frac{m}{p_y} \times \frac{p_x}{m} = \frac{p_x}{p_y}.$$

Notice that the slope is the price of the good on the horizontal axis divided by the price of the good on the vertical axis. What interpretation can we place on p_x/p_y? A numerical example will be helpful. Let $p_x = \$10$ and $p_y = \$5$, so that $p_x/p_y = 2$. If good X costs twice as much as good Y, the consumer can substitute two units of good Y for a unit of X and still spend the same amount. Thus, p_x/p_y tells us how much of good Y the consumer must give up to buy one more unit of good X. The ratio p_x/p_y has the dimensions of "y units per unit of X." For example, if $p_x = \$10$ per gallon and $p_y = \$5$ per pound, $p_x/p_y = 2$ pounds of Y per gallon of X.

The equation for the budget line can be derived as follows. Inequality (1) can be written in equation form as:

$$p_x x + p_y y = m. \tag{2}$$

Dividing through by p_y and solving for y:

$$y = \frac{m}{p_y} - \frac{p_x}{p_y} x. \tag{3}$$

The first term is the y-intercept, and the coefficient of x is the slope of the equation.

CONSUMER EQUILIBRIUM

Rational economic agents maximize satisfaction or profit. Applying this principle of action to our theory of consumer behavior, we assume that each agent will choose the commodity bundle that maximizes utility along his or her budget constraint.

Figure 4-2 illustrates how the consumer maximizes satisfaction subject to constraint. Four representative indifference curves for a consumer—U_1, U_2, U_3, and U_4—are shown in relation to the consumer's budget line, B. The consumer prefers to be on a higher indifference curve, because goods X and Y yield positive marginal utility *(MU)*; thus any point on, say, U_4 is preferred to any point on, say, U_2. Unfortunately, the consumer is limited by the budget constraint and can only choose points such as a, b, e, or d. (The consumer could choose points below the budget line; but with nonsatiation, such points would be considered inferior to some point on the budget line.) The consumer is in equilibrium at point e, where the budget line is tangent to an indifference curve. When indifference curves are convex to the origin,

PRACTICE EXERCISE 4-1

Q. If two goods are perfect substitutes, a given amount of one good will always interchange for a certain amount of the other good. The indifference curve will be a straight line with a constant marginal rate of substitution, MRS_{yx}. Can you still use the rule that $MRS_{yx} = p_x/p_y$? If not, what is the proper rule?

A. No. The proper rule is simple. Remember, MRS_{yx} is how much of good Y the consumer is willing to substitute for 1 unit of good X, whereas p_x/p_y is how much of good Y the consumer must pay for good X. If $p_x/p_y < MRS_{yx}$, the consumer will spend everything on good X. Without a diminishing marginal rate of substitution, there is no stopping the consumer at some balanced bundle. Thinking in terms of dollars rather than good Y makes it even simpler. If you are willing to pay $5 (the MRS) for a good that costs $3, you'll continue to buy the good as long as the MRS exceeds $3—eventually, all income is devoted to the good. Geometrically, Figure A shows the action. The indifference curves are parallel straight lines. If $p_x/p_y < MRS_{yx}$, the budget line B is flatter than the indifference curves. Clearly, point n on the budget line reaches the highest indifference curve, U_3.

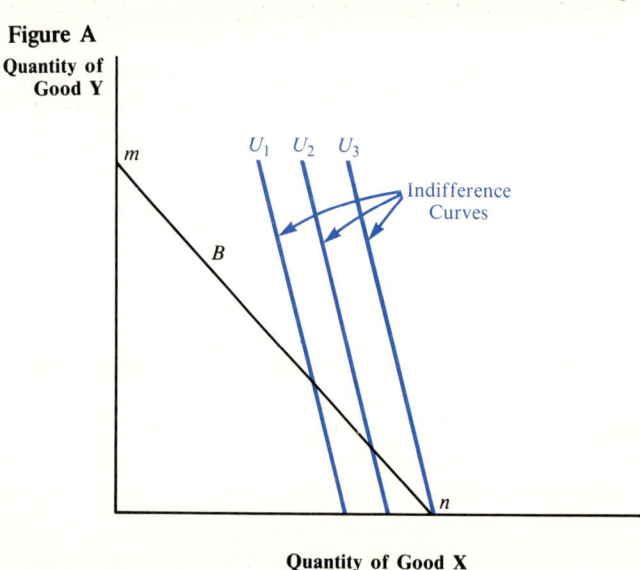

Figure A

Quantity of Good Y (vertical axis), *Quantity of Good X* (horizontal axis). Budget line B from m to n. Indifference curves U_1, U_2, U_3 shown as parallel straight lines.

the indifference curve that is tangent to the budget line is higher than any other indifference curve touching the budget line. At the point of tangency, the consumer is in equilibrium because a move away from e along the budget line is a move away from the highest possible curve, U_3. At point e both the indifference curve and the budget line have the same slope, and, thus, the equilibrium condition is $MRS_{yx} = p_x/p_y$.

Another way of understanding the equilibrium condition is to consider an arbitrary point such as a on the budget line. In Chapter 3, we learned that the absolute slope of the indifference curve at some point is the marginal rate of substitution of good Y for good X—the rate at which the individual is just willing to substitute good Y per unit of good X. At point a in Figure 4-2, the MRS of Y for X exceeds the absolute slope of the budget line, p_x/p_y, which is the rate at which the individual *must* give up some quantity of good Y to buy a unit of X in the marketplace. Thus, the individual is willing to substitute more Y for good X than he or she must give up in the marketplace. In other words, the consumer at point a values good X more highly than the market does. As a consequence, the consumer finds that buying more X and less Y is beneficial. For example, suppose $MRS_{yx} = 4$ and $p_x/p_y = 2$. The consumer considers four units of Y to be the equivalent of one unit of X but only has to give up two units of Y to buy it. Imagine that the consumer, thus, moves to point b. Notice that point b is on a higher indifference curve, U_2 rather than U_1. The consumer's utility has increased. But the same is true at b as at a: $MRS_{yx} > p_x/p_y$. Again, more of good X will be purchased at the expense of good Y. Should the consumer move as far as point d, the opposite is true: $MRS_{yx} < p_x/p_y$. At a point such as d, the marginal benefit of buying X is less than its cost, so less of good X is purchased. The consumer will gravitate towards point e where the slope of the indifference curve equals the slope of the budget line. We are led to the same conclusion: consumer equilibrium is reached where $MRS_{yx} = p_x/p_y$.

In marginal-utility terms, the consumer-equilibrium conditions can be rewritten in an illuminating fashion. As we saw in Chapter 3, $MRS_{yx} = MU_x/MU_y$. Thus, at the tangency point e in Figure 4-2, we can write either Equation (4) or Equation (5).

$$MU_x/MU_y = p_x/p_y. \tag{4}$$

$$MU_x/p_x = MU_y/p_y. \tag{5}$$

Equation (5) states that consumers equate the marginal utility per dollar for each good. The ratio MU/p is expressed in units of utility per dollar. If the marginal utility of milk is 10 utils and the price of milk is \$2 a gallon, then MU/p is "5 utils per dollar." At point a in the figure, $MU_x/p_x > MU_y/p_y$. Because the extra utility of another dollar spent on good X exceeds that of another dollar spent on good Y, spending more on X and less on Y will increase total utility. By spending more on good X and less on good Y, MU_y rises relative to MU_x until the condition in Equation (5) is satisfied.

The consumer is choosing the optimal or utility-maximizing commodity bundle when, first, $m = p_x x + p_y y$ and, second, $MRS_{yx} = MU_x/MU_y = p_x/p_y$.

The above two rules provide two equations to solve for unknown values of x and y. Generally speaking, n equations are needed to solve for n unknowns. As we can see in Figure 4-2, the equilibrium values of x and y—labeled x_e and y_e—depend on the parameters of the problem. The param-

PRACTICE EXERCISE 4-2

Q. Consider a consumer whose marginal-utility schedules for goods X and Y are given in Table A. The consumer's income is $10, $p_x = \$2$, and $p_y = \$1$. What is the consumer's demand for goods X and Y?

A. When $x = 3$ and $y = 4$, Equations (2) and (5) are satisfied. The consumer is spending $10 [= \$2(3) + \$1(4)]$ and $MU_x/p_x = 16/2 = MU_y/p_y = 8/1$.

Table A

Quantity of Good X	Marginal Utility of Good X, MU_x	Quantity of Good Y	Marginal Utility of Good Y, MU_y
1	20	1	11
2	18	2	10
3	16	3	9
4	14	4	8
5	12	5	7
6	10	6	6

eters of this consumer's problem are m, p_x, and p_y. Thus, the equilibrium values of x and y depend on money income, the price of good X, and the price of good Y.[1] We can express these values as the functions

$$x = x(p_x, p_y, m) \quad \text{and} \quad y = y(p_x, p_y, m) \quad (6)$$

---

[1]. The equilibrium conditions can be derived mathematically. We must choose quantity X of good X and quantity Y of good Y so as to maximize the utility function $u = u(x,y)$ subject to the income constraint $m = p_x x + p_y y$. A powerful indirect approach to constrained maximization is to write out the Lagrangian function:

$$L = u(x,y) + \lambda(m - p_x x - p_y y). \quad (A)$$

This method works because when L is maximized, so is u; because when the constraint is satisfied, $L = u$. The variable λ is called the Lagrangian multiplier. We now have three variables: x, y, and λ. The method of Lagrange is to take the partial derivatives of Equation (A) with respect to these variables and set each equal to zero. By the definition of marginal utility, we know that $MU_x = \partial u/\partial x = MU_y = \partial u/\partial y$. Hence, we obtain the three equations:

$$\partial L/\partial x = MU_x - \lambda p_x = 0. \quad (B)$$

$$\partial L/\partial y = MU_y - \lambda p_y = 0. \quad (C)$$

$$\partial L/\partial \lambda = m - p_x x - p_y y = 0. \quad (D)$$

These three equations can be used to solve for x, y, and λ. Equations (B) and (C) imply that $MU_x/p_x = MU_y/p_y = \lambda$. Thus λ can be interpreted as the extra utility per additional dollar or the marginal utility of money to the consumer. Equations (B) and (C) then have a straightforward economic meaning: the consumer is in equilibrium when marginal utility equals marginal sacrifice; λp_x, for example, is the utility sacrificed by buying a unit of good X.

PRACTICE EXERCISE 4–3

Q. Assume that the marginal-utility schedules for goods X and Y are independent and subject to the law of diminishing marginal utility. Can either good X or good Y be an inferior good?

A. No. When income increases, $MU_x/p_x = MU_y/p_y$. A bit more income devoted to good X causes MU_x/p_x to be less than MU_y/p_y because of the law of diminishing marginal utility. Thus, more must be spent on good Y, too, in order to bring about equal MUs per dollar. Both goods must be normal. This result extends to any number of goods. For this reason, economists abandoned the assumption that marginal-utility schedules are independent—in the real world, some goods are inferior.

These equations are the consumer's *demand functions* for good X and good Y.

It may be useful to consider an example of deriving a demand function from a utility function. Let $u = xy$ be the utility function. Since in this case $MU_x = y$ and $MU_y = x$, Equation (4) becomes $y/x = p_x/p_y$. But this means that $p_x x = p_y y$; dollar expenditures on each good are equal, so that exactly one half of all income is spent on each good. This means that the demand function for good X is $x = m/2p_x$; the demand function for good Y is $y = m/2p_y$. In this highly special case, the demand for each good does *not* depend on the price of the other good.[2]

The consumer equilibrium conditions are powerful. It might be thought that the idea of consumers choosing bundles to maximize utility is just empty rhetoric; whatever people do could be considered the utility-maximizing strategy. But the axioms of consumer behavior permit only certain actions. As a consequence, the consumer-equilibrium conditions impose restrictions on how consumer demand will respond to changes in prices and income. (See Example 4–1 for an application of this concept to food stamps.)

CHANGES IN INCOME

Inferior and Normal Goods

A **normal good** is one for which demand increases when income increases, holding prices constant.

When income changes, the demand for a good normally changes. Indeed, when income increases, we expect the demand for **normal goods** and services to increase as well. As income increases, however, consumers *reduce*

---

2. The marginal utility of income, λ, is easy to calculate in this example. As derived in footnote 1 above, $\lambda = MU_x/p_x = y/p_x$. Substituting $y = m/2p_y$ yields $\lambda = m/2p_x p_y$.

FIGURE 4-3 The Income/Consumption Curve

Increases in income cause parallel shifts in the budget line. As income increases from m_1 to m_2 to m_3, the budget line shifts from B to B' to B''. The sequence of consumer equilibrium points forms a curve called the income/consumption (*IC*) curve.

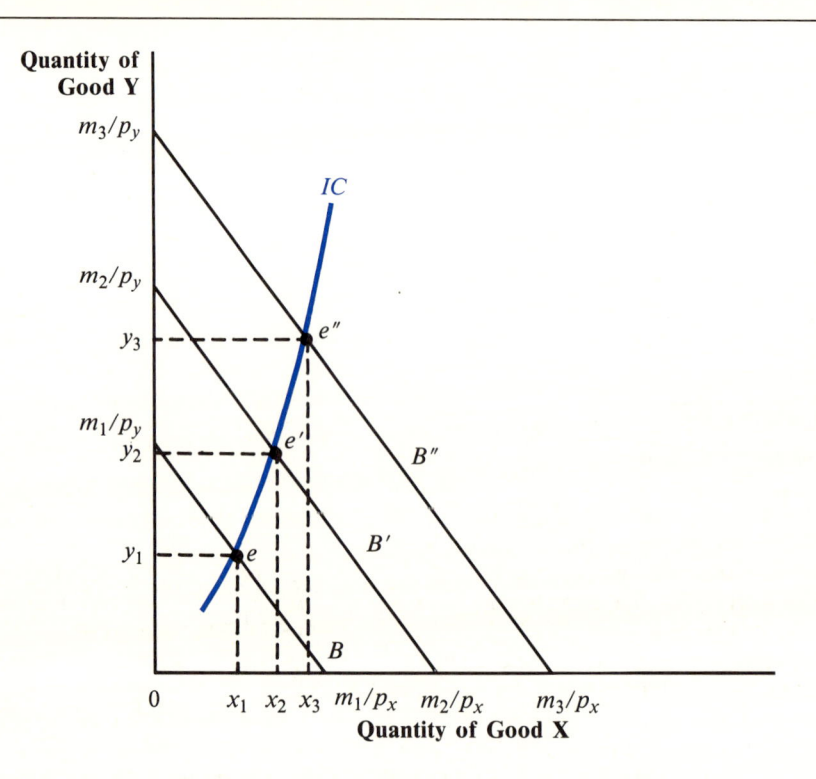

[Graph: Quantity of Good Y on vertical axis with markings m_3/p_y, m_2/p_y, y_3, m_1/p_y, y_2, y_1; Quantity of Good X on horizontal axis with markings x_1, x_2, x_3, m_1/p_x, m_2/p_x, m_3/p_x. Three parallel budget lines B, B', B'' with equilibrium points e, e', e'' connected by the IC curve.]

An **inferior good** is one for which demand decreases as income increases, holding prices constant.

their demand for **inferior goods** and services. For example, as income goes up, a particular consumer may buy fewer potatoes and less hamburger meat.

Notice that calling a good *inferior* does not imply the good is of inferior quality—the potatoes or meat may be of the highest quality. If goods are defined narrowly enough, there are many goods that are inferior for particular consumers. For example, as income rises, a person's demand for a Cadillac may fall while his or her demand for a Mercedes-Benz rises—to that person, the Cadillac is the inferior good, even though for the market as a whole a Cadillac is a normal good.

The Income/Consumption Curve

Figure 4-3 shows what happens to the demand for normal goods when income increases. Suppose income is initially m_1. The budget line is then B, and consumer equilibrium is achieved at point e. Now let income rise from m_1 to m_2. Because m_2 is greater than m_1, the maximum amounts of goods X and Y that can be purchased increase in proportion to the increase in income. There is, thus, a shift in the budget line from B to B'. Because prices have remained constant, the slopes of both budget lines are equal to the same p_x/p_y ratio. Thus, changes in income cause parallel shifts in the budget line. The equilibrium consumption bundle shifts from e to e', so the demand

EXAMPLE 4–1   How to Give Away Food Stamps

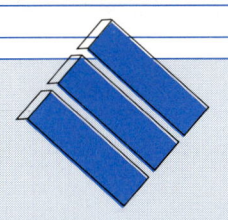

In 1983, about 19 million Americans received food stamps (vouchers for the purchase of food) totaling $10.3 billion. Thus, each of the recipients of food stamps was given an average of $45 per month during 1983.

Prior to 1977, food-stamp recipients had to pay for a monthly allotment of food stamps. The amount they had to pay was in inverse proportion to family income. Since 1977, the food stamps have been simply given away, with the amount varying inversely to income.

The difference between the old system and the new is illustrated by the following hypothetical example. Consider a consumer with a monthly income of $500 who (without food stamps) devotes $200 per month to food consumption. Suppose that the government wishes to increase the consumer's food expenditures. Let's say that in the pre-1977 system, the consumer might be given $250 worth of food stamps for $200—a net cost of $50. Then, in the post-1977 system, the consumer would simply be given $50 worth of food stamps. It may appear that the systems are equivalent, but they are not. The new system gives the consumer higher utility! The accompanying diagram shows why. Food items are measured horizontally, and the nonfood items are measured vertically. Food items and nonfood items are assumed to cost $1 per unit to the consumer. Thus, with a monthly income of $500, the budget line is *ab*. The equilibrium consumption combination (before food stamps) is point *e*, where $300 is devoted to nonfood items and $200 is devoted to food items. Now, assume the consumer is given the option of paying $200 for $250 worth of food stamps. After buying the food stamps, the consumer's budget line is *cedf*, a segment of which runs along *gf*. The consumer is obviously better off than before—consuming at point *d* rather than at point *e*. The pre-1977 system raises utility from U_1 to U_2.

In the post-1977 system, the consumer is simply given $50 worth of food stamps, which shifts the budget line horizontally by $50 from *ab* to *agf*. The consumer equilibrium would then shift from point *e* to point *h*—and utility would increase from U_1 to U_3. The old system of giving out food stamps forced the consumer (short of going to the black market for food stamps) to increase his or her food consumption by $50. In other words, the old system of handing out food stamps did not allow the consumer to allocate income freely between food and nonfood items; the new system is more permissive.

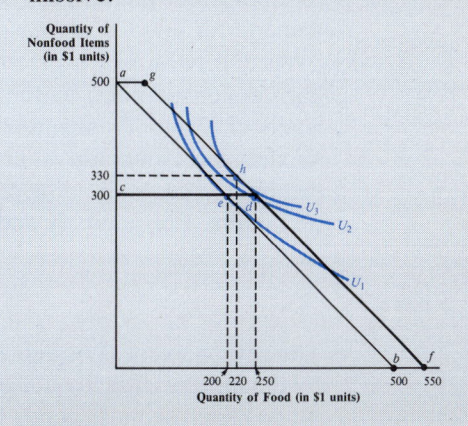

Sources: Kenneth Clarkson, "Welfare Benefits of the Food-Stamps Program," *Southern Economic Journal* 43 (1976): 864–78. Edgar and Jacquelene Browning, *Public Finance and the Price System* (New York: Macmillan, 1979), ch. 4.

FIGURE 4–4   Engel Curves

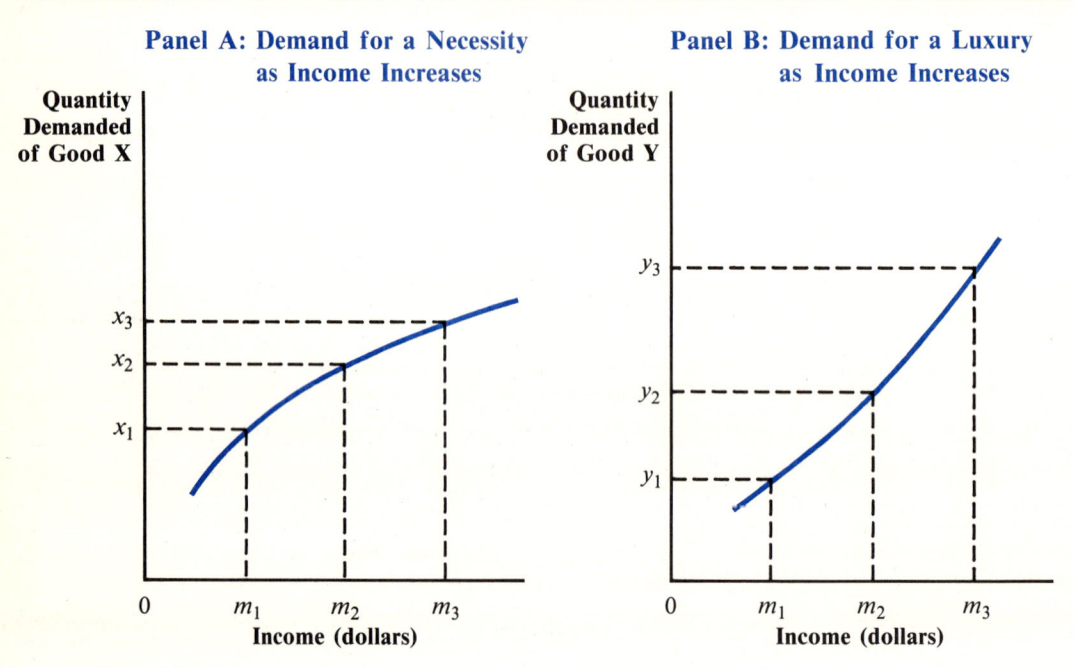

Panel A: Demand for a Necessity as Income Increases

Panel B: Demand for a Luxury as Income Increases

Panel A shows the Engel curve for a necessity (Good X); Panel B shows the Engel curve for a luxury (Good Y). Both are based on the income/consumption curve in Figure 4–3.

The **income/consumption (IC) curve** shows the locus of equilibrium commodity bundles as income changes, holding commodity prices constant.

for both goods increases. The demand for good X increases from x_1 to x_2; the demand for good Y increases from y_1 to y_2.

As the consumer's income increases further, from m_2 to m_3, the equilibrium consumption pattern shifts again, to point e''. The new equilibrium levels of X and Y consumption are now x_3 and y_3. The sequence of utility-maximizing commodity bundles, such as e, e', and e'' that are chosen as income increases, holding prices constant, make up the **income/consumption (IC) curve**. For goods X and Y in Figure 4–3, this is the curve IC.

Income Elasticity

The responsiveness of demand to changes in consumer income is measured by the **income elasticity of demand** (η_m). The income elasticity of demand will be positive for most goods because the higher are their incomes, the more consumers demand of most goods. If the income elasticity equals unity, a 1 percent increase in income will lead to a 1 percent increase in the demand for the good. The fraction of income devoted to, say, good X is $p_x x/m$. In this case, the consumer would continue to spend the same fraction of income on the good as before income increased. If the income elasticity exceeds 1, the

CHANGES IN INCOME

The income elasticity of demand (η_m) is the proportional (or percentage) change in demand for a product divided by the proportional (or percentage) change in income, holding all prices fixed.

consumer will spend a larger fraction of income on the good as income rises, because x rises faster than m. If the income elasticity for some good is less than 1, the consumer will spend a smaller fraction of income on a good as income increases, because x rises more slowly than m.

Necessities and **luxuries** can be defined using the income-elasticity concept. Using this criterion, goods such as food are usually considered necessities, while recreational vehicles and fur coats are considered luxury items. Notice that the economist allows these terms to be defined by objective market choices rather than by individual perceptions as to what is "necessary."

Engel Curves

Necessities are goods whose income elasticity of demand is less than 1.

Luxuries are goods whose income elasticity of demand is greater than 1.

An **Engel curve** shows the relationship between the quantity demanded of a good and the consumer's income level.

The **adding-up rule** is that the sum of all income elasticities, weighted by the relative importance of each good in the budget, must be unity.

Panel A of Figure 4–4 plots the level of income and the demand for good X from Figure 4–3's income/consumption curve. The resulting curve is called an **Engel curve** in honor of the Prussian statistician Ernst Engel, who in the mid-19th century noted a universal tendency for the percentage of family income devoted to food to decline as income rises. Notice that the Engel curve in Panel A is concave to the horizontal axis; the income elasticity of demand for good X is less than unity. Panel B plots the Engel curve for good Y in Figure 4–3. It is convex to the horizontal axis, meaning that the income elasticity of demand for good Y exceeds unity.

In a two-good world it is a necessary mathematical fact that if good X has an income elasticity less than 1, good Y has an income elasticity greater than 1. If income changes holding prices constant, from the budget constraint it must be that

$$\Delta m = p_x \Delta x + p_y \Delta y. \tag{7}$$

Dividing both sides of Equation (7) by Δm yields the **adding-up rule** for income elasticities:

$$\begin{aligned} 1 &= \frac{p_x \Delta X}{\Delta m} + \frac{p_y \Delta Y}{\Delta m} \\ &= p_x \left(\frac{x}{m}\right)\left(\frac{\Delta x}{\Delta m}\right)\left(\frac{m}{x}\right) + p_y \left(\frac{y}{m}\right)\left(\frac{\Delta Y}{\Delta m}\right)\left(\frac{m}{y}\right) \\ &= \left(\frac{p_x x}{m}\right)\eta_m^x + \left(\frac{p_y y}{m}\right)\eta_m^y. \end{aligned} \tag{8}$$

Because the fractions $p_x x/m$ and $p_y y/m$ add to unity, Equation (8) implies that if X is a necessity, Y must be a luxury. This relationship is shown geometrically by the IC curve in Figure 4–3. If the IC curve bends toward the x-axis, it must bend away from the y-axis!

Inferior Goods and the Income/Consumption Curve

All goods are normal over some range of income. After all, if a good is purchased at all, demand for it must increase as income rises from zero to the current level. Thus, if at the current level of income a good is inferior,

FIGURE 4-5 Good X as a Normal and as an Inferior Good

When income is less than m_c, good X is normal. After income level m_c is reached, good X becomes inferior, and the *IC* curve bends toward the y-axis. All inferior goods are normal over some range of income.

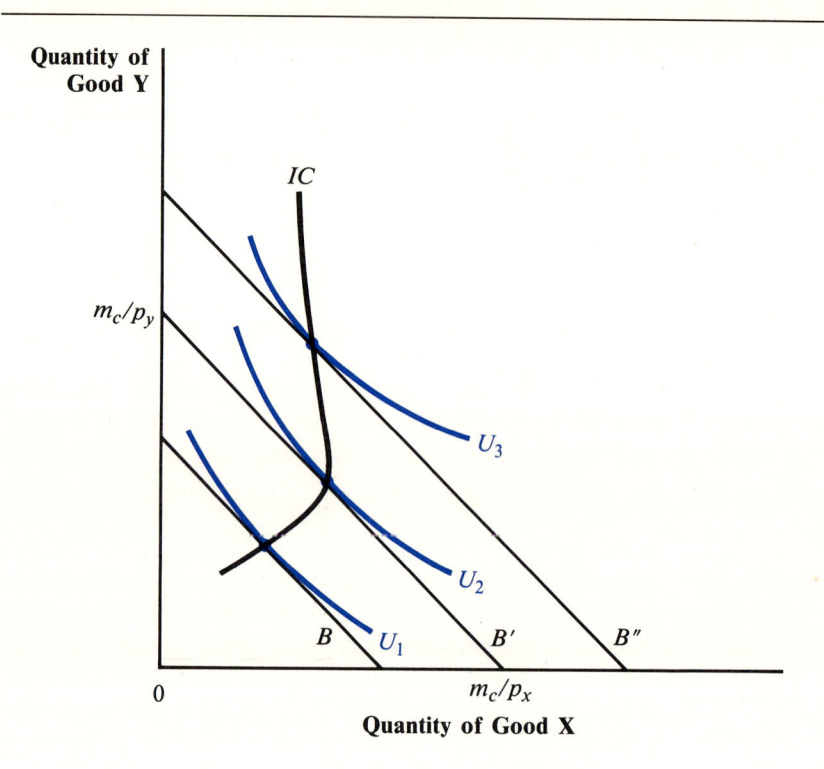

[Figure: Graph with Quantity of Good Y on vertical axis and Quantity of Good X on horizontal axis. Budget lines B, B′, B″ with intercepts m_c/p_y and m_c/p_x. Indifference curves U_1, U_2, U_3. IC curve bends backward toward y-axis at higher income.]

there must be lower levels of income for which the good would be normal. Figure 4-5 graphs indifference curves and budget lines similar to those in Figure 4-3. In Figure 4-5, however, the income/consumption (*IC*) curve for goods X and Y is affected when, after income reaches a certain critical level m_c, good X becomes inferior. When income is greater than m_c, the *IC* curve bends backward. When income is below level m_c, good X is normal.

The Absence of Money Illusion

Money illusion occurs when an equal or proportionate change in all money prices and money income causes a change in demand.

If money income and all prices doubled, relative prices and real income would remain unchanged. Presumably, any consumer aware of these purely monetary changes would continue to buy the same goods as before. Unless tastes change, the equilibrium commodity bundle will not shift as long as the budget line remains the same. A fundamental implication of utility-maximization theory and the assumption that tastes (that is, the indifference map itself) are invariant to prices and income is that demand functions do not reflect **money illusion**. (See Example 4-2.)

Figure 4-6 shows that there is no money illusion when consumer demand

CHANGES IN INCOME

FIGURE 4-6   **Proportionate Change in Income and Prices**

A doubling of both money prices and income leaves the budget constraint the same as before. If the consumer is not subject to a money illusion, choices of goods will be unaffected and will remain at point e.

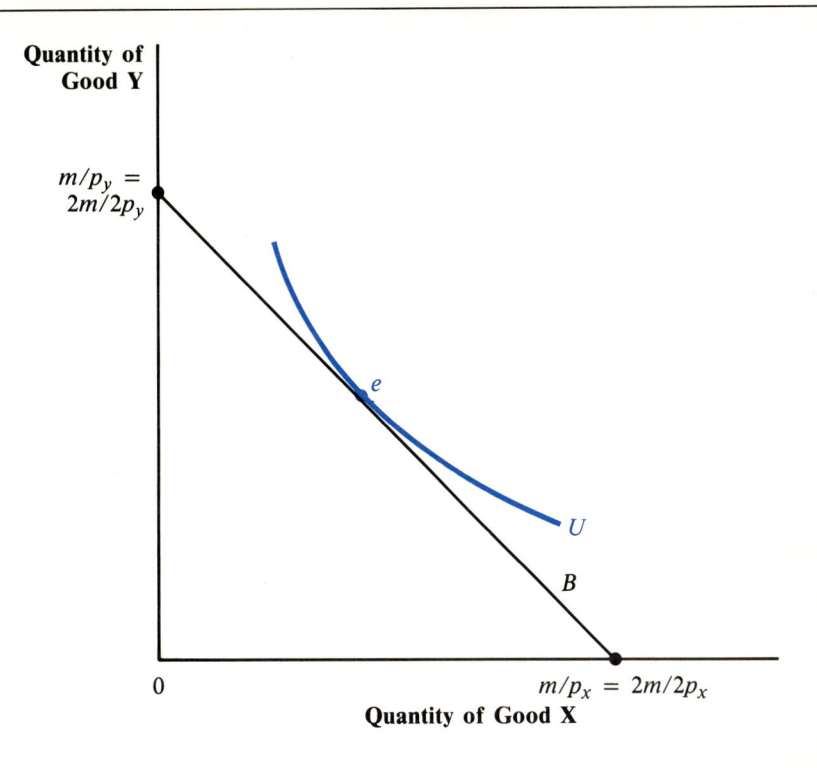

functions reflect rational, utility-maximizing behavior. Suppose m doubles to $2m$, p_x doubles to $2p_x$, and p_y doubles to $2p_y$. Obviously, the budget line B remains the same, so the set of affordable bundles has not changed at all. Nothing has changed in real terms, so the equilibrium commodity bundle remains at point e. In general terms, in the absence of money illusion, demand functions have the following property:

$$x(p_x, p_y, m) = x(\mu p_x, \mu p_y, \mu m) = x. \qquad (9)$$

This simply says that if all prices and money income are multiplied by any positive number μ, nothing happens to demand. In effect, only real values matter.[3] (See Example 4-3.)

---

3. When a function has the property displayed in Equation (9), it is said to be *homogeneous of degree zero* in the mathematics literature. Equation (9) implies that only real values matter in the following sense. Because the condition holds for all μ, let $\mu = 1/p_y$. Thus, we can write

$$x = x(p_x/p_y, 1, m/p_y) \equiv x(p_x/p_y, m/p_y).$$

The demand for X just depends on the relative price of X, p_x/p_y, and income measured in units of good Y, m/p_y.

FIGURE 4-7 Price/Consumption Curve

The price/consumption curve (*PC*) shows how the equilibrium quantities of goods X and Y vary as the price of good X changes, holding the price of good Y and money income, *M*, constant. When the price of good X falls, the budget line shifts outward, from *B* to *B'* to *B"*, generating the equilibrium points *e*, *e'*, and *e"*.

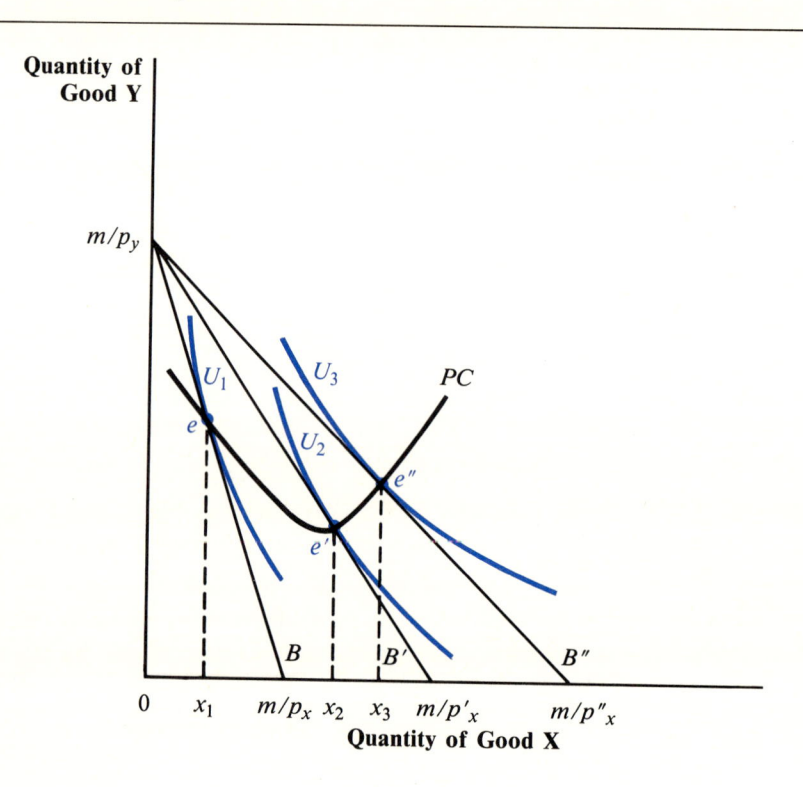

CHANGES IN PRICE

We claimed in Chapter 2 that the *price* of a good coordinates the separate supply and demand decisions of producers and consumers of the good. It is, therefore, important to investigate in more detail the impact of a change in price on the quantity demanded of a good. The relationship between a good's price and quantity demanded is called the **demand curve** or **demand schedule**.

The **demand curve** or **demand schedule** shows how the quantity demanded of a good varies with its price, holding other prices and income constant.

The alert reader will recall that we use the phrase "change in demand" to describe what happens when income changes, and the phrase "change in quantity demanded" to describe what happens when the price of the good itself changes. A *change in quantity demanded* is a movement along the demand curve; a *change in demand* is a movement of the entire curve.

The Price/Consumption Curve

To derive the demand curve for good X we must change the price of X, holding income, *m*, and the price of Y, m/p_y, constant. Figure 4-7 carries out this experiment. The budget line is initially *B*, when the price of good X is p_x. The equilibrium commodity bundle is *e*. Now let the price of X fall, to p'_x and

FIGURE 4-8   The Law of Demand

The demand curve, D, is derived by plotting the prices of Good X and the associated quantities of X demanded on the price/consumption curve in Figure 4-7. The demand curve is downward-sloping, reflecting the law of demand.

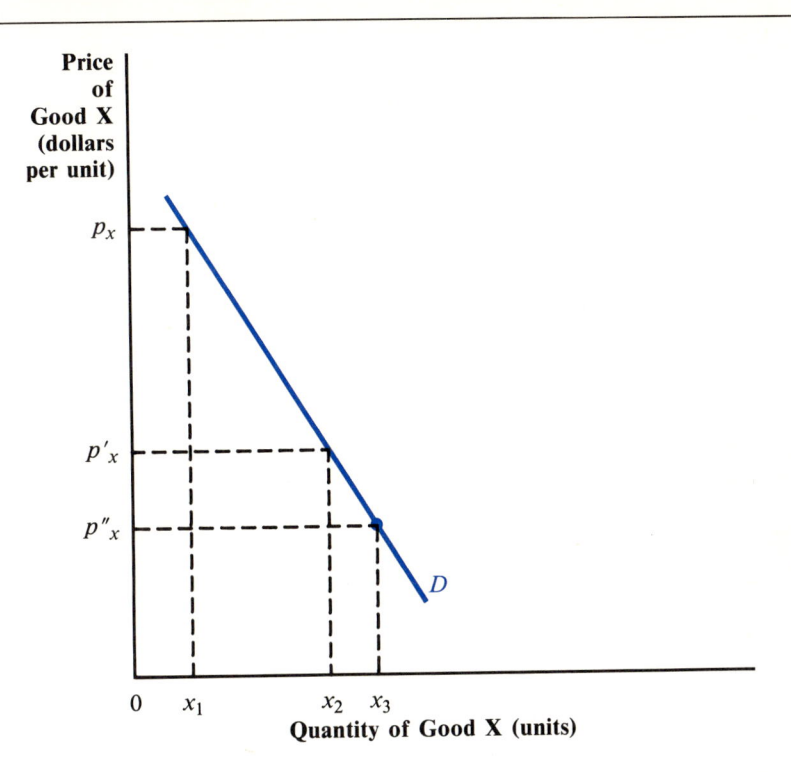

[Figure: Price of Good X (dollars per unit) on vertical axis with p_x, p'_x, p''_x marked; Quantity of Good X (units) on horizontal axis with x_1, x_2, x_3 marked; downward-sloping demand curve D.]

A **price/consumption (PC) curve**—sometimes called an *offer curve*—shows the locus of equilibrium commodity bundles for both goods as the price of one of the goods changes, holding the price of the other good and money income constant.

The **law of demand** states that the price of a good and the quantity demanded are inversely related; that is, the demand curve is downward-sloping.

p''_x successively. Because the maximum amount of good X that can now be purchased with the same income has increased, the budget line shifts outward, to B' and B'' successively. Correspondingly, the equilibrium commodity bundle shifts to e' and e''. The line connecting all of the equilibrium points is called the **price/consumption (PC) curve**.

Figure 4-8 plots the demand curve for good X from the *PC* curve in Figure 4-7. Each price is associated with a particular quantity of X demanded. The prices p_x, p'_x, and p''_x are associated with x_1, x_2, and x_3, respectively. Notice that the demand curve is downward-sloping: the lower is the price, the higher is the quantity demanded. The inverse relationship between price and quantity demanded is called the **law of demand**.

The law of demand shows that the everyday concept of need is not a very useful concept in economics. To "need" something implies that one cannot do without it, but when the price of something changes, quantity demanded changes. A recent example is provided by government subsidies of tobacco production in the United States, which have the effect of lowering the price of cigarettes to consumers. Tobacco farmers argue that the subsidies do not cause one more cigarette to be smoked. This argument is in direct conflict with the law of demand.

EXAMPLE 4–2   Studying Money Illusion

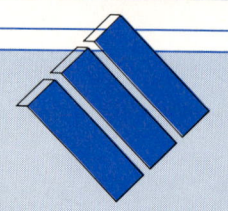

According to the theory of consumer behavior, if all incomes and prices rise (or fall) by the same percentage, nothing will happen to the pattern of consumption. This implication has been tested a number of times, and each time the data fail to conform to the theory! So far, economists have not been too concerned about the failure of the theory because there are still some problems with the tests that have been undertaken.

A recent study by Angus Deaton and John Muellbauer—two English economists—shows that a uniform proportional increase in all prices and incomes will decrease real expenditures on food and clothing and increase real expenditure on housing, transportation, and communication. The changes involved are not large. For example, a 10 percent increase in all prices and incomes was estimated to reduce the percentage of income devoted to food by only 0.33 percent (1/3 of 1 percent!) and increase the percentage devoted to housing by only about 0.5 percent.

Two explanations have been advanced: habit and price expectations. Habit gives the appearance of money illusion because consumers respond sluggishly to changes in prices and incomes—time may be needed to figure out what happens to relative prices or real income. The effects of price expectations are quite apparent. If inflation of all prices causes people to expect further inflation, they may decide to purchase more durable goods, such as housing, and to purchase less food. Thus, the appearance of money illusion in some statistical studies is so far not too disturbing. If money illusion persists in future studies, the theory may have to be revised.

Source: Angus Deaton and John Muellbauer, "An Almost Ideal Demand System," *American Economic Review* 70 (1980): 312–26.

Substitution and Income Effects

There are two reasons for the law of demand. First, when the price of any product goes up, people will try to find substitutes for that product. If the price of gasoline rises, drivers will cut back on less essential driving, and more people will carpool, take the bus, walk, or ride their bicycles to work. People who consume goods have a universal tendency to substitute other goods and services when the price of a good goes up.

Second, for normal goods, people also tend to buy less of a good as its price goes up because they feel poorer. If a person buys 6 pairs of socks a year at $2 per pair (total cost $12), and the price goes up to $3 per pair, the person would need an extra $6 (the total cost is now $18) in yearly income just to maintain the old standard of living. In effect, real income has fallen by

CHANGES IN PRICE

approximately $6. This drop tends to reduce the demand for socks as well as the demand for other normal goods.

In 1915 the Russian economist E. E. Slutsky devised a method for measuring the different effects of a change in price. Slutsky's work appeared in an obscure Italian journal and was not widely known. More than a decade later, British economists R. G. D. Allen and J. R. Hicks independently devised an equivalent method. The method is really quite brilliant, because it allows economists to test the theory of consumer behavior. We will here present the graphical method introduced by Hicks (see Problem 9 at the end of chapter for the Slutsky method).

Slutsky's insight came from two observations. First, in principle we can measure the impact of a change in price on quantity demanded and the impact of a change in income on demand. In other words, statistical methods can be used to estimate the demand function for good X. Second, every price change has an equivalent income change in terms of what happens to utility. In the example of a consumer buying 6 pairs of socks per year, a dollar increase in price was like a $6 reduction in income. Giving the consumer an extra $6 would compensate for the price change. In general, if x is the amount of good X consumed and Δp_x is a change in the price (positive or negative), $\Delta p_x x$ is the compensating change in income that is required to keep utility approximately constant.[4]

Now let us try to apply these principles. When a price changes, the change in quantity demanded holding utility constant is the **substitution effect**; the change in quantity demanded arising from the compensating change in income arising from the price change is the **income effect**.

> The **substitution effect** is the change in the quantity of good X demanded that occurs when the price of good X changes and the consumer is compensated to keep utility constant.
>
> The **income effect** is the change in quantity demanded that is attributable to the real income change that accompanies the price change.

---

4. The compensating change in income to a price change can be made precise when changes are infinitesimally small. In general, the change in utility is

$$du = MU_x dx + MU_y dy = MU_y[(MU_x/MU_y)dx + dy] \quad \text{(A)}$$

Equation (A) is always true. Utility maximization implies that $MU_x/MU_y = p_x/p_y$. Substitution into (A) yields

$$du = (MU_y/p_y)(p_x dx + p_y dy). \quad \text{(B)}$$

Now we know that $m = p_x x + p_y y$. If p_x changes, the change in income that would permit x and y to change by dx and dy is

$$dm = p_x dx + p_y dy + x dp_x. \quad \text{(C)}$$

Substituting Equation (C) into (B) yields

$$du = (MU_y/p_y)(dm - x dp_x). \quad \text{(D)}$$

We have, thus, derived the change in utility that occurs when the price of good X and income change at the same time! Obviously, in order to keep utility constant the compensating change in income is

$$dm = x dp_x. \quad \text{(E)}$$

This equation is sometimes called *Shepherd's Lemma*. Another important equation follows from (D). If $dm = 0$, we have

$$\partial u/\partial p_x = -\lambda x, \quad \text{(F)}$$

where λ is the marginal utility of income ($= MU_y/p_y$). Equation (F) is called *Roy's Identity*.

FIGURE 4-9 Substitution and Income Effects for a Normal Good

When the price of Good X falls from p_x to p_x', holding income constant at m, the equilibrium shifts from e to e' as the budget line shifts from B to B'. The substitution effect is obtained by drawing a budget line, C, parallel to the new budget line and just tangent to the initial level of utility, U_1. The move from e to s is the substitution effect; the move from s to e' is the income effect. For a normal good, the one effect reinforces the other.

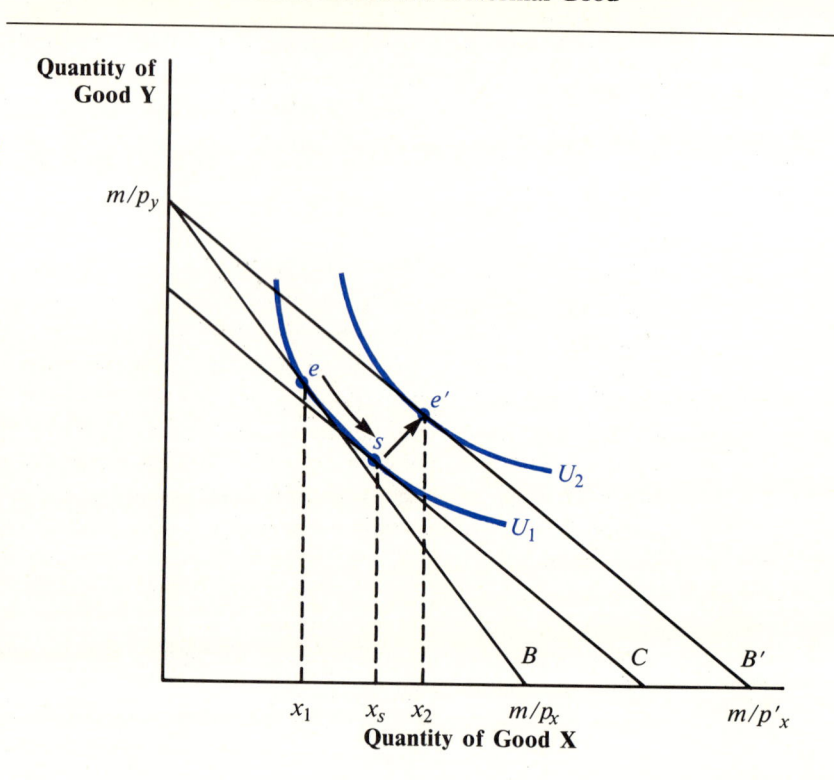

In Figure 4-9, the initial budget line is B, and the initial equilibrium point is e. When the price falls from p_x to p_x', the new equilibrium point is e' as the budget line swings outward to B'. The total change in quantity demanded is $x_2 - x_1$. We now wish to divide this increase into the substitution and income effects. To keep the consumer's utility or real income constant, we can pretend to take away income so that the new budget line is C, tangent to the initial indifference curve, U_1. The new budget line C is parallel to B'. The substitution effect is the movement from e to s along the indifference curve U_1 (that is, the change in quantity demanded $x_s - x_1$). Now, if we restore the initial level of income to the consumer, the budget line shifts back to B'. The movement from s to e' is the income effect of the price change (that is, the change in quantity demanded $x_2 - x_s$).

When only the substitution effect is considered, the association between quantity demanded and price is always negative—as the price of X rises, quantity demanded falls; as the price of X falls, quantity demanded rises. The substitution effect is, thus, said to be always negative. When good X is normal, the income effect reinforces the substitution effect. In Figure 4-9, for example, the total change in the quantity of X demanded—$(x_2 - x_1)$—is larger than the change in quantity demanded attributable to the substitution effect—$x_s - x_1$.

FIGURE 4-10 Substitution and Income Effects for an Inferior Good

If Good X is inferior, the income effect works against the substitution effect. Hence, point e' is to the left of point s.

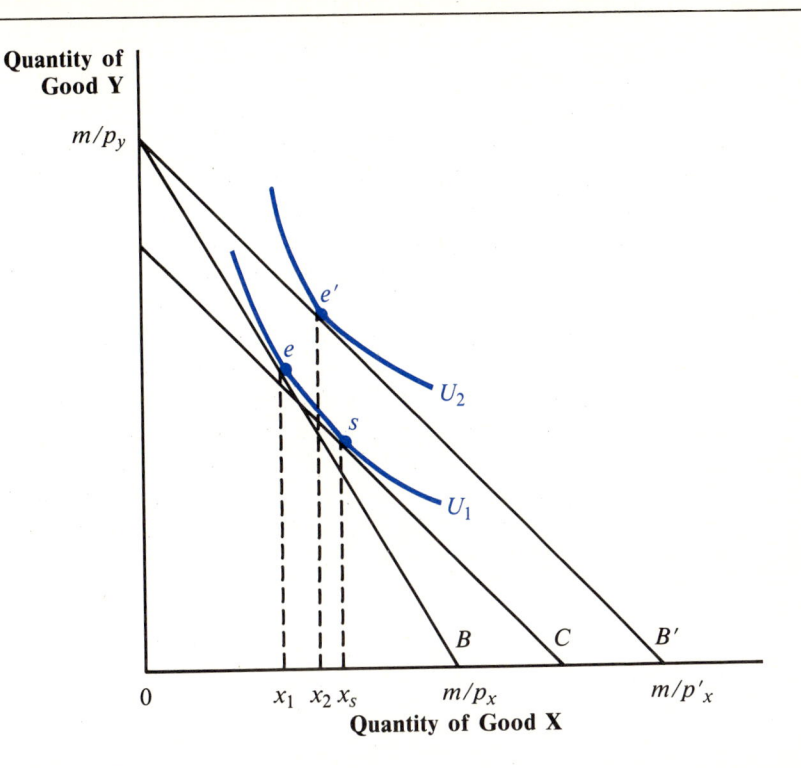

[Figure: Indifference curve diagram with Quantity of Good Y on vertical axis and Quantity of Good X on horizontal axis. Vertical intercept at m/p_y. Budget line B with horizontal intercept m/p_x, budget line B' with horizontal intercept m/p'_x, and compensated budget line C parallel to B'. Initial equilibrium e on U_1 at x_1; new equilibrium e' on U_2 at x_2; substitution point s on U_1 at x_s. Note $x_2 < x_s$.]

In the case of an inferior good, the income effect works against the substitution effect. A price reduction is like an increase in income, which discourages the consumption of an inferior good. Figure 4–10 illustrates this case. Again, we hold income constant at the level m and reduce the price of good X from p_x to p'_x. The budget line shifts from B to B'. To determine the substitution effect, we draw C parallel to B' and tangent to U_1, the initial indifference curve. The substitution effect increases the quantity of good X demanded from e to point s; the income effect lowers the quantity of good X demanded from s to e'. In this case, the total change in the quantity of good X demanded is from x_1 to x_2. The income effect partially offsets the substitution effect.

Giffen Goods

A **Giffen good** is a good for which the quantity demanded falls when the price falls.

Once one realizes that the income effect can work against the substitution effect, one can see that it is possible for a price reduction to cause a reduction in quantity demanded—which is the case for a **Giffen good**, named after a 19th-century English economist, Sir Robert Giffen. Of course, Giffen goods must be inferior. This reduction in quantity demanded can occur if the

FIGURE 4-11 Substitution and Income Effects for a Giffen Good

Good X is a Giffen good: when the price of good X falls, point e' is to the left of point e, indicating that the quantity of X demanded falls as well. In this case, the income effect from s to e' is larger than the substitution effect.

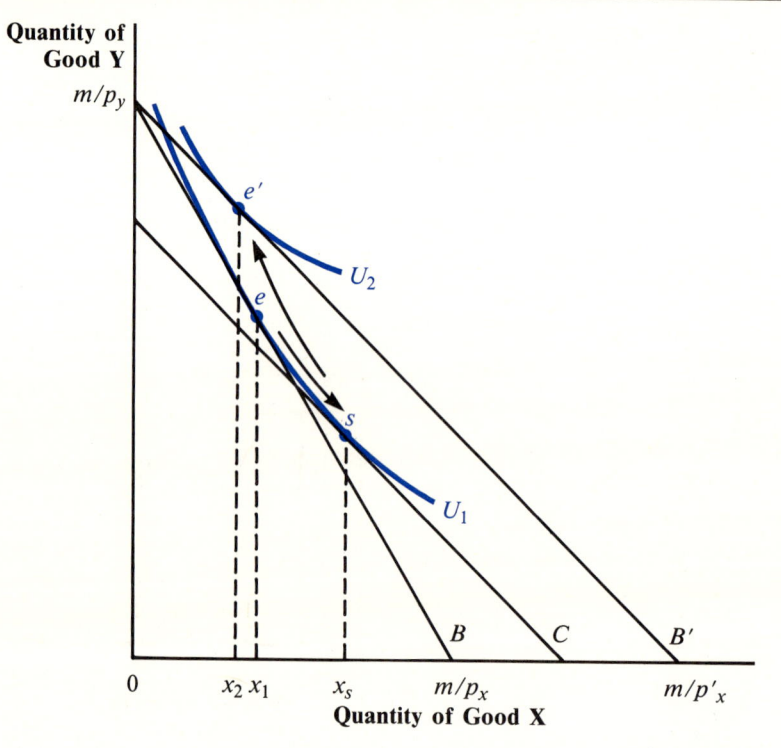

income effect is large while the substitution effect is relatively small. Figure 4-11 illustrates Giffen's case.

A classic example of a Giffen good is the potato during the Irish potato famine in 1845. Potatoes were a mark of poverty among Irish families, and a larger income would reduce their demand. In such families, where potatoes were a huge portion of their budgets, an increase in the price of potatoes would have a large income effect. With potatoes being inferior, the income effect of the price increase could increase quantity demanded by more than the reduction resulting from the substitution effect.[5]

---

5. The proper test of the theory of consumer behavior is derived from Slutsky's equation. Let the demand function for x be $x = x(p_x, p_y, m)$. Differentiate with respect to p_x and M simultaneously. Thus:

$$dx = (\partial x/\partial p_x)dp_x + (\partial X/\partial M)dM. \tag{A}$$

If we wish to hold utility constant, Equation D of footnote 4 shows we must set $dm = xdp_x$. Substituting Equation (E) of footnote 4 into Equation (A) of this footnote and dividing by dp_x yields *Slutsky's equation*:

$$(\partial x/\partial p_x)\, du = 0 = \partial x/\partial p_x + x\partial x/\partial m. \tag{B}$$

All that is required by the theory of consumer behavior is that the left-hand side (the substitution effect) be negative. The two terms on the right can be computed if we know the demand function. If these two terms sum to a positive number, the theory of consumer demand is contradicted. Giffen's case does not contradict the theory. Rearranging Equation (B), we can write

$$\partial x/\partial p_x = (\partial x/\partial p_x)du = 0 - x\partial x/\partial m \tag{C}$$

The first term is the substitution effect, and the second term is the income effect of the price change.

CHANGES IN PRICE

FIGURE 4-12 Compensated Versus Ordinary Demand

The compensated demand curve is steeper than the ordinary demand curve in the case of a normal good because the income effect reinforces the substitution effect.

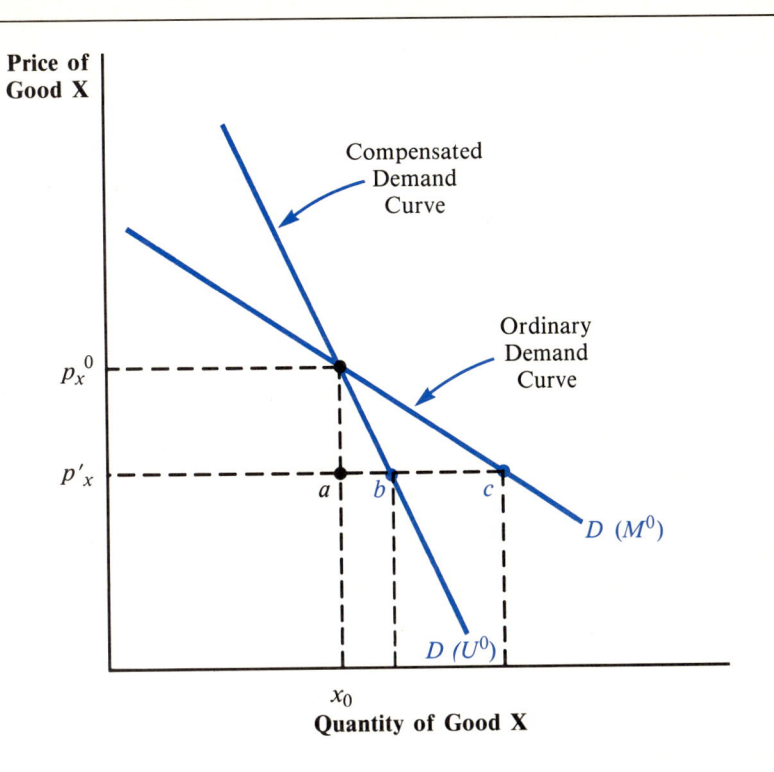

George Stigler has called into question the existence of Giffen goods. Giffen's own example was bread consumption by poor families. Stigler studied the English demand curve for wheat in the 1890s and found it to be downward-sloping. Giffen goods are reflected only in certain ranges of individual demand curves and need not hold for the market-demand curve. No important theoretical issues are involved because such goods do not contradict the fundamental theorem of consumer demand: the substitution effect is negative.

The Compensated-Demand Curve

A compensated-demand curve is a demand curve for a given level of real income.

So far we have studied the ordinary demand curve, which holds other prices and money income constant. The substitution effect holds utility constant. The demand curve that holds utility, or real income, constant is the **compensated-demand curve**.

Figure 4-12 illustrates the compensated-demand curve for a normal good. The ordinary demand curve is labeled $D(M^0)$. At price p_x^0, the quantity of X demanded is x_0. The corresponding level of utility is U^0. Along the ordinary demand curve, utility decreases as price rises above p_x^0 and decreases as price falls below p_x^0. To hold utility constant, it is necessary to compensate the consumer—giving money when the price goes up and taking money

FIGURE 4–13   The Price/Consumption Curve and Price Elasticity of Demand

When the price/consumption curve is downward-sloping—prior to point q—the demand for good X is price elastic; when the PC curve is upward-sloping, the demand for good X is price inelastic.

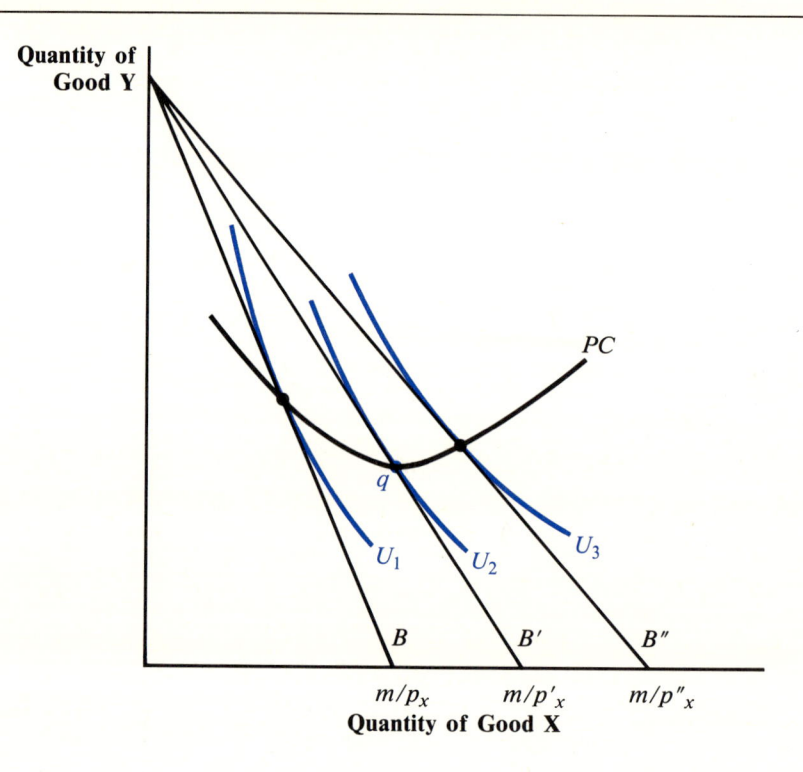

away when the price falls. Suppose price falls to p'_x. The substitution effect is the distance ab. The substitution effect is the change in quantity demanded when the price of X falls and income is taken away to just keep utility constant at the level U^0. When the income is given back, demand increases by the income effect bc. Thus, we can see that as long as good X is normal, the compensated demand curve—labeled $D(U^0)$—is steeper than the ordinary demand curve.

If a change in money income did not affect the demand for a particular good (a zero income elasticity), the compensated demand curve would coincide with the ordinary demand curve. A good example is coffee. As income rises, people do not consume more coffee, as a general rule.

Price Elasticity of Demand

The responsiveness of quantity demanded to price is measured by the **price elasticity of demand** (η_p). What happens to the total expenditures of a consumer on a good ($p_x x$) as the price changes depends on the price elasticity of demand. The numerical or absolute value of the price elasticity

APPLICATIONS

*The **price elasticity of demand** (η_p) is the proportional (or percentage) change in quantity demanded for a product divided by the proportional (or percentage) change in the price of the good itself, holding other prices and income constant. The price elasticity will be negative for non-Giffen goods.*

can be interpreted as the percentage *increase* in quantity demanded per 1 percent *decrease* in price—or, equivalently, as the percentage *decrease* in quantity demanded per 1 percent *increase* in price.[6] Along a demand curve, price and quantity demanded move in opposite directions. Although a fall in price tends to lower dollar spending, a rise in quantity demanded tends to raise dollar spending. If the numerical price elasticity equals unity, the percentage rise in quantity demanded just equals the percentage fall in price. Total spending will remain unchanged. If the numerical price elasticity exceeds unity, the percentage increase in quantity demanded will exceed the percentage fall in price. Total spending on the good will rise. If the numerical price elasticity is less than unity, the percentage increase in quantity demanded will be less than the percentage fall in the price. Total spending on the good will then fall. Thus, as the price falls, total spending rises if $|\eta_p| > 1$, remains constant if $|\eta_p| = 1$, and falls if $|\eta_p| < 1$. Demand is said to be price *elastic* or *inelastic* as the price elasticity exceeds or falls short of unity. (Chapter 5 contains a more detailed discussion of these relationships.)

Demand is *price elastic* if $|\eta_p| > 1$; demand is *price inelastic* if $|\eta_p| < 1$; and demand is *unit elastic* if $|\eta_p| = 1$. Spending on a good and its price move in opposite directions if demand is price elastic and in the same direction if demand is price inelastic.

In Figure 4-13, demand for good X is price elastic on the downward-sloping section of the price/consumption curve. In that portion of the *PC* curve, as the price of X falls, less of good Y is purchased and, thus, more dollars must be spent on good X. Hence, the demand for X must be price elastic in that range. When the price/consumption curve turns upward, after point *q*, the demand for good X becomes price inelastic: more units of Y are purchased as the price of X falls—so less must be spent on good X. The general rule that price elasticity falls as price falls will tend to hold if consumption of X can be driven to zero by a sufficiently high (finite) price and if the individual can become satiated at a finite quantity (with a zero price).

APPLICATIONS

The above theory of consumer demand has many applications. Two important ones are the costs of different types of government subsidies and the problem of measuring changes in consumer well-being (price indices).

---

6. Economists often refer to the absolute or numerical value of the price elasticity rather than the (negative) algebraic value because it is convenient to refer to larger price elasticity of demand as a *larger* numerical value. It is cumbersome to refer to a larger price elasticity of demand as a *smaller* algebraic value.

EXAMPLE 4–3 Evidence for the Law of Demand

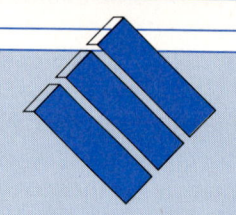

The evidence for downward-sloping demand curves—the main implication of the theory of consumer behavior—is both broad and deep. According to empirical studies of demand, in the vast majority of cases, the higher is the price of the good, the lower is the quantity demanded when other factors are held constant. While there are occasional studies that show the reverse is true, there has so far been no systematic evidence that the demand for any particular good or class of goods violates the law of demand.

The law of demand also emerges in laboratory experiments with animals, mental patients, and alcoholics. In all cases, as the price rises, the quantity demanded falls. The price sometimes has to be measured in terms of effort (for example, a pigeon may have to press two levers rather than one). Thus, the household need not be sane, smart, or sober (or even human!) in order for the basic law of demand to hold. One suspects that the law of demand is compatible with a far more general theory than the economists' theory of a rational individual bent on maximizing utility.

Professor John Kagel of the University of Houston and his associates argue that it is appropriate to study nonhuman species on the Darwinian grounds that animal behavior as well as structure vary continuously from one species to another. Accordingly, Kagel and associates study white male albino rats under strict laboratory conditions.

In one set of experiments, root beer and Tom Collins mix could be "purchased" by the rats. Under baseline conditions, 300 lever presses were alloted to each rat as "income." Root beer could be purchased by pressing the left lever; Tom Collins mix could be purchased by pressing the right lever. Prices could be changed merely by changing the amount of liquid dispensed by a single lever press. It was discovered that there was no significant difference between using the left or the right lever for either root beer or Tom Collins mix. Their experiments showed that laboratory animals change quantity demanded in inverse proportion to the price of the product.

Source: John Kagel *et al.*, "Experimental Studies of Consumer Demand Using Laboratory Animals," *Economic Inquiry*, 1975, pp. 22–38.

The Costs of Subsidies

Imagine that a government unit wishes to subsidize a group of responsible households in the cheapest possible way. More precisely, the government unit wishes to maximize the benefits the households receive from any given expenditure of public funds. The study of a single household will suffice for this purpose. Two methods will be studied: a lump-sum subsidy, in which the consumer would be given a fixed dollar payment, and a per-unit subsidy based on the number of units purchased by the consumer (that is, a price subsidy).

APPLICATIONS

FIGURE 4-14   The Effect on Utility of a Lump-Sum Price Subsidy

The budget line with a price subsidy is B_S; the budget line without a price subsidy is B. With the price subsidy, the consumer chooses point a, receiving a total subsidy of amount ac. With a lump-sum subsidy of dc, the budget line is B_L (parallel to B because relative prices are the same as with no price subsidy). The equilibrium point with a lump-sum subsidy is a'; the same utility is achieved at a smaller cost (distance dc is less than distance ac).

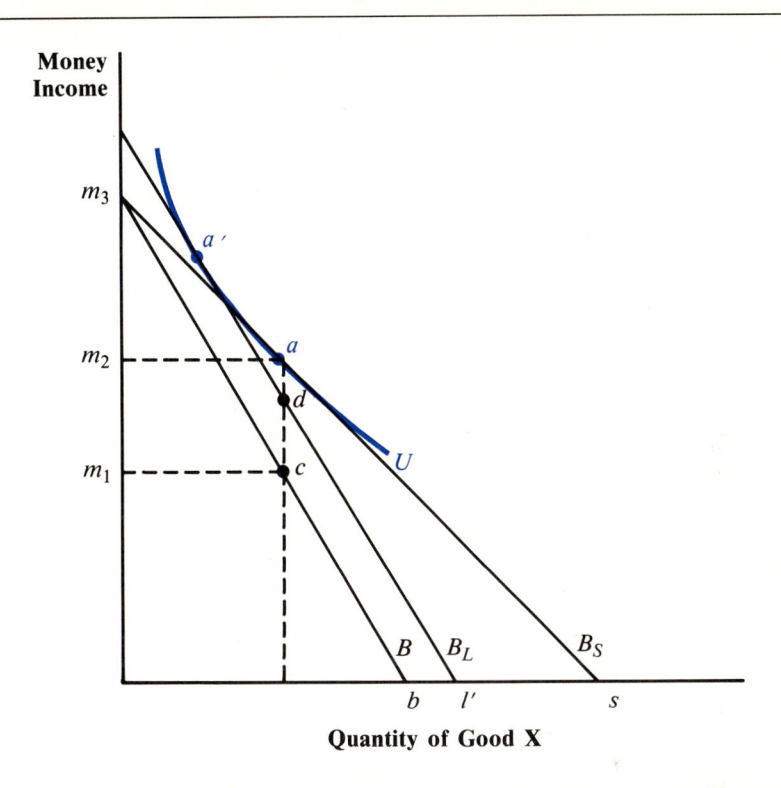

Figure 4-14 measures good X along the horizontal axis and measures money income (m) along the vertical axis. If we assume the prices of all goods but X are constant, m can be thought of as the amount of income devoted to goods other than good X. For simplicity, we shall think of the price of a bundle of these other goods as $1. Because the prices of these other goods are given, we can draw the usual indifference curves between m and good X consumption. Suppose the price of good X is subsidized. The budget line B_S is the budget line with a price subsidy; the budget line B is the budget line without the subsidy (the slope is the supply price, p_x). The subsidized consumer is in equilibrium at point a. The total subsidy received is the amount ac because the consumer spends only $m_3 - m_2$ of his or her own money, but the price of the good is still p_x to sellers. Hence, sellers must receive $m_3 - m_1$. The difference is the total subsidy paid to the consumer ($ac = m_2 - m_1$).

Now suppose the consumer is not given a price subsidy but instead is given a lump-sum subsidy. This causes a parallel shift in B to the right instead of a rotation of the budget line around the point m_3. Suppose that a lump-sum subsidy of exactly dc is given, so that the budget line shifts to B_L. The consumer reaches the new equilibrium a'. We have deliberately chosen a' to be on the same indifference curve as a. Thus, we see that the same level of utility can be achieved at a smaller cost. The cost of the lump-sum subsidy is only dc, while that of the price subsidy is the greater amount ac.

Typically, when consumers are subsidized, price subsidies are given. Examples: (1) The pre-1977 food-stamp program, where poor families were given food stamps that cut the cost of food purchases; (2) housing supplements; and (3) the school hot-lunch program, where children receive subsidized lunches to insure an adequate diet. The above exercise suggests that these programs cost more than was necessary. Society could have reaped the same benefits by handing out lump-sum subsidies at a smaller cost. Why are price subsidies favored by politicians? There are two reasons: first, lump-sum subsidies do not benefit any particular producers. Price subsidies have a broader political support because they are supported by both the subsidized consumers and the producers selling the subsidized good; second, politicians and the general public may assume (without solid evidence) that the poor lack enough intelligence to be rational (would the extra income be spent on beer instead of milk for the children?).

Price Indices and Revealed Preferences

Revealed Preferences

Imagine we observe a consumer at two points in time. The consumer has a (possibly) different income and (possibly) faces different relative prices. The problem is to decide whether the consumer is better or worse off. If we could observe indifference curves, there would be no problem making such a determination, but indifference curves are unobservable. All that can be observed are prices and quantities. If we use the theory of consumer behavior, we can postulate that the consumer's tastes have remained constant and that he or she is maximizing utility. What conclusions about welfare can be drawn?

Figure 4-15 shows an initial budget line B between two goods, X and Y. The equilibrium solution is e. Now consider two additional budgetary situations: budget lines B' and B'', the former passing through point e and the latter passing below point e. It is clear that e'—the new equilibrium with B'—is preferred to e. On the other hand, the new equilibrium with B'' is worse than e, because e'' lies below the indifference curve tangent to point e. The interesting point to be made about Figure 4-15 is that the indifference curve is needed to determine if e'' is worse than e, but the indifference curve is not needed at all to determine that e' is better than e. What is the difference between the two situations? When the budget line is B', the consumer could have purchased e but didn't. Thus, if the consumer is maximizing utility at e', we know that e' is on a higher indifference curve. On the other hand, when the budget line is B'', the consumer could not have purchased bundle e (bundle e lies above B''). Thus, e'' may or may not be preferred to e, depending on the location of the indifference curve itself.

Considerations such as these led Paul A. Samuelson to an alternative

FIGURE 4-15 **Revealed Preferences**

Commodity bundles e, e', and e'' are the optimum bundles chosen by a consumer for the three budget situations. The indifference curve is needed to determine that e'' is worse than e but is not needed to show that e' is preferred to e because e' will be chosen over e when e could have been purchased at the budget situation B'. Under these circumstances, e' is said to be a revealed preference to e.

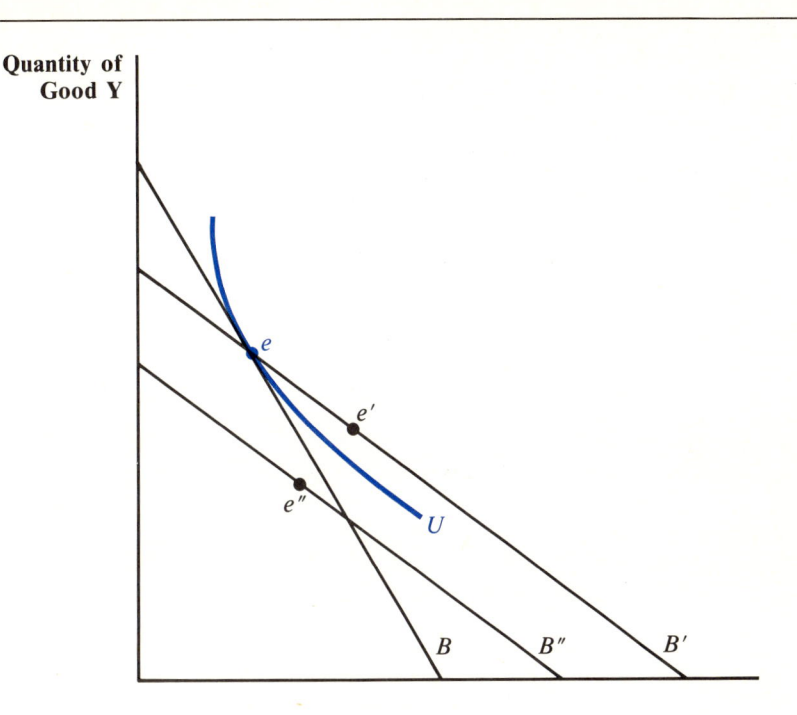

Quantity of Good Y (vertical axis), *Quantity of Good X* (horizontal axis). Budget lines B, B'', B' with optimum bundles e, e', e'' and indifference curve U.

approach to the theory of consumer behavior called the *revealed-preference approach*. According to this theory, bundle b is a *revealed preference* to bundle a if bundle b is chosen when bundle a could be afforded. Samuelson proposed the axiom that if bundle b is a revealed preference to bundle a, then bundle a must never be a revealed preference to bundle b.

One can construct the entire theory of consumer behavior from this perspective without indifference curves. For example, in Figure 4-15, the budget line B' passes through the chosen bundle e on budget line B. We observe e and the budget lines B and B'. According to Samuelson's axiom, none of the points to the northwest of e on B' can be chosen because they were affordable when e was selected to be the optimum bundle. Hence, the equilibrium with B' must be with some bundle that could not have been purchased in situation B (that is, must lie southeast of e on B'). Thus, the substitution effect is negative.

Price Indices

The same information used in revealed-preference theory is used to create price indices. Suppose per-capita income rises by 10 percent. If some price index rises by more than 10 percent, the average consumer is thought to be

FIGURE 4–16   Price-Level Changes

Budget line B represents initial income and prices. If income changes by as much as the Laspeyres index, the new budget line is B'—meaning that bundle e can still be just purchased. Because the consumer's welfare would be the same with the lower budget line B'', the Laspeyres index overestimates the change in the true cost of living.

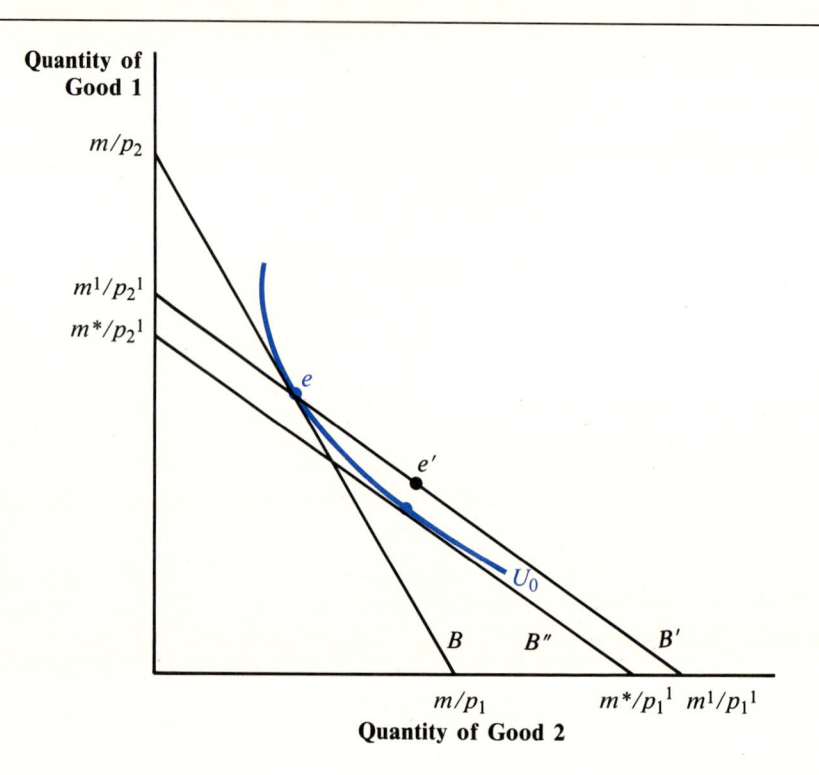

worse off; if the price index rises by less than 10 percent, the average consumer is thought to be better off. Can these conclusions be justified?

Let (x_1^0, x_2^0) be the commodity bundle purchased in period 0 and let (x_1^1, x_2^1) be the bundle bought in period 1. The cost of the period 0 bundle is $\Sigma p_i^0 x_i^0$; the cost of the period 1 bundle is $\Sigma p_i^1 x_i^1$. The relative change in expenditure is

$$I = \Sigma p_i^1 x_i^1 / \Sigma p_i^0 x_i^0. \tag{10}$$

A **price index** is a measure of the general level of prices in relation to the price level in some base year.

A **price index** shows how a market basket of goods in one year compares in cost to the same market basket in another year. If period 0 is the initial year and period 1 the later year, two indices can be used. The *Laspeyres price index* (named after Etienne Laspeyres) uses the cost of the initial market basket as a base:

$$L = \Sigma p_i^1 x_i^0 / \Sigma p_i^0 x_i^0. \tag{11}$$

The *Paasche price index* (after Hermann Paasche) uses the cost of the later market basket as the reference:

$$P = \Sigma p_i^1 x_i^1 / \Sigma p_i^0 x_i^1. \tag{12}$$

We can conclude that the consumer is better off if $I \geq L$. Comparing Equations (10) and (11) we find that

$$\Sigma p_i^1 x_i^1 / \Sigma p_i^0 x_i^0 \geq \Sigma p_i^1 x_i^0 / \Sigma p_i^0 x_i^0$$

or, more simply,

$$\Sigma p_i^1 x_i^1 \geq \Sigma p_i^1 x_i^0. \tag{13}$$

Thus we see that commodity bundle 0 could be afforded in period 1. It must be that the period 1 bundle is preferred to the period 0 bundle.

Notice the inequality in Equation (13) is "greater than or equal to." In other words, even if income rises at the same rate as prices as measured by the Laspeyres index, the consumer is better off. The reason for this is that the Laspeyres index represents an overestimate of the increase in the cost of living. Figure 4-16 can be used to show the extent that this bias is dependent on the curvature of the indifference curve (the substitutability of the two goods). The initial budget line is B, and the consumer is in equilibrium at point e. If both income and prices change in such a manner that $L = I$, the consumer can still purchase the original bundle e. Thus, the new budget line is B' going through point e. Clearly, the consumer is better off at the new equilibrium e'. If the consumer's new level of income were m^*, the budget line would be B'', and the level of utility would be the same as in the initial situation (U_0). The true cost of living index is really m^*/m. By experimenting with Figure 4-16 one can readily see that the bias is larger the less convex is the indifference curve (that is, the more substitutable are the goods).

In practice, the upward bias in the Laspeyres index over the true index is not as large as one might think from Figure 4-16. Steven Braithwait—an economist with the U.S. Bureau of Labor Statistics—estimated that from 1958 to 1973 the use of the Laspeyres index overestimated the true cost of living by only 1.5 percent. In other words, over the 15-year period, the Laspeyres index erred by only 0.1 percent each year![7]

By similar reasoning, we can conclude that the consumer is worse off if $I \leq P$. In that case, substitution shows that

$$\Sigma p_i^0 x_i^0 \geq \Sigma p_i^0 x_i^1. \tag{14}$$

Hence, the period 0 bundle is preferred to the period 1 bundle as the latter could have been purchased but was not in period 0. The Paasche index can be used to indicate only a deterioration in welfare because it is an underestimate of the change in the true cost of living. If income rises by the same amount as the Paasche index, welfare falls. While the L measure overestimates the change in the cost of living by assuming people do not adjust current consumption to changes in relative prices, the P measure underestimates the change in the cost of living by assuming people consumed the same amounts in earlier years.

---

[7]. Steven D. Braithwait, "The Substitution Bias of the Laspeyres Price Index," *American Economic Review* 70 (1980): 64-77.

FIGURE 4-17 From Individual to Market Demand

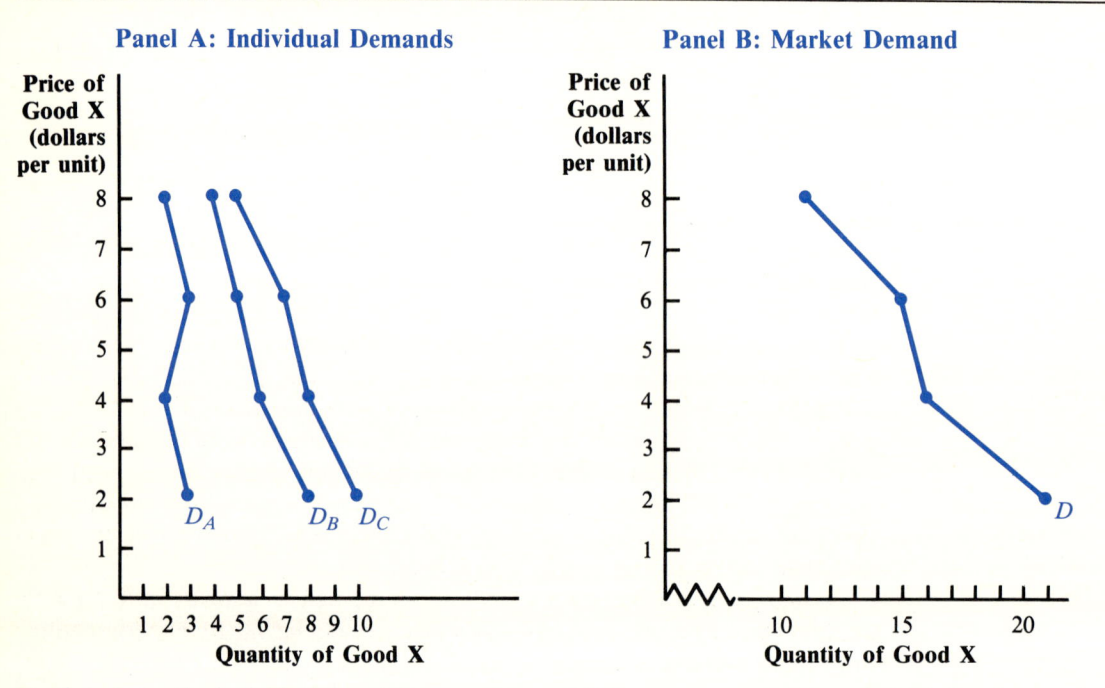

Panel A: Individual Demands

Panel B: Market Demand

Panel A shows the individual demand curves for good X for consumers A, B, and C. Notice that good X is a Giffen good between prices $6 and $4 for person A. The market-demand curve in Panel B is the horizontal summation of the individual demand curves at each price and is downward-sloping throughout the range of prices.

Nothing can be concluded in the situation in which $P < I < L$. In that case, the Paasche index indicates an improvement in welfare, whereas the Laspeyres index indicates a deterioration in welfare. Neither bundle is revealed preferred to the other, because inequalities (13) and (14) are reversed.

TABLE 4-1 Individual and Market Demand in a Three-Consumer World

Price (dollars per unit)	Quantity Demanded by Consumer A	Quantity Demanded by Consumer B	Quantity Demanded by Consumer C	Quantity Demanded by Market
8	2	4	5	11
6	3	5	7	15
4	2	6	8	16
2	3	8	10	21

The Paasche index can be used to indicate a reduction in welfare because it underestimates cost of living changes; the Laspeyres index can be used to indicate an increase in welfare because it overestimates cost of living changes.

MARKET DEMAND

The **market-demand curve** shows the total quantities demanded by all consumers in the market at each price and is the horizontal summation of all individual demand curves in the market.

So far we have focused on individual demand curves, but prices are established in markets, and the individual consumer is only a small part of the total market. Individual demand curves must be combined to determine the **market-demand curve** for a particular good.

For simplicity, imagine there are three consumers in a particular market. Call the consumers A, B, and C. Table 4–1 shows their quantities demanded for the product at four prices. Notice that for person A, the good is a Giffen good between the prices $6 and $4 because at the lower price, the quantity demanded is smaller. But the product is not a Giffen good for any other price pair or consumer. By adding across all three consumers for each price, the total market demand is shown in the last column and is represented by the downward-sloping curve in Figure 4–17.

A market with only three consumers is unrealistic, but it does serve to illustrate the way in which market-demand curves are the horizontal summation of the individual demand curves.

CONSUMER SURPLUS

Consumer surplus is the excess of the total consumer benefit that a good provides over what the consumer—or consumers in a market— actually have to pay.

When a consumer purchases a good, he or she enjoys a surplus above and beyond what is paid for the good. People in effect pay less than they would be willing to pay rather than go without the good itself. For example, most people would pay far more for the right to use water in their home than their current monthly water bill. This inducement to participate in the market is called **consumer surplus**.

Alfred Marshall introduced the consumer-surplus concept into economics. The concept is important because it provides economists with a technique for measuring the benefits of a particular good to the economy. It provides the foundation for measuring such things as the costs and benefits of tariffs, excise taxes, and various government projects (such as dams). We shall here follow the simplified approach pioneered by Alfred Marshall.

Consider the market demand curve in Figure 4–18. At the market price p_0, the market will purchase the maximum quantity of x_0 of good X. Alternatively, we can think of the demand curve as showing the maximum price the market is willing to pay to take any particular quantity off the market. The demand price for quantity x_0 is p_0.

When the price is p_0, the market is willing to pay the higher demand prices along the demand curve up to the quantity x_0. Thus, the demand price for

FIGURE 4–18 Consumers' Surplus

When the market price is p_0 consumers are willing to pay the demand prices along the demand curve up to the quantity x_0. Because the demand prices exceed p_0 up to that quantity, the color shaded area is the excess of what consumers are *willing to* pay over what they actually do pay— their *consumers' surplus*.

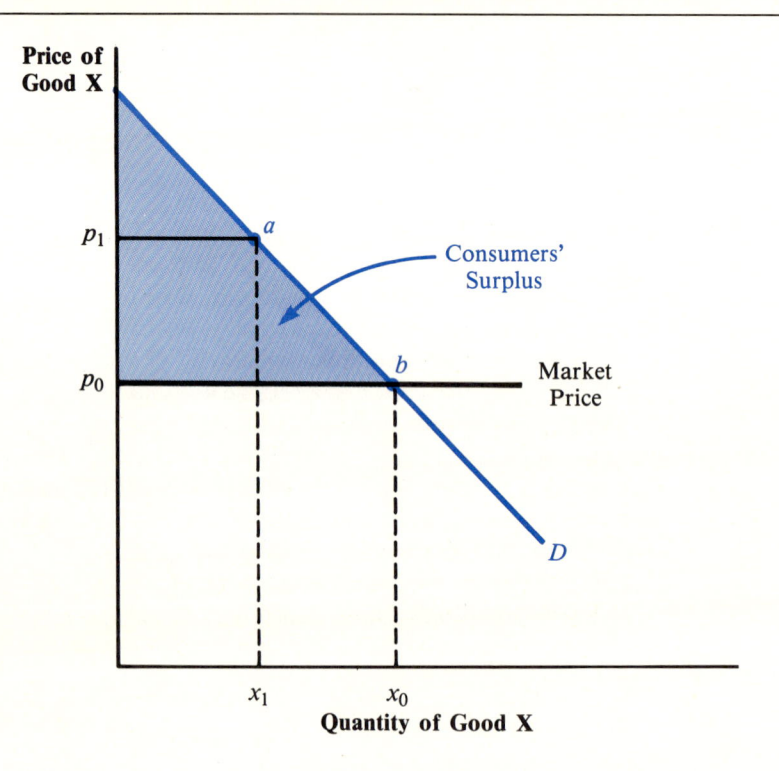

quantity x_1 is p_1, but consumers have to pay only p_0—the market price. Thus, $p_1 - p_0$ is the surplus the market enjoys on the x_1th unit. Accordingly, the consumer's surplus on the entire x_0 units purchased is the shaded area above the market price and below the demand curve.

The procedure can be strictly justified if we follow Marshall and assume that the marginal utility of income (λ) is constant. Since MU/P is the same for all goods, for any good $MU/P = \lambda$. If λ is constant, it follows that $P = MU/\lambda$, so that the price of the good is strictly proportional to its marginal utilty. Thus, in a free market, the price is an exact dollar measure of the marginal benefits of any good. The total benefits of consuming such a good would then be simply the sum of all the demand prices.[8]

---

8. When will λ—the marginal utility of income—be constant? The precise conditions are as follows. Recall Roy's identity from footnote 4 that $\partial u/\partial p_x = -x\lambda$. Now differentiate with respect to M, obtaining

$$\partial^2 u/\partial p_x \partial m = \partial^2 u/\partial m \partial p_x = [\partial(\partial u/\partial m)/\partial p_x] = \partial \lambda/\partial p_x$$
$$= -x\partial\lambda/\partial m - \lambda\partial x/\partial m.$$

It is clear that the marginal utility of income will be constant with respect to p_x if $\partial x/\partial m = \partial\lambda/\partial m = 0$. From consumer equilibrium we know that $MU_x = \lambda p_x$ or $p_x = MU_x/\lambda$. If λ is constant, p_x is a perfect measure of MU_x. Hence, the area under the demand curve and above the market price is the excess (in dollars) of total benefits over consumer expenditure. The above conditions imply that the compensated and ordinary demand curves coincide.

SUMMARY

1. The budget constraint shows the combinations of commodity bundles the consumer can buy with his or her limited income. It is $p_x x + p_y y \leq m$. If the quantity of good X is measured on the horizontal axis, the absolute slope is p_x/p_y and measures the rate at which the consumer can substitute good Y for good X in the market.

2. The consumer is in equilibrium when the commodity bundle is at a point where the budget line is tangent to an indifference curve, where $MRS_{yx} = p_x/p_y$ and income is spent. Alternatively, in marginal-utility terms, $MU_x/MU_y = p_x/p_y$ or $MU_x/p_x = MU_y/p_y$. The solution to the equilibrium conditions is the consumer's demand functions for goods X and Y.

3. The income/consumption curve shows how the optimum commodity bundles respond to a change in income, holding prices constant. A normal good is one where demand increases when income increases; an inferior good is one where demand falls when income increases. An Engel curve shows the relationship between the demand for a good and income, holding prices constant. A good is a necessity if the income elasticity of demand is less than unity. A good is a luxury if the income elasticity exceeds unity.

4. A price/consumption curve shows how the optimum commodity bundles change when income is constant, the price of good Y is constant, and the price of good X changes. From the price/consumption curve, the demand curve for X can be derived by plotting the various quantities of good X demanded against the corresponding price of good X. When a price changes, the change in quantity demanded can be decomposed into a substitution effect and an income effect. The substitution effect is the change in the quantity of good X demanded that occurs when the price of X changes and utility is constant. The substitution effect reflects the slope of the compensated demand curve. The income effect is the change in quantity demanded attributable to the real income change that accompanies the price change. If a good is normal, the income effect reinforces the substitution effect, and the demand curve must be downward-sloping. A Giffen good is the exceptional case of an inferior good in which the income effect more than offsets the substitution effect.

5. The theory of consumer behavior can be used to show that a lump-sum subsidy is a more efficient way of increasing a consumer's welfare than a price subsidy. Price indices can be used to determine whether a consumer's welfare has increased or decreased. They may be based on current-year quantities (the Paasche index) or base-year quantities (the Laspeyres index). Paasche *underestimates* cost-of-living changes; Laspeyres *overestimates* cost-of-living changes.

6. Market demand is the horizontal summation of individual demand curves.

7. Consumers' surplus is the excess of what people would be willing to pay for a good over what they actually pay. Marshall's measure of consumers' surplus is the area under the demand curve and above the price.

QUESTIONS AND PROBLEMS

1. Draw the budget line for a consumer whose income is $m = \$1,000$ weekly and who faces prices for ale and bread of $p_a = \$5$ and $p_b = \$2$.
   a. Show how the budget line shifts when income rises to $1,500.
   b. How does the budget line shift when $m = \$1,000$, $p_b = \$2$, and p_a rises from $5 to $10? When p_a falls from $5 to $4?

2. Draw a consumer in equilibrium with $m = \$1,000$, $p_a = \$5$, $p_b = \$2$, and with demand for ale equal to 160 units. What is the consumer's bread consumption? Now raise the price of bread to $3 and give the consumer an additional $100 in income. Draw the new budget line. Can bread consumption increase?

3. Assume $MU_x = a/x$ and $MU_y = b/y$, where a and b are positive constants. Derive the demand functions for x and y.
   a. When p_x changes, plot the price/consumption curve.
   b. Plot the income/consumption curve.
   c. What are the price and income elasticities of demand?

4. Assume $MU_x = ay$ and $MU_y = bx$, where a and b are positive constants. Derive the demand functions for x and y.
   a. When p_x changes, plot the price/consumption curve.
   b. Plot the income/consumption curve.
   c. What are the price and income elasticities of demand?

5. This chapter derived the price/consumption (PC) curve when p_y remained constant and p_x was varying. Now derive the PC curve when p_x is constant and p_y is varying. Why is this PC curve different than the one in the chapter? Derive the demand curve for y from this experiment.

6. Suppose the Engel curve for a good is $x = a + bm$, where m is income and a and b are constants. Assume b is positive. In the following cases, indicate whether the income elasticity of demand for x exceeds unity, equals unity, or falls short of unity.
   a. The parameter a is negative.
   b. The parameter a is positive.
   c. The parameter a is zero.

7. Alice's utility function for sandwiches is $u = \min(X_h, X_c)$, where h and c denote ham and cheese. With this utility function, ham and cheese are perfect complements. Assume Alice always spends m on sandwiches.

a. Compare and contrast the price/consumption and income/consumption curves.
b. When the price of ham falls, what is the substitution effect?
c. Derive the demand curve for ham when $m = \$100$ and the price of cheese is $3 per pound. Plot the demand curve for the ham prices of $1, $2, $3, $5, and $7 per pound. Is the demand curve elastic or inelastic?

8. From time to time politicians propose high gas taxes combined with a rebate of other taxes. Suppose a consumer's income is $200, gas is $1 a gallon, and nongas items are also $1 per unit. Assume that in equilibrium the consumer buys 100 gallons of gas. Now impose a $1 per gallon gas tax. Show what happens to a consumer's consumption if he or she is given a lump-sum rebate (fixed independently of the consumer's own actions) of $100. In other words, taking the effects of the rebate into account, does the consumer economize on gas consumption compared to the initial situation?

9. This chapter defined the substitution effect in terms of holding utility constant—following Hicks. Slutsky proposed compensating the consumer by giving him $\Delta m = x\Delta p_x$. In this case, the consumer's purchasing-power is held constant because the original bundle can still be purchased (compared to Problem 2). Divide up the effects of a change in the price of good X into the substitution and income effects using the Slutsky method. Is the substitution effect larger or smaller for normal goods? Why?

10. A consumer is observed consuming food and clothing in year 1 and in year 2. In year 1, the consumer buys 50 units of clothing and 50 units of food at prices of $1 per unit for food and $1 per unit for clothing. In year 2, the consumer buys 40 units of clothing at $4 each and 70 units of food at $2 each. Use the axiom of revealed preference or index-numbers theory to determine what happens to the consumer's welfare from year 1 to year 2.

11. A consumer purchases n distinct goods. The marginal utility of each good is independent of the other goods and, of course, subject to the law of diminishing marginal utility. Suppose that the demand for good 1 is price inelastic. Show that an increase in the price of good 1 must lower the demands for every other good. Is this result realistic?

SUGGESTED READINGS

Henderson, James M., and Richard E. Quandt. *Microeconomic Theory*, 2nd ed. New York: McGraw-Hill, 1971, chap. 2.

Hicks, John R. *Value and Capital*. London: Oxford University Press, 1939, chap. 3.

Layard, P. R. G., and A. A. Walters. *Microeconomic Theory*. New York: McGraw-Hill, 1978, chap. 5.

Stigler, George. "Notes on the History of the Giffen Paradox." *Journal of Political Economy*, 1947.

CHAPTER 5

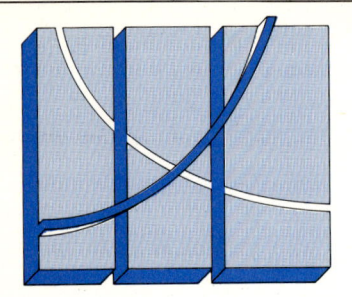

THE CHARACTERISTICS OF MARKET DEMAND

Chapter 4 described consumer demand as the rational consequence of utility maximization subject to an income or budget constraint. When the budget constraint changes, so do the equilibrium quantities purchased by the consumer. This chapter studies the various elasticities of demand, the relationship between price elasticity and revenue, and the way in which demand functions are estimated in practice. An appendix describes the basic statistical methods used in estimating demand (or supply) functions.

THE MARKET-DEMAND FUNCTION

Goods X and Y are said to be **complements** *if raising the price of good Y lowers the demand for good X.*

Goods X and Y are said to be **substitutes** *if raising the price of good Y raises the demand for good X.*

Goods X and Y are **independent goods** *if raising the price of one does not affect the demand for the other.*

The market demand for a good depends on the price of the good, the prices of other goods, the tastes of the consumers in the market, and the incomes earned by the various consumers in the market. We learned in Chapter 4 how to aggregate from an individual's demand curve to the market: one simply adds each individual's quantity demanded at each price to obtain the quantity demanded by the market at each price.

Price is the first determinant of the demand for a good. The principle of utility maximization implies that there is a law of demand: the higher is the price of normal goods, the lower is the quantity demanded. The only exception to the law of demand is the case of a Giffen good, which by necessity must be inferior. Because no commodity can be inferior for all levels of income, the demand curve for even a Giffen good will have downward-sloping sections.

The prices of other goods also influence the demand for a particular good. We can classify other goods as **complements**, **substitutes**, or **independent goods**.

FIGURE 5-1 The Effects of a Price Increase on the Demand for Complements and Substitutes

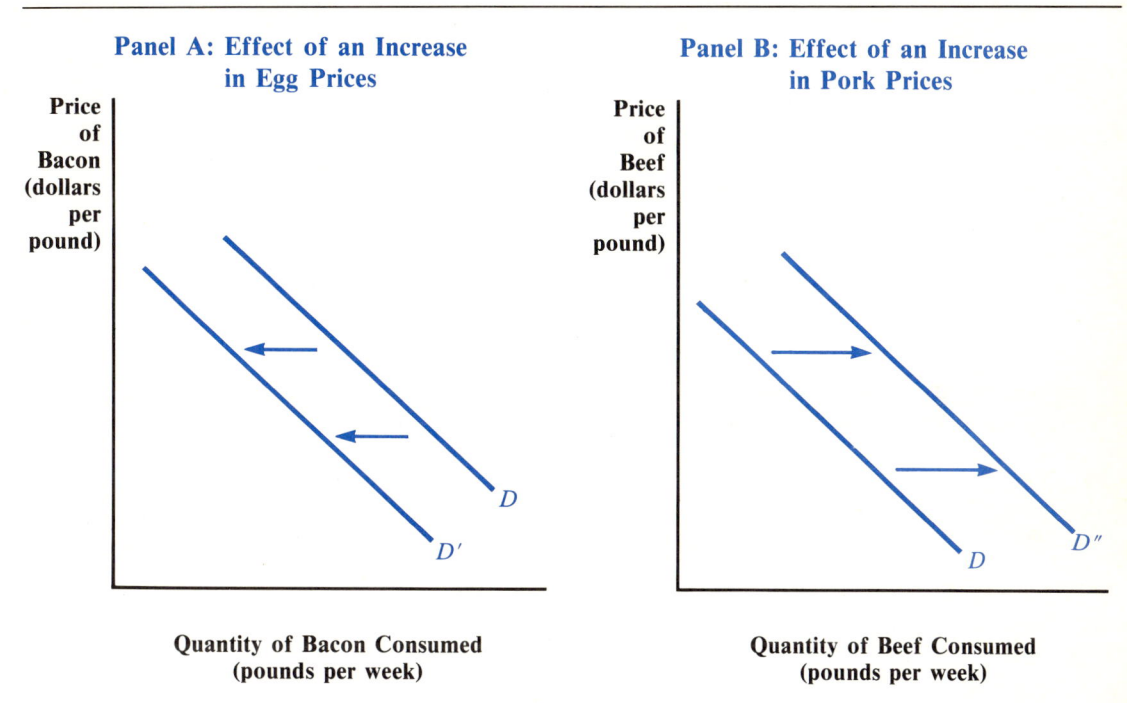

Panel A: Effect of an Increase in Egg Prices

Price of Bacon (dollars per pound)

D
D'

Quantity of Bacon Consumed (pounds per week)

Panel B: Effect of an Increase in Pork Prices

Price of Beef (dollars per pound)

D
D''

Quantity of Beef Consumed (pounds per week)

Panel A shows the effect of an increase in the price of eggs on the demand curve for a complement: bacon. Demand *decreases* from D to D'. Panel B shows the effect of an increase in the price of pork on the demand curve for a substitute: beef. Demand *increases* from D to D''.

Examples of complements would be eggs and bacon, peanut butter and jelly, car tires and gasoline, strawberries and cream. Examples of substitutes would be autos and airline tickets, television programs and movies, tea and coffee, wheat and barley, gasoline and diesel fuel, beef and pork, bacon and sausage.

Panel A of Figure 5-1 shows what happens to the demand curve for bacon as the price of eggs rises. Because eggs and bacon are complementary in consumption, the higher price of eggs will reduce the quantity demanded of eggs and lower the demand for bacon, thus shifting the demand curve for bacon leftward from D to D'. Panel B of Figure 5-1 shows what happens to the demand curve for beef as the price of pork rises. Because beef and pork are substitutes, the higher price of pork lowers the quantity demanded of pork and increases the demand for beef, thus shifting the demand curve for beef rightward from D to D''.

The third factor affecting demand is consumer tastes, or preferences. When tastes change, the demand curve will shift either to the left (a decrease in demand) or to the right (an increase in demand) depending on whether the taste for the good has deteriorated or intensified. A critical assumption of the theory is that tastes are stable. This assumption must be made because tastes cannot be directly measured. If all changes in demand that cannot be attributed to changes in prices or incomes (which are measurable) are attributed to changes in tastes, then no conceivable empirical observation could be considered inconsistent with the theory of demand. To add empirical content to the theory of demand, we must assume that tastes are relatively stable.

When long time periods are considered, taste changes do occur. In some cases, these taste changes can be identified. If the number of such taste changes is small relative to changes in prices or income, empirical analysis can still proceed by breaking the time period up into various subperiods. For example, World War II is widely known to have transmitted American tastes for such things as candy bars, chewing gum, Coca-Cola, whiskey, and hamburgers, to Europe and Japan.

The fourth determinant of demand is income. As we saw in Chapter 4, when income increases the demand for normal goods increases and the demand for inferior goods decreases. Here we should consider both the total level of consumer income as well as its distribution. Strictly speaking, if a given total of consumer income is redistributed from rich consumers to poor consumers, the demand for necessities (such as food) will increase and the demand for luxury goods (such as mink coats) will decrease. But if the distribution of income is not changing very much over the period of study, we can simply assume the demand for the good depends on total consumer income. Researchers involved in the estimation of demand functions have had no success in finding a significant role for income distribution or demographic variables.[1]

PRICE ELASTICITY OF DEMAND

The **price elasticity of demand** (η_p) for a product is the percentage change in quantity demanded per 1 percent change in the price of the good, holding other prices, income, and tastes constant:
$\eta_p = (\Delta Q/q)/(\Delta P/p)$
$= (\Delta Q/\Delta P)(p/q)$

The responsiveness of demand to any of the above determinants is its *elasticity*. In general, an elasticity of demand is the percentage change in demand for every 1 percent change in the variable in question (the good's own price, some other price, or income). If Q is quantity demanded and X is the variable in question, the elasticity of demand with respect to X is:

$$(\Delta Q/Q)/(\Delta X/X) = (\Delta Q/\Delta X)(X/Q).$$

Thus, a 10 percent change in Q produced by a 5 percent change in X would be an elasticity of "2," which literally means that demand increases by 2 percent for every 1 percent change in X. Why not simply use the slope, $\Delta Q/\Delta X$? The difficulty with slope is that its value is dependent on the units of

---
1. See Louis Philips, *Applied Consumption Analysis* (Amsterdam: North Holland, 1974), pp. 99–100.

FIGURE 5-2 Arc Elasticity of Demand

The arc elasticity formula must be used if only two points (*a* and *b*) on the demand curve are known.

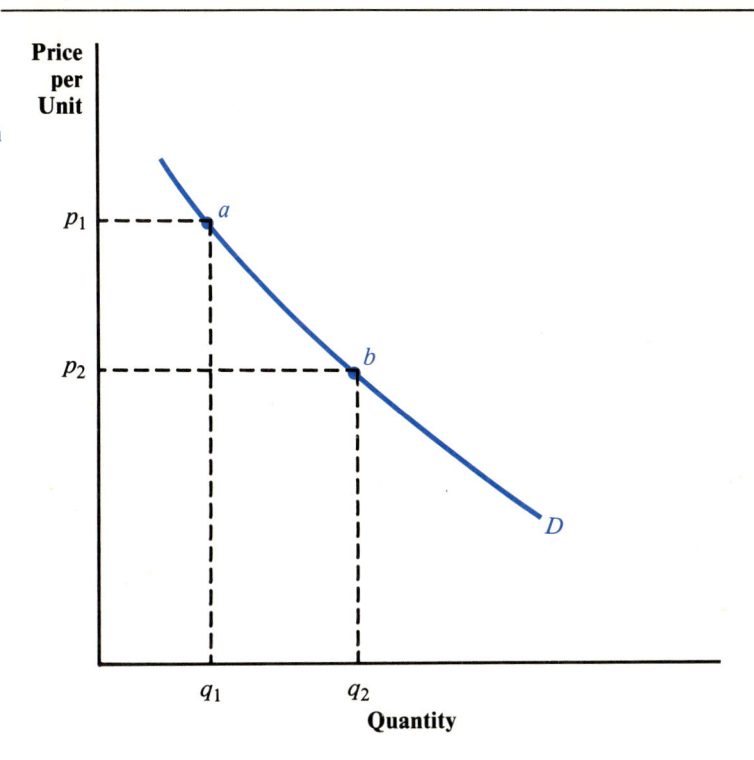

measurement for Q and X. Elasticity, however, is the same whether quantity demanded is measured in pounds or tons and whether X is measured in pennies or dollars.

The **price elasticity of demand** (η_p) (or indeed any elasticity) can be measured (1) between two separate points on a demand curve (forming an arc) or (2) at a particular point on a demand curve.[2]

Arc Elasticity

Suppose we have information on only two sets of prices and quantities. In Figure 5-2, all we know are the combinations (p_1, q_1) at point *a* and (p_2, q_2) at point *b*. The demand curve *D* need not be known. Because it is necessary to compute the percentage changes in quantity demanded and price, which of the two prices or quantities should be chosen as the base? Let us look at three possible rules for measuring arc elasticity:

---

2. Because the price elasticity measures the responsiveness of the quantity demanded of a good to its *own* price, some prefer to use the term *own-price elasticity of demand*.

PRACTICE EXERCISE 5-1

Q. The quantity of shirts demanded at the price of $10 is 8; the quantity of shirts demanded at the price of $8 is 12. Calculate the price elasticity of demand.

A. Based on the midpoints formula, the price elasticity is:

$$\eta_p = -(4/\$2)[(\$10 + \$8)/(8 + 12)] = -2(9/10) = -1.8.$$

Based on the larger quantity and the larger price, the elasticity is

$$\eta_p = -(4/\$2)(\$10/12) = -2(5/6) = -1.67.$$

Based on the smaller quantity and the smaller price, the elasticity is

$$\eta_p = -(4/\$2)(\$8/8) = -2.$$

All three of the above arc elasticities are correct.

---

1. Use the average price and quantity as the base.
2. Use the initial price with the final quantity (or the final price and initial quantity) as the base.
3. Use the initial price with the initial quantity (or final price with the final quantity) as the base.

Rule (1) is easy to justify. The computed price elasticity should not depend on whether the price is raised or lowered. Suppose, for example, that we have a price of $5 per unit when the quantity demanded is 30 units and a price of $6 when the quantity is 25 units. The numbers have been chosen deliberately so that the same dollar amount ($150) is spent. Using rule (1) the price elasticity is:

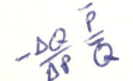

$$\eta_p = -(5/1)(5.5/27.5) = -27.5/27.5 = -1.$$

As we would expect, when the price elasticity is unitary, a change in price does not affect total expenditure on a good as price and quantity move in exact inverse proportion. The price elasticity formula using rule (1) is called the *midpoints formula*:

$$\eta_p = (\Delta Q/\Delta P)[0.5(p_1 + p_2)/0.5(q_1 + q_2)]. \tag{1}$$

According to rule (2), the price elasticity is either

$$\eta_p = (\Delta Q/\Delta P)(p_1/q_2) \text{ or } (\Delta Q/\Delta P)(p_2/q_1). \tag{2}$$

Rule (2) works because it always tells us what happens to revenue (PQ), just

PRICE ELASTICITY OF DEMAND

as the midpoints formula does. In the above numerical example, rule (2) shows that

$$\eta_p = -(5/1)(5/25) = -1 \text{ or } -(5/1)(6/30) = -1.$$

Rule (2) implies that we can use either the larger quantity and price or the smaller quantity and price. (See Practice Exercise 5-1.) Later in this chapter we will examine the algebraic link between revenues and price elasticity, which fully justifies both formula (1) and formula (2).

Rule (3), which uses either the initial price/quantity combination or the final price/quantity combination as the base, is the least reliable. Consider once again the simple numerical example. If the initial price and quantity (of $5 and 30 units) are used as the base, the elasticity is:

$$\eta_p = -(5/1)(5/30) = -5/6.$$

If the final price and quantity (of $6 and 25 units) are used as the base, the elasticity is:

$$\eta_p = -(5/1)(6/25) = -6/5.$$

Thus, using either the initial or final price/quantity combination either underpredicts or overpredicts the price elasticity. The price elasticity should be -1 in this case because total expenditures remain the same.

Point Elasticity

If the changes in prices and quantities are "small," the problem of choosing a base for calculating percentages does not arise. For example, if the price is $5 when the quantity demanded is 1,000 units and $5.01 when the quantity is 999 units, then using rule (3) with the initial price and quantity gives a price elasticity of $\eta_p = -(1/0.01)(5/1,000) = -0.5$; using rule (3) with the final price and quantity gives a price elasticity of $\eta_p = -(1/0.01)(5.01/999) = -0.5015$. The difference is slight. If the prices and quantities were even closer together, the error would be even smaller, but if we calculate the elasticity at a point there is no error at all. The formula for measuring *point elasticity* is:

$$\eta_p = (\Delta Q/\Delta P)(p/q), \tag{3}$$

where ΔQ and ΔP are very small.[3]

---

3. If $Q = D(p)$ is the demand curve, the point-elasticity formula is simply:

$$\eta_p = (\Delta Q/\Delta p)(p/Q) = D'(p)(p/Q).$$

For example, if $Q = p^{-b}$ (where $b > 0$), the elasticity is:

$$\eta_p = -bp^{-b-1}(p/Q) = -bp^{-b-1}(p/p^{-b}) = -b$$

FIGURE 5-3   Point Elasticity of Demand

The point elasticity of demand at any point, *a*, on the demand curve *D* is determined by drawing the tangent line *bc*. The price elasticity is then either $0p/bp$ or $qc/0q$.

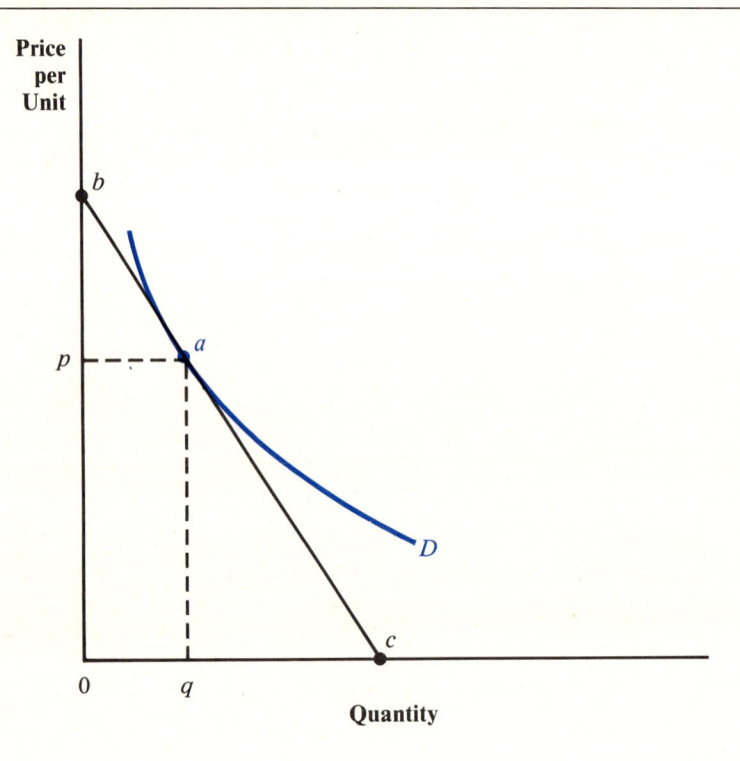

Figure 5-3 illustrates the geometric meaning of the point-elasticity formula. If one draws the tangent *bc* to the demand curve *D* at the point *a*, where it is desired to calculate the price elasticity, the slope $\Delta Q/\Delta P$ with respect to the vertical axis is clearly $-0c/0b$. Thus, the elasticity is $\eta_p = -(0c/0b)(0p/0q)$. By similar triangles, $0c/0b = pa/bp$. Because $pa \equiv 0q$, $pa/bp = 0q/bp$; substituting $0q/bp$ for $0c/0b$ leads to:

$$\eta_p = -0p/bp. \tag{4}$$

Formula (4) measures the price elasticity along the vertical (price) axis. (See Practice Exercise 5-2.) The price elasticity can also be measured along the horizontal (quantity) axis. Again, by similar triangles $0c/0b = 0c/qa$. Because $qa = 0p$, $0c/qa = 0c/0p$; substituting $qc/0p$ for $0c/0b$ leads to:

$$\eta_p = -qc/0q. \tag{5}$$

Either formula (4) or formula (5) gives the price elasticity of demand at the point *a* on demand curve *D*. Using the price version of point-elasticity formula (4), it is obvious that the demand for the good will be elastic or inelastic as $0p$ exceeds or falls short of the distance bp in Figure 5-3.

FIGURE 5-4   Changing Versus Constant Elasticity of Demand

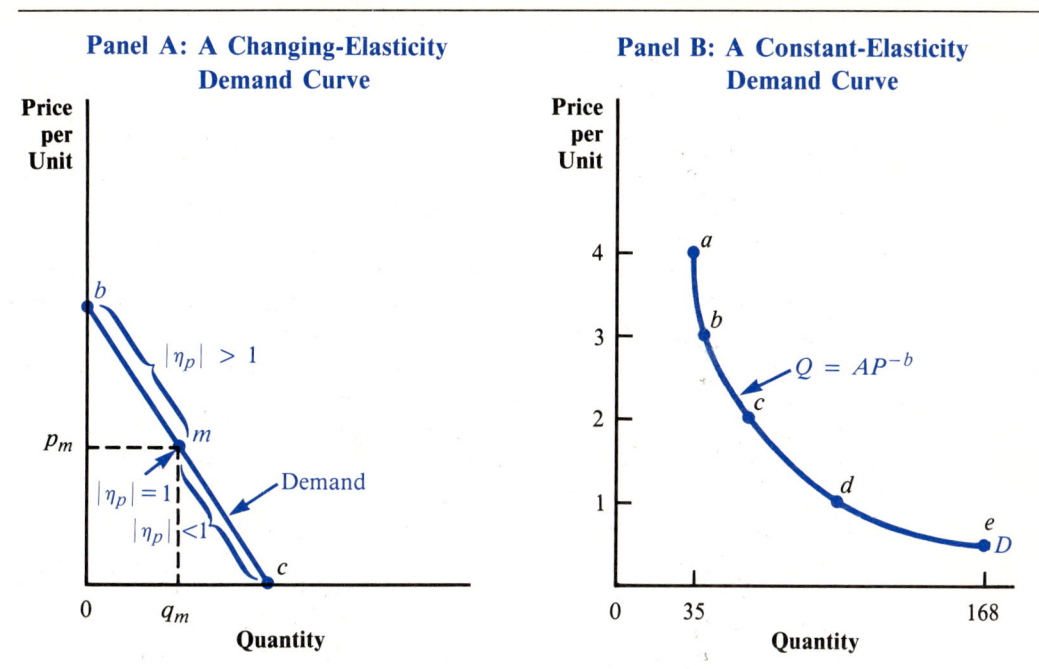

Panel A: A Changing-Elasticity Demand Curve

Panel B: A Constant-Elasticity Demand Curve

$Q = AP^{-b}$

Panel A shows that a straight-line demand curve is unit elastic at the midpoint, m, elastic above m, and inelastic below m. The elasticity varies from infinity at point b to zero at point c. Panel B shows a constant-elasticity demand curve.

Constant Slope Versus Constant Elasticity

The point-elasticity formula dramatically illustrates the difference between the *elasticity* and the *slope* of a demand curve. In Panel A of Figure 5-4, the demand curve is assumed to be a straight line. Consider the price p_m corresponding to the midpoint m on the demand curve. Using formula (4) it is clear that for any price above p_m, demand is elastic; for any price below p_m, demand is inelastic. (Demand is unit elastic at the price p_m.) If the price of the good is zero, the formula tells us that the price elasticity is zero; if the price of the good is such that the quantity demanded approaches zero (as at point b), then the price elasticity is infinity.

A constant-elasticity demand curve is shown in Panel B of Figure 5-4. The slope must continuously decline (in absolute value) in order to keep the elasticity constant. As price falls, the ratio of price to quantity falls and $\Delta P/\Delta Q$ must likewise fall to keep the ratio constant. The constant-elasticity demand curve has the form, $Q = AP^{-b}$, where $-b$ is the price elasticity.[4]

---

4. See footnote 3 for a calculus proof.

PRACTICE EXERCISE 5-2

Q. Suppose the demand curve for a product is $Q = 60 - 3P$. What is the price elasticity of demand when $P = \$15$?

A. When $P = \$15$, $Q = 15$. Thus, the point price elasticity is

$$\eta_p = -(3)(\$15/15) = -3.$$

Alternatively, by using the geometric formula (4), the vertical intercept of the demand curve is $20. The formula then states that the price elasticity is $-0p/bp$, where $0p$ is the price and bp is the difference between the intercept and the price. Thus, $\eta_p = -\$15/\$5 = -3$.

OTHER ELASTICITIES OF DEMAND

The Income Elasticity of Demand

The **income elasticity of demand** (η_m) is the percentage increase in the demand for a product per 1 percent increase in income:
$\eta_m = (\Delta Q/q)/(\Delta M/m)$
$= (\Delta Q/\Delta M)(m/q)$

Income elasticity of demand (η_m) was introduced in Chapter 4, which defined luxury goods as those having an income elasticity greater than 1 and necessities as those having an income elasticity less than 1. Figure 5-5 shows two Engel curves. Panel A shows a luxury good; Panel B shows a necessity. The elasticity of these curves at any point can also be computed by drawing a tangent at point c (in both panels). The tangent bc has a vertical-axis intercept at point b. The income elasticity can be calculated as

$$\eta_m = (\Delta Q/\Delta M)(m/q) = (qb/qc)(qc/0q) = qb/0q. \quad (6)$$

Clearly, in the case of Panel A, the ratio $qb/0q > 1$, and in the case of Panel B, the ratio $qb/0q < 1$.

The Cross-Price Elasticity of Demand

The **cross-price elasticity of demand** (η_{xy}) measures the percentage change in the demand for one good in response to a 1 percent change in the price of another good:
$\eta_{yx} = (\Delta Y/y)/(\Delta p_x/p_x)$
$= (\Delta Y/\Delta p_x)(p_x/y)$

When the price of any good changes, it not only affects the quantity of the good demanded, it also affects the demands for substitutes and complements. If the price of good X rises, the demands for its complements fall, and the demands for its substitutes increase. The relative responsiveness of the demand for one good to the price of another is measured by the **cross-price elasticity of demand** (η_{xy}).

A positive cross-price elasticity of demand between two goods indicates that they are substitutes. A negative cross-price elasticity of demand indicates that they are complements. If goods X and Y are perfect substitutes, the cross-price elasticity of demand would be infinity. Thus, the size of the

FIGURE 5-5 Income Elasticity Along an Engel Curve

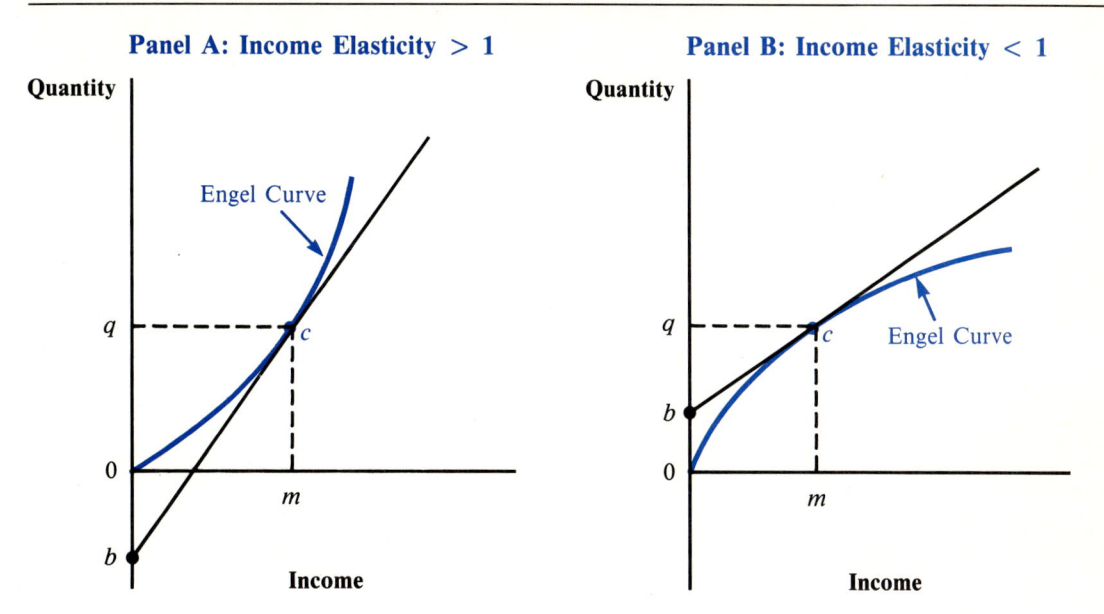

Panel A: Income Elasticity > 1

Panel B: Income Elasticity < 1

The income elasticity at any point on an Engel curve is determined by drawing a line tangent at that point and intersecting the vertical axis to form the ratio $qb/0q$. The income elasticity exceeds 1 in Panel A and is less than 1 in Panel B.

cross-price elasticity can be used to determine the extent to which two goods are close substitutes. While there is no universally agreed-upon criterion, a cross-price elasticity of demand close to unity would indicate that two goods were extremely good substitutes. Indeed, in statistical studies it is difficult to find cross-price elasticities greater than unity. For example, the cross-price elasticity of demand between butter and margarine has been estimated to be in the range of 0.67 to 0.81.[5]

The Aggregation of Elasticities

Market elasticities of demand are the consequence of the elasticities of demand of all the individual buyers in the market. If q_i is the quantity of some good demanded by agent i, it is clear that the change in total quantity is the simple sum of the changes in the individual quantities demanded by all agents:

$$\Delta Q = \sum_{i=1}^{n} \Delta q_i, \tag{7}$$

---

5. See Herman Wold, *Demand Analysis* (New York: John Wiley and Sons, 1953).

> **EXAMPLE 5-1**   Cross-Price Elasticities for Coal and Oil
>
> When the price of oil quadrupled in 1974, the demand for coal increased substantially. The resulting increase in the price of coal was also substantial. The accompanying table shows that the price of bituminous coal (in cents per BTU) more than doubled between 1972 and 1980—a direct result of the fact that coal and oil are substitutes and have a significant cross-price-elasticity coefficient. Those who owned coal mines in 1972 received a substantial windfall increase in their incomes after 1974. The television program "60 Minutes" even devoted a segment to how the owners of coal mines spent their newfound wealth.
>
> | Year | Price of Coal (in 1972 dollars) |
> |---|---|
> | 1972 | 31.90 |
> | 1974 | 57.80 |
> | 1976 | 63.50 |
> | 1978 | 64.70 |
> | 1980 | 64.90 |
>
> Source: *Statistical Abstract of the United States, 1981*, 102nd ed., p. 582.

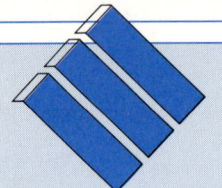

when there are n buyers in the market. Now suppose that the changes in the q_is are caused by a change in the price of the good. If we divide Equation (7) by ΔP and multiply both sides by p/q, we see that

$$(\Delta Q/\Delta P)(p/Q) = \sum_{i=1}^{n} (\Delta q_i/\Delta P)(p/q_i)(q_i/Q). \tag{8}$$

Notice on the right-hand-side of Equation (8) that we have written p/Q as $(p/q_i)(q_i/Q)$. Breaking p/Q down in this way allows us to put everything in elasticity form:

$$\eta_p = \sum_{i=1}^{n} (\eta_p^i)(q_i/Q) \tag{9}$$

Equation (9) states that the market price elasticity of demand is a *weighted* average of the individual price elasticities of demand. For example, if agent 1 has a price elasticity of -1 and buys 40 percent of the good, and if agent 2 has a price elasticity of -2 and buys the remaining 60 percent of the good, the market price elasticity is $-1.6 = (-1)(0.4) + (-2)(0.6)$. As a weighted average, the market price elasticity will be trapped between the lowest and highest individual price elasticities. If all individuals have the same price elasticity, the market price elasticity is equal to the common value. This should be obvious from the definition of price elasticity: if a 5 percent increase in the price of eggs reduces each person's quantity of eggs demanded by 1 percent, the quantity of eggs demanded by the entire market will fall by 1 percent as well.

COMPENSATED PRICE ELASTICITY OF DEMAND

Slutsky's Equation

We saw in Chapter 4 that if the change in money income equals the change in the cost of a given commodity bundle—that is, if $\Delta M = x\Delta P_x$—then the consumer's welfare is not diminished by the change in the price of good X. This makes intuitive sense because the consumer can just afford to buy the old bundle and still has the opportunity to make utility-raising commodity substitutions.[6] Under these circumstances the consumer is *compensated* for the change in the price of good X.

A consumer is compensated for the change in the price of good X if $\Delta M = x\Delta P_x$, where x is the quantity of good X.

If we assume that both the price of good X and total consumer income change, then the proportionate change in the demand for good X is:

$$\Delta X/x = \eta_p \Delta P_x/p_x + \eta_m \Delta M/m. \tag{10}$$

The first term is the proportionate change arising from the change in the price of good X, and the second term is the proportionate change arising from the change in income. If consumers are compensated, it follows that

$$\Delta X/x = \eta_p \Delta P_x/p_x + \eta_m \Delta P_x x p_x/p_x m$$
$$= [\eta_p + \eta_m(p_x x/m)](\Delta P_x/p_x). \tag{11}$$

Dividing both sides by $\Delta P_x/p_x$ yields *Slutsky's equation*:

$$\eta_p^c = \eta_p + \eta_m(p_x x/m), \tag{12}$$

where η_p^c is the **compensated price elasticity of demand.**

Compensated price elasticity of demand (η_p^c) is the price elasticity measured along a compensated demand curve (that is, holding real income constant).

Compensated price elasticities will be lower in absolute value than ordinary price elasticities because the second term in Slutsky's equation is positive for normal goods. (See Practice Exercise 5-3.) For example, the (long-run) price elasticity of demand for automobiles and parts has been

---

6. With small price changes, utility-raising substitutions are limited; with large price changes, utility-raising substitutions are abundant. For example, if you buy a new $10,000 car every year and the price goes up by $0.01, being compensated by $0.01 hardly increases your utility. But if the price goes up by $10,000, being compensated by $10,000 allows you to buy a much better car.

PRACTICE EXERCISE 5-3

Q. The ordinary price elasticity of demand for good X is -3. The income elasticity for X is 2, and 50 percent of the household budget is devoted to X. What is the compensated price elasticity?

A. Use Slutsky's equation: $-3 + 2(0.50) = -2$.

---

estimated to be -1.35, and the income elasticity has been estimated to be 1.65.[7] Using 0.0545 as the proportion of income devoted to automobiles and parts, the compensated price elasticity is -1.26; that is, using Equation (12),

$$-1.26 = -1.35 + 1.65(0.0545).$$

Slutsky's equation may be used to test the theory of consumer behavior. According to the theory, the compensated price elasticity is negative. Slutsky's equation gives us a method of recovering the compensated price elasticity from empirical estimates of the ordinary price elasticity, the income elasticity, and budget shares. Suppose $\eta_p = 1$, $\eta_m = 4$, and the share of the good in income was 0.3. Then, according to Slutsky's equation, even though the ordinary demand curve is downward-sloping, this hypothetical example contradicts the theory of consumer behavior because $\eta_p^c = +0.2 = -1 + 4(0.3)$.

Slutsky's equation gives us a method of recovering the compensated price elasticity from empirical market-demand functions because $\eta_p^c = \eta_p + \eta_m (p_x x/m)$. It may be used to test the prediction that the substitution effect is negative.

The factors governing the size of the price elasticity of demand are the substitution and income effects: the bigger are those effects, the larger is the price elasticity. A useful way of rewriting the Slutsky equation is to use the absolute values

$$|\eta_p^c| = -\eta_p^c \text{ and } |\eta_p| = -\eta_p.$$

Substituting into Equation (12) yields

$$|\eta_p| = |\eta_p^c| + \eta_m(p_x x/m). \tag{13}$$

We can conclude from Slutsky's equation that:

---

[7] Philips, *Applied Consumption Analysis*, p. 195.

1. The more substitutes there are for a good, the higher is the numerical price elasticity (the substitution effect is larger).
2. The more time the consumer has to adjust his or her consumption to the new price, the higher is the numerical price elasticity (the substitution effect is larger).
3. The more important is the good in the consumer's budget, the higher is the numerical price elasticity (the income effect is larger).
4. The higher is the income elasticity of demand for the good, the higher is the numerical price elasticity (the income effect is larger).

We would, therefore, expect that something like salt would have a low price elasticity, while a good like fur coats would have a high price elasticity.

Substitutes and Complements

A more general version of Slutsky's equation is obtained if, instead of examining the change in the demand for good X, we look at the change in the demand for good Y when the price of X changes. The compensation is still the quantity $\Delta M = \Delta P_x x$. The compensated cross-price elasticity of demand between Y and X can be written as:

$$\eta^c_{yx} = \eta_{yx} + \eta^y_m (p_x x/m) \qquad (14)$$

The compensated cross-price elasticity η^c_{yx} may have a different sign than the uncompensated cross-price elasticity η_{yx}.

Substitutes and complements may be defined in terms of the uncompensated or compensated cross-price elasticities. Two goods are called **net substitutes** if the demand for one increases in response to an increase in the price of the other, holding *real income* constant. Two goods are called **net complements** if the demand for one decreases when the price of the other increases, holding *real income* constant. When *nominal income* is held constant, substitutes and complements are referred to as **gross substitutes** or **gross complements**.

The advantage of the net definition over the gross definition is that by purging the cross-price elasticity of income effects one obtains a purer estimate of the substitution possibilities. To illustrate, suppose a consumer buys goods X and Y. If good X is price elastic and Y is price inelastic, then good Y must be a gross substitute for good X. Raising the price of good X will lower dollar expenditures on X and, thus, increase the demand for Y. At the same time, good X must be a gross complement with good Y because raising the price of Y will increase dollar expenditures on Y and, thus, lower the demand for X. If the gross measure is used, goods X and Y may appear to be substitutes or complements, depending on which price is increased. If the net measure is used, then there is no such ambiguity.

Equation (14) reveals that for normal goods there is a tendency toward net substitution. Because the second term is then positive, the first term would

<aside>Goods X and Y are **net substitutes** if η^c_{yx} (the compensated cross-price elasticity) > 0; they are **net complements** if $\eta^c_{yx} < 0$. Good Y is a **gross substitute** for good X if η_{yx} (the uncompensated cross-price elasticity) > 0; good Y is a **gross complement** for good X if $\eta_{yx} < 0$.</aside>

FIGURE 5-6   Total and Average Revenue

The firm's total revenue per period is the rectangle $0pcq$ when the price is $0p$. Because all units are sold at the same price, the average revenue (AR) also equals price. Thus, the demand curve, D, can also be labeled the AR curve.

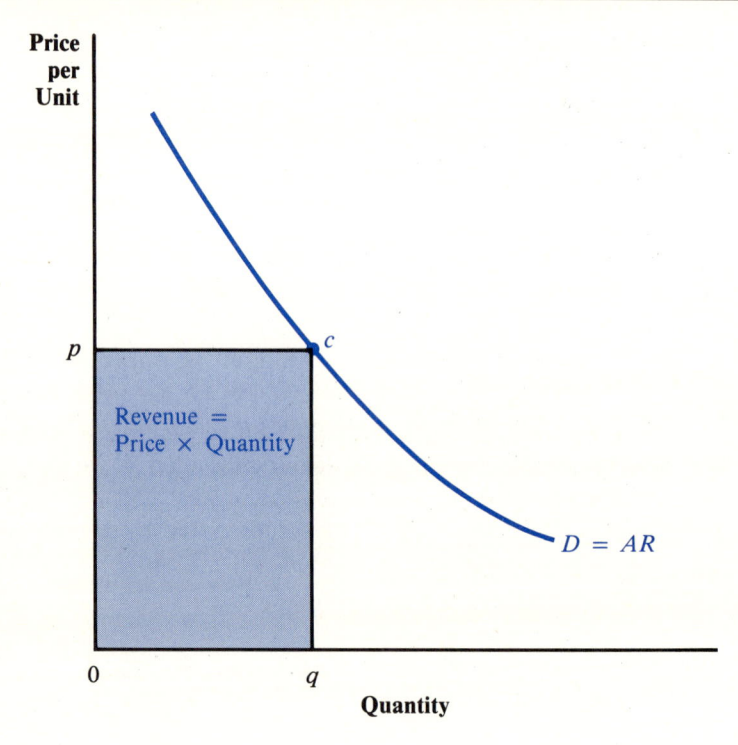

[Figure: Demand curve labeled $D = AR$ downward sloping, with rectangle $0pcq$ shaded showing Revenue = Price × Quantity]

have to be both negative and large in absolute value (strong complements) in order to cause net complementarity.[8]

PRICE ELASTICITY AND TOTAL REVENUE

The price elasticity of demand is related to the extra revenue generated by the firm trying to sell one more unit of its product. In general, a low numerical elasticity indicates that a sharp reduction in price is necessary to sell an additional amount of the good; a high numerical elasticity means that an additional unit can be sold with a comparatively smaller reduction in the price. As a consequence, the increase in revenue will tend to be larger the

---

8. There is a conceptual difficulty with this definition: if there are only two goods, both cannot be net complements. The definition is loaded against generalized net complementarity. An improved definition of substitutes and complements has been offered by Paul A. Samuelson, in "Complementarity—An Essay on the 40th Anniversary of the Hicks-Allen Revolution in Demand Theory," *Journal of Economic Literature* 12 (December 1974): 1255–89.

PRICE ELASTICITY AND TOTAL REVENUE

FIGURE 5-7 Perfectly Elastic and Perfectly Inelastic Demand

Panel A: Perfectly Elastic Demand

$P = MR$
$\eta_p = -\infty$

D

Quantity

Panel B: Perfectly Inelastic Demand

$MR = -\infty$
$\eta_p = 0$

D

Quantity

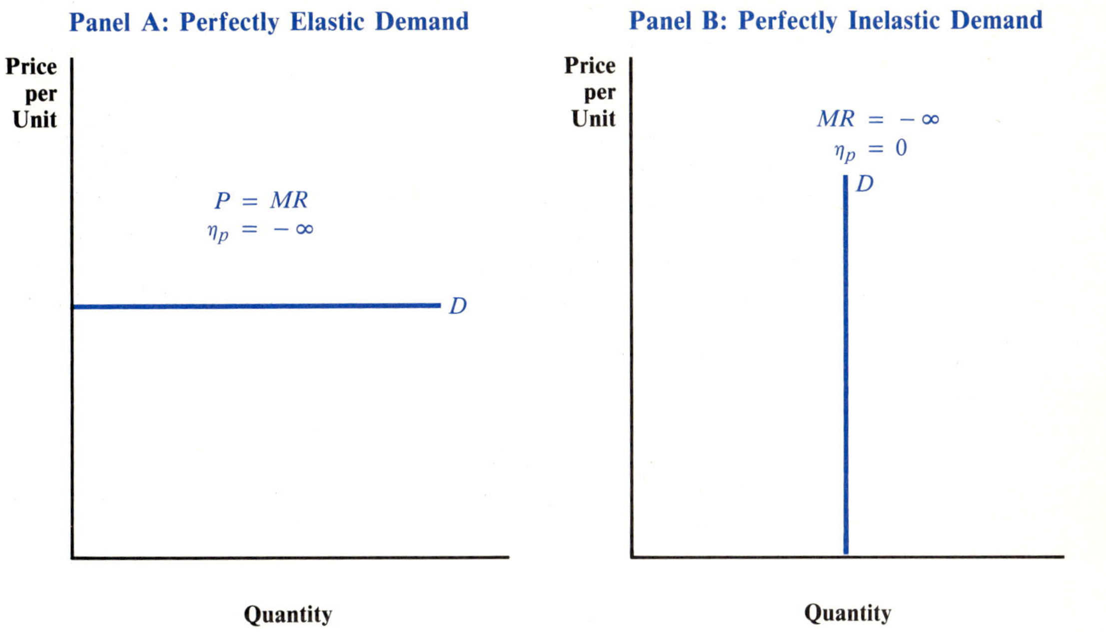

Panel A shows a perfectly elastic demand curve (an infinite price elasticity). In this case, marginal revenue equals price. Panel B shows a perfectly inelastic demand curve (a zero price elasticity). In this case, marginal revenue is infinitely negative.

Marginal revenue (MR) is the increase in revenue (R) per unit increase in the quantity of a good sold (Q) per unit of time; that is, $MR = \Delta R/\Delta Q$.

larger is the numerical price elasticity. The extra revenue associated with selling one more unit of a good is called **marginal revenue (MR)**.

Figure 5-6 shows a standard demand curve facing a firm. If the firm's price is p it will sell q units per period. Clearly, the firm's revenue per period is $R = p \times q$, or the rectangle $0pcq$. Because all units of the good are sold at the same price, the firm's average revenue (AR) is the same as price. Thus,

$$AR = R/q = (pq)/q = p. \tag{15}$$

How are average revenue (or price), price elasticity, and marginal revenue related?

Price, Marginal Revenue, and Elasticity

Two polar cases indicate the sensitive nature of the link between price elasticity and marginal revenue. Panel A of Figure 5-7 shows a perfectly elastic demand curve, where the price elasticity of demand is infinite. When $\eta_p = -\infty$, no reduction in price is required to sell an additional unit of a good. Hence, the price would be the marginal revenue.

Panel B of Figure 5-7 shows a perfectly inelastic demand curve, where

FIGURE 5-8　The Effect of a Price Change on Total Revenue

When price is lowered from p_1 to p_2, the net change in revenue is the rectangle G minus the rectangle S.

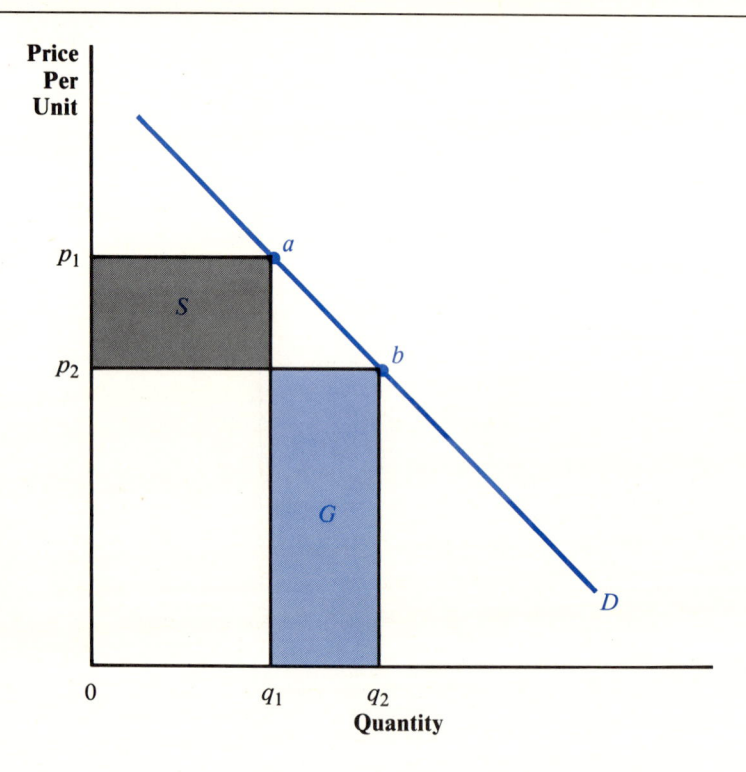

any reduction in price has no impact on quantity demanded. In this case, the price elasticity of demand is zero. Because ΔQ is zero and revenue must fall when the price is reduced, $MR = \Delta R/\Delta Q = -\infty$.

What is the general rule? Figure 5-8 shows the general case of a downward-sloping demand curve. When the price falls from p_1 to p_2, revenue changes from $p_1 q_1$ to $p_2 q_2$. The firm loses the gray shaded area S, and gains the color shaded area G. The area S is lost because the firm can no longer sell the first q_1 units at the price p_1 when the firm sells q_2 units per period. In effect, when the firm decides to sell the higher quantity q_2, instead of the lower quantity q_1, it must spoil the market on the first q_1 units sold by having to lower the price. The net increase in revenue will be the area G minus the area S. Because area S is $(p_1 - p_2)q_1$ and area G is $(q_2 - q_1)p_2$, the net change in revenue is:

$$\Delta R = (q_2 - q_1)p_2 - (p_1 - p_2)q_1.$$

Because $\Delta P = p_2 - p_1$ and $\Delta Q = q_2 - q_1$, we can write:

$$MR = p_2 + q_1(\Delta P/\Delta Q). \tag{16}$$

It is clear from Equation (16) that p_2 (the new price) must exceed marginal

TABLE 5-1   **The Revenue Test: The Effect on Revenue of a Price Rise or Fall When Demand Is Elastic, Unit Elastic, or Inelastic**

	Elastic Demand, $\|\eta_p\| > 1$	Inelastic Demand, $\|\eta_p\| < 1$	Unit-Elastic Demand, $\|\eta_p\| = 1$
Price rises	$\Delta R < 0$	$\Delta R > 0$	$\Delta R = 0$
Price falls	$\Delta R > 0$	$\Delta R < 0$	$\Delta R = 0$

revenue because the second term is negative. The first term is the gain in revenue attributable to selling an extra unit at the new price; the second term is the loss in revenue (the spoiling-of-the-market effect) attributable to having to sell the first q_1 units at a lower price. If we use the arc-elasticity formula,

$$\eta_p = (\Delta Q/\Delta P)p_2/q_1,$$

substitution into Equation (16) yields a general relationship between price (P), marginal revenue (MR), and price elasticity (η_p):

$$MR = P(1 + 1/\eta_p). \tag{17}$$

Formula (17) precisely reflects the quantitative relationships between price, marginal revenue, and the price elasticity.[9]

1. The higher is the (numerical) value of the price elasticity, the higher will be the marginal revenue for any given price.
2. What happens to total revenue as the price changes can be used as a test to determine the elasticity of demand. Marginal revenue is positive, zero, or negative as demand is elastic ($|\eta_p| > 1$), unit elastic ($|\eta_p| = 1$), or inelastic ($|\eta_p| < 1$). Table 5-1 summarizes the revenue test. The rule is that if demand is elastic, price and revenue move in different directions; if demand is inelastic, price and revenue move in the same direction.
3. Price exceeds marginal revenue as long as the price elasticity of demand is finite. If η_p is infinite, $P = MR$. The price elasticity can be infinite if the demand curve is perfectly elastic or if the quantity demanded is 0.

---

9. The relations between price, marginal revenue, and price elasticity are easily derived using calculus. Because $R = P \times Q$, MR is simply the derivative

$$MR = \Delta R/\Delta Q = P + Q\Delta P/\Delta Q.$$

Because $\eta_p = (\Delta Q/\Delta P)(P/Q)$, we can write:

$$MR = P(1 + 1/\eta_p)$$

TABLE 5-2   Revenues from the Sale of Mineral Spring Water

Quantity (liters), Q	Price (dollars per liter), P	Total Revenue (dollars), $R = P \times Q$	Marginal Revenue (dollars), MR
(1)	(2)	(3)	(4)
0	4	0	
1	3	3	3
2	2	4	1
3	1	3	−1
4	0	0	−3

Table 5-2 gives the quantity sold per week of water from a particular mineral spring. When the price is $4 per liter, quantity demanded per week is zero; when the price falls to $0 per liter, quantity demanded is 4 liters per week. The demand curve is linear because every $1 reduction in the price of mineral water raises quantity demanded by exactly 1 unit. Column (3) of Table 5-2 shows the revenue schedule; column (4) shows the marginal-revenue schedule. The marginal revenue of the first unit sold is $MR_1 = \$3$; $MR_2 = \$1$; $MR_3 = -\$1$; $MR_4 = -\$3$. Because marginal revenue is the addition to total revenue of one more unit sold, the total revenue of selling any quantity is simply the sum of the successive marginal revenues. For example, the revenue from selling 3 units in Table 5-2 is $3:

$$R_3 = MR_1 + MR_2 + MR_3$$
$$\$3 = \$3 + \$1 + (-\$1)$$

In general, if n units are sold, the relationship between revenue and the successive marginal revenues is:[10]

$$R_n = MR_1 + MR_2 + \ldots + MR_n = \sum_{i=1}^{n} MR_i \tag{18}$$

Figure 5-9 graphs the demand and the marginal-revenue schedules from Table 5-2. The figures for marginal revenue have been plotted midway

---

[10]. If $R(Q)$ is revenue, then the fundamental theorem of calculus states that $R(b) - R(a) = \int_a^b R'(Q)\delta Q$, where $R'(Q)$ is marginal revenue. If $a = 0$ and $R = 0$, it follows that for any output Q^*

$$R(Q^*) = \int_0^Q R'(Q)\delta Q.$$

FIGURE 5-9   Plotting the Marginal-Revenue Curve

The demand and marginal-revenue schedules of Table 5-2 are shown here. Each figure for marginal revenue has been plotted midway *between* the successive output levels. A straight line drawn through the dots shows the price or marginal revenue for any output level.

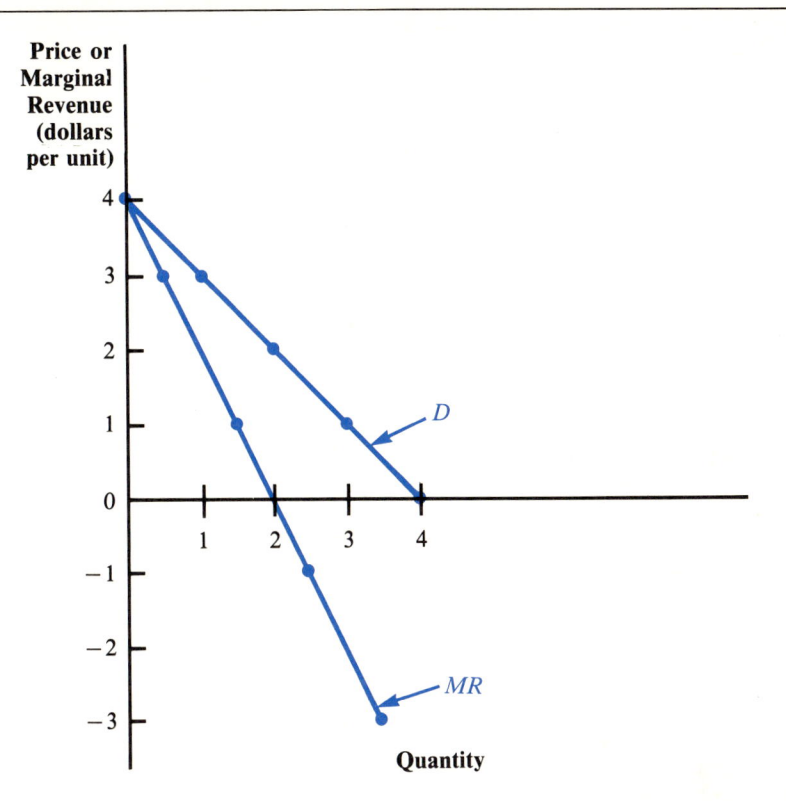

The **halfway rule**: If the demand curve is a straight line, the MR curve is twice as steep or lies halfway between the vertical axis and the demand curve.

between the successive output levels. For example, the marginal revenue between output levels of 1 unit and 2 units is $1 whether output is increased or decreased. Therefore, the marginal revenue of $1 is plotted at 1.5 units of output. A straight line drawn through the dots shows the price and marginal revenue for any level of output or sales. Notice that each time quantity increases by 1 unit, price falls by $1 and marginal revenue falls by $2, or by twice as much.

This example reveals a general rule: whenever the demand curve is a straight line, marginal revenue falls twice as fast as price. Consider Figure 5-10. The demand curve, D, is a straight line. Because $MR = P + Q(\Delta P/\Delta Q)$, the marginal-revenue curve is also a straight line. The trapezoid $0afq$ is the sum of the successive marginal revenues. Because revenue is the sum of the successive marginal revenues, we know that the revenue rectangle $0pcq$ = the trapezoid $0afq$. It follows that triangle pae = triangle ecf. Because the triangles have the same area and are also similar triangles, they are identical; thus, $pe = ec$. This series of observations proves that the MR

FIGURE 5-10 Marginal Revenue in Relation to Demand

The *MR* curve is a straight line if the demand curve is a straight line. Because total revenue is either 0*pcq* or the trapezoid 0*afq*, it follows that *pe = ec* or that the *MR* curve is exactly halfway between any straight-line demand curve and the vertical axis.

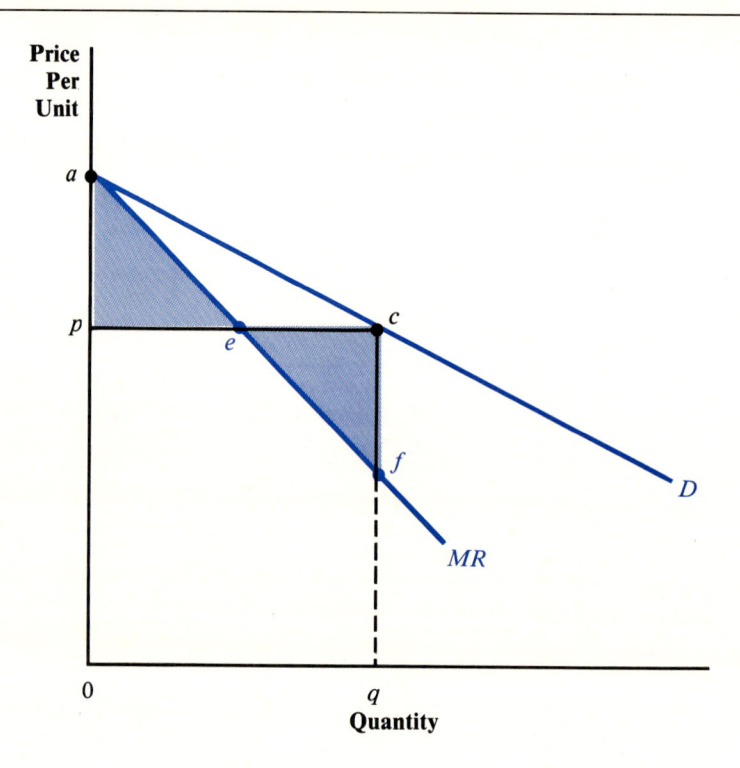

curve falls twice as fast as the demand curve or, equivalently, that the *MR* curve is exactly halfway between the vertical axis and the demand curve.[11]

The **halfway rule** is convenient because it allows us to quickly identify the *MR* curve in numerical examples. While a straight-line demand curve is unrealistic, it can serve as a useful approximation.

The Average/Marginal Rule

The relationship between price and marginal revenue is a special case of an important general rule: the relationship between average values and marginal values. If T is the total amount of some variable (revenue, cost, utility,

---

11. If $P = A - BQ$, it follows that
$$R = PQ = AQ - BQ^2.$$
Because MR is simply $\Delta R/\Delta Q$, we have
$$\Delta R/\Delta Q = MR = A - 2BQ.$$
This immediately proves that the marginal-revenue curve is twice as steep as the demand curve for any straight-line curve.

TABLE 5-3   **The Relationship Between Marginal Values (M) and Average Values (A)**

Quantity of First Variable, N	Total Amount of Second Variable, T	Average Value, $A = T/N$	Marginal Value, $M = \Delta T/\Delta N$
1	5	5	
			7
2	12	6	
			6
3	18	6	
			2
4	20	5	

output, number of hits) that is brought about by the quantity N of some other variable (sales, output, consumption, input, times at bat), the average (A) is defined as

$$A = T/N. \tag{19}$$

The marginal value (M) of changing N is the change in T per unit change in N, or

$$M = \Delta T/\Delta N. \tag{20}$$

The relationship between average values and marginal values is illustrated by Table 5-3. Notice that the average rises when N changes from 1 to 2, stays constant when N changes from 2 to 3, and falls when N changes from 3 to 4. When the average rises, the margin is above it; when the average stays constant, the margin equals the average; when the average falls, the margin is below the average. We can think of the marginal value as pulling up or pushing down the average as it exceeds or falls short of the previous average value.

From Equation (19), we can write $T = AN$. It follows that when N changes, the new value of T is

$$\begin{aligned} T + \Delta T &= (A + \Delta A)(N + \Delta N) \\ &= AN + A\Delta N + N\Delta A + \Delta A \Delta N \end{aligned} \tag{21}$$

Subtracting $T = AN$ from both sides and dividing both sides by ΔN, we can write

$$\Delta T/\Delta N = M = A + (\Delta A/\Delta N)(N + \Delta N). \tag{22}$$

If we let $N' = N + \Delta N$, we can rewrite Equation (22) as:

$$M = A + (\Delta A/\Delta N)N'. \tag{23}$$

Equation (23) shows the exact relationship between an initial average value, A, the change in the average, the new quantity N', and the marginal value of changes in N. For example, in Table 5-3, when N changes from 3 to 4, $M =$

2 = 6 +(−1)4. The formula shows that the average rises when the margin exceeds the average, falls when the margin is less than the average, and remains constant if the margin equals the average.

The relationship between marginal values (M) and average values (A) is that the average rises as M exceeds A, falls as M falls short of A, and remains constant when M equals A.

The marginal/average rule holds for all quantitative relationships. For example: your grade-point average rises when your last (marginal) test score exceeds your previous average; the baseball player's batting average falls when his or her (marginal) daily batting average falls short of the average; marginal revenue lies below average revenue because the latter declines with quantity.

EMPIRICAL DEMAND ANALYSIS

Regression Analysis

The relationship between consumer demand and income can be studied by taking a cross section of households at any particular time. Because the households at that time face approximately the same prices, variations in demand across households can be attributed to such factors as income, age, family size, or sex. To study the effects of prices on consumer demand, it is usually necessary to follow a group of households through time by collecting a time series of their demands, prices, and incomes. Price effects can be studied between households if they are located in different regions and face different prices, as in a cross-section analysis.

Whether one uses a cross-section or time-series analysis, variations in demand will be accompanied by simultaneous changes in all the explanatory variables. How does one sort out the effects of a change in the price of a good from the effects of, say, changes in income? The statistical method for holding all other factors constant is called a *multivariate regression*.

To understand a multivariate regression, we must first understand the concept of a *regression equation*. A regression equation is the equation that best fits a number of empirical observations. For example, in Figure 5-11 the dots correspond to various empirical observations of variables Y and X. Each dot might represent, for example, a particular family's consumption of butter (Y) and family income (X). We will assume that the dots are generated by the equation,

$$Y = a + bX + e,$$

where a and b are unknown parameters and e is an unobservable error term. It is assumed that the dots are generated by changes in e and observed changes in Y.

FIGURE 5-11 Regression Analysis

Each dot represents an empirical observation of a pair (X, Y). The collection of dots forms a scatter diagram. A regression equation is the best fit in the sense that the deviations e_1, e_2, e_3, etc. between each point and the regression line have the smallest possible dispersion as measured by the variance of the deviations.

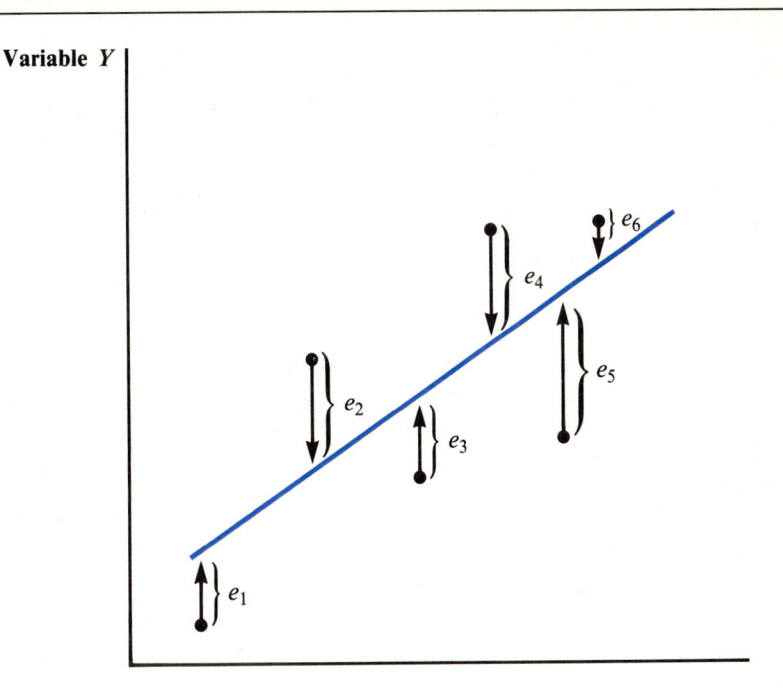

How should we determine the parameters a and b? Following two principles will lead us to a unique equation. The first principle is to choose a and b so that, *on the average*, the error terms—the *es*—are zero. Thus, on the average, the fitted equation turns out to be right. The second principle is to make the error term e independent of the explanatory variable X. Why? The error is presumed to arise from the fact that our theory has not omitted any other explanations (other than X) of the variable Y. It is supposed, therefore, that the errors arise from a succession of independent random events. Each time a pair (Y, X) is observed, it does not fall on the straight line because the error term e causes "noise." The theory of linear regression argues that if the error term is like the random wanderings of a gas molecule or like your winnings from a coin flip (heads you win, tails you lose), then the parameters a and b can be chosen in such a way as to give the minimum variance fit. Appendix 5A (which follows this chapter) describes the basic theory of such regressions.

Multivariate regressions follow exactly the same principles, except that more than one variable is assumed to explain the endogenous variable Y. We might hypothesize that

$$Y = a_0 + a_1 X_1 + a_2 X_2 + e,$$

EXAMPLE 5–2 The Measurement of Substitution and Income Effects

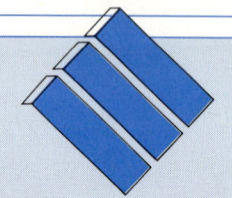

Table 5–5 showed that price and income elasticities are highly correlated. One reason is that higher income elasticities increase the income effect of a price change and, thus, indirectly contribute to a higher price elasticity. Another reason is that higher income elasticities are associated with higher *compensated-price* elasticities. In other words, the substitution effect itself might be larger the larger is the income elasticity of demand. At least three separate studies of consumer demand in Australia, Belgium, and the United States have reported this empirical phenomenon. The data are presented in the accompanying tables.

The intuitive reason why the rankings of compensated-price elasticity and income elasticities are related is that the goods with high income elasticities tend to be small proportions of the budget when incomes are not too high. The compensated-price elasticity, however, will tend to be relatively high because the base for computing the elasticity is small. Necessities (such as food) have a large base and, hence, tend to have a smaller compensated-price elasticity.

Belgium	Compensated-Price Elasticity	Income Elasticity
Travel abroad	−1.57	3.51
Services	−0.73	1.88
Durables	−0.62	1.83
Recreation	−0.46	1.06
Tobacco	−0.44	0.93
Clothing	−0.38	0.86
Housing	−0.28	0.69
Food and drinks	−0.21	0.55

Australia	Compensated-Price Elasticity	Income Elasticity
Transportation	−0.38	2.39
Fuel	−0.35	1.88
Housing	−0.34	2.07
Household durables	−0.26	1.46
Tobacco and drinks	−0.11	0.6
Clothing	−0.07	0.36
Services	−0.04	0.37

United States	Compensated-Price Elasticity	Income Elasticity
Other durable goods	−1.47	1.88
Automobiles and parts	−1.26	1.65
Household operation	−1.26	2.23
Gasoline and oil	−1.12	1.76
Housing	−0.99	3.49
Clothing and shoes	−0.88	1.04
Furniture and household equipment	−0.84	0.92
Transportation	−0.84	1.03
Other nondurables	−0.81	1.21
Food and drinks	−0.39	0.58

Sources: Louis Philips, *Applied Consumption Analysis*, p. 129 and p. 195 (Belgium data based on work of R. Sanz-Ferrer; U.S. data based on work of D. Weiserbs); Australian data from Alan A. Powell, *Empirical Analytics of Demand Systems* (Lexington, Mass.: D.C. Heath, 1974), p. 54.

where the *a*s are assumed to be constant parameters and *e* is again assumed to have a zero mean as well as be independent of the explanatory variables X_1 and X_2. These principles allow us to most accurately estimate the parameters.

Estimation Problems in Economics

The branch of economics that combines statistical estimation with the testing of economic theories is called *econometrics*. There are a number of econometric problems that plague the estimation of demand functions (or supply functions or any economic relationship), among which are data problems and the identification problem.

Data Problems

There are two serious data problems. First, the data that economists have are often subject to many errors. For example, the economist may collect posted or "official" prices rather than actual transaction prices; the prices that are collected may represent the price only at a particular time of the day (such as the closing price of General Motors common stock) rather than the price at which most transactions took place.

Second, there is often insufficient data available. The study of demand functions has been seriously hampered by the problem of having more variables to study than there are observations. There should always be more observations than variables. For example, in Figure 5-11 if there were only two dots (two observations), then the equation that fit these two dots would be totally unreliable; if there were only one observation no equation at all could be fitted! In a major study of consumer demand, Hendrik Houthakker and Lester Taylor studied 81 commodity categories using annual time series. Unfortunately, the time series began in 1929 and could not cover more than 81 years. Thus, there were far more variables than observations. Hence, it was impossible for Houthakker and Taylor to study the effect of any one of the prices on the demand for any one of the other goods. As a consequence, the study of cross-price elasticities has been limited to the study of large aggregations of goods (for example, food versus clothing), or the detailed study of one good against a few others (wheat versus corn or butter versus margarine). As time passes, the problem of too few observations will become less severe.

The Identification Problem

When a parameter (such as income or price elasticity of demand) cannot be estimated regardless of the quantity and quality of data available, there is said to be an *identification problem*. A parameter may not be identifiable simply because the usual laboratory of economics is such that empirical observations are generated as the equilibrium solutions to supply and demand. Controlled experiments with a random sample of the population

FIGURE 5-12   **Simultaneous Shifts in Supply and Demand**

If both the supply and demand curves shift simultaneously, the equilibrium pattern of price/quantity combinations will follow neither a supply nor a demand curve.

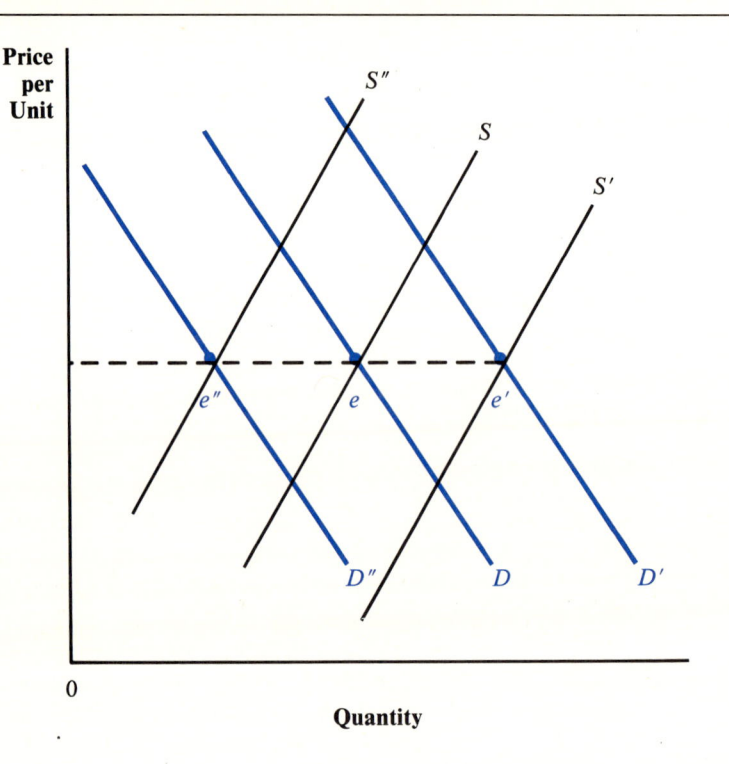

would simply be too expensive to carry out, although economists can carry out controlled experiments with laboratory animals.

Figure 5-12 shows a market in which both the supply and demand curves are shifting for the same reason (for example, a change in the price of corn could affect both the supply and demand for soybeans). If both demand and supply depend on the same factors, then neither function can be identified. When the demand curve shifts from D to D', the supply curve shifts from S to S'; when D shifts to D'', S shifts to S''. Thus, the equilibrium shifts from e to e' to e''. Clearly, the prices and quantities do not conform to either a supply curve or a demand curve. Figure 5-12 shows price/quantity combinations (e, e', e'') that lie along a horizontal line, but the equilibrium pattern could slope upward or downward or have no discernible pattern.

To be able to identify the supply and demand curves, certain conditions must hold. Panel A of Figure 5-13 shows a situation in which the supply curve shifts while the demand curve remains relatively stationary. In this case, supply depends on some factor (such as rainfall) that does not influence the demand for the good. The generated pattern of price/quantity combinations follows the average demand curve, D. Thus, if the supply curve shifts relative to the demand curve, the latter can be identified. Panel B shows a situation in which the demand curve shifts more than the supply curve, allowing the latter to be estimated. In the Panel B case, the demand

FIGURE 5-13 Identifying Demand and Supply

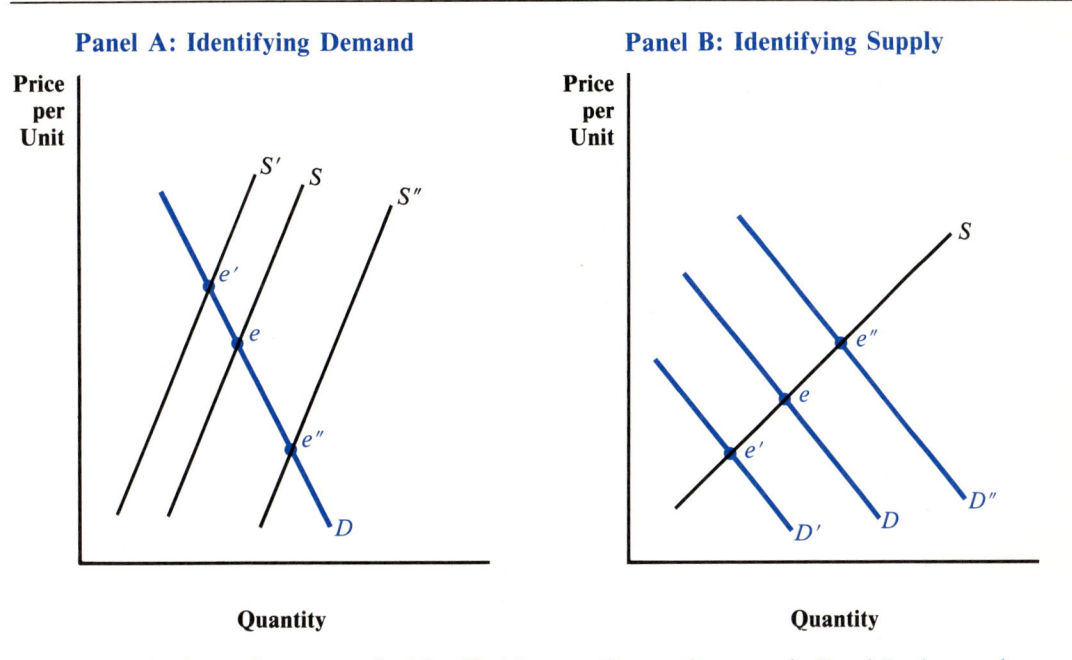

Panel A: Identifying Demand

Panel B: Identifying Supply

In Panel A, the demand curve can be identified but not the supply curve; in Panel B, the supply curve can be identified but not the demand curve.

curve depends on some factor (such as consumer income) that does not influence supply.

Both the demand and supply curves can be identified if supply depends only on rainfall and demand depends only on income. Statistical methods then allow the econometrician to sort out the effects of price and rainfall on supply and the effects of price and income on demand.[12]

Elasticity Estimates

The first estimates of demand functions examined the relationship between demand and incomes. In the 1850s, the Prussian statistician Ernst Engel collected cross-section data on different families and discovered that:

1. Food was the most important item in the budget.

---

12. The identification problem was originally raised in a classic paper by E. J. Working, "What Do Statistical Demand and Supply Curves Show?" *Quarterly Journal of Economics* 61 (1927), reprinted in *Readings in Price Theory*, G. J. Stigler and K. E. Boulding, eds. (London: Allen and Unwin). A lucid introduction can be found in David A. Katz, *Econometric Theory and Applications* (Englewood Cliffs, N.J.: Prentice-Hall, 1982), chap. 7.

TABLE 5-4 Elasticities of Demand for Food Versus Nonfood Items

Budget Category	Price Elasticity of Demand	Cross-Price Elasticity with Other Category	Income Elasticity
Food Items	−0.34	0.085	0.26
Nonfood Items	−1.03	−0.199	1.22

Source: George E. Brandow, "Interrelations Among Demands for Farm Products and Implications for Control of Market Supply," *Pennsylvania Agricultural Experiment Station Bulletin* 680 (1961): 17.

2. The proportion of income devoted to food declined as income increased—providing evidence that the income elasticity of demand for food is less than unity.
3. The proportion of clothing and housing in the budget appeared relatively constant, while that of luxury items increased.

Engel's law is that the income elasticity of demand for food is less than 1.

Today, **Engel's law** is the generalization that as income rises, the demand for food increases less than proportionately. Table 5-4 gives some estimates of various elasticities for food and nonfood items in the budget. The price elasticity of demand for food is −0.34, while that of nonfood is −1.03. The income elasticity of demand for food is 0.26, confirming Engel's law, and that for nonfood is 1.22. Because the demand for food is inelastic, an increase in the price of food must lower expenditures on nonfood items. Hence, the cross-price elasticity of nonfood with respect to food prices is negative (−0.199). Because the demand for nonfood is (slightly) elastic, an increase in the price of nonfood items must raise the demand for food (the cross-price elasticity is 0.085). Thus, food is a gross substitute for nonfood, but nonfood is a gross complement to food.

Table 5-5 presents some detailed estimates of long-run price and income elasticities. From Slutsky's equation it follows that demand is more elastic the greater is the number of substitutes and the larger is the income effect. Goods with high income elasticities, *ceteris paribus*, ought to have higher price elasticities. Moreover, there is a tendency for the substitution effects themselves to be larger when income elasticities are large (see Example 5.2). For example, food has a low substitution effect and a low income elasticity; foreign travel has a high substitution effect and a high income elasticity. The items with the 11 highest price elasticities have an average income elasticity of 1.9; the items with the 11 lowest price elasticities have an average income elasticity of 0.8. Large substitution effects would tend to explain the elastic demands for turkey and chicken; small substitution effects would tend to explain the inelastic demands for jewelry, stationery, and theater tickets. It is often said that smokers "need" tobacco or that people "need" electricity and gasoline; yet the demands for these goods (in the long run) have been estimated to be price elastic.

TABLE 5-5 Selected Price and Income Elasticities

Item	Price Elasticity	Income Elasticity	Source
Motion-picture tickets	−3.7	3.4	H
Toilet articles	−3.0	3.7	H
China, glassware, etc.	−2.6	0.8	H
Electricity	−1.9	1.9	H
Tobacco	−1.9	0.9	H
Foreign travel	−1.8	3.1	H
Turkey	−1.4	0.5	B
Automobiles and parts	−1.4	1.7	P
Owner-occupied housing	−1.2	2.5	H
Chicken	−1.2	0.4	B
Gasoline and oil	−1.2	1.8	P
Toys (nondurable)	−1.0	2.0	H
Clothing and shoes	−1.0	1.1	P
Beef	−1.0	0.5	B
Medical insurance	−0.9	2.0	H
Furniture	−0.9	0.9	P
Butter	−0.9	0.3	B
Margarine	−0.8	0	B
Pork	−0.8	0.3	B
Jewelry and watches	−0.7	1.7	H
Stationery	−0.6	1.8	H
Lard	−0.4	−0.1	B
Theater and opera tickets	−0.3	1.3	H
Eggs	−0.3	0.2	B
Water	−0.1	0.6	H

Sources: H - H. S. Houthakker and L. D. Taylor, *Consumer Demand in the United States: Analyses and Projection*, 2nd ed. (Cambridge: Harvard University Press, 1970), pp. 166–67; P - L. Philips, *Applied Consumption Analysis* (Amsterdam: North-Holland, 1974), p. 195, based on a doctoral dissertation by D. Weiserbs; B - George Brandow, "Interrelations Among Demands for Farm Products and Implications for Control of Market Supply," *Pennsylvania Agricultural Experiment Station Bulletin* 680 (1961).

Table 5-6 shows some typical cross-price elasticities between related goods: beef, pork, chicken, and fish. Notice that fish is nearly independent of the other meat products. Because beef is the most important meat product in the household budget, a change in the price of beef affects the demand for pork and chicken more than a change in the prices of those goods affect the demand for beef.

TABLE 5-6   Own-Price and Cross-Price Elasticities of Demand (retail prices)

Good Demanded	Beef	Pork	Chicken	Fish
Beef	−0.95	0.10	0.07	0.004
Pork	0.13	−0.75	0.07	0.005
Chicken	0.23	0.16	−1.16	0.004
Fish	0.02	0.003	0.007	−0.65

Source: George Brandow, "Interrelations Among Demands for Farm Products and Implications for Control of Market Supply," *Pennsylvania Agricultural Experiment Station Bulletin* 680 (1961).

SUMMARY

1. The major determinants of the market demand for a good are: the price of the good, the prices of substitutes and complements, tastes, and income.

2. The price elasticity of demand for a product is the percentage change in the quantity demanded per 1 percent change in the price of the good, holding other prices, tastes, and income constant.

3. The income elasticity of demand for a product is the percentage increase in demand per 1 percent increase in income, holding all prices and tastes constant. Income elasticity for luxury goods is greater than 1; income elasticity for necessities is less than 1. The cross-price elasticity of demand measures the percentage change in the demand for one good in response to a 1 percent change in the price of another good, holding other factors constant. The market elasticity of demand is the weighted average of the elasticities of each individual in the market, where the weights equal the shares of each individual in total demand.

4. Slutsky's equation shows how the compensated price elasticity can be recovered from the ordinary price elasticity and the income elasticity of demand. For normal goods, the absolute value of the compensated elasticity is smaller than the ordinary price elasticity. Goods X and Y are net substitutes if the compensated cross-price elasticity is positive; they are net complements if the compensated cross-price elasticity is negative. Good X is a gross substitute for good Y if the demand for X rises when the price of Y rises (*ceteris paribus*); good X is a gross complement to Y if the demand for X falls when the price of Y rises (*ceteris paribus*).

5. Marginal revenue (*MR*) is the increase in revenue per unit increase in quantity sold. Demand is elastic when the absolute value of the price elasticity coefficient ($|\eta_p|$) is greater than 1, inelastic when $|\eta_p| < 1$, and unit elastic when $|\eta_p| = 1$. The marginal revenue is positive when demand is elastic; $MR = 0$ when demand is unit elastic; *MR* is negative when demand is inelastic. When the demand curve is a straight line, the mar-

ginal-revenue curve lies halfway between the vertical axis and the demand curve, and the *MR* curve is twice as steep as the linear demand curve. The relationship between average values and marginal values is that the average rises when the margin exceeds the average, the average remains constant when the margin equals the average, and the average falls when the margin falls short of the average.

6. A regression equation gives the best fit to a collection of observations. Econometrics is plagued by two major problems: inadequate data and the identification problem.

QUESTIONS AND PROBLEMS

1. Calculate the price and income elasticities of demand for the data in Table A.

2. Suppose that there are 100 identical people each with the demand curve $Q = 10 - 2P$.
   a. What is the market-demand curve?
   b. Compute the equilibrium price when supply is fixed at $S = 400$.
   c. Compute η_p for each person and the market at the equilibrium price.
   d. Draw the market-demand curve.

3. Suppose the demand function for good X is:

$$X = 13 + 0.1M - 0.4P_x + 0.05P_y.$$

When income $(M) = \$100$, $P_x = \$10$, and $P_y = \$20$, calculate the price, cross-price, and income elasticities of demand.

4. Assume the demand curve for a good is $Q = 100/P$. Draw the demand curve by plotting the quantities demanded when $P = \$100, \$50, \$25, \$10$, and $\$5$. Use the revenue test to determine the price elasticity of demand. Does the elasticity depend on the price?

5. Assume the demand for a good is $Q = A/P + B$, where A and B are constants (A is a positive number; B is either positive or negative).

Table A

Price	Quantity Demanded at Income of $9,000	at Income of $10,000
$5	100 units	105 units
$10	60 units	62 units

Using the revenue test, what determines whether the demand for the good is elastic or inelastic? Is the curve elastic (or inelastic) at any price?

6. Example 5-2 showed evidence that the substitution effect is stronger the higher is the income elasticity of demand. How would you explain this fact?

7. Consider the demand curves $Q = 10 - P$ and $Q = 10 - 0.5P$. Use the point-elasticity formula to determine which demand curve is most elastic at any particular price. Which demand curve is most elastic at any particular quantity?

8. Suppose the marginal revenue a firm gains from selling a good is $5. If the price of the good is $15, is it possible to determine the price elasticity of demand from this information? If so, what is the elasticity? If not, what information is needed?

9. Suppose the marginal revenue a firm gains from selling a particular good is −$5. Given the price elasticity of −0.5, what is the price of the good? Should the firm raise or lower its price and why?

10. Use Slutsky's equation and the data in Table 5-4 to calculate the compensated price elasticity of demand for food. Assume that food expenditures are 23 percent of expenditures.

11. The price elasticity of demand for good Z is −0.3, the income elasticity is 2, and the good makes up 20 percent of the budget. Calculate the compensated price elasticity of demand for good Z. Is it a Giffen good? Is demand for this good consistent with the theory of consumer behavior? What might explain these empirical results?

12. (Calculus required.) Calculate the price and income elasticity of demand for a good with a demand function of the form,

$$Q = AP^\alpha M^\beta,$$

where A, α, and β are constants.

SUGGESTED READINGS

Houthakker, H. S. and L. D. Taylor. *Consumer Demand in the United States: Analyses and Projections*, 2nd ed. Cambridge: Harvard University Press, 1970.
Kelejian, H. and W. Oates. *Introduction to Econometrics*. New York: Harper and Row, 1981.
Robinson, Joan. *The Economics of Imperfect Competition*. London: Macmillan, 1933, chap. 2.
Stigler, G. *The Theory of Price*, 4th ed. New York: Macmillan, 1987, chap. 3.

APPENDIX 5A

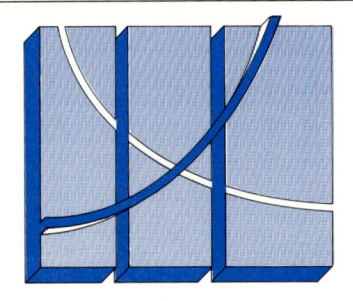

STATISTICS

This appendix explains how to estimate the coefficients α and β of the linear equation $y = \alpha + \beta X$ when the Xs and Ys are real-world observations that are supposed to be related.[1] You will learn how to run a **linear regression**—that is, determine the straight line that gives the best fit to a scatter diagram of paired Xs and Ys (see again Figure 5–11). While many personal calculators perform these calculations routinely, it is useful to know how the underlying mechanism works.

A **linear regression** gives the best linear unbiased equation that fits a set of observations.

Basic Concepts

Recall (from Chapter 3) that a random variable is simply a variable that can take on different values according to some specified probability. The expected value of X is simply

$$E(X) = \sum_{i=1}^{n} X_i \pi_i, \qquad (1)$$

where π_i is the probability that the value X_i will occur.

The dispersion of a random variable about its expected value, or mean, is called its **variance**, which is defined by

$$\text{Var}(X) = E\{[X - E(X)]^2\}. \qquad (2)$$

The **variance** of a random variable is a measure of its spread.

If X never varied from the mean, the variance of X would be zero. Because the deviations from X are squared, deviations above and below the mean are positive numbers weighted by their probabilities.

---

1. My colleague, Badi A. Baltagi, suggested the approach followed here. A textbook exposition of this approach can be found in Harry Kelejian and Wallace Oates, *Introduction to Econometrics* (New York: Harper & Row, 1981), pp. 40–51.

140   APPENDIX 5A   STATISTICS

*The **covariance** of random variables X and Y is a measure of their statistical relationship.*

The relationship, or **covariance**, between two random variables, X and Y, which is simply

$$\text{Cov}(X,Y) = E\{[X - E(X)][Y - E(Y)]\}. \quad (3)$$

Unlike the variance, the covariance can be either positive or negative. A negative covariance indicates that the variables are negatively related.

For example, suppose that the random variable X takes on the values $X_i = 1, 2, 3, 6$ with equal probabilities. When a random variable takes on particular values with the equal probabilities $1/n$, where n is the number of observations, the expected value and variance are:

$$E(X) = \left(\sum_{i=1}^{n} X_i\right)/n$$

$$\text{Var}(X) = \left\{\sum_{i=1}^{n} [X_i - E(X)]^2\right\}/n$$

Thus, the mean $E(X) = 3$. The variance is: $\text{Var}(X) = [(1-3)^2 + (2-3)^2 + (3-3)^2 + (6-3)^2]/4 = 14/4 = 3.5$.

Suppose we observe the following (X, Y) pairs—each with equal probabilities: $(1,2), (2, 2), (3, 4),$ and $(6,8)$. The covariance formula when each (X, Y) combination occurs with equal probabilities is:

$$\text{Cov}(X, Y) = \{\Sigma[X_i - E(X)][Y_i - E(Y)]\}/n,$$

where to simplify notation the index $i = 1$ to n has been suppressed. The mean of X is $E(X) = (1 + 2 + 3 + 6)/4 = 3$; the mean of Y is $E(Y) = (2 + 2 + 4 + 8)/4 = 4$. The covariance is $\text{Cov}(X, Y) = [(-2)(-2) + (-1)(2) + 0 + (3)(4)]/4 = 18/4 = 4.5$.

Linear Regression

The linear-regression model makes the assumption that the observations Y_i and X_i are related by the following linear equation for each time period i:

$$Y_i = \alpha + \beta X_i + u_i, \quad (4)$$

where it is assumed that the unobserved disturbance term, u_i, has a zero mean—that is, $E(u) = 0$—and that the independent variable, X, and u are unrelated—that is, $\text{Cov}(X, u) = 0$. Equation (4) should be interpreted as follows. There is a fixed sample of X_is (n in number). Each time the observation X_i is made, a drawing is made from the probability distribution of the random variable u. The particular drawing, u_i, then combines with Equation (4) to determine the observation Y_i. From the two principles that $E(u) = \text{Cov}(X, u) = 0$, we can derive the *ordinary least squares (OLS)*— estimators of the parameters α and β.

If we denote the estimates of α and β by a and b, the assumption that $E(u) = 0$ implies that [using Equation (4)]:

$$E(Y) = a + bE(X). \quad (5)$$

Because $E(Y)$ and $E(X)$ are simply the means of the observations Y_i and X_i,

THE LEAST-SQUARES PROPERTY

Equation (5) is one equation in the two unknowns a and b. One more equation is needed to pin down the estimates. Before writing the next equation, let us simplify Equation (4) by defining the deviations from $E(Y)$ and $E(X)$:

$$y_i = Y_i - E(Y) \text{ and } x_i = X_i - E(X)$$

Equation (4) can now be written as:

$$y_i + E(Y) = a + b[x_i + E(X)] + u_i,$$

where the estimates a and b have replaced α and β. Because Equation (5) holds, which is the same as $E(u) = 0$, we can now write:

$$y_i = bx_i + u_i. \tag{6}$$

The assumption that the $\text{Cov}(X, u) = 0$ now means $\text{Cov}(x, u) = 0$. In this form, the second assumption means:

$$\text{Cov}(x,u) = E(xu) = \Sigma(x_i u_i)/n = 0,$$

where the summation notation suppresses the index $i = 1$ through n (in all cases considered the same indexing is used). If we multiply both sides of Equation (6) by x_i and sum, we obtain:

$$\Sigma y_i x_i = b\Sigma x_i^2 + \Sigma x_i u_i.$$

Because $\Sigma x_i u_i = 0$,

$$\Sigma y_i x_i = b\Sigma x_i^2 \text{ or}$$
$$b = \Sigma y_i x_i / \Sigma x_i^2 = \text{Cov}(Y, X)/\text{Var}(X). \tag{7}$$

Inserting b and the means of X and Y into Equation (4) determines the estimate a.

The Least-Squares Property

The explanatory power of a linear regression is indicated by the closeness of the fit. When the parameters are estimated, the unexplained portion or residual is simply

$$u_i = y_i - bx_i \tag{8}$$

for each observation. By assumption, the u_is average out to zero. The deviations of the u_is from zero is measured by the *sum of the squared deviations*, or *errors*, *(SSE)*:

$$SSE = \Sigma(u_i^2) \tag{9}$$

The estimator b in Equation (7) has the property that it minimizes *SSE*—hence, linear regressions are often called *ordinary-least-squares (OLS) estimators*. From Equation (8), it is clear that $\partial u_i/\partial b = x_i$. Now if b is chosen to minimize *SSE*, we set $\partial (SSE)/\partial b = 0$:

$$\partial(SSE)/\partial b = 2\Sigma[u_i (\partial u_i/\partial b)] = -2\Sigma(u_i x_i) = 0.$$

PRACTICE EXERCISE 5A-1

Q. Estimate the demand for chicken in the United States. Table A presents actual data on the per-capita consumption of chicken in the United States from 1948 to 1963 and the price of chicken in constant 1957–59 dollars.
A. Assume that the demand function is:

$$Q_t = \alpha + \beta P_t + u_t,$$

where Q_t is the per-capita consumption of chicken in year t, P_t is the price in cents, and u_t is the disturbance term. From Table A the average quantity demanded was 24.66 and the average price was 53.99 cents. It follows that the estimates a and b must satisfy

$$24.66 = a + b53.99.$$

To determine b, Equation (7) directs us to calculate the variance of P and the covariance of Q and P. Because these are straightforward (but tedious)

Table A

Year	Consumption of Chicken Per Capita (pounds)	Deflated Price Per Pound (cents)
1948	18.3	75.4
1949	19.6	71.8
1950	20.6	68.0
1951	21.7	66.0
1952	22.1	65.0
1953	21.9	62.8
1954	22.8	56.4
1955	21.3	58.7
1956	24.4	50.4
1957	25.5	47.6
1958	28.2	45.8
1959	28.9	41.4
1960	28.2	41.4
1961	30.3	37.0
1962	30.2	38.6
1963	30.6	37.6

Note: Price is deflated by the consumer price index (1957–1959 = 100).
Source: Frederick V. Waugh, *Demand and Price Analysis—Some Examples from Agriculture* (Washington, D.C.: U.S. Department of Agriculture, Technical Bulletin 1316, Nov. 1964), Table 5-1, p. 39.

THE LEAST-SQUARES PROPERTY

calculations, we leave it to the reader to show that $\text{Cov}(Q, P) = -53.42$ and $\text{Var}(P) = 171.66$. Thus, we find that

$$b = \text{Cov}(Q,P)/\text{Var}(P) = -53.42/171.66 = -0.31.$$

Next, we determine that

$$a = 24.66 - b53.99 = 24.66 + 0.31(53.99) = 41.466.$$

Hence, the regression we seek is:

$$Q = 41.466 - 0.31P.$$

Because the elasticity coefficient depends on the point selected on the above linear demand curve, it is common practice to choose the average quantity and average price. The price elasticity of demand for chicken is

$$\eta_p = -(0.31)(53.99/24.66) = -0.678.$$

Because the other factors that influence the demand for chicken (the price of beef, income, etc.) have been ignored, the above estimate of the price elasticity of demand for chicken should only be taken as illustrative.

However, this is exactly the property $\text{Cov}(X, u) = 0$ that was used to derive the estimate b in the first place. Thus, the sum of squared errors has been minimized.

We have, thus, chosen the best-fitting linear equation through the collection of observations (X_i, Y_i). The goodness of fit is measured by the measure called R squared.

$$R^2 = [\Sigma(y_i^2) - \Sigma(u_i^2)]/\Sigma(y_i^2).$$

If $R^2 = 1$, the fit is perfect; if $R^2 = 0$ there is no fit at all.

CHAPTER 6

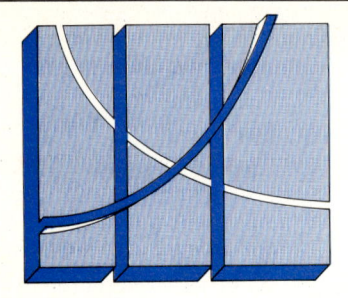

SPECIALIZATION AND EXCHANGE

Each person in our economy has the opportunity to specialize in certain goods and then trade for a staggering variety of goods and services. This chapter studies the gains from specialization and exchange by studying the theory of a pure-exchange economy and the law of comparative advantage.

This chapter focuses on *general-equilibrium economics*. In *partial-equilibrium economics*, a particular market is studied and other markets are neglected by assuming that all other prices are fixed. In a general-equilibrium model, it is necessary to spell out the ingredients of an entire economy—its resources, its technology, and its people. Although this is indeed a tall order, by focusing on sufficiently simple models, it is possible to study general-equilibrium economics without complex mathematics.

In the nine chapters following this one, we will shift our analysis to partial-equilibrium economics, but we shall return to general-equilibrium models in Chapter 16.

THE THEORY OF EXCHANGE

A **pure-exchange economy** is an economy in which participants enter with fixed endowments of goods and then trade with others to achieve a more desirable consumption pattern.

A **pure-exchange economy** is one in which people enter the world with fixed endowments of goods and then trade with others to achieve a more desirable pattern of consumption. When there is no production, exchange is the only economic activity. Analyzing a pure-exchange economy is useful because it enables us to focus on the exchange of goods between people without the additional complications arising from the production side of the economy—that is, the linkages between an economy's resources and what it produces.

Strictly speaking, a pure-exchange economy can be used only to analyze the allocation of fixed quantitites of various commodities among different

FIGURE 6-1   The Edgeworth Box

Person A's quantities are read relative to origin 0_A; person B's quantities are read relative to the northeast origin 0_B. Thus, the coordinates of the single point, d, measure the allocation of goods X and Y between person A and person B.

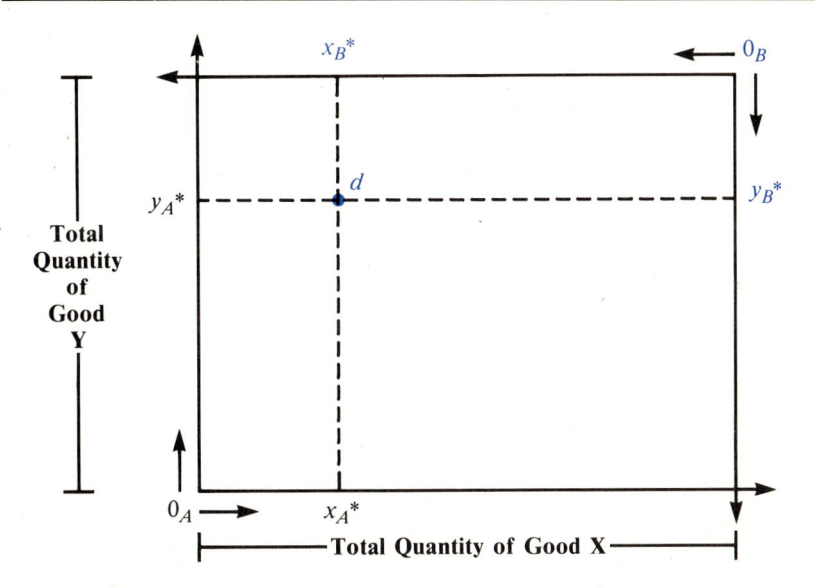

[Figure 6-1: Edgeworth box diagram showing origin 0_A at lower left and 0_B at upper right, with point d having coordinates x_A^*, y_A^* from 0_A and x_B^*, y_B^* from 0_B. Vertical axis labeled "Total Quantity of Good Y"; horizontal axis labeled "Total Quantity of Good X".]

individual agents. However, a pure-exchange economy also exhibits many of the essential problems of an economic system. While analyzing such an economy cannot shed light on what determines the distribution of income or what causes national wealth or poverty, the model can be used to illustrate (1) the meaning of economic efficiency, (2) the relationship between efficiency and competitive equilibrium, (3) the existence of a general competitive equilibrium, and (4) the stability of the general-equilibrium solution.

The Edgeworth Box

The simplest possible pure-exchange economy that can be imagined is one with only two agents and two goods. British economist Francis Edgeworth (1845–1926) devised an ingenious method for graphically depicting a two-agent, two-good economy. While very simple, the Edgeworth model does illustrate some general principles.

Figure 6-1 illustrates the Edgeworth box diagram. The vertical height of the Edgeworth box measures the total quantity of good Y available to persons A and B; the horizontal width of the box measures the total quantity of good X available to persons A and B. All the quantities that pertain to person A are measured from the origin marked 0_A; all the quantities that refer to person B are measured from the origin marked 0_B. When reading A's consumption or holdings of goods X and Y, the Edgeworth box is read just like any other diagram depicting consumer tastes. When reading B's consumption or holdings of goods X and Y, however, it is necessary—in one's mind's eye—to turn the diagram upside down.

FIGURE 6–2   Indifference Curves in the Edgeworth Box

Higher utility levels for B are indicated by moving away from origin 0_B toward origin 0_A. If d is the initial-endowment point, the shaded area represents the set of *feasible trades*. At point d, A values an extra unit of X more than B values it because $MRS^A > MRS^B$.

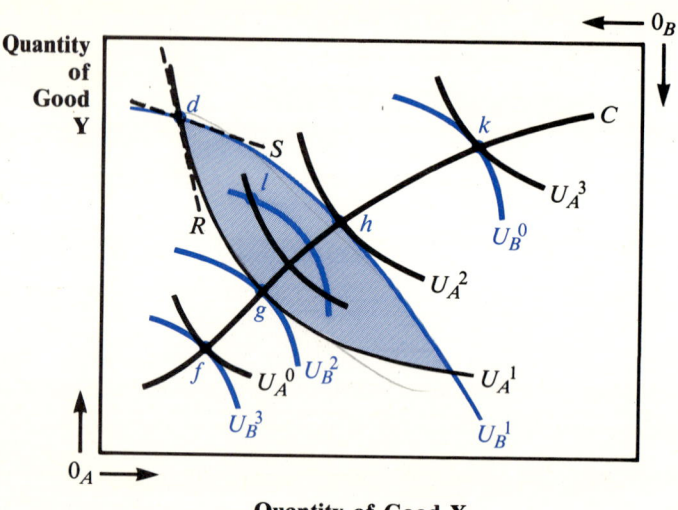

Quantity of Good X

A *feasible state* of an exchange economy is simply an allocation of the two goods between A and B such that their total consumption of each good does not exceed the available supply. Thus, any commodity bundles (x_A, y_A) and (x_B, y_B) that satisfy the equations

$$x_A + x_B = x^0 \tag{1}$$

$$y_A + y_B = y^0 \tag{2}$$

are feasible allocations. The useful property of an Edgeworth box is that any point in the box can represent a feasible allocation. For example, point d in Figure 6–1 describes a particular allocation between person A and person B. A has the bundle (x_A^*, y_A^*), and B has the bundle (x_B^*, y_B^*). Just by virtue of being inside the box, the allocation d has the property that the total amounts of X and Y received by the two agents sum to the total amount available. Reading horizontally, the quantity x_A^* on the lower horizontal axis plus the quantity x_B^* on the upper horizontal axis sum to the horizontal width of the box. Similarly, reading vertically, y_A^* on the left axis plus y_B^* on the right axis sum to the vertical height of the box.

Voluntary Exchange

Let us assume that person A and person B each enter our economy with a certain endowment of the two goods and that each enters with certain tastes. Imagine that each period the two traders receive a fresh endowment of the

THE THEORY OF EXCHANGE

two goods and that the two goods are highly perishable so that each period everything must be consumed. It is highly unlikely for the two traders to receive the goods in the exact proportions that would satisfy their tastes most efficiently. Thus, under normal circumstances, the two agents will trade until they reach a final contract. Clearly, as long as trade is mutually beneficial a deal will be made.

Figure 6–2 adds indifference curves to the Edgeworth-box diagram. Person A's indifference curves are convex to the origin 0_A. As always, the indifference curves U_A^0, U_A^1, U_A^2, and U_A^3 portray, respectively, higher and higher levels of satisfaction for A. Person B's indifference curves must be read upside down and, hence, are convex to the origin 0_B. B is made better off moving in the southwest direction. For example, U_B^1 represents a higher level of satisfaction than U_B^0 for person B. Thus, the indifference curves U_B^0, U_B^1, U_B^2, and U_B^3 portray, respectively, higher and higher utility levels for B. Thus, A is made better off moving toward B's origin, and B enjoys greater satisfaction moving toward A's origin.

Assume point d in Figure 6–2 represents the initial endowment of the two goods received by A and B. Before any trade takes place both consumers are at point d and are destined to enjoy the initial utility levels U_A^1 and U_B^1, which are simply the indifference curves passing through their endowments. Person A would refuse any trade moving to an indifference curve worse than U_A^1, such as U_A^0; B would refuse any trade moving to an indifference curve worse than U_B^1, such as U_B^0. A is better off as long as he or she is above U_A^1, while B is better off as long as he or she is above (relative to origin 0_B) U_B^1. Any allocation in the shaded area—say, l—is on a higher indifference curve for A and for B than point d. Obviously, both are better off only in the shaded region. Because voluntary trade requires mutual benefit, the shaded region bounded by the two initial indifference curves represents the set of **feasible trades**.

A feasible trade makes neither party to a trade worse off and makes at least one party better off than would have been the case in the absence of trade.

The set of feasible trades is the set of allocations bounded by the indifference curves passing through the initial endowment point in an Edgeworth box.

Figure 6–2 depicts the incentives to trade in more ways than one. Consider each agent's marginal rate of substitution of good Y for good X, MRS_{yx} at the endowment point d. Recall that the marginal rate of substitution is the rate at which a person is just willing to give up good Y for one more unit of X and is measured by the absolute slope of the tangent to an indifference curve. Line R is the tangent to person A's indifference curve at point d; line S is the tangent to B's indifference curve at point d. Clearly, $MRS^A > MRS^B$; in other words, A places a higher valuation on an extra unit of good X than does B. For example, A might regard another unit of X as worth 5 units of Y while B might be willing to sacrifice a unit of X for as little as 2 units of Y. Thus, there is ample room for a mutually beneficial exchange: A is willing to pay more for X than B is willing to accept as a seller.

EFFICIENCY OR PARETO OPTIMALITY

An exchange equilibrium exists when there is no further incentive for both parties to trade—that is, when all mutual benefits from trade are exhausted.

The contract curve in the Edgeworth box represents the set of potential exchange equilibria.

If the units of goods are perfectly divisible, and if the indifference curves are strictly convex as in Figure 6-2, people will trade as long as their marginal rates of substitution differ.[1] Trade always requires different marginal evaluations by the buyer and the seller. If both buyer and seller value an extra unit of a good exactly the same, there is no room for mutually beneficial exchange. In the Edgeworth box, an **exchange equilibrium** can occur at points such as f, g, h, and k where A's indifference curves are tangent to B's indifference curves. The C curve represents all the allocations in which A's marginal rate of substitution is equal to B's—that is, where $MRS^A = MRS^B$.[2] Only an allocation on this **contract curve** has any chance of being an exchange equilibrium. Of course, with the initial endowment at d the possible exchange equilibria are restricted to the points along C from g to h. But the contract curve represents all the potential exchange equilibria in the economy because the initial-endowment point can be anywhere in the box. (See Example 6-1.)

In an exchange equilibrium, traders have the same marginal rate of substitution if their indifference curves are strictly convex.

Any point off the contract curve represents an exchange opportunity because by definition MRS^A is *unequal* to MRS^B anywhere off the contract curve. Thus, each party can be made better off by a simple exchange of the two goods at some price ratio between their respective marginal rates of substitution. If transaction costs are zero, traders will exchange until the contract curve is reached.

The situation is quite different on the contract curve. A movement from one point to another on the contract curve must make one party better off and the other worse off. For example, in a move from point g to point h in Figure 6-2, person A is made better off and B is made worse off. For this reason the contract curve has sometimes been called the *conflict curve*, as any move that helps one party hurts the other.

The contract curve, however, has an even more important property: any move from a position on the contract curve that makes one person better off must hurt the other person. In Figure 6-3, point e represents any point on the contract curve C. To make A better off requires a reallocation of the two

---

[1]. One exception to this rule occurs when the marginal rates of substitution differ, but further trade is impossible because each consumer has a zero quantity of the good the other person wants.

[2]. This rule does not always hold; there are two exceptions. The first exception can occur when the contract curve coincides with all or part of one of the edges of the Edgeworth box. The second exception occurs when the indifference curve is not strictly convex; if there are "kinks" in the indifference curves, the marginal rate of substitution may not even be uniquely defined. These problems, however, mean only that different types of mathematical tools need to be used. No critical issues are involved. For an illuminating discussion, see Tjalling Koopmans, *Three Essays on the State of Economic Science* (New York: McGraw-Hill, 1957).

FIGURE 6–3 Pareto Optimality on the Contract Curve

Point *e* is any point on the contract curve. Point *e* is the Pareto optimum because any move that improves A's welfare must move into the shaded region where B is worse off.

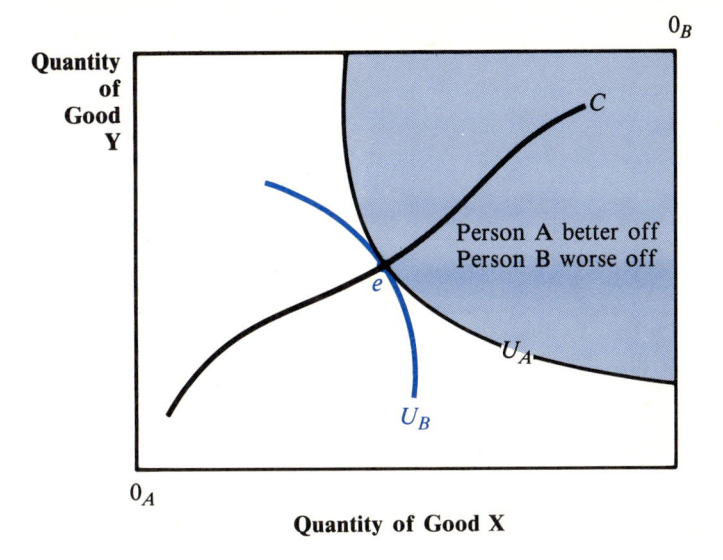

Quantity of Good Y (vertical axis), *Quantity of Good X* (horizontal axis). Origin O_A at lower left, O_B at upper right. Contract curve runs from O_A through e to C near O_B. At point e, indifference curves U_A and U_B are tangent. Shaded region to the upper right of e labeled "Person A better off, Person B worse off."

Pareto optimality exists whenever any resource reallocation that makes one person better off must make some other person worse off. In other words, in a Pareto-optimal allocation of resources, it is impossible to make everyone better off. A condition for Pareto optimality is $MRS^A = MRS^B$ for every pair of consumers and every pair of goods.

goods so that A moves into the shaded region. Obviously, any allocation in the shaded region moves B onto a lower indifference curve. In other words, point *e* has the property of being an allocation of resources that is so efficient that it is impossible to make one person better off without hurting the other person by any reallocation of resources. Any such allocation of resources is called **Pareto optimality**, or *Pareto efficiency*—named after the celebrated Italian economist and sociologist Vilfredo Pareto (1848–1923).

The concept of Pareto optimality allows us to define efficiency in a world of any number of persons or any number of goods or, indeed, any degree of complexity. If an economic system is inefficient, it must be possible to squeeze a bit more out of the economy in such a way as to make it possible to improve everyone's welfare.[3] If an economic system is efficient, so much is being squeezed out of the system that you cannot help one person without giving someone else a smaller piece. The Pareto criterion of efficiency is defined independently of distribution questions. It is not necessary to weigh the worth of person A compared to person B, which is clearly impossible in positive economics. If an economy cannot make both A and B better off, it is efficient; if it can, it is inefficient! The Pareto criterion requires unanimity.

The relationship between profitable exchanges and efficiency is dualistic. Whenever there are mutually profitable exchanges possible, the economy is

---

3. If it is possible to make person A better off without hurting person B, then as long as goods are divisible and people are nonsatiated, both A and B can be made better off just by taking a bit from A and giving it to B.

> **EXAMPLE 6–1**   Indian Giving and Silent Exchange as Exchange Mechanisms
>
> There are more ways of exchanging goods and services than can be imagined. In close-knit societies where everybody knows everybody else, such as in small tribes of native American Indians or among numerous nonliterate groups, exchanges may take place in the form of gifts: person A gives cattle to person B; later B gives wheat to A. These are not gifts in the usual sense, because B is obligated to return a gift of comparable value to A.
>
> Such gift giving is just another form of exchange to the observing economist, although the anthropologist may see other functions of gift giving. Early American colonists erroneously interpreted the practices of native Americans who had a highly developed gift-exchange system. If native American A wanted B's prize horse, A would tender a gift to B with obvious but subtle hints. If B did not give A the prize horse in return, A would demand that the original gift be returned. This practice of "Indian giving" was considered petty or cheap among Europeans and American colonists. Among native Americans, however, the practice was a primitive way of honoring property rights and the requirement that trade be mutually beneficial.
>
> Another type of exchange mechanism used by primitive economies is the practice of silent trade. Tribe A would deposit goods in a particular spot and then retreat. Tribe B would then advance and inspect the goods. If tribe B found the goods acceptable, they would leave other goods in their place. If tribe A did not find tribe B's payment adequate, B's goods would be left in place. Tribe B would thereupon return the original goods. This mechanism demonstrates that the long-term gains from continuous trade far exceed the short-term gains from not playing by the rules of the game.
>
> **Source:** Melville J. Herskovits, *Economic Anthropology* (New York: W.W. Norton, 1952), pp. 164–68, 185–87.

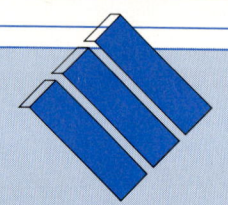

inefficient. The profitable exchanges are then carried out until the system moves to the contract curve. When no mutually profitable exchanges are possible, the economy is efficient. Thus, efficiency implies exchange equilibrium, and vice versa.[4]

---

[4] The link between Pareto optimality and competitive equilibrium is explored in more detail in Chapter 16, which shows that a competitive equilibrium is Pareto optimal under certain conditions, but that Pareto-optimal allocations need not be sustainable as competitive equilibria unless more stringent conditions are met.

COMPETITIVE EQUILIBRIUM

FIGURE 6-4   **The Offer Curve**

The utility-maximizing consumption bundles corresponding to different budget lines—representing different price ratios—going through the original-endowment point, d, determine the offer curve, or the price/consumption path, PC.

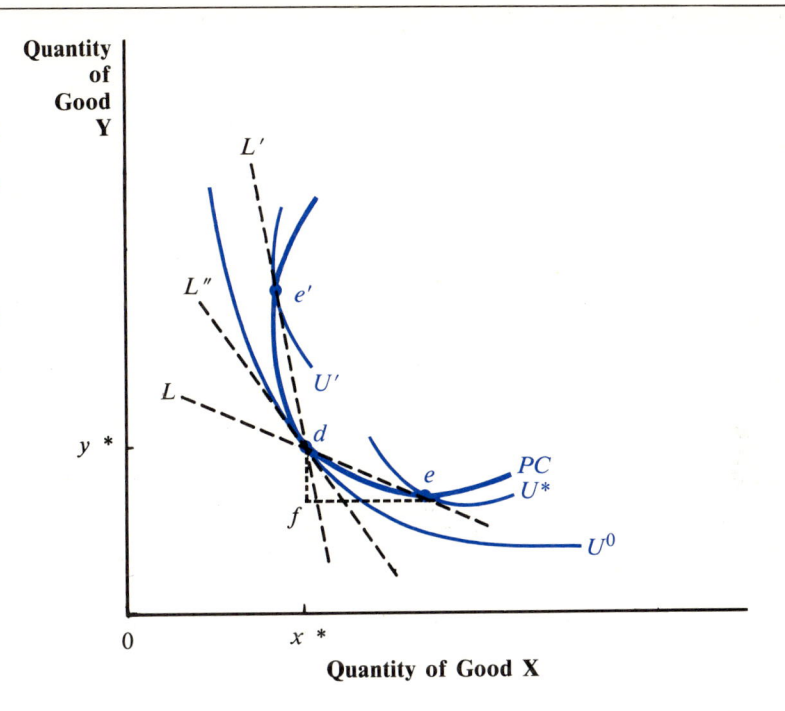

Any allocation of resources that is *not* on the contract curve of an Edgeworth box is inefficient and represents potential profitable exchanges; any allocation of resources that is on the contract curve is efficient, and mutually profitable exchanges do not exist.

COMPETITIVE EQUILIBRIUM

When people face so much competition that they take the market price as fixed, they are *price takers*. Figure 6-4 shows a price-taking consumer in a pure-exchange economy. The consumer's initial endowment is point d, consisting of x^* units of good X and y^* units of good Y. Given the market prices of X and Y, the consumer's income consists of the market valuation of his or her endowment. Thus, the consumer's budget constraint is simply

$$p_x x^* + p_y y^* = p_x x + p_y y. \tag{3}$$

In Figure 6-4, the budget constraint must pass through the original endowment point d, because regardless of prices the consumer can still purchase his or her original endowment.

Let us now consider the response of a single consumer to different price ratios. Segments of three representative budget lines, labeled L, L', and L'',

FIGURE 6-5   The Competitive Equilibrium and the Core

The competitive equilibrium is achieved at point t, where the budget line, L, through the endowment point d allows each consumer to maximize utility at stated prices and where demand equals supply. The offer curves must intersect on the contract curve along segment hg, which is the *core*.

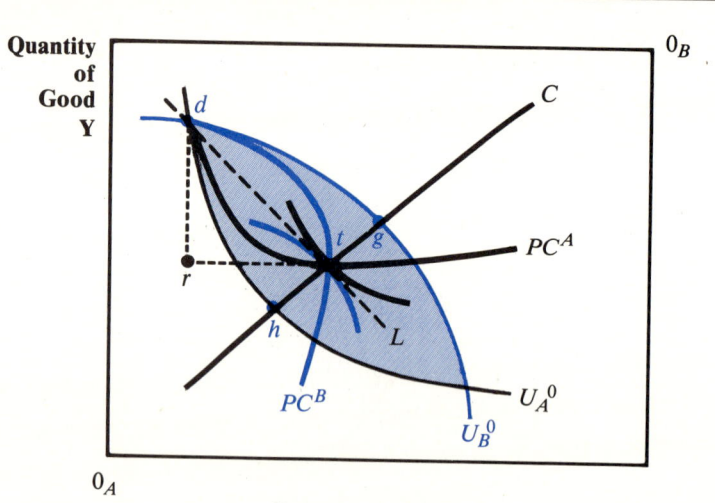

The **offer curve** shows the utility-maximizing consumption bundles at different price ratios for a competitive price-taking consumer whose only income is a fixed endowment of goods; it is the price/consumption curve for a consumer in a pure-exchange economy.

A **competitive equilibrium** is a set of prices and an allocation of resources such that (1) each price-taking agent maximizes utility subject to his or her budget constraint, and (2) supply equals demand for each and every good.

are shown in Figure 6–4. The budget line L'' is assumed to have the same slope as the indifference curve U_0 at the endowment point d; L has a smaller (absolute) slope; L' has a larger (absolute) slope. The price ratio, p_x/p_y, measures the absolute slope because it indicates how much of good Y is required to buy a unit of good X. If the price ratio is the same as the initial marginal rate of substitution at point d, the consumer chooses point d. If p_x/p_y is lower than the initial MRS, as in the case of budget line L for indifference curve U^*, the consumer chooses point e. If the price ratio is higher than the initial MRS, as in the case of budget line L' for indifference curve U', the consumer chooses point e'. The series of tangency points of budget lines with indifference curves, represented by the heavy line PC, is the **offer curve**. The offer curve is a generalized version of the price/consumption curve studied in Chapter 4.

The price/consumption path is an offer curve in this case because if the original-endowment point is subtracted from the desired consumption point, we are left with the offer of one good for the other good. For example, when the price ratio equals the absolute slope of L, df units of good Y are offered, or traded, for fe units of good X. The offer curve must lie wholly above the initial indifference curve U_0 because a regime of voluntary exchange implies that a rational consumer will not accept a trade that reduces his or her welfare.

Now suppose a price-taking consumer becomes one of the participants in a pure-exchange economy consisting of two or more agents. The economy will be in **competitive equilibrium** when a set of prices is found that allows each utility-maximizing agent to fulfill his or her desired trade.

COMPETITIVE EQUILIBRIUM

The concept of a competitive equilibrium may be illustrated in an Edgeworth box. In Figure 6-5, the initial-endowment point is d. Regardless of prices, persons A and B can always buy their endowment. Thus, as before, a budget line must go through the point d. The absolute slope of a budget line is the ratio of the price of X to the price of Y. Clearly, the budget line L results in a competitive equilibrium. Each consumer maximizes utility by choosing the point t. Person A is buying rt units of good X and selling dr units of good Y. Person B is selling rt units of good X and buying dr units of good Y. Thus, the definition of a competitive equilibrium is satisfied for the point t and the price ratio given by the slope of budget line L. The competitive equilibrium occurs at the intersection of A's offer curve, PC^A, and B's offer curve, PC^B. The offer curves must intersect on the contract curve, C, because line L is tangent to both consumers' indifference curves at the point t.

The offer curves can be used to show that a competitive equilibrium exists. Person A's offer curve, PC^A, must lie above U_A^0. Person B's offer curve, PC^B, must lie above U_B^0 (relative to the northeast origin, 0_B). Clearly, these restrictions put the two offer curves on a collision course, and they must intersect somewhere in the set of feasible trades. Indeed, the offer curves can intersect any number of times! In other words, the competitive equilibrium need not be unique.

Strictly speaking, in a two-person economy competitive price-taking behavior would be unlikely; however, the Edgeworth box is a simple way to visualize general-equilibrium relationships. Using equations, it is easy to extend the simplified model to any number of consumers or goods.

To illustrate the use of equations, let us describe a competitive equilibrium for two persons and two goods.[5] Let u_i^j be person j's (j = A, B) marginal utility of good i (i = X, Y). A competitive equilibrium requires (1) that both consumers maximize their utility:

$$u_x^A/u_y^A = u_x^B/u_y^B = p_x/p_y \qquad (4)$$

$$(p_x/p_y)\, x_j^* + y_j^* = (p_x/p_y)\, x_j + y_j \; (j = A, B) \qquad (5)$$

---

[5]. The equations of a competitive equilibrium may be easily generalized to include any number of consumers and any number of goods. For example, if there are n consumers and two goods, X and Y, the conditions are:

$MRS^i = p_x/p_y \quad i = 1, \ldots, n$
$x_i^*(p_x/p_y) + y_i^* = x_i(p_x/p_y) + y_i \quad i = 1, \ldots, n$
$\Sigma x_i^* = \Sigma x_i$ or $\Sigma y_i^* = \Sigma y_i$

There are $2n + 1$ equations to determine the $2n + 1$ unknowns, $x_1, \ldots, x_n, y_1, \ldots, y_n$, and p_x/p_y. (The x_i^*s and y_i^*s are the given endowments and need not be determined.) For a further discussion of the mathematics of a general competitive equilibrium, see James M. Henderson and Richard E. Quandt, *Microeconomic Theory: A Mathematical Approach*, 2nd ed. (New York: McGraw-Hill, 1971), chap. 5. For the philosophical viewpoint of general equilibrium, see Robert E. Kuenne, *The Theory of General Economic Equilibrium* (Princeton, N.J.: Princeton University Press, 1963), chap. 1.

PRACTICE EXERCISE 6-1

Q. Assume both Sally and George have identical preferences for goods X and Y. Let $MRS = y/x$ denote each person's marginal rate of substitution of good Y for another unit of good X. Assume Sally owns 100 units of X and 50 units of Y and that George owns 50 units of X and 400 units of Y. What is the competitive equilibrium?

A. A competitive equilibrium is defined by two characteristics: each person is maximizing utility subject to their budget constraints and subject to the condition that demand equal supply for both goods. Sally's income is $m^S = 100p_x + 50p_y$. George's income is $m^G = 50p_x + 400p_y$. Sally is maximizing utility when

$$y^S/x^S = p_x/p_y \text{ and } x^S(p_x/p_y) + y^S = m^S$$

It follows that Sally's demand for good Y is:

$$y^S = m^S/2p_y = (100p_x + 50p_y)/2p_y = 50(p_x/p_y) + 25$$

George's demand for good Y is:

$$y^G = m^G/2p_y = (50p_x + 400p_y)/2p_y = 25(p_x/p_y) + 200.$$

When total demand of $y^G + y^S = 450$ (total supply), the market is in equilibrium; that is,

$$50(p_x/p_y) + 25 + 25(p_x/p_y) + 200 = 75(p_x/p_y) + 225 = 450$$
$$75(p_x/p_y) = 225.$$

Thus, in equilibrium, $p_x/p_y = 3$. Sally consumes 175 units of good Y and George consumes 275 units of Y. Because $y^i/x^i = 3$, $x^S = 175/3$ and $x^G = 275/3$. The market for good X also clears because the only market for X is where good Y trades for good X.

---

and (2) that supply equals demand for both goods:

$$x_A + x_B = x_A^* + x_B^* \tag{6}$$

$$y_A + y_B = y_A^* + y_B^*, \tag{7}$$

where x_j^* and y_j^* are initial endowments for the jth consumer. Note that only one of the Equations (6) or (7) need be used, because with two goods there is only one market where good X trades for good Y. Chapter 16 will show that when the budget constraints are added, one of Equations (6) or (7) is implied by the other. (See Practice Exercise 6–1.)

The Core

The core is an allocation of resources such that no person, or coalition of persons, acting on their own (that is, trading with no other person or coalition) can do any better.

Now instead of considering competitive trades between the agents, let us assume that the agents are free to enter into any bilateral trade. The only constraint faced by such exchanges has been that any trade make at least one person better off. In Figure 6–5, starting from point *d*, any point between *h* and *g* could be reached. The set of possible exchange equilibria is restricted to the *hg* portion of the contract curve because when exchange is voluntary, people will not accept a lower level of welfare than they can attain under *autarky* (economic self-sufficiency or independence). With bilateral bargaining, it is impossible to say where the economy will end up between the points *h* and *g*. Point *h* is where the economy would move if A agreed to whatever B proposed; point *g* is where the economy would move if B agreed to whatever A proposed. Presumably, the final solution under bilateral bargaining might depend on the relative bargaining skills of the traders.

Imagine now that some allocation of resources has been reached along the line segment *hg*. Any such solution has the property that any allocation cannot be improved upon by A or B acting independently. Such an allocation of resources is called the **core**.

By definition, the core is contained in the set of Pareto-optimal allocations. With zero transaction costs in an economy, the core is where the economy will end up. People will continue to exchange until the allocation ends up in the core; otherwise, there will be some advantage to moving to some other allocation. In Figure 6–5, the core is the set of points along the segment *hg*. In the present case, the core is much smaller than the set of Pareto optima represented by the contract curve *C*.[6]

The contract curve is the set of all Pareto-optimal allocations and can be thought of as all potential exchange equilibria. The core can be thought of as all possible exchange equilibria given that people start off with given endowments and can always assure themselves of some minimum level of utility by simply refusing to trade. A competitive equilibrium represents the exchange equilibrium when people behave competitively. The competitive equilibrium belongs to the core; the core belongs to the set of Pareto-optimal allocations.

---

6. The core can be defined formally as follows. Let x_i represent the *i*th agent's consumption bundle. There are n agents, $i = 1, 2, \ldots, n$. Let e_i be the *i*th agent's endowment vector of goods. Let S be any coalition of the n agents. For example, S could be the entire set of agents or a small group consisting of, say, agents 1 and 7. An allocation x_i ($i = 1, \ldots, n$) is in the core if for every coalition S there does *not* exist another allocation x_i^* such that

$$u_i(x_i^*) > u_i(x_i) \qquad i \in S$$
$$\Sigma_{i \in S} x_i^* = \Sigma_{i \in S} e_i$$

If the set S is the set of all persons, the above definition is just the definition of Pareto optimality. Thus, an allocation is Pareto optimal if there does not exist another allocation that can make everybody better off.

A competitive equilibrium is both in the core and a Pareto-optimal allocation.

Core allocations place very few restrictions on the deals that can be struck between parties—anything goes, short of stealing. Aside from theft, only the imagination of the individual traders limits the kinds of deals that can be made.

Obviously, the core is a wild place. The competitive equilibrium is contained in the core because competitive behavior represents constrained exchange. With competition, agents are forced to accept whatever terms the market dictates. Normally, there will be competitive behavior on the part of sellers if each seller is small relative to the universe of buyers; there will normally be competitive behavior on the part of buyers if each buyer is small relative to the universe of sellers. In a small economy, the core is (usually) much bigger than the set of competitive equilibria. In a large economy, it can be shown (as Edgeworth showed) that the core collapses to the set of competitive equilibria. In other words, if there are enough people in the economy, the core and the set of competitive equilibria are one and the same thing.[7]

Competitive Stability

One of the critical questions about a competitive economy is whether the competitive equilibrium can be achieved by market forces. Chapter 2 argued that with a downward-sloping demand curve and an upward-sloping supply curve, the equilibrium price is stable. Does a similar result hold for the Edgeworth model?

To study stability, we must consider the market forces at a price ratio p_x/p_y for which supply is not equal to demand. In Figure 6-6, the absolute slope of budget line L' is the equilibrium relative price of good X. Consider a smaller price of good X, as represented by the absolute slope of the budget line L (which is flatter than L'). Person A chooses point m and person B chooses point n (or they at least attempt to do so). A handy feature of the Edgeworth box is that if the two agents choose different points, supply cannot equal demand. In the present case, there is an excess demand for good X and an excess supply of good Y. The excess demand for good X equals the overlap of the horizontal components of points n (read relative to 0_B) and m (read relative to 0_A)—that is, the distance rs. The excess supply of good Y is equal to the shortfall of the vertical components of points n and m—that is, the distance wu. Stability is assured because the excess demand

---

7. See Francis Edgeworth, *Mathematical Psychics* (New York: Kelly and Milman, 1881). For a modern discussion of Edgeworth's discussion of how the core reduces to the competitive solution with many agents see Peter Newman, *The Theory of Exchange* (New York: Prentice-Hall, 1965), chap. 5.

FIGURE 6-6 Stability

When the relative price of good X is too low for equilibrium (when the slope of budget line L is less than the slope of budget line L'), there is an excess demand for good X (equal to distance rs) and an excess supply of good Y (equal to distance wu). The relative price p_x/p_y will rise until the equilibrium price ratio is restored. Thus, stability is assured in the above case.

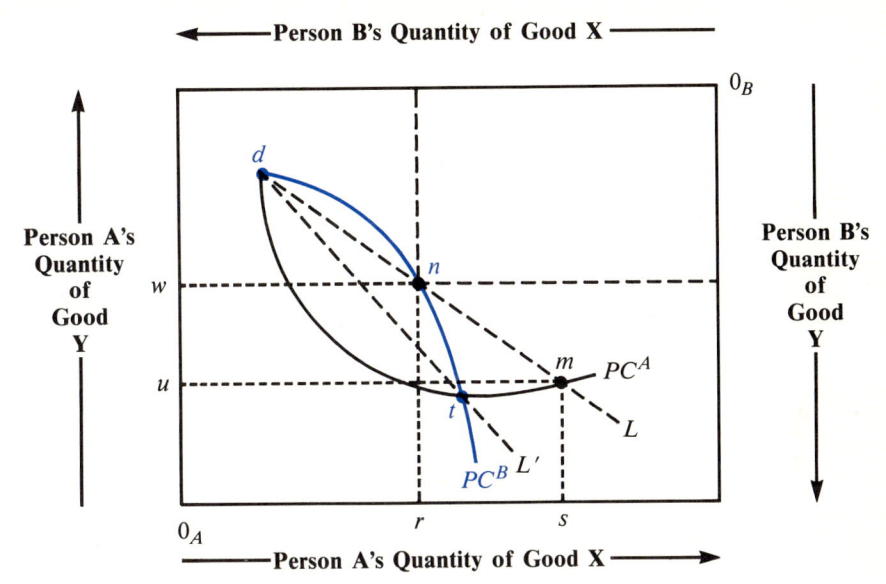

for good X will cause p_x/p_y to rise (or the excess supply for good Y will cause p_y/p_x to fall) until the equilibrium price ratio is restored.

THE LAW OF COMPARATIVE ADVANTAGE

The **law of comparative advantage** states that people (or countries) specialize in those goods in which they have the greatest advantage or the least disadvantage compared to other people (or countries).

The above analysis assumes that persons A and B have endowments such that the former sells good Y and the latter sells good X. If there is no production, no explanation for specialization is possible. Why people (or countries) specialize is explained by the **law of comparative advantage**, discovered by the English economist David Ricardo (1772–1823).

Imagine that a person is superior to everyone else in all activities. This person would clearly choose to specialize in that activity in which his or her margin of superiority was the greatest. Likewise, a person inferior to everyone else in all activities would choose that occupation in which his or her margin of inferiority was the smallest. If people simply choose their income-maximizing occupation, they will obey the law of comparative advantage.

An implication of the law of comparative advantage is that absolute levels of productivities are irrelevant in determining specialization patterns. A lawyer may be the fastest typist in town but makes more income preparing deeds than typing deeds. The best check-out clerk may be working as a computer scientist someplace. Comparative, not absolute, advantages determine where we work or how we use our resources.

FIGURE 6-7 Production-Possibilities Frontiers in the Case of Self-Sufficiency

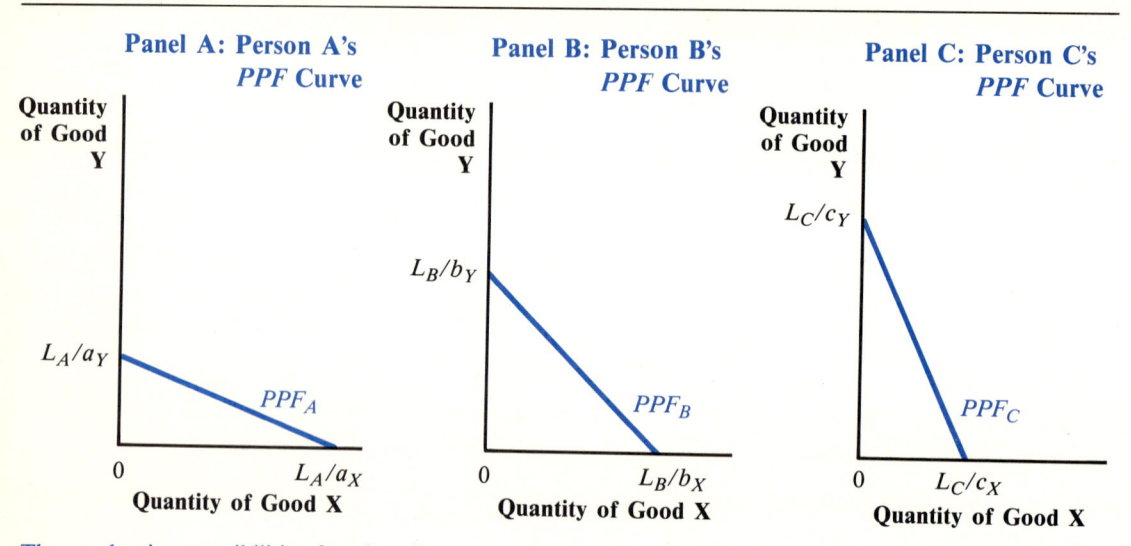

Panel A: Person A's PPF Curve

Quantity of Good Y

L_A/a_Y

PPF_A

0 — L_A/a_X

Quantity of Good X

Panel B: Person B's PPF Curve

Quantity of Good Y

L_B/b_Y

PPF_B

0 — L_B/b_X

Quantity of Good X

Panel C: Person C's PPF Curve

Quantity of Good Y

L_C/c_Y

PPF_C

0 — L_C/c_X

Quantity of Good X

The production-possibilities frontiers for person A, person B, and person C show what each can consume under *autarky*, or self-sufficiency. The absolute slopes represent the opportunity cost of producing good X. Clearly, A has the smallest opportunity cost of good X, and C has the highest opportunity cost of good X.

The Ricardian Model of Comparative Advantage

The law of comparative advantage can best be understood in the simplified setting that Ricardo originally pioneered (although Ricardo applied the idea to international rather than interpersonal trade). Imagine an economy consisting of three people: persons A, B, and C. Assume that:

1. each person works a fixed number of labor hours, L_j (j = A, B, C);
2. labor is the only input into production;
3. only two goods, X and Y, are produced;
4. each person is indifferent between producing good X or good Y as long as the wage is the same per hour;
5. each person behaves competitively by treating the price ratio, p_x/p_y, as a parameter;
6. each person's output per labor hour is constant and independent of the number of hours worked.

Let the lowercase letters a_i, b_i, and c_i (i = X, Y) denote the labor costs per unit of output for persons A, B, and C, respectively. Thus, a_X is how many labor hours it takes person A to produce 1 unit of good X. The inverse, $1/a_X$, represents A's output of good X per labor hour worked—that is, A's productivity. For example, if a_X = 2 labor hours per unit of good X, then each labor hour worked yields 0.5 unit of X. These labor costs—or productivities—are taken as given. Without loss of generality we can assume that:

$$a_X/a_Y < b_X/b_Y < c_X/c_Y. \tag{8}$$

The ratio a_X/a_Y, for example, has the interpretation of being A's opportunity cost (or relative cost) of producing good X. If A lived alone on a desert island, a_X/a_Y would be how many units of good Y person A would have to sacrifice per unit of good X consumed. For example, if $a_X = 2$ and $a_Y = 6$, then $a_X/a_Y = 1/3$. Thus, one third of a unit of Y must be sacrificed for each unit of X produced by A. In other words, one third of a unit of Y and one unit of X use the same amount of A's labor. Assumption (8) means that A has the lowest opportunity cost of good X and that C has the highest opportunity cost of good X; equivalently, A has the highest opportunity cost of good Y and C has the lowest opportunity cost of good Y.

Figure 6-7 shows the individual opportunity sets when each person lives alone and must be a jack-of-all-trades. The amounts of goods X and Y producible by A, for example, are given by the equation

$$L_A = x_A a_X + y_A a_Y. \tag{9}$$

A term such as $x_A a_X$ is how many hours A must work producing good X. Thus, Equation (9) states that the total available labor hours to A must equal the total amount of time spent producing good X and good Y. A similar equation holds for B and for C. Panels A, B, and C of Figure 6-7 show the production possibilities for each person. In Panel A, for example, L_A/a_X is the maximum amount of good X person A can produce, and L_A/a_Y is the maximum amount of Y person A can produce. The ratio of the vertical and horizontal intercepts,

$$\frac{L_A/a_Y}{L_A/a_X} = \frac{a_X}{a_Y},$$

is the opportunity cost of good X for A. Given the assumption in Equation (8), person A's production-possibilities frontier will be flatter than B's and B's *PPF* curve will be flatter than C's.

Now we will assume that a market opens up for goods X and Y. The price of good X in terms of Y is p_x/p_y. By considering different relative prices for good X, we can derive good X's (or good Y's) supply curve. If $p_x/p_y < a_X/a_Y$, person A will have no incentive to produce good X and will devote all energies to producing good Y. For example, if $a_X/a_Y = 4$ and $p_x/p_y = 2$, the market offers A half as much for good X as it costs A to produce X—in which case, it is better to produce Y and try to buy X. Similarly, persons B and C (who have an even higher opportunity cost of producing X) will devote their energies to producing good Y, resulting in no good X at all being produced. By analogous reasoning, no good Y will be produced if $p_x/p_y > c_X/c_Y$. In order for the economy to produce some of good X and some of good Y it must be that $a_X/a_y \le p_x/p_y \le c_X/c_Y$.

EXAMPLE 6–2   The Comparative Advantage of Fishers

An important implication of the theory of comparative advantage is that absolute advantage is irrelevant. A recent illustration is provided by data on the productivity of fishers in the Texas shrimp industry. When individual fishers are followed through time, do they appear to have roughly the same productivities, or are there wide disparities in their productivities? Economists Ronald Johnson and Gary Libecap found that professional fishers exhibit large differences in fishing ability, as is known by Texas shrimpers. Fishers differ in their knowledge of how to set nets, the location of shrimp, and the correct trawling speed. While the more productive fishers had slightly better equipment, Texas laws restrict the size and number of nets that can be used.

The differences in productivity are significant. In a study of 29 full-time shrimpers, good fishers may average between 500 and 1,100 pounds per week, average fishers may catch between 300 and 650 pounds per week, and poor fishers may catch an average of only 150 to 500 pounds per week. Naturally, because of random factors, sometimes a poor fisher catches more than a good fisher, but over time good fishers were consistently more successful. Johnson and Libecap classified 2 of the shrimpers as good, 6 as poor, and 21 as average.

The poor fishers and the average fishers could still compete with the superior fishers by earning lower wages. The poor fisher had no absolute advantages in shrimping and, in all likelihood, was probably unable to fish as well as a number of weekend fishers. Shrimping affords the poor fishers an opportunity to maximize their income by exploiting their comparative, not their absolute, advantages.

Source: Ronald N. Johnson and Gary D. Libecap, "Contracting Problems and Regulation: The Case of the Fishery," *American Economic Review* 72 (December 1982): 1005–1022.

Figure 6–8 shows the market supply curve of good X. The supply curve is horizontal at each step corresponding to one agent's opportunity cost. For example, if $p_x/p_y = a_X/a_Y$, then A is indifferent between producing good X or good Y.

Another way of seeing how people specialize in good X or good Y depending on the comparison of the cost ratio with the price ratio is to look at wages. If $p_x/p_y < b_X/b_Y$, then it is also true that $p_x/b_X < p_y/b_Y$. As indicated earlier, $1/b_i$ is the output of good i that B obtains by working one labor hour in that activity. If a unit of labor yields $1/b_i$ units of good i, which has the dollar value of p_i per unit, then p_i/b_i is the dollar earnings of a unit of B's labor in good i production. Because $p_x/b_X < p_y/b_Y$, B will earn more working in industry Y!

The benefits of specialization are obvious. The standard of living of

FIGURE 6-8   Ricardian Market Supply

In the Ricardian model, the market-supply curve is a step function, with each step corresponding to a particular agent's opportunity cost of producing good X.

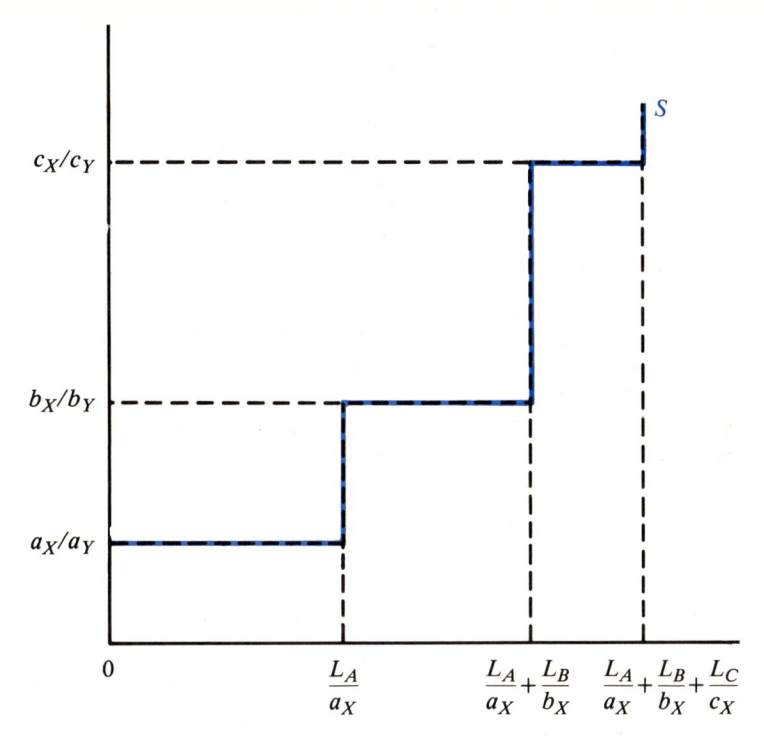

(Figure: step function supply curve S with steps at heights a_X/a_Y, b_X/b_Y, c_X/c_Y on the vertical axis, and breakpoints at $\frac{L_A}{a_X}$, $\frac{L_A}{a_X}+\frac{L_B}{b_X}$, $\frac{L_A}{a_X}+\frac{L_B}{b_X}+\frac{L_C}{c_X}$ on the horizontal axis.)

advanced societies is much higher than in poor, semiliterate countries, where the degree of specialization is far less.

Absolute Advantage Is Irrelevant

Notice that the allocation of labor between activities does not depend directly on the absolute values of a_i, b_i, and c_i—only *relative* values matter. For example, when $p_x/p_y < b_X/b_Y$, a doubling of b_X and b_Y would still lead B to specialize in good Y. The principle of comparative advantage, in the simple Ricardian world, is that absolute advantage is irrelevant. (See Example 6-2.)

William Shakespeare actually observed this principle several centuries before David Ricardo when one of his characters remarked, "There is place and means for every man alive." Basically, the law of comparative advantage implies that there is a job for everyone in a world of scarcity.

The real world appears to depart from the law of comparative advantage in several ways. First, not everyone can find a job—partly because everyone does not have perfect information about his or her comparative advantage. In the real world, jobs and people are hard to match because of information difficulties.

Second, the free working of the law of comparative advantage requires that there be no lower limit on wages. A person with no absolute advantages over anyone would have to receive lower wages than anyone in order to profit from his or her comparative advantage. In 1984, the minimum wage was $3.50 an hour. Minimum-wage laws may be interpreted as making illegal the comparative advantages of all those individuals whose incomes are maximized at wages of *less* than $3.50 an hour.

The law of comparative advantage illustrates the futility of trying to raise wages to socially acceptable levels. While the intention of those who desire higher wages for the poor is admirable, the effects of such policy may be to limit the employment opportunities of the most disadvantaged members of society.[8]

Third, the Ricardian model supposes that people are not supported by government welfare programs or unemployment insurance.

SUMMARY

1. An exchange equilibrium exists when there is no incentive for people to engage in further trades—that is, when all mutual benefits of trade are exhausted—and usually occurs when marginal rates of substitution are equalized. In the Edgeworth box, the contract curve represents the set of possible exchange equilibria.

2. Pareto optimality exists whenever any resource reallocation that makes one person better off must make some other person worse off. In the Edgeworth-box diagram, Pareto optimality is achieved along the contract curve, defined (generally) by the condition that the marginal rates of substitution for the two persons are equalized.

3. A competitive equilibrium in an exchange economy is achieved when (1) each consumer is maximizing utility and (2) supply equals demand for each good at some set of prices. The *core* is an allocation of resources such that no person or coalition of persons acting on their own can do any better. A competitive equilibrium belongs to the core; the core belongs to the set of Pareto-optimal allocations.

4. The law of comparative advantage states that each person will specialize in that activity in which his or her advantage is the largest or in which his or her disadvantage is the smallest. The law implies that absolute advantages are irrelevant in determining the allocation of labor between different jobs.

---

8. The empirical evidence for the proposition that minimum wages reduce employment opportunities for low-wage groups is persuasive. For a well-balanced survey of about 100 studies, see Charles Brown, Curtis Gilroy, and Andrew Kohen, "The Effect of the Minimum Wage on Employment and Unemployment," *Journal of Economic Literature* 20 (June 1982): 487–528. See also Timothy Tregarthen, "Minimum Wage: Time for a Boost?" *The Margin* 2 (January 1987): 8–9, for a good summary of theory and facts.

QUESTIONS AND PROBLEMS

1. Thinking only in terms of economics, would you rather live in a society in which all people were the same as you or one in which others were different from you? Explain your answer.

2. Consider Sally and George in a two-good, pure-exchange economy. If their tastes are identical, can there be any trade? How?

3. Ron and Betty have identical endowments of goods X and Y. Is it possible for Ron and Betty to make profitable exchanges? How?

4. Assume 20 units of good X and 40 units of good Y are available to Paul and Marie. Let Paul have 10 units of X and 15 units of Y; give Marie 9 units of X and 23 units of Y. Show each person's allocation in an Edgeworth box. How many points are needed? How would you describe the allocation?

5. Assume (again) that 20 units of X and 40 units of Y are available to Paul and Marie. Paul wants 10 units of X and 15 units of Y; Marie wants 8 units of X and 30 units of Y. Show these wants in an Edgeworth box. How many points are needed? Can these wants be satisfied by the economy?

6. Assume that 20 units of X and 40 units of Y are available to Paul and Marie. Both Paul and Marie have identical preferences described by $MRS = y^i/x^i$. Illustrate the contract curve in an Edgeworth box. For any endowments given to Marie and Paul, what do you expect the competitive equilibrium, p_x/p_y, to be? Why?

7. Tom has an endowment of 50 units of X and 50 units of Y; Mary has an endowment of 50 units of X and 250 units of Y. Both have the same preferences described by $MRS = y^i/x^i$.
   a. Who will sell X? Who will sell Y?
   b. What is the competitive allocation and p_x/p_y in equilibrium?
   c. Draw the contract curve in the Edgeworth box. Does the competitive equilibrium p_x/p_y depend on the way in which the 100 units of X and 300 units of Y are initially distributed to Tom and Mary?

8. If Ralph and Betty have the same endowments and the same preferences, what is the core of the economy? How does the core correspond to the competitive equilibrium? What is the price ratio in equilibrium?

SUGGESTED READINGS

Alchian, Armen and William R. Allen. *Exchange and Production: Theory in Use.* Belmont, California: Wadsworth Publishing Co., 1969, chaps. 3 and 10.

Newman, Peter. *The Theory of Exchange.* New York: Prentice-Hall, 1965.

Ricardo, David. *The Principles of Political Economy and Taxation* (1817), chap. 7.

CHAPTER 7

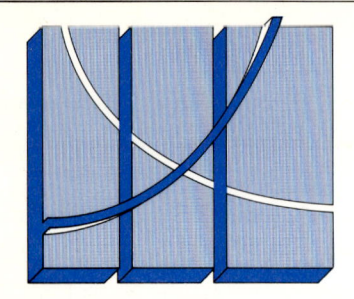

THE TECHNOLOGY OF PRODUCTION

Production is organized within entities known as business firms. Producing any good or service requires the correct combination of the factors of production. A manager must determine the mix of land, labor, and capital. This chapter examines the laws governing the relationship between outputs and inputs. The next chapter looks at the optimum mix of inputs and the corresponding costs of production.

In 1980, some 16.8 million businesses filed tax returns in the United States. About 12 million of these firms had annual business sales of less than $50,000 and were operated on a part-time basis or were just starting up. About 2.7 million (16 percent) of these firms were corporations, 1.4 million (8 percent) were partnerships, and 12.7 million (76 percent) were sole proprietorships—but 60 percent of our goods and services are produced by corporations.

The corporation, as a form of business organization, has the advantage of offering business owners limited liability and a perpetual life. Large sums of financial capital can be raised from thousands or even millions of investors, who risk only their initial investment. The corporation exists independently of the individual men and women who constitute its management. If a management team is incompetent, it can be easily replaced without dissolving the business firm.

Firms are islands of *managerial coordination* in a sea of *market coordination*. Within the business firm, a management team allocates resources by assigning tasks to different inputs. Between firms, markets allocate resources by setting equilibrium prices. Firms exist because market coordination is costly: contracts must be negotiated, information about alternative sources of supply must be gathered, and prices must be fixed. Managerial coordination reduces the costs of these transactions when the firm is dealing with its familiar activities—assembling a car, producing paper, making a hamburger, or marketing whatever is the product or service in which the firm has a comparative advantage.[1]

The central purpose of the business firm is production. Inputs may be gathered from all over the globe to generate some type of output. Generally speaking, production of an airplane, a car, a television set, or a restaurant meal requires a mixture of inputs—a combination of different types of labor, land, and physical capital under the central direction of a manager. Each input is assigned a task. For example, in 1978 the General Motors Tarrytown plant (just north of New York City) produced X-type cars—the Chevrolet Nova, Pontiac Phoenix, and Buick Skylark—at a 97-acre plant facility. On any given shift, about 2,000 workers assembled about 5,000 parts in about 1,000 separate work stations, each operated by one or two workers. The job of each work station in the plant had to be completely specified by industrial engineers.

Adam Smith pointed out the enormous advantages of large-scale production within a business firm. He used the example of a pin factory in the late 18th century. Smith estimated that each worker in a fully equipped pin factory could produce about 4,800 pins a day. But if each employee worked independently and separately, according to Smith, a worker certainly could not have made 20 pins a day, and perhaps not even one. The Tarrytown auto plant provides a modern example. With a shift of 2,000 workers turning out about 500 cars per shift (one a minute), the equivalent of 4 days' work was required to produce a car.[2] Working in one's own garage, one might require a month to assemble 5,000 parts into a working automobile.[3] The advantages of assembly-line production are enormous: little time is lost in going from task to task, and workers can specialize in a thousand different activities such as spot-welding, mounting engines, applying primer or paint, door hanging, and mounting wheels.

---

1. The reasons firms exist are explored by Ronald Coase in "The Nature of the Firm," *Economica* (1937), pp. 386–495; and by Armen Alchian and Harold Demsetz in "Production, Information Costs, and Economic Organization," *American Economic Review* 57 (December 1972): 777–95. A critical review of this literature is found in David S. Evans and Sanford J. Grossman, "Integration," in D. S. Evans, ed., *Breaking Up Bell* (New York: North-Holland, 1983).

2. Based on 1978 data gathered by Roger W. Shmenner, *Production/Operations Management: Concepts and Situations* (Chicago: Science Research Associates, 1981), chap. 5. In 1978, the Tarrytown plant had 3,700 production workers and 500 salaried workers and operated two shifts for 18 hours a day. The plant turned out about one car per minute. Robots and a new emphasis on quality have changed the old-fashioned assembly line. For a description of new methods, see "An Assembly-Line Revolution," *New York Times*, September 3, 1985, p. 31. The General Motors Saturn plant in Lansing, Michigan, now has automated vehicles carrying the engine from location to location, and workers have the option of varying the amount of time required to complete a task.

3. Assembling a car from kits provided by companies such as Classic Motor Carriages of Miami, Florida, requires about 200 hours of work even when the full drivetrain is provided.

THE PRODUCTION FUNCTION

Physical and chemical laws govern the relationships between outputs and inputs. *Engineering* (but not economic) *efficiency* can be defined in terms of maximum output for a given input, or a minimum of some input for a given output. *Economic efficiency* is defined in terms of dollar costs instead of physical inputs; it is studied in the next chapter.

The **production function** shows the maximum output that can be achieved from any prescribed set of inputs. It also shows the minimum amount needed of one particular input, given the level of output and prescribed levels of the remaining inputs.

The best information the firm possesses about all the various ways in which its product can be produced is captured by the economic concept of the **production function**, which describes the maximum output that can be achieved from any given combination of inputs and also the minimum of any one input needed given the output and the remaining input levels. Thus, the production function reflects all the technological information available to the firm. If Q is the output of the firm and A, B, C, etc., are the various inputs, then the production function can be represented by the equation

$$Q = F(A, B, C, \ldots) \tag{1}$$

Marginal and Average Products

The **average product** of input A is the quantity of output divided by the quantity of A; that is, $AP_A = Q/A$.

There can be no output without inputs. The ratio of total output to the amount of one particular input is the **average product** of that input.

The concept of average product of an input is useful because it serves as the basis for learning how costly it is to use that input. To illustrate, consider an auto plant that produces 1,000 cars a day with 4,000 workers. The average product of a worker is 1/4 of a car. The reciprocal of the average product of an input is the amount of the input used per unit of the output. If 4 worker days are needed per car and workers earn $200 to $300 a day, the labor-cost component of a car is $800 to $1200 per car.

If inputs are useful, more inputs imply more outputs. The production function governs the relationship between total output, or product, and total input usage, as well as the relationship between input usage and the **marginal product** of any particular input.[4]

The **marginal product** of input A for the production function $Q = F(A, B, C, \ldots)$ is the extra output generated per unit of change in input A; or, $MP_A = \Delta Q/\Delta A$ when all other inputs are held constant.

There are as many physical examples of the concept of marginal products as there are combinations of products and inputs. As a farmer adds more feed, holding all other inputs constant, the output of livestock or eggs or milk will increase. If two more pounds of feed cause a farmer's hens to produce one more egg, then the marginal product of feed will be $\Delta(\text{eggs})/\Delta(\text{feed}) = 1/2$ egg per pound. Corn is produced by combining the inputs of labor, land, seed, fertilizers, and rainfall. Increasing the application of fertilizer per acre from 0 to 40 pounds, holding all other inputs constant, might increase the

---

4. For $Q = F(A, B, C, \ldots)$, the marginal product of input A is simply $MP_A = \partial Q/\partial A$. Example: if $Q = K^{0.25}L^{0.75}$, then $\partial Q/\partial L = 0.75 K^{0.25} L^{-0.25} = 0.75(K/L)^{0.25}$.

THE PRODUCTION FUNCTION 167

output of corn by 66 bushels per acre. Thus, the marginal product of fertilizer would be 66/40 = 1.65 bushels per pound.[5]

The marginal product of any input depends on the quantities of the other inputs being held constant. For example, the marginal amount of corn produced by added fertilizer might fall to 1.3 bushels per pound if the amount of rainfall were cut in half. Similarly, the marginal product of even a skilled auto worker would be much higher on a modern assembly line than when working with simple wrenches, pulleys, and blowtorches in a small garage.

The Short Run and the Long Run

The **short run** is a period of time so short that existing plant and equipment cannot be varied. Additional output can be produced only by expanding the variable inputs of labor and raw materials.

The **long run** is a period of time long enough to vary all inputs.

A business firm expands the volume of its output by hiring or using additional resources. The level of some resources can be adjusted immediately; the levels of others require considerable time to change. Inputs such as labor and raw materials can be adjusted quickly. If the firm needs to increase output in the next few weeks, it may be able to obtain more raw materials and work its existing labor force more intensively simply by asking each employee to work overtime. But installing a new machine or building a new plant may take considerable time. Economists distinguish between **the short run** and the **long run** by considering the time available to change levels of **fixed inputs** or **variable inputs**.

The long run is not a specified amount of calendar time. It may be as short as a few months for a fast-food restaurant, or as long as a couple of years for a new automobile plant, or as long as a decade for an atomic power plant. Generally speaking, engineering complexity determines whether the long run is a matter of weeks, months, or years.

The Law of Diminishing Returns

Fixed inputs cannot be varied in the short run.

Variable inputs can be varied in the short run.

Whenever a variable input is increased, holding all the other inputs constant, the marginal product of that input must eventually decline. This *law of diminishing returns* is an empirical regularity characterizing every production process. The law holds because as the variable input is increased, the fixed inputs are spread thinner and thinner, giving each unit of the variable input fewer fixed inputs with which to work.

Notice there is nothing in the law that requires the marginal product to eventually become zero, or negative. Marginal product can increase at first, but it must eventually fall. It may reach zero or become negative, but it can decline forever without becoming negative as long as it declines at a slow enough rate!

---

5. These examples are drawn from Earl O. Heady and John L. Dillon, *Agricultural Production Functions* (Ames, Iowa: Iowa State University Press, 1961), pp. 568–73.

THE LONG-RUN PRODUCTION FUNCTION

In the long run, all inputs are variable. In the short run, some inputs are fixed. To simplify our discussion of the production function, we will suppose that there are only two inputs: labor (L) and capital (K). Labor will be treated as the variable input in the short run; capital will be treated as the fixed input in the short run. The long-run production function can then be written as

$$Q = F(L, K). \qquad (2)$$

A sample production function is shown in Table 7–1. The table lists units of output for each combination of labor and capital input. For example, when 6 machine hours of capital are combined with 4 worker hours, output is 87 units. When 4 machine hours are combined with 2 worker hours, output is 50 units.

Constant returns to scale are present when a given percentage increase in all inputs increases output by the same percentage.

Table 7–1 makes two assumptions. First, it assumes that the law of diminishing returns applies. When the capital input is 4 machine hours, increasing worker hours from 1 to 2 to 3 and so on increases output from 35 to 50 to 61 and so on. Thus, the marginal product of the second worker is 15 units of output, while the marginal product of the third worker decreases to 11 units, and so on. Second, the table assumes **constant returns to scale**. There are constant returns when a given percentage increase in inputs increases output by the same percentage. For example, if output is 53 units

TABLE 7–1   A Hypothetical Production Function

Output per Unit of Time

Capital Input (machine hours), K								
8	50	71	87	100	112	122	132	141
7	47	66	81	94	105	115	124	132
6	43	61	75	87	97	106	115	122
5	40	56	68	79	88	97	105	112
4	35	50	61	71	79	87	94	100
3	31	43	53	61	68	75	81	87
2	25	35	43	50	56	61	66	71
1	18	25	31	35	40	43	47	50
	1	2	3	4	5	6	7	8

Labor Input (worker hours), L

FIGURE 7-1 Production Isoquants

Each isoquant shows all the combinations of labor and capital that produce a given level of output. (See Table 7-1.) The isoquants are convex to the origin. The marginal rate of technical substitution (*MRTS*) of capital for labor diminishes as more labor is substituted for capital: from point *a* to point *b*, the *MRTS* is 2/1 = 2 and from point *b* to point *c*, the *MRTS* is only 2/2 = 1.

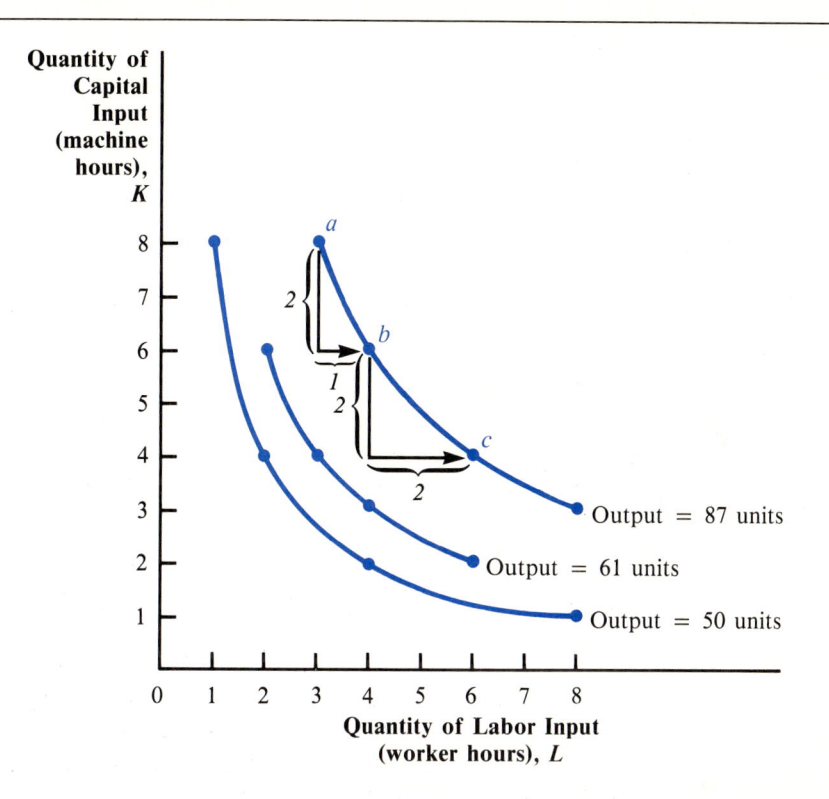

A **production isoquant** for any production function is the graph of all the combinations of two inputs that will produce a particular level of output.

when the input combination (L, K) is $(3, 3)$, a constant return to scale means that output will be 106 units when inputs are doubled to $(6, 6)$.

The production function $Q = F(L, K)$ exhibits constant returns to scale if $\lambda Q = F(\lambda L, \lambda K)$ for any $\lambda > 0$.

The properties of constant returns to scale will be examined in detail later.

Table 7-1 shows different ways of producing various levels of output. For example, 50 units of output can be produced by at least four different combinations of capital and labor: when $(L, K) = (1, 8), (2, 4), (4, 2),$ and $(8, 1)$.

In the long run, all controllable inputs are variable. The firm will choose that combination of inputs which minimizes the cost of achieving any particular level of output. Thus, the theory of cost minimization (studied in the next chapter) rests on the various input combinations that will produce any particular level of output. The production function for any good or service can in fact be characterized by its corresponding set of **production isoquants**.

Figure 7-1 shows three production isoquants for the production function given in Table 7-1. If labor and capital are divisible into any real number, there will be an infinity of isoquants—one for every output level. Thus, each production function can be associated with an *isoquant map*. The isoquants in Figure 7-1 have three properties:

1. higher isoquants represent higher output levels;
2. each isoquant is downward-sloping;
3. each isoquant is convex to the origin.

Higher isoquants represent higher levels of output simply because inputs have positive marginal products. Thus, the isoquant for an output level of 61 units in Figure 7-1 is farther from the origin than the isoquant for an output level of 50 units.

An isoquant is typically downward-sloping because inputs usually have positive marginal products. More output can be produced by using more labor or more capital. Because output (Q) is constant along any given isoquant, adding a quantity of labor implies that less capital must be used (or adding a quantity of capital implies the need for less labor). Indeed, the trade-off of labor for capital will depend on the relative magnitudes of the marginal products of labor (MP_L) and capital (MP_K). In general, $\Delta Q = \Delta L \cdot MP_L + \Delta K \cdot MP_K$, where the first term ($\Delta L \cdot MP_L$) is the extra output resulting from the change in labor input and the second is the extra output resulting from the change in the capital input. Along an isoquant, $\Delta Q = 0$; accordingly,

$$0 = \Delta L MP_L + \Delta K MP_K. \qquad (3)$$

Rearranging terms, we find that the slope of the isoquant is:[6]

$$\frac{\Delta K}{\Delta L} = \frac{-MP_L}{MP_K} \qquad (4)$$

The numerical value of the slope of an isoquant is called the **marginal rate of technical substitution** ($MRTS_{KL}$) of capital for labor because it shows the rate at which capital can be substituted for another unit of labor without sacrificing any output.

Equation (4) shows that if either MP_L or MP_K is negative, the slope of the isoquant is positive rather than negative. We shall return to this case shortly.

Why is the production isoquant convex? Convexity simply means that the $MRTS$ of capital for labor declines as more labor is substituted for capital along an isoquant. In Figure 7-1, the slope, or $MRTS$ from point *a* to point *b* is greater (2/1) than it is from point *b* to point *c* (2/2). (See Example 7-1.)

The meaning of convexity is illustrated in Figure 7-2. Production process *a* is relatively capital-intensive; production process *b* is relatively labor-intensive. Now consider a linear mixture of processes *a* and *b*: production process *c* is a weighted average of *a* and *b*. When the isoquant is convex to

The **marginal rate of technical substitution** ($MRTS_{KL}$) of capital for labor is $-\Delta K/\Delta L = MP_L/MP_K$; that is, it is the rate at which a unit of capital can be substituted for a unit of labor and still keep output constant.

---

6. If $Q = F(L, K)$, the total differential is $dQ = F_L dL + F_K dK$, where $F_L = \partial F/\partial L$ and $F_K = \partial F/\partial K$. When $dQ = 0$, we obtain $0 = F_L dL + F_K dK$ or

$MRST_{KL} = -dK/dL = F_L/F_K$.

FIGURE 7-2 Isoquant Convexity

When isoquants are convex to the origin, any weighted average of input bundles *a* and *b*, such as bundle *c*, will increase output. Balanced input combinations are preferable to extreme input combinations. Convexity also means that the marginal rate of technical substitution of capital for labor declines from point *a* to point *b*, as indicated by the smaller absolute slope at point *b*.

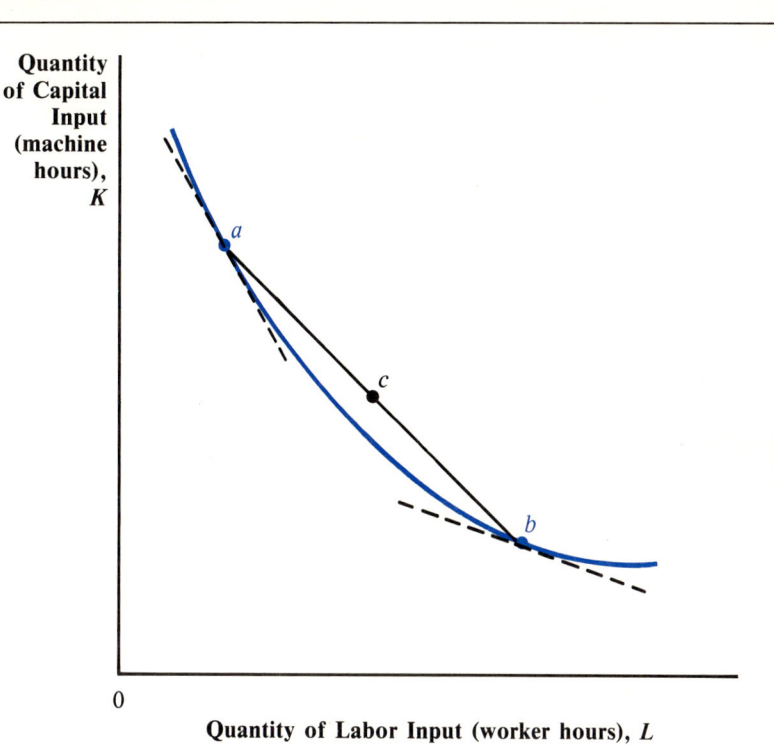

[Graph: Quantity of Capital Input (machine hours), K on vertical axis; Quantity of Labor Input (worker hours), L on horizontal axis. A convex isoquant curve passes through points a and b, with point c on the straight line connecting a and b, lying above the isoquant.]

the origin, point *c* is above it. Because adding more labor or capital implies more output, process *c* corresponds to a larger volume of output than either process *a* or *b*. Thus, convexity can be interpreted as meaning that a more "balanced" mixture of any two production processes will yield more output. In other words, nature abhors extremes when it comes to production functions.

Convexity is a fundamental characteristic of all production functions.

The **law of diminishing marginal rate of technical substitution ($MRTS_{KL}$)** states that the marginal rate of technical substitution of capital for labor diminishes as more labor is used, holding output constant.

Convexity of the production isoquants is also explained by the **law of diminishing marginal rate of technical substitution ($MRTS_{KL}$)**.

The law of diminishing returns states that the marginal product of an input eventually declines as more of it is added, holding other inputs constant. In other words, the marginal product of a factor falls when production processes become more intensive or "extreme" in the use of that input factor.

While convexity, or the law of diminishing *MRTS*, is related to diminishing marginal productivity, they are not the same thing. In a sense, diminishing *MRTS* is more fundamental. Diminishing *MRTS* means that the ratio of marginal products, MP_L/MP_K, falls as the ratio of capital to labor, K/L, falls along a given isoquant. If the quantity of labor input is rising and the quantity of capital input is falling, MP_L might fall and MP_K might rise if marginal products fall as more of an input is used (or rise as less of an input is used). If there are economies of large-scale production, however, the substitution of labor for capital (holding output constant) might raise the marginal product of labor by less than the marginal product of capital is rising.[7]

Returns to Scale

The *scale* of the firm refers to how large the firm is for any given proportion of labor to capital. For example, if all inputs are increased by 10 percent, the scale of the firm is increased by 10 percent. There is no general rule, such as the law of diminishing returns, to cover the relationship between outputs and inputs when all inputs are increased by the same proportion. Instead, economists refer to three general cases: *constant*, *increasing*, and *decreasing* returns to scale.

Constant Returns to Scale

Constant returns to scale occur when a percentage increase in all inputs increases output by the same percentage. Equivalently, constant returns to scale means that an increase in the scale of the firm (holding the ratio of labor to capital constant) does not affect the average product of any input.

There are two implications of constant returns to scale. The first, for output Q and marginal products MP_L and MP_K, is called *Euler's equation*:

$$Q = L(MP_L) + K(MP_K). \qquad (5)$$

A simple proof of Euler's equation follows. Suppose the inputs of labor and capital are increased by ΔL and ΔK. Then, by the definition of marginal productivity [see the text development of Equation (3)], the change in output would always be

$$\Delta Q = \Delta L MP_L + \Delta K MP_K. \qquad (6)$$

If there are constant returns to scale, $\Delta L/L = \Delta K/K = \mu$ implies that output increases by the same proportion; that is, $\Delta Q/Q = \mu$. But then Equation (6)

---

[7]. Let $F_L = MP_L = \partial F/\partial L$, $F_K = MP_K = \partial F/\partial K$, and $F_{LK} = \partial^2 F/\partial L \partial K$. It can be shown that $dMRTS_{KL}/dL < 0$ if and only if

$$D = (F_K)^2 F_{LL} + F_L^2 F_{KK} - 2F_K F_L F_{LK} < 0.$$

Thus, F_{LL} or F_{KK} may be positive if $F_{LK} > 0$. One possibility with economies of large-scale production would be for $F_{LL} < 0$, $F_{KK} > 0$. Now consider the change in F_L and F_K along an isoquant, where $dK/dL = -F_L/F_K$; totally differentiating F_L yields

$$dF_L/dL = F_{LL} + F_{LK}(dK/dL) = F_{LL} - F_{LK}F_L/F_K.$$
$$dF_K/dK = F_{KK} - F_{KL}F_K/F_L.$$

If both of these are negative, F_L falls and F_K rises as more labor is substituted for capital.

implies that $\mu Q = \mu L M P_L + \mu K M P_K$, which becomes Equation (5) when both sides are divided by μ.

A second implication of constant returns to scale is that the marginal products of labor and capital depend *only* on the ratio of capital and labor. Mathematically, this follows from the definition. If $\lambda Q = F(\lambda L, \lambda K)$ for all λ, it also holds for $\lambda = 1/L$. Thus, $Q/L = F(1, K/L)$. Accordingly, the average product of labor depends only on the capital-to-labor ratio. Because the average product of labor depends only on K/L, so too does the marginal product of labor (or capital). Intuitively, one can see that constant returns to scale mean that a large firm is just like an equivalent number of smaller firms given that they have the same ratio of capital to labor. Thus, an additional unit of labor (or capital) will have the same impact on output whether it is added to one of the smaller firms or to the larger firm.[8]

An example of constant returns to scale is the well-known Cobb-Douglas production function, Equation (7). Charles W. Cobb, a mathematician, and Paul H. Douglas, an economist who later became a U.S. senator from Illinois, argued that aggregate production data for the U.S. economy approximately followed the form:

$$Q = L^{0.25} K^{0.75}.$$

The Cobb-Douglas production function is of the general form:

$$Q = CL^a K^{1-a}. \tag{7}$$

where C is some constant and $0 < a < 1$. Table 7–1 is based on the Cobb-Douglas production function $Q = 17.7(LK)^{0.5}$. Why does this function exhibit constant returns to scale? Suppose labor input (L) is changed to λL and capital input (K) to λK. Then output will be

$$(\lambda L)^a (\lambda K)^{1-a} = L^a K^{1-a} \lambda^a \lambda^{1-a} = Q\lambda.$$

In other words, the initial level of output Q is changed to $Q\lambda$ and the definition of constant returns to scale is satisfied.

It turns out that, given constant returns to scale plus diminishing returns, the production isoquant must be convex. Recall that convexity means that the marginal rate of technical substitution falls from point a to point b in Figure 7–2; thus, convexity means by definition that the slope MP_L/MP_K is greater at point a than at point b. The slope of a ray drawn from the origin to point a would be steeper than that of a ray drawn to point b; accordingly, K/L is higher at a than at b. We argued earlier that with constant returns to scale, the marginal products of labor and capital depend only on the ratio K/L. The higher is K/L, the lower will be MP_K and the higher will be MP_L.

---

8. Because $Q = LF(1, K/L)$, the marginal product of capital is $\partial Q/\partial K = LF_K(1, K/L)(1/L) = F_K(1, K/L)$. Similarly, the marginal product of labor is $\partial Q/\partial L = F(1, K/L) + LF_K(1, K/L)(-K/L^2) = F(1, K/L) - (K/L)F_K(1, K/L)$.

FIGURE 7-3 Returns to Scale

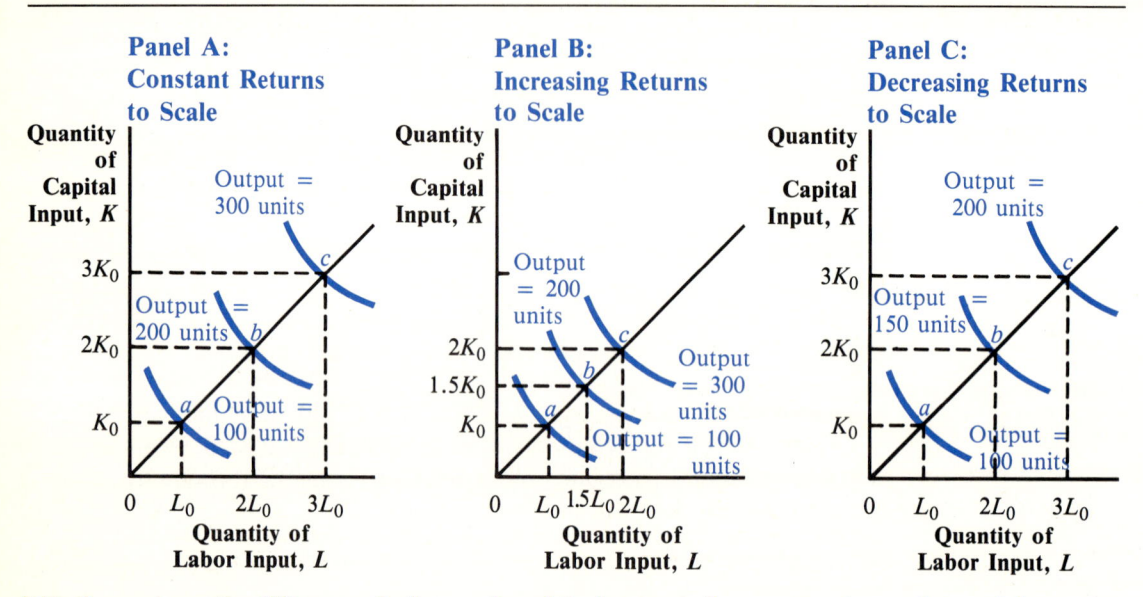

Panel A: Constant Returns to Scale

Panel B: Increasing Returns to Scale

Panel C: Decreasing Returns to Scale

This figure shows the differences in the spacing of the isoquants for constant, increasing, and decreasing returns to scale.

Because the ratio K/L is higher at point a than at point b, MP_L/MP_K must be higher at a than at b.

Some economists have argued that if inputs are perfectly divisible, constant returns to scale would be a law of production. With perfectly divisible inputs, workers and machines could be infinitely augmented or infinitely reduced without increasing or decreasing their usefulness or productivity. One worker could spend 25 percent of the time being a lawyer, 25 percent being an accountant, and 50 percent being an engineer without rendering any of the work less useful. A small assembly line would be just as effective as a large one: with a proportionately smaller number of workers, a 1-acre assembly line would be just as effective as a 100-acre assembly line.

Increasing Returns to Scale

Increasing returns to scale, or **economies of scale**, are present when increasing all inputs by a certain percentage increases output by a larger percentage.

Inputs are not usually perfectly divisible. When the scale of a firm is increased, workers and machines can be specialized. Nonspecialized generalists are replaced by well-trained accountants, lawyers, mechanical engineers, electrical engineers, managers, and machine operators. General-purpose machines are replaced by intricate ones designed for special purposes. Larger firms may find that it is possible to maintain smaller inventories of materials per unit of sales. Thus, increasing all inputs by a certain percentage may increase output by an even greater percentage. **Increasing returns to scale** are also called **economies of scale**, because certain economies are achieved when the size of the firm is increased.

Decreasing Returns to Scale

As the scale of a firm is increased, it is likely that it will first run into increasing returns to scale as the benefits of specialization are reaped. Eventually, the benefits of further specialization become exhausted. Once the limit point of specialization is reached, returns to scale become constant. Eventually, however, constant returns may run out as output is increased indefinitely. When a firm gets larger and larger, problems of coordination and management may begin to raise their troublesome heads. When the firm is too large, information cannot be efficiently passed from one part of the firm to another. At this stage, the firm runs into **diseconomies of scale**, or **decreasing returns to scale**.

Decreasing returns to scale, or **diseconomies of scale**, prevail when increasing all inputs by a certain percentage increases output by a smaller percentage.

In the long run, all inputs over which the firm has control are *variable*—but not all inputs affecting production can be controlled. For example, the farmer cannot vary the amount of rainfall or sunshine received during any given period. Some inputs are not available at any price. The fact that some inputs may be fixed and noncontrollable means that ultimately the law of diminishing returns will apply to long-run production functions as well. In this case, it might be expected that the production function would exhibit increasing returns to scale, constant returns to scale, and then decreasing returns to scale.

Figure 7–3 illustrates the spacing of the isoquants when constant, increasing, and decreasing returns to scale prevail. Panel A illustrates constant returns to scale. From point *a* to point *b*, output doubles when input doubles; and from point *b* to point *c*, output increases by 50 percent when input increases by 50 percent. Panel B illustrates increasing returns to scale. From point *a* to point *b*, output doubles when inputs increase by 50 percent; and from point *b* to point *c*, output increases by 50 percent when inputs increase by 33 percent. Finally, Panel C illustrates decreasing returns to scale. From point *a* to point *b*, output increases by only 50 percent when inputs double; from point *b* to point *c*, output increases by only 33 percent when inputs increase by 50 percent.

Homothetic Production Functions

A **homothetic production function** is one in which the marginal rate of technical substitution depends only on the ratio of capital to labor.

One of the most interesting production functions is the class of **homothetic production functions**. Simply put, a production function is homothetic if the marginal rate of technical substitution, $MRTS = MP_L/MP_K$, depends only on the ratio of capital to labor, K/L.

Constant returns to scale constitute a special case because both the marginal product of labor (MP_L) and the marginal product of capital (MP_K)

FIGURE 7-4   A Homothetic Production Function

A production function is homothetic if the *MRTS* remains the same for a constant capital/labor ratio. In this case, it is assumed that there are increasing returns from *a* to *b*, constant returns from *b* to *c*, and decreasing returns from *c* to *d*.

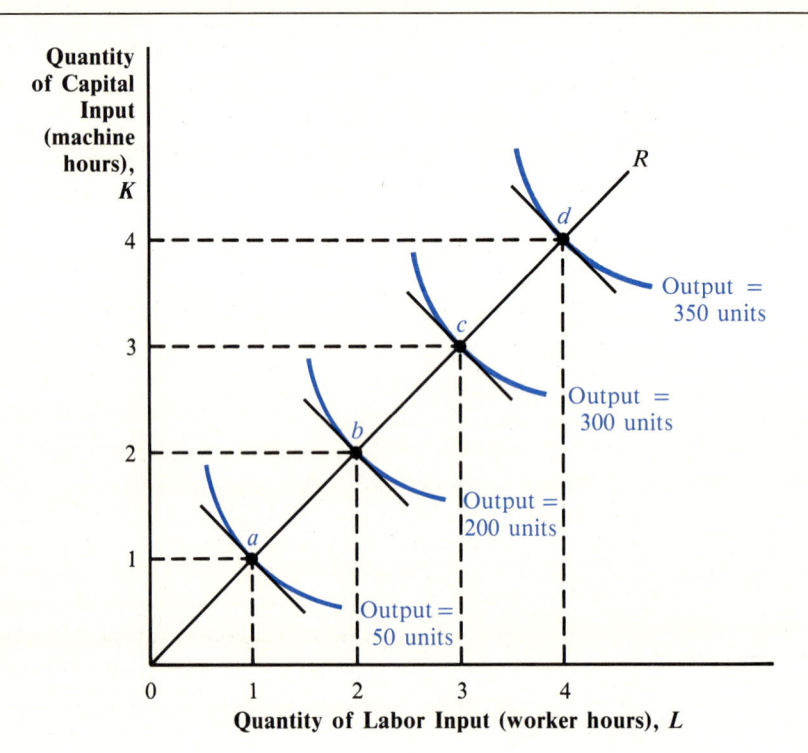

depend only on the ratio of capital to labor (K/L). Figure 7-4 shows the production isoquants of a homothetic function. Any ray *R* has the property that it intersects each isoquant at points *a*, *b*, *c*, *d*, . . ., where the rates of substitution are the same. The slopes of the tangents at points *a*, *b*, *c*, and *d* are parallel.

The beauty of a homothetic function is that it is the simplest case consistent with increasing, constant, and decreasing returns to scale. Figure 7-4 illustrates this case for a homothetic production function where the range of outputs from 50 to 200 units exhibits increasing returns to scale, the range of outputs from 200 to 300 units exhibits constant returns to scale, and the range of outputs above 300 units exhibits decreasing returns to scale.

THE SHORT-RUN PRODUCTION FUNCTION

We now turn to a detailed study of the short-run production function, in which some inputs are fixed. If $Q = F(L, K)$ is the long-run production function, the short-run production function is defined by

$$Q = F(L, K_0) = f(L), \tag{8}$$

EXAMPLE 7-1 — An Isoquant for Oil Pipelines

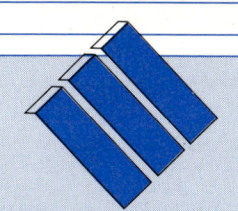

Frederick T. Moore has reported the production isoquant for pumping 125,000 barrels of oil at least 1,000 miles through a pipeline. The inputs are the outside diameter of the pipe and the horsepower used at the pumping station. The isoquant in the accompanying diagram is convex to the origin and is relatively flat, showing that it is easy to substitute the two inputs. The *MRTS* of pipe diameter for horsepower varies between 500 and 7,500, while the horsepower/diameter ratio varies from 67 to 2344. Because the horsepower/pipe diameter ratio varies by 35 times and the *MRTS* varies by 15 times, the elasticity of substitution averages out to be greater than unity.

Studies show that economies of scale are also present in the pumping of oil through a pipeline (up to about 200,000 barrels per day) because increasing the diameter of a pipeline by a given percentage increases the volume of the pipeline by twice that amount.

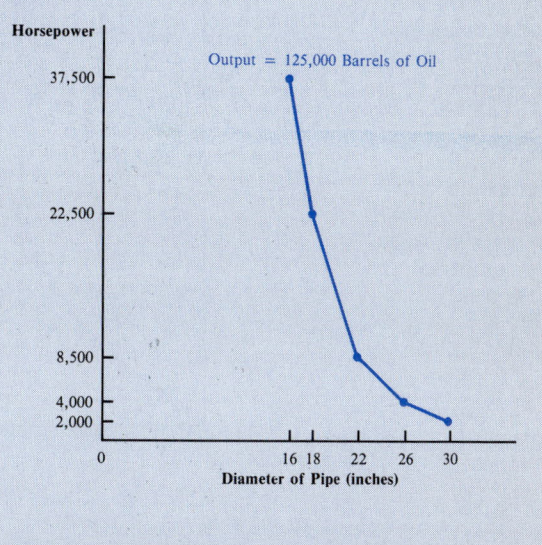

Source: Frederick T. Moore, "Economies of Scale: Some Statistical Evidence," *Quarterly Journal of Economics* 74, (1959).

where K_0 is the fixed level of the capital input. Practice Exercise 7-1 gives an example of deriving a short-run production function from the long-run function. Example 7-2 describes a real-world short-run function.

PRACTICE EXERCISE 7-1

Q. Assume the production function is $Q = L^{0.75}K^{0.25}$. From calculus we know that the marginal product of labor is $MP_L = 0.75(K/L)^{0.25}$. Let $K = 10,000$ units in the short run. What is the short-run production function? Show that average product AP_L is greater than marginal product MP_L.

A. $Q = L^{0.75}K^{0.25} = 10L^{0.75}$, because the fourth root of 10,000 is 10. The $AP_L = Q/L = 10/L^{0.25}$ and $MP_L = 7.5/L^{0.25}$. Because $10 > 7.5$, $AP_L > MP_L$.

FIGURE 7-5 A Short-Run Production Function

The typical short-run production function is convex at first (up to point *i*), when production is increasing at an accelerating rate; it then becomes concave, when production increases at a decreasing rate (the law of diminishing returns); finally, production may reach a maximum (at point *s*), when the number of variable inputs is so large as to actually block production.

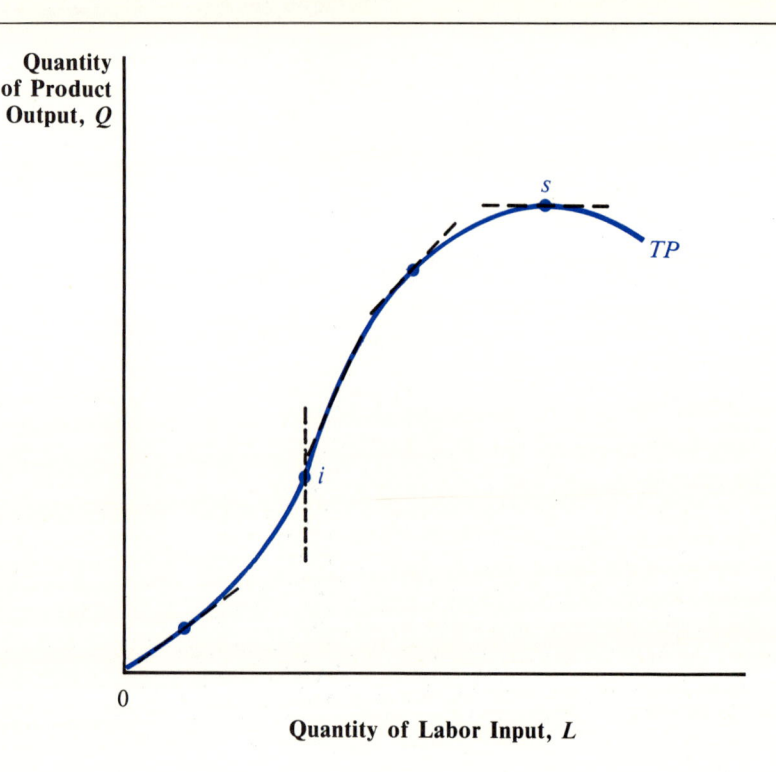

[Graph: Quantity of Product Output, Q on vertical axis; Quantity of Labor Input, L on horizontal axis. Curve labeled TP rises convexly through a point, then through inflection point i, continues concavely up to maximum point s.]

The Total-Product Curve

Figure 7–5 illustrates a typical short-run production function. Total product per unit of time, Q, is measured along the vertical axis; labor input per unit of time, L, is measured along the horizontal axis. Units of product output might be bushels of wheat per growing season; and units of labor input might be hours of labor per growing season. The slope of the production function at any point is the marginal product of labor, $MP_L = \Delta Q/\Delta L$. Notice that the total-product curve is convex at first, up to the inflection point *i* (where the slope is maximized) and concave from *i* to *s* and thereafter. Up to point *i*, the marginal product of labor is increasing; after point *i*, the marginal product decreases. Beyond point *s*, output actually decreases—the marginal product of labor is negative.

The shape of the short-run production function is explained by variations in the amount of labor input per unit of fixed input. When the labor input is increased, each unit of labor has less of the fixed capital input with which to work. Thus, in the short run, additional labor means that the fixed factor is being used more intensively. At first there may be too much of the fixed factor per unit of labor; labor is spread too thinly. So the first few increases

EXAMPLE 7-2 A Production Function for Eggs

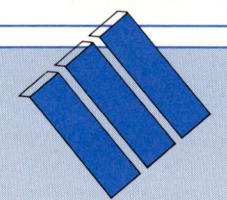

Agricultural economists Earl Heady and John Dillon studied 140 record-keeping egg farms in the 1950s. The production function for eggs was estimated to be:

$$Q = 26.23(X_1^{.3853} X_2^{.1132} X_3^{.2504} X_4^{.1368} X_5^{.0670})$$

The output, Q, is the number of dozens of eggs produced per farm per year, X_1 is the number of hens, X_2 is the number of square feet of housing, X_3 is the number of weeks of labor (where a week is defined as 50 hours of labor) per year, X_4 is the number of pounds of corn, and X_5 is the number of pounds of 26 percent protein-concentrate equivalent. Fixing the levels of all inputs except labor at their geometric averages over the 140 farms, the short-run production function for eggs is: $Q = 3,542 (X_3^{.2504})$.

The accompanying table shows how many dozen eggs a hypothetical farm of fixed size, holding the number of hens and the other factors constant, could produce per week of labor applied per year. Notice that for one week of labor per year, total output is 3,542 dozen. If 10 weeks of labor are applied, egg output increases by a little more than 60 percent. Thus, as might be intuitively obvious, beyond a certain point added labor becomes relatively ineffective. The marginal benefit of extra cleaning and care diminishes quite rapidly beyond five or six labor weeks.

Labor Input (weeks/year)	Egg Output (dozens/year)	Marginal Product (dozens/year)
1	3,542	3,542
2	4,115	573
3	4,493	378
4	4,782	289
5	5,018	236
6	5,220	202
7	5,397	177
8	5,556	159
9	5,699	143
10	5,831	132

The average farm surveyed used about five weeks of labor per year; at that point, an extra week of labor would increase total output by 202 dozen eggs. If eggs were worth $0.75 a dozen in the 1950s, a week's extra labor would have added roughly $151.50 to a farm's gross revenue.

Source: Earl O. Heady and John L. Dillon, *Agricultural Production Functions* (Ames, Iowa: Iowa State University Press, 1961), pp. 568–73.

---

in labor may cause enormous increases in output. Imagine a few workers operating an automobile assembly plant. With more than 1,000 work stations, those few workers would be wasting a lot of time shifting from station to station: "jacks of all trades and masters of none." Extra workers would

FIGURE 7-6 **Relationships Between Curves**

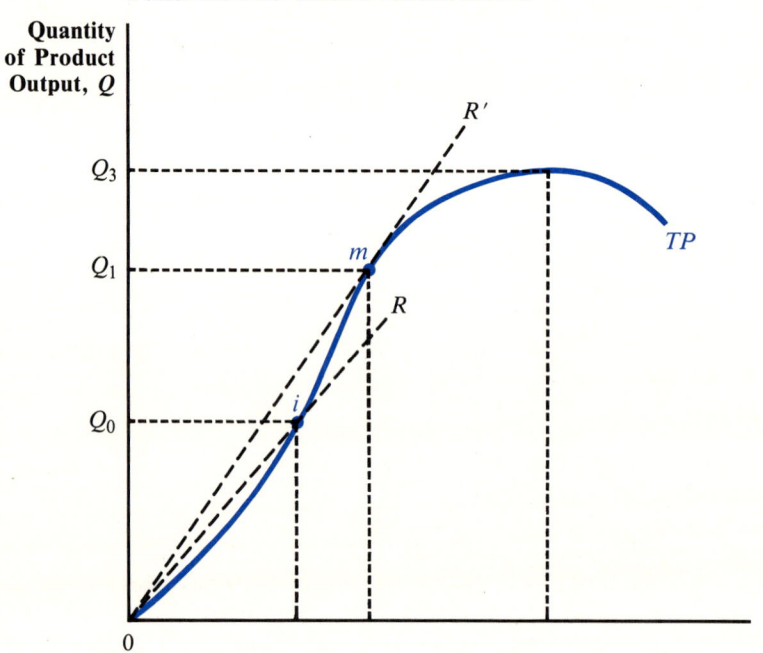

Panel A: The Total-Product Curve

Panel B: Marginal-Product and Average-Product Curves

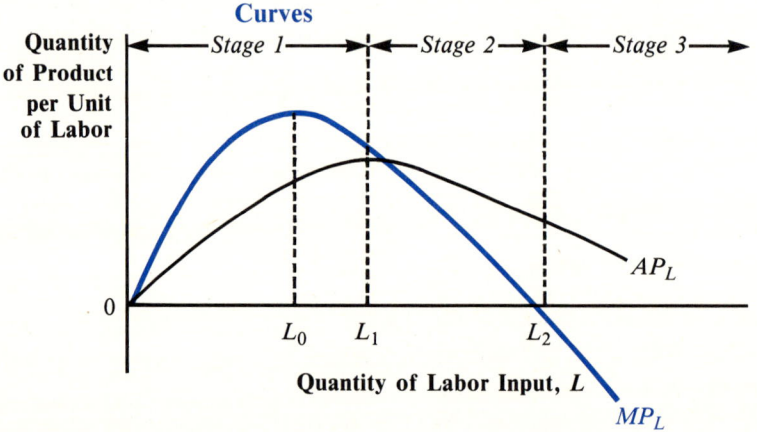

Panel A graphs the short-run production function TP. The slope of ray R is the average product of labor at point i. Average product reaches a maximum at point m on ray R'. In Panel B, the average-product curve is AP_L. Because the marginal product of labor is the slope of the TP curve at any point, it is also equal to the average product of labor at a labor-input level of L_1 (the labor input level corresponding to point m on the TP curve). The MP_L curve initially rises, reaching a peak when labor input is L_0 (the labor-input level corresponding to inflection point i on the TP curve) and then declines. Stage 1 is the range of labor input up to L_1, Stage 2 is the range up to labor input L_2, and Stage 3 is the range after L_2.

prove extremely beneficial; doubling the number of workers from 1 to 2 would cut in half both the time involved in moving between job stations and the number of specialized tasks. The benefits of going from 2 to 3 workers might be larger yet. Doubling the workforce from 500 to 1,000 would also be extremely beneficial, because each worker could specialize in one task and no one need run around from job station to job station. As more workers were added, they would start doubling up at work stations. This would also add output at first, as more than one task might be required at each station. But as more and more workers were added, the extra output generated by each worker would become smaller and smaller. Eventually, in a fixed automobile-assembly plant, there could be so many workers as to clog the production process. Eventually—say, with 300,000 workers in a plant suited for 2,000 workers—automobile production would grind to a halt. Thus, the marginal product of labor should at first rise, then reach a maximum, and then decline.

The Three Stages of Production

Figure 7-6 illustrates the relationships between the total-product curve, the average-product curve, and the marginal-product curve. Panel A shows the total-product curve, TP. We know that the marginal product of labor, MP_L, is given by the slope of the TP curve at any point. The average product of labor, AP_L can be determined for any level of labor input by drawing a ray from the origin to the corresponding point on the TP curve. For example, the slope of ray R, drawn from the origin through inflection point i, is the average product of labor for L_0 units of labor because $Q_0/L_0 = AP_L$.

The maximum average product of labor is shown by the steepest ray, R', touching the TP curve at point m. The average product of labor at point i (or at any point below m) will be less than the marginal product of labor at that point, because the slope of a ray through any point below m is smaller than the slope of the short-run production function at that point. Thus, in Panel B, we show that for all labor inputs up to L_1, MP_L is greater than AP_L. When the labor input equals L_1, at the point where a ray from the origin is just tangent to the total product curve (point m in Panel A), then $AP_L = MP_L$. At point m, the slope of the ray is identical to the slope of the TP curve. When the labor input is L_0, the marginal product of labor is at its maximum. Point i (the inflection point) corresponds to the maximum marginal product of labor.

The entire range of inputs from 0 to L_1 is known as the *first stage of production*. Stage 1 is characterized by an increasing average product of labor, with the marginal product of labor necessarily exceeding the average product. In this stage, there is too much of the fixed factor and too little of the variable factor. In effect, the variable factor is spread too thinly over the relatively large amount of the fixed factor. In this stage, the marginal product of the fixed factor is likely to be negative (and must be negative if there are constant returns to scale).[9] For example, a single worker trying to produce cars in a modern assembly plant would be so busy going from station to station that it could take as much as a year to produce a single car. But the same worker might be able to produce a car in a month working with the proper equipment in a small garage.

When the average product of labor reaches its maximum, the marginal product equals the average. Any additional labor inputs are associated with a marginal product of labor less than the average. The average product of labor, thus, falls when the labor input is increased beyond the input level L_1. The *second stage of production* begins where the average product of labor exceeds the marginal product of labor. Eventually, it is even possible (but by no means necessary) for the marginal product of labor to become negative. In Figure 7-6, it is assumed that $MP_L = 0$ at input level L_2. The range of Stage 2 is from input level L_1 to level L_2. The second stage of production is the economically relevant stage, because in the other stages the marginal products of labor or capital are negative.

In the *third stage of production*, the marginal product of labor is negative. This stage occurs when there is too much labor relative to capital: labor is spread so overabundantly over the fixed stock of capital that the production process becomes clogged with workers. The third stage is symmetrical with the first stage, where there is too much capital relative to labor.

The relationships between the average and marginal products of labor in the three stages are:

Stage 1: $AP_L < MP_L$.
Stage 2: $AP_L > MP_L$.
Stage 3: $AP_L > 0 > MP_L$.

Recall from Chapter 5 that, according to the average/marginal rule, the average product of labor must be rising in Stage 1 because labor's marginal product exceeds it; labor's average product must be falling in Stages 2 and 3 because labor's marginal product falls short of it.

The Economic Region of Production

What does the isoquant map look like when one of the marginal products becomes negative? Because the slope of an isoquant is $\Delta K/\Delta L = -MP_L/MP_K$, the isoquant will be positively sloped in the third stage, where MP_L is negative.

---

9. Euler's equation in footnote 7 can be used to prove that if the marginal product of labor exceeds the average product of labor, the marginal product of capital must be negative when there are constant returns to scale. Euler's equation can be rewritten as $AP_L = MP_L + (K/L)MP_K$ by dividing both sides of the equation by L. Obviously, $MP_L > AP_L$ can only take place if $MP_K < 0$.

FIGURE 7-7 The Economic Region of Production

When the marginal products of labor or capital become negative, the isoquants are positively sloped in the regions where one is negative and the other is positive. Along isoquant Q_1, for example, MP_L is zero at point b and negative to the right of b; and MP_K is zero at point a and negative to the left of point a. The lines H and G—called *ridge lines*—enclose the area of economically relevant production.

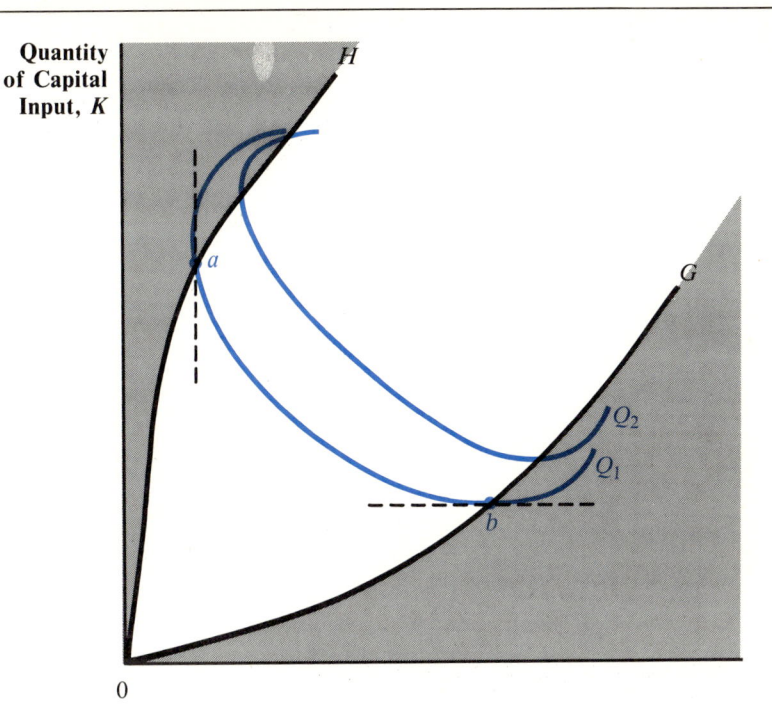

Figure 7-7 is an isoquant map on which the shaded regions represent negative marginal products for either labor or capital. Along the Q_1 isoquant, the marginal products of labor and capital are both positive between points a and b. Thus, the slope of the isoquant is negative. This situation corresponds to Stage 2 production. At point b, however, MP_L equals zero; any additional labor has a negative marginal product. Therefore, beyond point b, in the shaded area, MP_L is negative and MP_K is positive. This situation corresponds to Stage 3 production. The isoquant Q_1 is positively sloped in the shaded area. By similar reasoning, MP_K equals zero at point a and MP_K is negative to the left of a. Thus, the isoquant begins to bend backward as it enters the first or third stage of production.

The **economic region of production** requires positive, or at least nonnegative, marginal products. The curves G and H connect all those points for which $MP_L = 0$ and $MP_K = 0$, respectively. The marginal rate of technical substitution of capital for labor is zero along line G and infinity along line H, as shown by the dashed tangents. These *ridge lines* G and H, enclose the area of economically relevant production (the unshaded area). In the long run, a firm does not have to produce where marginal products are negative, because all inputs are variable.

The **economic region of production** is that range of input combinations for a given level of output where the marginal products of the inputs are positive.

FIGURE 7-8　　A Leontief Production Function: No Substitution

If capital and labor cannot be effectively substituted for one another, the isoquants will be right-angled at the fixed proportion of capital to labor.

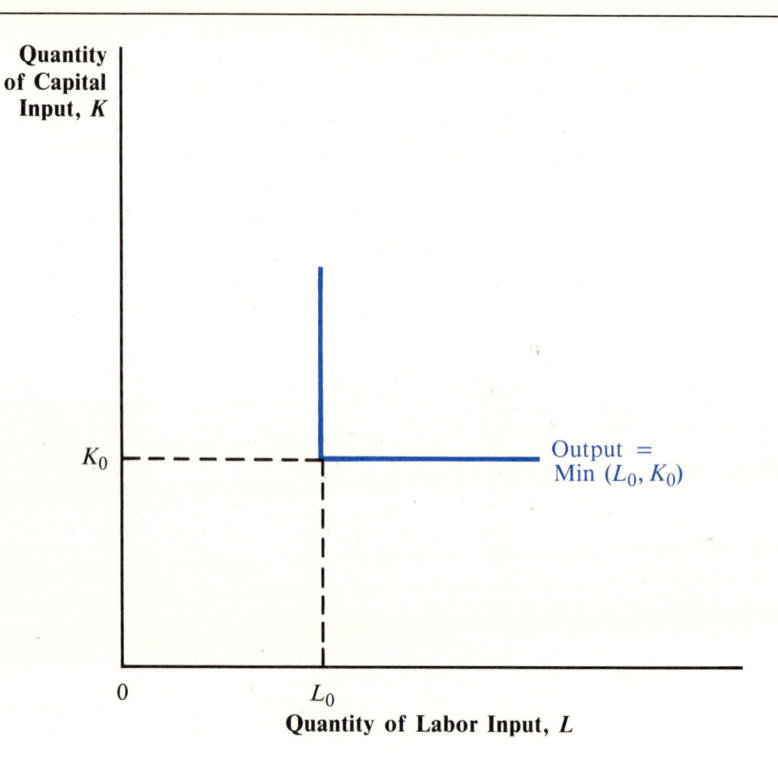

[Graph: Quantity of Capital Input, K on vertical axis; Quantity of Labor Input, L on horizontal axis. A right-angled isoquant with corner at (L_0, K_0), labeled Output = Min (L_0, K_0).]

THE ELASTICITY OF SUBSTITUTION

The curvature of the production isoquants indicates the ease with which one input can be substituted for another. The more convex the curve, the harder it is to substitute one input for another; the less convex the curve, the easier it is to substitute one input for another.

Figure 7-8 illustrates the extreme case, in which substitution of capital for labor is the most difficult. Capital and labor are used in fixed proportions. Assume that every unit of capital requires one unit of labor (for example, one shovel and one digger). This type of production function is described by the following formula:

$$Q = \text{Min}(L, K).$$

Such a production function is called a *Leontief production function* in honor of Wassily Leontief, who described the American economy in such terms.

This particular Leontief function states that output equals the minimum of the labor or capital input, so that no additional unit of either capital or labor

FIGURE 7-9 Perfect Substitution

When inputs are perfect substitutes, the isoquants are straight lines. The marginal rate of technical substitution of capital for labor is constant.

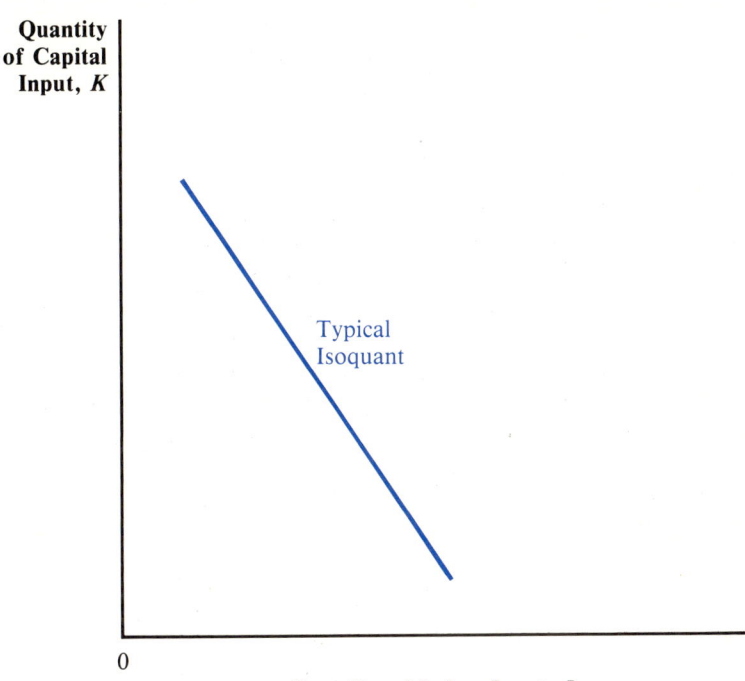

[Graph: Quantity of Capital Input, K on vertical axis; Quantity of Labor Input, L on horizontal axis; a downward-sloping straight line labeled "Typical Isoquant"]

will have any impact on output. For example, two diggers with one shovel will be no more productive than one in digging ditches (discounting rest periods). The isoquants for this function form a right angle at the fixed proportion of capital to labor, and the Leontief production function exhibits constant returns to scale.

If, at the opposite extreme, units of capital and labor are perfectly substitutable for each other, the isoquants will be straight lines. In Figure 7-9, the marginal rate of technical substitution (*MRTS*) is constant and does not fall as the capital-to-labor ratio (*K/L*) changes. An example of such substitutability is the use of women or men in a particular activity. If women are better at the activity than men, three men may be needed to do the same job as two women. The effectiveness of men versus women, however, may not depend at all on the ratio of men to women used. Another example of substitutability is a situation in which two types of fertilizer in agricultural production may be perfect substitutes.

Notice that in Figure 7-8 any *MRTS* is compatible with the same, fixed *K/L* ratio; and in Figure 7-9 one *MRTS* is compatible with any *K/L* ratio. The two cases are polar extremes.

FIGURE 7-10 Elasticity of Substitution

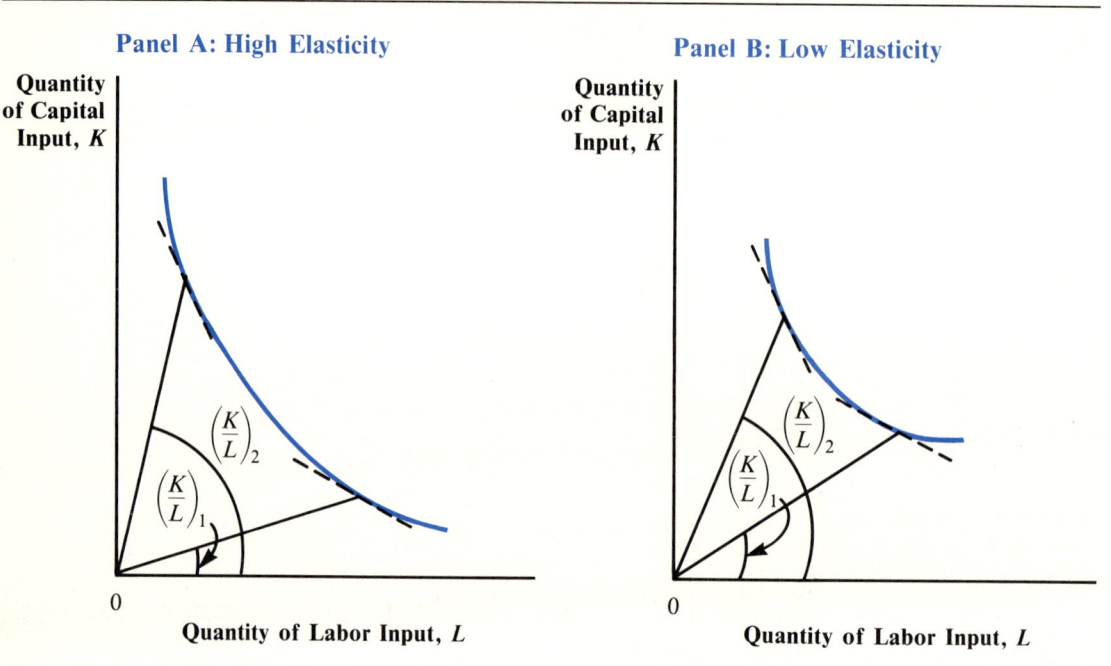

Panel A: High Elasticity

Panel B: Low Elasticity

The elasticity of substitution is greater in Panel A than in Panel B. In Panel A, a small change in *MRTS* is associated with a large change in *K/L*; in Panel B, the same change in *MRTS* is associated with a small change in *K/L*.

PRACTICE EXERCISE 7-2

Q. Assume that a production function is $Q = L^{0.75}K^{0.25}$. It can be shown by calculus that $MP_L = 0.75(K/L)^{0.25}$ and $MP_K = 0.25(L/K)^{0.75}$.

1. Show that the law of diminishing returns holds.
2. Because the function exhibits constant returns to scale, apply Equation (5).
3. Calculate the marginal rate of technical substitution of capital for labor.
4. What is the elasticity of substitution?

A. 1. The law of diminishing returns holds because if L increases, holding K constant, K/L falls and, therefore, $0.75(K/L)^{0.25}$ also falls.
2. $Q = 0.75(K/L)^{0.25} L + 0.25(L/K)^{0.75}K = 0.75K^{0.25}L^{0.75} + 0.25L^{0.75}K^{0.25} = L^{0.75}K^{0.25}$.
3. $MRTS = MP_L/MP_K = 0.75(K/L)^{0.25}/0.25(L/K)^{0.75} = 3(K/L)$.
4. The elasticity of substitution equals unity because when $MRTS = 3(K/L)$, a 1 percentage point rise in *MRTS* must cause K/L to rise by 1 percentage point.

EXAMPLE 7–3 The Substitutability of Capital and Labor

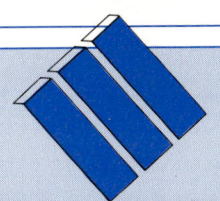

The elasticity of substitution gives a measurement of the flexibility of production methods. The Cobb-Douglas production function assumes that the elasticity of substitution between inputs is unity; the Leontief production function assumes it is zero, which means there is no flexibility. Some selected estimates are shown in the accompanying table. Production methods appear to be flexible in all the industries shown, with the exception of apparel production. But even there, elasticity of substitution is still significantly different from zero.

Source: K. Arrow, H. B. Chenery, B. Minhas, and R. M. Solow, "Capital/Labor Substitution and Economic Efficiency," *Review of Economics and Statistics* 43 (August 1961): 225–50.

Industry	Elasticity of Substitution of Capital for Labor
Metal mining	1.41
Agriculture	1.20
Paper	1.14
Nonferrous metals	1.10
Iron and steel	1.00
Fishing	0.94
Coal mining	0.93
Processed food	0.93
Textiles	0.80
Apparel	0.42

The **elasticity of substitution (σ)** is the percentage change in the capital/output ratio divided by the percentage change in the marginal rate of technical substitution along a given isoquant.

In the ordinary case, each *MRTS* will be associated with a particular *K/L* ratio along any given isoquant. The higher is the *MRTS*, the higher will be the *K/L* ratio. In Panel A of Figure 7–10, a relatively small change in *MRTS* causes a large change in *K/L*; in Panel B of Figure 7–10, a relatively large change in *MRTS* causes a small change in *K/L*. The **elasticity of substitution (σ)** measures the responsiveness of the *K/L* ratio to the *MRTS*. It is measured by dividing the percentage change in the capital/labor ratio by the percentage change in the marginal rate of technical substitution. (See Practice Exercise 7–2.)

In Panel A of Figure 7–10, elasticity is high; in Panel B, it is low. In Figure 7–8, there is no elasticity; in Figure 7–9, elasticity is infinite. Economists have estimated elasticities of substitution for various industries (see Example 7–3). When inputs are aggregated into the two broad categories of labor and capital, the estimated elasticities tend to be around unity.

SUMMARY

1. The production function describes the maximum output that can be produced from a given set of inputs. There are increasing, constant, or decreasing returns to scale as a given percentage increase in all inputs causes output to increase by a larger percentage, the same percentage, or a smaller percentage, respectively. The marginal product of an input is the change in output per unit of change in the input. The law of diminishing returns states that the marginal product of an input eventually declines as more of the input is added, holding all other inputs fixed.

2. An isoquant shows the combinations of inputs yielding the same output and is convex to the origin. The marginal rate of technical substitution (*MRTS*) of capital for labor is the rate at which capital can be substituted for labor without affecting output. Convexity has also been called the law of diminishing marginal rate of technical substitution as labor is substituted for capital along an isoquant.

3. In the short run, input levels are fixed. The shape of the short-run production function is explained by variations in the amount of labor per unit of fixed input.

4. The elasticity of substitution is the percentage change in the *K/L* ratio for each one percent change in the marginal rate of technical substitution. Elasticity is the ease with which units of capital and labor input can be substituted for each other.

QUESTIONS AND PROBLEMS

1. Define the production function when more than one output is produced (think of the myriad of products derived from petroleum).

2. Consider the production function in Table A, which lists the output quantity for each combination of capital and labor inputs.

Table A

Units of Output

Capital Input (machine hours), K	1	2	3	4
4	30	53	73	92
3	24	42	58	73
2	17	30	42	53
1	10	17	24	30

Labor Input (worker hours), L

Table B

Quantity of Labor Input (worker hours), L	Quantity of Output (units), Q
0	0
1	10
2	25
3	45
4	60
5	70
6	78
7	84
8	88

    a. Sketch the Output = 30 isoquant.
    b. Does the law of diminishing returns apply?
    c. Are there increasing, constant, or decreasing returns to scale?
    d. Draw the total-product (TP) curve for Output = 2; the average-product curve AP_L; and the marginal-product curve MP_L.

3. Construct an output table similar to the one in Problem 2 for the production function $Q = 10(LK)^{0.5}$. Are there constant returns to scale? Draw a typical isoquant.

4. Draw the isoquants for the production function $Q = 2L + K$ and the production function $Q = \text{Min}(2L, K)$.

5. Explain why $MRTS = MP_L/MP_K$.

6. Consider the short-run production function in Table B.
    a. Draw the TP, AP_L, and MP_L curves.
    b. Where does AP_L reach its maximum?

7. Suppose $Q = CL^aK^{1-a}$, where $C > 0$ and $0 < a < 1$. It can be shown that $MP_L = aC(K/L)^{1-a}$ and $MP_K = (1-a)C(L/K)^a$.
    a. What is the $MRTS_{KL}$?
    b. What is the elasticity of substitution? Is the production function homothetic?

8. Suppose MP_K is never zero but $MP_L = 0$ whenever L exceeds or equals K. Draw the isoquant map and the economic region of production.

SUGGESTED READINGS

Arrow, K., H. B. Chenery, B. Minhas, and R. M. Solow. "Capital/Labor Substitution and Economic Efficiency." *Review of Economics and Statistics* 43 (August 1961).

Douglas, Paul H., "Are There Laws of Production?" *American Economic Review* 38 (March 1948): 1–41.

Ferguson, C. E. *The Neoclassical Theory of Production and Distribution*. New York: Cambridge University Press, 1969.

Walters, A. A. *An Introduction to Econometrics*. New York: W.W. Norton, 1970, chap. 10.

CHAPTER 8

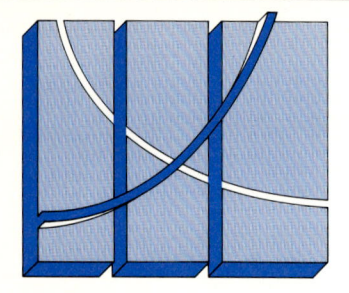

THE COSTS OF PRODUCTION

The last chapter examined the laws of production. The costs of producing goods and services reflect (1) the productivity of the inputs, (2) the opportunity costs of the inputs, and (3) the economic efficiency with which the inputs are used. This chapter examines the costs of production in both the short run and the long run. Since similar laws govern costs for all firms, this chapter forms the foundation for the chapters on competition, monopoly, and oligopoly.

OPPORTUNITY COSTS

To make correct business decisions, the firm must look at both revenues and costs. If either revenue or cost is misunderstood, the firm can make incorrect or poor decisions. The concept of cost is particularly elusive. If costs are underestimated, the firm will do too much; if costs are overestimated, the firm will do too little. What are the appropriate costs of doing business? Logical analysis suggests that the appropriate concept of cost is the notion of **opportunity costs.** Any action involving scarce resources involves sacrifices. The value of those sacrifices constitutes the cost of the action. What makes the concept of opportunity cost elusive is that some costs are not explicit.

The **opportunity cost** of any activity is the value of the best forgone alternative.

Generally speaking, the price that is paid for anything reflects its opportunity cost. In order for a firm to attract resources, it must pay for those resources. Opportunity cost is not always the same as the original money cost. For example, in inflationary times the replacement cost of a good exceeds its original money cost. Following the principle of paying attention to opportunity cost, the current cost rather than the historical cost is used as a basis for pricing items in a wide range of businesses. Many shoppers have had the experience of buying a product in the grocery store with a "stack"

EXAMPLE 8–1 Opportunity Cost

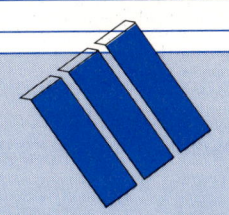

A dramatic example illustrates the difference between accounting cost and opportunity cost. Imagine that a machine used in the production of some product lasts forever and that new machines are exactly the same as old ones. These assumptions allow us to concentrate on opportunity cost without the complicating factors of depreciation or "lemons" (products that do not work well). Under these circumstances, there will be a market for such machines, and all such machines will sell for the same price.

Assume that you have discovered a use for the machine that will generate for you $1,500 a year in net revenue (after paying for any necessary labor and raw materials). Whether it is worthwhile to buy the machine or not depends on the cost of using the machine. What is that cost?

Suppose you purchase the machine for $20,000 from a particular dealer but immediately discover that the machine's market value is only $10,000. The dealer ripped you off for $10,000. If there is no legal recourse, what is your optimal action? Under these circumstances, you have only two options: use the machine or sell it. If you sell the machine, you will receive its replacement cost, $10,000, which you can put in a bank for $1,000 per year (assuming the interest rate is 10 percent per year). If you use the machine, you can earn $1,500 per year. Clearly, it is better, by the amount of $500 per year, to keep the machine. The opportunity cost of using the machine is the sacrificed interest—namely, $1,000 a year. Notice that what you paid for the machine has absolutely no relevance to the correct economic decision. In this case, the original money cost of the machine does not correspond to either its replacement cost or its opportunity cost.

---

of price tags on it, reflecting the fact that when the good was bought the grocery store paid less than the current opportunity cost for the good. (See Example 8–1.)

Explicit and Implicit Costs

A great many costs that the business firm incurs are explicit: labor costs, raw-material costs, interest charges, taxes, rents, and so forth. Explicit costs are often called *accounting costs* because these highly visible costs are the focus of accounting procedures. But a number of opportunity costs are implicit: the sacrificed wages of the entrepreneur's own time; the sacrificed interest for the entrepreneur's own capital; depreciation (the fall in value of capital goods as they are used). Whenever the term *costs* is not otherwise defined, we mean opportunity costs, which include both explicit and implicit costs.

Accounting Profit Versus Economic Profit

Economic profit is revenue minus opportunity cost.

Accounting profit can be defined as revenue minus accounting costs, where accounting costs include explicit costs and depreciation. Accounting profit should be sharply contrasted to **economic profit**, the difference between revenue and opportunity cost. In general, economic profit equals accounting profit minus the value of the entrepreneur's time and capital. For example, Walt the grocer has yearly accounting profits of $40,000. But he could have earned $30,000 working as a manager elsewhere, and his $50,000 worth of personal capital could have earned, say, $4,000 in interest. Without any changes in the replacement costs of his inventories, his economic profit is $40,000 − $34,000 = $6,000. In normal circumstances, accounting profit will exceed economic profit. Indeed, if accounting profit is zero, a business firm may be on its way to bankruptcy; if economic profit is zero, the firm is earning exactly what its resources could earn in their best alternative employment.

LONG-RUN COSTS

The firm interested in maximizing its profit must, of course, minimize its cost of production for any given volume of output. Suppose that the long-run production function is $Q = F(L, K)$. Because in the long run all inputs are variable, the firm will choose that combination of labor (L) and capital (K) inputs that minimizes costs for any given output (Q).

Labor is paid per unit of time, explicitly; capital may be purchased all at once rather than being rented. To put labor and capital on the same basis, the price of capital should be expressed as the opportunity cost of using the capital per unit of time. The opportunity cost of capital is the sacrificed interest on the dollars tied up in capital goods (such as machines), plus the depreciation of the capital goods over the relevant time period. (In exceptional circumstances, capital goods may appreciate, and the appreciation must be deducted from the sacrificed interest to obtain the opportunity cost of capital.) In the following sections, the price of capital will be denoted by the equivalent rental price, r, per unit of time. The wage rate will be the explicit wage rate, w, per unit of time.

Isocost Curves

The cost, C, of any bundle of inputs (L, K) is

$$C = wL + rK, \tag{1}$$

where L represents the number of worker hours and K represents the number of machine hours. It will be assumed in this chapter that whatever quantity of capital or labor the firm uses, the factor prices, w and r, remain the same. In other words, the firm behaves like a perfect competitor in factor markets by taking factor prices as given.

LONG-RUN COSTS

FIGURE 8-1   An Isocost Curve

The isocost line, *TC*, for a given level of total costs is a straight line with the absolute slope *w/r*, where *w* is the wage rate and *r* the rental price of capital. The vertical intercept is at *C/r* units of capital input; the horizontal intercept is at *C/w* units of labor input.

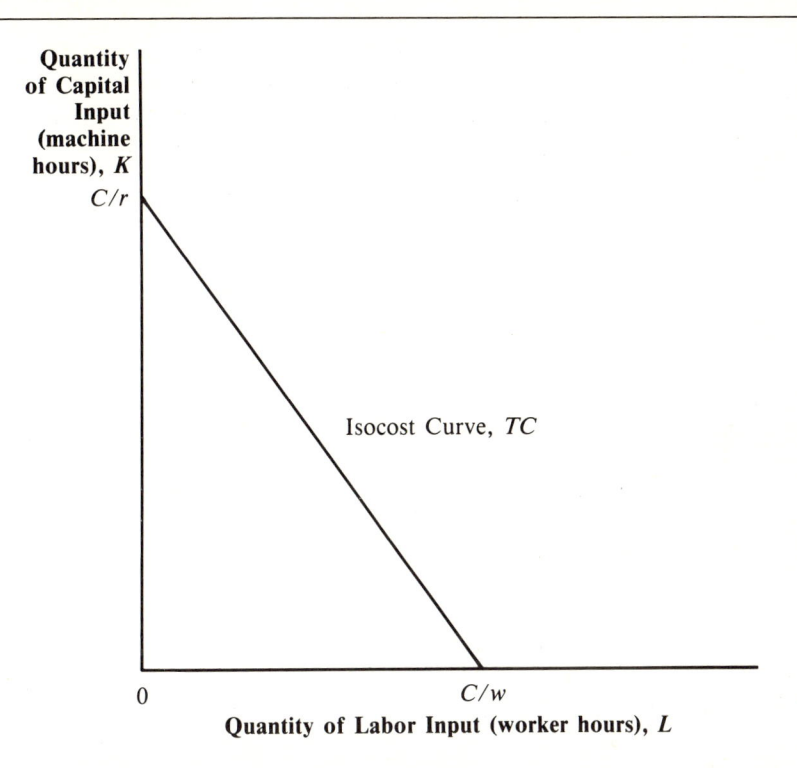

Quantity of Capital Input (machine hours), K

C/r

Isocost Curve, *TC*

0   *C/w*

Quantity of Labor Input (worker hours), L

The **isocost line** represents all the combinations of inputs that cost the same amount.

Figure 8-1 illustrates an **isocost line**, the graph of various combinations of labor and capital inputs that cost the same. The isocost line is linear if wages and rents are independent of the quantities of labor and capital hired by the firm. Solving Equation (1) for *K*, the equation for the isocost curve corresponding to cost level *C* is:

$$K = C/r - (w/r)L. \qquad (2)$$

It is clear that if $L = 0$ hours, then $K = C/r$; if $K = 0$ hours, then $L = C/w$. In Figure 8-1, the vertical intercept is *C/r* and the horizontal intercept is *C/w*. The intercept points indicate, respectively, the maximum number of hours of capital or labor that can be used without exceeding the budget, *C*. For example, assume that costs, *C*, are $2,160. If $w = $240 per worker per week and $r = $180 per machine per week, then the maximum number of workers per week that can be used without exceeding the budget is $2,160 ÷ $240 = 9 workers, and the maximum number of machines that can be used per week is $2,160 ÷ $180 = 12 machines.

The absolute slope of an isocost line measures the rate at which units of capital can be substituted for units of labor without changing costs. Costs are constant along an isocost curve. If the quantities *K* and *L* change and *C* does not change, then

FIGURE 8-2   A Family of Isocost Curves

The isocost curves shift upward as total cost increases from *TC* to *TC'* to *TC''*. For a given wage/rent pair (*w*, *r*), the upward shift is parallel.

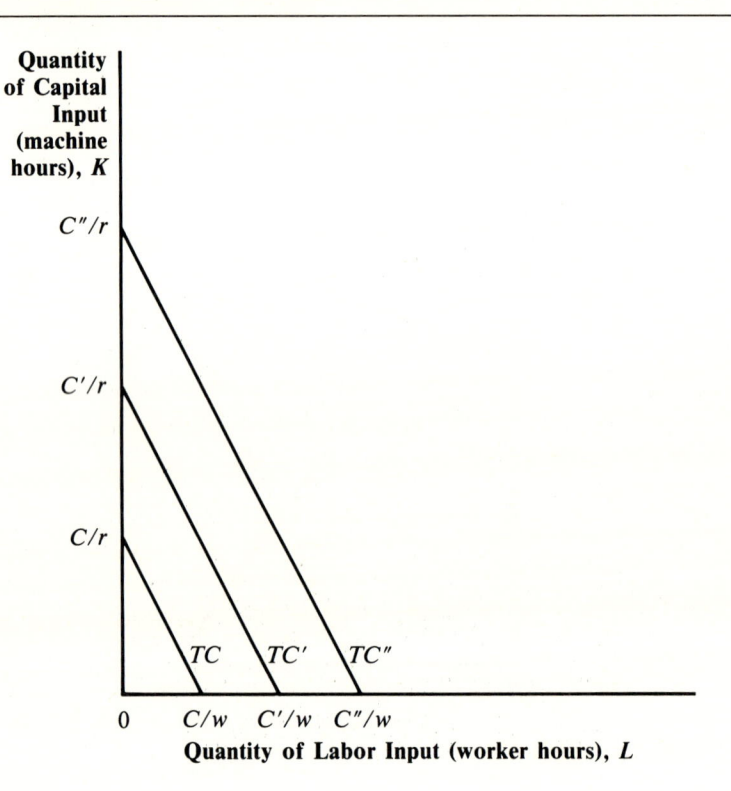

Quantity of Capital Input (machine hours), K — intercepts *C/r*, *C'/r*, *C''/r*; horizontal intercepts *C/w*, *C'/w*, *C''/w*; curves labeled *TC*, *TC'*, *TC''*.

Quantity of Labor Input (worker hours), *L*

$$\Delta C = 0 = w\Delta L + r\Delta K, \tag{3}$$

or, rearranging terms,

$$\Delta K/\Delta L = -w/r. \tag{4}$$

Thus, the absolute slope of the isocost curve in Figure 8–1 is w/r, or the relative price of labor in terms of capital. When $w = \$240$ and $r = \$180$, $w/r = 1.33$, which means that 1.33 machine hours cost the same as 1 worker hour. The absolute slope of an isocost curve can also be determined from the ratio of the vertical and horizontal intercepts,

$$\frac{C/r}{C/w} = \frac{C}{r} \times \frac{w}{C} = \frac{w}{r}. \tag{5}$$

For any given wage/rent pair, there is an entire family of isocost curves, one for every level of cost. Figure 8–2 shows that the higher is the overall cost, the greater is the distance from the corresponding isocost curve to the origin. When $C'' > C' > C$, the horizontal intercepts are C''/w, C'/w, and C/w. Because the slope of each isocost curve is the same ratio w/r, the isocost curves are parallel.

LONG-RUN COSTS

FIGURE 8–3   Minimizing Cost for a Given Output

The minimum cost of producing output level Q' is achieved at point e, where the isoquant Q' is tangent to the lowest isocost curve, TC. Point e represents the optimal input combination (K_0, L_0). Input combinations d and f lie on higher isocost curves.

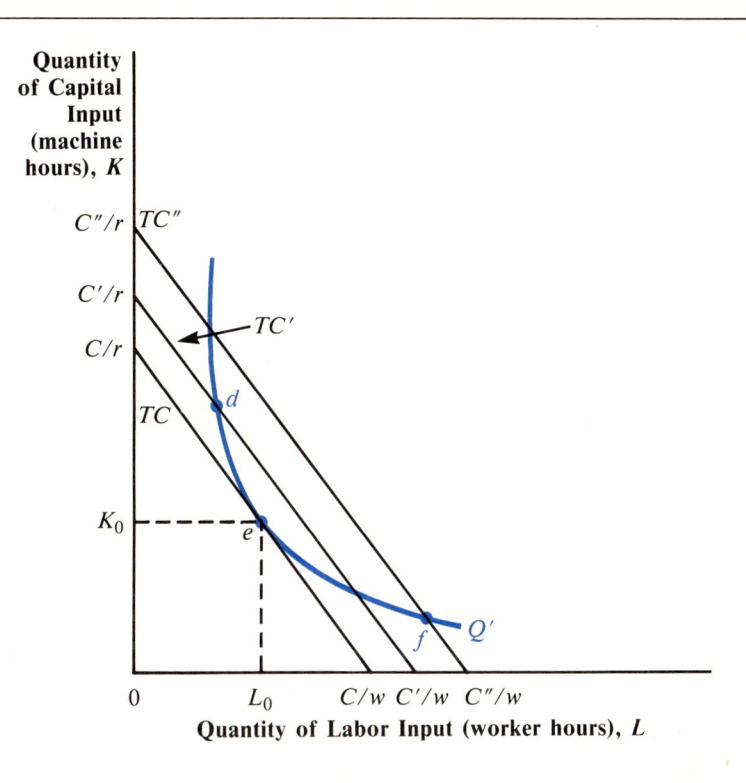

The Optimal Combination of Inputs

Consider now the problem of choosing the optimal combination of inputs. The objective of the firm is to maximize profits. On the cost side of its equation, it must either minimize the cost of producing any given output or maximize the output from any given cost expenditure.

Minimizing the Cost of a Given Output

Let us begin by analyzing the problem of minimizing the cost of achieving some particular level of output, Q'. In Figure 8–3, Q' is the isoquant (see Chapter 7) for that quantity of output. Now superimpose a family of isocost curves on this lone isoquant. The lowest isocost line compatible with producing Q' units of output is clearly TC. The firm will choose the input combination (L_0, K_0), which lies on both isoquant Q' and isocost line TC. Any other input combination will cost more. For example, input combinations d and f cost C' and C'', respectively, which correspond to the higher isocost curves TC' and TC''.

The least cost of producing a given output is achieved when the slope of the isoquant equals the slope of the lowest isocost curve. As discussed in

FIGURE 8-4   Maximizing Output for a Given Cost

Maximum output is achieved for the given isocost line, *TC*, by moving to point *e* on line *TC* where the isocost line is tangent to the highest production isoquant, *Q'*.

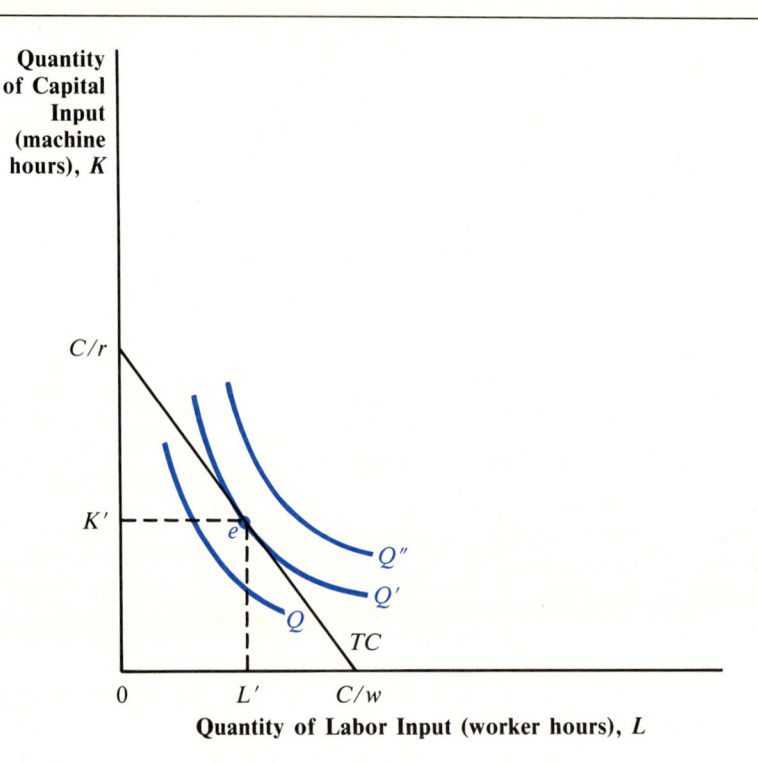

Chapter 7, the absolute slope of an isoquant is the marginal rate of technical substitution (*MRTS*) of capital (*K*) for labor (*L*), which equals the ratio of the marginal products of these inputs: $MRTS_{KL} = MP_L/MP_K$. Since the absolute slope of an isocost line is w/r, the least cost of producing quantity *Q'* is achieved when

$$MRTS = MP_L/MP_K = w/r \qquad (6)$$

PRACTICE EXERCISE 8-1

Q. Suppose the total-cost budget is $C = \$2,000$ per week, wages (w) are $400 per worker per week and rental (r) on capital is $200 per machine per week. What is the isocost line? Show how the isocost line would shift if r fell to $100. In each case, what is the slope in absolute terms?

A. When $w = \$400$ and $r = \$200$, the isocost line is a line running from $K = 10$ to $L = 5$. When r falls to $100, the isocost line runs from $K = 20$ to $L = 5$. The absolute slope increases from 2 to 4, because w/r increases from 2 to 4.

LONG-RUN COSTS

for the function

$$Q' = F(L, K). \tag{7}$$

These two equations determine the optimal input combination (L, K) that minimizes cost for the output level Q'.

Maximizing Output from a Given Cost Outlay

To approach the optimal combination from a different standpoint, suppose the firm is working with a fixed budget for costs. Economic efficiency requires that output be maximized. Figure 8-4 shows a family of isoquant curves in relation to isocost curve TC from Figure 8-3. Maximum output is obtained by allocating labor and capital along isocost line TC until it is tangent to the highest possible isoquant, Q'. The optimal input combination (K', L') is located at point e. The only difference between the two approaches is that the second satisfies the following equations:

$$MRTS_{KL} = MP_L/MP_K = w/r \tag{8}$$

$$C = wL + rK. \tag{9}$$

Equations (6) and (8) are the same. Equation (7) represents a given isoquant, while Equation (9) represents a given isocost line. Clearly, if the maximum output arising from Equations (8) and (9) is the same as the output for which Equations (6) and (7) determine minimal cost, both approaches lead to the optimal input combination.

The intuition behind the condition $MP_L/MP_K = w/r$ can be seen by rewriting it as

$$MP_L/w = MP_K/r. \tag{10}$$

The **least-cost rule** states that to maximize output for a given cost outlay or to minimize total cost for a given output, the marginal product per wage dollar (MP_L/w) must equal the marginal product per capital-rent dollar (MP_L/r).

Equation (10) is the **least-cost rule**, which states that to maximize output for a given cost outlay or to minimize total cost for a given output, the extra output per wage dollar (MP_L/w) must equal the extra output per capital-goods dollar (MP_K/r). If, for example, MP_L/w is greater than MP_K/r, the firm could switch a dollar of spending from capital to labor and increase output by the difference, $MP_L/w - MP_K/r$. Such a substitution of labor for capital would continue until the least-cost rule was satisfied.

The Output Expansion Path

It is probably most useful to think of the firm as minimizing the cost of achieving any given level of output. The corresponding level of cost depends on the output quantity Q and the wage/rent pair (w, r). Indeed, the solution e in Figures 8-3 and 8-4 depends on the three factors, Q, w, and r. The higher is the output quantity, the higher are the costs; the higher are input prices, the higher are costs.

FIGURE 8-5 Expansion Paths

Panel A: Output-Expansion Path for a General Production Function

Panel B: Output-Expansion Path for a Homothetic Production Function

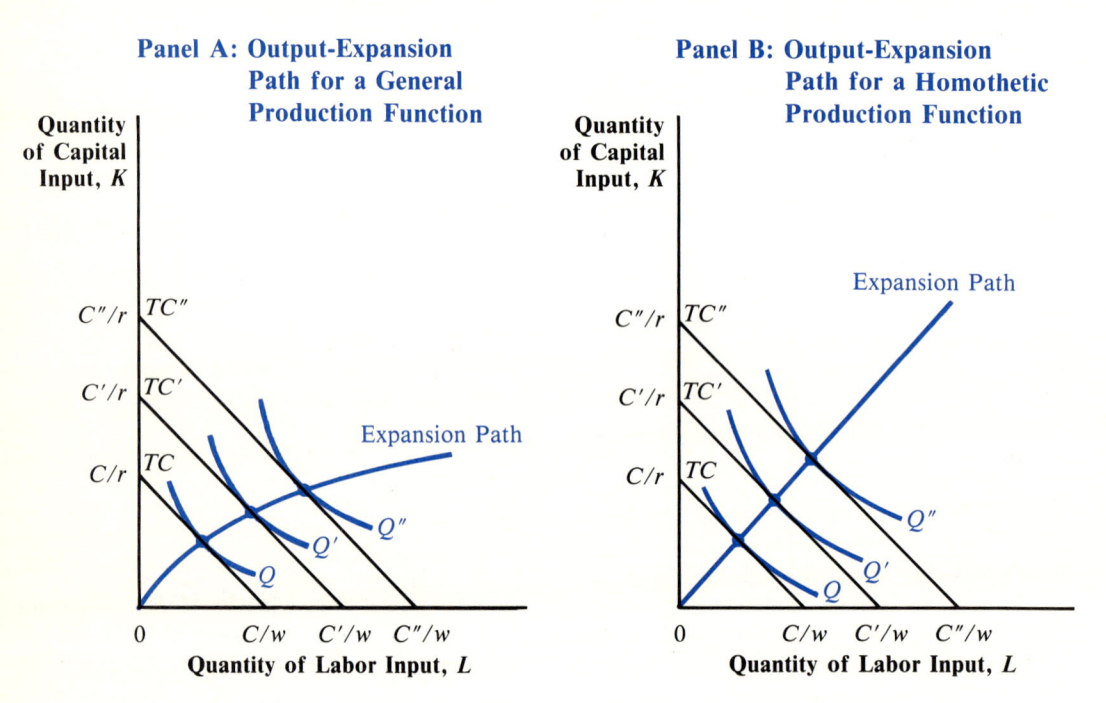

In general, the demand for capital and labor inputs may not be proportional to output. Panel A shows the expansion path for a general production function, while Panel B shows an *EP* curve for a homothetic production function, where quantities demanded do remain proportional. The resulting *EP* curve in Panel B is a straight line from the origin.

The **expansion path** (*EP*) shows the optimal combinations of labor and capital as output expands for any given wage/rent pair (w, r).

Figure 8-5 shows how the optimum input combination and the level of cost respond to higher output levels. The path followed by the various optimal combinations of labor and capital inputs is called the **expansion path** (*EP*).

Panel A of Figure 8-5 shows the expansion path, *EP*, for any general production function. The *EP* curve normally slopes upward, but it can be concave, convex, or concave and convex; it can even bend backward in unusual cases. In Panel A, the *EP* curve shows that as output expands, the input demands need not increase proportionately. Panel B shows the *EP* for any homothetic production function, which is a straight line through the origin. The expansion path for this function shows that as output expands, holding w/r constant, the demands for all inputs increase proportionately.

Long-Run Cost Curves

Notice that for each level of output along each expansion path in Figure 8-5 there is a unique level of cost, given a particular wage/rent pair. For exam-

FIGURE 8-6 Determining a Long-Run Total-Cost Curve

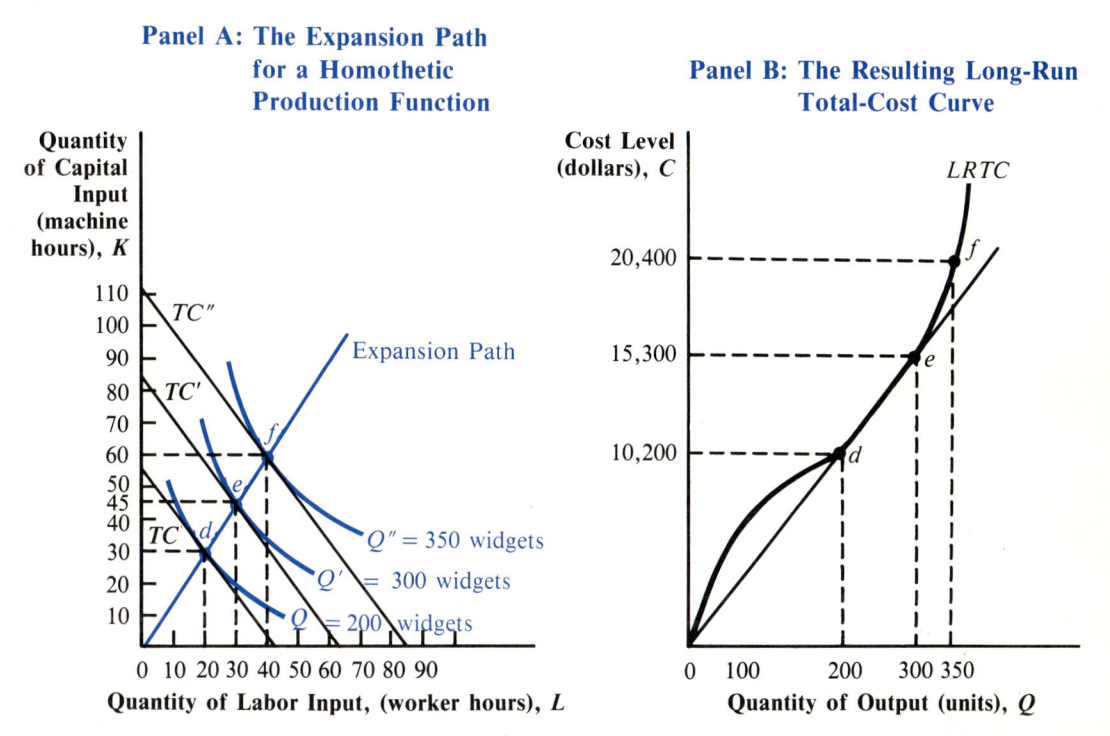

Panel A: The Expansion Path for a Homothetic Production Function

Panel B: The Resulting Long-Run Total-Cost Curve

Panel A shows the expansion path for a homothetic function in which there are increasing returns to scale up to point *d*, constant returns from *d* to *e*, and decreasing returns from *e* to *f*. In Panel B, the resulting long-run total-cost (*LRTC*) curve is graphed by plotting the association between output quantity and cost for each optimal input combination in Panel A.

The **long-run cost function** is the minimum cost of production for a given level of output and a given wage/rent pair. It may be written as $C = C(w, r, Q)$.

ple, the isoquant Q is associated with the isocost curve *TC*, which determines the pair of intercepts, C/r and C/w. The function relating w, r, and Q to costs is called the **long-run cost function**.[1]

Figure 8-6 illustrates how a long-run cost function can be determined. Panel A demonstrates the case of increasing returns to scale from the origin to point *d* along expansion path *EP*, constant returns to scale from point *d* to point *e*, and decreasing returns to scale from point *e* to point *f*. From *d* to *e*, inputs and output increase by 50 percent, but from *e* to *f* inputs increase by one third and output increases by one sixth. To determine the actual cost level, assume that $w = \$240$ per worker and $r = \$180$ per machine. When

---

1. The cost function is defined by

$$C = C(w, r, Q) = \underset{L, K}{\text{Minimum}} \; [wL + rK : F(L, K) = Q].$$

FIGURE 8-7   A Long-Run Average-Cost Curve

This long-run average cost (*LRAC*) curve is plotted for the hypothetical data used in Figure 8–6. The *LRAC* curve declines when there are increasing returns to scale (up to $Q = 200$), is constant when there are constant returns (from $Q = 200$ to $Q = 300$), and rises when there are increasing returns (after $Q = 300$). The minimum efficient scale (*MES*) is the output level of 200 units.

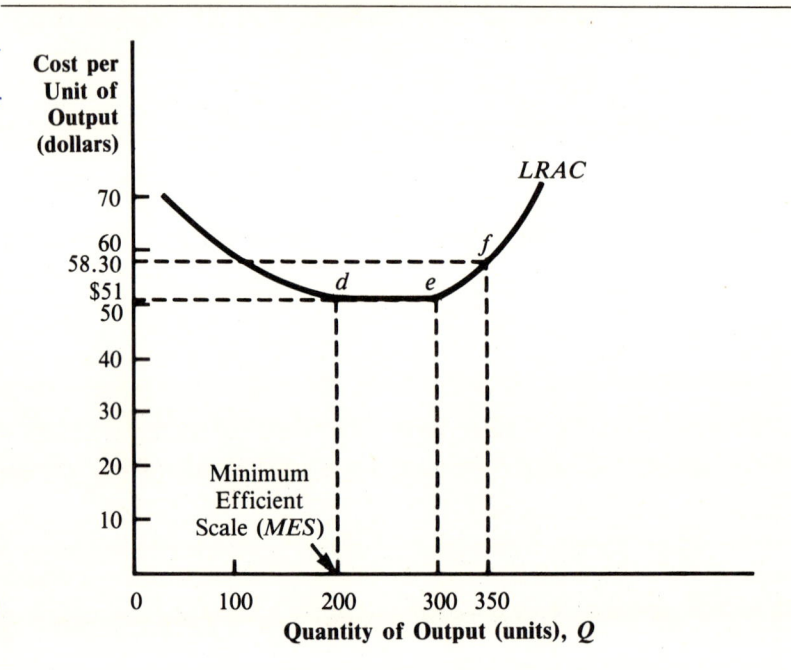

output is 200 units, cost is $10,200; when output is 300 units, cost is $15,300; when output is 350 units, cost is $20,400. Panel B shows the association between costs, *C*, and output, *Q*. Because wages and rents are held con-

---

PRACTICE EXERCISE 8–2

Q. Suppose $Q = A(LK)^{0.5}$. It is known (by calculus) that $MP_L = 0.5A(K/L)^{0.5}$ and $MP_K = 0.5A(L/K)^{0.5}$. What is the cost function for the wage/rent pair (w, r)?

A. The firm minimizes cost by equating *MRTS* with w/r. In this case, $MRTS = MP_L/MP_k = K/L$. It follows that $w/r = K/L$, or, multiplying out, $wL = rK$. The total level of costs is always $C = wL + rK$. But optimization requires that $wL = rK$. Eliminating K shows that $0.5C = wL$, and eliminating L shows that $0.5C = rK$. Substituting these back into the production function yields

$$Q = A(C/2w)^{0.5} (C/2r)^{0.5}.$$

Thus, solving for C, $C = 2Q(wr)^{0.5}/A$.

stant, the association of C and Q is called the long-run total-cost (*LRTC*) curve.[2]

The increasing, constant, and decreasing returns in Panel A of Figure 8-6 are reflected in the shape of the *LRTC* curve in Panel B. When there are increasing returns to scale, up to an output of 200 units, output increases at a faster rate than costs. Thus, up to 200 units of output, the *LRTC* curve is concave to the horizontal axis. During the range of constant returns to scale, from output of 200 to output of 300 units, output and cost increase at the same rate, and the *LRTC* curve is linear. Finally, when there are decreasing returns to scale, at output levels beyond 300 units, the *LRTC* curve is convex to the horizontal axis, because output increases at a rate slower than costs.

Long-Run Average Cost

The long-run average-cost (*LRAC*) curve shows the minimum cost of production per unit for each level of output. Implicit in any expansion path is a corresponding *LRAC* curve based on the formula

$$LRAC = LRTC/Q = \text{Min} \frac{(wL + rK)}{Q}. \tag{11}$$

From Equation (11) it is clear that increasing returns imply that long-run average cost falls as output increases (since costs increase proportionately less than Q); constant returns imply that the *LRAC* is constant (since costs increase in the same proportion as Q); decreasing returns imply that the *LRAC* increases as Q increases (since costs increase in a larger proportion than Q). Figure 8-7 shows the *LRAC* curve implicit in Figure 8-6. Thus,

---

2. The long-run cost function for the Cobb-Douglas production function discussed in Chapter 7, $Q = AL^a K^{1-a}$, can be derived in a straightforward way. First, the partial derivatives of the production function are $\partial Q/\partial L = aA(K/L)^a$ and $\partial Q/\partial K = (1 - a)A(L/K)^{1-a}$. Cost minimization requires that $MRTS = w/r$. Since in this case $MRTS = (\partial Q/\partial L)/(\partial Q/\partial K) = aK/(1 - a)L$, it follows that

$$w/r = aK/(1 - a)L. \tag{A}$$

For any L and K, costs are:

$$C = wL + rK = wL[1 + (r/w)(K/L)]. \tag{B}$$

Substituting Equation (A) into Equation (B) and eliminating K yields:

$$C = wL[1 + (r/w)(1 - a)w/ar] = wL[(a + 1 - a)/a] = wL/a. \tag{C}$$

Thus $aC = wL$. Labor costs are exactly the proportion a of total costs C. By symmetry, it is also true that if Equation (A) is substituted into Equation (B) and L is eliminated,

$$(1 - a)C = rK. \tag{D}$$

Substituting Equations (C) and (D) into the production function yields

$$Q = A[aC/w]^a [(1 - a)/r]^{1-a} = ACa^a(1 - a)^{1-a}/w^a r^{1-a}.$$

Rearranging terms yields

$$C = Qw^a r^{1-a}/Aa^a(1 - a)^{1-a}.$$

Notice that this cost function is very similar to the form of the Cobb-Douglas production function. The complex coefficient of Q in the final equation is simply long-run average cost; it is also long-run marginal cost, since the average is a constant.

when output is 200 units, long-run average cost per unit is $10,200 ÷ 200 = $51; when Q = 300 units, $LRAC$ = $15,300 ÷ 300 = $51; when Q = 350 units, $LRAC$ = $20,400 ÷ 350 = $58.30. The long-run average cost declines until Q = 200 units, is constant from Q = 200 to Q = 300 units, and rises after Q = 300 units.

The $LRAC$ curve in Figure 8-7 may be regarded as a typical, real-world cost curve because there is a fairly large range of outputs over which there are constant returns to scale. Indeed, in practice, constant returns may prevail almost everywhere. The minimum output level consistent with the lowest $LRAC$ is called the **minimum efficient scale** (**MES**). In Figure 8-7, the MES is 200 units. As Example 8-2 shows, the MES differs from industry to industry.

The concept of a minimum efficient scale is important because it has been hypothesized that the degree of competition in an industry may depend on the MES specific to that industry. In particular, it has been conjectured that the larger is the MES for a given industry, the smaller will be the degree of competition. The evidence for this hypothesis will appear in Chapter 13.

*The **minimum efficient scale** (**MES**) is the lowest level of output at which long-run average costs are minimized.*

Long-Run Marginal Cost

Long-run marginal cost ($LRMC$) is defined as the increase in long-run total cost per unit of change in output; that is,

$$LRMC = \Delta(LRTC)/\Delta Q. \tag{12}$$

Figure 8-8 shows the long-run marginal-cost curve for a highly simplified case. (The $LRAC$ curve does not have a flat bottom.) As discussed in Chapter 5, the marginal cost exceeds, equals, or falls short of the average cost as the average is rising, constant, or falling. Accordingly, the $LRMC$ curve must be below the $LRAC$ curve when $LRAC$ is in the range of economies of scale; the $LRMC$ curve must intersect the $LRAC$ curve at its minimum point; the $LRMC$ curve must rise above the $LRAC$ curve in the range of diseconomies of scale, or rising $LRAC$. Notice that the $LRMC$ curve intersects the $LRAC$ curve at two points: where output is zero and where the $LRAC$ is minimized. When Q = 0, the marginal cost and the average cost are equal for the first small increment of output.

Every point on the $LRAC$ curve corresponds to the ratio of total costs to output along the expansion path. How is the $LRMC$ curve related to the EP curve? Along the expansion path, $MP_L/MP_K = w/r$, or, rearranging,

$$\frac{w}{MP_L} = \frac{r}{MP_K}. \tag{13}$$

This equation is the same as the least-cost rule, Equation (10), except that both sides have been inverted. Consider the meaning of w/MP_L: the wage rate per unit of marginal product of labor. Because MP_L is $\Delta Q/\Delta L$, substitution shows that

LONG-RUN COSTS

FIGURE 8-8   The Long-Run Cost Curves

The *LRAC* curve shown here is *U*-shaped. The long-run marginal-cost (*LRMC*) curve intersects the *LRAC* curve at two points: when output is zero and at the minimum average cost. At any level of output Q_0, *LRMC* equals $w/MP_L = r/MP_K$, point *m*, because at point *a* costs are minimized.

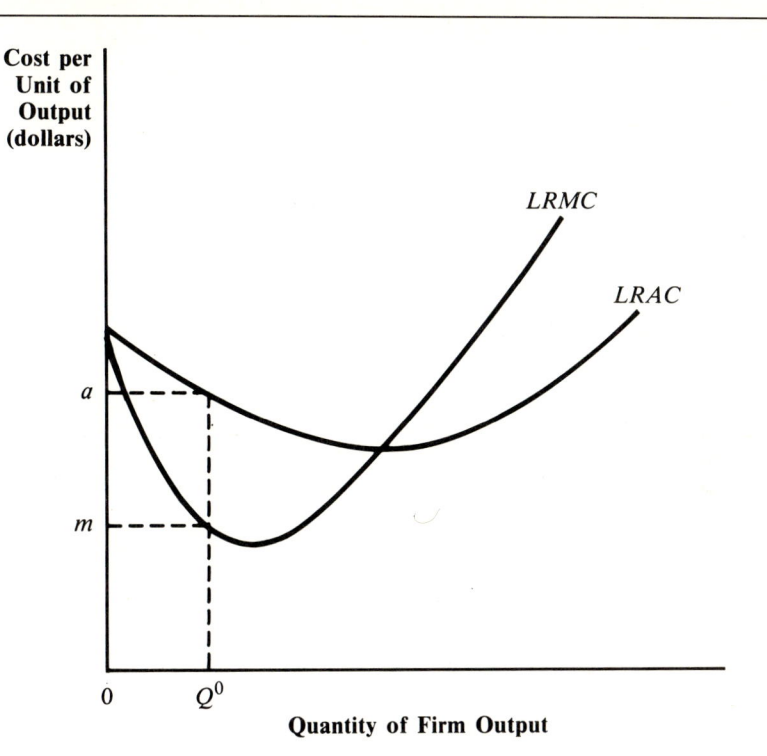

$$\frac{w}{MP_L} = \frac{w}{(\Delta Q/\Delta L)} = \frac{w\Delta L}{\Delta Q} = \frac{\Delta C}{\Delta Q}. \tag{14}$$

The ratio w/MP_L is the marginal cost of increasing output by increasing labor. Similarly, r/MP_K is the marginal cost of increasing output by increasing capital. Costs are minimized for a given output when the condition in Equation (13) is met: the marginal cost incurred by increasing labor input is exactly the same as the marginal cost incurred by increasing capital input. If $w/MP_L > r/MP_K$, the firm can lower its costs for any given volume of output by increasing the capital input and lowering the labor input. Thus, when the two marginal costs are equated,

$$\frac{w}{MP_L} = \frac{r}{MP_K} = LRMC. \tag{15}$$

Because every point on the *LRAC* curve is associated with minimizing the cost of producing that volume of output, an equation such as Equation (15) must hold. For example, in Figure 8-8, when the firm produces Q_0 units of output and average cost is *a*, the marginal cost at that level of output must equal *m*, the common value $w/MP_L = r/MP_K$.

SHORT-RUN COSTS OF PRODUCTION

What Is the Short Run?

Every point on the *LRAC* curve corresponds to an optimal use of inputs where $MP_L/MP_K = w/r$. For any output, $LRMC = w/MP_L = r/MP_K$.

The firm cannot always have the luxury of varying all inputs in order to arrive at the optimal input combination. It takes time to change inputs. Very little time is needed to change some inputs; changing others requires a great deal of time. Unskilled labor and certain common raw materials can be hired or purchased and put to use quickly, but building a plant or installing a complicated piece of machinery may take a long time.

The *long run* is a period so long that all inputs can be varied. The *short run* is a period of time in which at least one of the inputs is fixed in supply. Because the firm uses many inputs, and changing each input may require a different time span, there are many short runs. For example, it may take a few days to vary unskilled labor, a few weeks to vary skilled labor, and a few months to vary managerial labor. The short run would be a few days if only unskilled labor were to be varied, but it would be a few months if managerial labor were the varying input.

We will assume that there is only one short run, because we are following the convenient assumption that labor and capital are the only inputs. In this case, it is plausible to assume that capital is the fixed input in the short run and that labor is the variable input. This convenient assumption will simplify the discussion but will not change the fundamental character of the analysis.

Short-Run Costs and the Production Function

By definition, the short run is a period so short that the firm cannot vary its capital input. In Panel A of Figure 8-9, the firm's plant size is reflected in the size of its capital stock, K_1. The expansion path, *EP*, goes through point *b*, which indicates where the firm would be in the long run for the output level Q_1. The *LRTC* curve in Panel B shows how costs vary along the *EP* curve in Panel A. Because the firm cannot vary capital in the short run, output can be increased to Q_2 or decreased to Q_0 only by moving along the horizontal line at K_1 to input combinations *f* or *a*. If the firm is initially at point *a*, one can draw an isocost line through point *a* to see that the firm's cost of producing Q_2 must be higher than it is at point *d*, which is on the expansion path. Similarly, the firm's cost of producing Q_0 must be larger at point *f* than it is at point *g*, which is on the *EP*. Thus, the firm's short-run total-cost curve for the capital stock K_1, labeled $SRTC_1$ in Panel B, must lie above the *LRTC*

FIGURE 8-9 Short-Run and Long-Run Costs

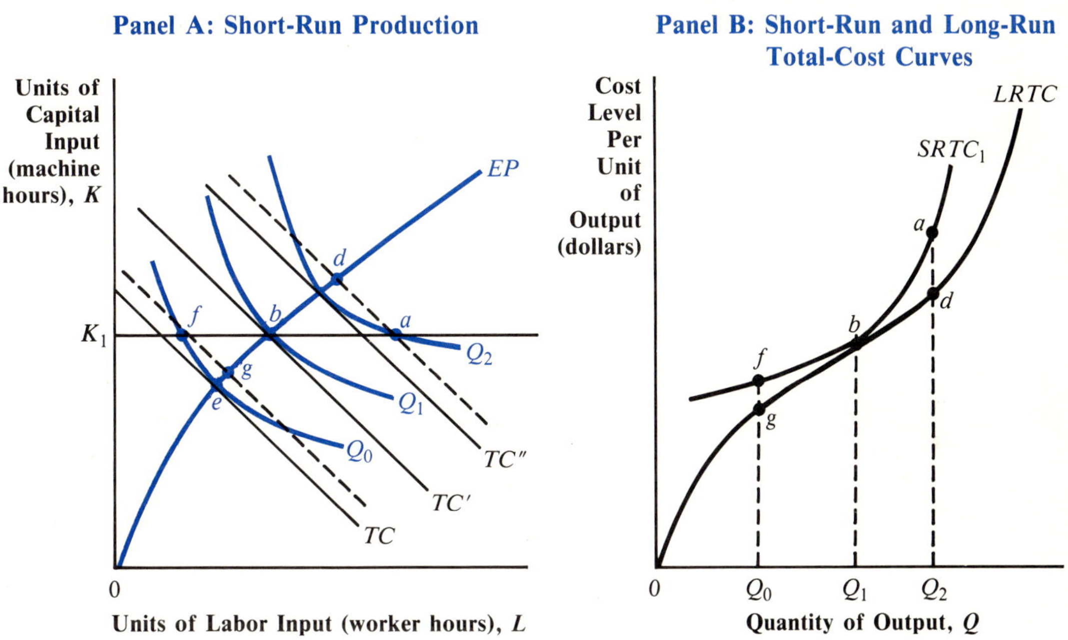

Panel A: Short-Run Production

Panel B: Short-Run and Long-Run Total-Cost Curves

Panel A illustrates the long-run expansion path for a firm whose capital input is fixed at K_1. In the short run, the firm cannot produce output Q_2 at point d because d does not lie along line K_1. Production at points such as a and f is inefficient. Panel B shows the corresponding costs (a, b, d, f, g) on the short-run and long-run total-cost curves. The short-run total-cost curve, $SRTC_1$, is tangent to the long-run total-cost ($LRTC$) curve at an output of Q_1 but lies above the $LRTC$ curve for all other output levels because short-run costs for producing more or less output are higher than long-run costs.

curve when output is above or below Q_1. When output equals Q_1, the $SRTC_1$ curve is tangent to the $LRTC$ curve. The points a, b, etc., in Panel A correspond to the points a, b, etc., in Panel B.

Fixed Cost and Variable Cost

Fixed costs (FC) are costs that do not vary with the level of output.

Variable costs (VC) are costs that do vary with the level of output.

The costs of fixed inputs in the short run are called **fixed costs (FC)**; the costs of variable inputs in the short run are called **variable costs (VC)**. The sum of the fixed costs and variable costs is the **total cost (TC)**: $FC + VC = TC$.

In Figure 8-9, when the capital input is K_1, the firm's fixed cost would be rK_1, and its variable cost would be wL, assuming capital and labor are the only inputs,

$$FC = rK_1 \text{ and } VC = wL.$$

TABLE 8–1 Short-Run Production Costs When Capital Input Is Fixed at 10 Machines

Quantity of Labor Input (workers), L (1)	Quantity of Output (units), Q (2)	Fixed Costs (dollars), FC (3)	Variable Costs (dollars), VC (4)	Total Costs (dollars), TC (5)	Marginal Cost (dollars), MC (6)	Average Fixed Cost (dollars), AFC (7)	Average Variable Cost (dollars), AVC (8)	Average Total Cost (dollars), ATC (9)
0	0	1,800	0	1,800		...	...	...
					4.80			
1	50	1,800	240	2,040		$36.00	$4.80	$40.80
					3.43			
2	120	1,800	480	2,280		15.00	4.00	19.00
					4			
3	180	1,800	720	2,520		10.00	4.00	14.00
					4			
4	230	1,800	960	2,760		7.83	4.17	12.00
					6			
5	270	1,800	1,200	3,000		6.67	4.44	11.11
					8			
6	300	1,800	1,440	3,240		6.08	4.80	10.80
					12			
7	320	1,800	1,680	3,480		5.63	5.25	10.88
					24			
8	330	1,800	1,920	3,720		5.45	5.82	11.27

Note: It is assumed that the wage rate is $240 per worker per week.

EXAMPLE 8–2 Long-Run Cost Curves and Minimum Efficient Scale

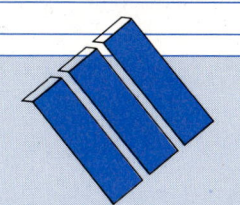

Empirical evidence shows that the typical *LRAC* curve looks like the one in the accompanying diagram. The curve exhibits increasing returns up to the minimum efficient scale (*MES*), and then constant returns to scale. It is difficult to find evidence of decreasing returns to scale, simply because firms avoid producing where the *LRAC* curve is upward-sloping.

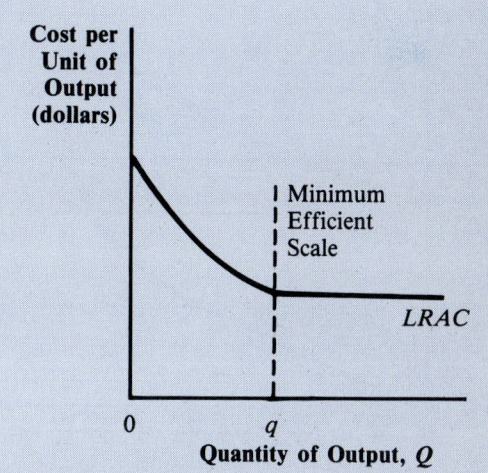

Economies of scale differ substantially among industries. Some industries experience economies of scale that are a substantial fraction of industry sales; others experience economies of scale only up to a small fraction of industry sales. Economies of scale are measured by various techniques. The first technique is *engineering estimates*: engineers are asked what the optimal plant size is and by how much costs will rise as plant size departs from this optimum. The second method is *statistical cost studies*. This approach examines actual cost data of firms in an industry from year to year or for different firms at the same point in time. Such studies cannot discover diseconomies of scale unless firms actually run into increasing long-run costs. The third approach is the *survivor technique*. Records kept for an industry over time establish whether the sizes of firms are staying the same or increasing. If the sizes of some firms increase, firms of a smaller size will not be able to survive or coexist with the larger firms.

Source: William G. Shepherd, *The Economics of Industrial Organization* (Englewood Cliffs, N.J.: Prentice-Hall, 1979), chap. 12.

Total costs (*TC*) are the sum of fixed and variable costs: *TC* = *VC* + *FC*.

Consider a hypothetical firm facing weekly machine rental costs of $180 per machine and weekly wage costs of $240 per worker. If $K_1 = 10$ machines, then *FC* = $1,800. Columns (1) and (2) of Table 8–1 show the short-run production function of this firm. Column (3) shows the firm's fixed costs, column (4) shows variable costs, and column (5) shows total costs. For

FIGURE 8-10   Short-Run Cost Curves

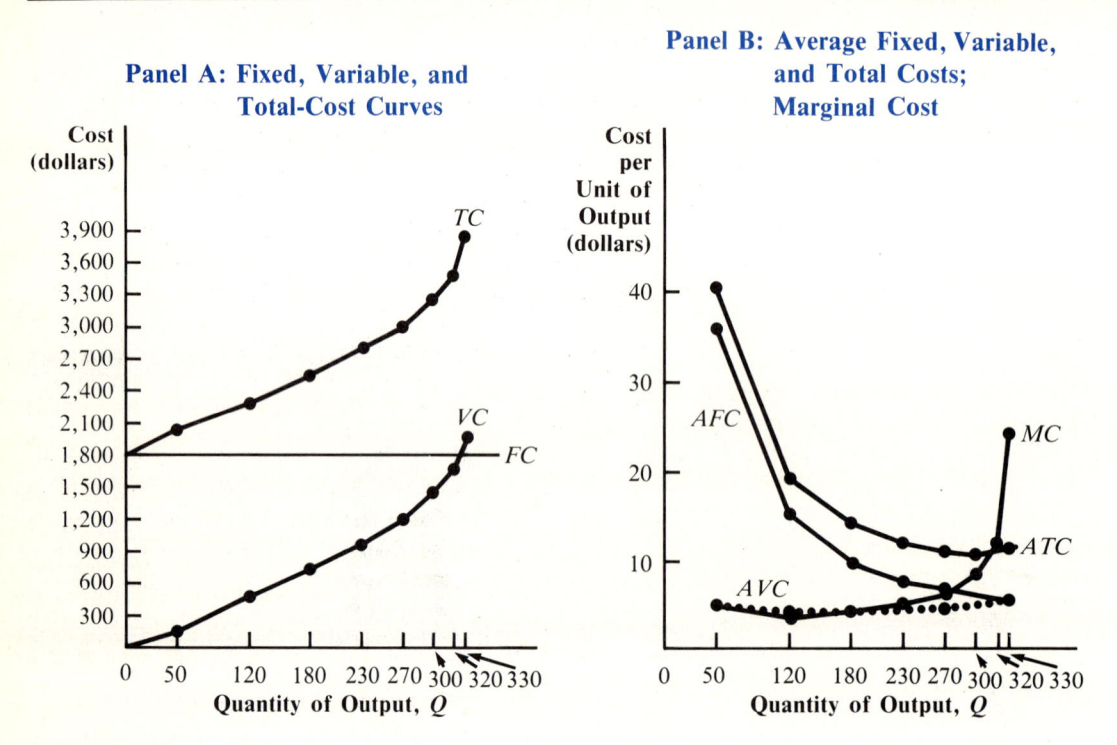

Panel A: Fixed, Variable, and Total-Cost Curves

Panel B: Average Fixed, Variable, and Total Costs; Marginal Cost

In Panel A, fixed cost is constant at $1,800 because capital input is assumed fixed at 10 machines and r = $180. Because total cost increases by the same amount as variable cost for each output quantity, the curves are similar. Panel B shows that the *AFC* curve declines steadily as fixed cost is spread over more units of output. The *ATC* curve declines and then begins to rise slightly, as the average variable cost begins to increase because of diminishing returns for added inputs of labor. The marginal cost per unit of output rises more sharply at higher levels for the same reason. The *MC* curve intersects the *AVC* and *ATC* curves at their lowest points. (This figure graphs the data from Table 8-1.)

example, when $L = 2$, $VC = \$240 \times 2 = \$480$. Thus, $TC = \$1,800 + \$480 = \$2,280$.

Average Fixed Cost, Average Variable Cost, Marginal Cost

Average fixed costs (*AFC*) equal fixed costs divided by output: $AFC = FC \div Q$.

Fixed cost and variable cost can be divided by the output quantity (Q) to obtain **average fixed costs (*AFC*)** and **average variable costs (*AVC*)**. The sum of *AFC* and *AVC* is **average total costs (*ATC*)**.

$$FC/Q + VC/Q = AFC + AVC.$$

Columns (7), (8), and (9) of Table 8-1 show, respectively, average fixed, average variable, and average total costs for our hypothetical firm with fixed capital input of 10 machines.

Average variable costs (AVC) equal variable costs divided by output: $AVC = VC \div Q$.

Average total costs (ATC) equal average fixed costs plus average total costs: $ATC = FC/Q + VC/Q = AFC + AVC$.

Marginal cost (MC) is the extra variable or total cost per unit of a change in output: $MC = \Delta TC/\Delta Q = \Delta VC/\Delta Q$.

The incremental cost, or **marginal cost (MC)**, of an extra unit of output is defined as the extra variable cost or total cost per unit of change in output:

$$MC = \Delta TC/\Delta Q = \Delta VC/\Delta Q.$$

Notice that marginal cost is either the change in total cost or the change in variable cost because the increase in total cost always equals the increase in variable cost because the change in fixed cost is always zero, as illustrated in columns (4) and (5) of Table 8-1. Marginal cost is calculated simply by dividing the increase in cost by the increase in output. For example, the marginal cost of increasing output from 0 units to 50 units is $4.80, because costs rise by $240 and output rises by 50.

Figure 8-10 plots the cost figures in Table 8-1. The *FC*, *VC*, and *TC* curves are plotted in Panel A; Panel B plots the *AFC*, *AVC*, *ATC*, and *MC* curves. Notice that the *AFC* curve declines throughout the range of output levels. The *AVC* curve at first declines and then rises; the *ATC* curve also declines and then rises. The *MC* curve intersects the *AVC* and *ATC* curves at their minimum points because the average/marginal rules apply: the average falls when the margin is below it and rises when the margin is above it. When the average cost is minimized (or maximized), the marginal cost equals the average cost.

The Economics Behind Short-Run Cost Curves

The shapes of the *AVC*, *ATC*, and *MC* can be explained in general terms. Given that $AVC = VC/Q$ and that $VC = wL$, it follows that $AVC = wL/Q$. But wL/Q can also be written as $w/(Q/L)$:

$$AVC = \frac{w}{Q/L} = \frac{w}{AP_L} \qquad (16)$$

PRACTICE EXERCISE 8-3

Q. If $Q = A(KL)^{0.5}$, what is the short-run cost function when $K = 100$? What is the *MC* curve?

A. Fixed cost is $100r$, and variable cost is wL. The short-run production function is $Q = 10AL^{0.5}$. If both sides of the short-run production function are squared, we have $Q^2 = 100A^2L$. Because $VC = wL$, we can simply write $VC = wQ^2/100A$. The short-run cost function is, therefore, $C = 100r + wQ^2/100A$ and $ATC = 100r/Q + wQ/100A$. To obtain the *MC* curve, note that $AVC = wQ/100A$. Now, recall from Chapter 5 that the *MR* curve is twice as steep as any straight-line demand curve. The same rule holds for any straight-line average curve. Thus, $MC = 2wQ/100A$. Calculus can also be used: $dC/dQ = MC = 2wQ/100A$.

FIGURE 8-11   Marginal and Average Costs of Production in Relation to Labor Productivity

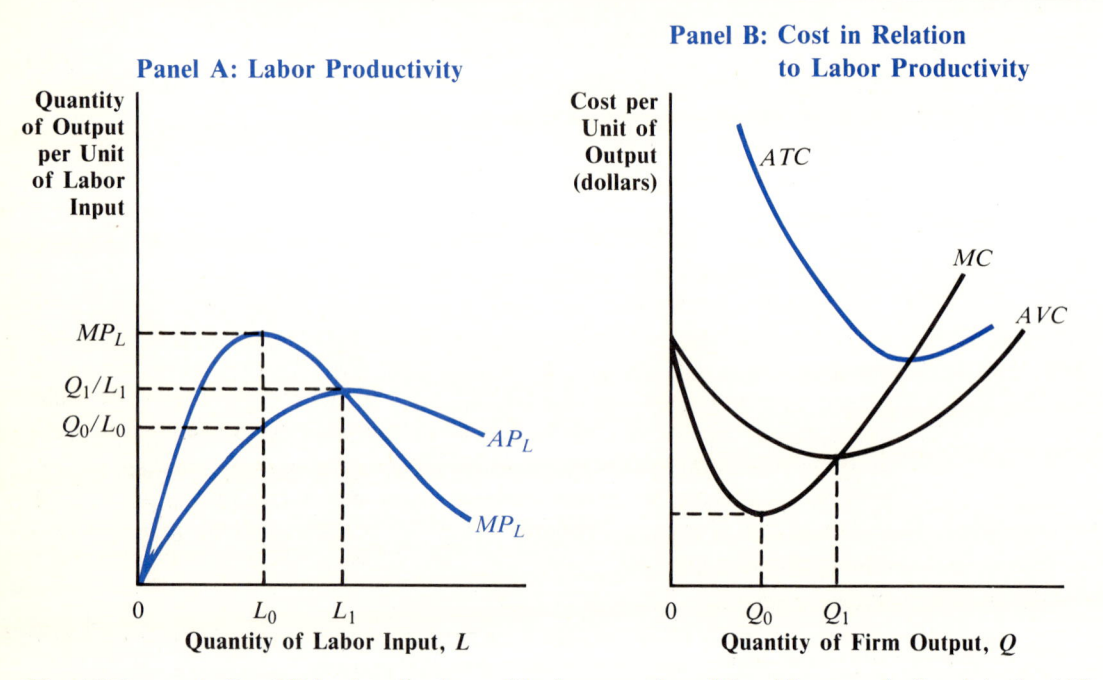

Panel A: Labor Productivity

Panel B: Cost in Relation to Labor Productivity

The AVC curve in Panel B is virtually the upside-down version of the AP_L curve in Panel A; the MC curve in Panel B is the upside-down version of the MP_L curve in Panel A. They are linked because $AVC = w/AP_L$ and $MC = w/MP_L$. When one is maximized, the other is minimized. The MC curve intersects the AVC and ATC curves at their minimum points.

Because AVC is proportional to the reciprocal of AP_L, an increase in AP_L will reduce AVC, and vice versa—a decrease in AP_L will increase AVC. Similarly, as shown earlier,

$$MC = \frac{w}{MP_L} \tag{17}$$

Thus, MC is proportional to the reciprocal of MP_L. When MP_L increases, MC decreases, and vice versa.

Panel A of Figure 8–11 shows a standard AP_L curve with its associated MP_L curve. Panel B shows the corresponding AVC and MC curves, using Equations (16) and (17). At the level of labor input L_0 in Panel A, the MP_L curve reaches its peak; at the level of labor input L_1 in Panel A, the AP_L curve reaches its peak. Suppose now that $Q_1 = f(L_1)$ and $Q_0 = f(L_0)$. In Panel B, the MC curve reaches its lowest point where output is at the level Q_0, and the AVC curve reaches its lowest point at an output of Q_1. The MC

curve is virtually an upside-down version of the MP_L curve, except that it is in the space measuring cost in relation to output rather than in the space measuring output in relation to input. Similarly, the AVC curve is the inverse of the AP_L curve. In Panel A, the MP_L curve intersects the AP_L curve at its maximum point; correspondingly, in Panel B, the MC curve intersects the AVC curve at its minimum point.

To obtain the ATC curve in Panel B of Figure 8–11 it is necessary only to add the AFC curve (not shown) to the AVC curve. Because average fixed cost grows smaller as output expands, the ATC curve approaches the AVC curve as output grows. Because marginal cost is marginal to both total and variable costs, the MC curve intersects both the AVC and ATC curves at their minimum points.

Notice that the MC curve intersects the AVC curve to the left of its intersection of the ATC curve. At the output level Q_1, average variable cost is at a minimum and is stationary (neither rising nor falling). But average fixed cost is still falling. Therefore, average total cost is *declining* at the output level Q_1 because it is the sum of a curve with a zero slope at that point (the AVC curve) and one with a negative slope (the AFC curve). The arithmetic is likewise compelling: at output level Q_1, *marginal* cost is less than *average* total cost and must, therefore, be pulling the average down.

The short-run cost curves have the following properties: (1) the AFC curve declines throughout; (2) the ATC curve approaches the AVC curve as output grows; (3) the MC curve intersects the AVC and ATC curves at their minimum points; (4) necessarily, the minimum point on the AVC curve occurs at a smaller output level than the minimum point on the ATC curve; and (5) the AVC and MC curves are upside-down versions of the AP_L and MP_L curves, respectively.

LONG-RUN AND SHORT-RUN COST CURVES

Short-run cost curves are drawn on the assumption of a fixed input of capital. When capital input is increased, the short-run cost curves will shift. Because long-run cost curves allow the size of the plant to vary, there must be a link between short-run and long-run cost curves.

Figure 8–9 touched on the connection between the short-run total-cost curve and the long-run total-cost curve. The long-run cost curve is a mapping from the expansion path into the corresponding level of cost and output. At every point along the EP curve, there is a specific capital input and a specific set of short-run cost curves. Thus, any point on the long-run cost curve can be associated with a short-run cost curve. We will now examine the link in detail.

FIGURE 8-12 Long-Run Costs with Constant Returns to Scale

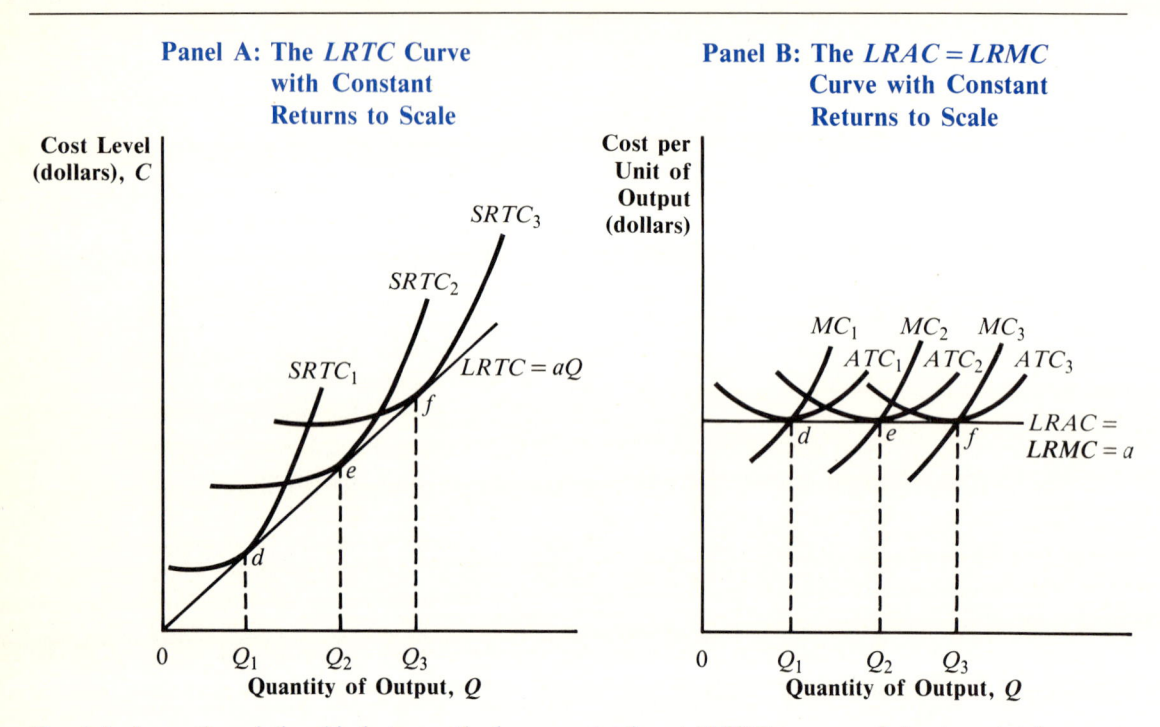

Panel A: The $LRTC$ Curve with Constant Returns to Scale

Panel B: The $LRAC = LRMC$ Curve with Constant Returns to Scale

Panel A shows the relationship between the long-run total-cost ($LRTC$) curve and short-run total-cost ($SRTC$) curves when there are constant returns to scale. Panel B shows the relationships between the short-run average-total-cost (ATC) and marginal-cost (MC) curves and the long-run average-cost and marginal-cost curves corresponding to the $LRTC$ curve in Panel A. The $LRAC$ curve is the envelope of an infinite number of short-run ATC curves. The input combination at each point, such as d, e, or f, is an optimal combination in the long run; hence, in the short run, plant efficiency is maximized when $ATC = LRAC$ and $MC = LRMC$ at every output level in the case of constant returns to scale.

Constant Returns to Scale

Figure 8-12 shows that the long-run cost curve is an envelope of all the short-run cost curves. To simplify, we assume constant returns to scale. Panel A shows the relationship between the short-run TC curves and the long-run total-cost ($LRTC$) curve. With constant returns to scale, $LRTC = aQ$, where a is some positive constant depending on the productivity of the inputs and the prevailing set of factor prices. Constant returns to scale mean that doubling inputs, holding factor prices constant, must double output and costs. Thus, the $LRTC$ curve is a straight line from the origin. Panel B shows the $LRAC$ curve for the same $LRTC$ curve. With constant returns, the $LRAC$ curve is a straight horizontal line. Because the average is constant, $LRMC = LRAC = a$.

Consider now the short-run curves. Panel A shows the short-run TC curves for various levels of capital input. Each TC curve touches the $LRTC$

FIGURE 8-13   Long-Run Costs with Increasing and Decreasing Returns to Scale

The *LRAC* curve is the envelope of all the *ATC* curves. When the optimal input combination is used to produce output Q_1, Q_2, or Q_3, short-run marginal cost equals long-run marginal cost. With increasing returns, the capital input at point *d* is too small for higher output levels. With decreasing returns, the capital input at point *f* is too large for lower output levels.

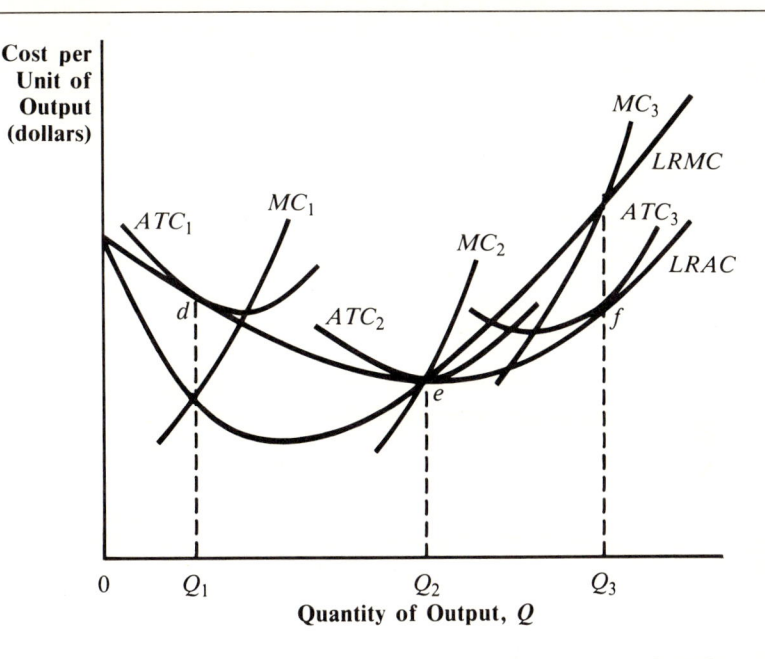

curve at one point and lies above it elsewhere. $SRTC_1$, $SRTC_2$, and $SRTC_3$ are the short-run total-cost curves corresponding to the capital inputs K_1, K_2, and K_3 associated with the output levels Q_1, Q_2, and Q_3. Panel B shows the short-run *ATC* curves corresponding to the capital-input levels K_1, K_2, and K_3. For example, when the capital input is K_1, the ATC_1 curve must lie above the *LRAC* curve for any output not equal to Q_1. The associated marginal-cost curve, MC_1, cuts the ATC_1 curve at its lowest point. In the case of constant returns, when the *ATC* curve is minimized, short-run marginal cost equals long-run marginal cost because the optimal use of the plant K_1 is exactly the same as the optimal plant when output is Q_1. Because there is an infinite number of plants, there is an infinite number of short-run curves. The long-run curve is the envelope of an infinite number of short-run curves.

Increasing and Decreasing Returns to Scale

In Panel B of Figure 8-12, the minimum point on each *ATC* curve is tangent to the *LRAC* curve. In other words, because this industry has constant returns to scale, the optimal or minimum-cost use of any given level of capital input is the optimal plant size for the given level of output. In all other cases, the minimum cost of operating any given plant exceeds the minimum cost of producing that output. In other words, in the general case, the optimal use of any given level of capital input in the short run is not the best level of capital input for producing that particular output in the long run!

Figure 8-13 shows the *LRAC* curve of a firm facing increasing returns to scale from output levels 0 to Q_2 and decreasing returns thereafter. For example, at output level Q_1, there are increasing returns to scale. The associated level of capital input, K_1, corresponds to the short-run ATC curve labeled ATC_1; note that ATC_1 is above the $LRAC$ curve for any output level but Q_1. Notice, however, that the minimum point on the ATC_1 curve is to the right of Q_1 and above the $LRAC$ curve. In other words, the K_1 level of capital input is not efficient for any higher output level. How can we prove this result? When output is Q_1, the $LRAC$ is declining (by assumption); accordingly, by the average/marginal rule, the $LRMC$ curve must be below the $LRAC$ curve. At output Q_1 the firm is minimizing its costs with capital-input level K_1; therefore,

$$LRMC = r/MP_K = w/MP_L. \qquad (18)$$

Because short-run $MC = w/MP_L$, however, marginal cost must be less than average total cost at output level Q_1. Because of the average/marginal rule, the ATC_1 curve must be declining at output level Q_1. Thus, the MC_1 curve must intersect the $LRMC$ curve at output level Q_1 and must also intersect the minimum point of the ATC_1 curve. It follows that the optimal use of any given plant in the short run is not optimal in the long run. When there are increasing returns to scale, any given plant size is too small for a larger volume of output.

Now consider output level Q_3, where the firm faces decreasing returns to scale. Here the firm uses a level of capital input of K_3. In this case, the ATC curve again will be tangent to the $LRAC$ curve. Because the $LRMC$ curve lies above the $LRAC$ curve at that output, it follows that MC_3 intersects the $LRMC$ curve at that point (again, because at output level Q_3, $MC = LRMC$). Because MC_3 lies above ATC_3 at the output level Q_3, it must be that the ATC_3 curve is rising at that point. Accordingly, the minimum point on ATC_3 occurs to the left of the output level Q_3. Thus, the optimal use of any plant in the short run again is not optimal for any given output in the long run because with decreasing returns to scale, smaller plants are efficient for smaller outputs.

Notice that the $LRAC$ curve is tangent to the various short-run ATC curves and touches the minimum point on the associated ATC curve only if there are constant returns to scale. In Figure 8–13, the ATC curve for output level Q_2 is ATC_2, which is perfectly nestled at the minimum point of the $LRAC$ curve.[3]

---

3. The classic paper on cost curves is Jacob Viner's "Cost Curves and Supply Curves" in American Economic Association *Readings in Price Theory* (Homewood, Ill.: Richard D. Irwin, 1952), chap. 10. This paper, reprinted from the original 1931 article, made a famous mistake. Viner instructed his draftsman to draw the $LRAC$ curve through the minimum points on the ATC curves. It is intuitively clear that if a U-shaped $LRAC$ is the envelope of all the short-run ATC curves, the $LRAC$ cannot intersect the minimum points. If it did, it would necessarily pass above sections of the ATC curves in the increasing or decreasing returns sections—a fact which contradicts the minimum-unit-cost property of the $LRAC$ curve. The draftsman objected, but Viner still forced him to draw the $LRAC$ curve incorrectly.

FIGURE 8-14   Effect of a Change in Factor Prices on the Expansion Path

When the wage/rent ratio increases, the (K/L) ratio increases and the expansion path shifts from EP to EP'.

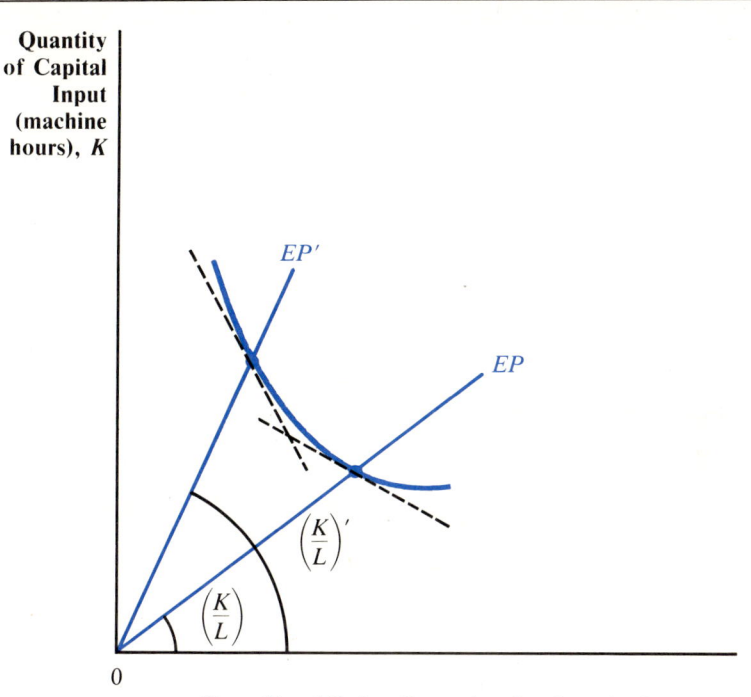

[Figure: Graph with Quantity of Capital Input (machine hours), K on vertical axis and Quantity of Labor Input (worker hours), L on horizontal axis. Shows two expansion paths EP' (steeper) and EP, with (K/L)' ray steeper than (K/L) ray.]

When there are increasing returns to scale, the *LRAC* curve is tangent to the left of the minimum point on the *ATC* curve. When there are constant returns to scale, the *LRAC* curve is tangent to the minimum point on the *ATC* curve. When there are decreasing returns to scale, the *LRAC* curve is tangent to the right of the minimum point on the *ATC* curve.

CHANGES IN FACTOR PRICES

When factor prices change, the expansion path and the corresponding cost curves change. If wages rise relative to rents, cost-minimizing business firms will substitute capital for labor; they will become more capital-intensive. If wages rise while the rental on capital stays the same, the *LRAC* curve will shift up. But how much will the curve shift? What will happen to the minimum efficient scale?

The Effect of Changes in Factor Prices on the Expansion Path

Figure 8-14 shows what happens to the expansion path (*EP*) as the wage/rent ratio increases. When *w/r* rises, the firm minimizes the cost of producing any given output at a higher *K/L* ratio. In other words, the firm economizes by shifting from labor to capital because labor has become relatively more expensive. The expansion path shifts upward, from *EP* to *EP'*. Because $w/r = MRTS_{KL}$, the extent to which the *K/L* ratio changes depends on the elasticity of substitution. The higher is the elasticity, the more the firm can escape the increase in labor costs by substituting capital for labor.

Shepherd's Lemma

When the expansion path shifts, the cost curves shift. The wage/rent ratio can increase because wages rise or because capital rental falls. Let us consider the impact of an increase in wages. (The effect of an increase in rents is analogous.) We know that $C = wL + rK$, where *L* and *K* are the inputs at each point on the expansion path. At each point along the expansion path,

$$w/r = MRTS_{KL} = -\Delta K/\Delta L. \tag{19}$$

By multiplying both sides of Equation (20) by *r* and ΔL, we obtain

$$w\Delta L + r\Delta K = 0. \tag{20}$$

Now consider the change in costs that occurs when wages change. By definition,

$$\Delta C = L\Delta w + w\Delta L + r\Delta K, \tag{21}$$

where the first term, $L\Delta w$, is the change in costs resulting from the change in wages, the second term is the change in costs resulting from the change in the labor input, and the third term is the change in costs resulting from the change in capital input. But Equation (20) shows that the sum of the second and third terms in Equation (21) is zero. Accordingly, we obtain the basic result that (for small changes only)

$$\Delta C/\Delta w = L, \tag{22}$$

which is called **Shepherd's lemma**.[4] By similar reasoning,

$$\Delta C/\Delta r = K. \tag{23}$$

Shepherd's lemma is the equation that states that each dollar increase in wages (or rents) increases the cost of producing any given volume of output by the quantity of labor (or capital) used to produce that volume of output.

What is remarkable about Shepherd's lemma is that the increase in costs is the same as if *K* and *L* did not change—but *K* and *L* do change. If *K* and *L* do not change optimally, Equation (21) governs the change in costs, but

---

4. Shepherd's lemma states that $\partial C/\partial w = L(w, r, Q)$, or that, $\partial C/\partial r = K(w, r, Q)$. The proof follows the same steps as in Equations (19) through (23) in the text. In other words, the partial derivatives of the cost function show the factor demands for given output and factor prices. As an example, consider the cost function derived in footnote 2.
Applying Shepherd's lemma, we obtain $\partial C/\partial w = L(w, r, Q) = Q(r/w)^{1-a}/A[(1 - a)/a]^{1-A}$.

when K and L change optimally, as in Equation (20), we obtain the much simpler expression in Equation (22).

It is clear that if wages (or rents) increase, the $LRAC$ curve will shift up. Shepherd's lemma tells us by exactly how much. Given that $LRAC = C/Q$, an increase in C for any given Q yields $\Delta LRAC = \Delta C/Q$. Using Shepherd's lemma shows that

$$\frac{\Delta LRAC}{\Delta w} = \frac{L}{Q}. \tag{24}$$

How does $LRMC$ change when factor prices change? This is a more complicated question, but Shepherd's lemma can again be used to show that

$$\frac{\Delta LRMC}{\Delta w} = \frac{\Delta L}{\Delta Q}. \tag{25}$$

A simple argument for Equation (25) would be that, because $LRMC = \Delta C/\Delta Q$,

$$\frac{\Delta LRMC}{\Delta w} = \Delta(\Delta C/\Delta Q)/\Delta w. \tag{26}$$

But by quick-and-dirty algebra, the right-hand side can be rewritten as $\Delta(\Delta C/\Delta w)/\Delta Q$. Substituting L for $(\Delta C/\Delta w)$, by Shepherd's lemma, yields Equation (25).[5]

The Role of the Expansion Path

The relative effects of an increase in wages (or rents) on $LRAC$ and $LRMC$ are determined by the shape of the expansion path. Consider the output elasticity of demand for labor,

$$\eta_{LQ} = \frac{\Delta L / L}{\Delta Q/Q} = \frac{\Delta L/\Delta Q}{L/Q}. \tag{27}$$

Using Equations (24) and (25), we see that

$$\eta_{LQ} = \frac{\Delta LRMC/\Delta w}{\Delta LRAC/\Delta w}. \tag{28}$$

If $\eta_{LQ} = 1$, the expansion path is a straight line from the origin, as in Panel A

---

5. By definition, $LRMC = \partial C/\partial Q$. Clearly,

$$\partial LRMC/\partial w = \partial^2 C/\partial Q \partial w.$$

But the order of differentiation does not matter, so that

$$\partial LRMC/\partial w = \partial^2 C/\partial w \partial Q = \partial(\partial C/\partial w)/\partial Q = \partial L/\partial Q,$$

given that $\partial C/\partial w = L$ by Shepherd's lemma.

FIGURE 8-15 The Output Elasticity of Demand for Labor and the Expansion Path

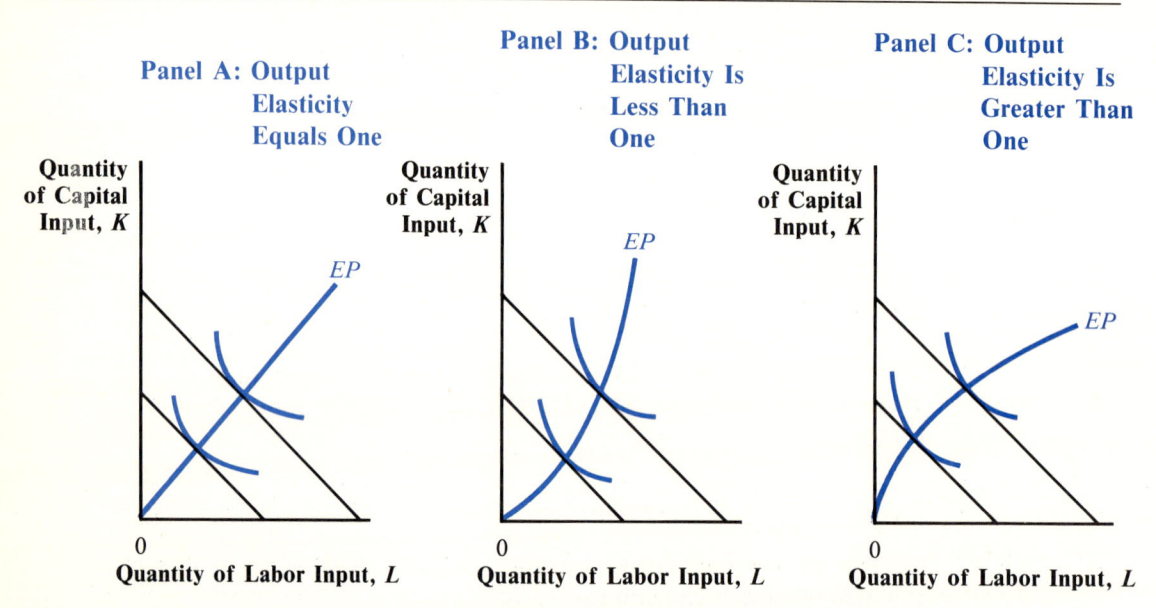

Panel A: Output Elasticity Equals One

Panel B: Output Elasticity Is Less Than One

Panel C: Output Elasticity Is Greater Than One

Each panel shows the result of an increase in output under the given elasticity of demand for labor. In Panel A, as output expands, capital and labor inputs keep the same relative importance. In Panel B, the capital input becomes more important. In Panel C, the reverse is true, and labor input becomes more important as output expands.

of Figure 8-15; that is, the production function is homothetic. In this case, an increase in wages increases *LRAC* and *LRMC* by the same amount. Panel B shows the case in which $\eta_{LQ} < 1$. Here the *EP* curve is convex to the labor axis as labor becomes relatively less important and capital becomes more important at higher output levels. Panel C shows the case in which $\eta_{LQ} > 1$. The *EP* curve is concave to the labor axis as labor becomes relatively more important at higher output levels.

Changing Factor Prices and the Optimal Output Level

The results illustrated in Figure 8-15 can be used to show how the optimal size of a firm (optimal output level) changes when the *LRAC* curve is *U*-shaped. The optimal firm size occurs where *LRMC* = *LRAC*. In Figure 8-16, the optimum output of the firm is Q_0 in each panel before wages increase. When wages increase, the initial *LRAC* and *LRMC* curves shift up to *LRAC'* and *LRMC'*. Panel A assumes that an increase in wages increases *LRAC* and *LRMC* by the same amount (so $\eta_{LQ} = 1$). Hence, *LRAC'* =

CHANGES IN FACTOR PRICES

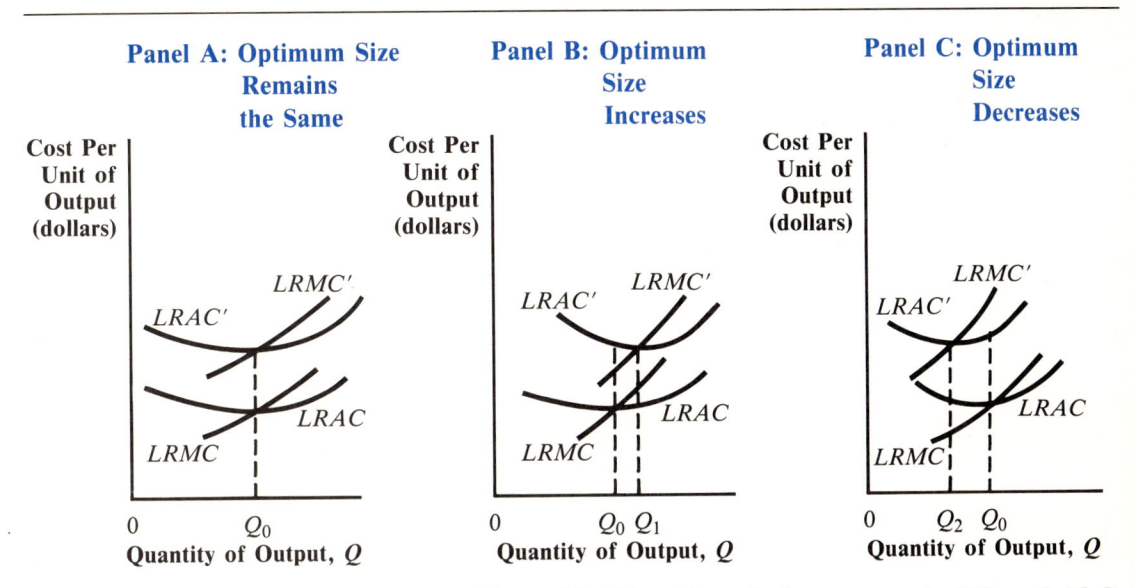

FIGURE 8–16 Optimum Size of the Firm as Wages Increase

Panel A: Optimum Size Remains the Same

Panel B: Optimum Size Increases

Panel C: Optimum Size Decreases

Each panel assumes the output elasticity of demand for labor shown in the same panel of Figure 8–15. It is assumed that wages increase. Panel A illustrates the case in which the optimal firm size stays the same, which occurs when the *LRAC* curve shifts upward by the same amount as the *LRMC* curve. Panel B illustrates the case in which the optimal firm size increases from an output level of Q_0 to Q_1, which occurs when the *LRAC* curve rises more than the *LRMC* curve. Panel C illustrates the case in which the optimal firm size decreases from an output level of Q_0 to Q_2, which occurs when the *LRAC* curve shifts upward by less than the shift in the *LRMC* curve.

LRMC' at the original output level Q_0. The optimal firm output remains at Q_0. Panel B shows the case in which an increase in wages shifts the *LRAC* curve up more than the *LRMC* curve (so $\eta_{LQ} < 1$). At output level Q_0, *LRAC'* > *LRMC'*; thus, *LRAC'* must be declining at Q_1. As illustrated in Panel B, the optimal output level becomes Q_1. Panel C assumes that an increase in wages shifts the *LRAC* curve up less than the *LRMC* curve. At output level Q_0, *LRAC'* < *LRMC'*; thus, the *LRAC'* curve must be rising at Q_2. As illustrated in Panel C the optimal output level falls to Q_2.

Consider the case represented by Panel B. When wages increase, the firm tries to economize by cutting back on the use of labor relative to capital. If the output elasticity of demand for labor is less than unity, the firm becomes relatively less dependent on labor as output grows. Therefore, higher wages will be associated with a larger optimal firm size because the expansion of output itself will help the firm to economize on labor.

SUMMARY

1. The opportunity cost of any activity is the value of the best forgone alternative. Economic profit equals accounting profit minus the value of the entrepreneur's time and capital.

2. The isocost curve shows the combinations of inputs (such as labor and capital) that have the same dollar cost. In the long run, the firm minimizes cost for a given output by moving to the lowest isocost curve tangent to the given isoquant, or the firm maximizes output for a given cost outlay by moving to the highest isoquant tangent to the given isocost line. At the tangency for either case, $MRTS_{KL} = MP_L/MP_K = w/r$, or $MP_L/w = MP_K/r$, which means the least-cost rule is satisfied. The output-expansion path (*EP*) shows the optimal combinations of labor and capital as output expands for any given wage/rent pair (w, r). The *EP* curve is related to the long-run cost function, which is defined as the minimum cost of producing any given output for a given wage/rent pair. In the long run, all inputs are variable. In the short run, at least one input is fixed.

3. The average-fixed-cost (*AFC*), average-variable-cost (*AVC*), average-total-cost (*ATC*), and marginal-cost (*MC*) curves are the critical short-run cost curves. There is one set of these curves for each plant size. The *MC* curve intersects the *ATC* and *AVC* curves at their minimum points. The *ATC* and *AVC* curves are U-shaped. The *AVC* and *MC* curves are inverse versions of the curves for the average and marginal products of labor.

4. The long-run average-cost (*LRAC*) curve is the envelope of all the short-run *ATC* curves, and it shows the minimum unit cost of producing any given output level. Generally speaking, the *LRAC* curve is U-shaped, but with a rather flat bottom.

5. Shepherd's lemma is an equation that shows how costs change in response to changes in factor prices. It can be used to show how the cost curves themselves shift.

QUESTIONS AND PROBLEMS

1. Draw the isocost line when $C = \$1,000$, $W = \$50$, and $r = \$100$. What is its slope?

2. Explain why costs are minimized for a given output level when $MP_L/MP_K = w/r$.

3. Why does $LRMC = w/MP_L = r/MP_K$?

Table A

Quantity of Output (units), Q	Variable Cost (dollars), VC
1	10
2	25
3	35
4	50
5	70
6	95

4. Explain why the MC curve is the upside-down version of the MP_L curve.

5. Explain the relationship between AVC and AP_L.

6. Assuming that FC = $15, draw the AVC, ATC, and MC curves for the cost data in Table A. (Suggestion: place each MC figure in the row between successive output levels.)

7. Suppose that a lump-sum tax of $100 is imposed on a firm. What happens to its MC curve?

8. Chapter 5 showed that the marginal/average relationship is $M = A + Q(\Delta A/\Delta Q)$, where M is the margin and A is the average. Using this rule, show that if $AVC = aQ$ (that is, if $VC = aQ_2$), then $MC = 2aQ$. (Hint: $\Delta AVC/\Delta Q = a$.)

9. Assume that FC = $1,000, $MC = 20Q$ and $AVC = 10Q$. Show that when ATC is minimized (where MC = ATC), Q = 10.

SUGGESTED READINGS

Clark, J. M. *The Economics of Overhead Cost*. Chicago: University of Chicago Press, 1923.
Friedman, Milton. *Price Theory: A Provisional Text*. Chicago: Aldine, 1962, pp. 93–107.
Silberberg, Eugene. *The Structure of Economics: A Mathematical Analysis*. New York: McGraw-Hill, 1978, chap. 7.
Viner, Jacob. "Cost Curves and Supply Curves." In American Economic Association *Readings in Price Theory*. Homewood, Ill: Richard D. Irwin, 1952, chap. 10.
Walters, A. A. "Production and Cost Functions." *Econometrica* 31 (January–April 1963): 1–66.

APPENDIX 8A

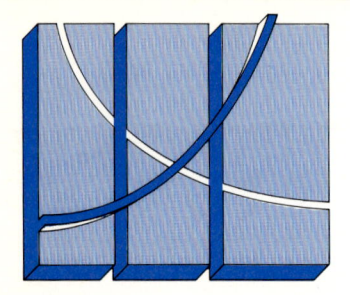

LINEAR PROGRAMMING

Economics is a science that studies problems of the following sort: achieving the greatest possible result with given means, or achieving given ends with the least possible means. Linear programming is a mathematical technique for calculating the best plan for achieving stated objectives in situations where resources are to be economized; both the objective function and the constraints are linear in nature. While linear programming is mathematical, it falls within the scope of economics because of its wide applicability to economic problems.

Linear programming is widely used in the world of business; it is a tool of analysis in industries as different as oil refining and farming. This appendix explains the basic concepts of linear programming, but it does not explain the methods of solution (for example, the simplex method) available to the potential business manager. In the modern world of computers, there are standard programs for solving linear-programming problems. For economists, the challenge is to understand the fundamental properties of these problems.

Choosing the Least-Cost Diet

A classic problem in linear programming is to minimize the cost of a given diet, subject to the constraints that certain nutritional requirements must be met. The diet problem is a practical version of a consumer's attempt to minimize the cost of attaining a given indifference curve or of a producer's efforts to minimize the cost of producing a particular output.

Suppose there are m different foods, $F_1, F_2, \ldots, F_m$. From these foods one must choose a *diet*, the amount of food of each type that will be consumed by a household (or, perhaps, by animals, in the case of farming).

Suppose there are n different nutrients, $N_1, N_2, \ldots, N_n$. The consuming unit requires at least c_j units of nutrient N_j. If this basic requirement is not met, the given ends are not satisfied.

The economic problem is to choose a least-cost diet that satisfies the specified nutritional ends. We need to know the prices, p_i, of each food and the amount of each nutrient contained in a unit of food. Let a_{ij} denote the amount of the jth nutrient contained by a unit of the ith food.

Imagine now that a diet has been chosen. It consists of y_1 units of F_1, y_2 units of F_2, and y_m units of F_m. How much of, say, nutrient N_1 is supplied by this diet? If a_{11} is the amount of N_1 contained in a unit of F_1, the amount of N_1 obtained from y_1 units of F_1 is $y_1 a_{11}$. Similarly, the amount of N_1 obtained from all units of F_2 is $y_2 a_{21}$. The total amount of N_1 contained in the diet $(y_1, y_2, \ldots, y_m)$ is

$$\sum_{i=1}^{i=m} y_i a_{i1} = y_1 a_{11} + y_2 a_{21} + \cdots + y_n a_{m1}.$$

In order for the given diet to satisfy the requirement of c_1 units of N_1, it must satisfy the condition

$$\sum_{i=1}^{i=m} y_i a_{i1} \geq c_1.$$

The diet must also satisfy a similar inequality for all n nutrients. Thus, n inequalities must be satisfied:

$$\sum_{i=1}^{i=m} y_i a_{i,j} \geq c_j \qquad j = 1, 2, \ldots, n. \qquad \textbf{(A-1)}$$

Any diet satisfying statement (A-1) is called a feasible diet. The above constraints are linear.

What is the cost of the diet? If p_i is the dollar price of a unit of F_i, the total cost is the sum

$$\sum_{i=1}^{i=m} p_i y_i = p_1 y_1 + \cdots + p_m y_m. \qquad \textbf{(A-2)}$$

The diet problem is to select from among all those diets satisfying statement (A-1) the diet (or set of diets) for which the linear function (A-2) is a minimum.

Determining the Least-Cost Method of Production

Consider now an economic system, such as a factory, producing goods G_1, $G_2, \ldots, G_n$, with resources $R_1, R_2, \ldots, R_m$. Suppose that the quantities of each resource are given as follows: r_1 of R_1, r_2 of R_2, and so on. The goods are produced by linear processes or activities which specify how much of each resource is used per unit of each good; that is, a_{ij} is the amount of R_i used to produce a unit of G_j. Each good has a dollar price, p_j. The problem is

FIGURE 8A-1 Solving a Primal Maximizing Problem

The feasible set is the shaded region. The highest iso-revenue line occurs at point e. Maximum revenue is $R^* = \$54$.

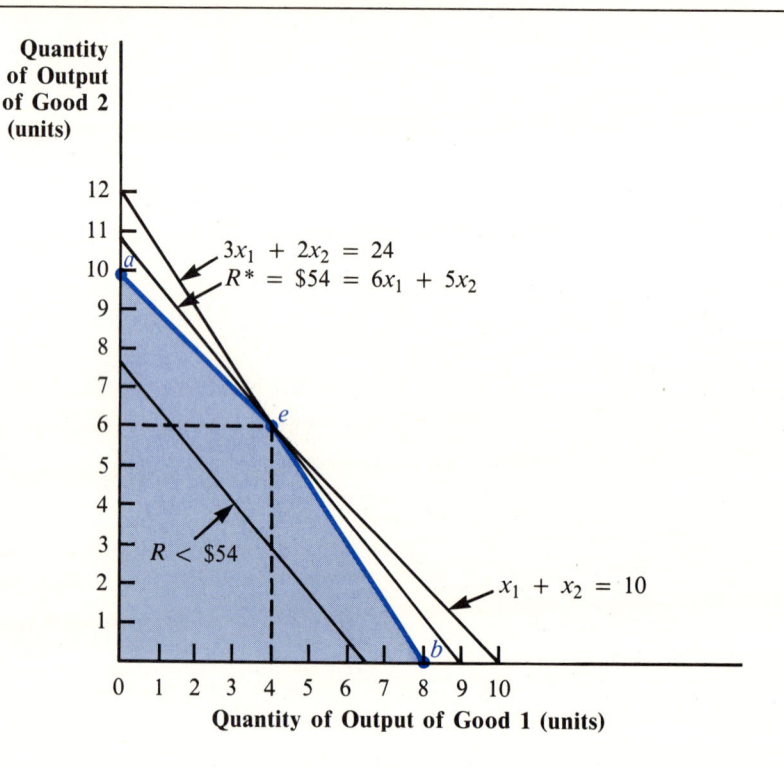

[Graph showing feasible region bounded by $3x_1 + 2x_2 = 24$, $x_1 + x_2 = 10$, and axes. Iso-revenue line $R^* = \$54 = 6x_1 + 5x_2$ tangent at point e. Points labeled a, e, b on boundary. Region marked $R < \$54$.]

to choose a production schedule—x_1 units of G_1, x_2 units of G_2, and so on—such that income is maximized. This is a linear-programming problem because both the *objective function* and the *constraints* are linear; that is, when the relationships are graphed, they are straight lines.

The revenue that the production schedule $(x_1, \ldots, x_n)$ generates will be

$$\sum_{i=1}^{i=n} p_j x_j = p_1 x_1 + p_2 x_2 + \cdots + p_n x_n. \tag{A-3}$$

The linear objective function, statement (A-3), must be maximized subject to certain constraints. The output x_1 of G_1 uses $x_1 a_{11}$ of resource 1, the output x_2 of G_2 uses $x_2 a_{12}$ of resource 2, and so forth. In general, $x_j a_{ij}$ is the amount of R_i used up in the production of G_j. Assuming that the production schedule cannot use more than the m available resources $(r_1, \ldots, r_m)$, the constraints are:

$$\sum_{j=1}^{j=n} x_j a_{ij} \leq r_i \quad i = 1, 2, \ldots, m. \tag{A-4}$$

A feasible production schedule satisfies all of the inequalities in statement (A-4). An optimal production schedule maximizes the objective function subject to these constraints.

A very simple numerical solution to the problem of choosing the best production schedule is illustrated in Figure 8A-1. Suppose the firm has 10 units of R_1 and 24 units of R_2 with which to produce goods G_1 and G_2. Suppose that the a_{ij}s (input of R_i into a unit of G_j) are:

$$a_{11} = 1;\ a_{12} = 1;\ a_{21} = 3;\ \text{and } a_{22} = 2.$$

The resource constraints are then

$$x_1 + x_2 \leq 10 \tag{A-5}$$

$$3x_1 + 2x_2 \leq 24 \tag{A-6}$$

Figure 8A-1 shows inequalities (A-5) and (A-6). The shaded areas represent all the combinations x_1, x_2 that satisfy both constraints; it is the feasible set of solutions. The absolute slope of line segment ae is 1; the absolute slope of line segment eb is 1.5.

Assume now that the prices of G_1 and G_2 are $p_1 = \$6$ and $p_2 = \$5$. The revenue generated by any production schedule is

$$R = 6x_1 + 5x_2. \tag{A-7}$$

Figure 8A-1 shows two isorevenue curves—(x_1, x_2) pairs consistent with constant revenue. Higher isorevenue curves represent higher revenues. Revenue is maximized at point e, where $x_1 = 4$ and $x_2 = 6$. The optimum solution occurs at that point because the absolute slope of an isorevenue line is $p_1/p_2 = 6/5 = 1.2$, which is between the absolute slopes of line segments ae and eb (1 and 1.5). The maximum revenue is $R^* = \$54$.

Defining the Dual Problem

A linear-programming problem can be formally defined as finding a set of nonnegative numbers $x_1, x_2, \ldots, x_n$ that either maximize or minimize the objective function

$$\sum_{j=1}^{i=n} c_j x_j = R, \tag{A-8}$$

where each c_j is a given constant and each x_j must satisfy the constraints

$$\sum_{j=1}^{i=n} x_j a_{i,j} \leq b_i \qquad i = 1, 2, \ldots, m. \tag{A-9}$$

Each b_i is a given constant. (The sense of the inequalities in (A-9) can be changed by multiplying both sides of each inequality by -1.) The optimal solution R^* will be called the *value* of the program.

Consider now the standard problem of maximizing (A-8) subject to the constraints in (A-9). In economic terms, the problem is to achieve the greatest possible result within given means (the constraints). But economic problems can also be stated in terms of minimizing means for any given end. Just as every economic problem can be converted from a maximizing to a

FIGURE 8A-2 Solving the Dual Minimizing Problem

The feasible set is the shaded region. The lowest isocost line occurs at point e'. Minimum cost is $C^* = \$54$.

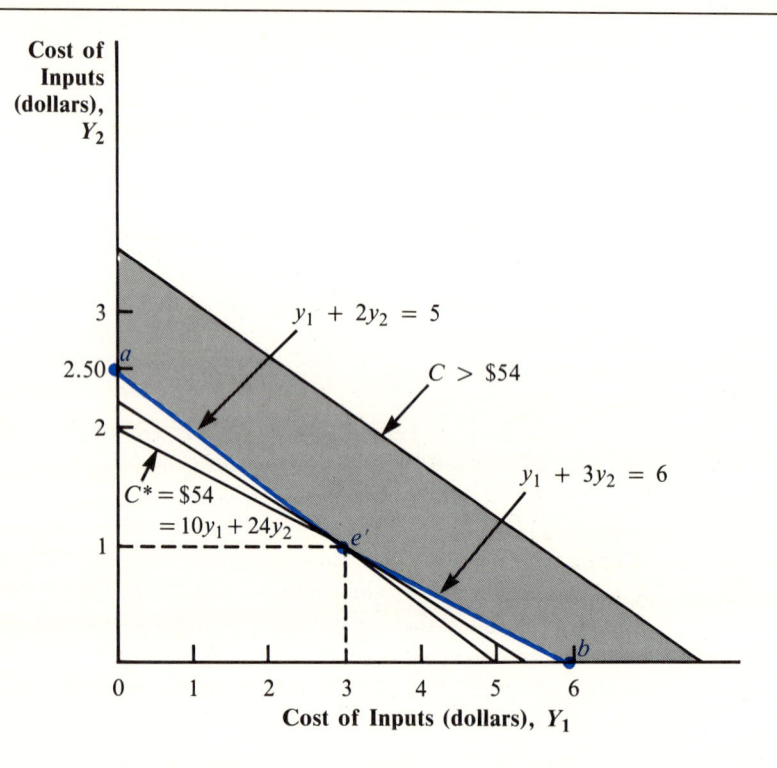

[Graph: Cost of Inputs (dollars), Y_2 on vertical axis; Cost of Inputs (dollars), Y_1 on horizontal axis. Constraints $y_1 + 2y_2 = 5$ and $y_1 + 3y_2 = 6$ shown. Isocost line $C^* = \$54 = 10y_1 + 24y_2$ at point e'. Points a at (0, 2.50) and b at (6, 0). Region $C > \$54$ indicated.]

minimizing problem, so can every linear-programming problem. Every linear-programming problem has a dual nature. The original problem can be called the primal problem.

Each primal problem involves choosing n variables subject to m constraints. The *dual problem* involves three elements: (1) introducing a dual variable for each constraint in the primal problem; (2) stating a new constraint for each variable in the primal problem; and (3) minimizing the new objective function if the primal problem is a maximum problem (or maximizing it if the primal problem is a minimum problem). Because there are m constraints in the primal problem, it is necessary to introduce m dual variables $y_1, \ldots, y_m$. The objective function is to find the nonnegative values of y_i that minimize

$$\sum_{i=1}^{i=m} b_i y_i = C, \tag{A-10}$$

where each b_i corresponds to a constraint in statement (A-9) in the primal problem. The values of y_i must satisfy the new constraints:

$$\sum_{i=1}^{i=m} y_i a_{i,j} \geq c_j \quad j = 1, \ldots, n, \tag{A-11}$$

where the values of c_j are the constants in the primal objective function, (A-8). Notice that the sense of the inequalities in (A-11) are the reverse of those in (A-9) of the primal problem. The optimum solution C^* is the value of the dual problem.

Solving the Dual Problem

We can now write and solve the dual problem to the linear-programming problem of maximizing (A-7) subject to inequalities (A-5) and (A-6). The dual problem is to minimize

$$10y_1 + 24y_2 = C, \qquad \text{(A-12)}$$

subject to

$$y_1 + 3y_2 \geq 6 \qquad \text{(A-13)}$$

$$y_1 + 2y_2 \geq 5. \qquad \text{(A-14)}$$

Think of y_i as the imputed value of a unit of resource i. Thus, the objective function is to minimize the value of the resources used in the problem. Because good 1 has a price of \$6, constraint (A-13) can be interpreted as stating that in a feasible program the value of the resources used in producing good 1 cannot be less than \$6. A similar interpretation applies to (A-14).

We can also solve this problem geometrically. The shaded area in Figure 8A-2 is the feasible set for the dual variables (y_1, y_2). The minimum isocost line occurs at e', where $C^* = \$54$ and $(y_1, y_2) = (1, 3)$.

It is no accident that the value of the dual problem, C^*, equals the value of the primal problem, R^* (both equal \$54). This result is an important theorem in linear programming.

The dual problem and the primal problem are intimately related, as stated in the main theorem of linear programming:[1]

Fundamental duality theorem: If a maximizing or minimizing problem and its dual counterpart have feasible solutions, then their optimal solutions have the same value. If either problem does not have a feasible solution, neither has an optimal solution.

The dual nature of linear-programming problems casts light on the dual nature of many economic problems. We saw in Chapter 8 that maximizing output for a given cost gives the same rule of optimal input use as minimizing the cost of producing a given output. In Chapter 6, we saw that a competitive equilibrium can also be interpreted in dual-efficiency terms.

---

1. This appendix draws on the excellent book by David Gale, *The Theory of Linear Economic Models* (New York: McGraw-Hill, 1960), chap. 1. A proof of the fundamental duality theorem is contained in Chapter 3.

CHAPTER 9

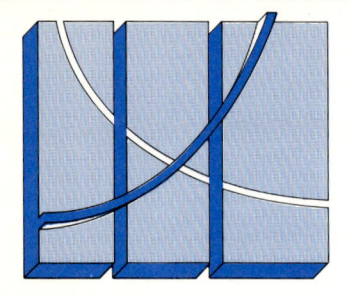

THE THEORY OF PERFECT COMPETITION

The last two chapters examined the technology of production and the theory of costs, forming the foundation for analyzing different types of markets. The three basic types of markets are: perfect competition, monopoly, and imperfect competition. Perfect competition prevails when many firms are **price takers** in an industry producing a homogeneous product; monopoly prevails when there is only one firm in the industry; imperfect competition prevails when the market is dominated by an oligopoly (a few firms) or by monopolistic competition (many firms selling a heterogeneous product).

This chapter explains and analyzes perfect competition. It represents the core of microeconomics because it brings together the preceding material on demand and costs into a complete theory of pricing and output for what is arguably the most important class of markets.

Price takers are agents with so little control over price that they must take the market price as given.

THE MEANING OF PERFECT COMPETITION

To say that an economic agent faces much competition means that the agent has very little control over the price of the good being bought or sold. The more competition an agent faces, the less control the agent has over the price being charged. **Perfect competition** is an idealized model of the competitive process that supposes each agent is a price taker—that is, one who has absolutely no control over the price. While this abstraction holds only in a handful of markets (for example, some agricultural markets, the New York Stock Exchange, and various commodities markets), the empirical relevance of perfect competition ranges over a large portion of the economic system. Indeed, some economists argue that perfect competition can be used to analyze the forces determining price and output in nearly all industries.

Perfect competition results from (1) a large number of buyers and sellers, (2) perfect information about product price and quality, (3) a homogeneous product, and (4) freedom of entry into and exit from the industry.

The conditions sufficient to bring about price-taking behavior are:

1. *There are many buyers and sellers.* There are so many buyers and sellers that each buyer or seller is small relative to the market and cannot, by his or her own actions, influence the market price of the good.
2. *Each buyer has perfect knowledge about the price and quality of the product.* If buyers operate in ignorance, a given seller may be able to charge a price higher than the market price. With perfect information, every buyer pays the same price, and the price of the product is uniform throughout the market.
3. *The product is homogeneous from seller to seller.* Buyers are indifferent about buying the product from different firms as long as the price is the same. As far as the buyer is concerned, firms are all the same with respect to the quality of the product, or even the location of the sales outlet.
4. *There is free entry into and exit from the market.* The theory of perfect competition addresses the case in which existing firms do not have an advantage over new firms. There are no licensing requirements; new firms have the same information as old firms; there are no patents blocking production of the good; new firms have as easy access to credit markets as old firms; the technology of production is accessible to all.

These assumptions are sufficient conditions for perfect competition, but they are not necessary conditions. Perfect competition may apply if there is enough free entry, if there is enough knowledge to insure that price is nearly uniform in the market, and if firms are approximately price takers. Thus, the empirical relevance of the theory extends beyond the limited scope indicated by the strict assumptions. In this regard, economics is no different from the physical sciences. For example, the theory of gravity assumes that there is a vacuum but applies to situations in which atmosphere does not significantly alter the attraction between two bodies. Precise assumptions render the analysis clear and straightforward. If a theory is a good one, the analysis will also be applicable to the real world.

The pricing of goods in an industry characterized by perfect competition can be analyzed in three distinct time periods: the market period, the short run, and the long run.

PRICING IN THE MARKET PERIOD

The **market period** is a period of time so short that the supply of a good cannot be changed.

The **market period** is a period of time so short that the supply of goods cannot be changed. Thus, the supply curve is vertical, as in Figure 9–1. The market period is a period of time shorter than the time required to produce a good. It may be very short in calendar time—a few weeks in the case of many manufactured goods—or very long—years or decades in the case of complicated goods like space shuttles and nuclear power plants. In the case of Rembrandt paintings, old coins and stamps, and antique furniture, the market period is indefinite.

FIGURE 9-1   Supply in the Market Period

In the market period, supply is fixed. The equilibrium price, P_0, simply clears the market. At that price, the existing supply of the good is demanded.

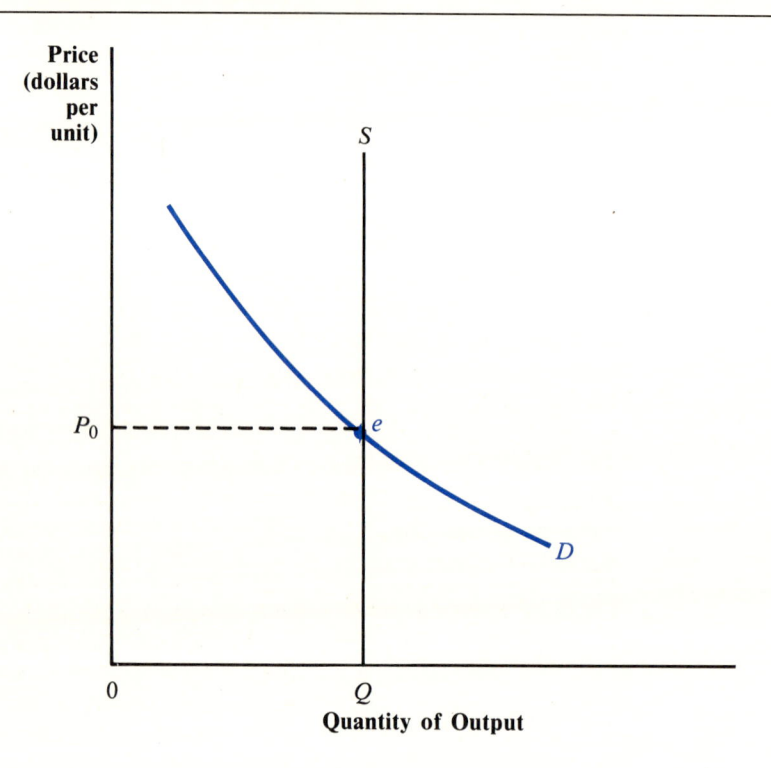

[Figure: Vertical supply curve S at quantity Q intersecting downward-sloping demand curve D at point e, with price P_0 on the vertical axis. Axes: Price (dollars per unit) vs. Quantity of Output.]

Pricing is simple in the market period. If the price is higher than P_0 in Figure 9-1, there is an excess supply and the price is bid down; if the price is lower than P_0, the price is bid up by excess demand.

The institutions in the economy for pricing goods that are fixed in supply are many. There are organized markets, such as the New York Stock Exchange or the Chicago Board of Trade. In many large cities, centralized produce markets must set equilibrium prices in order to prevent widespread spoiling of perishable vegetables. Many second-hand goods are auctioned off in a variety of types of auctions (see Example 9-1).

PRICING IN THE SHORT RUN

The **short run** is a period of time so short that at least one input is fixed in supply.

The theory of perfect competition in the **short run** explains the determination of price and output for both the firm and the industry in a period of time so short that new firms cannot enter and old firms cannot build new plants. What is different from the market period is that, in the short run, the firm has the option to produce more or less of the product. Thus, the firm must pay close attention to revenues and costs.

> **EXAMPLE 9–1**   **Auction Markets**

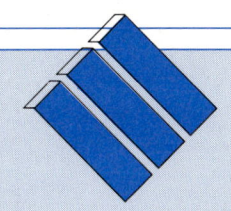

An auction market is a public or private sale of property to the highest bidder. The distinguishing feature of items sold at auction is that the supply of the product is irregular in quantity and quality. Manufactured goods tend to be homogeneous in quality and available on a continuous basis, but goods such as antiques and second-hand machinery along with certain types of basic commodities such as tobacco, wool, and fish are often traded on auction markets.

Two fundamental types of auction markets exist. The English auction is the most popular. In this well-known type, the auctioneer asks for ascending bids. When the highest bid is reached, the item is sold. The second most popular type is the Dutch auction, in which the auctioneer actually asks for descending bids. In the Dutch auction, the auctioneer starts at a relatively high price and quotes descending prices at fixed intervals (for example, $100, $95, $90, . . .). The successful bidder is simply the first bidder. Presumably, the first bidder places the highest value on the item in question.

The above schemes are single-sided auctions: the seller asks for bids from buyers. The New York Stock Exchange is an example of a double-sided auction. In such an auction, buyers submit bids and sellers submit offers. Would-be sellers submit supply prices, and would-be buyers submit demand prices. A binding contract occurs when any buyer accepts the offer of any seller or any seller accepts the bid of any buyer.

Economists have studied auctions, particularly the double-sided auction. Through experimental techniques, economists have learned that the competitive equilibrium is achieved very quickly and with very few buyers or sellers. On the basis of over 100 double-sided auction experiments, Vernon L. Smith reached the following conclusions: (1) The competitive equilibrium is achieved within three or four trading periods (or less) when the subjects are experienced with the auctioning method. (2) A competitive equilibrium can be achieved with six to eight agents. (3) Reaching a competitive equilibrium quickly does not require that the agents have complete information about the theoretical supply-and-demand conditions being studied.

Sources: Ralph Cassady, Jr., *Auctions and Auctioneering* (Los Angeles: University of California Press, 1967); Vernon L. Smith, "Microeconomic Systems as an Experimental Science," *American Economic Review* 72 (December 1982).

Price, Marginal Revenue, and Costs

It is assumed that the competitive firm tries to maximize profit. Profit is defined as

$$\pi = TR - TC, \tag{1}$$

FIGURE 9-2 Revenue and Demand Curves Under Perfect Competition

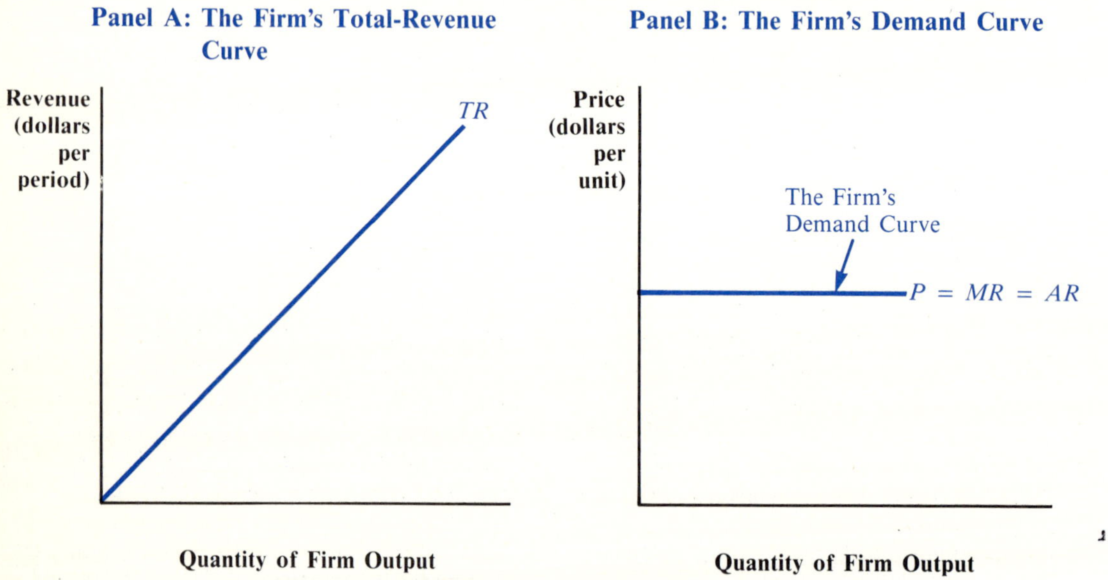

Panel A: The Firm's Total-Revenue Curve

Panel B: The Firm's Demand Curve

$P = MR = AR$

Panel A shows the total-revenue curve for a perfectly competitive firm. Panel B shows the demand curve for this type of firm. Because the slope of the *TR* curve = *P*, price, marginal revenue, and average revenue are equal: $P = MR = AR$.

where *TR* is total revenue and *TC* is total cost. Total revenue for a firm, in turn, is defined as

$$TR = P \times q, \qquad (2)$$

where *P* is the price of the product and *q* is the quantity sold.[1] Because price is fixed for the individual firm, the firm's marginal revenue (*MR*) is equal to the price; that is,

$$MR = \Delta TR/\Delta q = P. \qquad (3)$$

Because all units are sold at the same price, the firm's average revenue (*AR*) is the same as price; that is,

$$AR = TR/q = Pq/q = P. \qquad (4)$$

Chapter 5 showed that the relationship between marginal revenue and price was given by the formula:

$$P = MR(1 + 1/\eta_p), \qquad (5)$$

where η_p is the price elasticity of demand for the product. In the case of perfect competition, the firm can sell all it wants at the going market price.

---

1. Throughout this chapter, *q* denotes the output quantity of an individual firm and *Q* denotes the output of an entire industry.

FIGURE 9-3　Profit Maximization

Profit is maximized when the vertical difference between the *TR* and *TC* curves is at a maximum. The slopes of these curves are the same at q^*; when profit is maximized, marginal revenue equals marginal cost.

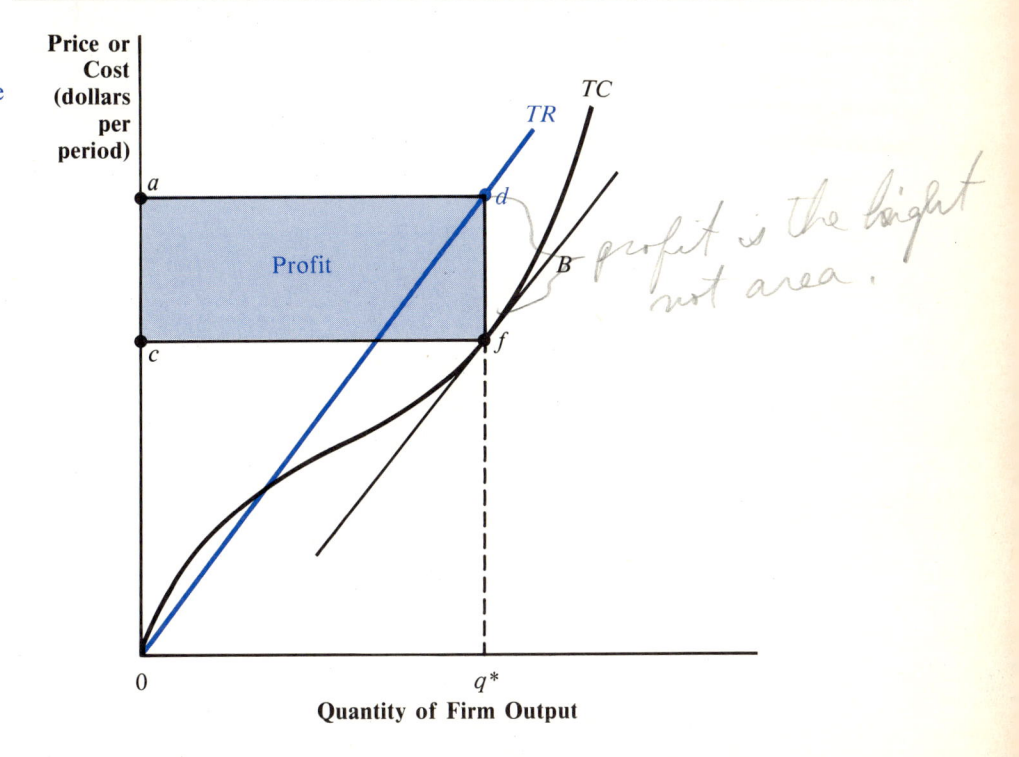

[Handwritten annotation on figure: "profit is the hight not area."]

In other words, the firm faces a perfectly elastic demand curve. Accordingly, $\eta_p = -\infty$ for each perfectly competitive firm. Thus, again, we see that $P = MR(1 - 1/\infty) = MR(1 - 0) = MR$.

Figure 9-2 shows the *TR* curve and the demand curve facing a perfectly competitive firm. In Panel A, the *TR* curve is a straight line from the origin; its slope is *P* at every point. In Panel B, the demand curve is a horizontal line with a height equal to the price of the product. We can label the demand curve *P*, *MR*, or *AR*; they are all the same.

Profit Maximization

Profit can be measured as the difference between total revenue and total cost or as the profit per unit sold multiplied by the number of units sold. Given that $TR = P \times q$ and $TC = (ATC)q$,

$$\pi = (P \times q) - (ATC \times q) = (P - ATC)q. \tag{6}$$

The term $(P - ATC)$ is the profit per unit.

How can the firm maximize profit? From a global perspective, the firm need only select that output at which the difference between total revenue and total cost is maximized. For example, in Figure 9-3 profit is maximized

FIGURE 9-4 Profit Maximization and the Marginal Rule

Profit is maximized at that output level, q^*, where price equals marginal cost. Price equals marginal revenue in the case of perfect competition. The maximum profit is the color shaded rectangle. Point e_0 is on the firm's supply curve.

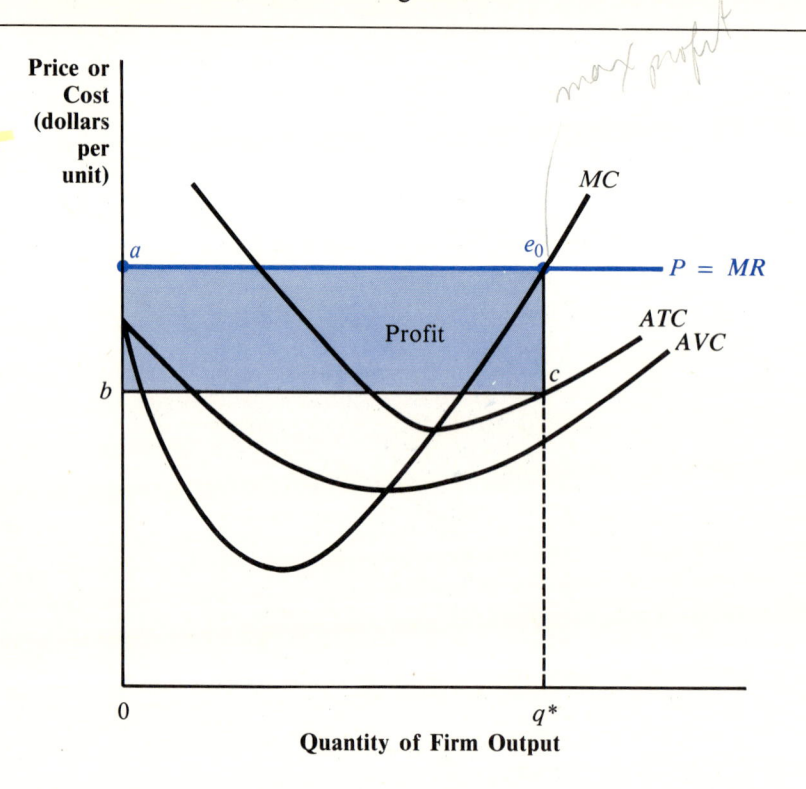

by producing at quantity q^*. The optimal, or profit-maximizing, output q^* occurs where the slope of the TC curve is the same as the slope of the TR curve. In Figure 9-3, line B is parallel to the TR curve and just tangent to the TC curve at level q^*. When output quantity is either less than or greater than q^*, profit is smaller than at the optimal level.

When profit is maximized, the slope of the TR curve equals the slope of the TC curve. In other words, $MR = MC$. Thus, an alternative way to represent profit maximization is to examine the behavior of marginal revenue and marginal cost. From this perspective, the firm locally searches for the output level that maximizes profit by comparing MR with MC. What is the logic behind this comparison? Given that $\pi = TR - TC$, it follows that

$$\Delta\pi = \Delta TR - \Delta TC. \tag{7}$$

Dividing both sides by Δq, we obtain the change in profit per unit of change in q, that is,

$$\Delta\pi/\Delta q = MR - MC. \tag{8}$$

Accordingly, the difference between marginal revenue and marginal cost measures marginal profit—the change in profit per unit of increase in output.

FIGURE 9-5   Prices, Cost Curves, and the Supply Curve

When price is less than minimum average variable cost, at a price level such as p_1, the firm minimizes losses by shutting down. When price is greater than minimum AVC, at a price level such as P_2, the firm minimizes losses by producing at the level where price equals marginal cost. At this point, e_2, there is an excess of revenue over variable cost. The firm's supply curve is the part of the MC curve that lies above the AVC curve.

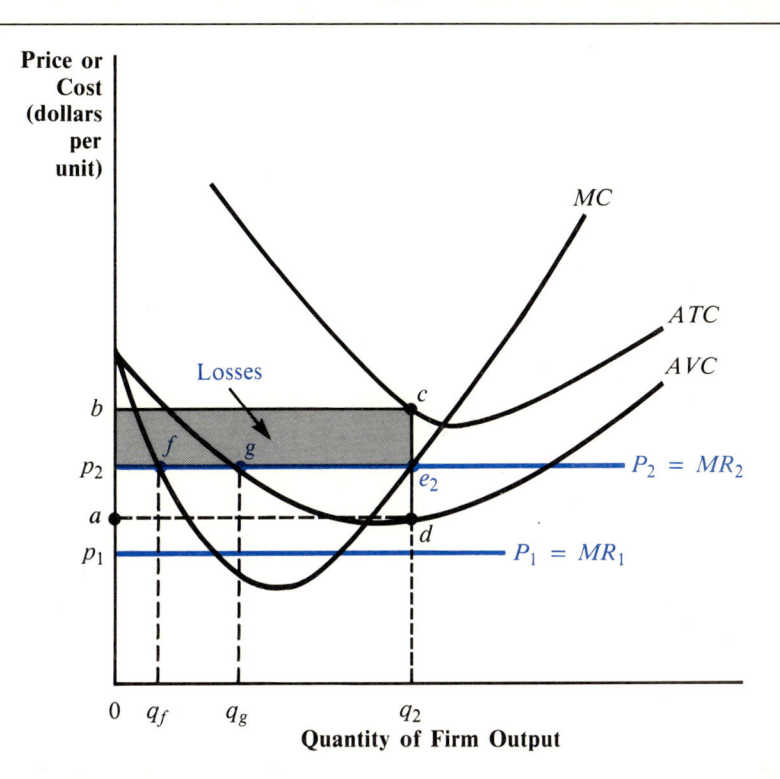

If *MR* is greater than *MC*, profit increases when output is increased and falls when it is decreased. If *MR* is less than MC, profit decreases when output is increased and rises when it is decreased.

Figure 9-4 shows the $MR = MC$ rule for the case of a perfectly competitive firm (where $MR = P$). In the short run, the firm's cost curves are MC, AVC, and ATC. The figure shows that as long as output is less than q^*, $MR > MC$. Profit can be increased whenever $P > MC$ by expanding output. Thus, profit is maximized when output is q^*, where $P = MC$. The firm's profit is shown by the shaded rectangle, which equals $(P - ATC)q^*$, or profit per unit multiplied by the number of units sold.

The Firm's Supply Curve

For any given price, the competitive firm pushes up output until marginal cost equals price. Point e_0 in Figure 9-4 is a point on the firm's supply curve, because by definition a supply curve shows various quantities supplied at different prices. This suggests that at least part of the firm's *MC* curve is also the firm's supply curve.

Figure 9-5 superimposes various prices on the same set of cost curves.

FIGURE 9-6 Cost Curves and the Short-Run Supply Curve

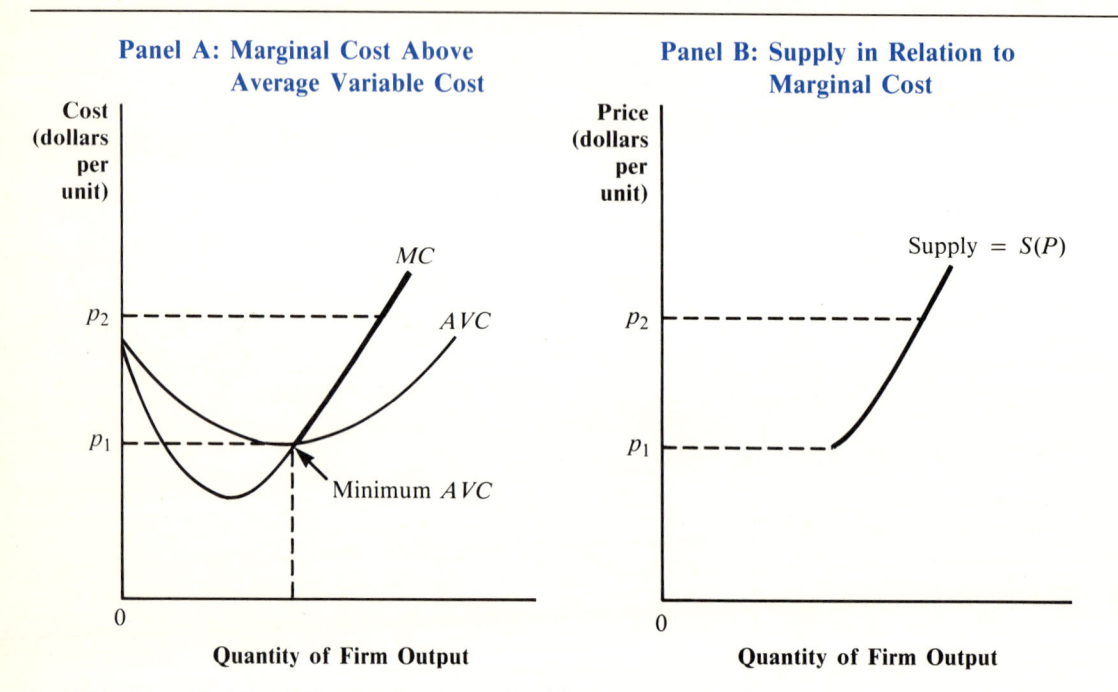

Panel A: Marginal Cost Above Average Variable Cost

Panel B: Supply in Relation to Marginal Cost

Panel A shows that the *MC* curve intersects the *AVC* curve at its minimum point. The short-run supply curve, isolated in Panel B, is the portion of the *MC* curve above that intersection.

First, notice that the firm's profit is:

$$\pi = (P - ATC)q = (P - AVC)q - (AFC)q$$
$$= (P - AVC)q - FC. \qquad (9)$$

Equation (9) tells us that profit is the excess of revenue over *variable cost* minus *fixed cost*. Consider price p_1 in Figure 9-5, which is less than the minimum *AVC*. Because $P_1 < AVC$ for all output quantities it follows that variable cost exceeds revenue at any output level. If the firm produces at all, it loses not only its fixed cost but also some portion of variable cost. By shutting down, the firm loses only its fixed cost. At this price level, the firm's **shutdown rule** takes effect.

Suppose now that the price settles between the minimum *ATC* and the minimum *AVC*, along a price line such as P_2. At what output level should the firm produce? If the firm shuts down, it loses its fixed costs. Imagine that the firm produces at point *f*, where $P_2 = MC$ and the *MC* curve is downward-sloping. At point *f*, the firm loses even more than fixed costs, because $P_2 < AVC$ at that point. The firm might try a larger output level, for example, at point *g*, where $P_2 = AVC$. At this point, the firm is losing precisely its fixed costs, because it is just covering variable costs. But the firm can do better. At point *g*, $MR = P_2 > MC$. Accordingly, any increase in output will raise

The **shutdown rule** is that the firm should produce no output if price is less than minimum average variable cost. By shutting down, the firm loses only its fixed cost.

PRACTICE EXERCISE 9-1

Q. A firm's variable cost is $VC = 75q - 10q^2 + q^3$. How much will the firm produce if $p = \$40$? (*Hint*: AVC is minimized when $q = 5$.)

A. The optimal firm output is zero, because $AVC < P$. By direct computation,

$$AVC = \frac{VC}{Q} = \frac{75q - 10q^2 + q^3}{q} = 75 - 10q + q^2.$$

Given that AVC is minimized at $q = 5$, minimum $AVC = 75 - 10(5) + 5^2 = \$50$, which is greater than the price, \$40. The firm should shut down in the short run and lose only its fixed cost.

---

revenue more than cost and will cut the firm's losses below the level of fixed costs. Losses are minimized at point e_2, where $P_2 = MC$ at output level q_2. The firm's losses are represented by the shaded area, where the firm is losing $(ATC - P_2)$ per unit multiplied by the quantity of output, q_2. But these losses are smaller than the firm's fixed costs, since FC = the rectangle $abcd$ [$= (ATC - AVC)q = (AFC)q$].

The firm maximizes profit by producing no output if the price is less than average variable cost. If the price is greater than minimum AVC, the firm maximizes profit or minimizes losses by producing where $MC = P$ and where the MC curve is rising. The firm's supply curve is that portion of the MC curve that lies above the AVC curve.

Figure 9-6 shows the firm's short-run supply curve. Panel A shows the AVC and MC curves; Panel B shows the short-run supply curve, which is just that part of the MC curve above the AVC curve in Panel A.

PRACTICE EXERCISE 9-2

Q. Suppose $FC = \$1,000$, $MC = 20q$, and $VC = 10q^2$. What is the firm's shutdown point? What is its supply curve?

A. $AVC = VC/q = 10q$. Because the supply curve is that portion of MC above minimum AVC, the supply curve is the entire MC curve. The firm's shutdown point is $q = 0$, because AVC is at a minimum when $q = 0$. The firm's supply curve is simply $P = 20q$ or $q = P/20$.

FIGURE 9-7   Supply Curve for a Two-Firm Constant-Cost Industry

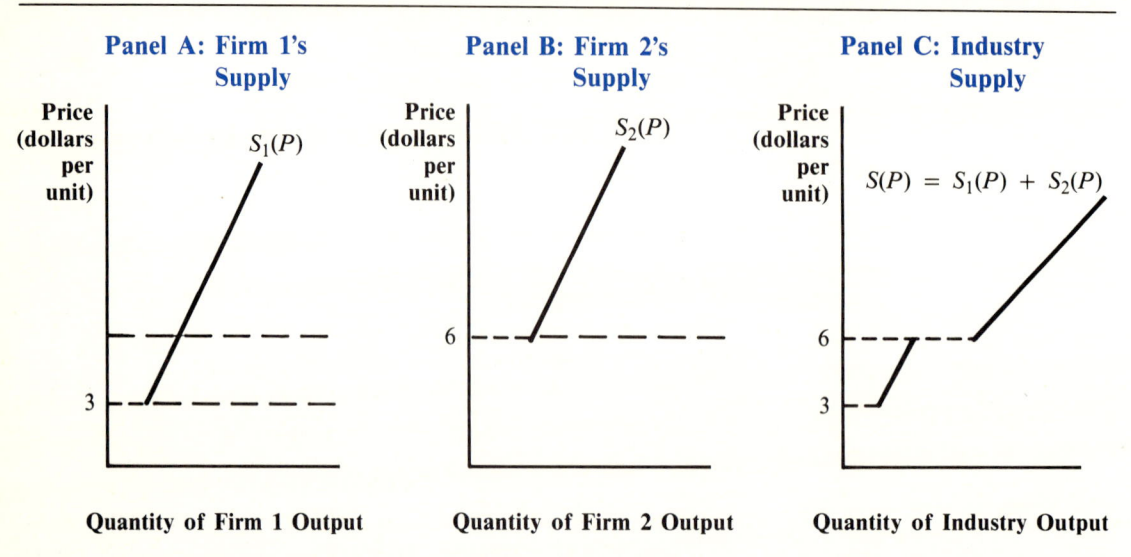

Panel A: Firm 1's Supply — $S_1(P)$, Price (dollars per unit) vs. Quantity of Firm 1 Output, with dashed lines at 3.

Panel B: Firm 2's Supply — $S_2(P)$, Price (dollars per unit) vs. Quantity of Firm 2 Output, with dashed line at 6.

Panel C: Industry Supply — $S(P) = S_1(P) + S_2(P)$, Price (dollars per unit) vs. Quantity of Industry Output, with dashed lines at 3 and 6.

In a constant-cost industry, the industry supply curve in Panel C is the horizontal sum of the supply curves of individual firms: $S(P) = \Sigma S_i(P)$ for any number of firms, i.

Short-Run Market Equilibrium

A **constant-cost industry** is one in which an increase in industry output does not affect factor prices.

An **increasing-cost industry** is one in which an increase in industry output raises the crucial factor prices paid by individual firms.

The individual firm in a competitive market takes the price as given. How is this price determined in the short run? The key feature of the short run is that the number of firms is fixed. Thus, the short-run equilibrium price equates the market demand and market supply of the existing firms. The market-demand curve is the horizontal summation of the individual-demand curves in the market (Chapter 4). The market-supply curve is likewise determined in relation to the horizontal summation of the individual firms' supply curves.

How the horizontal sum of each firm's supply curve is related to the market-supply curve depends on the extent to which the expansion of industry output affects the cost curves of the individual firms. A **constant-cost industry** is one in which an expansion of the industry has no impact on firms' cost curves. An **increasing-cost industry** is one in which an expansion of the industry raises the cost of production of the individual firms.[2]

---

2. There is a category of decreasing-cost industries that may be relevant in the long run. In the short run, it is hard to imagine that an increase in industry output could lead to a decrease in factor prices. However, this could happen in the long run if, say, an expansion in an industry gave rise to the development of transportation facilities that lowered the cost of production for each of the individual firms.

Constant-Cost Industry

A constant-cost industry is one that uses resources similar to those used by the rest of the economy. If Industry X expands, other industries necessarily contract in order to release the resources utilized by Industry X. When Industry X is a constant-cost industry, the resources absorbed by its expansion will be similar in quantity and composition to the resources released by the rest of the economy. Accordingly, increases in factor demand from Industry X will be matched by increases in factor supply, and there will be no need for the relative factor prices to change. For a constant-cost industry, the ATC, MC, AVC, and $LRAC$ curves remain the same in the face of changes in industrywide output.

The derivation of the short-run industry-supply curve for a constant-cost industry is shown in Figure 9–7. For simplicity, the figure depicts an industry comprising only two firms. The supply curves are $S_1(P)$ and $S_2(P)$ for Firms 1 and 2. Note that the two firms need not be the same. The industry-supply curve is the horizontal sum at each price: $S(P) = S_1(P) + S_2(P) = \Sigma S_i(P)$. This formula applies for any number of firms.

In the case of many firms, the short-run supply curve can be derived by algebraic methods. Suppose, for example, that each firm has the same supply curve: $S_i = bP$. The market-supply curve for N firms would then be $NS_i = NbP$.

There is a short-run competitive equilibrium for any industry if (1) each consumer of the product is maximizing utility, (2) each producer is maximizing profit or minimizing losses, and (3) market supply equals market demand.

In Chapter 4, we derived the demand curve for an individual consumer as the outcome of utility maximization at different prices for a good. The market demand for a good is the horizontal sum of all the individual demand

---

PRACTICE EXERCISE 9–3

Q. As in Practice Exercise 9–2, assume that $FC = \$1,000$, $MC = 20q$, and $VC = 10q^2$ for a representative firm in a constant-cost industry. The market demand curve is $D(P) = 1,200 - P$. If there are 80 firms ($N = 80$) in the industry, what are the short-run price/quantity combinations for the industry and the firm? Calculate profit, π, for each firm.

A. The short-run supply curve for the firm is $S_i = P/20$. The market-supply curve is $NS_i = S(P) = 80P/20 = 4P$. Accordingly, the equilibrium price occurs where $4P = 1,200 - P$ or $5P = 1200$. Thus, equilibrium $P = \$240$. Each firm produces where $P = MC$, or $\$240 = 20q$, or $q = 12$. Profit is $\$240(12) - 1,000 - 10(12)^2 = \$440$.

240 CHAPTER 9 THE THEORY OF PERFECT COMPETITION

FIGURE 9–8 **Competitive Equilibrium in the Short Run**

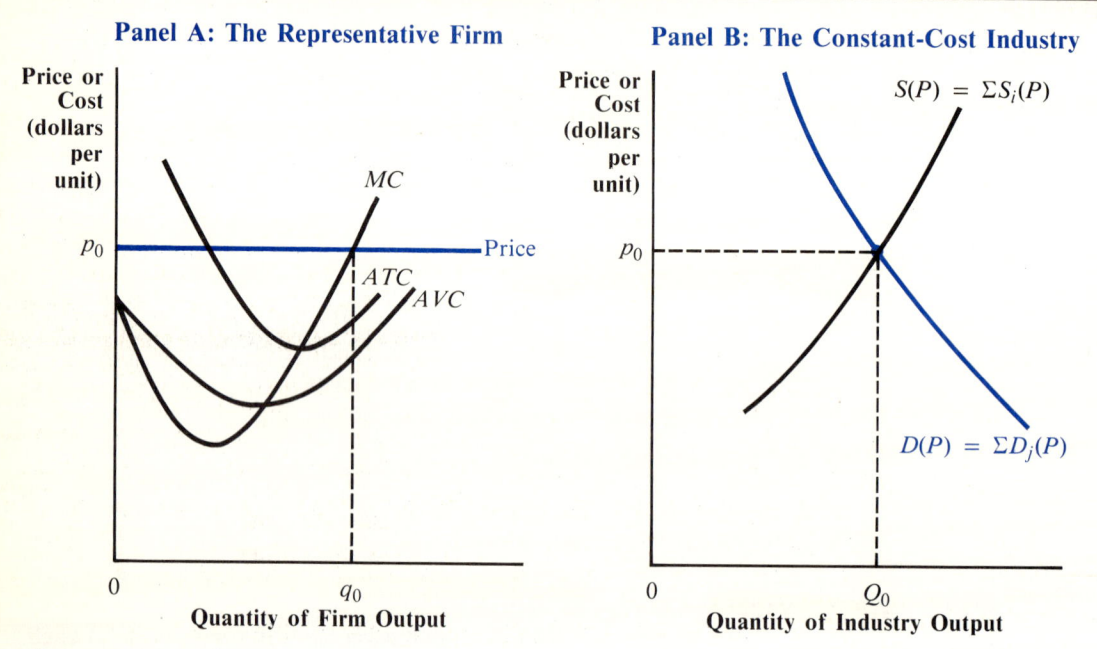

Panel A: The Representative Firm

Panel B: The Constant-Cost Industry

Short-run curves for a representative firm in a constant-cost industry are shown in Panel A. The firm's supply curve is the *MC* curve above the *AVC* curve. Supply and demand curves for the constant-cost industry are shown in Panel B; each is the horizontal sum of the individual curves for all sellers and buyers. The short-run equilibrium price is p_0 where industry output is Q_0 and the individual firm's output is q_0.

curves: $D(P) = \Sigma D_j(P)$. At each point along the $D(P)$ curve, each consumer in the market is maximizing utility subject to his or her budget constraint.

Figure 9–8 shows the short-run competitive equilibrium with particular attention paid to the individual firm. Panel A shows a representative, or average, firm. Panel B shows the market-demand curve, $D(P)$, and the market-supply curve, $S(P)$. The market-supply curve $S(P)$ is the horizontal sum of the supply curves of all the individual firms in the industry; in Panel A, the *MC* curve above *AVC* is a representative example of an individual firm's supply curve. At the market-equilibrium price p_0, industry output is Q_0, and the representative firm produces q_0 units of output. If N is the number of firms, then $Q_0 = Nq_0$. The price p_0 is the short-run competitive-equilibrium price because: each firm is maximizing profit (with $P = MC$), each consumer is maximizing utility, and supply equals demand.

The representative firm shown in Panel A of Figure 9–8 is making an economic profit at q_0 because $P > ATC$. The making of economic profit, however, it is not necessary in the short run; it is necessary only that the firm earn something in excess of variable cost in the short run because the

FIGURE 9-9   Supply Curve for an Increasing-Cost Industry

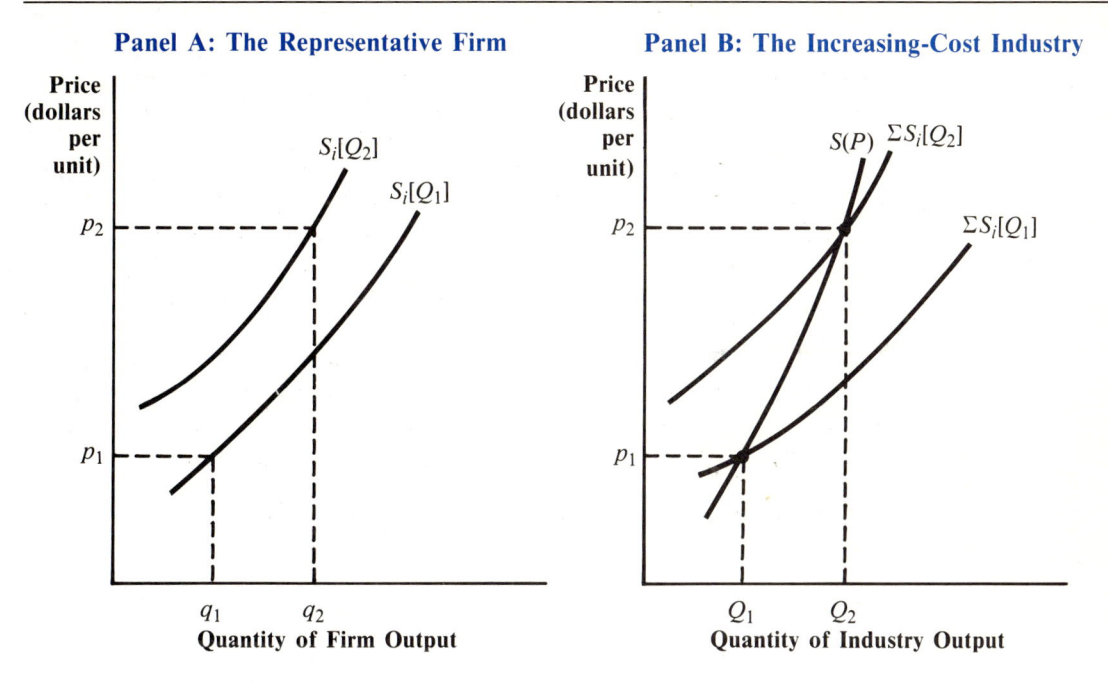

Panel A: The Representative Firm

Panel B: The Increasing-Cost Industry

Panel A shows that the representative firm's supply curve shifts to the left as industry output rises from Q_1 to Q_2. The higher output raises factor costs and, therefore, marginal costs. The industry supply curve is $S(P)$, where $\Sigma S_i(Q) = Q$.

firm must pay its fixed costs in any case. The firm could have short-run economic losses if $P < ATC$.

Increasing-Cost Industry

Let us now consider the industry-supply curve in the case of an increasing-cost industry, one using a resource mix dissimilar to that used by the rest of the economy. For example, Industry X might be capital-intensive while the rest of the economy is (on average) labor-intensive, or Industry X might use special resources, such as a certain type of agricultural land or certain minerals. When Industry X expands, it must draw resources from the rest of the economy. If Industry X is capital-intensive, when it expands it will try to absorb more capital and less labor than the rest of the economy is releasing at the original set of factor prices. As a consequence, the expansion of Industry X will raise the factor prices of the specialized resources upon which it depends, and the cost curves of individual firms will rise.

Figure 9-9 depicts the supply curve of an increasing-cost industry. While the individual firm's supply curve is still that portion of the *MC* curve above its *AVC* curve, the market-supply curve is steeper than the simple sum of the individual supply curves. In Panel A, $S_i(Q_1)$ is the supply curve (the *MC* curve above *AVC*) of the representative firm when industry output is Q_1, and $S_i(Q_2)$ is the supply curve when industry output rises to Q_2. The higher level of output increases costs by shifting up the individual *MC* curves. Panel B shows that the market-supply curve is the loci of intersections between each level of industry output and the appropriate horizontal sum ΣS_i. When output is Q_1, the horizontal sum is $\Sigma S_i(Q_1)$ and p_1 is the market-supply price for the industry output. When industry output is Q_2, the market supply price is p_2. The market supply curve $S(P)$ is steeper than the simple sum of all the firms' supply curves in the case of an increasing-cost industry.[3]

The increasing-cost-industry case illustrates the fallacy of composition in economics: what is true of each firm in an industry need not be true of all the firms taken together. If an economist were investigating the responsiveness of quantity supplied to price, a study based on the responses of individual firms would overestimate the market response.

In the short run, the number of firms is fixed. The firm's supply curve is that portion of the *MC* curve above the *AVC* curve. In a constant-cost industry, factor costs are independent of industry output, and the market-supply curve is simply the horizontal sum of all the individual supply curves. In an increasing-cost industry, factor costs increase when industry output rises, and the market-supply curve will be less elastic than the horizontal sum of all the individual supply curves.

The Price Elasticity of Supply

The price elasticity of supply is the percentage change in quantity supplied divided by the percentage change in the price of the product; that is,

$$\eta_s = \frac{\Delta Q/Q}{\Delta P/P}$$
$$= \left(\frac{\Delta Q}{\Delta P}\right)\left(\frac{P}{Q}\right).$$

The responsiveness of quantity supplied to price is measured by the **price elasticity of supply**. As with the elasticity of demand, the elasticity, rather than the slope, of the supply curve is used because the size of any change is better measured by the percentage change.

Supply is *elastic* or *inelastic* as η_s exceeds one or falls short of one. Supply is *perfectly elastic* or *perfectly inelastic* as η_s is infinite or zero.

Figure 9-10 shows how to measure the price elasticity of supply graphically. To measure elasticity at point e, a line is drawn tangent to the supply curve at that point. Then

$$\frac{\Delta Q}{\Delta P} = \frac{pe}{pa} = \frac{0Q}{pa} \tag{10}$$

---

3. The short-run supply curve is determined by $\Sigma S_i(P,Q) = Q$, where $S_i(P,Q)$ is the supply curve of the individual firm. A constant-cost industry is where $\partial S_i/\partial Q = 0$. An increasing-cost industry is where $\partial S_i/\partial Q < 0$, because an increase in industry output lowers the supply of the individual firm. By solving for Q as a function of P, the short-run supply curve is uniquely determined.

FIGURE 9-10   Price Elasticity of Supply

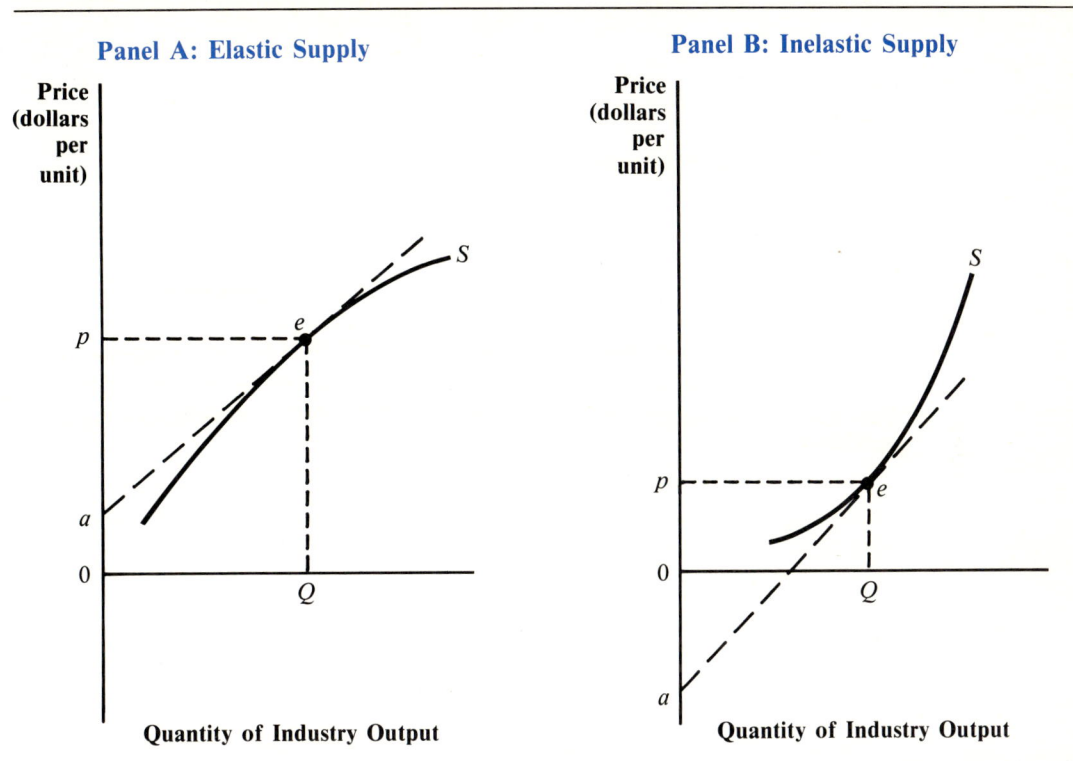

Panel A: Elastic Supply

Panel B: Inelastic Supply

The line tangent to the supply curve at point e intersects the vertical axis at point a. The elasticity of supply at price p is measured by the ratio $0p/pa$. In Panel A, the supply curve is elastic at point e because $0p/pa > 1$. In Panel B, the supply curve is inelastic at point e because $0p/pa < 1$.

Given that

$$\eta_s = \frac{0Q}{pa} \times \frac{0p}{0Q} \tag{11}$$

it follows that

$$\eta_s = \frac{0p}{pa} \tag{12}$$

In the case shown in Panel A, price elasticity exceeds unity because $0p > 0a$. If the tangent intersects the vertical axis above the origin, as in Panel A, the supply curve is elastic at that point. If the tangent intersects the vertical axis below the origin, as in Panel B, the supply curve is inelastic at that point, because $0p < pa$.

Suppose now that an industry consists of identical firms. If it is a constant-cost industry, the price elasticity of the individual firm's supply curves will equal the price elasticity of supply for the industry. But if the industry is

244 CHAPTER 9 THE THEORY OF PERFECT COMPETITION

an increasing-cost industry, the price elasticity of supply for the individual firm will exceed price elasticity of supply for the industry.

PRICING IN THE LONG RUN

The supply curve in the market period is perfectly inelastic. As time passes, the supply curve becomes more elastic or less inelastic. In the short run, the market-supply curve is related to the horizontal sum of all the existing firms' supply curves. What about the supply curve in the long run? There are two fundamental differences between the short run and the long run. First, in the long run, firms can minimize the cost of producing any given volume of output—that is, the firm is on the long-run average-cost (*LRAC*) curve. Second, in the long run, if there is freedom of entry into and exit from the industry, new firms can become established and old firms can quit the business.

The **long run** *is a period of time long enough to vary all inputs.*

Freedom of entry, of course, need not hold even with price-taking firms. The government can limit entry by issuing permits or licenses. For example, the number of taxicabs in New York City is determined by the number of permits issued; the number of private clubs in California is limited by the number of liquor licenses allowed. It is not surprising to learn that physicians, attorneys, and accountants are licensed by every state in the United States, but it is surprising that individual states license occupations such as dealers in scrap tobacco, pest controllers, tree surgeons, tile layers, potato growers, and many, many others.[4] In 1969, California licensed some 178 occupations, Pennsylvania about 165, New York about 130, and Texas only about 66. (See Example 9–2.)

Long-Run Competitive Equilibrium

If there is freedom of entry and exit, long-run economic profits in an industry must tend toward zero. Recall that economic profit is defined as revenue minus all opportunity costs. Because opportunity costs include what the entrepreneur could earn elsewhere for his or her capital and management inputs, economic profits signal that the assets used in a particular industry are earning above-normal accounting profits. Indeed, by the definition of opportunity costs, economic profits equal zero and prevail when accounting profits are competitive with those in other industries (see Chapter 8). If there are economic losses, they signal that the assets used in a particular industry are earning below-normal accounting profits. Thus, resources will enter an industry if there are economic profits and leave an industry if there are economic losses. The entry of new firms will drive profits down to zero by

---

[4]. For examples, see Walter Gelhorn, *Individual Freedom and Government Restraints* (Baton Rouge: Louisiana State University Press, 1956); Milton Friedman, *Capitalism and Freedom* (Chicago: University of Chicago Press, 1962), chap. 9.

EXAMPLE 9–2 Freedom of Entry

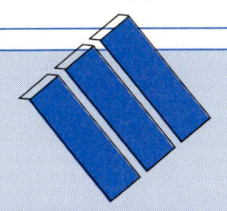

The freedom-of-entry assumption of perfect competition is not satisfied in many industries. The accompanying table shows the number of occupations licensed by each state in 1969. The data are approximate because of the lack of uniformity in the definition of an occupation. Nevertheless, the numbers are indicative of restrictions on entry. Every state regulates occupations such as insurance agents, real-estate agents, architects, attorneys, barbers, beauticians, dental hygienists, embalmers, engineers, practical nurses, nurses, optometrists, osteopaths, pharmacists, physiotherapists, physicians, elementary and secondary teachers, and veterinarians. Electricians are licensed in 30 states, plumbers in 39 states, contractors in 36 states, and funeral directors in 44 states. A few states license fortune-tellers, florists, ferry operators, and motor-vehicle mechanics. No state regulates professors or economists!

Source: Karen Greene, "Occupational Licensing and the Supply of Nonprofessional Manpower," Man Power Research Monograph No. 1, U.S. Department of Labor, 1969.

State	Occupations Licensed	State	Occupations Licensed
Alabama	117	Montana	74
Alaska	65	Nebraska	97
Arizona	83	Nevada	95
Arkansas	79	New Hampshire	78
California	178	New Jersey	100
Colorado	89	New Mexico	105
Connecticut	106	New York	130
Delaware	83	North Carolina	85
Florida	123	North Dakota	67
Georgia	129	Ohio	80
Hawaii	113	Oklahoma	76
Idaho	138	Oregon	96
Illinois	181	Pennsylvania	165
Indiana	88	Rhode Island	99
Iowa	73	South Carolina	69
Kansas	83	South Dakota	79
Kentucky	110	Tennessee	84
Louisiana	99	Texas	66
Maine	99	Utah	72
Maryland	94	Vermont	73
Massachusetts	106	Virginia	100
Michigan	147	Washington	95
Minnesota	114	West Virginia	63
Mississippi	94	Wisconsin	140
Missouri	68	Wyoming	131

FIGURE 9-11 Competitive Equilibrium in the Long Run

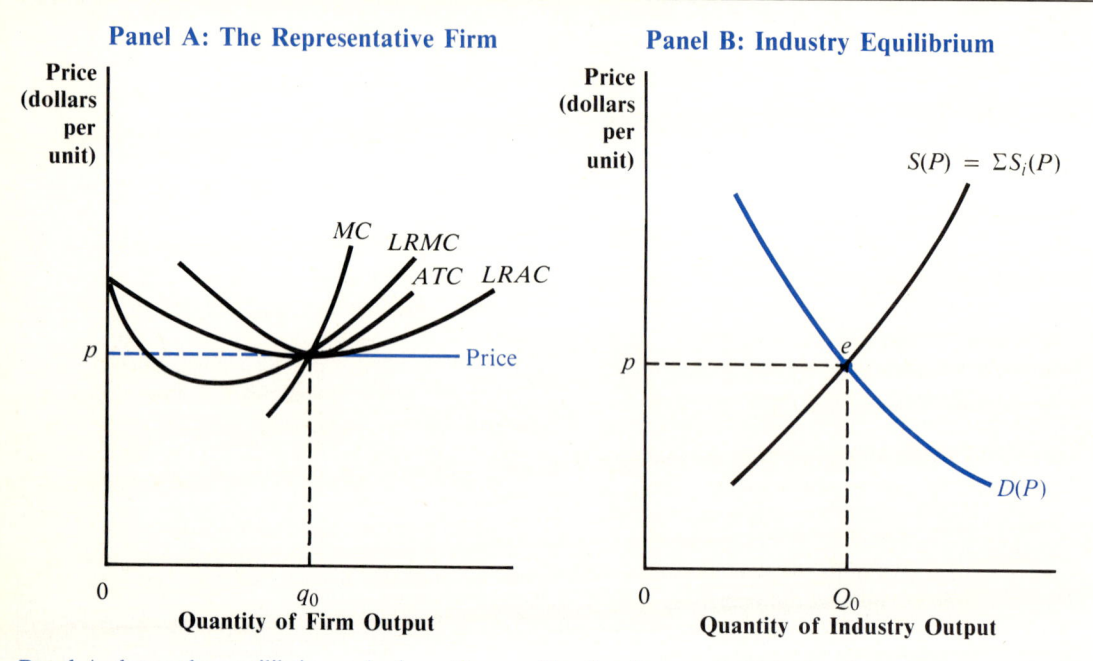

Panel A: The Representative Firm

Panel B: Industry Equilibrium

Panel A shows the equilibrium price/quantity combination for a representative firm. Profit must equal zero, and price must equal long-run marginal cost (*LRMC*). At the equilibrium point, $p = MC = ATC = LRAC = LRMC$. Panel B shows that the supply curve is the sum of the individual firms' supply curves. The number of firms in the industry must be such that $D(P) = \Sigma S_i(P)$.

increasing supply and lowering the price of the product; the exit of old firms will drive losses toward zero by decreasing supply and raising the price of the product.

Long-run competitive equilibrium requires that, first, the competitive firm must be maximizing profit in both the short run and the long run; that is, $P = MC$ and $P = LRMC$. Second, the representative firm must be earning zero profit; that is, $P = LRAC$. Third, the number of firms must be such that $D(P) = \Sigma \ S_i(P)$—that is, the industry must be in short-run equilibrium. Figure 9-11 shows the long-run competitive equilibrium for a representative firm and for its industry. The long-run equilibrium is also a short-run equilibrium in which the representative firm is operating where $P = LRAC = LRMC$. Because profit is zero when $P = LRAC$, there is no incentive for new firms to enter or old firms to leave the industry. The equilibrium number of firms, N, is $N = Q_0/q_0$.

The Behavior of the Firm in the Long Run

The behavior of the firm in the long run is fundamentally different when freedom of entry into the industry is limited or absent altogether. Let us first

FIGURE 9–12 Firm Behavior with and Without Freedom of Entry

With freedom of entry and rational expectations, the firm will treat p^* as a temporary price and will produce at point a with the optimum-sized plant. With absolute barriers to entry, however, the firm will attempt to produce at b, where $P = LRMC$, because p^* may then be considered permanent.

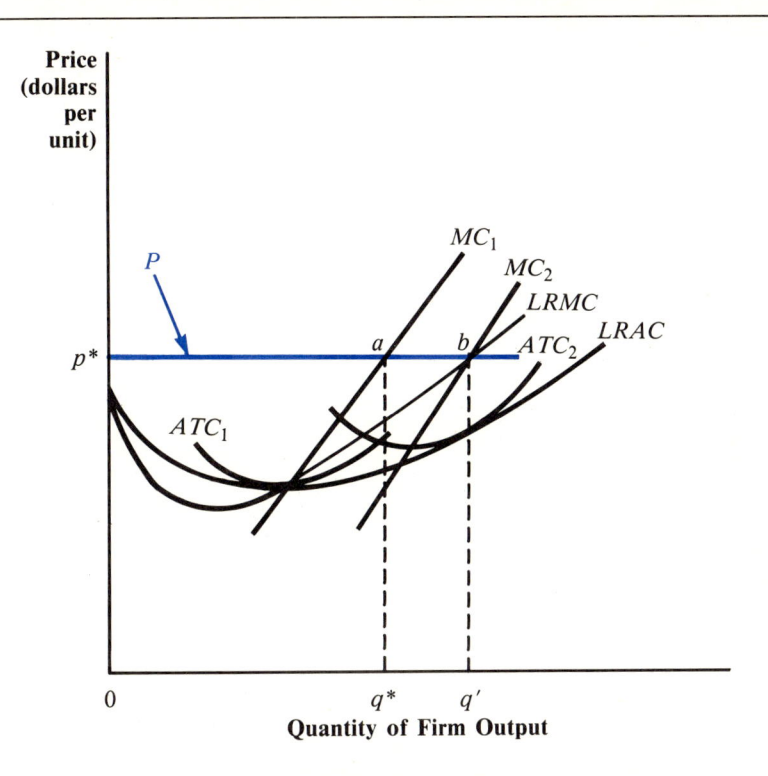

imagine that there is complete freedom of entry. Figure 9–12 shows a firm operating a plant at the minimum efficient scale (*MES*). If the price is p^*, the firm will, in the short run, produce quantity q^* where p^* equals short-run MC. What happens in the long run? If the firm could be assured that price p^* would prevail in the future, it would simply equate p^* with *LRMC* at point b to produce q' and operate the plant along cost curve ATC_2. However, with freedom of entry, the firm cannot treat p^* as a permanent price; a rational firm would consider such a price temporary because at price p^*, the representative firm is making an economic profit. An existing firm, or a new firm contemplating entry, would surely make a mistake by building a plant with costs represented by ATC_2 on the assumption that it would produce at point b. In the long run, new firms will enter and drive the price below p^*, making such a large firm economically unprofitable (because of the burden of diseconomies of scale).

Freedom of Entry

With complete freedom of entry, the rational firm will build a plant no smaller than the minimum efficient scale and not so large as to run into diseconomies of scale. A rational firm will certainly possess the information

FIGURE 9-13 Long-Run Supply: Constant-Cost Industry

Panel A: Representative Firm

Panel B: Constant-Cost Industry

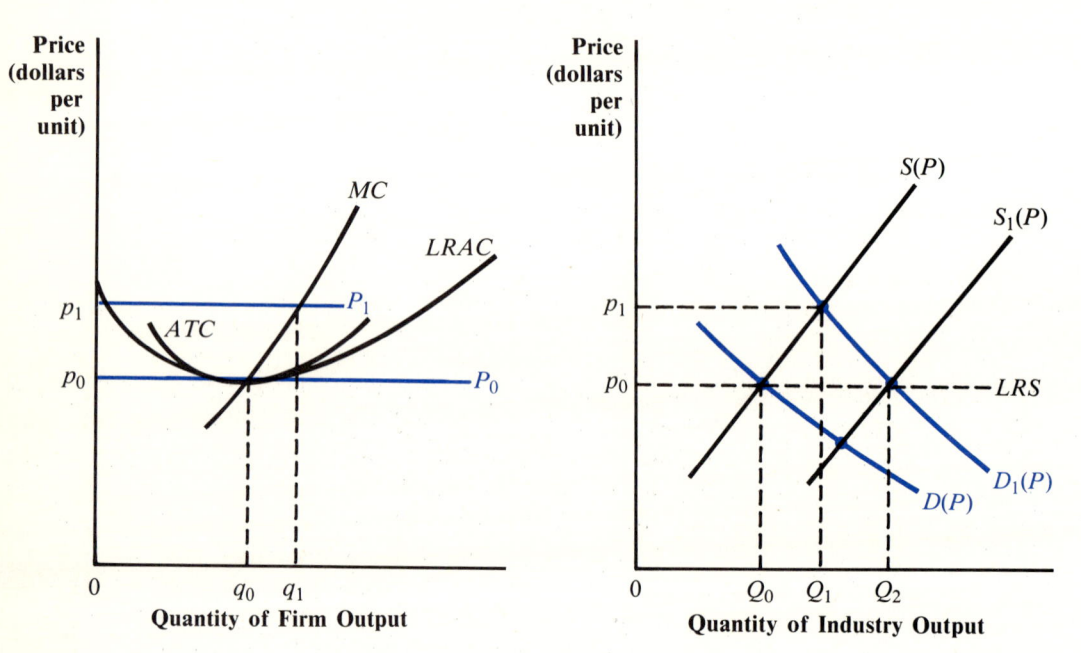

Initially, the supply and demand curves are $D(P)$ and $S(P)$ and the industry is in long-run equilibrium where P_0 equals MC and minimum $LRAC$. If the demand curve shifts upward to $D_1(P)$, the short-run equilibrium price rises to p_1. The representative firm produces q_1 in the short run and makes economic profits. In the long run, the profits attract new firms until the new short-run supply curve, $S_1(P)$, drives the price back down to p_0. Minimum $LRAC$ stays the same because this is a constant-cost industry. In the new long-run equilibrium, the number of firms is Q_2/q_0, which is larger than before.

that above-normal profits attract competition, making inefficient plant sizes unprofitable in the long run, as articulated in the **rational-expectations hypothesis**.[5]

Barriers to Entry

If there are absolute barriers to entry, the rational-expectations hypothesis implies that firms can be more optimistic when a price such as p^* in Figure 9-12 prevails. The firm will then find it profitable to expand until point b is

---

[5]. The rational-expectations hypothesis was introduced in the seminal article by John Muth, "Rational Expectations and the Theory of Price Movement," *Econometrica*, July 1971. For an application, see Thomas F. Cooley and Stephen J. DeCanio, "Rational Expectations in American Agriculture, 1867–1914," *Review of Economics and Statistics* 59 (February 1977): 9–17.

reached, where $p^* = LRMC$. If the price is less than minimum $LRAC$, however, the firm will go out of business. Thus, if there are entry barriers, the firm's long-run supply curve is simply that portion of the $LRMC$ curve above $LRAC$.

The Freedom-of-Entry Case

With freedom of entry, the price must equal the minimum point on the $LRAC$ curve in the long run. What is the long-run supply curve for each type of industry?

Constant-Cost Industry

Figure 9–13 illustrates the derivation of the long-run supply curve for a constant-cost industry. In Panel B, the demand curve is $D(P)$, and the short-run supply curve is $S(P)$. Panel A shows that at the equilibrium price, p_0, the representative firm is producing at the minimum points on both the ATC and $LRAC$ curves. Although the firm is maximizing profit in both the long run and the short run ($P_0 = MC = LRMC$), economic profit equals zero. The number of firms in the industry is $N = Q_0/q_0$, as in Figure 9–11.

Now suppose that the demand curve unexpectedly shifts upward, to $D_1(P)$. In the short run, the number of firms will remain the same, and the supply curve will remain at $S(P)$. The short-run equilibrium price will rise to p_1, creating short-run economic profit for the representative firm. These profits signal that returns on investments in this industry exceed returns in other industries. Consequently, new firms are enticed into this industry, shifting the supply curve to the right, from $S(P)$ to $S_1(P)$, because the supply curve is the horizontal sum of all individual MC curves above AVC. Ultimately, the price will be driven back down to the original price, p_0. Again, the firm is producing where the $LRAC$ and ATC curves are at their minimum points. Because this industry is a constant-cost industry, the expansion of industry output to Q_1 has no impact on firm costs, so minimum $LRAC$ remains the same. The new number of firms is Q_2/q_0.

The outputs Q_0 and Q_2 are both supplied at the same supply price, P_0, in the long run. Consequently, the long-run industry-supply curve is the horizontal line LRS. In a constant-cost industry, the long-run supply curve is perfectly elastic.

The **rational-expectations hypothesis** is the assumption that individual firms utilize all the information available to them to predict the future price of a product. In a world of perfect information, firms will know the $LRAC$ curve and be able to calculate the product's long-run equilibrium price.

Increasing-Cost Industry

Now consider the long-run supply curve for an increasing-cost industry. In this case, an expansion of industry output shifts the representative firm's $LRAC$ curve upward. The higher is industry output, the higher will be the minimum $LRAC$ for the representative firm. Because the industry is only in long-run equilibrium when price equals minimum long-run average cost, it

PRACTICE EXERCISE 9-4

Q. For the constant-cost industry in Practice Exercise 9-3, what is the long-run supply curve with free entry? Given the demand curve $D(P) = 1,200 - P$, what is the equilibrium number of firms, N?

A. Minimum ATC occurs where $ATC = MC$. Given $ATC = 1,000/q + 10q$ and $MC = 20q$, the firm's minimum ATC occurs when $10q = 1,000/q$, or $q^2 = 100$ or $q = 10$. Thus, minimum $ATC = 1,000/(10) + 10(10) = 20(10) = \$200$. In the long run, profit is zero, so $P = \$200$. The long-run supply curve will be a horizontal line at $P = \$200$. Because $D(P) = 1,200 - P$, the market output in the long run is 1,000. Because each firm produces $q = 10$ units, $N = 1,000/10 = 100$.

---

follows that the minimum $LRAC$ rises with industry output. Thus, the long-run supply curve must be upward-sloping.

Figure 9-14 illustrates the impact of an unexpected increase in the demand for the product of an increasing-cost industry. Initially, the industry is in long-run equilibrium at price p_0, with the short-run demand and supply curves $D(P)$ and $S(P)$ shown in Panel B. The representative firm's $LRAC$ curve is $LRAC_0$ because it depends on the output level q_0. Now the demand curve shifts to $D_1(P)$. In the short run, the price rises to p_2. We do not show the short-run equilibrium for the firm, because the MC curve shifts when industry output rises. But the increase in price means that there must be economic profits. New firms will enter the industry, causing the short-run supply curve to shift to the right, from $S(P)$ to $S_1(P)$. Economic profits are squeezed out as the price falls from p_2 to p_1, and the minimum $LRAC$ level rises to meet p_1. The long-run supply curve, LRS, is now upward-sloping, passing through the points (p_0, Q_0) and (p_1, Q_1).

Decreasing-Cost Industry

A **decreasing-cost industry** is one in which factor prices decline as output rises.

Are decreasing-cost industries possible? In a **decreasing-cost industry,** when industry output rises, the $LRAC$ curve of the individual firm shifts down. Increasing-cost industries arise from the pressure on factor prices when an industry expands: factor prices rise because the demands for inputs increase. Can factor prices decrease when industry output rises? In general, the answer must be no, but there may be special circumstances.

A decreasing-cost industry might be caused by economies of scale in the production of some of its inputs. It may be that an important input is produced by another industry in such small quantities as to still be subject to economies of scale. Greater output of the input may lower costs and, thus,

FIGURE 9-14 Long-Run Supply: Increasing-Cost Industry

Panel A: Representative Firm

Panel B: Increasing-Cost Industry

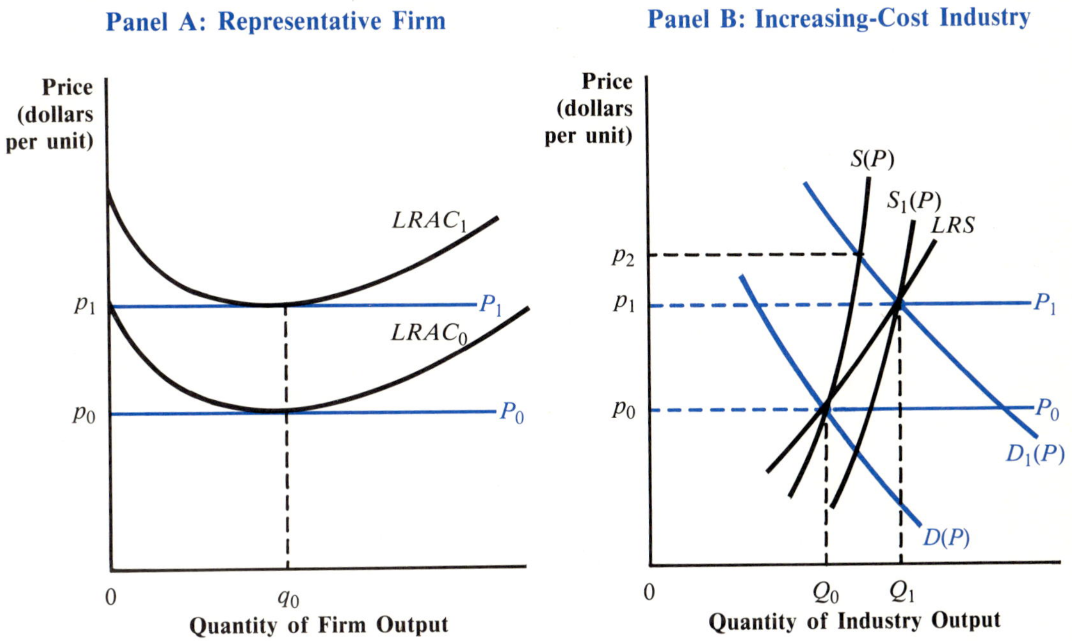

In an increasing-cost industry, the expansion of industry output shifts the firm's *LRAC* curve upward (Panel A). Initially, p_0 equals minimum $LRAC_0$, when market demand and supply are $D(P)$ and $S(P)$, as shown in Panel B. When demand rises from $D(P)$ to $D_1(P)$, the short-run equilibrium price rises from p_0 to p_1. In the long run, new firms enter and cause the supply curve to shift to $S_1(P)$. The new long-run equilibrium price, p_1, equals the minimum point on $LRAC_1$. Profit is squeezed to zero by falling prices and rising costs. The long-run supply curve, *LRS*, is upward-sloping.

lower the price to the decreasing-cost industry. The machines used in the early development of an industry may be adapted from other industries. But when an industry becomes larger, it may be able to use machinery that is more specifically designed to its particular needs.

The long-run supply curve for a competitive industry consists of the various long-run supply prices at different industry output levels. When there is freedom of entry and exit, the long-run supply price is simply the minimum *LRAC*. For a constant-cost industry, the long-run supply (*LRS*) curve is horizontal because minimum *LRAC* is independent of industry output. For an increasing-cost industry, the *LRS* curve is upward-sloping because minimum *LRAC* rises with industry output. For a decreasing-cost industry, the *LRS* curve is downward-sloping because minimum *LRAC* falls when industry output rises. Decreasing-cost industries are very rare.

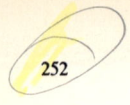

FIGURE 9–15 Long-Run Supply: Decreasing-Cost Industry

Panel A: Representative Firm

Panel B: Decreasing-Cost Industry

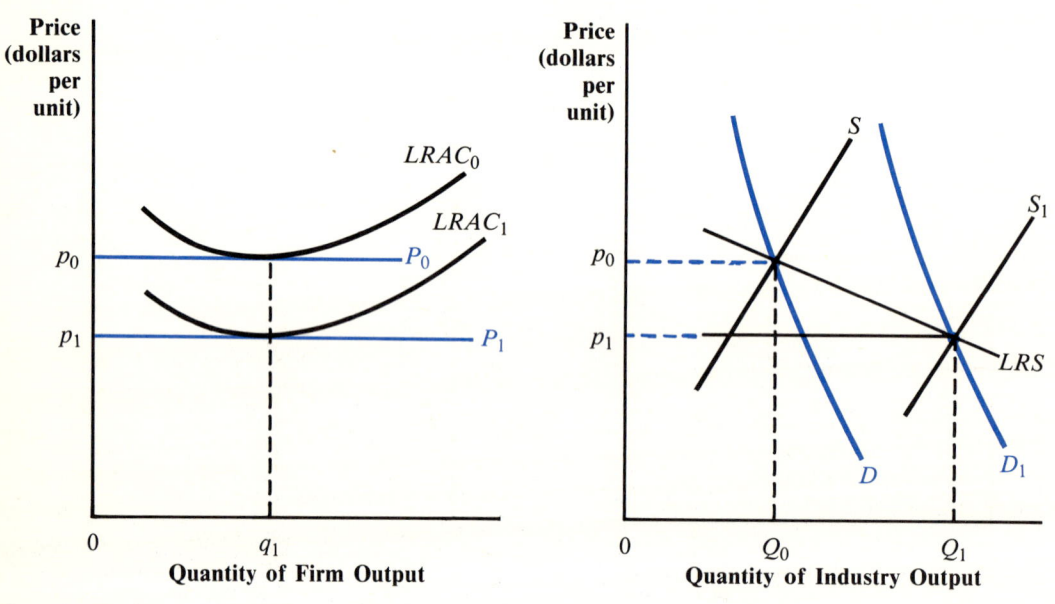

In a decreasing-cost industry, the long-run supply curve is downward-sloping because higher outputs are associated with reductions in *LRAC*. The minimum *LRAC* falls as industry output rises.

Figure 9–15 illustrates a decreasing-cost industry. As industry output rises, the *LRAC* curve shifts downward. When the demand curve shifts from D to D_1, the long-run equilibrium price falls from p_0 to p_1 because the *LRAC* curve shifts down from $LRAC_0$ to $LRAC_1$. The long-run supply curve *LRS* is now downward-sloping, because the minimum *LRAC* falls as industry output rises.

The Absence-of-Entry Case

So far, we have assumed new firms have free entry into an industry. In the absence of free entry, the long-run supply curve is quite different, because each firm can adjust its plant size until $P = LRMC$. For example, in the case of a constant-cost industry the long-run supply curve is the horizontal sum of each firm's *LRMC* above its *LRAC*.

The present value (see Chapter 2) of the stream of economic profits made by each firm in the long run is the value of absolute entry barriers (for example, licenses) to each existing firm. Indeed, the firm could be sold to outsiders for that capitalized value. In New York City, taxicab licenses are

PRICING IN THE LONG RUN

EXAMPLE 9–3 Price Controls

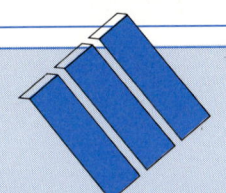

A clear prediction of the competitive model is that price ceilings cause shortages and that these shortages increase over time. In the accompanying figure, S and LRS are the short-run and long-run supply curves. The short-run and long-run equilibrium price is p_0. Now suppose a price ceiling of p_1 is imposed. Assuming that the price ceiling is effective, the quantity demanded will be Q_1 units. In the short run, the quantity supplied will be Q_2, causing a shortage of $Q_1 - Q_2$. In the long run, the quantity supplied will be even smaller, Q_3, so that the shortage is $Q_1 - Q_3$.

Many major cities have experimented with rent controls. San Francisco had rent controls after World War II; New York City has had rent controls since 1943. Stockholm, Sweden, tried rent controls during the 1950s. In each case, shortages occurred and grew worse over time. S. Rydenfelt measured the Stockholm housing shortage by estimating the average waiting time for an apartment in the city. Rydenfelt found that in 1950, when rent controls were imposed, the average waiting time was nine months. By 1958, after eight years of controls, the average waiting time had increased to 40 months!

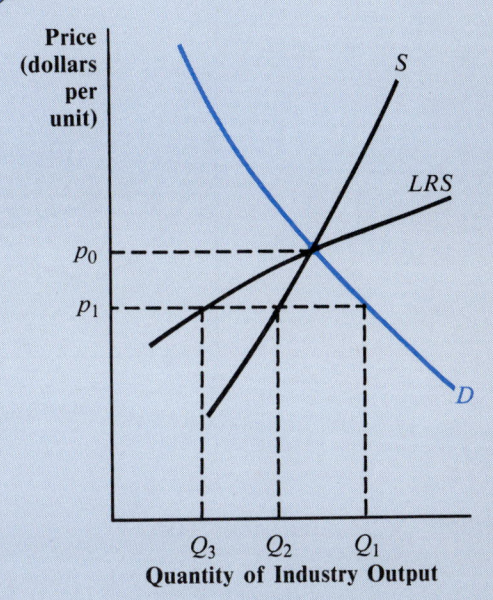

Sources: S. Rydenfelt, "Rent Controls Thirty Years On" in *Verdict on Rent Control* (London: Institute for Economic Affairs, 1972), p. 65; Milton Friedman and George Stigler, *Roofs or Ceilings?* (Irvington-on-Hudson, N.Y.: Foundation for Economic Education, 1946).

---

traded on the open market and sell for approximately the present value of the potential economic profits (in 1987, the price of a license was above $100,000). Naturally, newcomers to the industry earn zero economic profit, or normal accounting profit. The people who benefit from entry barriers are the owners or shareholders of the firms at the time the entry barriers are imposed.

FIGURE 9-16   Quasi Rent

Quasi rent is the excess of revenue over variable cost, or the rectangle *abcd*.

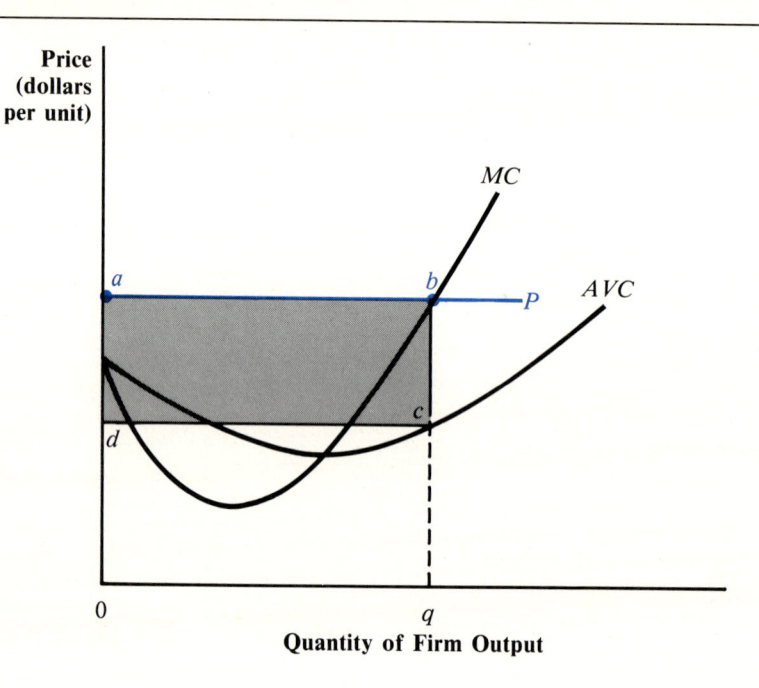

Ricardian Differential-Rent Theory

Economic Rent and Quasi Rent

Economic rent is the payment made for a resource over and above what is required to keep the resource in its current use.

The term **economic rent** refers to the payment made for a resource over and above what is required to keep the resource in its current activity. Such surplus payments are called *rents* because of the analogy to land rents: a given piece of land is fixed in supply, and whatever rent is received for it is by nature a surplus over what is needed to keep the land in use.

In the short-run theory of competitive pricing, the firm is willing to produce as long as revenue exceeds variable cost. The excess of revenue over variable cost is called **quasi rent**, because it is similar to an economic rent in the short run but not in the long run. For example, in Figure 9-16, the quasi rent is the area *abcd*. The quasi rent may be regarded as the short-run rent earned by the firm's fixed productive factors.

Differential Rents

Nearly every resource earns some economic rent (quasi or otherwise). A particularly important case is the economic rent earned by a superior resource. In a competitive industry, there is no need for all the resources to be

PRICING IN THE LONG RUN

FIGURE 9-17   **Costs for Two Firms with Different Rents**

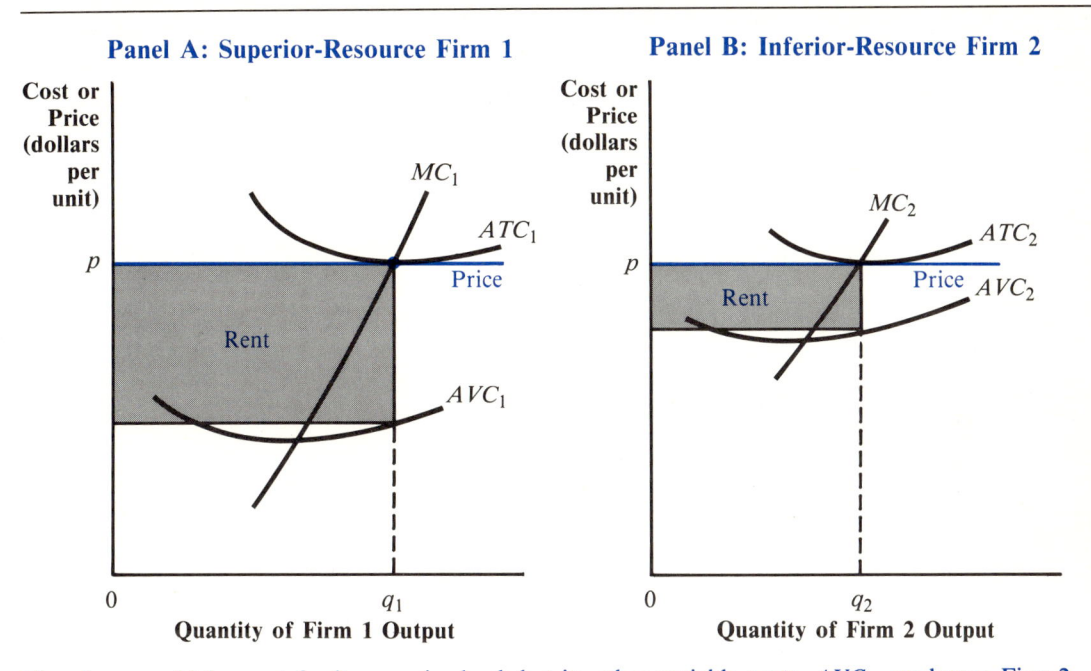

Panel A: Superior-Resource Firm 1

Panel B: Inferior-Resource Firm 2

Firm 1 pays a higher rent for its superior land, but its other variable costs, AVC_1, are lower. Firm 2 pays less rent but has higher variable costs, AVC_2, in working its inferior land. At price p, ATC_1 and ATC_2 have the same minimum point. The shaded areas represent the economic rent each firm must pay, or is willing to pay, at that price level.

Quasi rent is the short-run rent earned by the firm's *fixed* productive factors; that is, it is the excess of revenue over variable cost.

of uniform quality. For example, some farms will have access to fertile land; others will be situated on marginal lands. It is cheaper to extract coal from mines with rich veins of ore close to the surface than from marginal mines with veins of ore located deep underground.

Competitive firms will bid for superior resources. As a consequence, the superior resource will command a higher price in the marketplace. Thus, even though a firm uses the superior resource, its cost of production will be the same as the firm using the inferior resource. For example, Figure 9-17 shows the AVC curves of two different firms. Each AVC curve represents the average variable cost of production excluding the rent paid on the use of land. Firm 1 uses superior land. Thus, its other costs, represented by AVC_1, are lower than those of Firm 2, represented by AVC_2. When the price of the product is p, Firm 1 will be willing to pay the amount represented by the shaded rectangle as the rent on its land; Firm 2 will be willing to pay the amount represented by the smaller shaded rectangle as rent on its land. When the rents are combined with other costs, the average total costs (ATC) for the two firms have the same minimum level.

256   CHAPTER 9   THE THEORY OF PERFECT COMPETITION

FIGURE 9-18   Producers' and Consumers' Surpluses

Producers' surplus is the triangle *ceb*, the area below the price and above the supply curve. Consumers' surplus is the triangle *aeb*, the area below the demand curve and above the price. The value of the market is the sum, *aeb + ceb*.

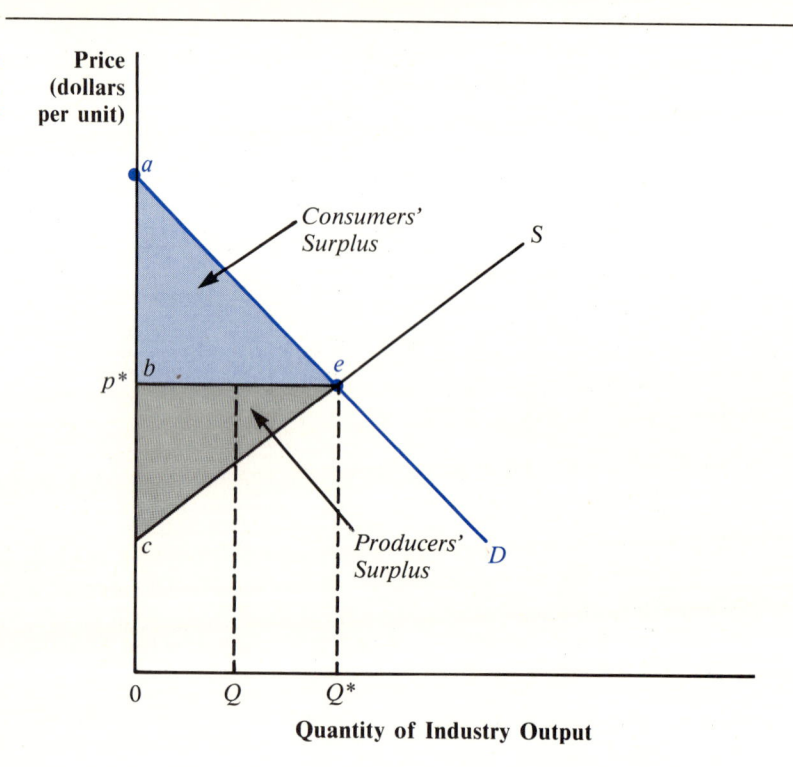

THE BENEFITS OF A MARKET: THE CASE FOR FREE TRADE

The theory of perfect competition can be used to demonstrate how both producers and consumers gain from voluntary exchange between many independent buyers and sellers. Chapter 6 described the benefits of exchange in general. This section explains how the benefits may be approximately measured.

Figure 9-18 represents a market that is in equilibrium when price is p^* and industry output is Q^*. The supply curve can be considered either a short-run or a long-run supply curve. At any given quantity, the supply curve shows the supply price for the product (the minimum price acceptable for an additional unit of the good). When the price is p^*, all Q^* units of the good are sold at p^*; thus, for output quantities less than Q^*, some sellers of the resources used in the industry are receiving more than their supply prices. All suppliers of this good, taken together, are getting a total surplus equal to the area of the triangle *ceb*. Alfred Marshall, the 19th-century British economist, called this area above the supply curve and below the price the **producers' surplus**. Obviously, producers' surplus and economic rent are

Producers' surplus is the excess of the amount suppliers receive over the minimum amount the suppliers would be willing to accept.

THE BENEFITS OF A MARKET

similar. While economic rent is the rent earned by a particular resource, producers' surplus consists of all the economic rents earned by the resources committed to the industry.

The interpretation of producers' surplus differs from the short run to the long run. If the supply curve in Figure 9–18 were the short-run supply curve for a constant-cost industry, producers' surplus would just be the total quasi rent earned by all firms in the industry. But if the supply curve were the long-run supply curve of an increasing-cost industry, producers' surplus would consist of the economic rents earned by the specialized resources used in the industry.

Chapter 4 introduced the concept of consumers' surplus, which is the excess of consumer benefits over cost. Consumers' surplus is measured by the area below the demand curve and above the price—triangle *aeb* in Figure 9–18.

The total value of the market is the sum of consumers' and producers' surpluses. In Figure 9–18, the market is worth the entire area *aec*. This area can be interpreted as the potential loss to society if this market were eliminated.

It is obvious that consumers benefit from the existence of producers and producers benefit from the existence of consumers. This simple principle is often overlooked. Consumers often blame high prices on producers, but such an analysis is incorrect in a competitive market. When prices are high, consumers have no one to blame but themselves. If more consumers enter the market, the old consumers are hurt because the equilibrium price rises. The higher is the equilibrium price, the lower is the consumer surplus for any group of consumers.

A much more subtle application of the analysis of market benefits is a comparison of the costs and benefits of protection. Sellers of a good often like to be protected from the competition of other sellers. For example, old sellers like to be protected from the competition of new sellers by licensing or prohibitions on advertising. By far the most important case of protection, however, is the desire of domestic sellers to be protected by means of tariffs or quotas from the competition of foreign sellers.

Clearly, any penalty imposed on foreign sellers of a product will benefit domestic sellers and hurt domestic consumers, but does the cost to domestic consumers exceed the benefit to domestic sellers? The answer is yes. Without the powerful tools of consumers' and producers' surplus, such an answer is far from obvious. Figure 9–19 shows the domestic demand curve for a good and two supply curves: S_d is the supply curve of domestic suppliers and S_t is the supply curve of the total world market, including both foreign and domestic suppliers. With free trade, the price of the good is p_f. Suppose now that foreign trade is prohibited. The price of the product becomes p_a (the price under autarky) in order to equate domestic demand with domestic supply. Domestic suppliers gain area *abce* in the figure, which is the gain in producers' surplus. But domestic consumers lose *abde*, the reduction in

FIGURE 9-19 The Case for Free Trade

D and S_d are the domestic demand and supply curves. S_t is the total supply curve of domestic and foreign sellers of the product. Protecting domestic suppliers from foreign competition reduces consumers' surplus by *abde* but raises producers' surplus by only *abce*—a net loss of *cde*.

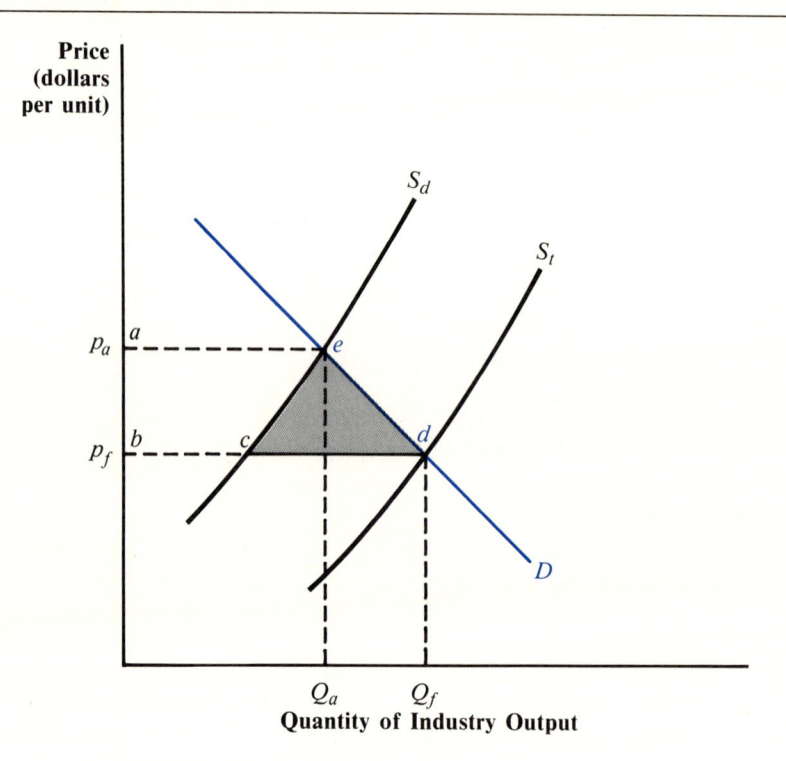

consumers' surplus. The loss in consumers' surplus exceeds the gain in producers' surplus by the triangle, *cde*. This result holds quite generally, because the demand and supply curves can have any slopes whatever. The brute economic fact remains: protection confers fewer benefits than it imposes in costs on society as a whole.

SUMMARY

1. Perfect competition is characterized by price-taking behavior by firms and consumers and is likely to exist when (a) there are many buyers and sellers, (b) each buyer has perfect information, (c) the product is homogeneous, and (d) there is free entry into and exit from the industry.

2. The market period is a period of time so short that the output of a good cannot be changed. The market price must be such as to just clear the market.

3. The short run is a period long enough for firms to adjust their output using variable factors such as labor and raw materials. The firm's short-run

QUESTIONS AND PROBLEMS

supply curve is the *MC* curve above *AVC*. In short-run equilibrium, the price must equate market demand with market supply.

4. In the long run, price must cover minimum *LRAC* if there is free entry. The long-run supply curve is horizontal for a constant-cost industry and upward-sloping for an increasing-cost industry.

5. The area above the supply curve and below the price is producers' surplus; the area below the demand curve and above the price is consumers' surplus. The sum of both surpluses is the value of the market and is maximized with a free market.

QUESTIONS AND PROBLEMS

1. The firm's variable-cost schedule is given in Table A. Calculate the firm's supply schedule.

2. Assume that the optimal-sized firm for a constant-cost industry has the following costs: $FC = \$45$, $MC = 10q$, and $VC = 5q^2$. The demand curve for the entire industry is $D(P) = 180 - P$.
   a. If the number of firms, $N, = 60$, what is the equilibrium price/output combination for the firm and industry? Is the output when $N = 60$ a long-run equilibrium? Why not?
   b. What is the long-run equilibrium number of firms? price? output?
   c. When there is free entry, what is the long-run supply curve?

3. "In a free-entry situation, the long-run market-supply curve has nothing to do with that portion of the *LRMC* curve that lies above the *LRAC* curve." Evaluate this statement.

Table A

Variable Cost (dollars), VC	Quantity of Firm Output (units), q
0	0
20	1
30	2
45	3
60	4
80	5
102	6
126	7
160	8

4. What is the critical difference between a constant-cost and an increasing-cost industry in the short run?

5. What is the critical difference between a constant-cost and an increasing-cost industry in the long run?

6. Calculate the amount of producers' surplus for a constant-cost industry in the long run.

7. If $VC = aq - bq^2 + cq^3$, where a, b, and c are positive constants, calculate the firm's supply curve. (*Hint*: $MC = d(VC)/dq$.) (Calculus required.)

8. If an industry is making economic profits, what would you predict about its future in the long run?

9. If an industry is experiencing economic losses, what would you predict about the future price and output?

10. Can perfect competition exist if some managers are smarter than others and achieve lower levels of costs? Why or why not?

11. If an industry is subsidized, the supply curve shifts down by the dollar amount of the subsidy. Will the increase in consumers' and producers' surplus combined exceed, equal, or fall short of the total amount of subsidy given to the industry?

SUGGESTED READINGS

Friedman, Milton. *Price Theory: A Provisional Text*. Chicago: Aldine, 1962, chap. 5.
Layard, P. R. G., and A. A. Walters. *Microeconomic Theory*. New York: McGraw-Hill, 1978, chap. 7.
Robinson, Joan. "Rising Supply Price." *Economica*, February 1941, pp. 1–8. Reprinted in Stigler, George and Kenneth Boulding, eds. *Readings in Price Theory*. Homewood, Ill.: Richard D. Irwin, 1952.
Stigler, George. *The Theory of Price*, 3rd ed. New York: Macmillan, 1966, chap. 10.
_____.*Capital and Rates of Return in Manufacturing Industries*. Princeton, N.J.: Princeton University Press, 1963, chap. 3 on "Competition and the Rate of Return."

CHAPTER 10

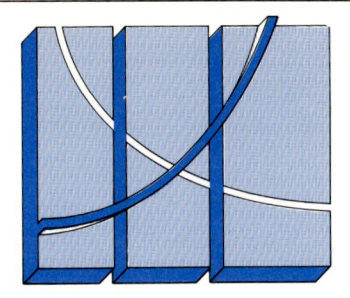

THE THEORY OF MONOPOLY

This chapter examines the theory of pricing and output decisions in a pure monopoly. (Literally, *monopoly* means "single seller.") The theory is then used to explain the various forms of price discrimination, two-part prices, and the social costs of monopoly.

THE DEFINITION OF MONOPOLY

A **pure monopoly** is a type of market structure in which (1) there is only one seller of a product that has no close substitutes; (2) the seller is free of external constraints; (3) the seller is protected by barriers to entry.

Monopoly as a market structure is the polar extreme from perfect competition. A **pure monopoly** exists when three conditions are satisfied: First, in a pure monopoly, there is only one seller in the market for some good or service that has no close substitutes. Such a firm is endowed with the power to be a **price maker**—that is, to set the price instead of acting as a price taker. Second, in a pure monopoly the seller is free of external constraints, such as price ceilings set by regulatory agencies. A pure monopolist, then, has complete freedom to maximize profit. Third, barriers to entry protect the seller from competition by new firms or entrants into the industry. With sufficiently high entry barriers, the profit stream of the monopolist can be more or less permanent.

Entry Barriers

A **price maker** is a seller that is able to control the price of the good it sells.

Monopoly arises from barriers to entry. The monopoly must exist because other firms perceive that entering the industry would be unprofitable. Presumably, potential competitors must face a cost disadvantage. There is a **barrier to entry** if costs or other disadvantages are incurred by new entrants that are not borne by the incumbent firm (or firms). Industrial-organization

FIGURE 10-1   Natural Monopolies

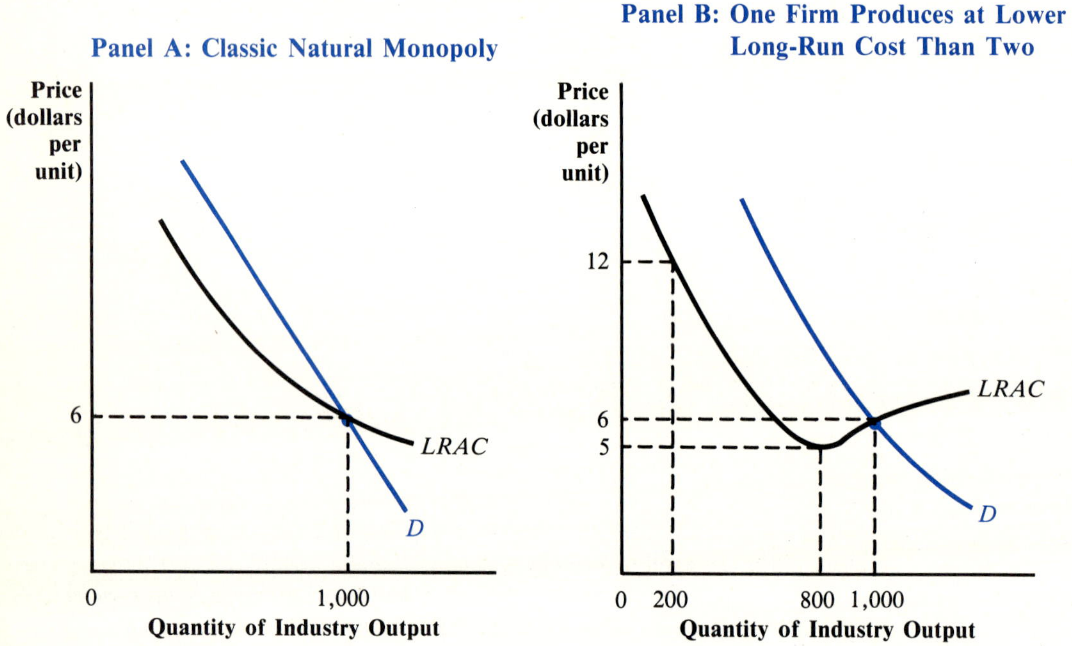

Panel A: Classic Natural Monopoly

Panel B: One Firm Produces at Lower Long-Run Cost Than Two

Both industries depicted here are natural monopolies because market demand at the break-even price, $6, can be met more cheaply by a single firm. Panel A illustrates a classic natural monopoly, but the industry in Panel B is also a natural monopoly; the cost of producing 1,000 units in one firm is $6,000 while the cost of producing 800 units in one firm and 200 in another is ($5 × 800) + ($12 × 200) = $6,400.

economists emphasize five types of entry barriers: sufficiently high economies of scale, limited access to raw materials, patents, government franchises, and large start-up, or *sunk*, costs.

Economies of Scale

A barrier to entry into a market exists if new entrants incur any disadvantages not facing the firms already in the market.

The classic definition of a **natural monopoly** is an industry in which, at the prevailing levels of industry demand, the firm faces economies of scale or declining long-run average costs. Modern economists have amended this definition to say that there is a natural monopoly if a single firm can meet market demand more cheaply than several firms can.

Figure 10-1 illustrates two natural monopolies. In Panel A, the LRAC curve is declining throughout. Given the market-demand curve, D, it is clear that a single firm can break even by producing 1,000 units at an average cost of $6 per unit. The total cost of production is $6,000. If two firms produced 1,000 units of output, the total cost would have to exceed $6,000 because the average costs of both firms would have to exceed $6.

A natural monopoly exists when it is cheaper for one firm to produce a product at the output level that meets demand than for two or more firms to do so.

The industry in Panel B is also a natural monopoly for the market-demand curve, D. Again, it costs a single firm $6,000 to produce 1,000 units, but the cost of producing the same 1,000 units in several firms exceeds $6,000. For example, to produce 200 units in one firm and 800 units in another costs ($12 × 200) + ($5 × 800) = $6,400. Economies of scale are present up to the minimum efficient scale (800 units), but costs for smaller outputs are exorbitant. A natural monopoly will not exist without economies of scale, but the output required to meet demand may require producing to the point where diseconomies of scale are encountered.

Is a natural monopoly a barrier to entry? The older industrial-organization literature assumed that because economies of scale are associated with large capital requirements, it would be difficult for new firms to enter. If new firms find it more difficult to borrow than old firms, because the capital markets treat incumbents better, then new firms face a cost disadvantage in the form of higher capital costs.

The modern industrial-organization literature questions whether economies of scale serve as a barrier to entry.[1] The modern corporation is a highly diversified institution. Many large companies are ready and able to enter new lines of business. For example, American Telephone and Telegraph (AT&T) is a new entrant in the electronic data-processing business. The R. J. Reynolds Tobacco Company is also in the food business. These examples can be multiplied a thousandfold. Thus, new entrants into a particular line of business may have even better access to capital markets than incumbent firms.

Access to Raw Materials

Established firms can control critical inputs and deny new firms access to these inputs. The best-known example is the case of the Aluminum Company of America (Alcoa), which controlled most of the high-grade bauxite reserves in the United States. The International Nickel Company of Canada owns virtually all of the world's nickel reserves.

Patents

Patents in the United States allow an inventor the exclusive right to use an invention for a period of 17 years. The main purpose of patents is to stimulate the invention or development of new products or processes. The cost of having a patent system is that it sets up a temporary monopoly in a particular product. For example, in the mid-1960s, the Pfizer Company sold its antibiotic, tetracycline, for about $30 (wholesale) per 100-capsule bottle.

---

1. George Stigler, *The Organization of Industry* (Homewood, Ill.: Richard D. Irwin, 1968), chaps. 6 and 10; David S. Evans, ed., *Breaking Up Bell* (New York: North-Holland, 1983), pp. 44–50; William Baumol, John Panzer, and Robert Willig, *Contestable Markets and the Theory of Industry Structure* (San Diego: Harcourt Brace Jovanovich, 1982).

FIGURE 10-2   Price and Marginal Revenue

The firm lowers the price by $-\Delta P$ in order to sell ΔQ additional units. To sell the extra output, the firm loses ΔP on the q units previously sold (the gray shaded rectangle) and gains $p\Delta Q$ (the color shaded area). Thus, $MR = p + q(\Delta P/\Delta Q)$.

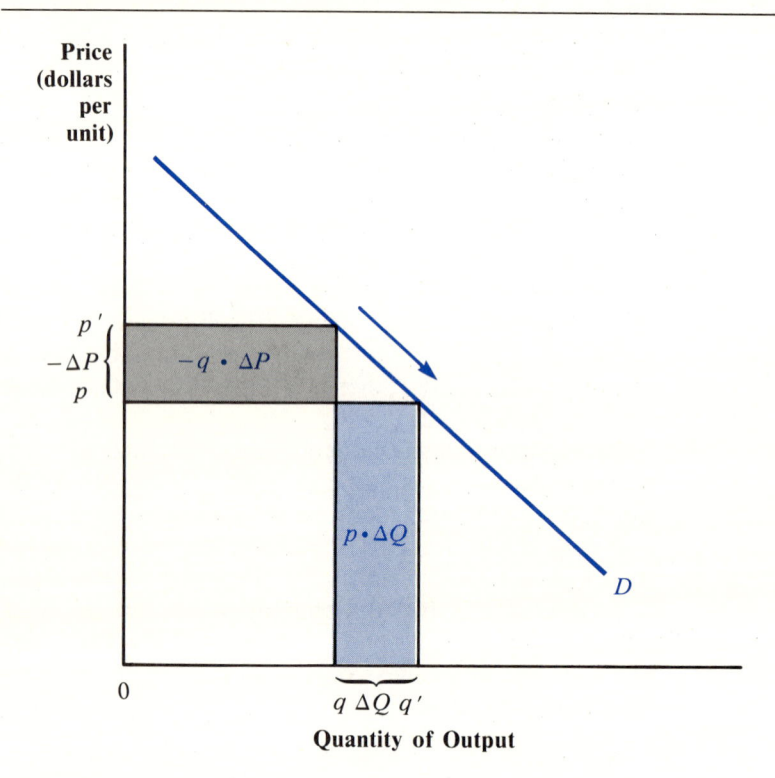

When the validity of the patents became questionable, new firms entered the market, selling tetracycline at approximately $2.50 per bottle wholesale. Valid patents, thus, serve as a substantial entry barrier.

Government Franchises

Governments create monopolies by erecting legal barriers to entry. British monarchs in the 17th and 18th centuries used to sell monopolies for trading with certain areas of the world to such corporations as the East India Company and the Virginia and Massachusetts Companies. In modern times, governmental units use franchises to control entry into industries that might otherwise be natural monopolies. The regulated public utilities (water, gas, electricity, and local telephone service) receive certificates of convenience and necessity from the state. The Federal Communications Commission controls entry into radio and television broadcasting. Before the Motor Carrier Act of 1980 that deregulated interstate trucking, the Interstate Commerce Commission controlled the entry of new trucking firms. Many cities grant exclusive franchises for such diverse industries as cable television and garbage collection.

THE DEFINITION OF MONOPOLY

Indeed, when examples of monopoly come to mind, they are often cases in which a government has granted an exclusive franchise to a particular person or group.

Sunk Costs

Economies of scale have often been associated with entry barriers because large firms may have large fixed costs. The newer industrial-organization literature, however, has emphasized that if fixed costs can be recovered, they do not constitute an entry barrier. An airplane is expensive and, in the short run, is a fixed cost to an airline, but in the long run the airplane can be sold. If the airplane could not be sold, the fixed cost would also be a **sunk cost**. In a world of uncertainty, sunk costs are an important barrier to entry. Any new business risks losses. The higher is the proportion of sunk costs, the larger are the potential losses. These potential losses motivate new firms to think twice before entering a market.

A **sunk cost** is a fixed cost that cannot be recovered, even in the long run.

There are many examples of sunk costs. New firms face setup costs, such as licensing fees, the hiring of attorneys to see if trademark or patent laws are being violated, and initial advertising expenses to make buyers aware of the new firm's presence. Even certain capital goods may represent sunk costs. The salvage value of a bridge may be very low. A machine built for exclusive use in one industry may have value only to the incumbent firm.

Monopoly Price and Marginal Revenue

A monopoly has its own demand curve. The basic difference between monopoly and perfect competition on the demand side is the relationship between marginal revenue (*MR*) and price (*P*). Recall that marginal revenue is the increase in total revenue per unit of increase in the quantity sold (*Q*). In perfect competition, marginal revenue and price are the same. In monopoly, except for the first unit sold, marginal revenue is less than price. Chapter 5 explained the relationships between price (or average revenue), marginal revenue, and elasticity. As presented in Chapter 5, the fundamental equation is

$$MR = P + Q(\Delta P/\Delta Q). \tag{1}$$

In perfect competition, $\Delta P/\Delta Q = 0$, so that $MR = P$. In monopoly, except when $Q = 0$, $MR > P$ because $\Delta P/\Delta Q < 0$.

The logic behind Equation (1) may be repeated here. If the firm sells an additional unit of the good per time period, it gains *P*. But to sell the additional unit, the price changes by $\Delta P/\Delta Q$ for each of the previous *Q* units sold. Thus, the firm gains *P* and spoils the market on the previous *Q* units by $Q \cdot (\Delta P/\Delta Q)$. Figure 10-2 diagrams these two components of marginal revenue.

Suppose now that the demand equation is a straight line, $P = A - BQ$.

FIGURE 10-3 Deriving the Marginal-Revenue Curve

For a straight-line demand curve, the MR curve is horizontally halfway between the demand curve and the vertical axis and twice as steep. The equation for the MR curve, $MR = A - 2BQ$, is obtained from the equation for the demand curve, $P = A - BQ$. Point r_0 shows the level of marginal revenue for quantity q_0 at price p_0.

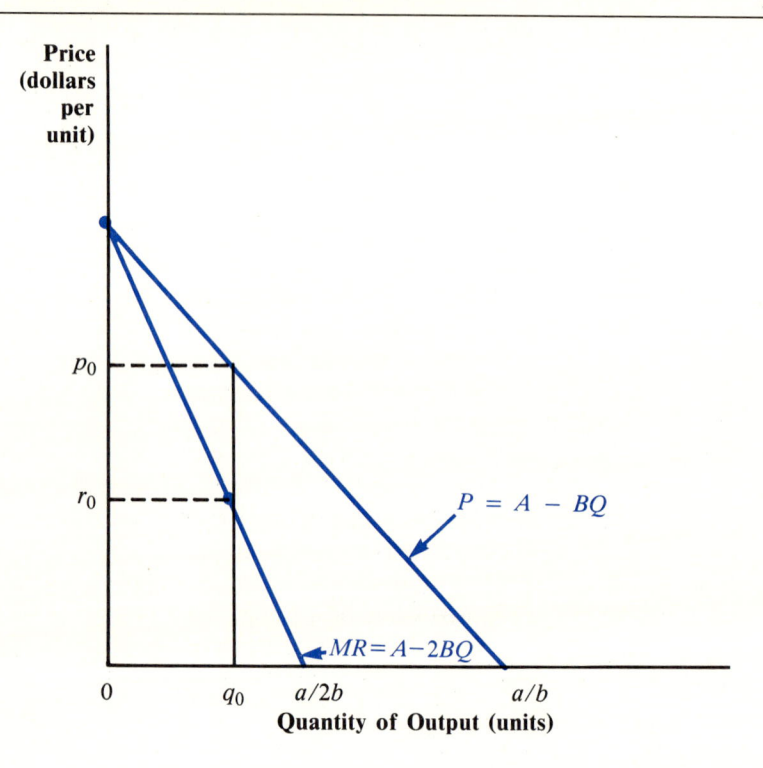

Figure 10-3 shows how to derive the MR curve for this demand curve using Equation (1). To sell an additional unit, the price must be reduced by $B. In other words, $\Delta P/\Delta Q = -B$. Thus, $MR = P + Q(-B)$, or

$$MR = A - BQ - BQ = A - 2BQ. \tag{2}$$

When the demand curve is a straight line, the MR curve is twice as steep. As Figure 10-3 shows, the MR curve is halfway between the vertical axis and any straight-line demand curve. (See Practice Exercise 10-1.) Marginal

PRACTICE EXERCISE 10-1

Q. Suppose $Q = 20 - 2P$. What is the marginal-revenue curve?

A. To use Equation (2) the demand curve must be in the form $P = A - BQ$. When $Q = 20 - 2P$, simple algebra shows that $P = 10 - 0.5Q$. Thus, $MR = 10 - Q$ because the MR curve is twice as steep.

TABLE 10-1   Price, Marginal Revenue, and Elasticity

Price (dollars), P (1)	Output (units), Q (2)	Total Revenue (dollars), TR (3)	Marginal Revenue (dollars), MR (4)	Price Elasticity of Demand, η (5)
6	0	0	6	$-\infty$
5	1	5	4	-5.0
4	2	8	2	-2.0
3	3	9	0	-1.0
2	4	8	-2	-0.5
1	5	5	-4	-0.2
0	6	0	-6	0

revenue for any given quantity, of course, is measured by the height of the MR curve at that quantity. For example, when output is q_0, marginal revenue is r_0, and price is p_0.

The halfway rule does not work for curvilinear demand curves. For example, if $D(P) = 10/P$, the price elasticity of demand equals -1 and $MR = 0$ everywhere.

Marginal Revenue and Elasticity

The ubiquitous Equation (1) can also be used to derive the relationship between marginal revenue and the price elasticity of demand, η. Briefly restating the development in Chapter 5, we can simply substitute the definition $\eta = (\Delta Q/\Delta P)(P/Q)$ into Equation (1):

$$MR = P(1 + 1/\eta) \text{ or } MR = P(1 - 1/|\eta|). \tag{3}$$

If demand is elastic, $|\eta| > 1$ and $MR > 0$. Intuitively, one can see that an elastic demand implies that a small reduction in price will increase the quantity sold by a relatively larger percentage, so that revenue rises (and marginal revenue is positive). If demand is inelastic, $|\eta| < 1$ and $MR < 0$. Intuitively, one can see that a large reduction in price will increase quantity sold by a relatively smaller percentage, so that revenue falls (and marginal revenue is negative).

Table 10-1 illustrates many of the points just made by assuming that the demand curve is $P = 6 - Q$. Columns (1) and (2) show the demand schedule of prices (P) and output quantities (Q). Column (3) shows total revenue: $TR = 6Q - Q^2$. The MR schedule is shown in column (4): $MR = 6 - 2Q$.

FIGURE 10-4 Marginal Revenue and Elasticity

Using the data from Table 10-1, Panel A shows the demand curve, $P = 6 - Q$, and the associated marginal-revenue curve, $MR = 6 - 2Q$. Panel B shows the total-revenue curve, $TR = 6Q - Q^2$. When demand is elastic, the TR curve is upward-sloping; when it is inelastic, the TR curve is downward-sloping.

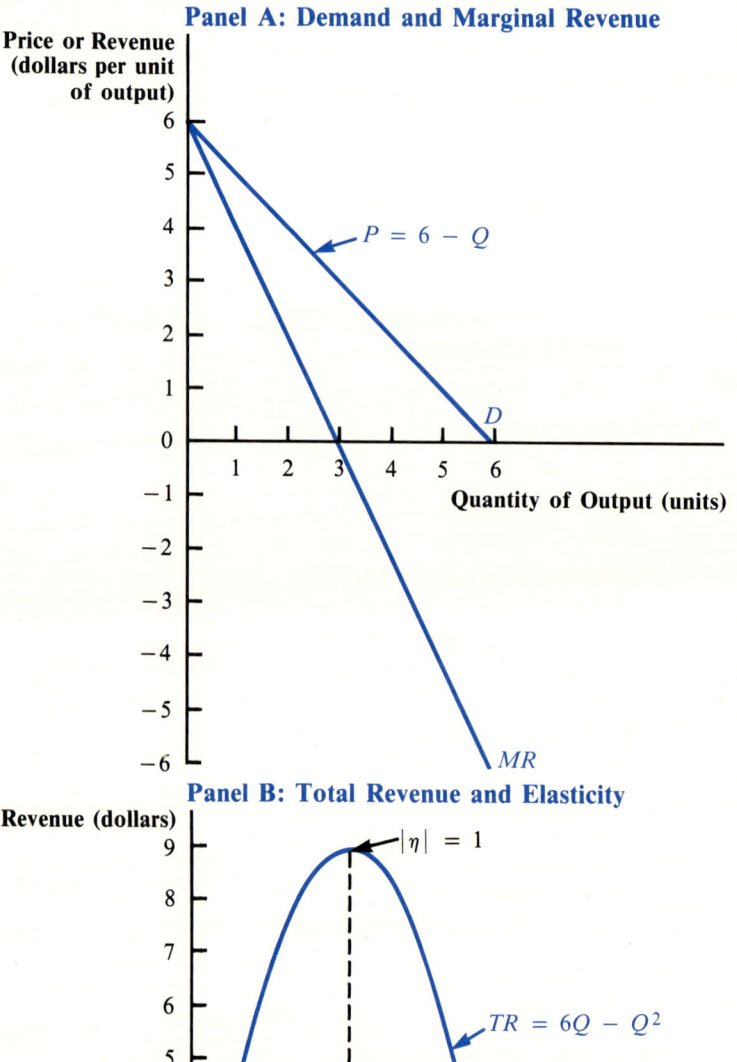

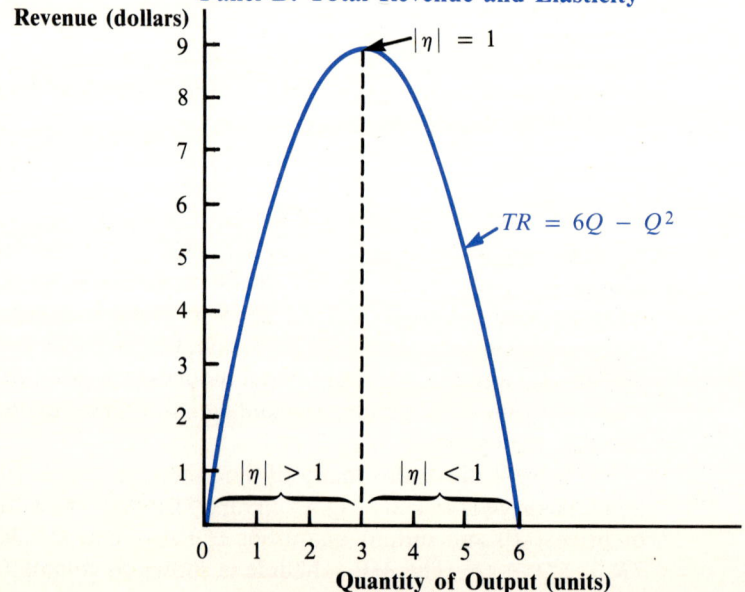

Panel A: Demand and Marginal Revenue

Panel B: Total Revenue and Elasticity

Column (5) shows the price elasticity of demand. Figure 10–4 shows the demand curve, the marginal-revenue curve, and the total-revenue curve for the data in Table 10–1. Notice that when demand is elastic, the total-revenue curve is upward-sloping; when demand is inelastic, the total-revenue curve is downward-sloping.

MONOPOLY PRICING AND OUTPUT IN THE SHORT RUN

The same general rules that govern profit maximization for a perfectly competitive firm apply to monopoly: The firm will choose that combination of output and price such that $MR = MC$ if $P \geq AVC$, or the firm will shut down if $P < AVC$. Because the demand curve for the monopolist is the entire market or industry demand, to determine the profit-maximizing combination of price and output requires matching market demand with the firm's cost conditions.

Short-Run Profit Maximization

Just as in the case of perfect competition, the conditions for maximum profit can be examined from either a global or a local perspective. Globally, profit is maximized when the difference, π, between the total-revenue and short-run total-cost functions is maximized.

$$\pi = TR - TC \tag{4}$$

Panel A of Figure 10–5 shows that profit is maximized when the vertical difference between the TR and TC curves is at a maximum. The tangents to the TR and TC curves (the dashed lines) drawn at the output level q^* show that when profit is maximized, $MR = MC$.

Panel B of Figure 10–5 shows profit maximization from the local perspective. The extra profit from another unit of output is

$$\Delta\pi/\Delta Q = MR - MC, \tag{5}$$

just as in perfect competition, except that $MR < P$ in monopoly. It pays the firm to expand output as long as $MR > MC$. In Panel B of Figure 10–5, when output is q_1, $MR > MC$. By increasing output by a marginal unit from output level q_1 to q^* profit *rises*. The last extra bit of profit is squeezed out, and profit is maximized at price p^* and output q^*, where $MR = MC$. The color shaded rectangle, $abcd$, shows the corresponding profit.

In Figure 10–5, the maximum profit is positive. In the short run, a monopolist can operate at a loss—as illustrated in Figure 10–6. Losses are minimized where $MR = MC$, provided that $P \geq AVC$. As long as price exceeds average variable cost, the monopolist can meet some of its fixed costs. If price is less than average variable cost, the monopolist would be better off shutting down and limiting its losses to fixed costs.

FIGURE 10-5 Short-Run Profit Maximization

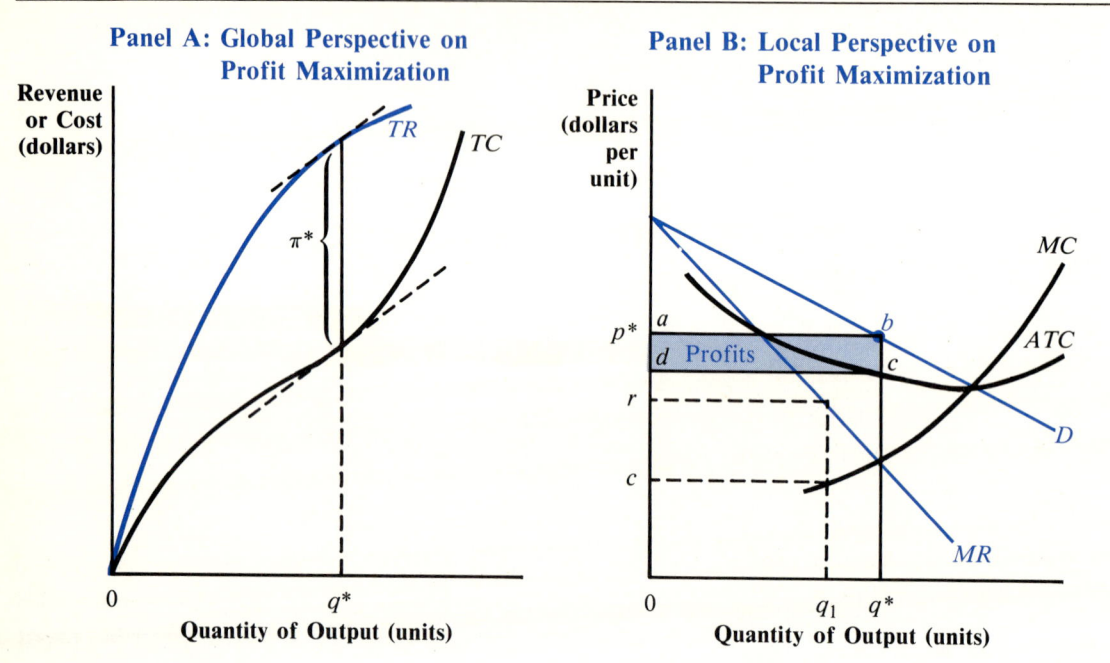

In Panel A, profit is maximized at the output level, q^*, where the difference between the TR curve and the TC curve is greatest. In Panel B, profit is maximized at the output level, q^*, where $MC = MR$, at a price of p^*. The color shaded area represents profits. At a lower output level, such as q_1, marginal revenue ($\$r$) is greater than marginal cost ($\$c$); it pays the firm to keep expanding output until it reaches level q^*.

The firm pictured in Figure 10-6 would presumably expect that demand or cost conditions could change in the future. While the firm would continue to operate at output level q^* in the short run, in the long run the firm should consider going out of business entirely unless it could anticipate making profits in the future.

Nothing guarantees the monopolist a profit. The only certainty the pure monopolist faces is the absence of free entry by competitors. Thousands of firms and individuals hold ironclad patents on products that have absolutely no market value.

The Second-Order Condition

The $MR = MC$ condition works only if a second-order, or secondary, condition is satisfied:[2] the MC curve must cut the MR curve from below. Mathematically, the slope of the MR curve must be less than the slope of the

FIGURE 10-6 Minimizing Losses in the Short Run

A monopolist can operate at a loss in the short run. Losses are minimized at an output of q*, where $MR = MC$, as long as $P \geq AVC$. If price is not greater than average variable costs, or if conditions do not improve, the firm should shut down.

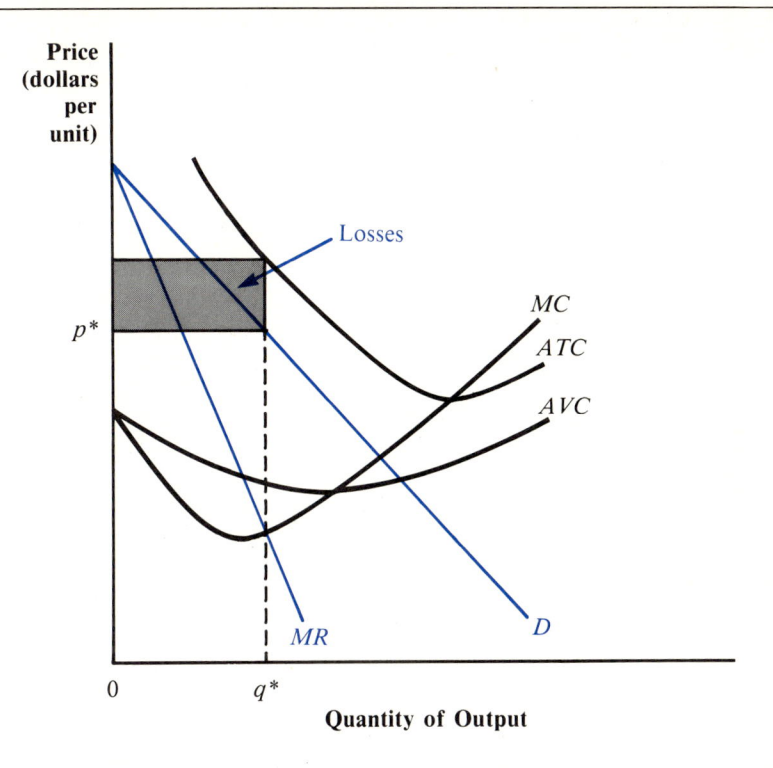

---

2. Let $R(Q)$ and $C(Q)$ be the revenue and cost functions. Profit is maximized when $d\pi/dQ = R'(Q) - C'(Q) = 0$, provided the second-order condition is satisfied. The second-order condition is that the function, $\pi(Q)$, being maximized is concave rather than convex. A function is concave if $\pi''(Q) < 0$ and convex if $\pi''(Q) > 0$. Given $\pi'(Q) = R'(Q) - C'(Q)$, the second-order condition is:

$$\pi''(Q) = R''(Q) - C''(Q) < 0$$

or, because

$$MR(Q) = R'(Q) \text{ and } MC(Q) = C'(Q),$$

$$MR'(Q) - MC'(Q) < 0.$$

Thus, the second-order condition is that the slope of the *MR* curve be algebraically smaller than the slope of the *MC* curve. The second-order condition can be restated in terms of the properties of the demand curve itself. Let $P = f(Q)$ be the inverse demand function. Then $R(Q) = f(Q)(Q)$. It follows that

$$R'(Q) = f(Q) + Qf'(Q) = P + Qf'(Q)$$

and

$$R''(Q) = 2f'(Q) + Qf''(Q).$$

The second-order condition is then

$$2f'(Q) + Qf''(Q) - C''(Q) < 0.$$

FIGURE 10-7 The Second-Order Condition for Profit Maximization

If the *MC* curve intersects the *MR* curve from above, the condition $MR = MC$ at q^* minimizes rather than maximizes profit. At all output levels above q^*, marginal revenues exceed marginal costs. Cutting output below q^* reduces marginal costs more than it reduces marginal revenue.

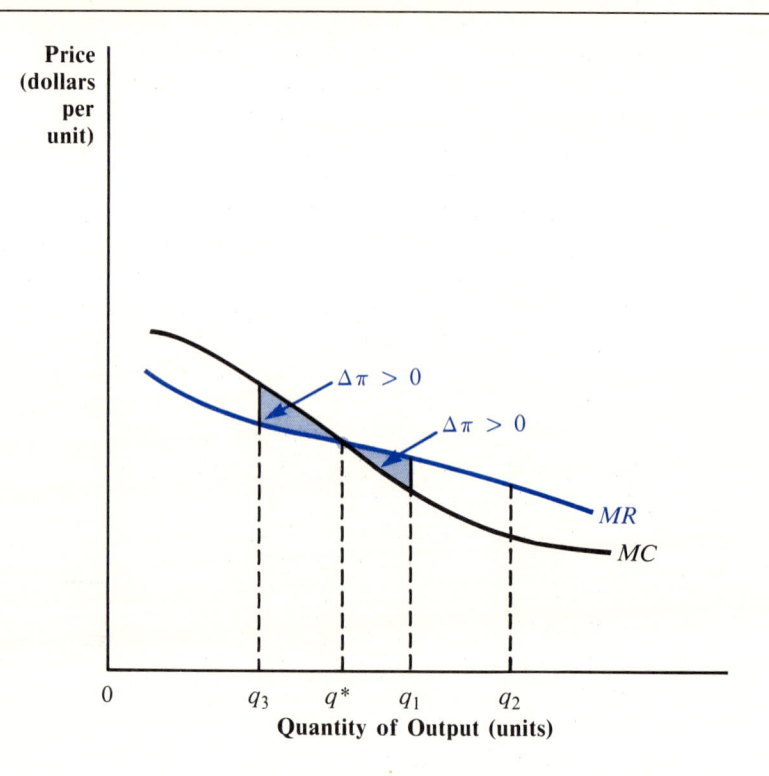

MC curve. Figure 10-7 shows the case where an *MC* curve has a slope *smaller* than the slope of the *MR* curve. In this case, when output is at q^*, it would pay the firm to expand to output levels q_1, q_2, and so on, because at those higher output levels $MR > MC$ (*MC* cuts *MR* from above) and profits would increase. Similarly, it would pay the firm to cut output back from q^* because at outputs such as q_3, $MC > MR$ and reductions in output would reduce costs more than revenues. Indeed, profit is at a local *minimum* at output level q^*.

It can be argued that the second-order condition must somewhere be satisfied in the case of monopoly. In Figure 10-7, the firm would wish to produce an infinite amount of output if the *MC* and *MR* curves continue as drawn. This level of output clearly makes no economic sense. Eventually, it would seem that the *MC* curve must either turn up and intersect the *MR* curve once again from below or that the *MR* curve must turn down and become zero or negative. If marginal cost is everywhere positive, if marginal revenue is anywhere zero, and if for some output $MR > MC$, there must be an intersection between the two curves at which the second-order condition is satisfied.

FIGURE 10-8 The Effect of Increased Demand

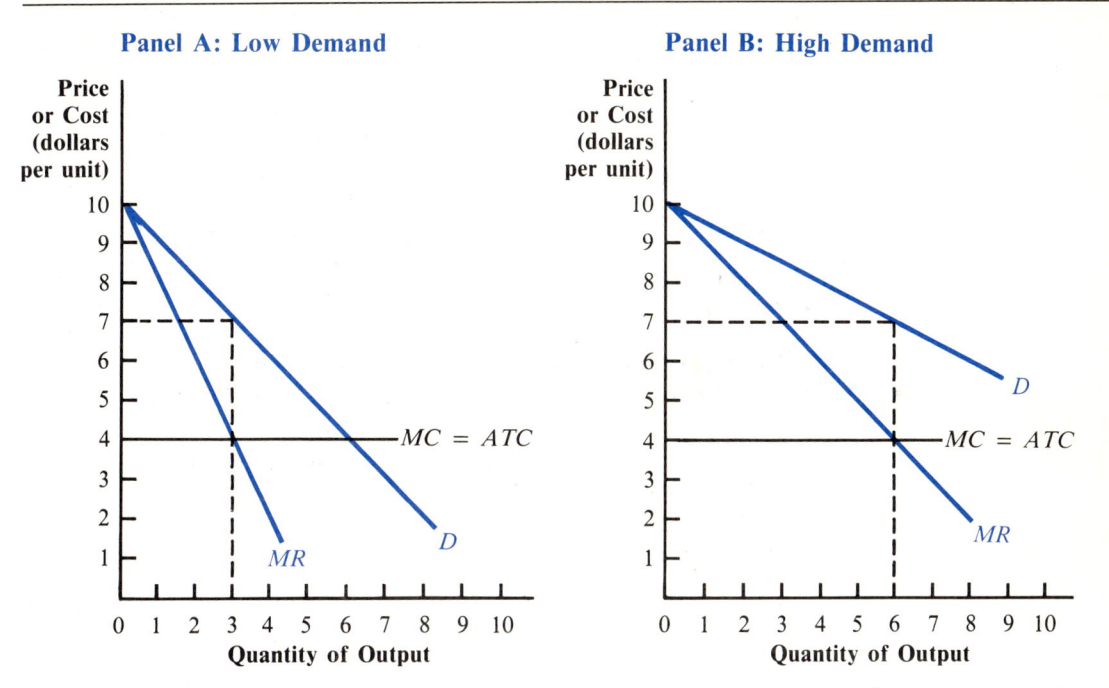

Panel A: Low Demand | **Panel B: High Demand**

In Panel A, monopoly profit is maximized at an output of 3 units and a price of $7. In Panel B, with the same costs but a different demand curve and with the same elasticity at each price, profit is maximized at an output of 6 units and a price of $7.

Monopoly Supply

The monopolist chooses a price p^* where $MR = MC$ as long as price exceeds average variable cost. In equilibrium, the condition can be written as:

$$P(1 + 1/\eta) = MC. \tag{6}$$

From this condition, it is clear that the profit-maximization output depends on three factors: price, elasticity of demand, and marginal cost. It follows that the level of output is not related simply to price without taking into account the market responsiveness of quantity demanded to price. If demand conditions change, the monopolist may produce a different output and sell it at the same price. Therefore, there is no supply curve in the theory of monopoly.

Figure 10-8 shows how two different demand curves can lead the same monopolist to sell two different levels of output at the same price. Both demand curves have the same elasticity of demand at each price. In Panel A,

FIGURE 10-9 Long-Run Profit Maximization

In the long run, a monopolist can earn the profit indicated by the color shaded area. The profit-maximizing output q^* occurs where $MR = LRMC$ and need not correspond to the minimum $LRAC$.

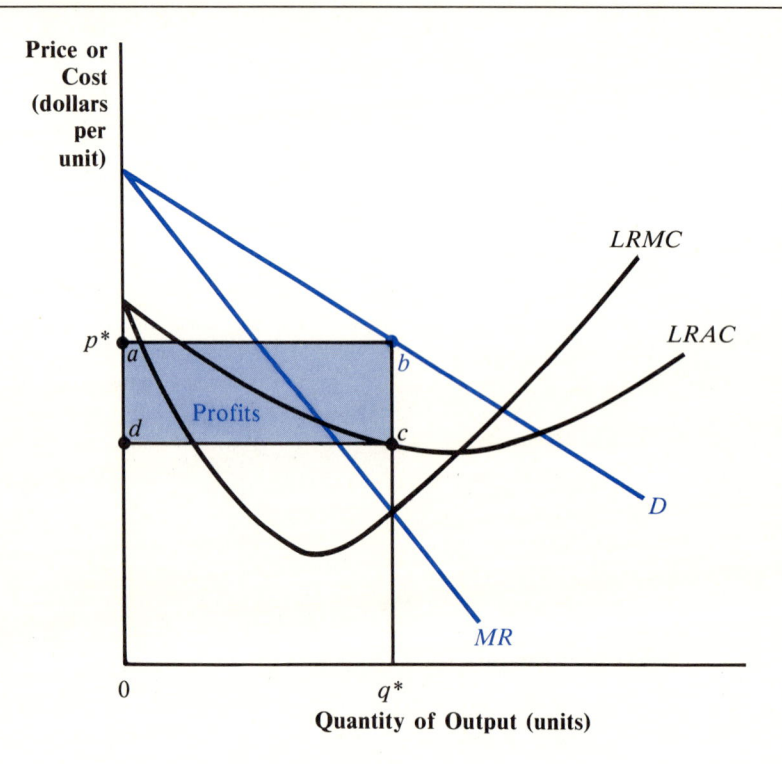

the demand curve is $P = 10 - Q$; in Panel B, the demand curve is $P = 10 - 0.5Q$. For simplicity, it is assumed that $MC = ATC = \$4$. In Panel A, $MR = 10 - 2Q$, and profit is maximized at an output of 3 units and a price of \$7 per unit. In Panel B, $MR = 10 - Q$, and profit is maximized at an

PRACTICE EXERCISE 10-2

Q. Suppose $P = 100 - 2Q$. If marginal costs and average costs are the same and $MC = AC = \$20$, what are the monopoly levels of price, output, and profit?

A. Because $MR = 100 - 4Q$, the solution is obtained by setting MR equal to MC and solving step by step. First, $\$20 = 100 - 4Q$ or $Q = 20$. Second, $P = 100 - 2Q = 100 - 2(20) = \$60$. Finally, $\pi = (60 - 20) \times 20 = \$800$.

output of 6 units and the same price of $7 per unit. Because demand elasticity and cost conditions are the same in both diagrams, it is clear that different outputs are being sold at the same price simply because demand conditions have changed.

MONOPOLY PRICING AND OUTPUT IN THE LONG RUN

In the long run, the monopoly firm need not fear competition from other firms. The monopolist can freely choose its plant size until long-run profit is maximized. A necessary condition for long-run profit maximization is that for any given level of output, costs are minimized—that is, the firm must be operating on its long-run average-cost (*LRAC*) curve. Because there is no free entry, the firm need not choose an optimum plant size.

Long-Run Profit Maximization

Figure 10–9 shows the marginal-cost and average-cost curves for a monopoly firm in the long run. To maximize long-run profit, the firm must choose a quantity, q^*, and a price, p^*, at which $MR = LRMC$. The color shaded area *abcd* represents long-run monopoly profit. This profit is a return above and beyond what the same resources could earn in other employments. Notice that at the profit-maximizing output q^*, the firm is using a plant that is smaller than the minimum efficient scale. Such a size is not necessary. Under different demand conditions, the firm might have chosen a plant larger than the most efficient size.

Multiplant Monopolies

We have so far assumed that the monopoly firm operates a single plant, but it may in fact operate many plants. For example, each plant might be associated with a unique source of raw material. In the U.S. economy, the four largest firms in each industry operate an average of six plants each. Multiplant operations, however, are the exception rather than the rule for the vast majority of firms.[3]

The economics of a multiplant monopoly is that it will operate each plant until long-run marginal cost is the same in each plant. In Panel A of Figure 10–10, $LRMC_A$ and $LRMC_B$ are the long-run marginal-cost curves for plants A and B. If $LRMC_A > LRMC_B$, it pays the firm to raise output at plant B and reduce output at plant A because total costs will fall. Panel B of Figure 10–10 shows that the firm's *LRMC* curve is simply the horizontal sum of the

---

[3]. See Edward M. Miller, "Size of Firm and the Size of Plant," *Southern Economic Journal* 44 (April 1978): 861–72.

FIGURE 10-10   Long-Run Costs for a Multiplant Monopoly

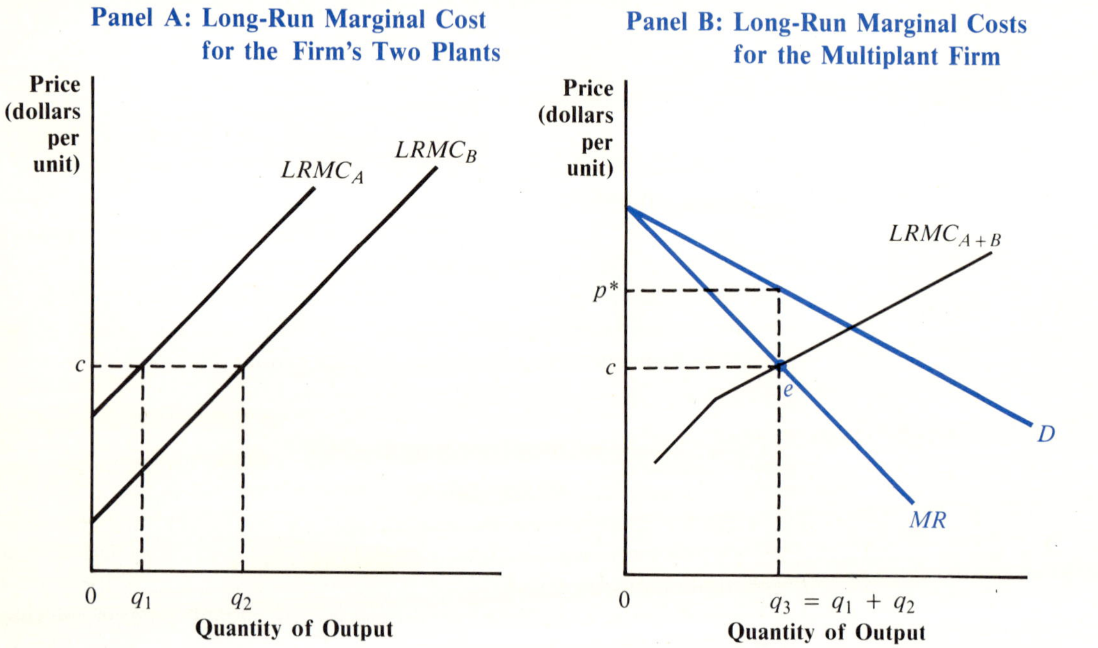

Panel A: Long-Run Marginal Cost for the Firm's Two Plants

Panel B: Long-Run Marginal Costs for the Multiplant Firm

Panel A shows long-run marginal costs for each of the firm's two plants. The $LRMC$ curve in Panel B is the horizontal sum of the curves in Panel A. Profit is maximized at output q_3 (the sum of the two plants' outputs) and price p^*. Profit maximization occurs at the output level where the firm's $LRMC$ is equal to its marginal revenue.

$LRMC$ curves for the two plants. For each industry output, it is necessary that the individual plants' marginal costs be equalized.

If there are N plants, the multiplant monopoly maximizes profit when

$$MR = LRMC_A = LRMC_B = \ldots = LRMC_N. \tag{7}$$

Because the firm's $LRMC$ curve is simply the horizontal sum of the individual plants' curves, the above conditions boil down to a single condition. Figure 10–10 illustrates for the case of 2 plants that profit is maximized at the output level $q_3 = q_1 + q_2$ because $MR = LRMC = LRMC_A = LRMC_B$ at point e at this output, where price is p^*.

CHARACTERISTICS OF MONOPOLY EQUILIBRIUM

The theory of profit maximization for a monopoly allows us to evaluate some misconceptions about monopolies.

Let us first examine some strategies that monopolies do *not* follow:

1. Monopolies do not charge the highest possible price. At the highest possible price, marginal revenue is likely to exceed marginal cost. The monopolist would, therefore, produce more output.
2. If economies and diseconomies of scale are present, monopolies do not produce where long-run average cost is at a minimum, except by accident. The profit-maximizing point where $MR = MC$ can occur anywhere along the *LRAC* curve. Monopolies are not likely to produce at the minimum efficient scale unless a large range of output is produced under constant returns to scale.
3. Monopolies do not maximize sales revenue. If the monopoly maximizes profit, it will produce at an output level that falls short of revenue or sales maximization. When profit is maximized, $MR = MC$, so that marginal revenue is necessarily positive. Thus, an increase in output would raise revenue but lower profits. Revenue maximization occurs when $MR = 0$. Such a monopoly would produce too much.
4. Monopolies do not maximize *profit per unit*; monopolies maximize *total profit*, which is profit per unit times total quantity. Total profit is maximized if and only if $MR = MC$. Profit per unit is maximized only by accident.

What strategies do monopolies follow?

1. Monopolies charge a price that is larger than marginal cost because at such a price $MR = MC$ and because $P > MR$ when a firm faces a downward-sloping demand curve. Because marginal revenue depends on both price and the elasticity of demand, monopolists do not have a simple supply curve relating output to price; they in fact have no supply curve.
2. Monopolies charge a price such that the demand for the good is price elastic. Demand is elastic because $MC = MR = P(1 + 1/\eta)$. Because MC is positive, elasticity must be less than -1. If demand were inelastic, it would pay the monopolist to raise the price because raising the price would increase revenue and lower costs (at a higher price, less output needs to be produced). The monopolist will continue to raise the price until it reaches the elastic portion of the demand curve, if such a portion exists.
3. Monopolies can make economic profits that persist through time if entry barriers can be maintained indefinitely. Not all monopolies make economic profits; but if they do, the profits can persist.
4. Monopoly profits are economic rents. Recall that economic rents are payments made for a resource that are above and beyond what is required to keep the resource in its present use. Monopoly profits are payments above what is necessary to keep the monopolist in business. For this reason, economists often refer to monopoly profits as *monopoly rents*. As a consequence, monopoly profits could be taxed without affecting the monopolist's price and output decisions. The price and output decision depends on the $MR = MC$ condition, and any profit tax that does not

affect marginal cost or marginal revenue will not affect the monopolist's optimal behavior.[4]

The monopolist charges a price where $MR = MC$ in both the short run and the long run. The price will necessarily exceed MC and, because marginal revenue is positive, demand must be elastic at the profit-maximizing price.

MONOPOLY AND PERFECT COMPETITION COMPARED

What is wrong with monopoly? If the achievement of monopoly is not the consequence of superior productivity, monopoly is economically inefficient. There are two basic sources of economic inefficiency: contrived scarcity and the resources absorbed by monopoly-rent-seeking behavior. A possible third source of monopoly inefficiency is Harvey Leibenstein's X-inefficiency, which is the possible failure of monopolists to minimize costs.

Sources of Inefficiency

Contrived Scarcity

The most powerful argument against monopoly is that monopolies maximize profits by restricting output to the level where marginal cost equals marginal revenue but where price exceeds marginal cost. This restriction of output is a **contrived scarcity** that leads consumers to restrict their consumption of the product more than the true scarcity of the good would require. In other words, setting a price higher than marginal cost creates an artificial scarcity of the good that leads people to economize too much on this good relative to other goods.

In Figure 10–11, the profit-maximizing position is the combination (p^*, q^*) represented by point b. It might appear that this price/output combination is not efficient because long-run average cost is not minimized. However, efficiency does not require that the firm produce the good at the lowest possible cost per unit. Indeed, the most efficient allocation of resources is the price/output combination (p_e, q_e) represented by point e.

When the monopolist produces q^* units, the excess of price over marginal cost is the amount measured by line bc. Recall from the theory of consumer demand that consumers adjust their consumption until the marginal benefit of the good just equals its price. Moreover, the marginal cost of production

Contrived scarcity is the restriction of output to the level where marginal cost equals marginal revenue but where price exceeds marginal cost.

---

4. Monopoly profit is $\pi = R(Q) - C(Q)$. If taxes $T = t\pi$ are imposed, the monopolist's profit after taxes is $(1 - t)\pi(Q)$, where t is the tax rate per dollar of profit. Maximizing after-tax profit implies that

$$(1 - t)\pi'(Q) = (1 - t)[R'(Q) - C'(Q)] = 0.$$

If $0 < t < 1$, after-tax profit is maximized if and only if $R'(Q) = C'(Q)$. Thus, the original $MR = MC$ condition is not disturbed by taxing profits.

FIGURE 10-11 The Social Costs of Monopoly

The price/output combination (p^*, q^*) is the profit-maximizing level for the monopoly but does not effectively meet social needs. Price/output combination (p_e, q_e) is the socially efficient one. At the lower output, area *bec* represents the social loss.

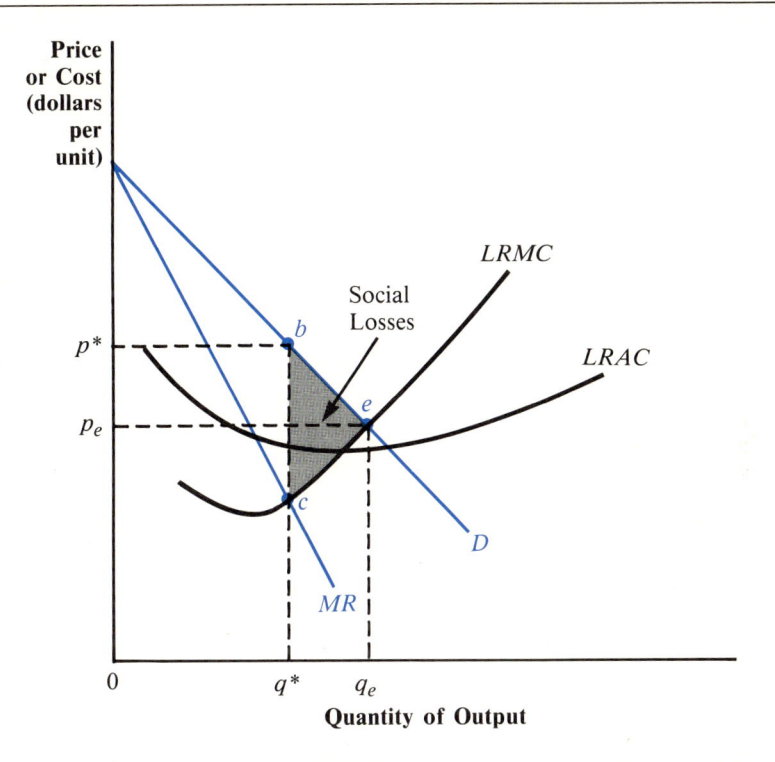

is what society must sacrifice in terms of other goods to produce one more unit of the good (remember that costs are always opportunity costs). Accordingly, $P - MC$ is the net social benefit of producing one more unit of the monopolized good. It therefore pays society to produce more of the good as long as $P > MC$. Because society gains $P - MC$ for producing an extra unit of output between output levels q^* and q_e, the area *bec* is the net gain society would enjoy if the monopolist produced at output level q_e instead of the output level q^*.

Monopoly is economically inefficient because there is a conflict between private optimization and social optimization when price is set to be greater than marginal revenue. The private gain from another unit of output is $MR - MC$; the social gain from another unit of output is $P - MC$. Under perfect competition, $P = MR$ and private gains coincide with social gains. Under monopoly, the firm does not produce enough from the social standpoint because when $MR = MC$, there are still social gains to be had from additional production. (See Practice Exercise 10–3.)

Monopolies are inefficient compared to perfect competition because they produce at an output level where price exceeds marginal cost. This signifies that the marginal value of the good to society exceeds the marginal cost; thus, output should be increased.

FIGURE 10–12 Perfect Competition Versus Monopoly

A competitive firm would operate at point *e*, setting price at p_c and output at q_c; a monopoly would operate at *b*, setting price at p_m and output at q_m. The move from competition to monopoly would provide the area *abcd* as monopoly rent to the producer while lowering output and increasing the price to the consumer, resulting in a deadweight loss of *bce*.

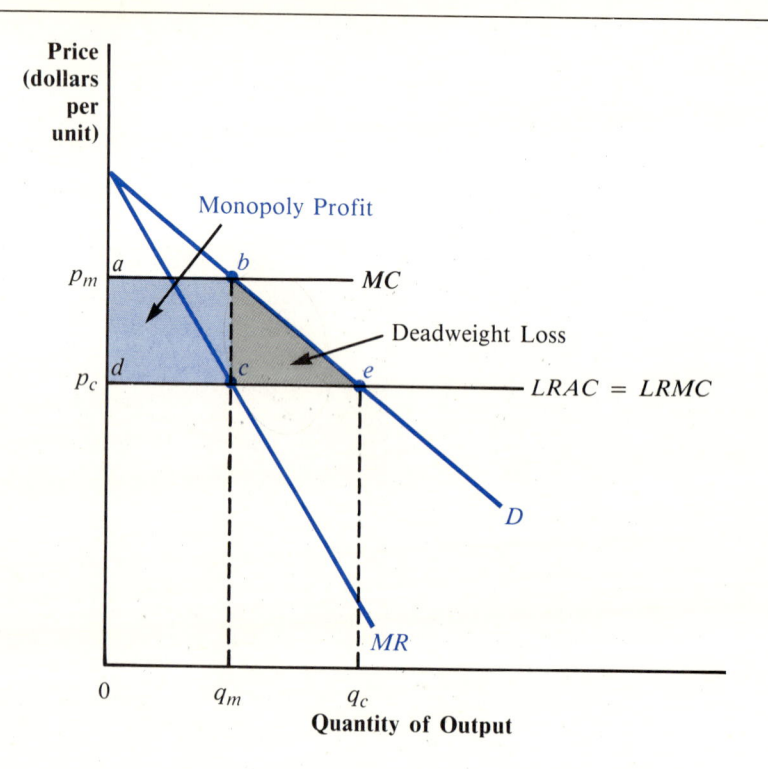

Monopoly-Rent-Seeking Behavior

Figure 10–11 showed an industry that could not be organized under perfect competition because the efficient-sized firm was so large relative to the market. Imagine now an industry that could be organized either as a monopoly or as a perfectly competitive industry. To make matters simple, assume that some constant-cost industry can produce its product with constant returns to scale. Figure 10–12 shows that the *LRMC* curve is horizontal and equal to the *LRAC* curve. The market-demand curve, *D*, can be shown on the same diagram. Under conditions of perfect competition, the firm would operate at point *e*, where the price and output would be p_c and q_c, because free entry would force price to fall to the minimum *LRAC*.

An important means of achieving monopoly power is **monopoly-rent-seeking behavior**, described by economists Anne Krueger and Gordon Tullock.[5] Decision makers in an industry may perceive that the industry could be organized as a monopoly if entry were restricted by, say, govern-

Monopoly-rent-seeking behavior is the effort made (through lobbying, persuasion, advertising) to organize an industry as a monopoly rather than as a competitive industry, in order to gain the extra profit, or rent, a monopoly can achieve.

---

5. See Anne Krueger, "The Political Economy of the Rent-Seeking Society," *American Economic Review* 64 (June 1974): 291–303; Gordon Tullock, "The Welfare Cost of Tariffs, Monopolies, and Theft," *Western Economic Journal* 5 (June 1967): 224–32.

PRACTICE EXERCISE 10–3

Q. In Practice Exercise 10–2, what are the monopoly rents and the consumer surplus? What is the deadweight loss of monopoly attributable to contrived scarcity?

A. Monopoly rent equals the monopoly profit of $800. Consumer surplus is the area above the price of $60 and below the demand curve, or 40 × 20 × 1/2 = $400. Under monopoly, consumer surplus plus monopoly rents = $1,200. Under perfect competition, consumer surplus would be ($100 − 20) × 80 = $1,600. Thus, the deadweight loss from contrived scarcity is $400.

ment franchising. As a monopoly, the industry would charge the price p_m in Figure 10–12 (where $MR = MC$) and sell the output q_m. The industry's potential monopoly profit, or rent, equals the color shaded area *abcd*. According to the Tullock-Krueger analysis, decision makers will be willing to devote real resources to acquiring monopoly power. The monopoly could be achieved or maintained by various vote-gathering activities (such as lobbying or advertising). For example, the textile industry advertises on television and in newspapers that it is the public's duty to support the American textile industry by encouraging the Congress to impose import limitations. The hiring of lawyers, advertising agencies, and lobbyists represents real social costs. It is possible that the entire amount of monopoly profit could be absorbed by monopoly-rent-seeking activities.[6] (See Example 10–1.)

If the industry in Figure 10–12 were converted from perfect competition to monopoly, consumers would lose the amount represented by area *abcd*. Without monopoly-rent-seeking behavior, the industry would gain *abcd*. The net **deadweight loss** of monopoly would then be the triangle *bec*. If the costs of achieving and maintaining the monopoly are close to the monopoly profit, area *abcd*, the conversion of an industry from competition to monopoly would result in simply the loss of consumer surplus, *abecd*. Under these circumstances, the greater cost of monopoly would be the cost of rent-seeking activities.

The importance of rent-seeking activities has not been estimated by economists. While they are potentially more important than the ordinary deadweight losses from contrived scarcity, no consensus exists about their relative size.

> **Deadweight loss** is a loss of consumers' or producers' surplus that is not offset by a gain on anyone's part.

---

6. Richard Posner, in "The Social Costs of Monopoly and Regulation," *Journal of Political Economy* 83 (August 1975): 807–27, argues that the entire monopoly rent may be absorbed by rent-seeking activities. For an appraisal of this argument, see Franklin M. Fisher, "The Social Costs of Monopoly and Regulation: Posner Reconsidered," *Journal of Political Economy* 93 (April 1985): 410–16.

EXAMPLE 10-1   How Important Is Monopoly?

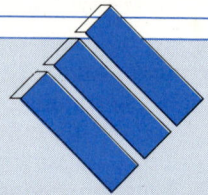

How much does the American economy lose from the monopoly power exercised by business firms? The pioneering research on this question was published in the 1950s by Arnold Harberger. The answer he gave was startling: that the economy lost about 0.1 percent of national income per year. Harberger assumed constant marginal costs, a price elasticity of demand for each industry equal to −1, and that monopoly profits were measured by above-average accounting profits. Industrial-organization expert Frederick Scherer characterized these losses in graphic terms: the per-capita cost of monopoly at that time was equivalent to the cost of a good steak dinner in a fine restaurant for every family every year. Because Harberger's study may have been somewhat on the low side, Dean Worcester later attempted to estimate the maximum cost of monopoly (measured as the loss from contrived scarcity). Worcester assumed that all economic activity was just as monopolized as the *Fortune* 500 list (the 500 largest industrial corporations). Worcester also corrected Harberger's assumption that price elasticities equal −1, because monopolies always produce where demand is elastic, and made some corrections for concealed monopoly profits in wages and advertising expenses. Given Worcester's liberal assumptions, he obtained a maximum permissible estimate of about 0.5 percent of national income for the years 1956–69. In 1984 terms, that would amount to about $70 per capita per year. Thus, Worcester put monopoly losses at several steak dinners per year!

Because Worcester studied firm data rather than industry data, he was able to identify the main culprits. He discovered that 31 percent of monopoly misallocation came from 30 firms. The list reads like an honor roll of American business: Xerox, Eli Lilly, Polaroid, Kodak, Maytag, IBM, Du Pont, R. J. Reynolds, and 22 other firms of sterling reputation. Interestingly enough, Worcester found no auto firms among his list of 30 monopolies. Because patents protect pharmaceuticals, it is not surprising to find 9 drug companies on the list. A subsequent study by John Siegfried and Thomas Tiemann confirmed the importance of monopoly in that sector but concluded that the automobile industry accounted for almost 44 percent of the losses from monopoly pricing. Siegfried and Tiemann used 1963 Internal Revenue Service data for industries, while Worcester used *Fortune* 500 data for the years 1956–69.

Almost all studies agree that monopoly losses from contrived scarcity are small. The only exception is that of David Kamerschen, who estimated the cost of monopoly to be about 6 percent of national income.

There has been virtually no work on the costs attributable to monopoly-rent-seeking activities. As pointed out by Richard Posner, these costs could dwarf the costs attributable to contrived scarcity.

Sources: Arnold C. Harberger, "Monopoly and Resource Allocation," *American Economic Review* 54 (May 1954); David R. Kamerschen, "An Estimation of the 'Welfare Losses' from Monopoly in the American Economy," *Western Economic Journal* 4 (Summer 1966); Dean A. Worcester, Jr., "New Estimates of the Welfare Loss to Monopoly, United States: 1956–1969," *Southern Economic Journal* 40 (October 1973); Richard A. Posner, "The Social Costs of Monopoly and Regulation," *Journal of Political Economy* 83 (1975).

Monopoly-rent-seeking behavior could cause losses much larger than the losses from contrived scarcity because firms might sacrifice a large portion of their monopoly profits in maintaining or securing the monopoly position.

X-Inefficiency

The *X-inefficiency* of monopoly is the organizational slack that results from the absence of competitive pressures.

The third loss from monopoly power has been called **X-inefficiency** by Harvey Leibenstein. The same basic idea was expressed many years ago by Sir John Hicks, a Nobel-prizewinning British economist, when he observed that "the best of all monopoly profits is the quiet life." According to Leibenstein, there is no competitive pressure in monopoly; hence, the monopolist may not minimize costs simply because managerial effort is required to do so.

There is empirical evidence that competition lowers the costs of production. Walter Primeaux compared electricity costs in those cities with a single supplier of electricity with costs in those cities served by at least two electric companies. He found that costs were about 11 percent higher for the monopoly suppliers.[7]

George Stigler has argued that *X*-inefficiency is not economic inefficiency even though competitive firms have lower costs than noncompetitive ones. The higher costs of a monopoly firm provide Hicks's "quiet life." These amenities have social value (to some members of society) and cannot be considered pure social loss, as are the losses from contrived scarcity or rent-seeking activities.[8]

The Measurement of Monopoly Power

The Lerner Index

Abba Lerner suggested that monopoly power be measured by the ratio, L:

$$L = \frac{P - MC}{P} \tag{8}$$

The advantage of the Lerner index is that it is zero in the case of perfect competition and presumably increases with monopoly power. Because $MC = MR$ when profits are maximized, and, according to Equation (3), $MR = P(1 + 1/\eta)$, substitution shows that

$$L = -1/\eta. \tag{9}$$

Thus, in principle at least, it is possible to use the Lerner index by simply determining the price elasticity of demand for a firm's product at its current

---

7. Walter Primeaux, "An Assessment of *X*-Efficiency Through Competition," *Review of Economics and Statistics* 59 (February 1977): 105–108.

8. George Stigler, "The *X*-Istence of *X*-Efficiency," *American Economic Review*, March 1976, pp. 213–16. See also Thomas J. DiLorenzo, "Corporate Management, Property Rights and the *X*-Istence of *X*-Inefficiency," *Southern Economic Journal* 48 (July 1981): 116–23.

EXAMPLE 10-2   Do Simple Profit Rates Capture Monopoly Profits?

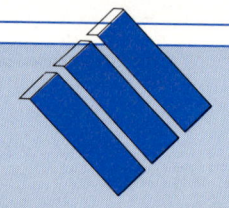

Many studies of monopoly profits assume that simple profit rates (profits divided by some measure of capital assets) adequately represent monopoly profits. Franklin Fisher, John McGowan, and Joen Greenwood have argued that only internal rates of return should be used to measure profit.

Imagine that $100 is invested in a machine that lasts forever. The machine generates no profit the first year and a profit of $39 per year thereafter. The accompanying table shows what happens if the firm buys one such machine every year. In the first year, the profit the machine generates is zero. In the second year, total profit is $39, but total assets are $200 (two machines have been purchased). The simple profit rate is 19.5 percent and will be 19.5 percent in each succeeding year, yet the firm's internal rate of return is 30 percent. If the interest rate is 30 percent, $39 per year is worth $130 ($39 ÷ 0.3). But the $39 profit is delayed by one year, so the investment of $100 today brings in an asset worth $130 in one year. Consequently, the internal rate of return is exactly 30 percent. When one such machine is bought every year, the simple profit rate varies from 0 to 19.5 percent and is unrelated to the internal rate of return.

This example illustrates the fact that to compute internal rates of return, it is necessary to have past and future information about each firm. Outside economists certainly do not have this information. How then should one measure monopoly power? The answer from Fisher, Greenwood, McGowan, and George Benston is to take a detailed history of the company and its industry, with emphasis on major events affecting the firm and industry (product innovations, marketing innovations).

The above argument appears devastating at first glance. However, it is still hypothetical. In 1984, Caterpillar Tractor had net losses of $428 million. In that same year, IBM made profits of $6.5 billion. Surely one is justified in concluding that IBM's internal rate of return was higher than Caterpillar Tractor's.

Sources: Franklin M. Fisher, John J. McGowan, and Joen E. Greenwood, *Folded, Spindled, and Mutilated: An Economic Analysis of* U.S. *v.* IBM (Cambridge, Mass.: MIT Press, 1983), pp. 234–42; George J. Benston, "The Validity of Profits-Structure with Particular Reference to the FTC's Line of Business Data," *American Economic Review* 75 (March 1985): 37–67; *Fortune*, April 29, 1985, p. 286.

Year	Profits (dollars)	Beginning-of-Year Capital Stock (dollars)	Profit Rate (percent)	Internal Rate of Return (percent)
1	0	$100	0	30
2	39	200	19.5	30
3	2 × 39	300	19.5	30
4	3 × 39	400	19.5	30

price. Because $|-\eta| > 0$, the Lerner index is higher the smaller is the absolute value of price elasticity. Generally speaking, the price elasticity of demand for a product is numerically larger when there are many substitutes. Thus, the fewer substitutes there are for a monopolized product, the greater is the monopoly power.

The disadvantage of using the Lerner index is that price elasticities are very difficult to obtain for a monopoly. Econometric studies of the price elasticity of demand assume that the supply curve shifts more than the demand curve shifts (see Chapter 5), but there is no supply curve in the theory of monopoly. The only solution would be to determine price elasticity by interview techniques, which have the shortcoming that the business manager has no incentive to give a correct or thoughtful answer.

Economic Profit

Because monopolies can earn above-average profits, it has been suggested by J. S. Bain that economic profits be used to measure monopoly power. To estimate economic profits, one must subtract an estimate of the competitive rate of return from the measured rate of accounting profits.

Some economists, however, seriously question the applicability of external measures of the profit rate. The profit rate in any particular year is profits divided by some measure of the firm's capital assets for that year. The conceptual difficulty with this measure is that some profits in any current year result from investments made in past years, and investments made in the current year will result in profits in some future year. In other words, investments take place over time. How should the profit rate be defined in an intertemporal setting? Economists have long held that the **internal rate of return** on any investment is the rate of interest that equates the present value of the future stream of profits to the cost of the investment. So defined, the internal rate of return may be poorly correlated with simple profit rates. Because the internal rate of return cannot be measured by an external observer, many researchers assume that simple profit rates give an adequate approximation. (See Example 10–2.)

> The **internal rate of return** is the interest rate that just equates the present value of the future stream of profits to the cost of an investment.

MULTIPLE-PRICING SCHEMES

The Conditions for Price Discrimination

This chapter has assumed thus far that the monopoly has a simple pricing policy, charging a single price to all of its customers. **Price discrimination** occurs if the same good is sold to different customers at different prices even though the firm's costs of selling are the same for each customer. Price discrimination is possible when: (1) perfect competition does not exist, (2) the seller can distinguish among classes of buyers, and (3) it is impossible for one buyer to sell to another buyer.

FIGURE 10-13 Profit Maximization and Price Discrimination

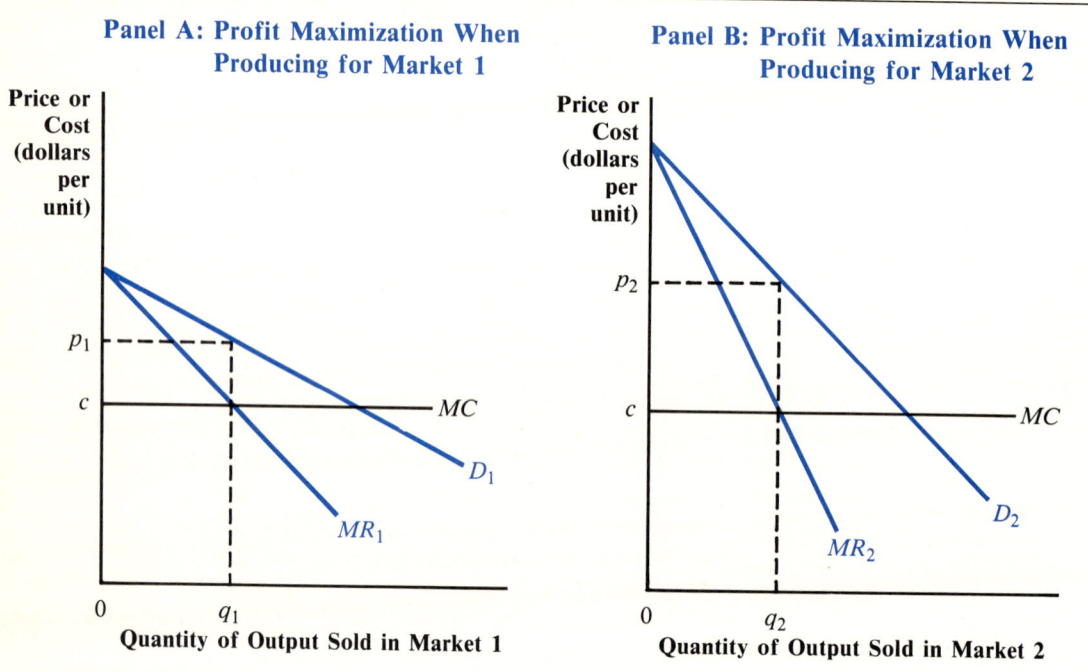

Panel A: Profit Maximization When Producing for Market 1

Panel B: Profit Maximization When Producing for Market 2

A monopoly discriminating between two markets maximizes profit by charging a higher price (p_2) in the market in which demand is less price elastic—Market 2.

Price discrimination exists if a seller charges different buyers different prices for the same good although the seller's costs for that good do not vary.

First, under conditions of perfect competition the demand for the good facing each seller is perfectly elastic. If there were different markets, each firm would sell its output where it could obtain the highest price. So, each market would eventually have the same price because if prices were different, sales would expand in the higher-priced market until prices were equalized in all the various markets.

Second, the seller must be able to distinguish between customers who are candidates for high prices and those who are candidates for low prices. Thus, buyers must have distinguishing characteristics. Sellers could use economic or occupational or age characteristics as screening devices. For example, public utilities have different rate schedules for industrial and residential buyers. Airlines, barbers, and theaters may charge children (or senior citizens) different prices than they charge younger adults.

Third, those who buy in the cheaper market must not be able to resell to those who buy in the dearer market; otherwise, competition would raise prices in the cheap market until they equaled prices in the dear market. Resale is impossible in the markets for services: shoeshines, haircuts, dental work, and medical treatment cannot be transferred from one buyer to another. Most physical goods, however, could be resold. To discriminate between high-paying and low-paying buyers of, say, oranges, the firm would need to find buyers separated by geography.

Why Price Discrimination?

Suppose that a monopoly firm could segment its markets and that the monopolist could determine the demand curve of each segment for the firm's product. If the monopolist sold its product at the same price in all market segments, it would be missing an opportunity to increase profits because marginal revenue would differ between market segments. If marginal revenue in Market 1, MR_1, exceeds marginal revenue in Market 2, MR_2, the firm could benefit from expanding output in Market 1 by one unit and reducing output in Market 2 by one unit. The firm's profit would then increase by $MR_1 - MR_2$. As long as MR_1 continued to be greater than MR_2, the firm would benefit from switching sales until MR_1 equaled MR_2. Of course, to expand sales to Market 1 at the expense of Market 2 would require that the firm lower the price in Market 1 and raise the price in Market 2.

Price discrimination is profitable because if the firm charges the same prices in different markets, marginal revenues will be higher in markets with higher price elasticity of demand. Recall from Equation (3) that $MR = P(1 + 1/\eta)$. Thus,

$$MR = P(1 - 1/|\eta|) \tag{10}$$

because $|\eta| = -1\eta$. For a given price, marginal revenue is higher whenever $|\eta|$ is higher. Because price elasticities are likely to differ between markets (calculated at the same price), price discrimination will normally be profitable if these conditions can be satisfied.

If there are, say, two markets, the monopolist will maximize profits whenever

$$P_1(1 - 1/|\eta_1|) = P_2(1 - 1/|\eta_2|) = MC. \tag{11}$$

To equate MR in both markets, it will be necessary to charge a lower price in the high-elasticity market. From Equation (11), because both MRs are equal to the same MC, it follows that $P_1 < P_2$ if and only if $|\eta_1| > |\eta_2|$.

Figure 10-13 illustrates profit maximization for a price-discriminating monopolist. For simplicity, it is assumed that marginal cost is constant. The demand curve, D_1, for Market 1 is more elastic than the demand curve, D_2, for Market 2 at any given price; the ratio of the price to the vertical intercept is larger (see the point elasticity formula in Chapter 5). When $MC = MR_1 = MR_2$, the firm is selling q_1 units in Market 1 at the price p_1, and q_2 units in Market 2 at the higher price p_2.

Perfect Price Discrimination

There is *perfect price discrimination* if each unit of a good is sold at a different price. To simplify the argument, suppose that each buyer buys

FIGURE 10-14　Perfect Price Discrimination

In the case of perfect price discrimination, each unit would be sold at a separate price. The demand curve would then also be the marginal-revenue curve, with the average-revenue curve above it.

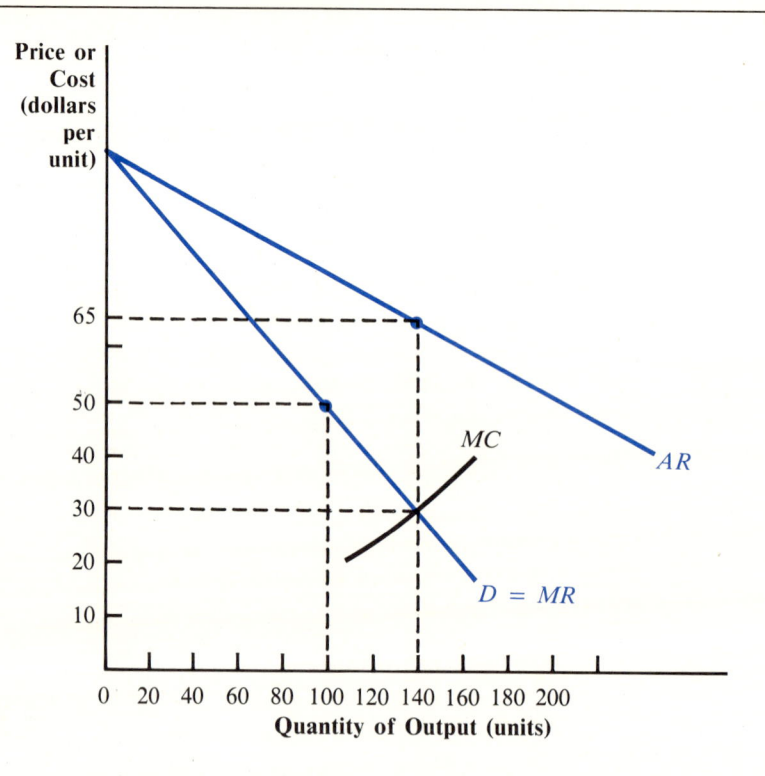

exactly one unit of the product. The demand curve can then be interpreted as the demand price of the marginal buyer. Such a demand curve is downward-sloping, because lower prices entice buyers who place smaller valuations on the good. For example, in Figure 10-14, the $50 price is the demand price of the 100th customer. If there were a uniform price of $50, the first 99 customers would obtain the good for less than their demand prices.

If the firm can engage in *perfect* price discrimination, the demand curve becomes the firm's marginal-revenue curve because to sell an additional unit, it is no longer necessary to lower the price on the preceding units sold. Thus, marginal revenue is just the price paid by the marginal buyer. The firm's average-revenue curve, *AR*, lies above the demand curve, *D*. (Because *D* is linear and represents *MR*, it must be twice as steep as *AR*.) Profits are maximized when $MR = MC$ at an output of 140 units and an average revenue of $65. The prices the firm charges are the demand prices arrayed along the demand curve up to the 140-unit quantity and the $30 price of the marginal buyer.

An important characteristic of perfect price discrimination is that the monopolist is socially efficient: the price paid by the marginal buyer is the social value of another unit of output. In equilibrium, this price equals marginal cost.

FIGURE 10-15   Two-Part Pricing

If a monopoly can charge each customer his or her consumer surplus, area *abe*, as an entry fee, profits are maximized by selling the product at the competitive price, p_c. Total profit will then equal the shaded area *ace* instead of the area, *efgh*, that would be achieved by a single-price monopoly.

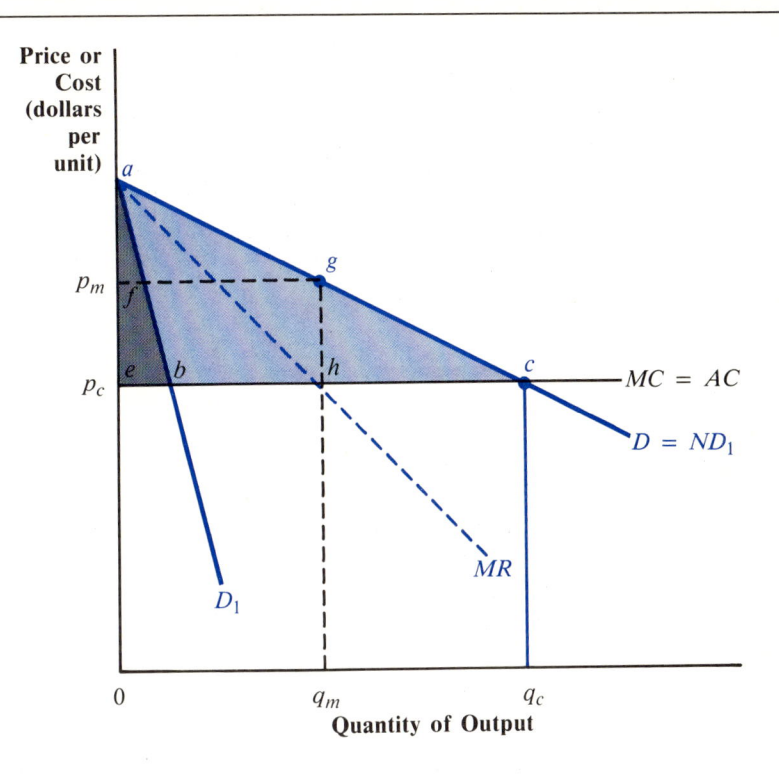

Two-Part Pricing

Perfect price discrimination would require a great deal of information on the part of the monopolist, but it is seldom encountered in the real world because it would be too costly for the firm to charge each customer a different price. Another type of pricing, however, is frequently encountered: two-part pricing where buyers pay an entry fee plus a price per unit of the good purchased. For example, nightclubs often charge a cover charge plus whatever the customer purchases. In Houston, Texas, Gilley's ("the world's largest nightclub") charges an entry fee depending on the quality of the entertainment, plus a competitive price for drinks purchased by customers. Many amusement parks have similar two-part pricing schemes.

To simplify the discussion, imagine that every buyer has the same demand curve for some product. Figure 10–15 shows a demand curve D_1 for the typical buyer as well as the market-demand curve, D, the horizontal sum of all such curves. If the firm knows each person's demand curve, a profit-maximizing monopoly will follow a two-part pricing scheme. Instead of charging price p_m, where $MR = MC$, the firm will charge each customer the competitive price p_c plus an entry fee. When the price is p_c, the firm can sell q_c units; its profits will equal the entry fees that can be collected. Each

> **EXAMPLE 10-3 Price Discrimination by Electric Utilities**
>
> Walter Primeaux and Randy Nelson have examined evidence of price discrimination between commercial and industrial users of electricity. Their evidence is consistent with the theory that customers with higher elasticities of demand pay lower prices. Industrial users have a more elastic demand for electricity than commercial users because they can always generate their own power. Measuring price discrimination by the ratio of price to marginal cost, Primeaux and Nelson found that the ratio averaged 2.6 for industrial users and 4.6 for commercial users.
>
> Source: Walter J. Primeaux, Jr., and Randy A. Nelson, "An Examination of Price Discrimination and Internal Subsidization by Electric Utilities," *Southern Economic Journal* 47 (July 1980): 84–99.

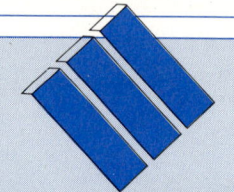

customer will be charged, at most, his or her consumer surplus. Recall that consumer surplus is the value the consumer places on the right to buy the good at some particular price. If it charges each consumer the entry fee *abe* (the consumer surplus of each customer), the firm's profits will be the shaded area *ace*, which is *abe* times the number of consumers. If the firm charged price p_m, as a single-price monopoly would do, its profits would be the standard rectangle *efgh*. With entry fees, price p_m could generate profits at most equal to *eagh*. Clearly, profits are maximized by charging the competitive price p_c plus an entry fee equal to consumer surplus. Because price equals marginal cost, such a monopoly is economically efficient.

If a monopoly firm can charge each customer his or her consumer surplus as an entry fee, profits are maximized by selling the product at the competitive price, $P = MC$. Such two-part pricing is economically efficient.

The Importance of Information Costs

The examples of two-part pricing and perfect price discrimination show that a monopoly need not be economically inefficient. In both cases, efficiency is achieved when the monopolist cleverly extracts all consumer surplus either by perfect price discrimination (charging each consumer his or her demand price) or by charging all consumers the competitive price plus their consumer surplus. Such pricing policies clearly depend on the monopoly's having extraordinary information about consumers. In practice, such information would be most difficult and costly to collect. The two examples do suggest, however, that economic efficiency can result if such information costs are zero.

Information costs, however, are not zero. When information costs are significant, the monopolist must expend resources to engage in either perfect price discrimination or perfect two-part pricing. Whatever resources are devoted to acquiring information about the consumer for the purpose of extracting consumer surplus are part of the social costs of monopoly. In short, if information is very costly, monopoly is inefficient.

SUMMARY

1. A pure monopoly exists when there is only one seller, when the firm can charge any price it chooses, and when there are barriers to entry from new competitors. Entry barriers include: economies of scale, limited access to raw materials, patents, government franchises or licenses, and sunk costs.

2. In either the short run or the long run, a monopoly maximizes its profit by charging a price where $MR = MC$. The relationship between price, marginal cost, and elasticity is: $MC = P(1 + 1/\eta)$. Because MC is positive, a monopolist always charges a price where demand is elastic.

3. In the long run, the monopolist can freely choose its plant size until long-run profit is maximized without fear of competition from other firms.

4. Profit-maximizing monopolies need not produce an efficient quantity of output and never maximize sales revenue.

5. The major social losses from monopoly are the deadweight loss incurred because price is set greater than marginal cost and the resources devoted to monopoly-rent-seeking behavior. The loss from contrived scarcity is the area above the marginal-cost curve, below the demand curve, and to the right of the monopolist's output level. The loss from monopoly-rent-seeking behavior could equal the potential profit from converting a competitive industry into a monopolized one. The losses from X-inefficiency are controversial. Monopoly power can be measured by the Lerner index or by profit rates. The Lerner index is seldom used, and the use of measured profit rates has been criticized by some economists.

6. Price discrimination can occur if perfect competition does not exist, if the firm can discriminate between segments of buyers, and if buyers cannot resell to one another. In the case of standard price discrimination, the monopoly equates marginal cost and marginal revenue in each market the firm faces, charging the lowest prices in those markets with the highest price elasticities of demand. In the case of perfect price discrimination,

every unit of the good is sold at its demand price, the demand curve becomes the marginal-revenue curve, and the firm extracts all the consumer surplus. Monopolists can also engage in two-part pricing, by charging an entry fee to extract the consumer surplus plus a competitive price. With zero information costs these practices result in economic efficiency; otherwise, the resources devoted to extracting consumer surplus are part of the social costs of monopoly.

QUESTIONS AND PROBLEMS

1. "A natural monopoly must produce where there are economies of scale in the production of the market supply." Evaluate this statement.

2. The demand curve for product Alpha is $Q = 50 - 5P$. Write an equation for the marginal-revenue curve.

3. The demand curve for product Beta is $P = 50 - 5Q$. Write an equation for the marginal-revenue curve.

4. Suppose $MC = AC = \$10$. Calculate the monopoly output (Q), price (P), and profit (π) for the demand curve $P = 50 - 5Q$. What is the price elasticity of demand (η) at the monopoly price? Check your answer by showing $MR = P(1 + 1/\eta)$.

5. Why are monopoly profits sometimes called *monopoly rents*?

6. Derive the formula $MR = P(1 + 1/\eta)$.

7. Suppose $MC = AC = C$ (a constant) and $P = A - BQ$ describes the demand curve. What are P, Q, and π in terms of the parameters A, B, and C?

8. For the monopoly in problem (4), what is the deadweight loss from contrived scarcity?

9. For the monopoly in problem (7), what is the deadweight loss from contrived scarcity?

10. Assume a monopolist sells a product in two separate markets. The demand curve in Market 1 is $P_1 = 10 - Q_1$ and the demand curve in Market 2 is $P_2 = 20 - Q_2$. If $MC = \$2$, determine the profit-maximizing levels of P_1, P_2, Q_1, Q_2, and total monopoly profit π.

11. Suppose the monopolist in problem (10) discovers a new market with the demand curve $P_3 = 20 - 2Q_3$. What would be the price and output for this market? Compare P_3 with P_2 and explain.

12. Suppose there are 100 identical consumers with the demand curve $Q = 10 - 0.01P$. The market-demand curve is then $Q = 1,000 - P$. For a monopoly that knows the demand curve for each consumer, calculate the optimal entry fee, price, output, and profit when $MC = \$10$. How do these results compare to the simple monopoly solution (no entry fees)?

SUGGESTED READINGS

Harberger, Arnold C. "Monopoly and Resource Allocation." *American Economic Review* 54 (May 1954): 77–87.

Henderson, J. M., and R. E. Quandt. *Microeconomic Theory: A Mathematical Approach*, 2nd ed. New York: McGraw-Hill, 1971, pp. 206–22.

Hicks, J. R. "Annual Survey of Economic Theory: The Theory of Monopoly." *Econometrica* 3 (1935): 1–20.

Robinson, J. *The Economics of Imperfect Competition*. London: Macmillan & Co., 1933, chaps. 3, 6, 15, 16.

Stigler, George. *The Theory of Price*, 3rd ed. New York: Macmillan, 1966, chap. 11.

CHAPTER 11

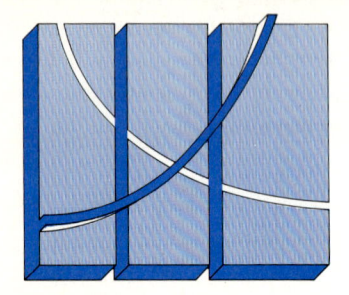

THE ECONOMICS OF INFORMATION

The previous chapters have generally supposed that information costs are small or zero, but information costs are a central factor in economics. While many years ago Nobel laureate George Stigler could write that "information occupies a slum dwelling in the town of economics," by the 1980s the economics of information became a centerpiece of economics. Most interesting economic problems arise because information is costly. With perfect information, the problem of allocating scarce resources among competing ends could be solved instantly by simply putting all the information about technology, resources, and individual preferences into a computer and letting some mathematical algorithm discover the set of prices that would equate supply and demand in all markets. With costless information, this setting of prices could be done on a minute-by-minute basis if necessary, but information is not costless to acquire or assimilate. Information is widely dispersed over millions of individuals; there is no single, controlling mind. In such a world, as Nobel laureate F. A. Hayek observed, the economic problem is "how to secure the best use of resources known to any of the members of society, for ends whose relative importance only these individuals know."[1]

This chapter will examine the role of information costs in the economy. We will study transaction costs, the economics of speculation, and the critical problems of adverse selection and moral hazard.

---

1. George Stigler, "The Economics of Information," *Journal of Political Economy*, June 1961, pp. 213–25; F. A. Hayek, "The Use of Knowledge in Society," *American Economic Review*, September 1945, pp. 519–30.

INFORMATION COSTS

Information is the most valuable of all commodities. If you knew the price of wheat tomorrow, you could speculate in the futures market and become wealthy beyond your wildest dreams. The discovery of an unexploited market—a new kind of television show (Dallas), a new kind of music (the Beatles), a new kind of restaurant (McDonalds), or a new kind of product (Apple computers or Sony videocassette recorders)—can make the discoverers a fortune. On a smaller scale, the consumer who discovers a higher quality product or a lower-priced consumer good increases his or her utility.

Information costs prevent people from exploiting all such economic opportunities. Examples of information costs include the costs of telephoning, shopping, collecting market data, reading ads and consumer reports, and inspecting goods.

Information costs are the costs agents face in finding out about markets.

Information is costly because human beings have a limited capacity to acquire, process, store, and retrieve facts and figures about prices, qualities, locations of products, the preferences of other individuals, and the technologies available to other individuals. Thus, each person accumulates information that is specific to each person's particular circumstances of time and place. Individuals who know a great deal about automobile production may know little about wheat production, and vice versa. Much of the knowledge about the economy is totally decentralized, unorganized, and highly valuable. As Hayek observed:

> . . . a little reflection will show that there is beyond question a body of very important but unorganized knowledge which cannot possibly be called scientific in the sense of knowledge of general rules: the knowledge of the particular circumstances of time and place. It is with respect to this that every individual has some advantage over all others in that he [or she] possesses unique information of which beneficial use might be made.

The price system allows people to specialize in information on a need-to-know basis. It is not necessary for the producer to know why people buy a particular product, although information about the preferences of people might be valuable to designing a particular product. It is not necessary for the consumer to know how a particular product is made. An equilibrium price coordinates quantities demanded and supplied without any cooperation among buyers, among sellers, or between buyers and sellers. There need not be an all-knowing mind. A dramatic example is the lowly pencil. It has been observed that no single person knows everything about making a simple pencil. If one thinks about the knowledge required to produce a pencil—about the growing of the trees that produce the wood, the making of the saws that fell the trees, the forging of the steel that makes the saws, the manufacture of the engines that run the saws, the harvesting of the hemp that makes the ropes that are necessary to tie down the logs, the training of the loggers, the mining of the graphite in Sri Lanka for the lead, the mining of

PRACTICE EXERCISE 11-1

Q. How can people buy and eat wheat without knowing anything about how to produce wheat?

A. The price of wheat is adequate to coordinate the supply and demand decisions of producers and consumers. At the equilibrium price, demand equals supply even though buyers and sellers are guided only by price. No information is needed about the other side of the market.

---

the zinc and copper for making the bit of metal holding the eraser, and the extraction of the rapeseed oil from the Dutch East Indies that is used in the eraser—it is clear that no single mind could comprehend all that information. The price of the pencil and the prices of its component parts economize on the information needed by any one person by the magic of an equilibrium price.[2]

Information is not exogenous. Economic agents must actively acquire information, as they do any other valuable economic commodity.

THE ECONOMICS OF SEARCH

Transaction Costs

Transaction costs are the costs of operating markets; they are the costs of bringing together buyer and seller.

Markets are costly to operate. **Transaction costs** include the costs of travel, the costs of negotiation, the costs of property-rights enforcement, and the costs of information. When brokers bring together buyers and sellers, the difference between the buyer's demand price and the seller's supply price is a payment for the resources committed to operating the market.

Different markets price transaction costs in totally different ways. Real-estate brokers often charge the seller 5 to 10 percent of the selling price as a brokerage commission. Retail stores charge customers a given markup over cost. Christies, an auction house, charges both buyers and sellers a 10 percent commission on used jewelry items sold for more than $3,000. Sotheby's, which auctions art, charges buyers 10 percent and sellers 20 percent for items sold for more than $500. Brokers for stocks, commodities, or foreign exchange will bid a certain price for an item and have a higher asking price. The bid/ask spread is higher the higher are the transaction costs. For example, a thinly traded stock on the over-the-counter (OTC)

---

[2]. See Milton and Rose Friedman, *Free to Choose* (New York: Harcourt Brace Jovanich, 1981) for the pencil example.

market for stocks might have a bid/ask spread of 12 or 13 percent, while an asset such as the British pound will have a bid/ask spread of only a few percentage points.

Centralized and Decentralized Markets

Some markets are centralized, while others are decentralized. A *centralized market* is one in which buyers and sellers of a particular product carry out their transactions in one location. Stocks, bonds, and commodities (like wheat or gold) are traded on centralized markets, such as the New York Stock Exchange or the Chicago Board of Trade. A *decentralized market* is one in which buyers and sellers carry out their transactions in a large number of different physical locations. Real-estate markets, retail stores, and wholesale houses are decentralized markets.

The perfectly competitive market of earlier chapters depicts a centralized market—where all buyers and sellers face exactly the same price—but many markets cannot be centralized. Consumers are spread out geographically. The retail markets for clothing, gasoline, food, and other goods must be located close to the consumer. Local department stores, grocery stores, and service stations reduce the consumer's shopping costs by packaging the goods in convenient sizes and selling them at convenient locations.

When a market is decentralized, prices can differ at each location, making perfect competition unlikely. Customers cannot know the prices charged at each location. Which store charges the lowest price? To know the answer to this question, the consumer would have to canvass every location. Because the consumer has imperfect information about the prices offered by different stores, and because different stores offer different degrees of convenience to any given consumer, prices can vary from store to store.

In a market with several locations, and with consumers facing significantly different costs of acquiring information, some price dispersion is likely. When information is imperfect, it is likely that some firms can exploit the customers who face higher information costs. Information costs give firms some monopoly power. Imagine, for example, that all firms charged the same price (equal to, say, the minimum point on each firm's *LRAC* curve). With significantly different information costs, some customers will be ignorant, and others will be well informed. If there are enough ignorant customers who do not know the prices charged by competitive firms, it might pay one or more of the firms to charge a higher price. Such a high-priced firm will lose informed customers, but it will be able to exploit the uninformed customers who by chance buy at the high-priced store rather than a low-priced store.[3]

---

3. For a detailed theoretical treatment, see Steven Salop and Joseph Stiglitz, "Bargains and Ripoffs: A Model of Monopolistically Competitive Price Dispersion," *Review of Economic Studies*, 1977, pp. 493–510. See also Tibor Scitovsky, *Welfare and Competition*, rev. ed. (Homewood, Ill.: Richard D. Irwin, 1971), chap. 23.

TABLE 11-1   **Calculating the Marginal Benefit of Search**

Lowest Price Sampled, s	Marginal Benefit of Search, MB
$1	0
$2	$0.25 = ($2 − $1)/4
$3	$0.75 = ($3 − $1)/4 + ($3 − $2)/4
$4	$1.50 = ($4 − $1)/4 + ($4 − $2)/4 + ($4 − $1)/4

The Optimal-Search Rule

Given that there will be some price dispersion in a decentralized market, what is the optimal amount of search a consumer should undertake? People will shop for a lower price as long as the expected marginal benefit of sampling one more store exceeds the shopping cost. When a person has found a price for which further shopping yields smaller expected marginal benefits than marginal costs, it pays to stop searching. Given the distribution of prices in the market and the costs of shopping, it is possible to calculate a **reservation price, r**. If the lowest price sampled exceeds r, the consumer should continue shopping; if the lowest price sampled is less than or equal to r, the consumer should stop shopping.

*The **reservation price**, r, is the highest price a buyer will pay or the lowest price a seller will accept.*

The optimal-search rule is that economic agents should search for a lower price for the things they buy, or a higher price for the things they sell, or a better-quality product, as long as the marginal benefits of searching exceed the marginal cost. If the marginal benefits of search fall short of the marginal cost, the agent should cut back on search activity. When the reservation price or quality is discovered, no further search need take place unless new information becomes available.

To calculate the reservation price, it is necessary to calculate the marginal benefit of searching. For simplicity, we will assume that:

1. there are many firms selling product X.
2. there are four different prices ($1, $2, $3, $4) charged by the various firms and each occurs with the same probability: 1 in 4.
3. each customer knows the probability distribution of possible prices; in other words, each customer knows that the prices of $1, $2, $3, and $4 can occur with equal probabilities.
4. the marginal cost of shopping at one more store is constant.

The above assumptions allow us to calculate the marginal benefit of searching in a simplified case. Suppose the customer has sampled various firms and has found that the lowest price is $$s$. Of course, s can be anything from $1 to $4. It is intuitively clear that the marginal benefits *(MB)* of search

EXAMPLE 11-1 The Optimal-Shopping Rule for Hamburgers

The optimal-shopping rule is simply that people will shop until they find a good whose price is less than their reservation price. The intuition behind the optimal-shopping rule should also hold for other kinds of information gathering. Suppose you are shopping for the best hamburger in town. Given your expectations about the distribution of hamburger quality among the various restaurants and about shopping costs, there is a reservation quality. If you find a hamburger at least as good as that quality, you have found that hamburger quality that maximizes your utility. It may not be the best hamburger, but it is not worthwhile to look for a better hamburger, given the expected benefits and costs.

will be higher the higher is s. Table 11-1 shows how to calculate MB. Clearly, when $s = \$1$, $MB_1 = 0$ because there are no lower prices. When $s = \$2$, the gain from finding a price of $1 is ($2 - $1). This occurs with probability 1/4; thus, the expected gain from sampling another store is $MB_2 = \$0.25$. When $s = \$3$, the searcher can gain ($3 - $2) and ($3 - $1) with probabilities 1/4 each; hence, $MB_3 = 2(1/4) + 1(1/4) = \$0.75$. Finally, when $s = \$4$, the marginal gain would be the expected value of ($4 - $3), ($4 - $2), and ($4 - $1); thus,

$$MB_4 = \$1(1/4) + \$2(1/4) + \$3(1/4) = \$1.50.$$

Whether or not the consumer will continue to search, however, depends on the cost of searching one more store. Suppose the marginal cost of search is $0.75. If the customer's lowest price is $4, he or she will continue searching because $MB_4 = \$1.50$. The marginal benefit of search exceeds the cost. Suppose further search turns up a price of $3. Now the marginal benefit of search exactly equals the marginal cost of search. The searcher will be indifferent between searching and not searching. The lowest price sampled of $3 is in fact the consumer's reservation price. The reservation price is the value of s that equates the marginal benefit to the marginal cost of search. If the marginal cost of search were $0.25, the consumer's reservation price would be $2. Clearly, the consumer would probably have to search longer if the reservation price were $2 instead of $3: the probability of finding a price lower than $3 is 1/2, and the probability of finding a price lower than $2 is only 1/4. In other words, the lower is the marginal cost of search, the more the consumer shops.

FIGURE 11-1 Determining a Reservation Price

The marginal benefit (*MB*) of search is higher the higher is the lowest price found from a given sampling of prices by the consumer. The consumer's reservation price, *r*, is the lowest sample price at which marginal benefit of search equals the marginal cost of search, *c*.

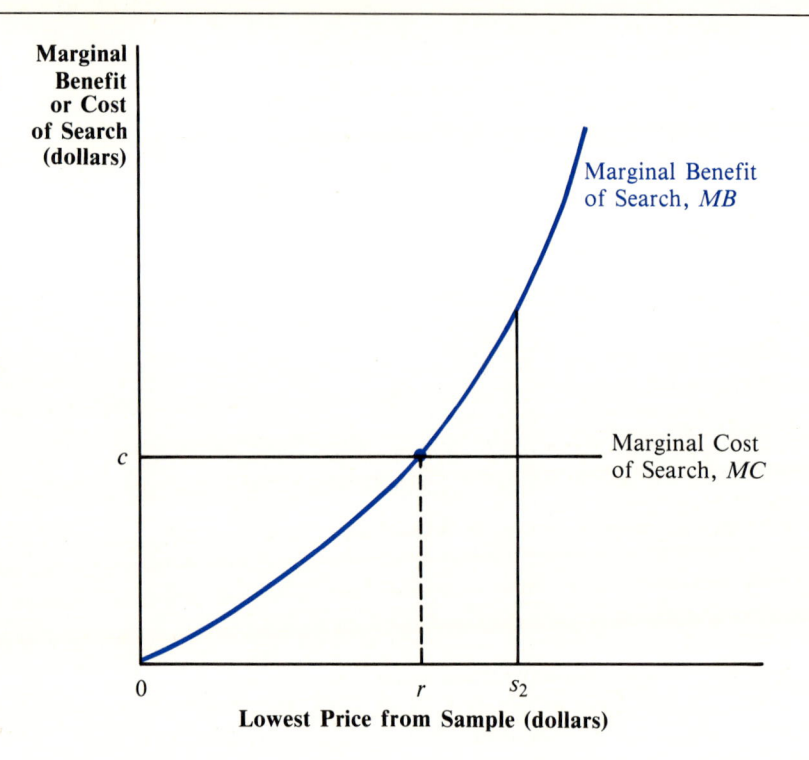

Figure 11-1 shows how the reservation price is determined in the general case. The *MB* curve shows the marginal benefit of search for the lowest price in each sample. When the lowest price from a given sample is s_2, for example, the marginal benefit of search at s_2 is greater than the marginal cost of search, *c*, so the consumer continues shopping. The reservation price, *r*, is that lowest price sampled at which the marginal benefit of search equals the marginal cost. Thus,

$$MB(r) = c. \qquad (1)$$

If the lowest price sampled is less than or equal to *r*, the consumer stops shopping; if the lowest price sampled is greater than *r*, the consumer continues to shop.

The smaller is the reservation price, the more a customer searches from a given dispersion of prices. The higher is the reservation price, the less a customer searches. Panel A of Figure 11-2 shows that a reduction in search costs from *c* to *c'* lowers the reservation price from *r* to *r'*. Thus, if search costs fall, the customer will have a lower reservation price. With a lower reservation price, it is necessary to search longer from a given distribution of prices.

FIGURE 11-2 The Effect on the Reservation Price of a Change in Search Costs or Benefits

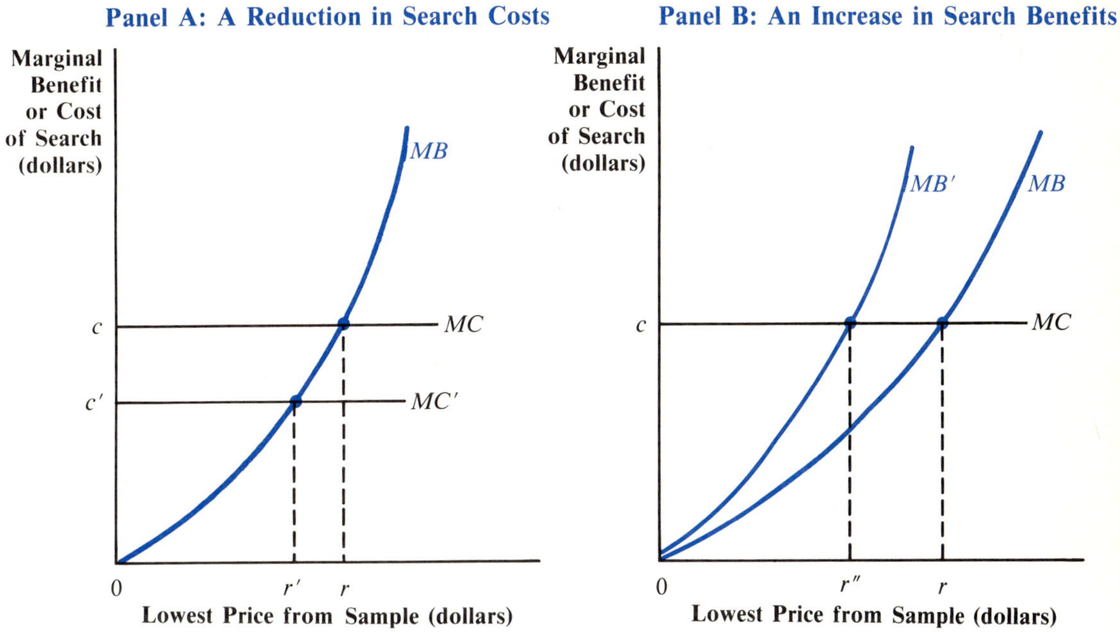

Panel A: A Reduction in Search Costs

Panel B: An Increase in Search Benefits

A reduction in search costs or an increase in the marginal benefits of search will lower the reservation price. In Panel A, when search costs fall from c to c', the reservation price falls from r to r'. In Panel B, an increase in the marginal benefits of search from MB to MB' reduces the reservation price from r to r''.

Panel B of Figure 11-2 shows that an increase in the marginal benefit of search, from MB to MB', decreases the reservation price from r to r''. With a lower reservation price, the customer will search more. An increase in the marginal benefit of search could be caused by an increase in the importance of the good in a consumer's budget. For example, Americans drink more coffee than tea; therefore, the marginal benefit of searching for the lowest price is higher for coffee than for tea. Thus, American consumers will do more comparison shopping for coffee than tea.

When a single consumer increases his or her search for the lowest price, the market's price dispersion will remain unaffected. But if all consumers increase the intensity of their search, market price dispersion will be reduced. For example, if search costs were zero or nil compared to benefits, price dispersion would have to be nil. Any firm that charged a higher price than the lowest-priced firm would have no business. In general, the smaller are search costs relative to benefits, the smaller are the sales of the high-priced firms relative to the low-priced firms. Lower search costs tend to reduce price dispersion in the market.

FIGURE 11-3 Profitable Speculation

With perfect speculation, p_0 is the price in both periods because speculators buy the amount of output represented by the distance between q_0 and q_1 in Period 1 and sell the amount represented by the distance between q_2 and q_0 in Period 2. (The supply curve in Period 1 is S_1 and in Period 2 is S_2.) In Period 1, the net gain to society is the area F; in Period 2, the net gain is area B.

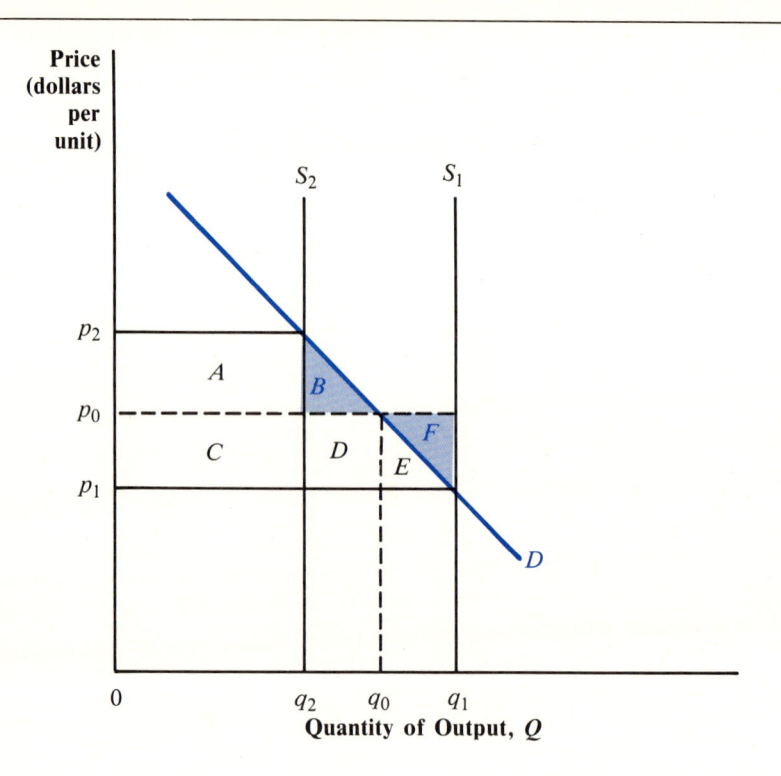

There is considerable evidence that market price dispersion falls when the benefits of search rise relative to search costs, including the three examples that follow.

1. The author collected the prices of a one-pound can of Folgers coffee and of a box of 48 Lipton tea bags in five Houston supermarkets (in January 1981). He found that the price of Lipton tea varied twice as much as the price of Folger's coffee. The ratio of the standard deviation to the mean was only 0.031 for coffee and 0.061 for tea. This result is not surprising because coffee is more important in American budgets than tea; thus, the marginal benefits of search are higher.
2. George Stigler, in his investigation of automobile and washing-machine prices, found that prices were less widely dispersed for identical makes of automobiles than for identical brands of washing machines.
3. Tibor Scitovsky observed that prices of consumer goods in Europe are less dispersed than in America. The reasons for this lower dispersion are twofold. The marginal benefits of search are relatively higher in Europe because American per-capita income is higher; search costs are lower in Europe because population density is higher in Europe than in America.[4]

---

4. See George Stigler, *The Theory of Price*, 4th ed. (New York: Macmillan, 1987), pp. 2–3; Tibor Scitovsky, *The Joyless Economy* (London: The Oxford University Press, 1976), pp. 178ff.

SPECULATION

When prices differ between markets or from seller to seller, people searching for the lowest price will reduce price dispersion to the smallest amount compatible with the costs of information and transportation between markets or firms. The practice of buying in cheap markets and reselling in expensive markets is *arbitrage*. Clearly, arbitrageurs reduce price dispersion.

Speculation is very similar to arbitrage. While the arbitrageur buys at one point and sells at another point in space, the speculator buys at one time and sells at another time. While arbitrage is a well-understood economic phenomenon—even tourists do it to a small degree—speculation is widely misunderstood by the general population. The only difference between arbitrage and speculation is that while prices in different locations can be obtained at a reasonable cost, future prices can never be known. The speculator must make an informed guess about what the future price of the good is going to be.

Profitable Speculation

The speculator is often considered to be a person who gains at the expense of other people. But what are the costs and benefits? Speculators try to make a profit by buying when a product is cheap and selling when the product is dear. Thus, profitable speculation raises prices when supplies are abundant (and prices cheap) and lowers prices when supplies are scarce (and prices dear). In other words, the speculator is smoothing out fluctuations in prices and quantities consumed.

If there were *perfect* speculation, people would perceive the future perfectly. Under these circumstances, the profits from speculation would have to be driven to zero as in any long-run competitive equilibrium. In Figure 11-3, S_1 is the supply of wheat in Period 1, and S_2 is the supply of wheat in Period 2. Thus, the harvest is plentiful in Period 1 and scant in Period 2. Without speculation, the prices of wheat would be p_1 in Period 1 and p_2 in Period 2, and consumers would be forced to consume enormous quantities when the harvest was plentiful and to ration themselves severely when the harvest was small.

If there were perfect speculation, speculators would buy the quantity $(q_1 - q_0)$ in Period 1 and sell the equal quantity $(q_0 - q_2)$ in Period 2. They would buy and sell at the price p_0. Compared to the situation without speculators, in Period 1, the price would be higher than otherwise (p_0 instead of p_1), but producers would gain areas $C + D + E + F$ while consumers would lose areas $C + D + E$—a net gain of area F. In Period 2, the price would be lower than without speculation (p_0 instead of p_2), and consumers would gain areas $A + B$ while producers would lose area A—a net gain of area B. Thus, speculation increases the net product of society by the sum of areas $B + F$. Goods are being transferred from a time when the

PRACTICE EXERCISE 11-2

Q. Suppose the demand curve for wheat in every period is $P = 10 - 0.5Q$. In Period 1, the supply of wheat is $S_1 = 8$ bushels; in Period 2, the supply of wheat is $S_2 = 4$ bushels. Assume zero storage costs. What is the price with perfect speculation? What are the net benefits of such speculation for society?

A. Without speculation, $P_1 = 10 - 0.5(8) = \$6$ and $P_2 = 10 - 0.5(4) = \$8$. The sum of consumer and producer surplus in Period 1 is the area under the demand curve down to the price of $6. By drawing the demand curve, it can be seen that the area to the left of the quantity of 8 bushels and below the demand curve is $64. The sum of consumer and producer surplus in Period 2 is $36. In both periods, the total surplus is $64 + \$36 = \$100$. With perfect speculation, the quantity supplied is 6 bushels in each period and the price is $7, because 2 bushels from Period 1 will be carried over to Period 2. The sum of consumer and producer surplus in each period would be $51, for a total surplus of $102. The net gain is $2.

marginal utility of consumption is low to a time when the marginal utility of consumption is high.

Profitable speculation takes place on a large scale in the world. Consider any agricultural product, such as wheat or corn. Wheat is harvested at definite times throughout the year; nothing is harvested while the wheat is growing. Clearly, if people did not speculate at all, there would be a binge of consumption at harvest times and near starvation at other times. Such an erratic consumption pattern does not occur.

Unprofitable Speculation

Perfect speculation adds to the net benefits of nonspeculators. What about unprofitable speculation? What if the speculator buys dear and sells cheap? In this case, the nonspeculator still gains, but the speculator loses *more*. As a consequence, unprofitable speculation lowers the net welfare of society (counting consumers, producers, and speculators). In Figure 11–4, the demand and supply curves, D and S, are constant from harvest to harvest. Without speculation, the price is p_0. Suppose speculators mistakenly buy $(q_0 - q_2)$ units at the price p_2 and sell the identical quantity $(q_1 - q_0)$ at the price p_1. When the price is p_2, nonspeculators gain area C (the difference between the gain in producer surplus and the loss of consumer surplus); when the price is p_1, nonspeculators gain area F (the difference between the gain in consumer surplus and the loss of producer surplus). Because the

FIGURE 11-4 Unprofitable Speculation

Unprofitable speculation can yield net benefits equal to the area of $B + C$ to nonspeculators but imposes net costs equal to the area of $A + B + C$ on speculators. The net cost to society is the area A.

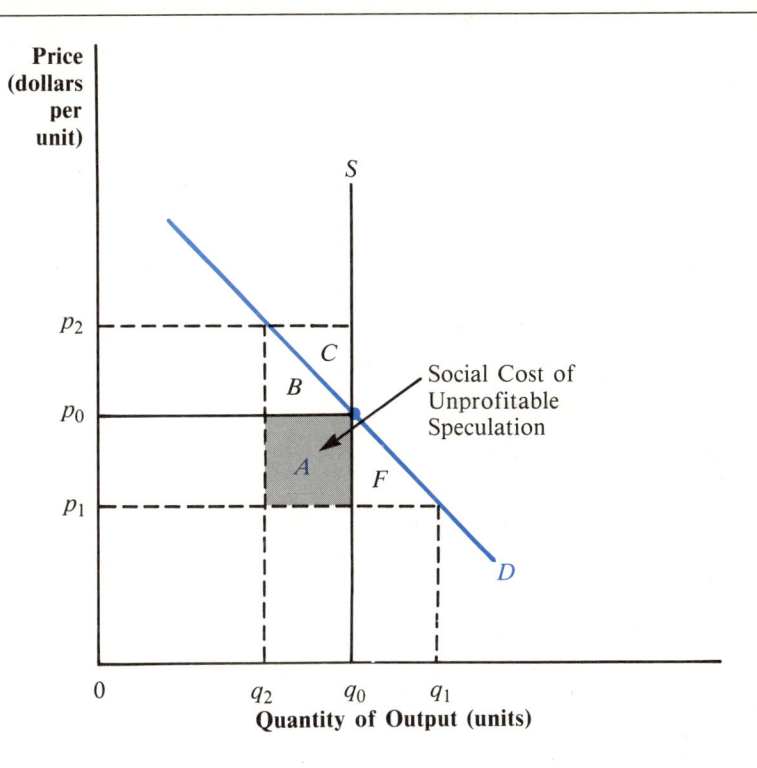

areas $F = C = B$, nonspeculators gain $B + C$, but the speculator loses the rectangle $A + B + C$—the loss per unit multiplied by the quantity purchased (or sold) by the speculators. Thus, counting everybody equally, the net loss to society is area A. Society incurs losses from unprofitable speculation because goods are being transferred from a time when marginal utility is high to a time when marginal utility is low. Consumption, in this case, is destabilized.

If speculation is profitable, consumption and prices will tend to be stabilized over time. If speculation is unprofitable, then consumption and prices will tend to be destabilized over time. The community as a whole will be better off with profitable speculation.

The Pattern of Prices Over Time

The above discussion is simplistic because it does not take into account the storage costs of commodities. When wheat is stored, the opportunity costs of storage must be paid: insurance, the sacrificed interest on the value of the wheat, deterioration, and the elevator operator's fee.

FIGURE 11-5   Agricultural Price Patterns

The ideal seasonal pattern of prices shows the price of wheat at its minimum at harvest time and at its maximum just before harvest time. The price rise reflects the cost of storage. If the harvest is instantaneously gathered, and if demand and supply are the same throughout the year, the above pattern of prices yields zero profits to speculators.

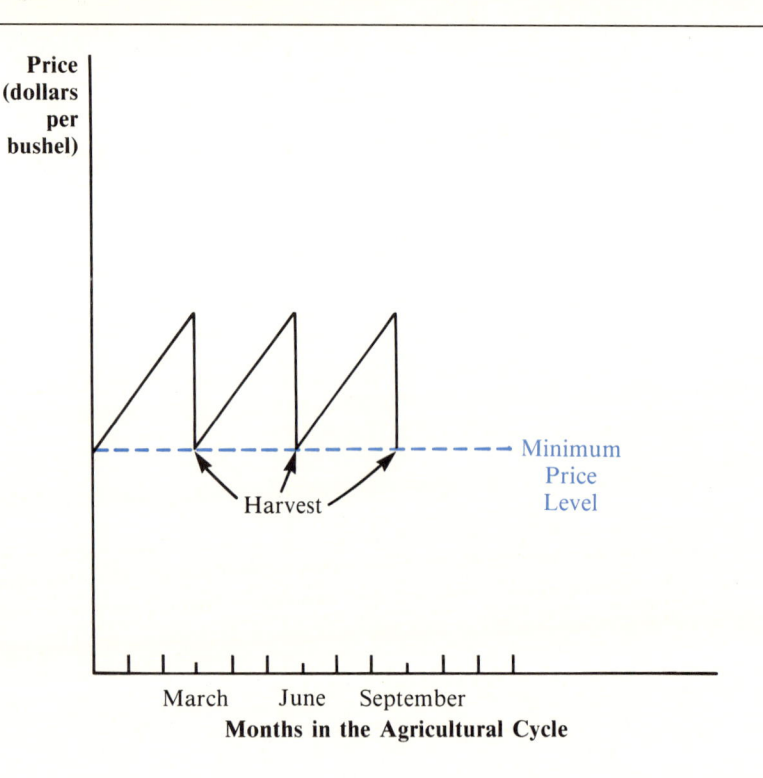

Price (dollars per bushel) vs. Months in the Agricultural Cycle (March, June, September), showing sawtooth pattern with drops at Harvest and a dashed Minimum Price Level.

To simplify the discussion of storage, consider the case where the demand and supply of wheat is the same from harvest to harvest. To keep matters even simpler, suppose all the harvest is gathered in an instant. Figure 11-5 shows the resulting pattern of prices over time when there is perfect speculation. The price of wheat rises from harvest to harvest in accordance with the costs of storage; the longer the wheat is stored, the higher are the storage costs. The price of wheat is at its maximum just prior to the harvest. When the harvest comes in, the price of wheat then sharply drops—then the process starts again. At any moment in time, the price of wheat just covers its production and storage costs in order to keep speculation profits equal to zero.

In the real world, things are not so simple. Supply and demand fluctuate from harvest to harvest, and people cannot predict the future perfectly. Indeed, in the real world, the business of speculation is so complicated that separate institutions arise for storage and speculation. How does speculation really take place?

The Futures Market

Speculators in wheat, corn, soybeans, cattle, and other commodities may never see a stalk of wheat or an ear of corn. They may not know anything

TABLE 11-2 Selected Transactions on the Futures Market and the New York Stock Exchange, January 7, 1986

Futures Market		Stock Exchange	
Commodities	Value	Stock	Value
Soybeans	$1.4 billion	IBM	$220 million
Corn	$400 million	GM	$ 29 million
Wheat	$120 million	Texaco	$ 64 million
Total	**$1.9 billion**	**Total**	**$317 million**

Source: *New York Times*, January 8, 1986.

about the storage business, except that it costs, say, $0.03 a bushel to store wheat for one month. The business of storage itself is complicated; one must know all the hazards of the business (insects, temperature variations, etc.) to stay competitive. Thus, markets arise in which people can speculate in commodities just by trading pieces of paper. These markets are called **futures markets**. The futures market is an arrangement in which a buyer and a seller agree now on the future price and quantity of a commodity to be delivered at some specified date in the future.

The futures market is to be contrasted with the **spot, or cash, market** in which agreements between buyers and sellers are made now for payment and delivery of the product immediately or shortly thereafter.

The way the futures market works is quite different from the way a spot market works. In a spot market, money changes hands now and purchases are made before sales. In a futures market, no money exchange takes place at the time the contract is struck; the contract is usually "closed out" before it is actually carried out, and agents can sell before they buy.

How large is the futures market? Table 11-2 gives some comparative statistics on the size of the futures market in certain commodities like soybeans, corn, and wheat and the size of the spot markets for IBM, GM, and Texaco shares. The total value of wheat, corn, and soybeans traded on the Chicago Board of Trade was $1.9 billion on January 7, 1986; the total value of IBM, GM, and Texaco shares traded on the same date was only $317 million. January 7, 1986, was also a day of hectic stock-market speculation, sparked by an attempt by Texaco to buy Getty Oil. On that day, stock-market news made the front page of the *New York Times*; futures-market news was buried in the back of the technical section of the newspaper. (Black Monday—October 19, 1987—would not be a fair comparison.)

In the futures market, traders are obligating themselves to buy or sell in the future. For example, in January, the buyer and seller of a futures contract for September wheat each commits to either buy or sell, say, 5,000 bushels of wheat in September at, say, $2.80 per bushel. The buyer (who is

---

Futures market is an arrangement in which a buyer and seller agree now on the future price and quantity of a commodity to be delivered at a specified date in the future.

Spot, or cash, market is an arrangement in which a buyer and seller agree now on price and quantity of a commodity to be paid for and delivered now.

said to *buy long* in wheat) expects the spot price of wheat in September to exceed $2.80; thus, he or she firmly establishes the buying price at a point below the expected selling price. The seller (who is said to *sell short* in wheat) expects the spot price of wheat in September to be less than $2.80; thus, he or she expects to buy wheat for less than $2.80 and has firmly established a selling price of $2.80. Sellers of futures contracts are *bearish* (they expect the price to fall); buyers of futures contracts are *bullish* (they expect the price of the good to rise).

In practice, the buyer and the seller of the futures contract (if they are speculators) will not actually wait until the contract is due before closing out their positions. For example, in the above case, suppose the price of September wheat rises from $2.80 to $2.90 per bushel. Should the buyer close out his or her position, he or she would simply sell 5,000 bushels of September wheat at $2.90. Since the buyer earlier bought 5,000 bushels at $2.80, a profit of $0.10 $\times$ 5,000 = $500 would be made. The seller of the original futures contract could buy 5,000 bushels at $2.90 per bushel and lose $500 because he or she has sold at $2.80. Whether a position is closed out or not, the speculator's account is credited or debited for the $500 profit or loss. In the stock market, profits or losses are considered "paper" losses until stocks are actually sold, but in the commodities market (except for tax purposes), paper profits and losses are real—the commodity-market speculator finds his or her money assets rising or falling as the price of the futures contract changes.

Hedging

Hedging is the temporary substitution of a futures-market transaction for an expected spot-market transaction.

There are two sets of traders in the futures market: speculators (who do not handle the physical commodity), and hedgers, such as merchants, farmers, and processors, who actually handle the physical commodity. **Hedging** can be thought of as the temporary substitution of a futures-market transaction for an intended spot-market transaction. Suppose a merchant has a stock of 100,000 bushels of corn. He intends, of course, to sell the corn on the cash market at some future time. By selling 100,000 bushels of corn on the futures market, the merchant is selling short in the futures market to offset a long position (holding corn) in the cash market. If spot prices and futures prices move together, the merchant hedges the risks because the gains in one market are approximately offset by losses in the other market. If the price of corn rises, the merchant loses on the short position but gains on the cash position; if the price of corn falls, the merchant wins in the futures market and loses in the cash market. It is clear that the merchant holding 100,000 bushels of corn can eliminate all risk by selling all 100,000 bushels in the futures market.

How does the futures market help allocate goods over time? Suppose, on a given day, traders learn that estimates of Brazil's future soybean harvest have dropped. This news will drive up the prices of soybean futures. As the prices of soybean futures rise, people in the business of storing soybeans will see that the profits from soybean storage will rise if spot soybean prices remain the same. Thus, spot soybeans will be purchased, driving up the spot price. In this manner, the supply of soybeans will be shifted from the present to the future. When the short Brazilian harvest comes due, there are more soybeans on the market because of the actions of speculators and spot-market traders. Note: People in the business of storing soybeans need not be concerned at all about the causes of the increase in futures prices. They need only buy spot soybeans and sell soybean futures, fixing their profits in advance. Correspondingly, people in the business of speculation need know nothing about how or where to store soybeans. The business of speculation and that of storage are effectively separated, and information is economized to the greatest extent possible. Hedgers and traders can specialize in information on a need-to-know basis.

Similarly, if people learn that the Brazilian soybean harvest will be larger than expected, futures prices will fall. The fall in futures prices will cause fewer soybeans to be stored today, as those holding current stocks of soybeans find the current spot price to appear favorable relative to the new futures price and the costs of storage. Soybean inventories will be liquidated until spot and futures prices are more in line with expectations and storage costs. Thus, inventories of soybeans should be lowered precisely because the harvest is expected to be larger.

If speculators are doing their job, there should be a powerful tendency for futures prices to move up and down in such a way as to stabilize consumption. Holbrook Working devoted his life to studying futures markets and concluded that the markets work efficiently. Thus, years of good crops tend to be followed by heavier carryovers of stock than years of poor crops.[5]

Hedging is most likely to be used by merchants and processors. The farmer, who faces considerable uncertainty about the size of his or her crop, cannot eliminate all risk by selling the expected crop. It is far easier to hedge a definite quantity than an uncertain quantity. If the farmer hedges an expected crop, and only half that crop is actually harvested, the farmer must purchase the entire harvest in the spot market in order to meet the futures-market obligation.

The Effects of Futures Trading

Generally speaking, the existence of a futures market increases the information available to all traders. First, information is costly. The futures market makes entry into the market easier for a class of agents—speculators—who specialize in information about future supply and demand. Because they have more information than hedgers, whose attentions are concentrated on

---

5. See Holbrook Working, "Theory of Inverse Carrying Charge in Futures Markets," *Journal of Farm Economics* 30 (1948): 1–28; "Futures Trading and Hedging," *American Economic Review* 43 (1953): 314–43.

other matters, the present spot price reflects more information about the future than otherwise.

A second reason futures markets make more information available is that they reduce transaction costs. Without a futures market, trading in forward-looking contracts would be decentralized, and speculators would face higher costs of locating potential traders. With a centralized market, the single futures price reflects all the available information.

Farmers, who seldom use futures markets, often argue that the existence of a futures market destabilizes commodity prices. When prices fall or rise rapidly because of the obvious actions of the speculator in the futures market, agricultural interests often identify the speculator as the culprit rather than blaming the underlying estimates of future supply and demand conditions.

As a result of public suspicion of futures-market speculators, many types of futures trading are tightly controlled. For example, futures trading in onions is prohibited. Futures trading in all other commodities is regulated by the Commodity Futures Trading Corporation. The most dramatic rule is that futures prices cannot fluctuate by more than a stated amount on any given day: a bushel of wheat cannot fluctuate by more than $0.20 a day.

Economists have studied the impact of futures trading on various commodities. Studies of futures trading of wheat, cotton, cattle, hogs, pork bellies, potatoes, frozen-concentrate orange juice, ground nuts, and linseed spot prices have found that the futures market stabilizes commodity prices. However, the effects are slight. For example, Charles Cox found that during a period of futures trading in cattle (December 1964 to July 1971), the standard deviation of estimated cattle prices was 2 percent of average cattle prices; during a period without futures trading in cattle (before December 1964), however, the standard deviation of estimated cattle prices was 2.7 percent of average cattle prices.[6]

THE MORAL-HAZARD PROBLEM

The **moral-hazard problem** arises when one or more parties to a contract engage in post-contractual opportunistic behavior because of an information imbalance between parties.

When does the fact that information about the present or future is costly cause problems? So far this chapter has discussed cases where information is symmetrically distributed. Everyone has access to information about the futures market or can search for the lowest price. Some people may have cheaper access, but everyone has access. In these cases, the market appears to work well. But what about cases where information is asymmetrically distributed? There are two classes of problems. The **moral-hazard problem** arises when one party to a contract cannot monitor the other party's performance because private actions are hidden from view. The **adverse-selec-**

---

6. On the effects of futures trading, see Charles C. Cox, "Futures Trading and Market Information," *Journal of Political Economy* 84 (December 1976): 1215–37. Cox also reviews the literature.

The **adverse-selection problem** occurs when one party engages in precontractual opportunistic behavior to lure the party at an information disadvantage into a disadvantageous contract.

tion problem arises when it is difficult to check the claims made by economic agents trying to secure favorable contracts because private information is hidden.

In many cases, economic agents find that they must have a contract (implicitly or explicitly) that spells out the terms of their future economic transactions. The employer hires an employee, paying wages for work. The insurance company insures risks, receiving a definite premium in return for an indefinite indemnity in the case of hazards. The seller implicitly or explicitly guarantees that a particular product will work a certain way. The owners of a house write a contract with a real-estate agent to sell their house in return for a certain commission. These contracts all involve expectations of future performance. If people were perfectly honest, writing these contracts would be an easy task—each party could feel sure that the other party would carry out the contract's terms.

Many people are opportunistic. Economic agents may be perfectly moral in most ways, but many will take advantage of situations when their behavior cannot be monitored and will not fulfill the expectation of future performance stipulated in a particular contract. Economic opportunism occurs when agents attempt to secure more utility or profit than would be permitted or anticipated by a particular contract by exploiting the imbalance in information existing between the two parties of the contract.

An **agent** acts for, on behalf of, or as a representative for a principal.

A **principal** has controlling authority when engaging services of an agent.

The *principal/agent problem* is one type of moral-hazard problem. An **agent** is a party that acts for, on behalf of, or as a representative of a **principal**, who has the controlling authority and engages the agent's service. Principals and agents often have different goals. For example, if you hired a real-estate agent to sell your house for a flat fee, you would run the risk that the agent would sell your house at a below-market price in order to minimize his or her selling effort. Thus, setting up multiple-listing contracts and establishing the fee as a percentage of the selling price minimizes this moral-hazard problem.

The Case of Disability Insurance

A classic example of the moral-hazard problem is the insurance policy. An insurance policy that would provide benefits if the policy holder suffered from certain hazards is harder to obtain in the private market because of the opportunistic behavior of people taking out insurance. An insurance company that pays out benefits if the policy holder gets sick, becomes disabled, or suffers damage to property must worry about policy holders who will take health risks or be negligent in caring for insured property after a policy is taken out. (See Example 11–2.)

Let us consider the case of disability insurance. The following model was developed by Peter Diamond and James Mirlees. To simplify the story, suppose that everyone is identical but that each person has a certain probability, θ, of becoming disabled. Income from work in the absence of disability is Y; consumption is C. The individual faces three situations: working

FIGURE 11-6   The Profit Constraint

The curve labeled I shows the combinations of indemnities and premiums consistent with zero expected profit, $E\pi = 0$. Insurance companies make negative or positive expected profits depending on whether they operate above or below the zero-expected-profit constraint.

Insurance Coverage or Indemnity (dollars to be paid to beneficiary), I

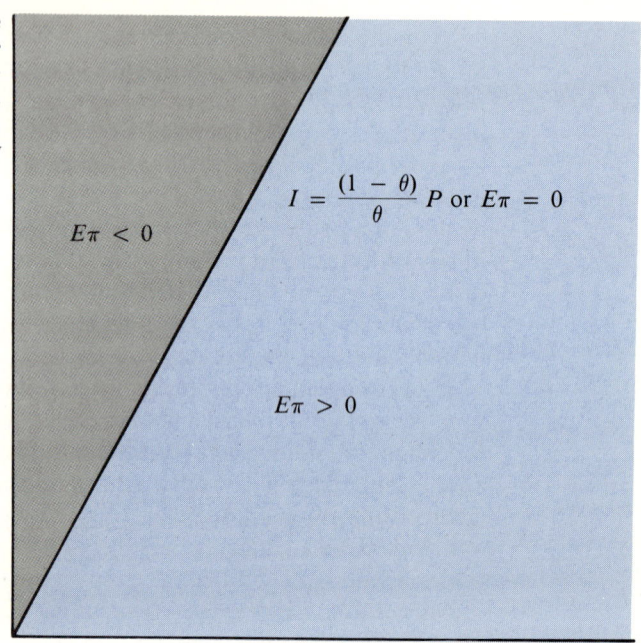

$E\pi < 0$

$I = \dfrac{(1 - \theta)}{\theta} P$ or $E\pi = 0$

$E\pi > 0$

Insurance Premium (dollars received from policy holder), P

and being able, not working and being able, and disability (and not working): $U_w(C)$ = utility of consumption level C when working; $U_l(C)$ = utility during leisure (when one is able-bodied); $U_d(C)$ = utility when one is disabled.

We shall assume that marginal utility (MU) in any state is positive but declining. To simplify, we will just consider working versus not working as an all-or-none choice; the worker cannot vary his or her hours of work. Because work is assumed to be distasteful, we assume that, if consumption were the same, utility would be higher when not working (but able) than when working. That is,

$$U_l(C) > U_w(C) \tag{2}$$

for all levels of consumption, C. The premium, P, for an insurance policy is what the worker pays when he or she is working. When not working because of disability, the worker receives an indemnity, I (net of any premiums). Thus, consumption when working, C_w, is

$$C_w = Y - P \tag{3}$$

and consumption when not working, C_l, is simply

$$C_l = I. \tag{4}$$

The indemnity, I, can be thought of as the individual's insurance coverage (minus any necessary premiums).

If the insurance industry faces a large number of independent risks, in the aggregate the risks will be very small, and we can assume that the insurance industry is risk-neutral. Recall from Chapter 3 that a risk-neutral person is one who is indifferent between a certain sum of money and a gamble with the same expected value. The expected profit in the insurance industry is the expected value of premiums, $E(P)$, minus the expected value of the indemnities, $E(I)$. (E is the expectations operator introduced in Chapter 3 and denotes the weighted average of all the possibilities.) Because $E(P) = (1 - \theta)P$ and $E(I) = \theta I$, expected profit is

$$E(\pi) = (1 - \theta)P - \theta I. \tag{5}$$

This equation ignores the cost of operating the insurance industry (the cost of writing policies and maintaining a sales force), but this complication would not affect our conclusions.

In the long-run competitive equilibrium, expected profits must be zero; accordingly, if the insurance industry offers a contract that represents some combination of premium and indemnity (P, I) to all comers, that contract must satisfy the equation

$$E(\pi) = 0 = (1 - \theta)P - \theta I. \tag{6}$$

Or, solving for I,

$$I = (1 - \theta)P/\theta. \tag{7}$$

Equation (5) or (6) shows the objective trade-off facing consumers when the insurance business is competitive; it is the zero-expected-profit constraint. Figure 11-6 shows that the zero-profit constraint is a straight line from the origin with a slope of $(1 - \theta)/\theta$. Above the line, indemnities are too high or premiums are too low so that $E(\pi) < 0$. Below the line, indemnities are too low or premiums are too high so that $E(\pi) > 0$.

Symmetrical Information

Information is symmetrical if all agents have access to it on the same terms. Symmetrical information is likely to exist in the insurance industry if a worker's disability is easily determined, as in the case of the loss of a limb. In this case, the expected utility (V) of each person is:

$$V(C_w, C_d) = E(U) = (1 - \theta)U_w(C_w) + \theta U_d(C_d), \tag{8}$$

which is simply the expected utility from working plus the expected utility from not working. Because $C_w = Y - P$ and $C_d = I$, we can write expected utility as a function of the premium and the indemnity; that is,

$$V(P, I) = E(U) = (1 - \theta)U_w(Y - P) + \theta U_d(I). \tag{9}$$

The term $(1 - \theta)U_w$ is the expected utility from working; the term θU_d is the expected utility when disabled and, of course, not working. The higher is the

FIGURE 11-7 Preferences for Insurance

The curves labeled V_0, V_1, and V_2 are typical indifference curves showing the combinations of coverage and premium among which the insured persons are indifferent. Utility is higher in the direction of the arrows. Indifference curves are convex to the horizontal axis.

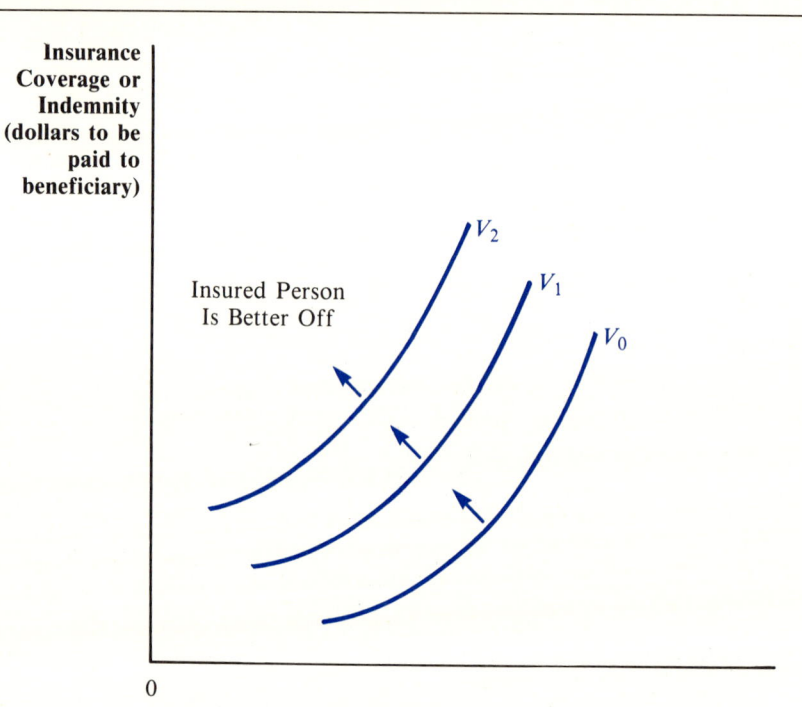

premium, P, the lower is expected utility; the higher is the indemnity, I, the higher is expected utility. Because an extra $1 of premium lowers consumption in the working state by exactly $1, the marginal expected utility of premiums is:

$$MU_P = -(1 - \theta)MU_w, \qquad (10)$$

where MU_w is the marginal utility of consumption when one is working. The marginal expected utility of indemnities is:

$$MU_I = \theta MU_d, \qquad (11)$$

where MU_d is the marginal utility of consumption when disabled. The amount of indemnity that just compensates the individual for an extra $1 of premium is the marginal rate of substitution,

$$MRS_{IP} = MU_P/MU_I = (1 - \theta)MU_w/\theta MU_d. \qquad (12)$$

Figure 11-7 shows the individual's indifference curves between the indemnity and premium payments. The curves are upward-sloping, because to maintain constant (expected) utility, additional indemnities must be promised for additional premiums. Expected utility is higher in the direction of the arrows—V_2 represents higher utility than V_1—because expected utility

FIGURE 11-8 Determining the Optimum Contract

The optimum contract, or combination of premium and indemnity, occurs where an indifference curve between indemnity and premium is just tangent to the zero-expected-profit constraint. This tangency occurs where the marginal utility of (MU_w) equals the marginal utility of (MU_d).

Insurance Coverage or Indemnity (dollars to be paid to beneficiary), I (vertical axis)

Insurance Premium (dollars received from policy holder), P (horizontal axis)

Curves shown: V^* (indifference curve) and $E\pi = 0$ (zero-expected-profit line), tangent at point b.

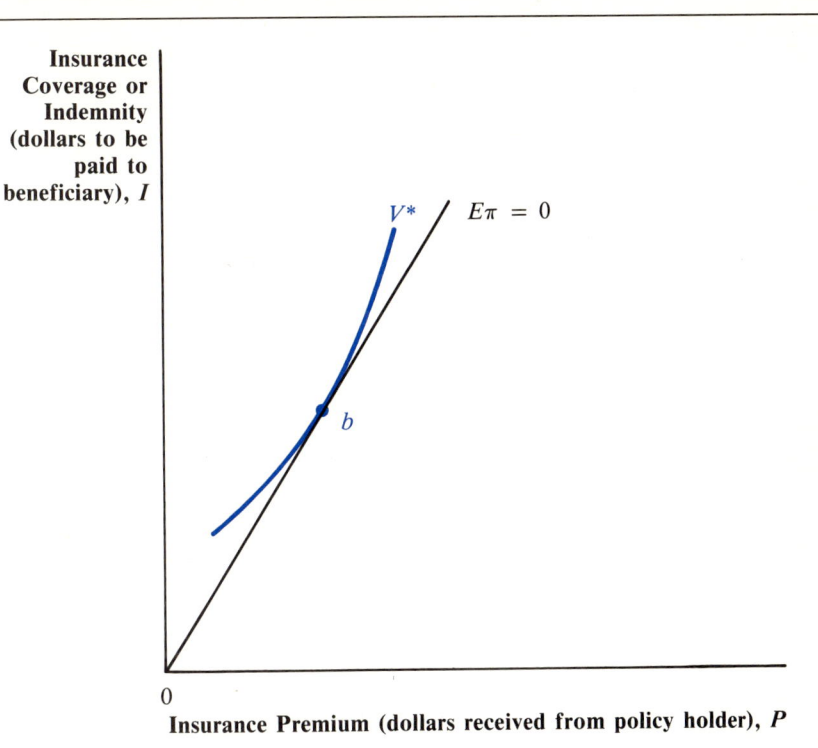

rises if the premium falls or if the indemnity rises. The marginal rate of substitution between receiving indemnities and paying premiums rises as one moves up a given indifference curve. Therefore, each indifference curve is convex to the horizontal axis. Convexity follows from the law of diminishing marginal utility: at higher premium levels, consumption while working, C_w, falls and raises the marginal utility of working, MU_w. At higher indemnity levels, consumption while disabled, C_d, rises and reduces the marginal utility of being disabled, MU_d. From Equation (12), MRS_{IP} must then rise as the individual moves up an indifference curve.

Figure 11-8 combines Figures 11-6 and 11-7. Competition drives the individual to maximize utility subject to the zero-profit constraint. Clearly, the optimum insurance contract occurs at point b, where the slope of the indifference curve equals the slope of the zero-profit constraint, $(1 - \theta)/\theta$. Because $MRS_{IP} = (1 - \theta)MU_w/\theta MU_d$, it follows that

$$(1 - \theta)MU_w/\theta MU_d = (1 - \theta)/\theta$$

or, canceling $(1 - \theta)/\theta$ from both sides and rearranging,

$$MU_w = MU_d. \tag{13}$$

In other words, the optimum insurance contract is reached when the con-

FIGURE 11-9   The Moral-Hazard Constraint

Line segment *mh* is the moral-hazard constraint: if insurance companies offer any contract inside *mh*, the worker will claim disability under any circumstance. Thus, the only contract that will be offered will be the one represented by point *c*.

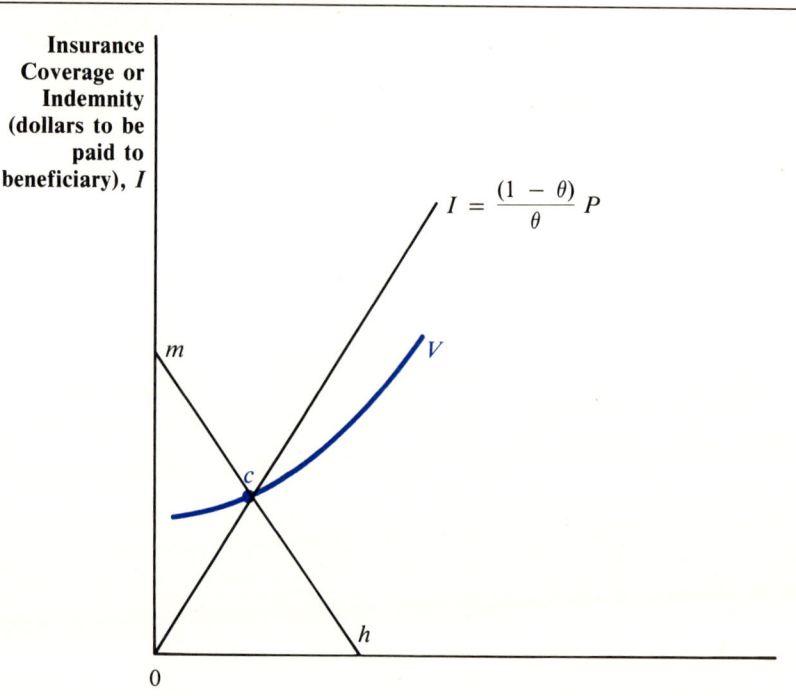

Insurance Coverage or Indemnity (dollars to be paid to beneficiary), I

$$I = \frac{(1-\theta)}{\theta} P$$

m, *V*, *c*, *h*

0

Insurance Premium (dollars received from policy holder), P

sumer's marginal utility of consumption is the same whether working or not working.

When possible consumption in each state yields the same marginal utility, it does not pay the consumer to buy any more insurance. The insurance contract offers a fair gamble to an otherwise risk-averse consumer. In this model, risk aversion is the same as the law of diminishing marginal utility. If a gamble is fair, its expected rewards equal its expected costs. With diminishing marginal utility, the expected utility of a dollar gained will fall short of the expected utility of a dollar lost. Along the zero-profit constraint, the amount of insurance coverage (the indemnity) equals its actuarial value. When MU_w equals MU_d, an additional dollar of insurance coverage lowers total utility because the increase in utility from greater insurance coverage is less than the decrease in utility from paying larger premiums.

Asymmetrical Information

In many types of disability (such as back problems), the worker can determine when he or she is disabled, but the insurance company cannot because information is asymmetrical. Obviously, if an insured person could buy as many policies as he or she wanted, the maximum utility would be achieved by purchasing infinite insurance coverage and then reporting a disability. In order for an insurance company to stay in business, it must be able to monitor the global insurance purchases of its customers. It is relatively easy for an insurance company to limit the global purchases of their customers; they need only monitor the claims made by their customers and pay only uncovered losses. In this case, the insured person has an incentive to buy only one policy, because the second and third policies will not pay any more than one policy will.

Given some policy (P, I) offered by an insurance company, when will opportunistic workers tell the truth? In the real world, some people are truthful, and some people are not. For the sake of simplicity, we will assume that the policyholder we are considering is completely opportunistic. Such a person will tell the truth if and only if the expected utility from truth telling exceeds the expected utility from misrepresentation (lying). The utility from truth telling is, as before,

$$V(P, I) = (1 - \theta)U_w(Y - P) + \theta U_d(I). \tag{14}$$

If the worker misrepresents being disabled, he or she will never have to work. Even when he or she is able to work, occuring with a probability of $(1 - \theta)$, this worker will report being disabled. The person's expected utility from lying, then, would be

$$L(I) = (1 - \theta)U_l(I) + \theta U_d(I), \tag{15}$$

where $U_l(Y)$ is the utility the worker obtains when able to work but receiving a disability pension (I). The worker will tell the truth if $V(P, I) \geq L(I)$. Thus, truth telling simply requires

$$U_w(Y - P) \geq U_l(I). \tag{16}$$

Inequality (16) is the moral-hazard constraint. Any contract offered by the insurance industry must satisfy (16); if it does not, all workers could report being disabled, and, of course, no insurance company could break even unless the indemnity, I, equals zero.

The moral-hazard constraint is the segment mh in Figure 11-9. At point h, the premium equals the worker's income, but the insurance coverage is zero. Clearly, the moral-hazard constraint will be satisfied. The moral-hazard constraint can also be satisfied with a zero premium, provided only that insurance coverage is not too high. Thus, point m represents that level of insurance coverage for which $U_w(Y) = U_l(I)$, or for which the utility from working and paying a zero premium equals the utility from the leisurely enjoyment of the indemnity. For any premium higher than zero, there must be a smaller indemnity by just an amount sufficient to induce truth telling. Any point inside mh will induce truth telling. The insurance industry is limited to offering contracts in the range, $0c$. Accordingly, people are limited in the amount of insurance coverage they can buy. The optimum contract— represented by point c—provides maximum utility subject to the zero-expected-profit constraint and the moral-hazard constraint. At point c, the slope of the indifference curve is less than the slope of the zero-expected-profit constraint. Thus,

$$(1 - \theta) MU_w/\theta MU_d < (1 - \theta)/\theta,$$

or

$$MU_w < MU_d. \tag{17}$$

When there is a moral-hazard problem, people cannot get enough insurance. The marginal utility of consumption in the able-to-work state will fall short of the marginal utility of consumption in the disabled state.

The moral-hazard problem limits the amount of private insurance in the real world. The above model predicts that if the government provided disability insurance and disregarded the zero-profit constraint, disability payments would likely grow. Economist Donald Parsons attributes the considerable withdrawal of prime-age males from the labor force from 1948 to 1976 to the Social Security disability program.

Moral hazard can result in people not being able to buy the products they could buy (such as insurance or any product for that matter) in a world of perfect information.

Strategies for the Moral-Hazard Problem

Because the moral-hazard problem arises where information is asymmetrical and where postcontractual behavior can be opportunistic, there is little the government can do about it. In the above example, the moral-hazard problem can be solved by simply offering very little insurance. In other cases, the insurance company (or government) must simply pay the information costs that will help reduce the information imbalance. Opportunistic behavior can also be limited by offering economic incentives for behaving as if information were symmetrical. For example, a person who obtains automobile insurance may be afraid that driving carelessly will increase his or her insurance premiums per dollar of insurance coverage. Insurance companies can control the moral-hazard problem by offering insurance contracts with deductibles; if full coverage of a health risk is impossible, anyone making an insurance claim must also pay a significant amount of the loss. Moral hazards are also involved in the way corporations protect themselves from hostile takeovers. (See Example 11–3.)

THE ADVERSE-SELECTION PROBLEM

Asymmetrical information and opportunism lead people to attempt to secure favorable contracts through misrepresentation. When buyers and sellers have different information about the product, it is possible for the one with the superior information to lure the other into entering a favorable contract

EXAMPLE 11-2 The Effects of Disability Payments on Labor-Force Participation

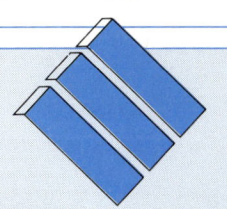

The Social Security system pays disability benefits to those individuals who can prove they are unable to work. About half of those who apply for disability benefits are rejected. Nevertheless, the disability program appears to have had a substantial impact on the labor-force nonparticipation rate. In the accompanying diagram, the upper line shows the nonparticipation rate of males aged 45–54. This rate is the number of males 45–54 who do not participate in the labor force divided by the number of males in that age group. In 1979, the nonparticipation rate was 8.6 percent. The lower line shows the Social Security *recipiency rate* for males in that age group. The recipiency rate is the ratio of male disability recipients 45–54 to the number of males 45–54 years of age. In 1979, the recipiency rate was 4.2 percent. Thus, about half of those who do not participate receive disability payments. The diagram shows that there has been an alarming increase in the nonparticipation of males and that this increase may be related to the Social Security program itself.

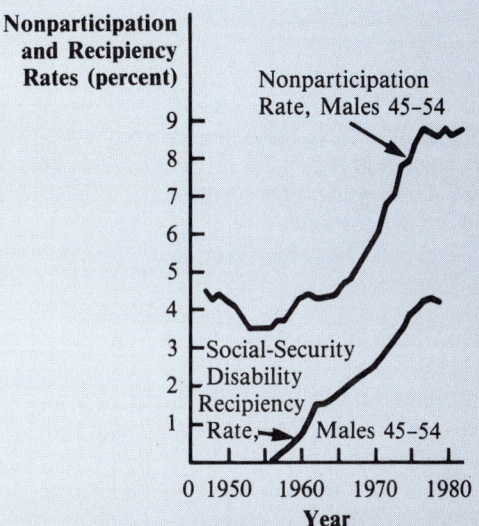

This development could be an illustration of the moral-hazard problem. Private insurance companies are constrained by the necessity to make a profit and, thus, must offer disability insurance that is not subject to much of a moral-hazard problem. The government is not so constrained; any shortfall in the Social Security system can be made up by raising taxes. Thus, to the extent that disability payments induce some people to represent themselves as disabled, there is a moral-hazard problem.

Source: Donald O. Parsons, "The Decline in Labor-Force Participation," *Journal of Political Economy* 88 (February 1980): 117–34; diagram from Donald O. Parsons, "Disability Insurance and Male Labor-Force Participation: A Response to Haveman and Wolfe," *Journal of Political Economy* 92 (June 1984): 542–49.

---

that would, with full information, be rejected. Whereas the moral-hazard problem arises after a contract is written, the *adverse-selection problem* arises when a party with an information advantage relative to another party lures the second party into entering a disadvantageous contract.

Insurance companies face the adverse-selection problem when the pol-

EXAMPLE 11-3 Golden Parachutes and Hostile Tender Offers

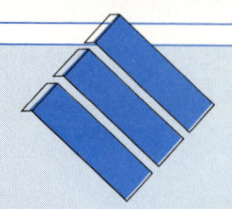

A *tender offer* to purchase a company's shares from the shareholders is considered hostile if an offer is made to the shareholders of a company without the approval of the target company's board of directors. In the 1970s and 1980s, hostile tender offers became a very popular method for changing the management of a corporation. In 1960, only 7 hostile tender offers were made for U.S. firms. By 1980, there were 123 tender offers.

A simple argument supporting hostile tender offers is that they may be the only way to remove an incompetent management. A tender offer is a mutually beneficial exchange between the shareholders and the acquiring firm.

One popular method of making hostile tender offers less likely is for a company to obstruct possible takeover attempts using a *golden parachute*—a contractual agreement to provide a substantial payment to a manager who is forced to or elects to leave the firm after a change of control. Because golden-parachute payments can be in the millions and represent a significant portion of a firm's assets, such an agreement lowers the value of a firm to a potential corporate raider.

Should golden parachutes be viewed as obstructing the free market? In other words, do they reduce the efficiency of the corporate-takeover market?

Managers have an incentive to behave opportunistically. Shareholders are interested in maximizing the present value of the firm; managers are interested in maximizing their own wealth. One technique for tying the interests of the manager to that of the company is the deferred-compensation package. A manager is offered low earnings in the beginning in return for very large earnings in the future. The continued employment of the manager is assured, and the manager wants to see the firm survive and prosper. A tender offer provides an avenue for shareholder opportunism. The tender offer allows the shareholders to replace the existing management. Once control changes hands, a manager may be discharged or not be paid the deferred compensation he or she was promised.

Golden parachutes eliminate the possibility of shareholder opportunism in relation to managers. By purchasing assets in a company with golden parachutes, the shareholders are in effect guaranteeing that they will not be opportunistic should a takeover occur.

Source: Charles R. Knoeber, "Golden Parachutes, Shark Repellents, and Hostile Tender Offers," *American Economic Review* 76 (March 1986): 155–67; Leonard Silk, "The Peril Behind the Takeover Boom," *New York Times*, December 29, 1985.

icies they write attract high-risk rather than low-risk policy holders. Buyers of used cars face the adverse-selection problem when sellers offer them "lemons" (cars that work poorly).

Detecting Lemons

The lemons problem illustrates how the adverse-selection problem results in poorly functioning markets. To simplify, suppose that everyone knows that there exist used cars in the market ranging (uniformly) in value from $1,000 to $6,000. We will assume that information is asymmetrical—that the buyer cannot determine the value of a car until it is purchased but that the seller knows the value of the car. How would such a market work if sellers were completely opportunistic and buyers could not rely on seller reputations? If a buyer offered $6,000 for a car, cars ranging in value from $1,000 to $6,000 would be offered on the market. On the average, the buyer would expect to buy a car worth $3,500 (the average value of the cars offered). A risk-neutral buyer would clearly lose by such an offer. What if the buyer offered $3,000? In this case, only cars ranging in value from $1,000 to $3,000 would be offered by profit-maximizing sellers. The buyer could expect to buy a car with an average value of only $2,000, because the cars with a value higher than $3,000 would be withdrawn from the market. Again, the buyer could expect to lose. The only cars that would trade in such a market would be the $1,000 cars—the lemons. The bad cars would have driven the good cars from the market.

When there is adverse selection, people will not offer deals that will result in personal losses. As when there is moral hazard, the contracts that are offered must take into account the maneuvering of buyers or sellers. In the lemons problem above, buyers should offer no more than $1,000 for a car. Firms can solve other types of adverse-selection problems by attempting to separate their customers into different quality or risk groupings.

The Case of Disability Insurance

The model of disability insurance used in the discussion of moral hazard can be used to analyze the adverse-selection problem. In this section, we will assume that:

1. there are two groups of individuals: a high-risk group, H, with a disability probability of θ_H, and a low-risk group, L, with a disability probability of θ_L. Thus $\theta_H > \theta_L$.
2. the insurance company can, at zero cost, determine whether someone is disabled or able. Thus, there is no moral hazard.
3. the individual knows the risk group to which he or she belongs.
4. insurance companies cannot tell whether a buyer of insurance is a high-risk or low-risk individual, but they do know the prevailing disability probabilities as well as the number of people of each type in the entire population.
5. everybody has the same utility function, which is known by insurance companies.
6. each insurance company can monitor the global insurance purchases of its customers.

FIGURE 11-10 Separating Low-Risk and High-Risk Policy Holders

Contracts represented by points *a* and *b* are a separating equilibrium. Low-risk people buy contract *a*, high-risk people buy *b*, and insurance companies make zero expected profit because *a* and *b* are each on the relevant zero-expected-profit line. Notice there is no incentive for high-risk people to pretend to be low-risk people.

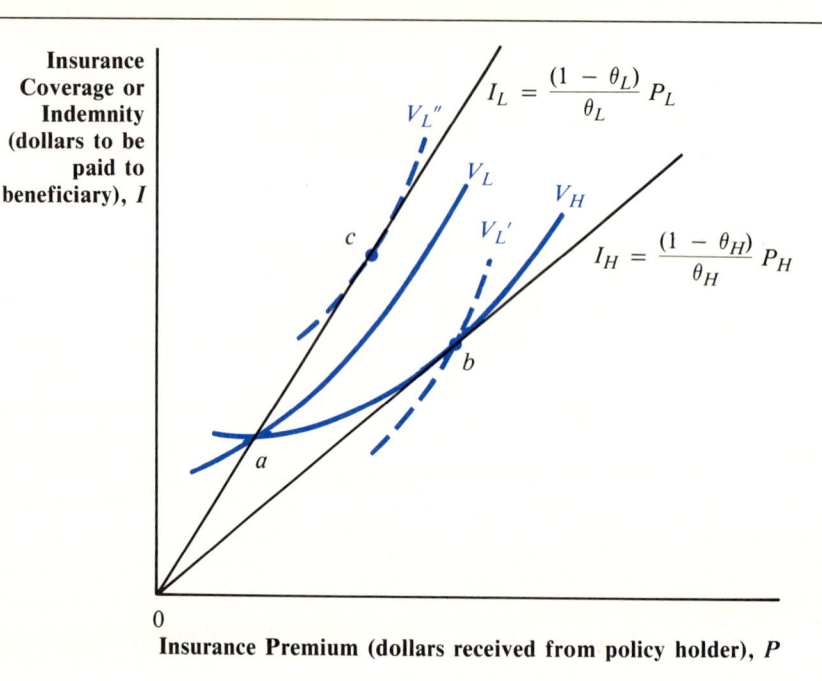

Insurance Coverage or Indemnity (dollars to be paid to beneficiary), I

$I_L = \dfrac{(1 - \theta_L)}{\theta_L} P_L$

$I_H = \dfrac{(1 - \theta_H)}{\theta_H} P_H$

Insurance Premium (dollars received from policy holder), P

There are two types of equilibria—or two types of contracts—that can occur: (1) at the *separating equilibrium*, each risk group buys a contract specifically tailored to that group; (2) at the *pooling equilibrium*, everybody must buy the same contract. Both types of contracts occur in the real world.

Separating Risk Groups

Figure 11-10 shows a separating equilibrium—a contract that separates risk groups. The line I_L denotes the zero-expected-profit line for the possible low-risk contracts, $I_L = (1 - \theta_L) P_L / \theta_L$; the line I_H denotes the zero-expected-profit line for the possible high-risk contracts, $I_H = (1 - \theta_H) P_H / \theta_H$. Because $\theta_H > \theta_L$, the high-risk-contract line must be flatter than the low-risk-contract line. Intuitively, for any given premium, the insurance companies can pay low-risk people a higher indemnity (or, for any given indemnity, must collect a higher premium from high-risk people).

Point *b* is the contract high-risk people would buy subject to the constraint of zero expected profit. Contract *b* maximizes the utility of the high-risk group. If this were the only contract offered, low-risk people would buy it as well, but that contract could not be an equilibrium contract because the insurance companies would be making positive expected profits out of their low-risk customers (because point *b* is below I_L). Another contract would have to be offered. At contract *a*, the indifference curve V_H just intersects I_L. The low-risk indifference curve, V_L, passing through point *a* must be steeper than V_H at that point because a low-risk person requires more indemnity per extra dollar of premium than a high-risk person, holding everything else constant. If the insurance industry offered both contracts a and b, the low-risk people would not buy b, because their indifference curve through that point (V_L') is lower than their utility level at a. The high-risk people would be indifferent between contracts a and b; thus, a slight move along I_L from a toward the origin would induce them to buy contract b only. Thus, a and b constitute a separating equilibrium. Profits are zero; everyone maximizes their utility, subject only to the constraint that there is no incentive for high-risk people to parade as low-risk people.

Notice that contract c could not be offered. While low-risk people would prefer c to a, high-risk people would also prefer c to b. Thus, all would choose c, and insurance companies would lose money because they would break even with their low-risk customers and lose money on their high-risk customers. Indeed, any contract between a and c along I_L will be preferred by high-risk people to contract b.

One property of a separating equilibrium should be observed. Although high-risk people are not hurt by the presence of low-risk people, low-risk people cannot be offered a sufficiently favorable contract to attract high-risk business; thus, low-risk people would be better off in the absence of high-risk individuals. The problem is that low-risk people cannot buy all the insurance or coverage they want. At point a in Figure 11-10, the MRS_{IP} for low-risk people falls short of the slope $(1 - \theta_L)/\theta_L$, so that, for low-risk people $MU_w > MU_d$. Just as in the case of the moral-hazard problem, in the case of adverse selection people with the lowest risks find that their marginal utility of consumption when working will exceed their marginal utility when not working because not enough insurance is available.

A separating equilibrium is achieved when an auto-insurance company offers one policy with a high penalty for accidents and another policy with a low penalty for accidents. A low-premium, high-penalty policy leads people with a low risk for accidents to choose that policy; a high-premium low-penalty policy will attract high-risk customers.

A second example of a separating equilibrium is the offering of collision-insurance policies with high or low deductibles. The *deductible* is that portion of the indemnity that the insured person must pay on any claim. A good driver is likely to ask for a low-premium, high-deductible policy, while a poor driver is likely to ask for a high-premium, low-deductible policy. Separating-equilibrium contracts motivate people to self-select themselves into the appropriate risk category.

Pooling Risk Groups

A pooling equilibrium is achieved when people in different risk classes buy the same contract. Assuming that only a single contract is offered, if the fraction λ of the people are high-risk individuals, the average probability of disability would be

FIGURE 11-11   Pooling Risk Groups

Point *d* represents a pooling equilibrium. Any move along the dashed line I_a from the origin beyond *d* will make one of the groups worse off, and expected profits are zero. A pooling equilibrium requires some transaction costs to prevent the introduction of a new contract, such as *f*, which will be profitable as long as a contract such as *d* is offered.

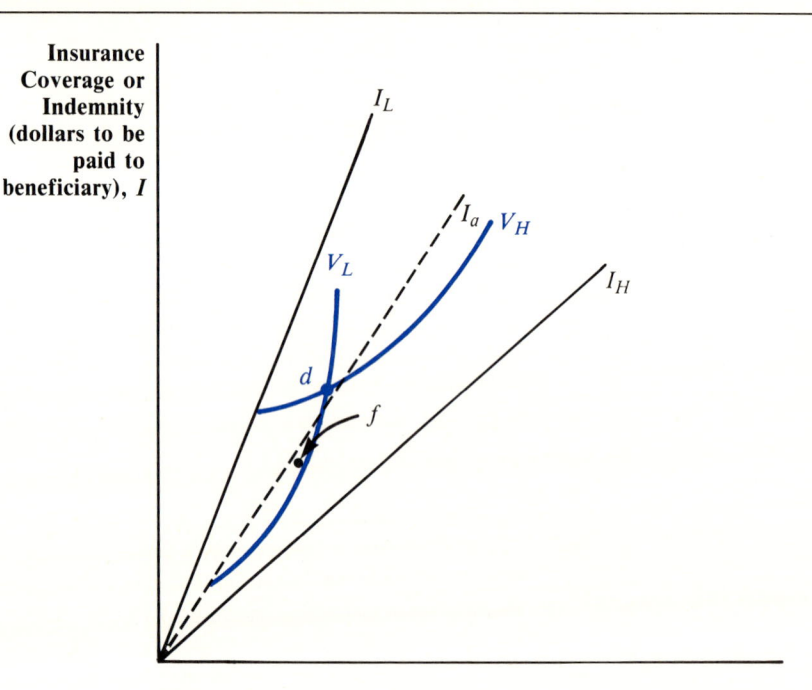

[Graph: Insurance Coverage or Indemnity (dollars to be paid to beneficiary), I on vertical axis; Insurance Premium (dollars received from policy holder), P on horizontal axis. Lines I_L, I_a, I_H emanate from origin; indifference curves V_L and V_H shown; points d and f marked.]

$$\theta_a = \lambda\theta_H + (1 - \lambda)\theta_L.$$

The zero-expected-profit condition is, then, simply

$$I_a = (1 - \theta_a)P/\theta_a,$$

where θ_a is the average risk in society. In Figure 11–11, I_L and I_H are still the zero-profit lines for high-risk and low-risk people separately, and I_a is the set of zero-profit contracts when the risk classes are pooled.

Consider the single contract, *d*, in Figure 11–11. Both high-risk and low-risk people prefer contract *d* to having no insurance at all (the origin). Any movement away from *d* that would keep expected profits zero (along I_a) would raise one person's utility at the expense of the other's utility. Is *d* an equilibrium? Economists Michael Rothschild and Joseph Stiglitz have argued that a point such as *d* could be a very unstable equilibrium. For example, if an insurance company offered contract *f*, low-risk people would prefer *f* to *d*. High-risk people would continue to buy *d*. The innovating company would make profits, because *f* is below I_L. But now only high-risk people would buy *d*, and those companies offering contract *d* would lose money (*d* is above I_H). In the end, either a separating equilibrium (such as the one discussed above) would be achieved or the economy would settle on another pooling equilibrium—but that pooling equilibrium would also be somewhat unstable.

Some economists have argued that if it is difficult to introduce new contracts, or if insurance companies realize that with free entry they really cannot do better than zero expected profits in the long run, any point such as d might be considered an equilibrium. Indeed, if one considers all the possible risk classes into which consumers might be grouped, the transaction costs of a separating equilibrium may be too high. Transaction costs include the costs of writing new contracts; presumably, new contracts are more expensive to write than old contracts. Moreover, people will have more difficulty understanding a new contract over an old contract. Thus, transaction costs and information costs will motivate insurance companies to necessarily pool different risk classes together. In the real world, pooling takes place because insurance companies offer far fewer contracts than there are risk classes. For example, there may be dozens of risk classes for automobile drivers. Low-risk people prefer low premiums and high deductibles; high-risk people prefer high premiums and low deductibles. Without transaction costs, there would be an entire range of such policies, but companies offer only a few choices.

Adverse selection results in insurance contracts that either pool high-risk people together with low-risk customers or give high-risk customers the perfect contract and low-risk customers inadequate coverage given what could be offered under perfect information. In the case of lemons, adverse selection can prevent the very best products from being sold because the price sellers can fetch is diluted by the existence of poor quality goods.

Product Information

The adverse-selection problem in insurance and labor markets arises because it is difficult to label people. In the case of products, which are produced by firms, it is possible to minimize the adverse-selection problem by relying on the reputations of the seller or on brand names.

As we saw in the case of the lemons model, when sellers have more information than buyers, and there are no brand names or seller reputations to guide the relatively ignorant buyer, only the lemons will be traded. Firms, thus, have an incentive to enter the market and develop a reputation for selling high-quality products that would allow all people to buy goods with the assurance that the quality is higher than they could find on their own.

One of the functions of intermediaries, such as Sears, Safeway, J. C. Penney, or car dealers, is to certify the quality of goods. The consumer is confronted with a vast array of goods, some of which are so complicated that the buyer is at an enormous information disadvantage relative to the producer. The number of producers is larger than the number of actual stores the consumer deals with. In such circumstances, the intermediary performs the function of certifying the quality of the good for the buyer. The customer is willing to pay a price for this valuable service; thus, the reputable intermediary can charge a higher markup over cost than a firm without any reputation.

SUMMARY

1. Information costs are the costs agents face in finding out about markets. They prevent people from exploiting all economic opportunities. The price system allows people to specialize in information on a need-to-know basis.

2. Transaction costs are the costs of operating markets; they are the costs of bringing together buyer and seller and involve the costs of transportation, the costs of writing contracts, enforcement costs, and the costs of negotiation. Because of information and transaction costs, prices of many goods differ from sales outlet to sales outlet. When the consumer shops for the lowest price, the optimal-search rule is to search whenever the lowest price sampled exceeds the reservation price. The consumer's reservation price is that price for which the marginal benefit of collecting one more price exactly equals the marginal cost.

3. Profitable speculation stabilizes prices and consumption; unprofitable speculation destabilizes prices and consumption. The ideal seasonal pattern of prices shows the price of agricultural products to be at a minimum at harvest times and to be at a maximum just before harvest. The rise in price reflects the cost of storage. In the futures market, traders are today establishing future prices and quantities. To sell a futures contract is to obligate oneself to sell a future quantity of a good at a fixed price. To buy a futures contract is to obligate oneself to buy a future quantity at a fixed price. Sellers of futures anticipate price reductions; buyers of futures anticipate price increases.

4. The moral-hazard problem arises when opportunistic persons alter their postcontractual behavior because the other party to the contract is unaware of their action. In the case of insurance, moral hazard means people cannot get enough coverage.

5. The adverse-selection problem arises when opportunistic persons with an information advantage engage in precontractual maneuvering to lure the other party into a disadvantageous contract. Generally speaking, firms solve the adverse-selection problem by offering contracts that give individuals incentives to self-select themselves into different risk groups. Insurance companies can separate low-risk customers from high-risk customers by offering different pricing packages.

QUESTIONS AND PROBLEMS

1. Discuss how the price system allows people to specialize in information on a need-to-know basis.

2. Why aren't prices uniform throughout each decentralized market?

3. Strictly speaking, can a perfectly competitive market be decentralized?

4. What is a person's reservation price in shopping for the lowest price?

5. Suppose many firms post three different prices, $1, $2, and $3 with equal (1/3) probabilities. If a firm's price cannot be known without shopping, what is the marginal benefit of search when the lowest price sampled is $1? $2? $3? If the marginal cost of search is $0.33, what is the reservation price?

6. The marginal benefit of searching for the lowest price increases the higher is the sampled price. Would the same be true of the marginal benefit of searching for the highest price (for example, a worker looking for the highest wage)?

7. Suppose you collect the prices of salt and sugar at different stores and discover that salt has a higher price dispersion. Explain why the dispersion of salt prices would be higher than that of sugar prices.

8. The demand curve of wheat is $P = 100 - Q$. In Period 1, 80 bushels are supplied; in Period 2, 60 bushels are supplied. Assuming zero storage costs, what are the net benefits of perfect speculation?

9. On February 27, 1986, the prices for soybean futures quoted on the Chicago Board of Trade are given in Table A. When do you think soybeans are harvested? What is the approximate cost of storage per bushel per month?

10. On July 1, you sell 5,000 bushels of December wheat for $3 a bushel. On July 10, December wheat is $3.20 a bushel. How much money have you made or lost?

Table A

Month	Price
July 1986	$5.32
August 1986	5.30
September 1986	5.15
November 1986	5.09
January 1987	5.20
March 1987	5.30
May 1987	5.39

11. On October 1, you buy 10,000 bushels of December corn for $2.40 a bushel. On October 30, December corn is $2.00. How much have you made or lost?

12. In the model of disability insurance, assuming there is a moral-hazard problem, why is it necessary to assume insurance companies can monitor the purchases of insurance coverage?

13. In the model of disability insurance with moral hazard, is it possible for the moral-hazard constraint to be irrelevant to the solution? If so, draw the appropriate diagram.

14. In the model of disability insurance with adverse selection, what would happen if the insurance companies could not monitor the global purchases of their customers?

15. Consider the separating equilibrium of the model with disability insurance and adverse selection.
    a. Show what happens to the welfare of the low-risk agents when the high-risk agents face higher probabilities of being disabled.
    b. Show what happens to the welfare of the high-risk agents when the low-risk agents face high probabilities of being disabled.

16. Might low-risk people be willing to pay a screening cost so that insurance companies could distinguish them from the high-risk people? Would that screening cost affect the welfare of the high-risk people in the model presented in this chapter?

SUGGESTED READINGS

Akerlof, G. "The Market for Lemons: Qualitative Uncertainty and the Market Mechanism." *Quarterly Journal of Economics* 90 (1970): 488–500.

Alchian A. A. and H. Demsetz. "Production, Information Costs, and Economic Organization." *American Economic Review* 62 (1972): 777–95.

Arrow, K. J. "Agency and the Market." In K. J. Arrow and M. D. Intriligator, eds., *Handbook of Mathematical Economics*, vol. 3. New York: North-Holland, 1986, pp. 1183–95.

Diamond, P. A. and J. A. Mirlees. "A Model of Social Insurance with Variable Retirement." *Journal of Public Economics* 10 (1978): 295–336.

McCall, J. J. "Economics of Information and Optimal Shopping Rules." *Journal of Business* 38 (1965): 113–26.

Rothschild, M. and J. E. Stiglitz. "Equilibrium in Competitive Insurance Markets." *Quarterly Journal of Economics* 90 (1976): 629–50.

Stigler, G. J. "The Economics of Information." *Journal of Political Economy* 69 (1961): 213–25.

CHAPTER 12

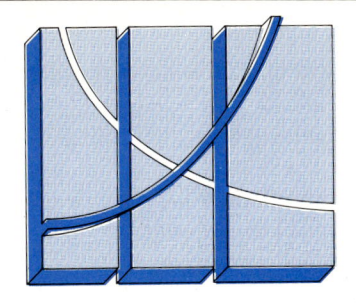

MONOPOLISTIC COMPETITION AND OLIGOPOLY

Chapters 9 and 10 dealt with the two extremes of perfect competition and monopoly. This chapter examines the market forms that fall between these extremes. The two intermediate market forms are *monopolistic competition* and *oligopoly*. The critical question is: How well do markets work in monopolistic competition or oligopoly? If perfectly competitive markets are efficient and monopolistic markets are inefficient, what can be said about the middle ground?

An industry is a collection of firms producing similar products. A given industry may be studied in terms of (1) the nature of the product, (2) the number of firms and their size distribution, and (3) the industry's barriers to entry.

1. Is the product homogeneous from firm to firm—as in the case of steel or aluminum? Is the product heterogeneous—as in the case of motor vehicles or cereals?
2. Presumably, the more firms there are, the more competitive an industry is. To what extent is the industry's output concentrated among the largest firms? A widely accepted hypothesis is that the larger is the share of the industry's output that is concentrated among the biggest firms, the less competitive the industry will be. As this chapter will point out, not all theories of industrial organization suggest this relationship between competition and concentration.
3. Chapter 10 discussed five barriers to entry: economies of scale or natural monopoly, access to raw materials, patents, government franchises, and sunk costs. The higher are the barriers to entry, the less competition there will be.

MEASURING CONCENTRATION

The *n*-firm concentration ratio measures the percentage of the top *n*-firms responsible for the domestic shipments in the industry.

The **Herfindahl index** is the total of the squared values of the market shares of all the firms in the industry.

The two basic measures of the degree of concentration in an industry are: the ***n*-firm concentration ratio** and the **Herfindahl index**. Table 12-1 shows the 4-firm concentration ratios for selected industries in 1977. Some industrial-organization economists presume that the higher is the concentration ratio, the smaller is the degree of competition as measured by the level of profits. There is definitely a simple correlation. For example, in the pioneering study of Joe S. Bain, 42 manufacturing industries were classified into those with an 8-firm concentration ratio exceeding 70 percent and those with a concentration ratio less than 70 percent. Bain found that in those industries for which the concentration ratio was less than 70 percent, the average after-tax profit rate was 7.5 percent, while those with a concentration ratio exceeding 70 percent had an average after-tax profit rate of 11.8 percent. Similar conclusions have been reached by most studies.[1]

Measurement Problems

Many concentration studies have been criticized on three major grounds: First, the concentration ratio may be an imperfect measure of monopoly power. Second, measured profit rates are unreliable. Third, the correlation between concentration and profit rates may just reflect the greater efficiency of large firms rather than enhanced monopoly power.

Limits of the Concentration Ratio

The concentration ratio is an imperfect guide to the extent of monopoly power for three reasons. First, concentration ratios do not reflect competition from foreign producers or from substitute products at home. For example, the U.S. automobile industry's 1977 4-firm concentration of 93 percent suggests enormous monopoly power, but competition from Japanese and German automobile companies has eroded its monopoly power significantly.

Second, concentration ratios may not measure concentration in the relevant market. The concentration ratio may be very small, but each firm may have a virtual monopoly in its local market (as in the case of local newspapers).

Third, concentration ratios do not measure *potential* competition. Imagine, for example, that all firms had access to a simple constant-returns-to-scale technology for producing bricks at $1 per brick (including a normal

---

1. For a summary, see F. M. Scherer, *Industrial Market Structure and Economic Performance* (Chicago: Rand McNally, 1971), chap. 7.

TABLE 12-1   **Selected Concentration Ratios in Manufacturing, 1982**

Industry	4-Firm Concentration Ratio (percent)	Number of Firms
Motor vehicles and car bodies	92	254
Cereal breakfast foods	86	32
Photographic equipment	74	723
Tires and inner tubes	66	108
Aircraft	64	139
Metal cans	50	168
Soaps and other detergents	60	642
Cookies and crackers	59	296
Radio and TV sets	49	432
Farm machinery	53	1,787
Blast furnaces and steel mills	42	217
Toilet preparations	34	596
Hardware	35	1,085
Gray-iron foundries	29	801
Men's footwear	28	129
Petroleum refining	28	282
Women's footwear	38	209
Periodicals	20	3,143
Mobile homes	24	261
Paper mills	22	135
Pharmaceutical preparations	26	584
Canned fruits and vegetables	21	514
Men's and boys' suits	25	443
Radio and TV equipment	22	2,083
Sawmills	17	5,810
Wood household furniture	16	2,430
Nuts and bolts	13	780
Valves and pipe fittings	13	944
Women's dresses	6	5,489
Ready-mixed concrete	6	8,163

Source: U.S. Department of Commerce, "Concentration Ratios in Manufacturing," 1982 *Census of Manufacturers*, MC82-S7.

return). With perfectly free entry, a single firm that sold the entire market could not raise the price of bricks above $1 without attracting new firms.

Difficulties of Measuring Profits

Economists define profit as the (economic) rate of return on the firm's investment. At this rate of return, the present value of the future profits from an investment equal its cost. This profit rate is difficult, if not impossible, to calculate by an external observer. Published profit rates are simply accounting profits divided by some measure of net assets—which, in some cases, may not be correlated with economic rates of return (see Example 10–2).

High Profits Need Not Mean Monopoly Power

Harold Demsetz has emphasized that industries with high concentration ratios have a larger than average share of highly efficient firms (for example, IBM in the computer industry or Ford in the automobile industry). These firms earn more profits not because of greater monopoly power, but because their costs are lower.

These three caveats do not prove that there is no relationship between profit rates and concentration or between monopoly power and concentration. What these caveats should suggest is that there are sound reasons for being skeptical about the relationship between concentration ratios and profits. However, skepticism does not necessarily mean disbelief.

Herfindahl Index

A more comprehensive measure of concentration, which still is subject to the same criticisms discussed above, is the *Herfindahl index* (named after Orris Herfindahl), which is calculated as the total of the squared values of the market shares of all the firms in the industry. If an industry consists of Firm 1 with a 60 percent share and Firm 2 with a 40 percent share, the Herfindahl index (H) is $(0.60)^2 + (0.40)^2 = 0.52$. The general formula is:

$$H = (S_1)^2 + (S_2)^2 + \ldots + (S_N)^2,$$

where the S_is are the market shares (totaling 1) of Firms 1 through N.

Because the market shares are squared, large firms have a much larger impact on the index than small firms. For example, both the telephone-equipment and lightbulb industries have 4-firm concentration ratios of 90 percent. But AT&T's dominance of the telephone-equipment industry leads to a Herfindahl measure of 0.5, while the lightbulb industry has a Herfindahl measure of only 0.2, because the dominant firms are more equal in size.

The Herfindahl index is of practical importance because it is used by the U.S. Justice Department to determine the government's policy on the mergers of two firms in an industry. The Herfindahl index can easily show the impact of a merger on concentration. If Firms 1 and 2 merge, the change in

TABLE 12-2   Trends in Concentration in American Manufacturing: Two Measures

Year	Percentage of Output by Firms with 4-Firm Concentration Ratio of 50 percent or Above (1)	Percentage of Output of 100 Largest Firms (2)
1895–1904	33	n.a.
1947	24	23
1954	30	30
1958	30	32
1972	29	33
1977	—	34

Sources: G. Warren Nutter, *The Extent of Enterprise Monopoly in the United States, 1899–1939* (Chicago: University of Chicago Press, 1951), pp. 35–48, 112–150; F. M. Scherer, *Industrial Market Structure and Economic Performance* (Boston: Houghton Mifflin, 1980), pp. 68–69; Concentration Ratios in Manufacturing, 1977 Census of Manufacturing, MC77-SR-9.

the Herfindahl index is simply the square of the market share of the new firm minus the squares of the market shares of the old firms; that is,

$$\Delta H = (S_1 + S_2)^2 - (S_1)^2 - (S_2)^2 = 2S_1S_2.$$

For example, if Firm 1 has a market share of 0.10 and merges with Firm 2, with a market share of 0.5, the Herfindahl index would increase by 0.1. If the Herfindahl index was originally 0.5, the increase in concentration would be 20 percent.

Has Concentration Increased?

Concentration ratios or Herfindahl indices may be used to answer the question: Has concentration increased or decreased in the American economy?

Table 12-2 shows the percentage of American manufacturing output produced by firms with a 4-firm concentration ratio of 50 percent or above. From 1895 to 1905, an estimated 33 percent of American manufacturing output was produced in concentrated industries. By 1972, about 29 percent of American manufacturing output was produced in concentrated industries. Thus, there may have been a slight tendency for concentration to decrease. On the other hand, Table 12-2 also shows that from 1947 to 1977 the percentage of America's manufacturing output produced by the 100 largest firms has increased from 23 percent to 34 percent.

Based on measures of concentration of *American* industries, it is difficult

FIGURE 12-1 Herfindahl Index of World Concentration in Four Industries, 1950–1970

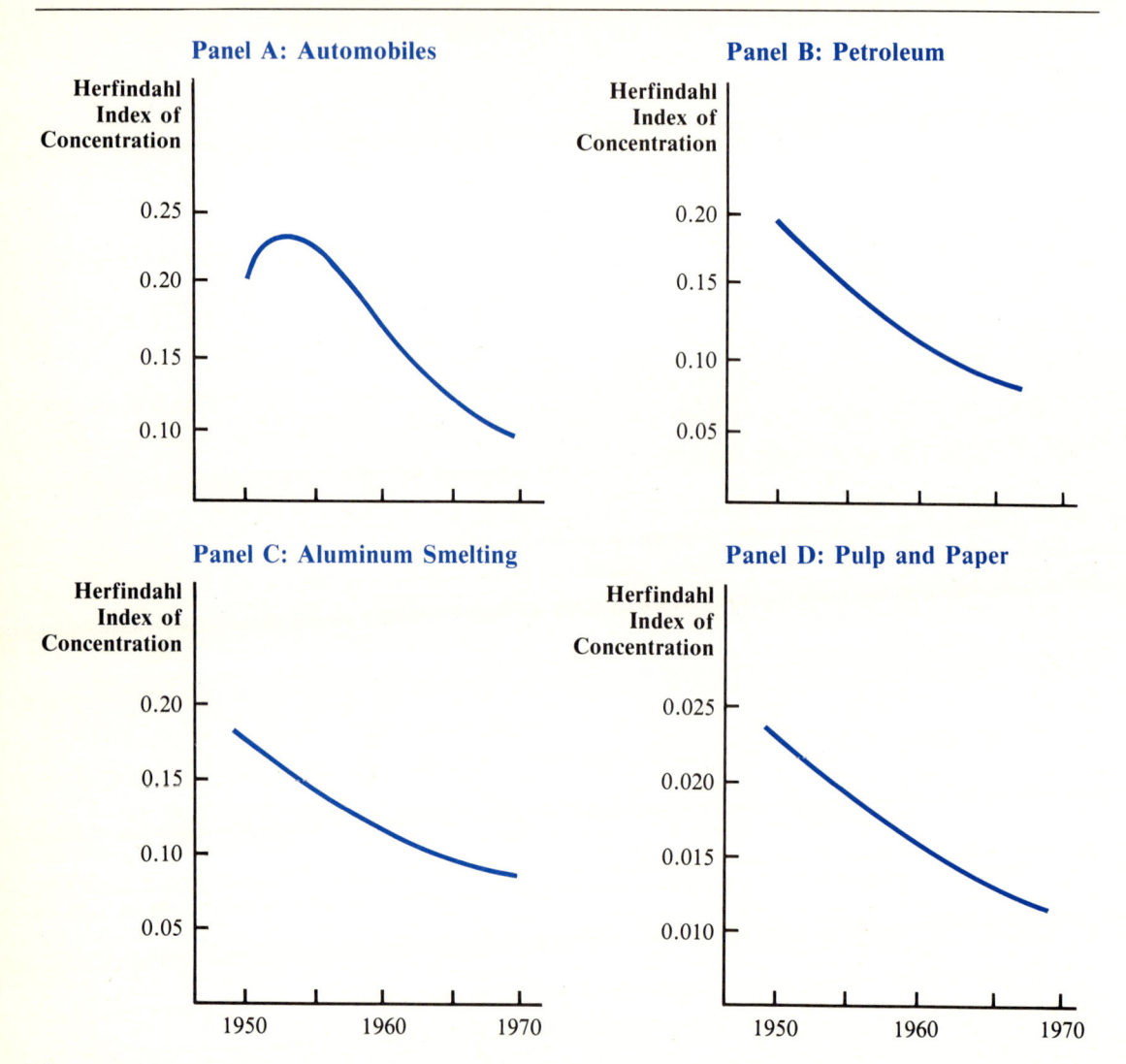

Panel A: Automobiles

Panel B: Petroleum

Panel C: Aluminum Smelting

Panel D: Pulp and Paper

Concentration, as measured by the Herfindahl index, has declined over the 20-year period from 1950 to 1970 in each of the four oligopolistic industries diagrammed.

Source: Raymond Vernon, "Competition Policy Toward Multinational Corporations," *American Economic Review* 64 (May 1974).

to say that competition has either increased or decreased. Since the end of World War II, however, advanced communication and cheap transport have allowed business firms to compete in many different countries. The multinational corporation is a company with production centers in many different countries. One would expect that competition in the postwar world should have been increasing on a *worldwide* basis.

This expectation is borne out in the Harvard Multinational Enterprise study by Raymond Vernon. Vernon examined the Herfindahl indices for the *world* automobile, petroleum, aluminum-smelting, and pulp-and-paper industries. Vernon discovered (apparently to his surprise) that the Herfindahl indices fell dramatically in each of these industries from 1950 to 1970 (see Figure 12-1).

The Equalization of Profit Rates

In the theory of perfect competition, resources are allocated between different industries until profit rates are equalized. Does this theorem hold in the real world? George Stigler has presented evidence to suggest that this theorem tends to hold in unconcentrated industries but not in concentrated industries. Another way to see that the theorem does not hold perfectly is to examine the rankings of industry profits over two different time periods. If profits tended toward equality, one would expect that the most profitable industries in year 0 would be uncorrelated with the most profitable industries in year 10. Example 12-1 shows that profits do not tend to equality for the *Fortune* 500 companies, which are heavily represented by concentrated industries.

MONOPOLISTIC COMPETITION

Monopolistic competition is characteristic of an industry in which (1) there are many small firms, (2) the product is differentiated, (3) there is free entry and exit, and (4) each firm has some control over the price it charges.

The theory of **monopolistic competition** was developed in the 1930s by the British economist Joan Robinson and the American economist Edward Chamberlain.[2] The theory of monopolistic competition shares with the theory of perfect competition the assumptions that profits tend toward zero in the long run and that individual firms behave *atomistically*—that is, they ignore their competitors. The theory of monopolistic competition shares with the theory of monopoly the assumptions that each firm can to some extent charge its own price and that price exceeds marginal revenue.

Perfect competition is impossible to achieve in many markets simply because the good produced by the industry is heterogeneous. The product may differ from firm to firm because of many factors: (1) the location of one firm may be superior to the location of other firms from the standpoint of some of the buyers; (2) the quality of the product may vary from firm to firm because one firm offers a high-quality product and another firm offers a low-quality product; (3) one firm's product may be tailored to the tastes of one group of people while another firm's product may be tailored to the tastes of another group of people (for example, different types of clothes); (4) consumers may think that the products of one firm are different from the products of another firm (for example, aspirin is aspirin, but people may

---

2. Joan Robinson, *The Economics of Imperfect Competition* (London: Macmillan, 1933); Edward Chamberlain, *The Theory of Monopolistic Competition* (Cambridge: Harvard University Press, 1933).

FIGURE 12-2 Long-Run Equilibrium for the Monopolistically Competitive Firm

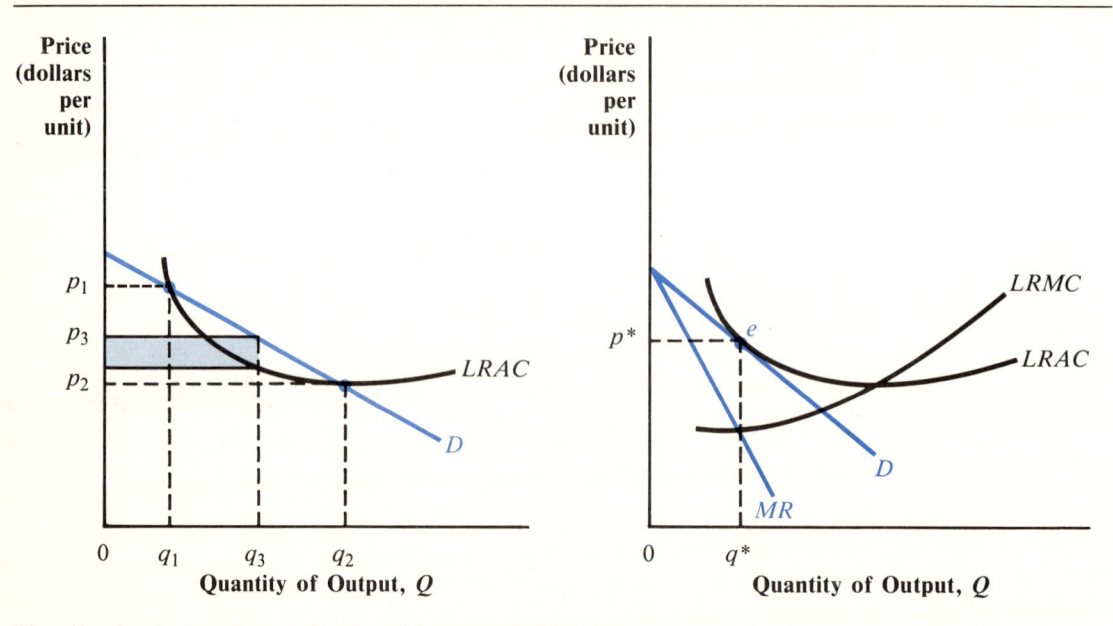

The situation in Panel A cannot be a long-run equilibrium for monopolistic competition because while profit is zero at prices p_1 and p_2, profit is not maximized. In Panel B, profit is both zero and at a maximum where the demand curve is just tangent to the $LRAC$ curve. At the profit-maximizing quantity, q^*, $MR = LRMC$ and $p^* = LRAC$.

think that one brand is different from another). In other words, some generic product will be differentiated if there is some significant basis—real or imagined—for distinguishing the product of one firm from that of another.

Monopolistic competition is characteristic of an industry in which the following assumptions are satisfied:

1. There are many small firms—so many that each firm assumes its actions will go unnoticed by its rivals.
2. The product is differentiated; consumers can distinguish among the products of each firm on grounds of quality, location, physical attributes, or imagined differences.
3. There is free entry and exit. New firms can produce close substitutes for existing products but not necessarily identical products.
4. Each firm faces a downward-sloping demand curve; thus, each firm has some control over the price it charges, and price necessarily exceeds marginal revenue.

In the short run, when no new firms can enter, monopolistic competition is analogous to monopoly. The firm produces where marginal cost equals marginal revenue (as long as price exceeds average variable cost) and may make a profit or loss. The firm's monopoly power may be weak, as measured by the ratio of price to marginal revenue, but the firm to all intents and purposes looks like a monopoly facing a very elastic demand curve.

Long-Run Equilibrium Under Monopolistic Competition

Monopolistic competition exhibits its particular characteristics in the long run. In monopolistic competition, potential competitors can produce a near-identical product. Any firm that is making economic profit will attract imitators. As more close substitutes are produced, the firm will face a more elastic demand for its product and its demand curve will decrease. In the long run, profit must be zero. Thus, it is essential that

$$P = LRAC. \qquad (1)$$

Each firm must also be maximizing profit. Thus, it must be true that:

$$MR = LRMC. \qquad (2)$$

Notice that it is necessary to use long-run costs in the above two equations because, in the long run, management can choose its optimal firm size.

The two conditions in Equations (1) and (2) will be satisfied only when the firm is producing that output for which the demand curve is just tangent to the $LRAC$ curve. In Panel A of Figure 12-2, the firm would satisfy condition (1) at either price p_1 or p_2. It would not satisfy condition (2) because the firm could, for example, charge the price p_3 and make a positive profit selling the quantity q_3. Thus, the demand curve facing the firm cannot intersect the $LRAC$ curve. Panel B shows a long-run equilibrium that satisfies both conditions (1) and (2). At the price p^* and the quantity q^*, profit is zero; profit is also at a maximum because at any price above *or* below p^*, profit would have to be negative.

Because profit is maximized at the price p^* in Panel B of Figure 12-2, it follows that at the quantity q^*, the MR curve intersects the $LRMC$ curve. In the vicinity of the tangency point, e, the $LRAC$ curve and the demand curve (which is just the average-revenue curve) have exactly the same slope; therefore, at that point, the marginal values on both curves must be the same. Recall that the marginal/average relationship is $M = A + Q\Delta A/\Delta Q$. Because at point e the expression $(A + Q\Delta A/\Delta Q)$ would be the same for either revenue or costs, the marginal values must be exactly the same.

In the long run, each monopolistically competitive firm produces at an output where long-run average cost exceeds minimum long-run average cost because the demand curve must be tangent to a U-shaped $LRAC$ curve.

The Welfare Aspects of Monopolistic Competition

Because, in the long run, the monopolistically competitive firm must produce at an output less than the minimum efficient scale, a slightly larger firm would produce the product at a lower unit cost. In a sense, each firm has

EXAMPLE 12–1   The Persistence of Oligopoly Profits

A characteristic of perfect or even monopolistic competition is that profits tend toward equality across industries. If profits are high in the publishing industry, and low in the motor-vehicle industry, prices will fall in the former and rise in the latter until profits are equalized. Thus, neither high nor low profits should persist. The accompanying table shows the return on equity (profits divided by stockholder equity) for the largest industrial corporations in various industries. The return on equity is ranked for the years 1970 and 1981. If profits are persistent, the two rankings should be correlated. Inspection shows that the rankings are remarkably similar. For example, pharmaceuticals were ranked second in both 1970 and 1981, and the motor-vehicle industry was ranked 21st and 22nd, respectively, in 1970 and 1971. On a scale of $+1$ to -1, the rank correlation coefficent between the two years is 0.90, which indicates that profits tended to persist over the 11-year period.

Source: *Statistical Abstract of the United States*, 1970 and 1981.

Industry	Return on Equity, 1981	Return on Equity, 1970	Rank 1981	Rank 1970
Tobacco	19.5	12.4	1	5
Pharmaceuticals	18.0	15.5	2	2
Mining/crude-oil production	17.6	13.8	3	3
Soaps, cosmetics	16.8	15.7	4	1
Petroleum refining	16.4	10.3	5	9
Publishing, printing	16.4	11.4	5	7
Apparel	16.2	10.9	7	8
Measuring, scientific equipment	15.6	13.1	8	4
Aerospace	15.0	8.5	9	15
Food	14.4	12.2	10	6
Transport equipment	14.4	9.8	10	12
Electronics, appliances	14.3	10.2	12	10
Metal products	14.1	10.1	13	11
Industrial and farm equipment	13.9	9.5	14	13
Chemicals	13.5	8.7	15	14

MONOPOLISTIC COMPETITION   339

FIGURE 12-3   Monopolistic Competition and Welfare Maximization

An all-knowing, welfare-maximizing dictator would determine the number of firms and varieties of products such that for each firm the price would just equal the minimum point on the *LRAC* curve.

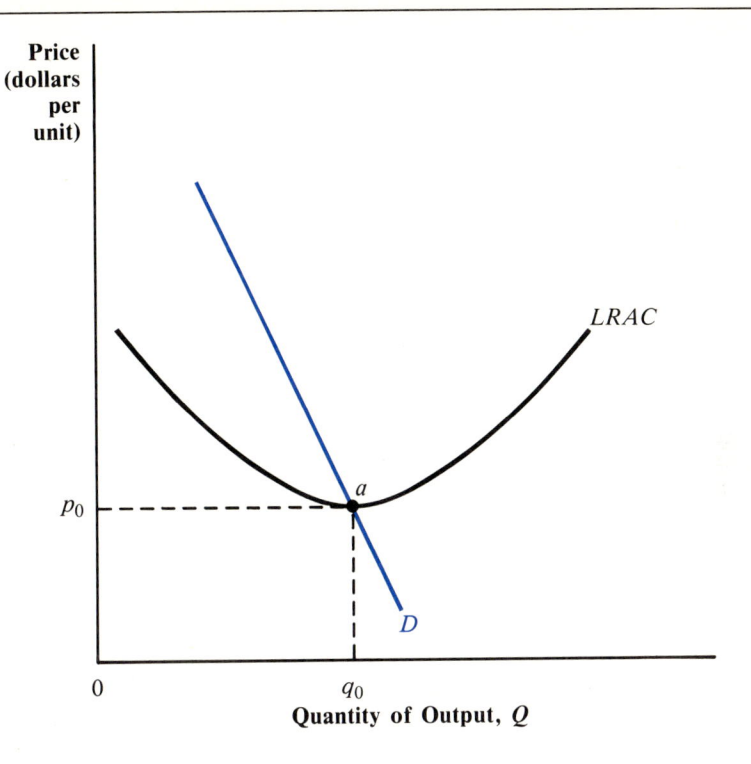

some excess capacity. In an ideal world, each monopolistically competitive firm should make zero profits and charge a price where $P = LRMC$. As long as price is greater than long-run marginal cost, it pays society (but not the firm) to produce another unit of the product. Figure 12-3 shows the solution that would be imposed by an omniscient, welfare-maximizing dictator. When each monopolistically competitive firm charges a price p_0 that equals minimum long-run average cost, where the demand curve facing the firm just intersects the minimum point on the *LRAC* curve, the outcome is efficient. The dictator is giving full scope to the principle of consumer sovereignty, but firms are not allowed to maximize profit (marginal revenue does not equal long-run marginal cost).

While Figure 12-3 shows the social optimum, few (if any) economists would recommend such a solution. In a world of decentralized information, no single mind has all the information that would be necessary to impose the solution depicted in Figure 12-3. The information costs would be prohibitive and would probably far exceed the gains that would be gathered by producing where $P = LRMC$.

Monopolistic competition is necessarily inefficient to an omniscient dictator, but it is probably not inefficient in the real world. The benefits of allowing individual firms the right to maximize profit by producing the varieties of the generic product that people demand probably far outweigh the losses arising from each firm producing with some excess capacity or where price is greater than long-run marginal cost. Whatever inefficiencies might be present under monopolistic competition may be regarded as the price society pays for the variety such an industrial organization provides.

COOPERATIVE OLIGOPOLY: CARTEL THEORY

The theory of monopolistic competition has two serious shortcomings when applied to some real-world industries. First, it supposes that each firm assumes that its rivals do nothing in response to its actions. In other words, along the individual firm's demand curve, the prices charged and varieties offered by its rivals are held fixed. But certainly General Motors pays attention to Ford, Boeing to McDonnell Douglas, and IBM to Xerox. A key feature of rivalry in the actual economy is *strategic behavior*.

Second, the theory of monopolistic competition supposes that there is free entry, which means that industry profits should tend to zero and that profits should not persist. As Example 12-1 showed, industry profits for the *Fortune* 500 companies do persist.

The theory of oligopoly is designed to fill the gap between monopolistic competition and monopoly. There are four characteristics of an industry that is an **oligopoly**:

An **oligopoly** is an industry with (1) a few relatively large firms, (2) modest or high entry barriers, (3) mutual interdependence of firms, and (4) similar or identical products.

1. A few relatively large firms dominate the market.
2. The ease of entry into the market is not perfect because there are modest or high entry barriers.
3. Each oligopolist follows specific strategies with respect to each of its rivals; there is mutual interdependence in the sense that each oligopolist must be aware of the market actions (output or price) of its rivals.
4. The products produced by each firm may be similar or identical. A homogeneous oligopoly produces identical goods—such as steel, rayon, or cement. A heterogeneous oligopoly produces close substitutes—such as cereals or automobiles.

Oligopoly is an umbrella term of considerable scope. Oligopoly behavior is rich and varied, presenting many puzzles that require solution. What forces determine oligopoly behavior? The key is the degree of mutual interdependence between the firms, with the strategy of each firm taking into account the total market and the expected strategies of its rivals.

Economists have a long tradition of being suspicious of oligopolies. According to Adam Smith, "People of the same trade seldom get together, either for merriment or diversion, but that the conversation ends in some conspiracy against the public." That sentiment was expressed more than 200 years ago. More recently, John Kenneth Galbraith expressed the same sentiment: "So long as there are only a few massive firms in an industry, each must act with a view of the welfare of all."

EXAMPLE 12-2 The Organization of Petroleum-Exporting Countries (OPEC) Cartel

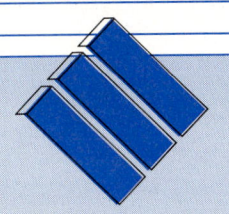

The 13 OPEC-member nations produced about two thirds of the total world output of oil in the latter part of the 1970s. During that period the cartel was strong. By 1986, the cartel produced only one third of total world output of oil. The incentive for each cartel member to cheat on the cartel agreement was far greater in 1986 than in the 1970s. As a consequence, the cartel members regularly exceed their assigned quotas, as vividly shown by the accompanying table for July 1986. Only Iran fell short of its quota because of its war with Iraq. In August 1986, the cartel reached an agreement to abide by the assigned quotas, but many analysts doubted whether the agreement would last.

Country	OPEC Quota (millions of barrels per day)	July Output (millions of barrels per day)
Saudi Arabia	4.353	5.125
Iran	2.300	2.200
**Iraq	1.200	1.900
Kuwait	0.900	1.425
U.A.E.	0.950	1.415
Qatar	0.280	0.400
Venezuela	1.555	1.700
Nigeria	1.300	1.550
Libya	0.990	1.200
Indonesia	1.189	1.400
Algeria	0.663	0.600
Gabon	0.137	0.170
**Ecuador	0.183	0.300
Total	**16.717**	**19.485**

Source: *Houston Chronical,* August 6, 1986, p. 1; "Oil Accord is Termed Temporary," *New York Times,* August 6, 1986, p. 25.

The Smith-Galbraith view is that oligopoly theory is simple: the oligopolists know each other, face the same set of problems, and can easily deduce the fact that they would each be better off if they acted as a shared monopoly, or **cartel**.

A cartel is simply an explicit collusive agreement among firms producing a particular product. The agreement may involve *market sharing* or *the setting of a common price*. Under market sharing, each firm might be assigned a particular production quota. For example, when the OPEC (Organization of Petroleum Exporting Countries) oil cartel was formed, each member country was assigned a production quota. When the cartel weakened in the mid-1980s, the members regularly exceeded their assigned production quotas (see Example 12–2).

A **cartel** is an explicit collusive agreement among firms producing a particular product to share the market or to set a common price.

FIGURE 12-4   Output Determination for a Cartel

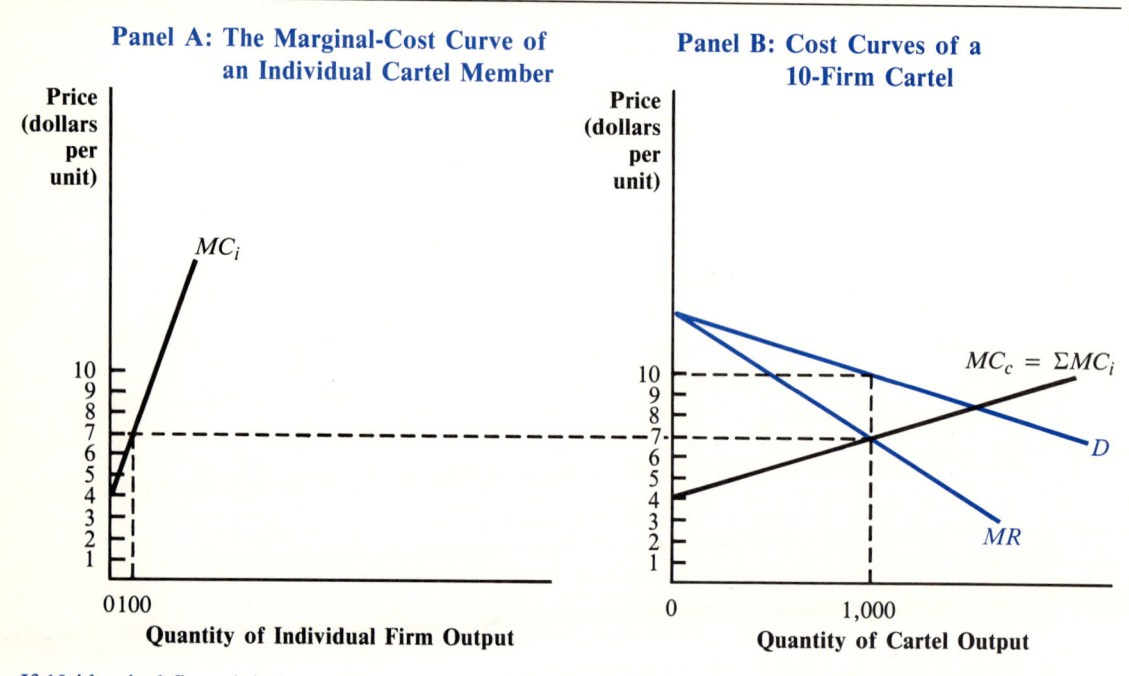

Panel A: The Marginal-Cost Curve of an Individual Cartel Member

Panel B: Cost Curves of a 10-Firm Cartel

If 10 identical firms jointly maximize their profits by forming a cartel, Panel A shows the marginal-cost curve for a typical cartel member. The cartel's marginal-cost curve, shown in Panel B, is the horizontal sum of the individual MC curves in Panel A. Cartel profit is maximized where the cartel's marginal-revenue curve, MR, equals the cartel's MC curve. The cartel price is $10; the cartel quantity is the number of firms multiplied by the individual-firm quantity—or $10 \times 100 = 1{,}000$ units in this case.

Under common-price setting, a minimum price is established for each firm. For example, from time to time drug companies have been charged with conspiring to fix identical prices on particular products, as in the antitrust case against Pfizer, American Cyanamid, and Bristol-Myers involving the tetracycline antibiotic. According to the government, the fact that an identical price was charged by all three companies to druggists and the fact that an identical (lower) price was charged by all three to the Veterans Administration (despite production costs far below the announced price) constituted circumstantial evidence of a conspiracy.

Joint Profit Maximization

According to the theory of joint profit maximization by members of a cartel, each firm simply produces that output for which its marginal cost equals the industry marginal revenue. Figure 12-4 diagrams a classical cartel. For simplicity, it is assumed that the firms produce a homogeneous product, that there are absolute barriers to entry, that each firm is identical, and that there are 10 such firms in the cartel. Panel A shows the marginal-cost curve facing each firm, MC_i. The cartel's marginal-cost curve is simply the horizontal sum of each firm's marginal-cost curve. Panel B shows the cartel's marginal-cost curve, MC_c. The profit-maximizing price/output combination is found where the industry's marginal revenue equals cartel marginal cost. Thus, each firm produces q_i units and charges the same price. This solution maximizes profit because

$$MR = MC_1 = MC_2 = \ldots = MC_{10}.$$

When the MC_i values are equated, it is impossible to produce the same output at a lower cost by simply rearranging output. If the MC_i values were unequal, industry costs for any given output could be lowered by assigning higher outputs to the low-cost firms and lower outputs to the high-cost firms.

Each member of a cartel, however, has an incentive to cheat. A key factor in cartel theory is that the price of the product exceeds each firm's marginal cost. Figure 12-4 shows the marginal revenue *to the cartel* of selling an additional unit, but what is the marginal revenue *to the firm* of selling an extra unit? The firm could probably sell an extra unit by simply shaving the price a bit from the cartel price (thereby attracting business from other cartel members). It may spoil the market for the rest of the cartel, but it need not spoil its own market very much at all. For example, suppose each firm sells 100 units at $10 per unit for a total revenue of $1,000. A defecting cartel member could charge $9.995 per unit and easily sell, say, 101 units. The marginal revenue of the defecting firm will be ($9.995 × 101) − $1,000 = $9.495. In other words, the cartel price itself need be only slightly higher than the marginal revenue to the cheating firm. Thus, each firm's marginal revenue exceeds its marginal cost. Therefore, the cartel price should be difficult to maintain over a long period of time.

Cartels have typically been unstable. The most powerful cartel in history—the OPEC cartel—could not sustain monopoly prices permanently. The OPEC cartel, established in 1960, showed its muscle in 1974 and began to decline 10 years later. It may recover, but economic theory predicts that it will weaken once again. Once one cartel member defected, all defected.

PRACTICE EXERCISE 12-1

Q. Firm A and Firm B both have a marginal-cost curve $MC = Q_i$. The market demand for their homogeneous product is $P = 10 - Q$. What is the cartel price and quantity?

A. The marginal-cost curve for the cartel is $MC = \frac{1}{2} \cdot Q$ because $Q_A = Q_B$ when costs are minimized. The cartel maximizes profit when $MR = MC$, or $10 - 2Q = \frac{1}{2} \cdot Q$ or $Q = 4$ and $P = 6$.

Lesser cartels have not been so fortunate.[3] If the cartel is clandestine, it may be even more difficult to maintain.

The factors that give rise to instability are many. A few of the most important are: product heterogeneity; a large number of firms; large fixed costs with low marginal costs; and low entry barriers. Heterogeneous products make it difficult to write agreements. A large number of firms makes it easier for any one firm to cheat. Low marginal costs increase the incentive to cheat. Low entry barriers reduce the advantage of joining a cartel because high cartel profits will attract new entrants.

Antitrust Laws

Cartels are, of course, illegal in the United States. If they exist, they must be clandestine. The basic federal antitrust law in the United States is the Sherman Act, passed in 1890 in response to charges of monopoly and cartelization. Section 1 of the act provides that "every contract, combination, . . . or conspiracy, in restraint of trade or commerce among the several States . . . is hereby declared to be illegal." Many court decisions have interpreted this section as saying that it is illegal *per se* to make an agreement among competing firms to fix prices, restrict or pool output, or share markets on some predetermined basis. Section 2 of the Sherman Act prohibits monopolization and conspiracies and attempts to monopolize.

Antitrust laws doubtless make cartels more difficult to organize. Meetings must be kept secret, and it is more difficult for the cartel to police the various schemes of the cartel members to evade the market-sharing rules.

NONCOOPERATIVE OLIGOPOLY

Oligopoly is not likely to result in simply a shared monopoly. The forces that bring the firms together are not as strong as the forces that blow them apart. It is, therefore, necessary to examine a different type of oligopoly equilibrium.

Cournot Oligopoly

The pioneering model of a noncooperative oligopoly was developed by the French economist, Augustin A. Cournot, in 1838. The difficulty with oligopoly theory is figuring out the appropriate degree of mutual interdependence between the firms. Firm A must guess about Firm B's policies, and vice versa. This extraordinarily difficult problem was solved by Cournot in

---

3. For examples of the instability of cartels, *see* George W. Stocking and Myron W. Watkins, *Cartels in Action* (New York: Twentieth Century Fund, 1946). For the most notorious case in U.S. history, see Richard Austin Smith, "The Incredible Electrical Conspiracy," *Fortune* (April 1961), pp. 132ff and (May 1961), pp. 161 ff.

FIGURE 12-5   The Demand Curve for a Cournot Firm

Panel A: Industry Demand

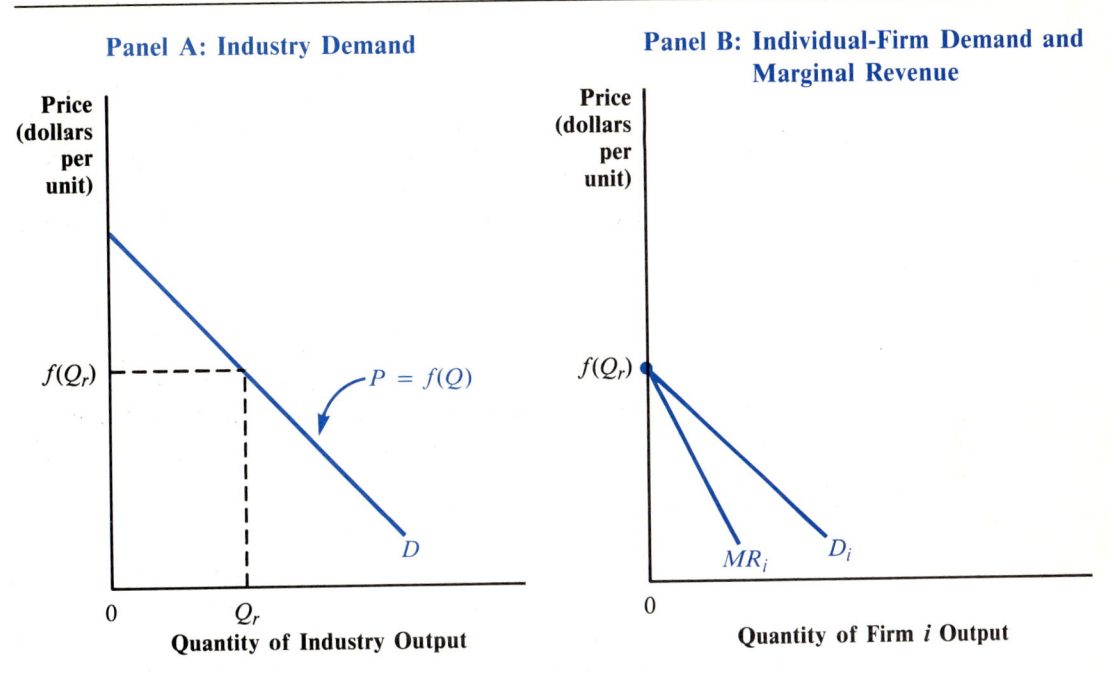

Price (dollars per unit) vs. Quantity of Industry Output; industry demand curve D with $P = f(Q)$; at rivals' output Q_r, price is $f(Q_r)$.

Panel B: Individual-Firm Demand and Marginal Revenue

Price (dollars per unit) vs. Quantity of Firm i Output; firm demand curve D_i starting at $f(Q_r)$, with marginal-revenue curve MR_i.

Panel A shows the industry-demand curve, D. The output of Firm i's rivals is Q_r. That portion of D to the right of Q_r is Firm i's demand curve, D_i, in Panel B, because Firm i assumes rivals maintain their output in the face of its decisions. The MR_i curve in Panel B is Firm i's marginal-revenue curve.

an ingenious fashion. Cournot made an apparently naive assumption: he assumed that each oligopolist takes the output of its rivals as *given*. In other words, each oligopolist assumes that it can vary its own output while its rivals maintain their outputs. While the Cournot assumption is unrealistic, the resulting model turns out to be stronger than the foundation on which it is built. Moreover, the Cournot model of oligopoly is the prototype for nearly all oligopoly models.

Cournot also assumed that the oligopoly produces a homogeneous output, that the number of firms is fixed, and that each oligopolist knows the total market-demand curve as well as the collective outputs of all its rivals. Figure 12-5 shows what the Cournot assumption means for any particular oligopolist. The output of all rivals, Q_r, is taken as given. Because the oligopolist knows the market-demand curve, D, as well as the rivals' output, Q_r, the demand curve facing the firm is taken to be that portion of D to the right of Q_r in Panel A—or the curve D_i in Panel B. Because D_i is an ordinary demand curve, the marginal-revenue curve facing this oligopolist is MR_i.

The calculation of MR_i follows the average/marginal rule (see Chapter 5). Suppose the demand curve facing the industry is $P = f(Q)$. The firm's

FIGURE 12–6 How a Cournot Firm's Output Is Determined

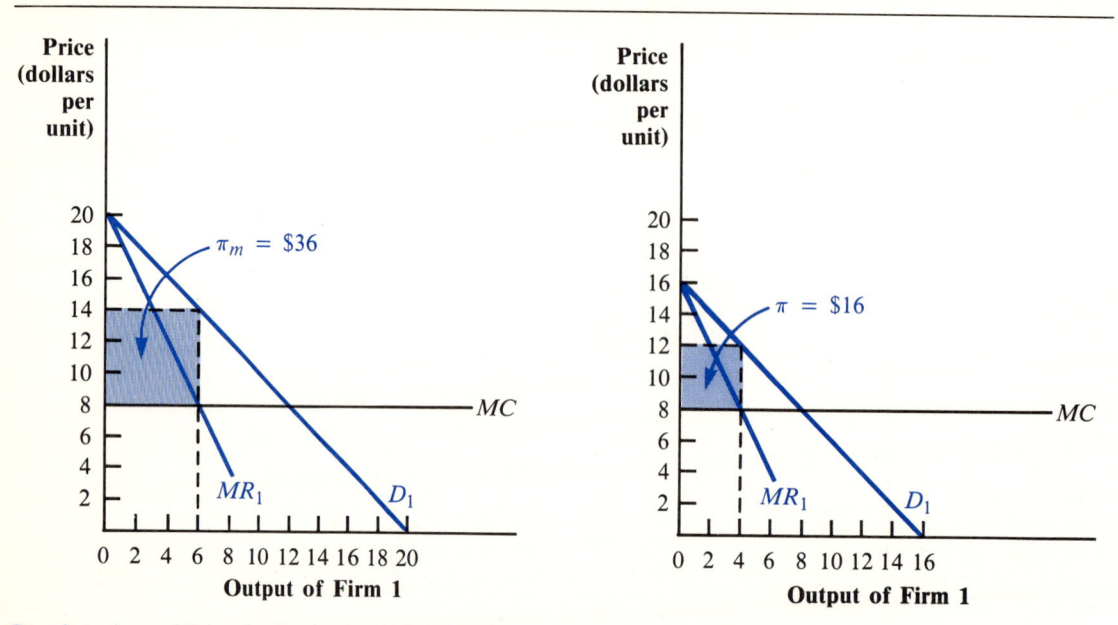

Panel A shows Firm 1's demand curve when Firm 2's output is zero; Firm 1's optimal output is the monopoly output, 6 units. Panel B shows Firm 1's demand curve when Firm 2's output is 4 units; Firm 1's optimal output is also 4 units.

output, denoted here by x_i, is the market that is spoiled when the firm increases its output. Thus, if $\Delta P/\Delta Q$ is the slope of the market-demand curve, the firm's marginal revenue is

$$MR_i = f(Q) + x_i \Delta P/\Delta Q. \tag{3}$$

The term $(x_i \Delta P/\Delta Q)$ is the loss of revenue attributable to having to reduce the price on all x_i units sold when an extra unit is sold. If the demand curve is $P = a - bQ$, then the marginal revenue facing the ith firm is:

$$MR_i = a - bQ - bx_i. \tag{4}$$

The **reaction curve** shows the profit-maximizing output of one firm as a function of the other firm's output; it is downward-sloping, because the higher is the output of the other firm, the lower is the firm's optimal output.

To illustrate how Cournot oligopoly works, consider the case in which there are only two firms: Firm 1 and Firm 2. A two-firm oligopoly is called a *duopoly*. We will assume that the marginal cost of production is constant and equals $8 for both firms. The market-demand curve is $P = \$20 - Q$. Cournot asked: what would be the optimal output for one firm given the output of the other firm? The response of each firm to the other's output is shown by a **reaction curve**.

Panel A of Figure 12–6 shows Firm 1's demand curve assuming Firm 2's output is 0 units (in other words, Firm 1 has a monopoly). In this case, Firm

FIGURE 12-7   Cournot Equilibrium

Curves R_1 and R_2 are the reaction curves of Firms 1 and 2; point e is the Cournot equilibrium and shows the point where both firms are producing their desired outputs.

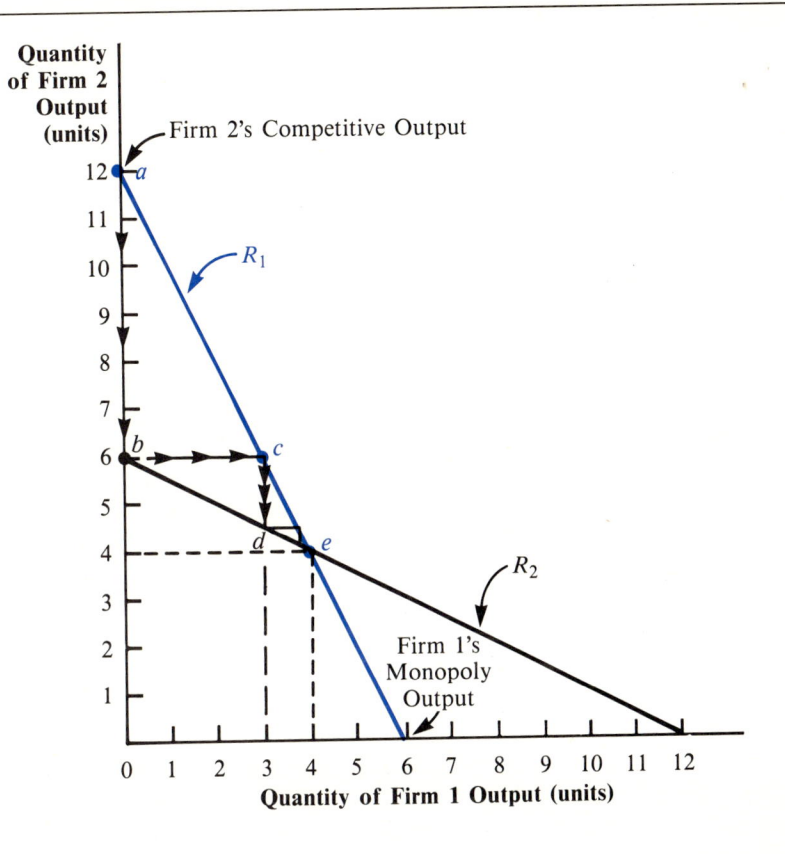

1's demand curve is just the market-demand curve. As always for linear demand curves, the marginal-revenue curve is twice as steep. If marginal cost is $8, Firm 1's profit-maximizing output is 6 units (the monopoly output) and price is $14. Monopoly profit is $36, because profit per unit is $6. Panel B shows Firm 1's demand curve when Firm 2's output is 4 units. In this case, Firm 1's demand curve is $P = 20 - (x_1 + x_2) = 20 - (x_1 + 4) = 16 - x_1$; the marginal-revenue curve is $MR = 16 - 2x_1$. Profit is maximized for Firm 1 where $MR = MC$, or at an output of 4 and price of $12. The firm's profit is now $16, because profit per unit is now only $4.

Firm 1's reaction curve showing Firm 1 output at all the different levels of Firm 2 output is labeled R_1 in Figure 12-7. When Firm 2 is producing 12 units, the price of the product is only $8, and there is no room for Firm 1. In this case, Firm 2 is producing the perfectly competitive output, because $P = MC = \$8$. Thus, when Firm 2 output is 12, Firm 1's optimal output is 0 units. The reaction curve R_1 is a straight line that cuts the vertical axis at Firm 2's competitive output of 12 units and cuts the horizontal axis at Firm 1's monopoly output (6 units). Firm 1's reaction curve is, thus, the curve $x_1 = 6$

A Cournot equilibrium is a set of outputs for which each firm is maximizing profit given the outputs of the remaining firms.

$- 0.5x_2$. Because Firm 2's production costs are identical, its reaction curve, R_2, is symmetrical; it is simply $x_2 = 6 - 0.5x_1$. The two curves intersect at point e where $x_1 = x_2 = 4$ units. A **Cournot equilibrium** is achieved when the expectations of each firm are realized. When $x_2 = 4$, Firm 1 wants to produce 4 units; when Firm 1 produces 4 units, Firm 2 wants to produce 4 units. At the Cournot equilibrium, each firm is maximizing its profits given the output of the other firm; therefore, there is no incentive for any firm to alter its output.

How do the firms arrive at the Cournot equilibrium, point e? If Firm 2 is producing 12 units, then Firm 1 will produce at point a, where Firm 1 output is 0. When Firm 1 is producing 0 units, however, Firm 2 has an incentive to produce 6 units (at point b). As Firm 2 cuts its output to 6 units, Firm 1 has an incentive to expand its output to 3 units (at point c). The process continues from c, to d and so forth until the equilibrium point, e, is reached.

The Cournot assumption that each firm adjusts its output in the expectation that the other firm holds output fixed has been criticized. This expectation is fulfilled only at the Cournot equilibrium point. For example, if Firm 2 happened to be producing 12 units, Firm 1 would choose to produce 0 units; but then Firm 2 would choose the monopoly output, 6 units (at point b). If Firm 1 were to produce no output, why wouldn't it assume Firm 2 would produce 6 units? In other words, why wouldn't Firm 1 know Firm 2's reaction curve, or vice versa?[4]

N-Firm Cournot Oligopoly

Even though the Cournot model makes a naive assumption, when viewed from the standpoint of an *N*-firm oligopoly, the model is extraordinarily useful. For example, consider the case where there are *N* identical firms. In this case, each firm will produce the same output, x (under most circumstances). The profit-maximizing condition $MR_i = MC$ then can be used to derive the Cournot model's predicted output/price combination for any number of firms. If $P = a - bQ$ and marginal costs of each firm are constant and equal to c, $MR = MC$ implies:

$$P - bx = a - bQ - bx = c. \tag{5}$$

Because $Q = Nx$, Equation (5) can be rewritten as

$$a - bNx - bx = c \quad \text{or}$$

$$x = \frac{a - c}{b(N + 1)}. \tag{6}$$

---

4. This assumption has been analyzed by Heinrich von Stackelberg; for an analysis, *see* William J. Fellner, *Competition Among the Few* (New York: Knopf, 1949).

TABLE 12-3 A Cournot Oligopoly

Number of Firms, N	Price (dollars per unit), P	Quantity of Firm Output (units), x	Quantity of Industry Output (units), Q	Firm Profit (dollars), π	Industry Profit (dollars), Σπ
1	14	6	6	36	36
2	12	4	8	16	32
3	11	3	9	9	27
4	10.4	2.4	9.6	5.76	23.04
5	10	2	10	4	20
6	9.71	1.71	10.29	2.94	17.63
7	9.5	1.5	10.5	2.25	15.75
8	9.33	1.33	10.67	1.78	14.22
9	9.2	1.2	10.8	1.44	12.96
10	9.09	1.09	10.91	1.19	11.90
20	8.57	0.57	11.42	0.33	6.53
∞	8	0	12	0	0

Note: Marginal cost is assumed to be constant at $8 per unit. The demand curve is described by the equation: $P = 20 - Q$.

Because $Q = Nx$,

$$Q = \frac{N(a-c)}{b(N+1)}. \tag{7}$$

The predicted price would be

$$P = a - \frac{N(a-c)}{N+1} = \frac{a+Nc}{N+1}. \tag{8}$$

The firm's profit per unit is $P - c$, or

$$\frac{\pi}{x} = P - c = \frac{a-c}{N+1}. \tag{9}$$

Using Equation (9), the firm's total profit is:

$$\pi = \frac{(a-c)^2}{b(N+1)^2}. \tag{10}$$

Table 12-3 shows how price, profit per firm, firm output, and industry output behave (for the case where $P = 20 - Q$ and where $MC = c = \$8$) as the number of Cournot oligopolists varies from $N = 1$ to $N = \infty$. When $N =$

PRACTICE EXERCISE 12-2

Q. Suppose a Cournot oligopoly consists of two firms, each of which faces a constant marginal cost of $1. The (inverse) market-demand curve is $P = 10 - Q$. What is each firm's marginal revenue? What is the Cournot equilibrium?

A. In equilibrium, both firms will produce the same output, x. $MR = P + x(\Delta P/\Delta Q)$, because each firm assumes price falls by the slope of the demand curve, and x is the individual firm's unit sales. Thus, $MR = 10 - Q - x$. In the Cournot equilibrium, $Q = 2x$. Thus, $MR = 10 - 3x$. Because $MC = \$1$, it must be that profits are maximized when $MR = MC$. Thus, $10 - 3x = 1$, or $x = 3$. It follows that $Q = 2x = 6$, and $P = \$4$.

1, there is monopoly. The price of the product is $14, and the firm earns a profit of $36. When $N = 2$, we obtain the duopoly case described earlier. Notice that in the case of duopoly, aggregate profits of $32 fall short of monopoly profits. When $N = 10$, the price of the product has fallen to $9.09. Notice how the price falls dramatically from monopoly to the case of 10 firms (a Herfindahl index of 0.1 and a concentration ratio of 40 percent). The competitive price is, of course, the minimum marginal cost, or $8. When $N = 20$, the price of the product is still $8.57. Thus, the first 10 firms unleash the forces of competition more than the next 90 firms (or even the next 1,000 firms).[5]

The lesson learned by a study of Cournot oligopoly is: If firms behave somewhat independently, as they do in Cournot oligopoly, relatively few firms are needed to reap the major benefits of competition.

Mergers and Cournot Oligopoly

Table 12-3 can also be used to study the economics of mergers. The last decade has witnessed massive merger movement in the United States. Two fundamental reasons for mergers would be: (1) a merger increases monopoly

---

[5]. The numerical example suggests that perfect competition is the limit of Cournot oligopoly. This conclusion holds only in the case of nondecreasing marginal costs. If the cost curve is U-shaped and if an infinite number of firms were possible, the limiting price would exceed the competitive price. With a U-shaped cost curve, Cournot oligopoly would approach perfect competition if the number of buyers tended to infinity and free entry prevailed. For a discussion, see Roy J. Ruffin, "Cournot Oligopoly and Competitive Behavior," *Review of Economic Studies* 38 (October 1971): 493–502. James W. Friedman, in *Oligopoly Theory* (Cambridge: Cambridge University Press, 1983), chap. 2, gives a good numerical example of a Cournot oligopoly with a U-shaped cost curve.

power and, therefore, the joint profits of the merged firms, and (2) the merger enables firms to enjoy greater profits through cost savings, or economies of scale. It can be argued that a merger that takes place to achieve lower costs would be beneficial to society while a merger that takes place between firms for the sole purpose of increasing monopoly power would not be beneficial.

Table 12-3 is based on the assumption that there are no economies of scale and that every firm is symmetrically situated with respect to every other firm. If two firms merge, then the number of firms simply drops by one; or if M firms merge, the number of firms drops by $M - 1$. In the present model, the new firm earns as much as any of the other firms. The main effect of a merger is to raise the product price and to raise the profit of each firm.

Does it pay to merge? If $N = 2$ firms, it pays the two firms in the industry to merge. Prior to the merger, they each earn $16 in profit for a total of $32. By merging, the two firms achieve a monopoly and earn $36 (see Table 12-3). Suppose, however, that there are 3 firms prior to merger. Each firm makes a profit of $9. If only two of the firms merge, there will be two firms in the market: the old firm and the new (merged) firm. The old firm's profit will rise to $16 and the merged firm's profit (by the symmetry assumption) will also be $16. The new firm is composed of two former firms, however, who jointly earned $18 prior to the merger. Accordingly, the new merged firm earns less than the two old firms earned prior to merger.

In the Cournot model, when there are no economies of scale, there is no incentive for any two firms to merge, unless it results in monopoly.

In other words, mergers for the sole purpose of increasing monopoly power are unlikely. The major benefits of the merger of two firms, when economies of scale are not involved, are likely to fall on those firms remaining *outside* the merger. When there are fewer firms, a higher price is charged. Because there is no incentive for two firms to merge without economies of scale being part of the story, the Cournot oligopoly model suggests that there is nothing to fear from a horizontal merger. To the extent, however, that mergers of firms leads to cooperative oligopoly—a cartel—such a conclusion might be questioned.

THE KINKED-DEMAND-CURVE MODEL

In the 1930s, economists became concerned about the apparent stability of oligopoly prices. While prices of goods in competitive markets appeared to fluctuate with supply and demand, the prices of oligopolized goods appeared relatively stable. In the light of these observations, Paul Sweezy advanced the theory of a **kinked-demand curve** of a heterogeneous oligopoly. According to this model, oligopolists match the price cuts of rivals but not their price hikes.

A **kinked-demand curve** is the demand curve of a firm whose rivals match price cuts but not price increases.

FIGURE 12-8   The Kinked-Demand Model of an Oligopolist

Because this firm assumes its rivals will match its price cuts, but not its price increases, the demand curve will have a kink at point c, the current price. The MR curve will have a vertical section below the current price. The current price, p_c, maximizes profit when the marginal-cost curve is either MC or MC'; the oligopoly price is relatively stable.

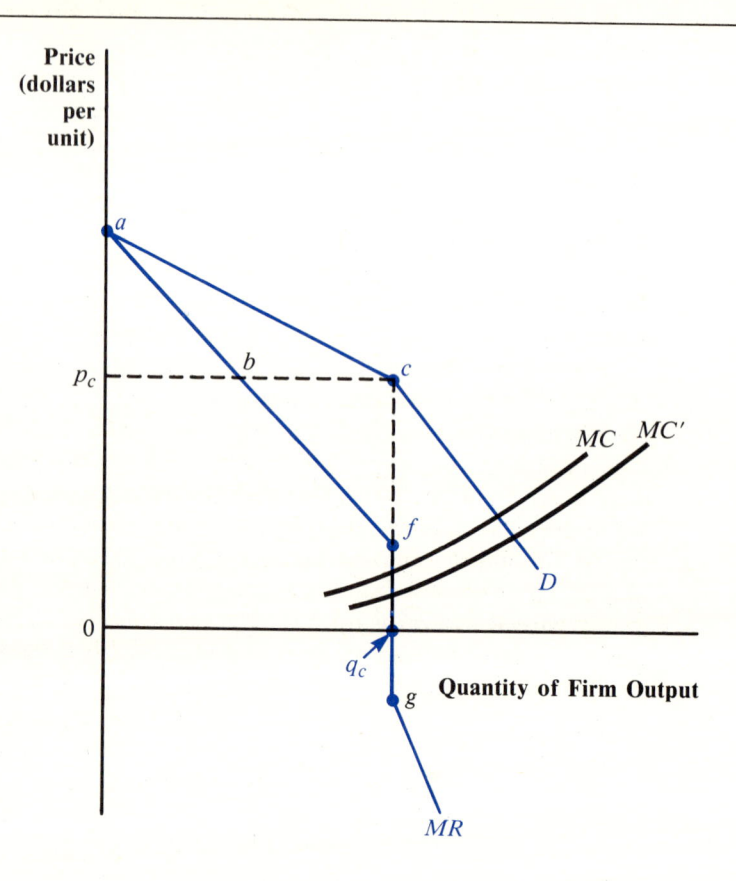

At one time the kinked-demand model was the most popular oligopoly model, but its popularity has suffered in recent years. Nevertheless, the kinked-demand model has been useful for two reasons. First, it serves as a simple introduction to oligopoly theory by bringing out the dramatic implications of mutual interdependence and the importance of the assumptions each firm makes about its rivals. Second, it has served as a focal point for empirical research.[6]

Figure 12-8 shows the kinked-demand curve of a single firm among several competitors. The firm's current price is p_c, and it sells the quantity q_c. If the firm raises its price, it assumes that its rivals will not also raise their prices; thus, the demand curve will be highly elastic above the price p_c. If the firm lowers the product price, it assumes that its rivals will also lower

---

[6]. Paul Sweezy, "Demand Under Conditions of Oligopoly," *Journal of Political Economy* 47 (August 1939): 568–73. Serious criticisms of the Sweezy model began with George J. Stigler, "The Kinky Oligopoly Demand Curve and Rigid Prices," *Journal of Political Economy* 55 (October 1947), reprinted in Stigler, *The Organization of Industry* (Homewood, Ill.: Richard D. Irwin, 1968), chap. 18.

their prices to be able to compete; thus, the demand curve will be less elastic below the price p_c than above that price. The demand curve D has a kink at point c.

When the demand curve has a kink in it, the marginal-revenue curve will have a vertical span at the current price. Because elasticity drops sharply below the current price, so does marginal revenue. The MR curve has a vertical section fg. The MR curve northwest of point f is marginal to the ac section of the demand curve; the MR curve southeast of point g is marginal to the lower section of the demand curve.

The oligopoly price will tend to be insensitive to costs. If the marginal-cost curve shifts from MC to MC' in Figure 12-8, the optimum occurs at the same output level as before the shift. As long as the MC-curve shifts stay within the fg range of the MR curve, price will remain stable. Moreover, price may remain stable in the face of small demand shifts as well.

Economists have criticized the kinked-demand model on two grounds. First, the kinked-demand model fails to explain how the current price is determined. Thus, the model cannot explain the exercise of monopoly power. In other words, the kinked-demand model is not a complete theory.

The second criticism is that the main prediction of the model seems false. Essentially, the model says that oligopoly will have more stable prices than either competition or monopoly will. But this prediction has not held up to close scrutiny. J. Fred Weston and Steven Lustgarten investigated price changes between 1954 and 1974 and found that, typically, the higher is the concentration ratio, the lower is the annual percentage change in price. This fact is not uniformly consistent with kinked-demand theory; according to the kinked-demand model, an increase in concentration from oligopoly to pure monopoly would reduce price stability, contrary to the empirical evidence.[7]

The Weston-Lustgarten evidence however, *is* consistent with the Cournot model. According to Equation (8), the predicted Cournot price is

$$P = \frac{a + Nc}{N + 1} = \frac{a}{N + 1} + \frac{cN}{N + 1}.$$

Notice in the second term c is multiplied by $N/(N + 1)$. Thus, a $1 change in costs increases P by the multiplier, $N/(N + 1)$:

$$\Delta P/\Delta c = N/(N + 1).$$

If $N = 1$, a $1 change in costs increases the price by only $0.50; if $N = 10$, a $1 change in price changes the price by $10/11 = \$0.91$. In other words, the higher is the degree of concentration, the smaller is the flexibility of prices in response to cost changes.

---

7. J. Fred Weston and Steven H. Lustgarten, "Concentration and Wage-Price Changes," in eds. Harvey J. Goldschmid *et al.*, *Industrial Concentration: The New Learning* (Boston: Little, Brown, 1974).

FIGURE 12-9 Limit Pricing

If c_m is the monopolist's average and marginal cost, and c_e is the marginal and average cost of potential entrants, the monopolist cannot charge a price exceeding c_e. The limit price is c_e.

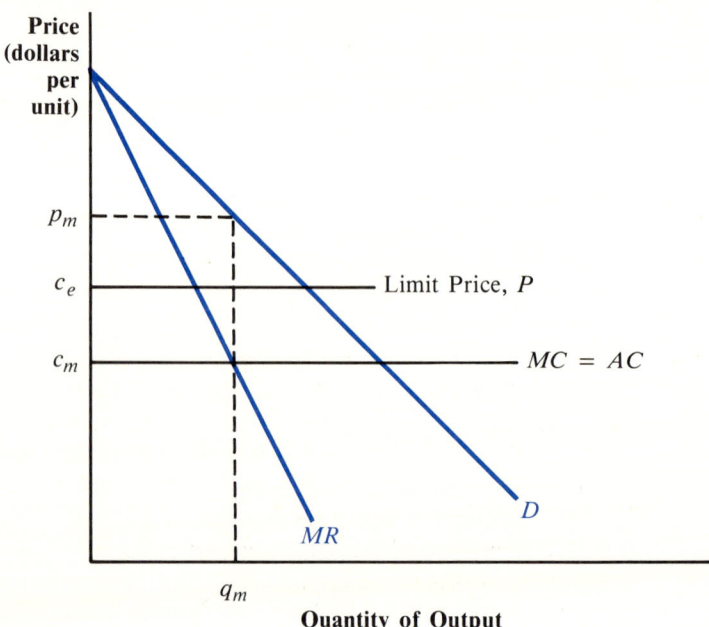

[Graph: Price (dollars per unit) vs. Quantity of Output. Horizontal lines at p_m, c_e (labeled "Limit Price, P"), and c_m (labeled "MC = AC"). Demand curve D and MR curve slope downward from the vertical axis. Dashed vertical line at q_m.]

POTENTIAL ENTRANTS

Oligopoly models often analyze the rivalry between existing firms, but another class of models analyzes the issue of potential entrants. The earliest model of potential entry is that of J. S. Bain, who argued that the price charged by monopolists must be limited by the potential competition invited by high prices. The Bain view is called the *limit-pricing model*. The latest model of potential entry is the *contestable-market model*, proposed by William J. Baumol, John C. Panzer, and Robert Willig.[8]

Limit Pricing

Assume a monopolist has a definite cost advantage over any other firms because of its superior access to raw materials or technology (by means of a patent). In Figure 12-9, the monopolist's marginal cost equals average cost equals c_m. If the monopolist did not have to worry about potential competitors, the monopoly price would be p_m, but suppose an indefinite number of firms had access to the technology at the higher average and marginal costs of c_e. The marginal cost of potential firms, c_e is the entry-preventing price. If price is greater than c_e, new firms will enter. If price is less than c_e, new firms will not enter. Clearly, under the postulated conditions, the

---
[8]. See William J. Baumol, "Contestable Markets: An Uprising in the Theory of Industry Structure," *American Economic Review* 72 (March 1972): 1–15.

FIGURE 12-10 Price Setting in a Natural-Monopoly Contestable Market

In a contestable market, a natural monopolist would charge the price p_c; any higher price would attract hit-and-run entrants.

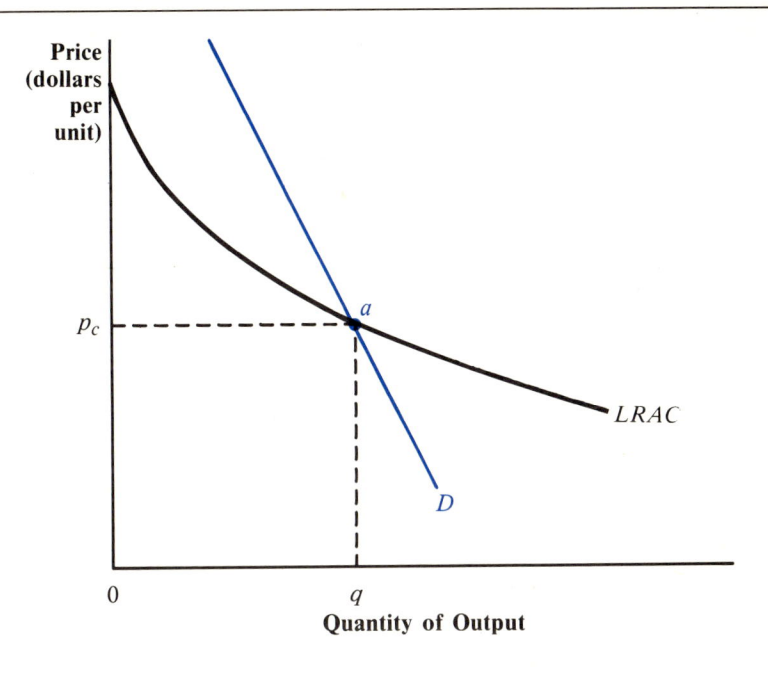

Price Setting in a Natural-Monopoly Contestable Market — graph showing demand curve D intersecting LRAC at point a, with price p_c and quantity q.

Limit pricing is the setting of a monopolist's price at or slightly below the marginal-cost level of potential entrants to the market.

monopolist will maximize its profit by practicing **limit pricing**, or setting the limit price at or slightly below c_e.

Limit-pricing models can become substantially more complicated than the one depicted in Figure 12-9. In dynamic limit-pricing models, for example, the firm's monopoly position erodes over time. The rate at which new firms enter may also depend very much on the gap between the price and the cost of production of potential entrants. F. M. Scherer has pointed out that if the "gap is very large, as when ballpoint pens costing $0.80 were sold at $12.50 in 1945, a veritable torrent of entry may be induced."[9]

Contestable Markets

Limit-pricing theory suggests that potential competition can constrain an industry to behave more competitively than it otherwise would when entry barriers are high. What if entry barriers were nonexistent? Baumol, Panzer, and Willig have argued that if entry and exit are ultrafree, *potential* competition has the same impact as *actual* competition on prices and output. Figure 12-10 shows the case for a natural monopoly.

---

9. F. M. Scherer, *Industrial Market Structure and Economic Performance* (Chicago: Rand McNally, 1970), p. 224. See also Joe S. Bain, "A Note on Pricing in Monopoly and Oligopoly," *American Economic Review* (March 1949), pp. 448–64; Paolo Sylos-Labini, *Oligopoly and Technical Progress* (Cambridge: Harvard University Press, 1962); D. W. Gaskins, Jr., "Dynamic Limit Pricing: Optimal Pricing Under Threat of Entry," *Journal of Economic Theory* (1971), pp. 306–22.

FIGURE 12-11 Price Setting in a Contestable Market That Is Not a Natural Monopoly

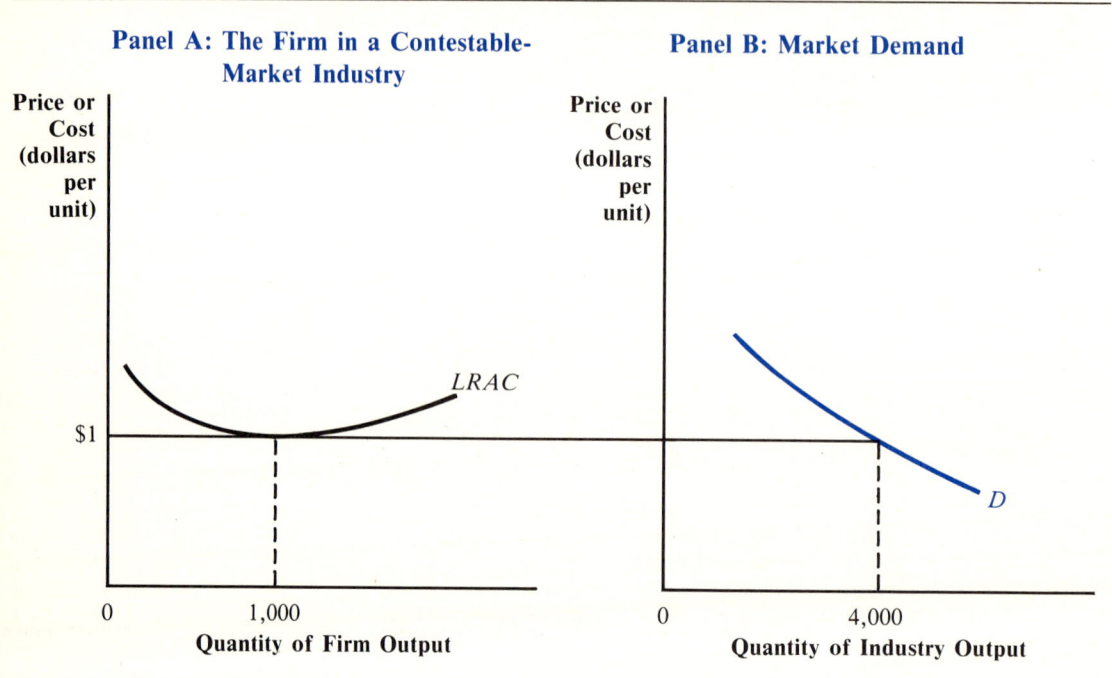

Panel A: The Firm in a Contestable-Market Industry

Panel B: Market Demand

If a contestable-market industry is not a natural monopoly, the price of the product will be set to equal the long-run competitive solution; any higher price invites hit-and-run entrants.

A contestable market is one in which (1) entry and exit by new firms is completely free, (2) new firms can produce with the same costs as the incumbent firms, (3) firms can easily escape their fixed costs by selling their fixed inputs elsewhere (in other words, fixed costs are not sunk costs and can be recovered), and (4) customers buy from the firm (or firms) that first posts the lowest price.

In a **contestable market**, there are no sunk costs, and entry can be hit-and-run. Economic profit is impossible, because a new firm could then enter, charge a slightly lower price, make a quick profit, and exit.

If a firm were a natural monopoly, it would be forced to charge a price equal to its long-run average cost. The firm's technology and costs can be duplicated by potential entrants; there is no advantage to being first. The natural monopolist's limit price, when the market is perfectly contestable, is determined where the market-demand curve intersects the LRAC curve, as in Figure 12-10.

Consider now an industry that requires several firms for economic efficiency, where all firms have access to the same U-shaped LRAC curve and where the cost curve reaches a minimum LRAC at $1 per unit and 1,000 units of output, as in Figure 12-11. To keep matters simple, assume that at the price of $1 exactly 4,000 units of the product are demanded. Efficiency clearly requires that each of the 4 firms produce 1,000 units and charge $1 per unit for the product. As a contestable market, the price of the product would also have to equal $1. If all four firms charged a higher price—say, $1.10—they would face hit-and-run entry. Another firm (or firms) would enter and charge, say, $1.05, make a profit, reduce profit to zero for incumbent firms, and exit. Thus, to prevent the entry of potential competitors, the four firms would produce 1,000 units each and charge exactly $1 per unit. Because the price equals the minimum long-run average cost in Figure 12-11, the price also equals long-run marginal cost—as it would in a perfectly competitive market.

How realistic is the case of contestable markets? The theory implies that such factors as concentration ratios have no bearing on the performance of an industry. Traditional industrial-organization economists sharply dispute the theory. Even in the airlines industry, which is the prototype of a contestable market, it has been found that concentration ratios still play an important role in the determination of the price charged by airlines.[10]

While contestable markets may not be a realistic description of actual industrial markets, the theory has focused attention on one of the weaknesses of concentration ratios: they do not take into account potential competition. Moreover, the shape of future empirical research will bear the mark of the theory of contestable markets. A key hypothesis, suggested by the theory, is that concentration ratios play a smaller role when sunk costs are low; this hypothesis is likely to inspire a number of empirical investigations.

GAME THEORY

When oligopolists do not collude, they must interact strategically. Oligopoly is like a game. As in sports, poker, chess, or war, each player must play in response to the strategies adopted by his or her opponent. In 1944, mathematician John von Neumann and economist Oskar Morgenstern together developed a general approach for studying the strategic interactions among individual agents. All games have certain elements in common: several players, payoffs to each of the players, payoffs to any one player dependent on the strategies followed by all the players. How should the game be played?

There are two types of games: a *zero-sum game* and a *nonzero-sum game*. In a zero-sum game, the players are dividing a constant total pie; thus, the payoff to any one player is at the expense of the other players. Poker and chess are examples of zero-sum games. The sum of the payoffs to each player is a constant, regardless of the strategies followed. In such games, there is pure opposition between the players; there is no incentive to collude.

In a nonzero-sum game, the sum of the payoffs to all the players will

---

10. For a critique of contestable-markets theory, see William G. Shepherd, "'Contestability' vs. Competition," *American Economic Review* 74 (September 1984): 572-87. Diana Strassmann, in "Potential Competition in the Deregulated Airline Industry," working paper, Institute for Policy Analysis, Rice University, November 1987, has found that the airline industry is not a contestable market, because the Herfindahl index is an important determinant of the price/cost margin.

TABLE 12-4   Payoffs in a Zero-Sum Game

		Firm 2 Strategies	
		A	O
Firm 1 Strategies	A	50	75
	O	25	50

depend on the strategies followed. Hence, there will be an incentive to collude or cooperate because the strategies that maximize the joint payoff are optimal from a group standpoint. Our previous examples of cartels and mergers certainly show that oligopoly is a nonzero-sum game. If the oligopolists form a cartel, their joint profits will exceed their profits from independent behavior. The puzzle is to develop a theory of individual behavior in nonzero-sum games.

A *game strategy* is a complete specification of actions on the part of one player. It indicates what the player will do in every particular instance. One of the difficulties of game theory is to specify games in extensive form, where the details concerning every move are exhibited. It is possible to study games such as tic-tac-toe, chess, and poker in terms of such extensive details, but the more difficult is the game, the more unmanageable is the problem. Thus, game theorists usually rely on a simpler method. Games are said to be in strategic form when all the various strategies are simply labeled (for example, 1, 2, 3 or A, B, C), with all the details of moves and countermoves suppressed.

Nash Equilibrium

In economics, an equilibrium usually requires that several players maximize their independent goals in a consistent fashion. Game theory complicates the problem by considering how the payoffs to any one player depend on the strategies followed by all the players. A **Nash equilibrium** (named after mathematician John Nash) has the property that each player maximizes his or her payoff given the strategies chosen by the opposing players.

A **Nash equilibrium** occurs when every player is maximizing his or her payoff given the strategies followed by all the opposing players.

In a Nash equilibrium, no player finds it advantageous to depart from his or her behavior pattern as long as the others continue to behave the way the player believes they are behaving. Because no player alters his or her behavior in such an equilibrium, each player's guess about the strategies of rival players will be correct.

An example of a Nash equilibrium is the famous **prisoners' dilemma game**. The setup for the game is that two bank robbers have been apprehended by

A prisoners' dilemma game is a game between two players in which the Nash equilibrium involves a smaller total payoff to the players than the cooperative solution.

the police; they are being interrogated in separate rooms. If both talk, both go to jail but with 5-year sentences. If one talks and the other remains quiet, the one who talks receives a 6-month sentence, while the silent bank robber gets a 20-year jail sentence. If neither talks, both get a 1-year sentence for carrying a concealed weapon. Each knows that if he or she keeps quiet, both get a light sentence *provided* the other remains quiet; but keeping quiet is risky, because the other prisoner might talk. A situation in which both prisoners keep quiet is *not* a Nash equilibrium because either one of them could improve his or her position if the other remained quiet. If both confess, a Nash equilibrium is achieved. If one confesses, the best the other can do is to also confess.

We have already examined two economic examples of a Nash equilibrium: a Cournot equilibrium and the kinked-demand model. In a Cournot equilibrium, each firm maximizes its profit given the outputs of all the other firms. Each firm supposes the other firms will hold output constant; this assumption will be ratified in equilibrium. In the kinked-demand model, it pays each firm to hold price constant because price cuts lead other firms to cut prices and price hikes are not followed by rivals.

When a Nash equilibrium does not prevail, it pays at least one player to deviate from his or her strategy given the strategies chosen by the remaining players. For example, in a cartel, each member is made better off by breaking the cartel if all the other firms stick to their assigned output shares. Cartels are not Nash equilibria and are, consequently, unstable. Notice that Nash equilibria have a self-enforcing property; it is not necessary to monitor the players, as it is in a cooperative cartel.

The Zero-Sum Game

We begin our study of game theory by examining the zero-sum game. Such games illustrate the critical concepts of payoffs, strategies, and the nature of equilibrium in a game context.

Table 12–4 shows a game in strategic form. There are two players, Firm 1 and Firm 2. Firm 1's strategies are listed along the left of the matrix as *A* and *O*. Strategy *A* is advertising at a certain level; strategy *O* means a zero advertising budget. Firm 2's strategies are listed along the top of the matrix. To obtain a zero-sum game, we assume that the firms are interested only in market share—profits are irrelevant. Thus, what one firm gains the other loses. The entry in each cell of the matrix is the market share of Firm 1 in each situation. For example, if Firms 1 and 2 both choose strategy *A* (advertising), then Firm 1's market share is 50 percent; if Firms 1 and 2 both choose strategy *O* (no advertising), then Firm 1's market share is also 50 percent. If Firm 1 advertises while Firm 2 does not, Firm 1's market share is 75 percent (and vice versa). To simplify, it has been assumed that Firms 1 and 2 are symmetrically situated, but this is not necessary.

What will the rational firm do? Suppose Firm 1 knows Firm 2's strategies in advance (but not vice versa). If Firm 2 advertises, Firm 1 maximizes its

TABLE 12-5 **The Minimax (or Maximin) Principle in a Zero-Sum Game**

		A_2	O_2	Row Minima	
Firm 1 Strategies	A_1	50	75	50*	← Firm 1's Maximin
	O_1	25	50	25	
Column maxima		50*	75		

Firm 2's Minimax ↗

market share by also advertising; if Firm 2 does not advertise, Firm 1 can achieve a 75 percent market share by advertising. Thus, if Firm 1 *knows* what Firm 2 is doing in advance, it will advertise. (Because the game is symmetrical, Firm 2 would also *always* choose to advertise.) However, if Firm 1 had to choose its strategy before knowing Firm 2's strategy, what would it do?

Von Neumann and Morgenstern suggested the **minimax (or maximin) principle of rational behavior:** players should maximize their minimum payoff or minimize their maximum loss. A reasonable way for people to behave is to try to gain as much as possible, or to lose as little as possible, from a skillful opponent whose goals are diametrically opposed. A prudent player should choose a strategy that maximizes the smallest possible gain or minimizes the largest possible loss.

The entries in Table 12-4 show the market shares of Firm 1 for each possible strategy pair. These are Firm 1's gains. Because Firm 2's market share is what is remaining out of 100 percent, the entries also represent Firm 2's *losses*. In Table 12-5, each row shows the possible consequences of any given action by Firm 1; each column shows the possible consequences of any given action by Firm 2. For example, if Firm 1 chooses action A, its market share will be either 50 or 75, depending on Firm 2's strategy. If Firm 2 also chooses action A, Firm 1's payoff is at a minimum—a 50 percent market share. The numbers in the last column of Table 12-5 show the row minima.

If Firm 2 chooses action A, its worst loss occurs when Firm 1 also chooses action A. The maximum in any one column is the worst loss for any action by Firm 2. The bottom row of Table 12-5 shows the column maxima.

Because Firm 2 wishes to minimize Firm 1's market share—and thereby minimize its maximum loss—Firm 2 will follow the minimax strategy—A_2—in Table 12-5. Firm 1 will follow the maximin strategy—A_1. The strategy pair (A_1, A_2) is called a *saddle point*. A saddle pointing in the north/south

*The **minimax (or maximin) principle of rational behavior** is that players in a game should maximize their minimum payoff or minimize their maximum loss.*

TABLE 12-6   **Payoffs in a Nonzero-Sum Game**

		Firm 2 Strategies	
		A_2	O_2
Firm 1 Strategies	A_1	**$10**, $10	**$30**, $0
	O_1	**$0**, $30	**$20**, $20

direction reaches a minimum along a north/south plane and a maximum along a west/east plane in the middle of the saddle. A saddle point is reached if the minimax of Firm 2 equals the maximin of Firm 1. The saddle point also happens to be a Nash equilibrium. Given that one firm advertises, the best response for the other firm is to also advertise.

The Nonzero-Sum Game

The zero-sum-game example may be criticized on the grounds that firms are more interested in profits than in market shares. When profits are used as the payoff, the game must be the nonzero-sum game. Again consider the case of advertising. Suppose advertising simply switches a fixed amount of business between two firms. To keep things simple, suppose that the gross profit available to both firms is $40 (without advertising costs) and that advertising costs $10 per firm. Table 12-6 shows the net profit payoffs (after advertising expenses) to Firms 1 and 2. In each cell, the boldface numbers indicate Firm 1's net profits; the lightface numbers indicate Firm 2's net profits. Again, strategies A and O indicate the advertising and no-advertising strategies of Firms 1 and 2. When both follow the same strategy, they split profits.

Because advertising is assumed not to add to the total amount of business, joint profits are maximized when both firms follow the strategy pair of no advertising: (O_1, O_2). Jointly, the worst situation is when they both advertise, because joint net profits are only $20. If only one firm advertises, joint profits are $30, but profits are asymmetrically distributed. What is the rational action? Firm 1 cannot choose its best strategy unless it knows Firm 2's strategy, and vice versa.

The maximum joint profit is not a Nash equilibrium because it pays each firm to advertise given that the other firm does not advertise. The Nash point is (A_1, A_2), where each firm is maximizing its profit given the strategy of the other firm. The advertising game in Table 12-6 is also equivalent to the prisoners' dilemma game, because both would be better off if they agreed not to advertise, just as two prisoners would be better off if they could somehow agree to remain silent.

SUMMARY

1. The n-firm concentration ratio shows the percentage of domestic shipments accounted for by the largest n firms in an industry. The Herfindahl index measures concentration as the sum of the squared market shares of all the firms in the industry. There have been no dramatic tendencies for concentration ratios to increase over the years. Measures of concentration do not take into account such factors as free entry and foreign competition.

2. In monopolistic competition, there is free entry into an industry producing a heterogeneous product. In the long run, industry profits tend toward zero. Thus, for each firm price must equal long-run average cost. This price is determined by the point where the firm's demand curve is just tangent to the $LRAC$ curve, where marginal revenue equals long-run marginal cost.

3. In a cartel, each firm must agree to cut its output to the point where for the firm $MR > MC$ but for the industry $MR = MC$. The individual firm's marginal revenue approximates the cartel price. Thus, each firm has an incentive to cheat. Cartels have a history of instability.

4. In Cournot oligopoly, a homogeneous product is produced by a fixed number of firms. Each firm assumes nonretaliation on the part of its rivals. The Cournot oligopoly price will tend to be between the competitive price and the monopoly price. There is no incentive for mergers in the Cournot-oligopoly model, unless the merger results in monopoly.

5. In the kinked-demand model, firms produce a heterogeneous product. Each firm assumes price cuts, but not price hikes, will be matched by rivals. The demand curve has a kink around the current price, which will be insensitive to cost increases. The empirical evidence appears to support the Cournot model more than the kinked-demand model.

6. In limit-pricing models, potential competition plays a role in determining market price. In the contestable-market model, hit-and-run entry keeps price equal to average production cost, and if there is no natural monopoly, price will equal the minimum $LRAC$.

7. A Nash equilibrium is achieved if there is no incentive for any individual player to deviate from his or her strategy given the strategies of the remaining players. In the prisoners' dilemma game, the cooperative solution is not a Nash equilibrium because the individual player can gain by acting independently, given that the other attempts cooperation.

Table A

Firm	Market Share
1	0.5
2	0.2
3	0.1
4	0.05
5	0.05
6	0.04
7	0.03
8	0.03

QUESTIONS AND PROBLEMS

1. What are some problems with n-firm concentration ratios and the Herfindahl index?

2. Using the data in Table A, calculate the 4-firm concentration ratio and the Herfindahl index.

3. Calculate the 4-firm concentration ratio and the Herfindahl index for an industry consisting of 10 equal-sized firms.

4. Two firms with market shares of 0.2 and 0.5 merge. What would happen to the Herfindahl index?

5. Compare and contrast monopolistic competition in the long run with perfect competition in the long run.

6. Discuss the inefficiencies involved in monopolistic competition and what the government can do to control them.

7. Firm 1 has the MC curve $MC_1 = 0.5Q_1$; Firm 2 has the MC curve $MC_2 = Q_2$; for Firm 3, $MC_3 = 1.5Q_3$. What is the MC curve for the cartel?

8. Consider a Cournot oligopoly with two firms. Each firm faces the constant marginal and average cost of production, $c = \$2$. If the market-demand curve is $P = 26 - 2Q$, draw the reaction curves and calculate the output for each firm, x, the industry output, Q, and the market price, P.

9. Consider the Cournot oligopoly in Table 12-3. Assume there are 5 firms. Assume 3 of the firms merge, so that the new oligopoly consists of 3 equal-sized firms. Is there any economic incentive for the 3 firms to merge? Explain.

Table B

	Firm 2's Strategies		
	A	B	C
Firm 1's Strategies I	$5	$1	$1
II	4	2	3
III	9	1	2

10. Why is price relatively stable in the kinked-demand model?

11. How does a Nash equilibrium relate to a Cournot equilibrium?

12. Why is a cartel not a Nash equilibrium?

13. What is the Nash equilibrium in a prisoners' dilemma game?

14. Firm 1's profits equal Firm 2's losses regardless of the strategies followed by the two firms. Are the firms involved in a zero-sum or non-zero-sum game? What is the Nash equilibrium for the payoff in Table B, which shows Firm 1's profits and Firm 2's losses?

15. In problem (14), is the Nash equilibrium the same as the minimax solution?

SUGGESTED READINGS

Baumol, W. J. "Contestable Markets: An Uprising in The Theory of Industry Structure." *American Economic Review* 72 (March 1972): 1–15.

Chamberlin, E. *The Theory of Monopolistic Competition*. Cambridge: Harvard University Press, 1933.

Fellner, W. J. *Competition Among the Few*. New York: Knopf, 1949.

Friedman, J. W. *Oligopoly Theory*. Cambridge: Cambridge University Press, 1983.

Robinson, J. *The Economics of Imperfect Competition*. London: Macmillan, 1933.

Ruffin, R. J. "Cournot Oligopoly and Competitive Behavior." *Review of Economic Studies* 38 (October 1971): 493–502.

Salant, S. W., S. Switzer, and R. J. Reynolds. "Losses from Horizontal Merger: The Effects of an Exogenous Change in Industry Structure on Cournot-Nash Equilibrium." *Quarterly Journal of Economics* 98 (May 1983): 185–99.

Scherer, F. M. *Industrial Market Structure and Economic Performance*. Chicago: Rand McNally, 1971.

Shepherd, W. J. "'Contestability' vs. Competition." *American Economic Review* 74 (September 1984): 572–87.

Stigler, G. J. "The Kinky Oligopoly Demand Curve and Rigid Prices." *Journal of Political Economy* 55 (October 1947). Reprinted in Stigler, *The Organization of Industry*, Homewood, Ill.: Richard D. Irwin, 1968, chap. 18.

CHAPTER 13

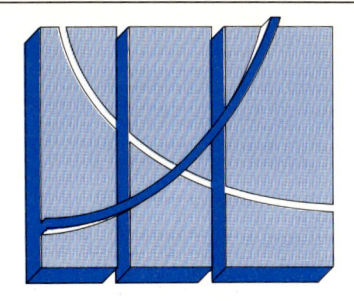

COMPETITIVE RESOURCE MARKETS

Preceding chapters have examined the markets for outputs, but outputs are produced by inputs, or resources. The major classes of productive resources are land, labor, and capital. The major differences between these resources are on the supply side: land comes from the bounty of nature; the supply of labor is determined by complex economic, social, and biological forces; capital is a produced resource. On the demand side, the theory of output determination examined in previous chapters also constitutes the theory of input determination. Any output decision is simultaneously an input decision. Thus, we have already implicitly taken into account the theory of demand for inputs. This chapter explicitly describes laws of demand and supply for inputs.

One important difference between input markets and output markets is that input markets tend to be more competitive. The reason is very simple: every industry uses land, labor, and capital. In competitive output markets, each firm faces competition from other firms in the industry, but in input markets, each firm faces competition from firms in every industry, except in cases where productive factors are industry-specific (for example, coal mining).

This chapter will focus on the general features of the demand and supply for input factors. The demand—whether for land, labor, or capital—is derived from the demand for outputs, and each input is hired to maximize the firm's profits. The first part of this chapter explains the theory of derived demand; the second part describes special features of the supply of land, and labor. Chapter 15 examines the special features of capital.

THE LAWS OF DERIVED DEMAND

The demand curve for an input is derived from the demand for the product itself: if demand for the product were zero, there would be no demand for any of its inputs.

We will assume a competitive industry composed of potentially many firms and, for simplicity, we will assume that every firm faces constant returns to scale. Under these circumstances, it makes no difference how many firms are in the industry—the number may be small or infinite. In Chapter 8, we proved a proposition known as Shepherd's lemma, which states that if the cost of an input (say, the wage rate, w, for a particular kind of labor) rises by a small amount, the increase in the total cost of producing the good, ΔC, rises by exactly the amount of the input being used (for example, L) times the increase in the price of the input, ΔW. Thus, Shepherd's lemma may be written as:

$$\Delta C = \Delta W(L). \tag{1}$$

Under constant returns to scale, the change in average costs, AC, will be:

$$\Delta AC = \Delta W(L/Q), \tag{2}$$

where Q is the output of the firm. Labor is only one of the inputs. Assume that labor costs are the proportion θ of total costs, so that $\theta = wL/C$. Rewriting that as $L = \theta C/w$ and substituting in Equation (2) yields

$$\Delta AC = \Delta W\left(\frac{\theta C}{w} \div Q\right) = \frac{\Delta W}{w} \times \theta\left(\frac{C}{Q}\right). \tag{3}$$

And because $C/Q = AC$, we can write

$$\Delta AC/AC = \theta(\Delta W/w). \tag{4}$$

In other words, Shepherd's lemma says that if wages increase by, say, 2 percent, the average unit costs of production will rise by a fraction of 2 percent equal to the share of total costs that are labor costs. The same is true of any input.

Alfred Marshall (and, later, Sir John Hicks) stated five laws of derived demand.

1. *The higher is the elasticity of demand for a product, the higher is the elasticity of demand for any input.* This law follows directly from Shepherd's lemma. The increase in the price of a product in long-run competitive equilibrium is the same as the increase in the average cost of production. According to Shepherd's lemma, then, the increase in product price is proportional to the increase in the cost of the input. Thus, when the cost of an input rises, the decrease in the quantity of the product demanded will depend on the price elasticity of demand for the product and the increase in the product's price.

2. *The more elastic is the supply of cooperating factors of production, the more elastic is the demand for a given input.* Suppose the price of

agricultural labor falls. Farmers will hire more labor input and attempt to expand output; the farmer's demand for farmland will also increase. If more farmland is available on fixed terms (if there is a perfectly elastic supply of farmland), the elasticity of demand for farm labor will be higher than if no additional farmland is available. When additional farmland cannot be hired without driving up land prices, average costs of production will not fall by as much; accordingly, the price of the product will not fall as much, which reduces the elasticity of demand for the inputs. The smaller is the elasticity of supply of farmland, the smaller is the elasticity of demand for farm labor.

3. *The easier it is to substitute one input for another, the larger is the elasticity of demand for the input.* This law simply reflects the fact that if there are many substitutes for something, a higher price will motivate demanders to shift to the substitutes. If secretaries are close substitutes for clerks, an increase in the wage rate for secretaries will motivate business firms to shift to hiring more clerks.

4. *The elasticity of demand for an input is larger in the long run than in the short run.* This principle follows from the fact that in the long run, the firm can partially escape an increase in the price of an input by substituting cheaper inputs. For example, if wages rise, machines can be substituted for labor in the long run.

5. *The greater is the proportion of an input's cost in the total costs of production, the larger is the elasticity of demand for the input, provided the elasticity of substitution is sufficiently small.* Alfred Marshall proved this law for the case in which inputs are used in absolutely fixed proportions. If θ is the share of labor cost in total costs then, from Shepherd's lemma, it follows that $\Delta AC/AC = \theta(\Delta W/w)$. The higher is θ, the higher will be the increase in average costs in response to an increase in wages. Since the increase in average costs equals the increase in wages, the larger is θ the larger will be the reduction in the demand for labor that results from an increase in wages. Hicks showed that Marshall's argument depended very much on his assumption that the elasticity of substitution was zero.[1]

PROFIT MAXIMIZATION ON THE INPUT SIDE

Suppose that a firm produces a single output by using several inputs, v_1, v_2, v_3, and so forth. The firm's output is governed by the following production function, where Q is the quantity of the output good and n is the number of inputs:

$$Q = f(v_1, v_2, \ldots, v_n). \tag{5}$$

---

1. John R. Hicks, *The Theory of Wages* (London: Macmillan, 1932), showed that the higher is the share of an input in total costs, the higher is the elasticity of input demand, provided that the elasticity of demand for the product exceeds the elasticity of substitution between the inputs. (See the Appendix to this chapter for a simplified proof.)

The marginal (physical) product (MP) of an input is the change in output divided by the change in the number of units of the input (holding other inputs constant).

Each input has a **marginal (physical) product** (*MP*) and

$$MP_i = \Delta Q / \Delta v_i. \tag{6}$$

The firm's output is sold on the market for some price, *P*, and generates a certain revenue, *TR*, so that

$$TR(Q) = P(Q)Q, \tag{7}$$

where $P(Q)$ is the inverse demand function for the firm's product. As always, the firm has a certain *marginal revenue* (*MR*):

$$MR = P(Q) + Q\Delta P/\Delta Q. \tag{8}$$

Finally, the firm faces costs for its inputs, $r_1, r_2, r_3, \ldots$, with r_i being the rental price of input v_i. The firm is assumed to face perfect competition on the input side, so that the rental costs are given parameters.

In previous chapters, we combined the production function and input costs into a cost function for output and showed that profit is maximized when marginal revenue equals marginal cost, or when $MR = MC$. Now, instead of deriving a cost function, let us consider the demand for inputs directly. The firm will hire each input until the marginal benefit of each input equals its marginal input cost. In the present case, the marginal input cost is r_i. What is the marginal benefit of an input?

Each extra input adds MP_i to the firm's output. This output is sold at a price, *P*. The **value of the firm's marginal product** (*VMP*) is then

The value of the firm's marginal product (VMP) is the price of the product multiplied by the marginal product of the factor input.

$$VMP_i = P(MP_i). \tag{9}$$

For example, if the marginal product of a unit of labor input is 10 bushels of wheat and wheat sells for $3 a bushel, the value of the marginal product of that input is $3 (10) = $30.

The marginal benefit of any input to the firm is the amount an extra unit of the input adds to the firm's revenue. The firm's **marginal revenue product** (*MRP*) for any input is defined:

The marginal revenue product (MRP) for any input is the marginal revenue for the product multiplied by the marginal product of the input.

$$MRP_i = \Delta TR/\Delta v_i. \tag{10}$$

But $\Delta TR = MR(\Delta Q)$. In other words, the change in the firm's revenue is always the product of its marginal revenue and the change in its output, because marginal revenue is the change in revenue per unit of change in output. Thus,

$$MRP_i = MR\Delta Q/\Delta v_i = MR(MP_i). \tag{11}$$

If the firm is competitive on the output side, the value of the marginal product is also the marginal revenue product. Using the wheat example, $MRP = MR(MP) = \$3 (10) = \$30$. But if the firm has monopoly power on the output side, so that $P > MR$, the firm's *VMP* will exceed *MRP* for every input.

$$VMP_i > MRP_i \text{ if } P > MR \tag{12}$$
$$VMP_i = MRP_i \text{ if } P = MR \tag{13}$$

THE ONE-INPUT CASE

The value of the marginal product, VMP, is $P \cdot MP$; the marginal revenue product, MRP, is $MR \cdot MP$. If the firm has a monopoly on the product market, $VMP > MRP$; if the firm is competitive in the product market, $VMP = MRP$.

The conditions for profit maximization from the input side are summed up in Equation (14) and are arrived at as follows. If MRP_i is greater than r_i, the firm should hire one more unit of input v_i. If the marginal revenue product of labor is $20 and the wage rate is $12, then an additional worker adds $20 to revenue and $12 to cost—or adds the difference, $8, to profit. The firm's increase in profit is the difference $(MRP_i - r_i)$. Analogously, if MRP_i is less than r_i, the firm is hiring too many units of input v_i. The firm is maximizing its profit when

$$MRP_1 = MR \cdot MP_1 = r_1,$$
$$MRP_2 = MR \cdot MP_2 = r_2,$$

and

$$MRP_N = MR \cdot MP_N = r_N, \qquad (14)$$

where N is the number of inputs.

The conditions for profit maximization boil down to the $MR = MC$ condition of previous chapters. Each line of Equation (14) can be rewritten as follows for every i:

$$MR = \frac{r_i}{MP_i}. \qquad (15)$$

But things equal to a common number are equal to each other; thus,

$$\frac{r_1}{MP_1} = \frac{r_2}{MP_2} = \ldots = \frac{r_N}{MP_N} = MC. \qquad (16)$$

The common value of r_i/MP_i is the long-run marginal cost of production (see Chapter 8). Combining Equations (15) and (16) shows that $MR = MC$, just as in earlier chapters.

Profit maximization on the input side requires that factor prices be equal to the marginal revenue product of each input and implies that marginal revenue equals marginal cost on the output side.

THE ONE-INPUT CASE

Assume that a firm produces a single output with a single input—say, labor. The firm's production function is $Q = f(L)$. Figure 13-1 shows curves for the average and marginal products of labor, as analyzed in Chapter 7.

FIGURE 13-1 The Relationship Between Average and Marginal Products

The MP_L curve intersects the AP_L curve at its maximum point.

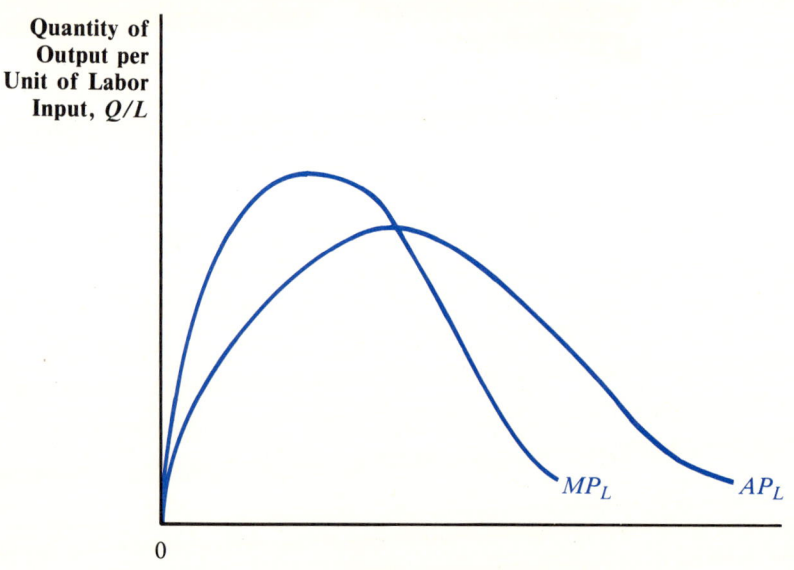

Quantity of Output per Unit of Labor Input, Q/L vs *Quantity of Labor Input, L*, showing MP_L and AP_L curves.

The **average revenue product** (*ARP*) of an input is total revenue divided by the total level of factor input.

The firm is competitive on both the input and the output sides, so the product price, P, equals marginal revenue. The price of the product measures the firm's average revenue—revenue per unit of output. The **average revenue product** (*ARP*) is defined as total revenue divided by total labor input:

$$ARP_L = \frac{P(Q)}{L}. \tag{17}$$

When a firm is competitive on the output side, we know that $MRP_L = VMP_L$. (The case in which a firm has a monopoly on the output market will be described in the next chapter.)

Figure 13-2 shows the same firm's average revenue product (ARP_L) and marginal revenue product (MRP_L) curves, which exactly reflect the average and marginal product curves in Figure 13-1. According to the average/marginal rule, the MRP_L curve intersects the ARP_L curve at its maximum point. If w is the wage rate, then according to the rule stated in Equation (14), the firm maximizes profit when $w = MRP_L$; that is,

$$w = MRP_L = MR \cdot MP_L = P \cdot MP_L. \tag{18}$$

Because $w/MP_L = MC$, it also follows that Equation (18) is exactly the same as $MC = P$, the profit-maximizing rule in the perfectly competitive case. In Figure 13-2, the profit-maximizing point is e, where the wage rate is w and the quantity of labor demanded is L_0. The firm's profit is the shaded area $abew$ because costs equal $w \times L_0$ and revenue is the rectangle $0abc$.

THE ONE-INPUT CASE

FIGURE 13-2   **Maximizing Profit with One Input**

This firm maximizes profit at point e, where $w = MRP_L$; the shaded area represents profit. The firm's demand curve for labor is the portion of the MRP_L curve below the ARP_L curve.

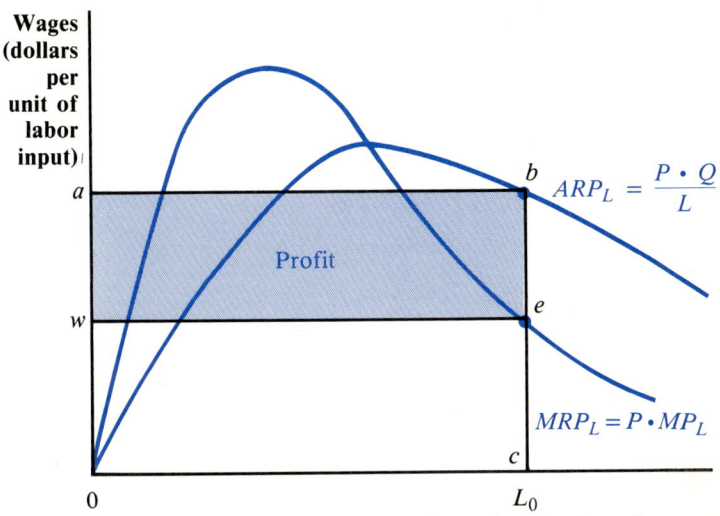

[Graph: Wages (dollars per unit of labor input) vs. Firm Quantity of Labor Input (worker hours). Shows $ARP_L = \frac{P \cdot Q}{L}$ curve and $MRP_L = P \cdot MP_L$ curve. Profit rectangle $abce$ shaded, with wage w intersecting MRP_L at point e at labor quantity L_0.]

The firm's demand curve for labor is the heavier portion of the MRP_L curve, below the ARP_L curve. If the wage rate exceeded the maximum ARP_L, as in Figure 13-3, it follows that for any input level the firm's variable costs, WL, will exceed total revenue. The firm would, therefore, lose that

FIGURE 13-3   **A Shutdown Case with One Input**

If the wage rate, w, exceeds the maximum average revenue product, costs exceed revenue and the firm should shut down. The firm loses the amount indicated by the shaded area if it hires L units of labor at wage rate w.

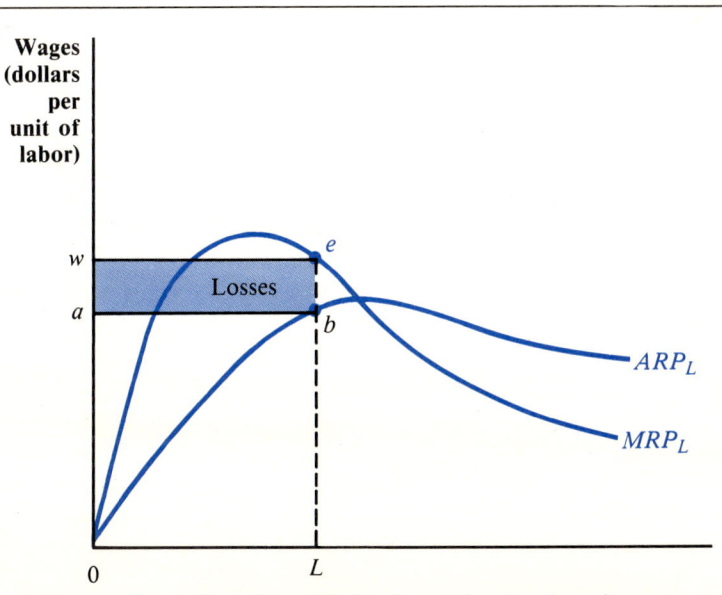

[Graph: Wages (dollars per unit of labor) vs. Quantity of Labor Input (worker hours). Shows ARP_L and MRP_L curves with wage line w above maximum of ARP_L. Losses rectangle shaded between points a, w, e, b at labor quantity L.]

PRACTICE EXERCISE 13-1

Q. A farmer produces wheat according to the production function given in Table A. The price of wheat is $3 per bushel.

a. Draw the ARP_L, MRP_L, and VMP_L curves.

b. How many workers would the firm employ if the wage were $29 per worker? How many if the wage were $17 per worker?

Table A

Quantity of Labor Input (worker hours), L	Quantity of Firm Output, Q
0	0
1	6
2	16
3	24
4	30
5	34
6	36

Table B

Quantity of Labor Input (worker hours), L	Revenue (dollars), $TR = P \cdot Q$	Average Revenue Product of Labor (dollars), ARP_L	Marginal Revenue Product of Labor (dollars), MRP_L
0	0	—	
			18.00
1	18.00	18.00	
			30.00
2	48.00	24.00	
			24.00
3	72.00	24.00	
			18.00
4	90.00	22.50	
			12.00
5	102.00	20.40	
			6.00
6	108.00	18.00	

A. See Table B. Multiplying Q by \$3 shows the revenue produced by labor. Because $P = MR$, $VMP_L = MRP_L$. If the wage (W) = \$29, the firm would hire no workers because \$29 exceeds ARP_L for any level of the labor input; the firm would lose money for any L. If W = \$17, the firm would maximize profit for $L = 4$, because the fourth unit of labor adds \$18 in revenue and the fifth adds only \$12.

portion of variable costs that exceeds total revenue plus any fixed costs. Notice that

$$W > ARP_L = P \cdot AP_L, \quad \text{or}$$
$$W/AP_L = AVC > P. \quad (19)$$

In other words, when the wage rate exceeds ARP_L, the situation is equivalent to revenue falling short of average variable costs: it pays the firm to shut down. If the firm in Figure 13-3 hired L units of labor, total revenue would be the rectangle $0abL$, and total costs would be larger by the shaded rectangle $weba$. Thus, only that portion of MRP_L below ARP_L should be considered.

THE TWO-INPUT CASE

The two-input case provides for a richer analysis of the demand for factors. In Chapters 7 and 8, we studied production isoquants. Figure 13-4 reviews the theory of cost minimization for the two-input case. If the firm wishes to produce output level Q_0, the minimum cost of production is achieved with the input combination (L_0, K_0). The firm's costs are C, with w being the wage rate of labor and r the rental rate on capital. At the cost-minimizing point e, the slope of the isoquant equals the slope of the isocost line, or:

$$MP_L/MP_K = w/r;$$
$$w/MP_L = r/MP_K = LRMC. \quad (20)$$

The common ratio is the level of long-run marginal costs, $LRMC$ (see Chapter 8).

The Elasticity of Substitution

In Figure 13-4 the optimal *capital/labor ratio* is K_0/L_0 for the given *wage/rent ratio*. When the wage/rent ratio rises, the capital/labor ratio also rises, and vice versa. Because w/r equals the marginal rate of technical substitution of capital for labor, the response of K/L to w/r measures the **elasticity of substitution** (see Chapter 7).

FIGURE 13-4   **Cost Minimization with Two Inputs**

Costs are minimized at point e, where the slope of the isoquant Q_0 equals the slope of the isocost curve, TC. Quantities K_0 and L_0 are the optimal amounts of the two inputs, capital and labor.

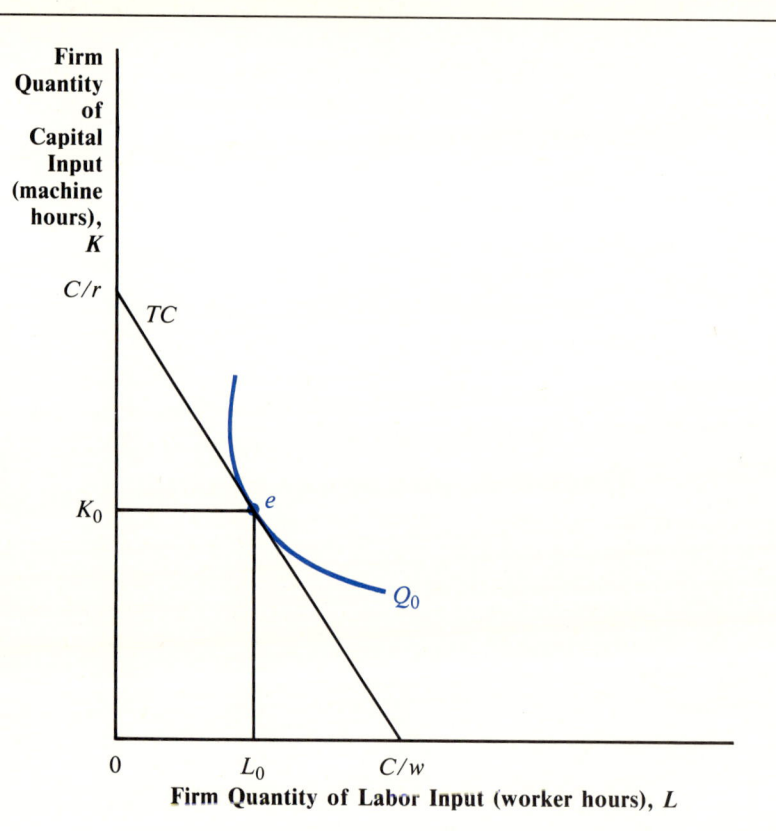

Firm Quantity of Capital Input (machine hours), K — vertical axis with C/r, TC, K_0, point e, isoquant Q_0.

Firm Quantity of Labor Input (worker hours), L — horizontal axis with 0, L_0, C/w.

The **elasticity of substitution** is

$$\sigma = \frac{\%\Delta K - \%\Delta L}{\%\Delta W - \%\Delta R},$$

where a term such as $\%\Delta K$ is defined as $\Delta K/K$, which is the proportionate or percentage change in a variable.

Figure 13-5 shows that the higher is the elasticity of substitution, the higher will be the elasticity of demand for an input because the substitution effect of a change in input prices is larger when elasticity of substitution is higher. In the theory of input demand, the substitution effect is the impact of a change in input cost on input demand, holding output constant. In Panel A of Figure 13-5, the elasticity of substitution is low; in Panel B, the elasticity of substitution is relatively high. When the cost of labor falls, the quantity of labor demanded increases from L_0 to L_1. The increase in labor demanded is larger in Panel B than in Panel A because the elasticity of substitution is higher.

The larger is the elasticity of substitution—that is, the easier it is to substitute one input for another—the larger is the elasticity of demand for an input.

FIGURE 13-5 Elasticity of Substitution of Capital for Labor

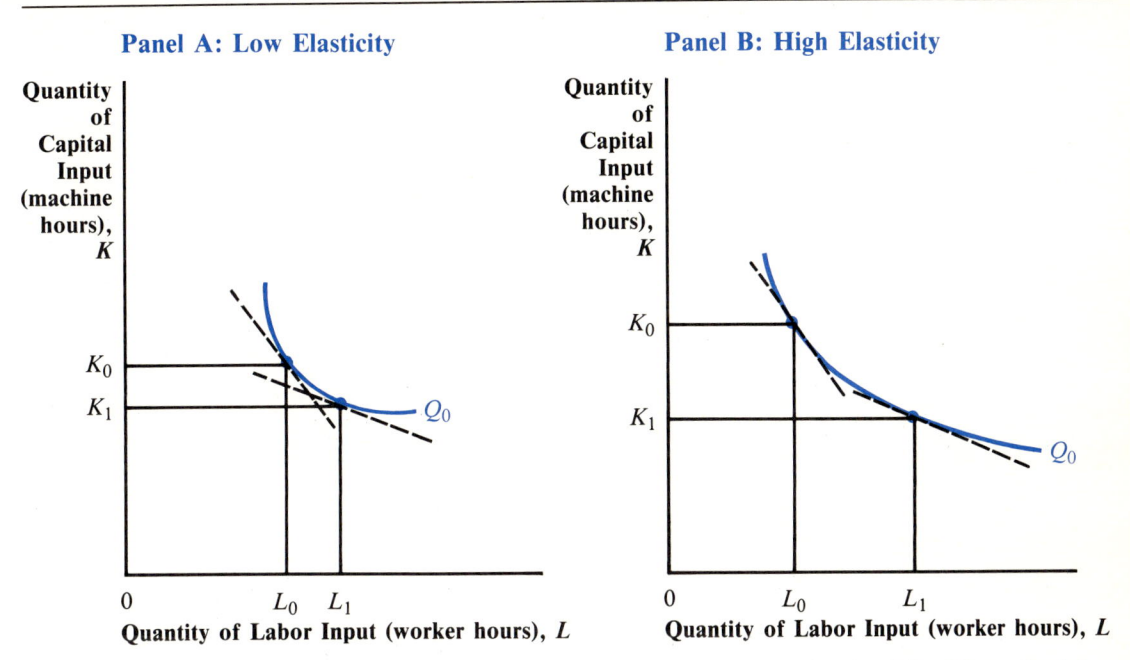

Panel A: Low Elasticity

Panel B: High Elasticity

When the wage rate for labor falls, the ratio w/r is reduced and the ratio K/L also falls. When elasticity of substitution is higher, as in Panel B, the effect of the wage reduction is an increase in quantity of labor demanded (the difference between L_0 and L_1) that is greater than the increase shown in Panel A, where elasticity is lower.

Relative Factor Shares

The elasticity of substitution is related to the relative shares of labor and capital as the elasticity of demand is related to total revenue. The relative share of labor income to capital income is

$$wL/rK \quad \text{or} \quad (w/r)(L/K). \tag{21}$$

As w/r rises, L/K falls (just as when P rises, Q falls). When $\sigma = 1$, the change in L/K just offsets the change in w/r, because the percentage change in K/L equals the percentage change in w/r. No change in wL/rK would occur when $\sigma = 1$. But in the case where $\sigma < 1$, the percentage change in K/L would be less than the percentage change in w/r, so that an increase in w/r would not be offset by the fall in L/K; accordingly, if w/r increased, wL/rK would increase. Finally, if $\sigma > 1$, then the percentage change in K/L would be greater than the percentage change in w/r. In this last case, an increase in w/r is more than offset by the fall in L/K, so that wL/rK then falls.

FIGURE 13-6 Profit Maximization and Long-Run Demand for Labor

Long-run demand for labor is more elastic than short-run demand, indicated by the MRP_L curves. Reducing the wage from w_0 to w_1 shifts the curve for the marginal revenue product of labor to the right as capital input increases from K_0 to K_1 and as labor input increases from L_0 to L_1. Optimal combinations like e_0 and e_1 form the curve representing long-run demand for labor.

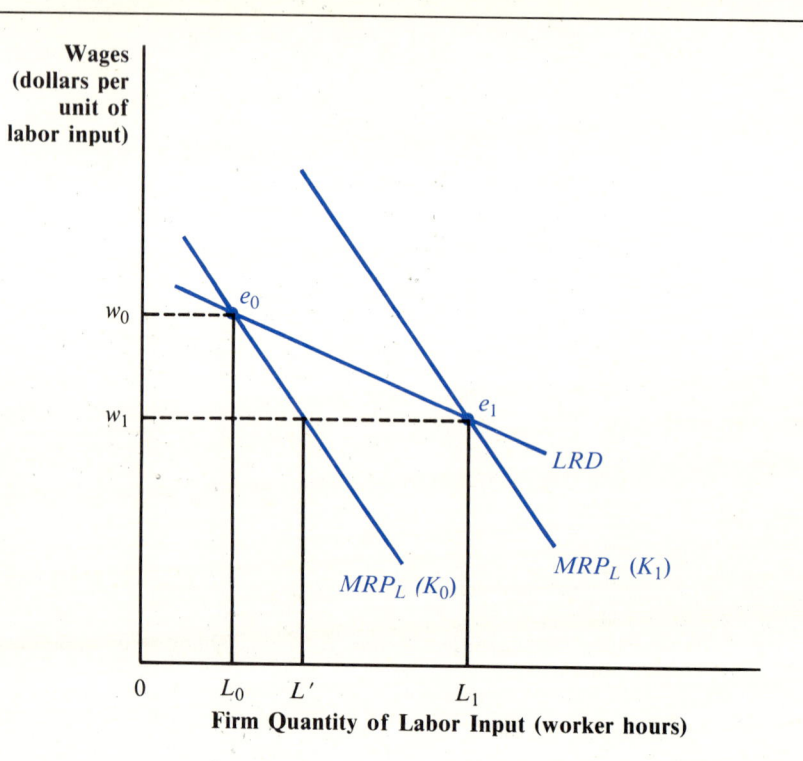

A simple application of the role of elasticity of substitution would be the consequences of a change in the relative supplies of labor and capital. Suppose a country allowed immigration of labor, so that the ratio L/K increased. What would happen to the share of income going to labor in the economy? If elasticity were less than one, the w/r ratio would fall so much that wL/rK, the relative share of labor income, would also fall.

The Long-Run Demand for Labor

Figures 13–4 and 13–5 showed how cost-minimizing inputs are chosen, given an output level. Allocating inputs is only half of the story; the firm must also choose the profit-maximizing level of output. For example, when the price of labor falls, costs will fall, and the firm must increase its output. Profit maximization requires that all inputs be adjusted until factor prices equal marginal revenue products. The firm chooses, say, a level of labor input, given the demand for its product. As we learned earlier, the firm maximizes profit by hiring both labor and capital until

$$MRP_L = w \quad \text{and} \quad MRP_K = r. \tag{22}$$

These two conditions must both be satisfied. If the marginal product of labor

> **EXAMPLE 13–1** Empirical Wage Elasticities of Demand

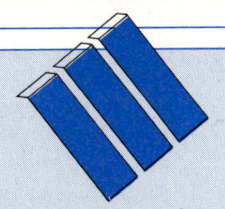

The wage elasticity of demand for labor for the economy as a whole is estimated at −0.3. In other words, the demand for labor is generally inelastic. At the industry level, wage elasticities vary widely. The accompanying table shows some representative estimates for coal mining, manufacturing, and retail trade. The estimates vary from a low of −0.09 to a high of −1.3. In general, retail trade has a more elastic demand for labor than manufacturing, which is part of the general phenomenon that there is greater substitutability between capital inputs and nonproduction labor than between capital inputs and production labor.

Industry	Long-Run Wage Elasticity of Demand
Coal mining	
Underground	−0.98
Surface	−0.86
Manufacturing	−0.09 to −0.62
Retail trade	−0.34 to −1.20
State and local government	
Employees in education	−1.06
Noneducation employees	−0.38

Source: Ronald G. Ehrenberg and Robert S. Smith, *Modern Labor Economics: Theory and Public Policy,* 2nd ed. (Glenview, Ill.: Scott, Foresman, 1985), pp. 99–102.

depends on the quantity of capital services utilized by the firm, one equation cannot be solved independently of the other.

Figure 13–6 compares long-run demand for labor with short-run demand for labor. Suppose that at wage rate w_0 and rental rate r_0, the firm hires L_0 and K_0 units of labor and capital and that profit is maximized at point e_0. The marginal revenue product of labor depends on the level of capital services, K_0. We assume that labor and capital are complements, in the sense that adding more capital increases the marginal product of labor and adding more labor increases the marginal product of capital. If the wage rate falls to w_1, holding the capital input constant, the firm increases its labor inputs to L' in the short run. But the increase in labor input will increase the marginal product of capital. Hence, in the long run, the firm's capital input increases from, say, K_0 to K_1. The MRP_L curve shifts to the right to $MRP_L(K_1)$. At the wage rate w_1, the firm's optimal quantity of labor is L_1. The long-run demand-for-labor curve, LRD, runs through the points e_0 and e_1 and is more elastic than the short-run demand-for-labor curves. (See Example 13–1.)

If labor and capital were substitutes, in the sense that more labor would

FIGURE 13-7 Industry Demand for an Input

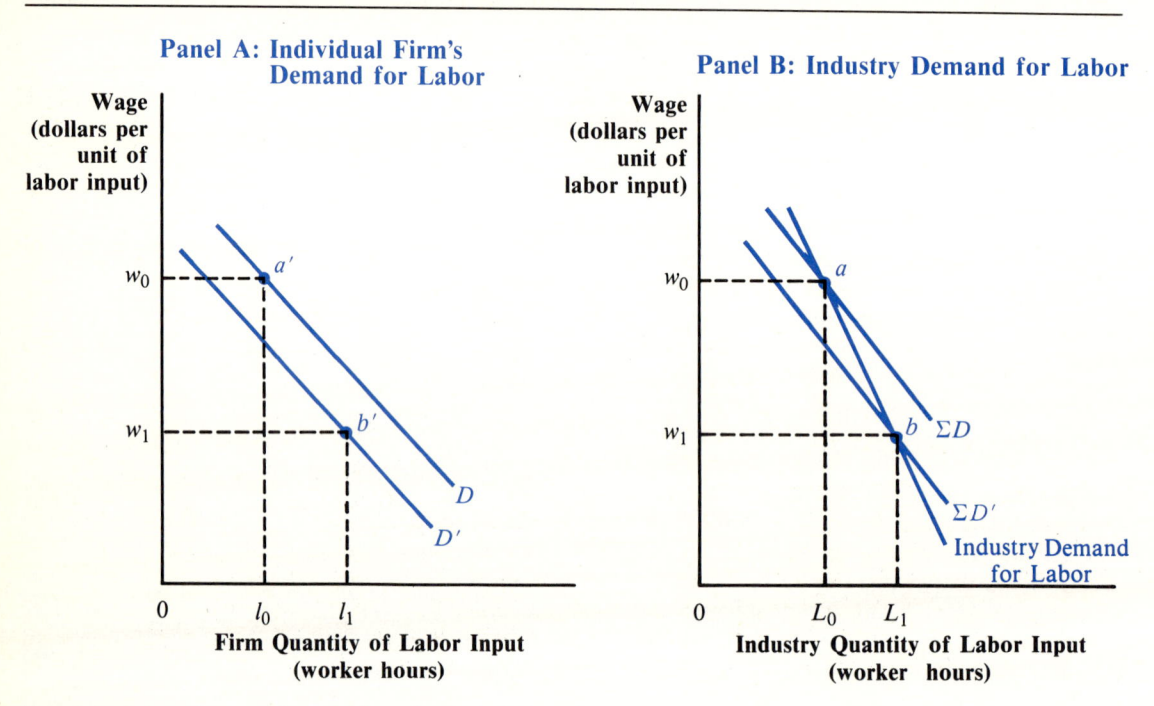

Panel A: Individual Firm's Demand for Labor

Wage (dollars per unit of labor input) vs. Firm Quantity of Labor Input (worker hours). Points a' at (l_0, w_0) and b' at (l_1, w_1) on curves D and D'.

Panel B: Industry Demand for Labor

Wage (dollars per unit of labor input) vs. Industry Quantity of Labor Input (worker hours). Points a at (L_0, w_0) and b at (L_1, w_1) on curves ΣD and $\Sigma D'$, with Industry Demand for Labor curve.

Panel A shows the quantity of labor demanded, l_0, when the wage rate is w_0 and the price of the output product is p. Panel B shows the sum of all such curves at price p, the price at which consumers will purchase the given level of industry output. The aggregate demand for labor at wage w_0 and price p is L_0, at point a. If the wage rate falls to w_1, the firm uses more labor (l_1) and produces more output. Product price falls to p' and the labor-demand curve shifts downward. Aggregate demand is then L_1, at point b in Panel B. The adjusted industry-demand curve is the locus of points such as a and b, where a given wage rate intersects the aggregate input-demand curve for a particular price. The adjusted demand curve is less elastic than any of the aggregate-demand curves.

reduce the marginal product of capital and more capital would reduce the marginal product of labor, the conclusion would be unaltered. In that case, capital input would decrease instead of increase, but a decrease in the capital input would also shift the MRP_L curve to the right.

The long-run demand curve for any input is more elastic than the short-run demand curve for the input.

INDUSTRY DEMAND FOR AN INPUT

In a competitive industry, how does a *firm's* elasticity of demand for an input compare to the *industry's* elasticity of demand? We showed in Chapter 5 that the market demand for a consumer good is just the aggregate demand of all the consumers in the market; the elasticity of demand for the market is just the average elasticity of each consumer. The same result, however, is *not* true of inputs! The demand for inputs is a demand *derived* from the sale of outputs. What one firm can do, all firms together cannot do. One firm can sell more of the good without lowering the product price; but when all firms try to sell more of the good, the price of the product must fall. A drop in the product price reduces the value of the marginal product to the industry faster than it reduces the value of the marginal product to the firm; thus, the industry's demand is less elastic than the firm's demand.

Figure 13-7 demonstrates how industry demand is related to the simple sum of firm demands. Assume the industry is perfectly competitive (so that $MRP = VMP$). The firm's demand curve D in Panel A of Figure 13-7 is based on a particular product price—say, p. The horizontal sum of the D curves of all firms in the industry is ΣD in Panel B.

In equilibrium, at the product price p and the prevailing wage rate, consumers just purchase the corresponding output that is produced. Suppose that quantity of output corresponds to the aggregate input level L_0 and the market wage w_0. When the wage rate is w_0, the representative firm hires L_0.

Now let us assume that the price of the input falls to w_1. As each firm attempts to move down demand curve D, more aggregate output is produced and the product price must fall from p to p'. The smaller is the price elasticity of demand for the product, the more the product price will fall. Accordingly, the individual firm's demand curve must shift to the left—say, to D'—to reflect the smaller product price. This shift in individual demand shifts ΣD to $\Sigma D'$. At the wage rate, w_1, therefore, only the aggregate input quantity L_1 is demanded. The industry demand curve for the labor input is the locus of points such as a and b and is less elastic than the simple, unadjusted horizontal sum of the individual firms' demand curves at any given price level.

The industry demand curve for an input will be more elastic the more elastic is the demand for the product labor helps to produce. When the price of an input falls, costs fall and more of the product is produced. The price of the product falls less the more elastic is the demand for the product. Hence, in a figure such as Figure 13-7, a highly elastic demand curve for the product will be associated with a smaller leftward shift in the individual demand curves.

The industry demand for an input is more elastic the greater is the price elasticity of demand for the product the input is used to produce.

CHARACTERISTICS OF INPUT SUPPLY

This chapter will examine the markets for the services of labor and land; the market for capital will be studied in Chapter 15.

FIGURE 13-8 The Consumption/Work Choice

Possible consumption is represented by the budget line, $C = a + wL$. Leisure time is the difference between time available, t, and hours of work, L_0.

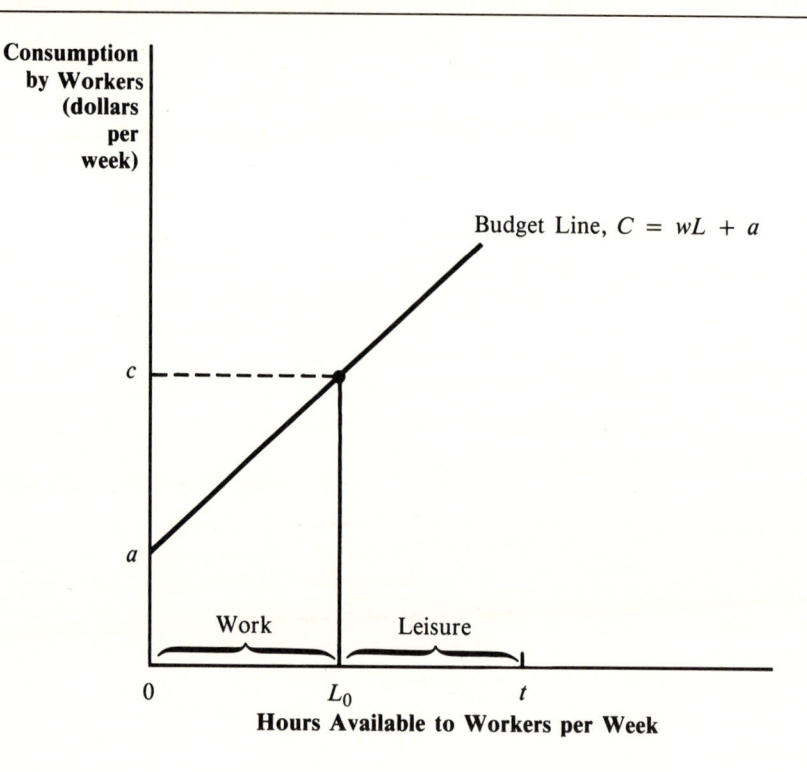

Consumption by Workers (dollars per week)

Budget Line, $C = wL + a$

c

a

Work Leisure

0 L_0 t

Hours Available to Workers per Week

The Supply of Labor Services

About 75 percent of national income in the United States is the compensation of employees—that is, payment for labor services. The principal fact about hours of work is that, over the years, the number of hours of work in the workweek has decreased. For example, in 1947, the average workweek for private nonagricultural workers consisted of 40.3 hours at an average hourly wage (in 1986 dollars) of $5.55. In 1986, the average workweek had fallen to 34.8 hours at an average hourly wage of $8.76.

A simple microeconomic explanation for why people work fewer hours per week when paid more is that the labor-supply curve is backward-bending, as we will illustrate later in this chapter. As wages increase, a point is reached where the quantity of labor supplied will diminish because of the interaction between substitution and income effects, explained in Chapter 4 on consumer demand.

The Consumption/Work Choice

Recall the classic consumer-choice problem: the consumer maximizes utility by choosing the commodity bundle along a given budget constraint that

FIGURE 13-9 Indifference Curves for the Consumption/Work Choice

The indifference curves are upward-sloping because providing labor service generates disutility (work is a "bad"). Moving from indifference curve U_0 to a higher curve, such as U_1, increases utility because although consumption remains the same, work decreases and leisure increases.

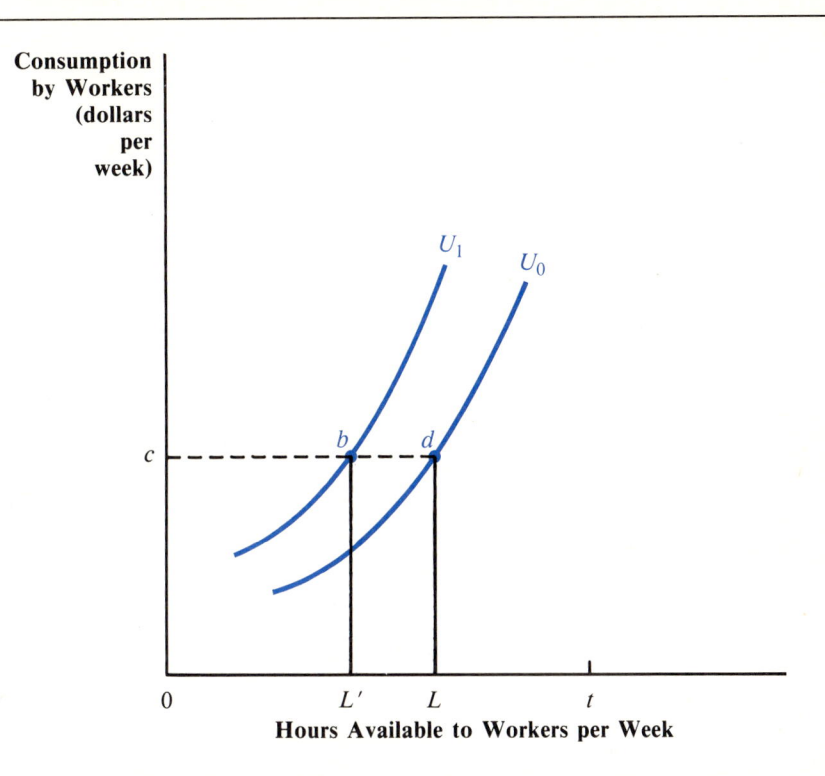

[Graph: Consumption by Workers (dollars per week) on vertical axis; Hours Available to Workers per Week on horizontal axis with points L', L, t. Two upward-sloping indifference curves U_1 (left) and U_0 (right), with horizontal dashed line at level c intersecting them at points b and d.]

reaches the highest indifference curve. Now suppose that a consumer is choosing among different bundles of consumption and work, subject to the constraint that income is primarily earned through work.

Suppose that the consumer earns $a from interest-earning or rent-paying assets. The consumer can also choose to work L hours at $w per hour. Abstracting from saving (studied in Chapter 14), the consumer's consumption, C, would be

$$C = a + wL. \tag{23}$$

Figure 13-8 shows the objective terms of trade between working and consumption. The amount of leisure enjoyed by the household is the difference between the amount of time, t, available in a week and the hours worked in a week. For example, if the household works L_0 hours, the amount of leisure is $t - L_0$. The slope of the budget line is the wage rate, w.

Figure 13-9 shows the consumer's indifference curves between consumption and work. These indifference curves are upward-sloping, because providing labor services increases a consumer's level of *disutility*. The more one works, the more consumption is needed to compensate for the extra work. A movement from point d on indifference curve U_0 to point b on the higher indifference curve U_1 is a lateral movement in the sense that the

FIGURE 13-10　Maximizing Consumer Utility

The consumer maximizes utility at point *e*, where the slope of the budget line, *W*, equals the marginal rate of substitution of consumption for labor. Point *e* is on the highest attainable indifference curve, U_0; points *f* and *g* are on a lower indifference curve.

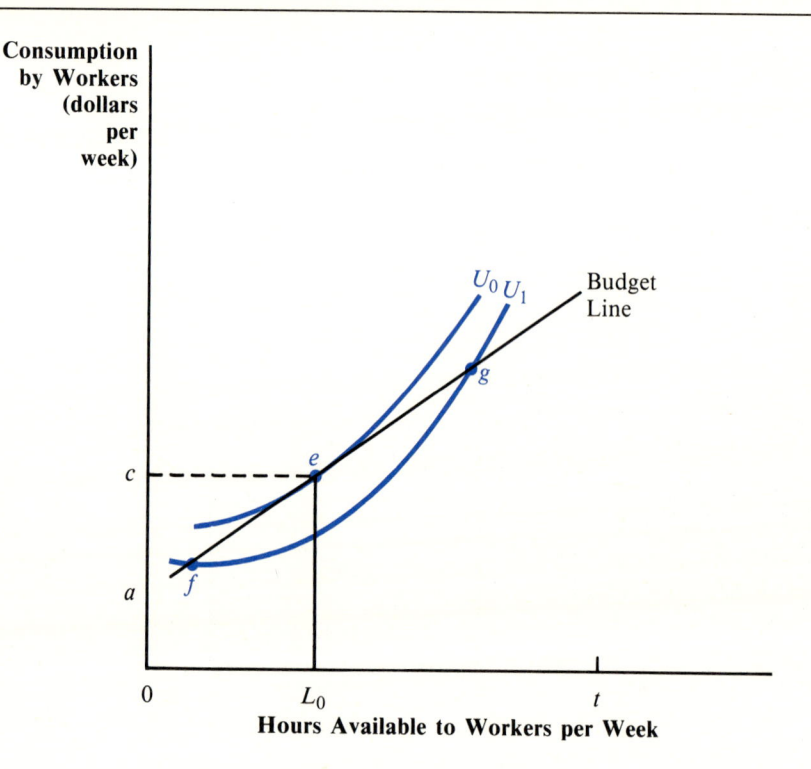

amount of consumption is the same. Although there is the same amount of consumption at point *b*, there is less work and more leisure than at point *d*. Because work is a "bad" and leisure is a "good," the indifference curve U_1 represents a higher level of satisfaction than indifference curve U_0.

The indifference curves in Figure 13-9 are convex to the horizontal axis, reflecting the basic convexity assumption of the theory of consumer behavior. As the consumer moves in the northeast direction along any given indifference curve, the marginal rate of substitution of consumption for work (MRS_{CL}) increases. The MRS_{CL} is the slope of the indifference curve, $\Delta C/\Delta L$. If the utility function is $U = U(C, L)$, along an indifference curve

$$\Delta U = 0 = MU_C \Delta C + MU_L \Delta L, \tag{24}$$

where MU_C and MU_L are the marginal utilities of consumption and labor, respectively. Rearranging Equation (24) shows that:

$$MRS_{CL} = \Delta C/\Delta L = -MU_L/MU_C. \tag{25}$$

Because labor services are irksome, $MU_L < 0$, so the above slope is positive.

Maximum utility is achieved by moving to the highest indifference curve compatible with the budget line, just as in the theory of consumer demand

FIGURE 13-11   Effect of an Increase in Nonlabor Income

When nonlabor income rises from a to a', the consumer's supply of labor falls from L_0 to L_1. Consumption increases from c to c'. Points e and e', the optimal consumption/work combinations, are on the income/consumption path.

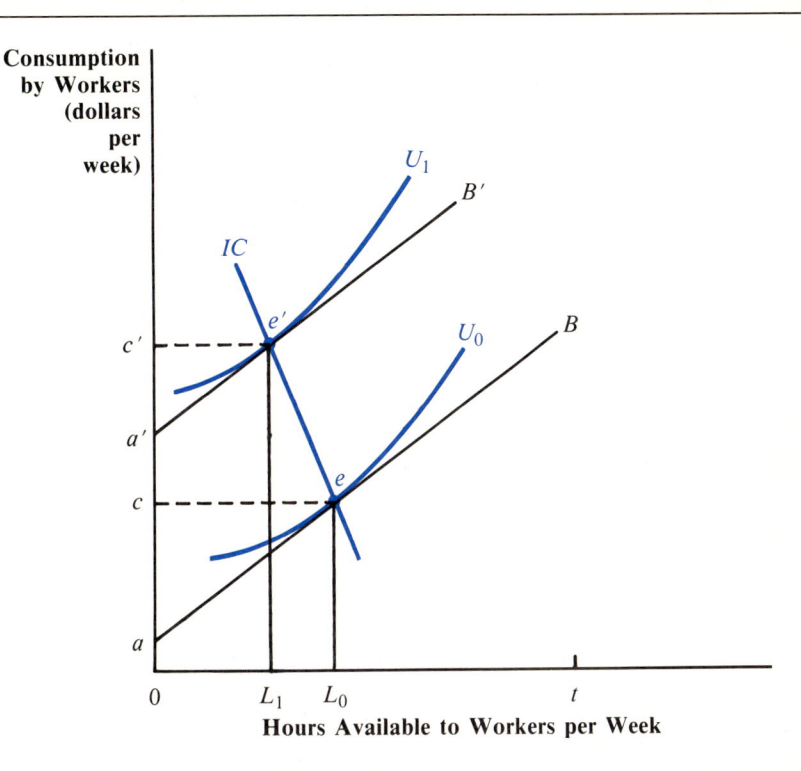

studied in Chapter 4. In Figure 13-10, the optimum combination of work and consumption is achieved at point e. Points f and g are feasible but result in lower utility. For example, point f is on a lower indifference curve than point e because, while it requires less work, it also requires too large a sacrifice of consumption; point g is on a lower indifference curve because, while it offers greater consumption, it requires too much work. The consumer benefits by moving from f to e (working more) because the marginal rate of substitution of consumption for labor is less than the wage; the consumer also benefits by moving from g to e (working less) because at point e, the MRS_{CL} exceeds the wage.

The Demand for Leisure

The optimal quantity of labor supplied in Figure 13-10, L_0, corresponds to an optimal quantity of leisure demanded, $t - L_0$, and an optimal quantity of consumption demanded, c. Suppose that the consumer discussed thus far receives an exogenous increase in nonlabor income that raises a to a'. The budget line then shifts in a parallel fashion from B to B' in Figure 13-11. Notice that if leisure is a normal good, the household will want to "consume" more of it at a higher level of utility (holding relative prices constant).

FIGURE 13-12 Offsetting Effects of a Wage Increase

The move from e_0 to e^* illustrates the substitution effect of an increase in wages on the quantity of labor supplied; the move from e^* to e_1 shows the income effect of the increase in wages.

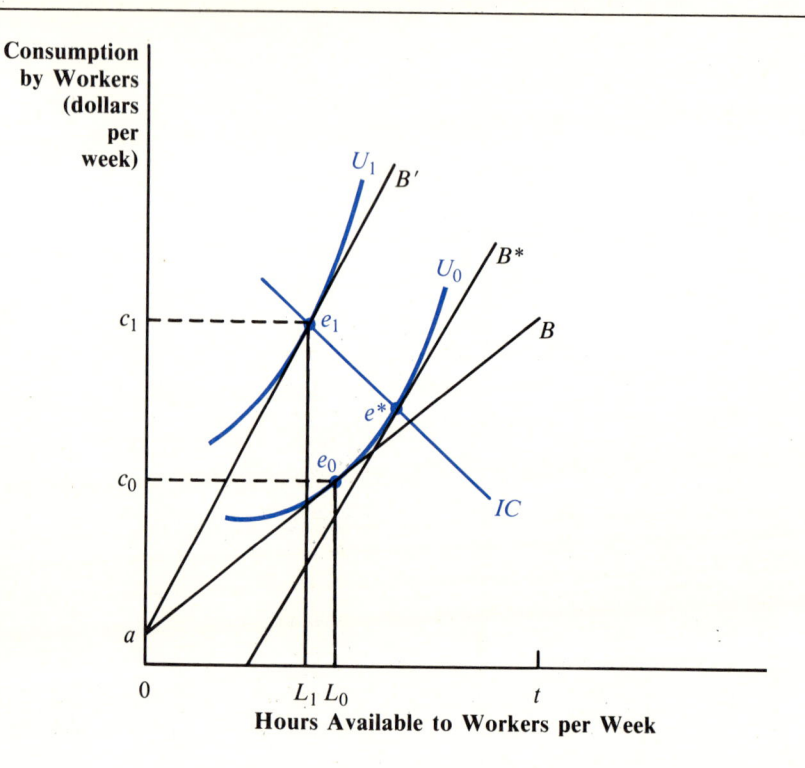

Normality implies that the household's supply of labor will decrease at a constant wage rate if nonlabor income increases. In Figure 13-11, the consumer's optimal response to the increase in a is to *lower* the quantity of labor supplied from L_0 to L_1, resulting in a corresponding *increase* in the quantity of leisure.

The Backward-Bending Labor-Supply Curve

Now suppose that the consumer we've been discussing gets a raise—an increase in the wage rate. First, a higher wage rate increases the opportunity cost of leisure; therefore, the substitution effect of a higher wage rate is an increase in the quantity of labor supplied (a decrease in the quantity of leisure demanded). Second, a higher wage rate also increases income; because leisure is a normal good, the income effect of a higher wage rate is an increase in the demand for leisure (a reduction in the quantity of labor supplied). Thus, a higher wage rate has two offsetting effects: the substitution effect increases the quantity of labor supplied; the income effect lowers the quantity of labor supplied.

Figure 13-12 shows the income and substitution effects in the case where the negative income effect more than offsets the positive substitution effect

FIGURE 13-13 The Labor-Supply Curve

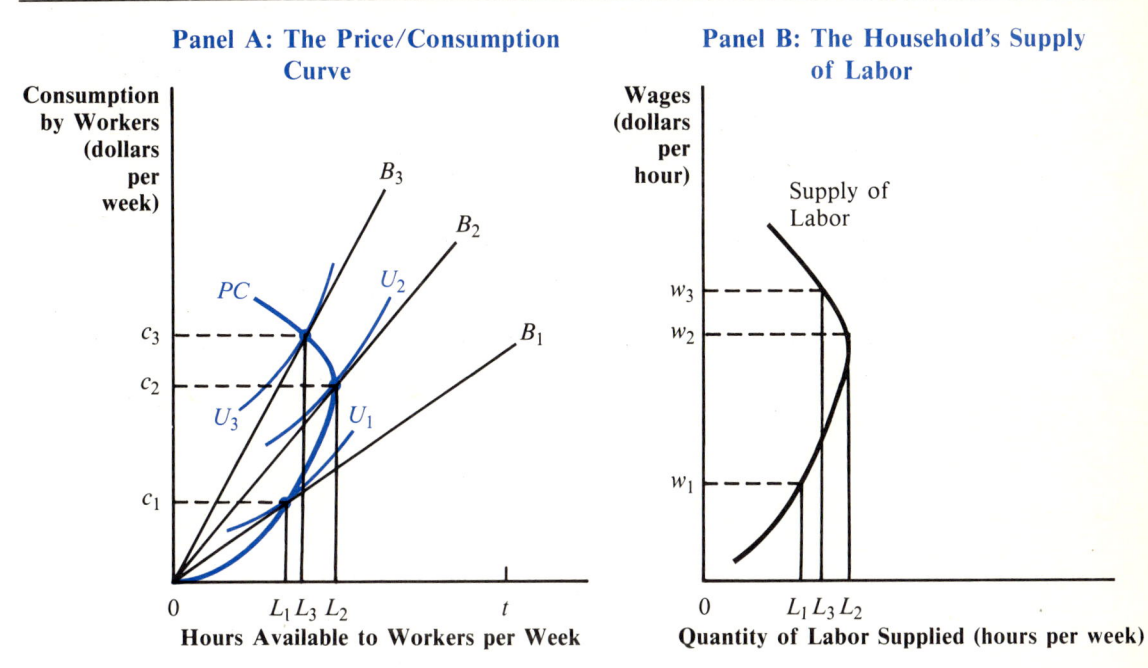

Panel A: The Price/Consumption Curve

Consumption by Workers (dollars per week) vs. Hours Available to Workers per Week

Panel B: The Household's Supply of Labor

Wages (dollars per hour) vs. Quantity of Labor Supplied (hours per week)

The labor-supply curve in Panel B is derived from the price/consumption curve in Panel A, which is composed of the utility-maximizing consumption/work choices at varying wage rates. The curve is backward-bending when the income effect outweighs the substitution effect, reducing the quantity of labor supplied at higher wage rates.

of an increase in the wage rate. The budget line shifts from B to B', indicating an increase in the wage rate. The equilibrium point shifts from e_0 to e_1. The substitution effect (the shift from e_0 to e^*) holds utility constant. The substitution effect is like a shift in the budget line from B to B^*: the wage rate rises but nonlabor income is hypothetically taken away when the opportunity cost of leisure rises until the consumer just reaches the original indifference curve, U_0. The income effect is like a shift in the budget line from B^* to the parallel line B', which moves the consumer from e^* to e_1 when the nonlabor income taken away earlier is returned.

To derive the consumer's labor-supply curve, we need to examine the utility-maximizing choices of the household for all possible wage rates. In Figure 13-13, Panel A shows the *price/consumption (PC) curve* for all possible wage rates: as the wage rate rises, the optimal labor choice first increases along the positively sloped segment and then decreases along the negatively sloped, or backward-bending, segment. Panel B plots the quantity of labor supplied at each wage rate, as derived from Panel A. When the curve is upward-sloping, the substitution effect dominates the income effect. As the quantity of labor supplied increases, the income effect (which works

EXAMPLE 13-2 Overtime Pay

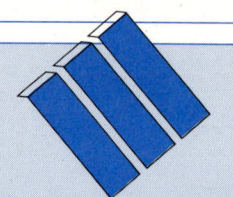

American workers appear to be in the backward-bending portion of their labor-supply curve, because the average workweek has fallen as real wages have risen. What about the phenomenon of overtime pay? To get workers to work additional hours, companies often pay them an overtime rate of pay (for example, time and a half). Is the enthusiastic response of workers to overtime opportunities inconsistent with the backward-bending supply curve?

The accompanying figure shows that overtime pay can always be expected to persuade workers to work extra hours. Assume that the standard wage rate is $10 an hour and the optimal quantity of work is 40 hours per week. If the firm offers the worker $15 an hour for overtime work (that is, for hours in excess of 40 hours), the worker's budget constraint will have a kink at 40 hours of work, where the slope of the budget line abruptly shifts from $10 an hour to $15 an hour. The worker's utility will now be maximized at point e', where he or she is working 45 hours a week. The worker's total pay is now $400 for straight time plus $75 overtime. Indeed, as long as the indifference curve is tangent at point e, the worker will always want to work overtime at any wage in excess of $10 an hour.

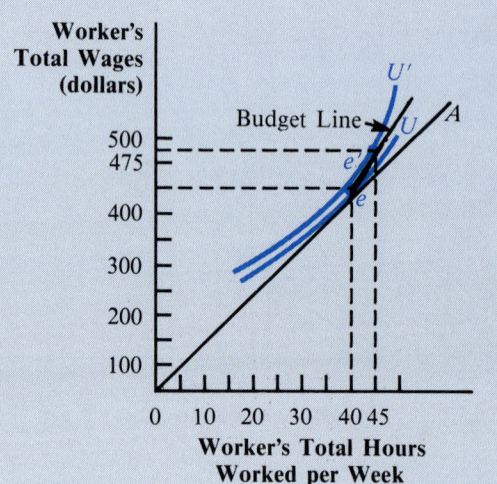

---

against the substitution effect) becomes larger. Eventually, in the general case, the income effect outweighs the substitution effect, and the quantity of labor supplied diminishes. (See Example 13–2.)

The labor-supply curve tends to be backward-bending because when wages are low, the substitution effect dominates the income effect, but when wages are high, the income effect dominates.

Labor-Market Equilibrium

The labor-market equilibrium wage rate occurs when the market quantity of labor demanded equals the aggregate quantity of labor supplied. Figure

FIGURE 13-14   Effect of Increased Demand for Labor on Quantity of Labor Supplied

With a backward-bending aggregate labor-supply curve, an increase in the market demand for labor can lower the quantity of labor supplied and increase the wage rate.

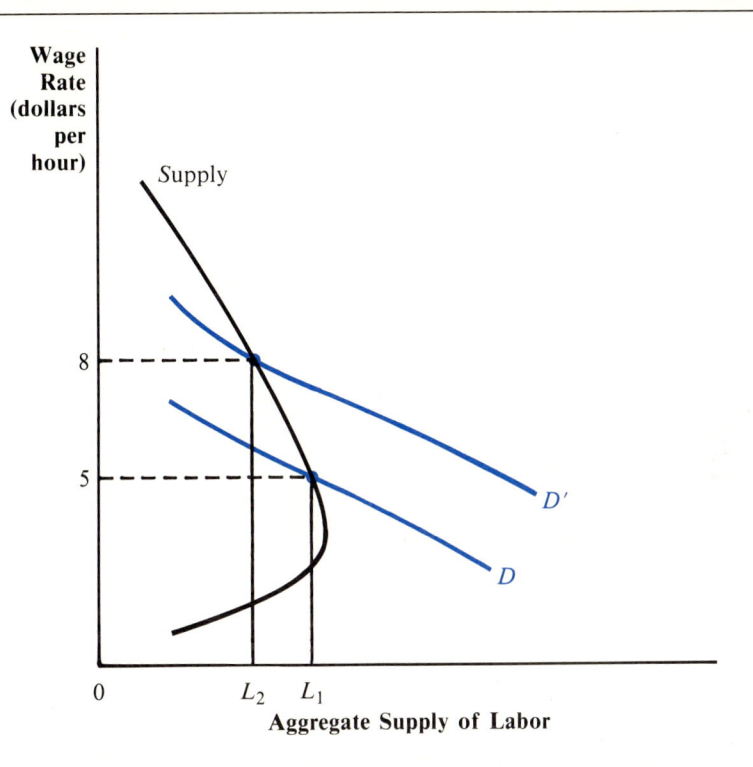

[Graph: Wage Rate (dollars per hour) on vertical axis, Aggregate Supply of Labor on horizontal axis. A backward-bending Supply curve intersects demand curve D at wage $5 and quantity L_1, and intersects D' at wage $8 and quantity L_2.]

13-14 illustrates the effect of an increase in the demand for labor on the wage rate in the case of a backward-bending labor-supply curve. The labor-market supply curve is the horizontal sum of each worker's supply curve. The original demand curve, D, intersects the labor-supply curve at the wage rate of $5. When the demand curve shifts from D to D', however, the wage rate rises to $8, and the aggregate quantity of labor supplied falls. Presumably, the shape of the labor-supply curve helps explain the downward trend in the number of hours in the average workweek in the United States.

The Supply of Land Resources

The supply of land resources differs dramatically from the supply of labor because it depends on nature's bounty. When unimproved land is cultivated with fertilizers and irrigation and improved by the removal of trees, shrubs, and rocks, it becomes a form of capital good, but land (or natural resources like coal) in its original state can neither be increased nor decreased in supply.

The value of land is differentiated by its location and its productivity. An acre of land in Manhattan is worth a fortune simply because of its location. An acre of Iowa farmland is worth more than an acre of farmland in Maine

FIGURE 13-15 The Supply of Land

The supply of land is perfectly inelastic. The shaded area represents economic rent to the owners of the land resource.

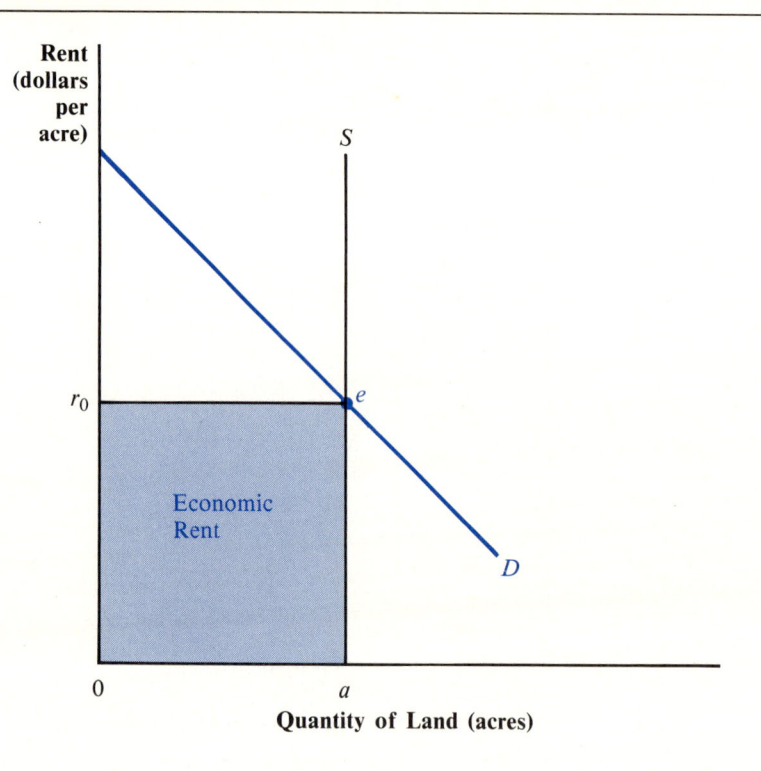

simply because Iowa land is more fertile. Chapter 10 presented the Ricardian theory of differential rents.

In the simple case where all land is uniform, the rent on land is determined by the intersection of the curves for market demand for land and market supply of land. Because the supply of land is perfectly inelastic, the supply curve for land is vertical, as shown in Figure 13-15. The rent that clears the land market, r_0, is such that the total returns exceed the payments needed to coax landowners to rent their land. When land is differentiated, the same analysis applies except that the vertical supply curve applies to a particular piece of land or land with a particular characteristic. The market price of the land is determined by the intersection of the demand curve with the vertical supply curve. The demand curve will be a function of the prices paid for competing units of land.

Recall that *economic rent* is that portion of any factor's return that is in excess of what is required to coax the factor into service. In the case of the inelastic supply of land, the entire factor payment is economic rent. But in general, economic rent is the area above a factor's supply curve and below its price, as shown in Figure 13-16.

Economic rents are everywhere in the economy. They are earned by politicians, musicians, baseball players, monopolists, landowners, and even economists.

FIGURE 13-16 Economic Rent for a Factor Input

In general, economic rent for any factor-supply curve is the shaded area above the supply curve and below the factor price.

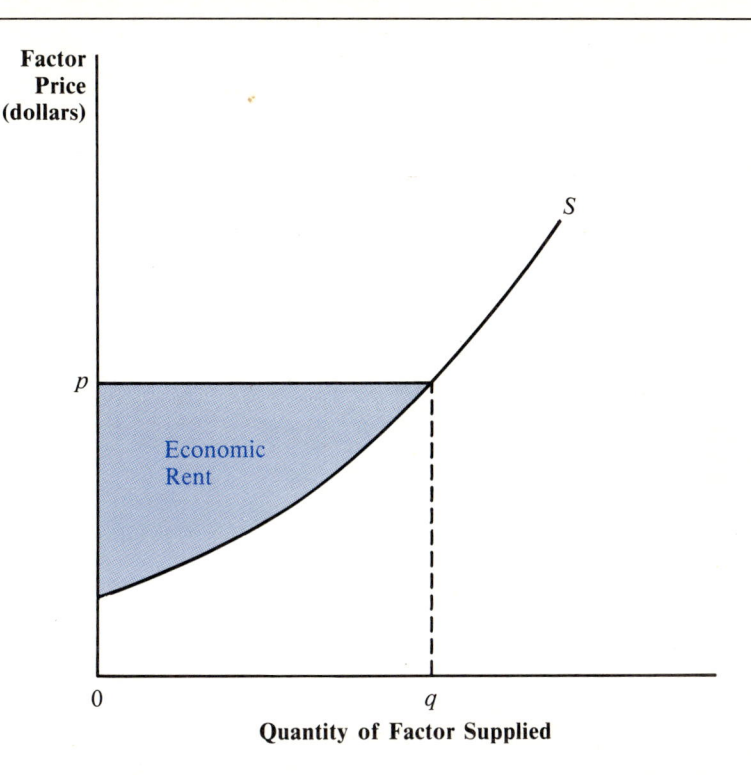

THE MARGINAL-PRODUCTIVITY THEORY OF DISTRIBUTION

This chapter has explained how factor prices are determined and how the total economic pie is distributed among the various factors of production. Factor prices equal marginal-revenue products; if there is competition in product markets, each factor price equals the value of the marginal product. In the case of a competitive product market, the wage is

$$w = P \cdot MP_L \quad \text{or} \quad w/P = MP_L, \tag{26}$$

so that the wage rate ("in kind," or in product terms rather than dollar terms) equals the marginal product of the factor.

Suppose an economy produces a single good with two factors, labor (L) and land (T). In the competitive case, land and labor would earn their marginal products (measured in terms of the product being produced). How can we be assured that all the product is used up in factor payments?

In the case of perfect competition, as we learned in Chapter 10, in the long run each firm produces in the constant-returns-to-scale region of the *LRAC* curve. For this reason, if we study the aggregate economy, it makes some sense to assume that the aggregate production function displays constant returns to scale.

FIGURE 13-17 Marginal Productivity Theory for Two Inputs, Labor and Land

Total wages are represented by the rectangle and equal the labor supply times the marginal product of labor. If constant returns to scale prevail, the area under the marginal-product-of-labor, or demand-for-labor, curve and above the wage rate is the rent paid to land (the other factor) and equals the supply of land times the marginal product of land.

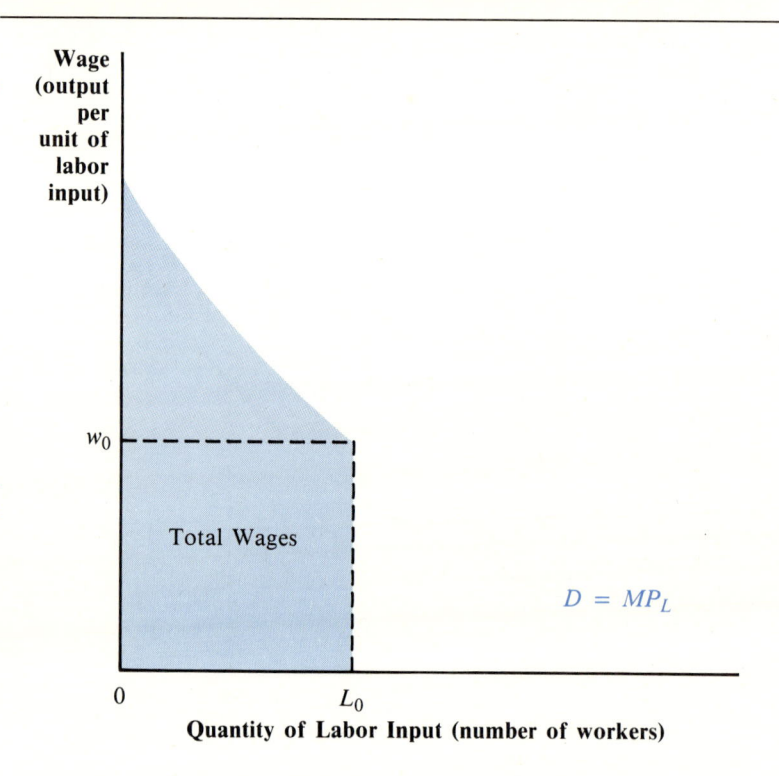

Phillip Wicksteed, a 19th-century English economist, applied a theorem in mathematics to this question. If the production function $Q = F(L, T)$ exhibits constant returns to scale, it is a mathematical fact that

$$Q = MP_L L + MP_T T. \tag{27}$$

This result, called Euler's theorem after the mathematician Leonhard Euler (1707–83), can be understood using the economic properties of production functions. We know that

$$\Delta Q = MP_L \Delta L + MP_T \Delta T, \tag{28}$$

simply because each term represents the increase in output resulting from the increase in labor and land, respectively. But with constant returns to scale, if $\Delta L/L = \Delta T/T = \lambda$, it follows that $\Delta Q/Q = \lambda$ as well. Accordingly, with constant returns to scale, when all inputs are increased at the same rate, we can write:

$$\lambda Q = MP_L \lambda L + MP_T \lambda T. \tag{29}$$

Dividing through by λ results in Euler's equation.

Euler's theorem states that the product is exactly distributed when factors are paid their marginal product. Labor earns $MP_L L$ and land earns $MP_T T$. The product is exhausted as long as there are constant returns to scale.

EXAMPLE 13-3 Immigration Winners and Losers

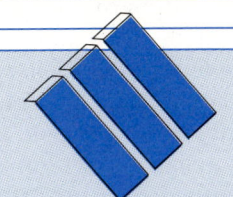

Who gains and who loses from the immigration of labor? Suppose that an economy's output is produced by labor and capital inputs only, under constant returns to scale. We can, therefore, apply Euler's theorem as shown in the accompanying figure. Before immigrants arrive, the total number of workers in the economy is L. The wage rate is w and capital investment earns a return equal to triangle abw. When the immigrants arrive (assuming they are workers of the same quality as the indigenous population), the supply of labor increases to L' and the wage rate falls to w'. The return to the owners of capital increases by $wbdw'$ to adw'. The original workers lose the amount represented by the rectangle $wbcw'$, which is less than the capitalists gain. Accordingly, the net gain to the economy is represented by the small triangle bdc. To the extent that workers own capital such as savings accounts, stocks, and bonds, they may not be worse off at all.

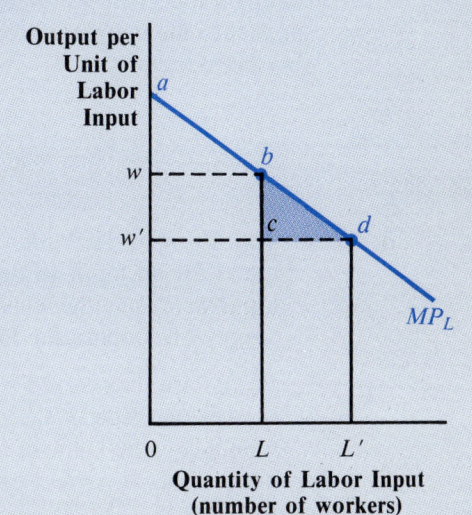

Figure 13-17 illustrates Euler's theorem. The demand curve for labor is D, which equals the marginal product of labor. Assume that workers are paid in kind, so that the wage rate is measured in terms of corn or whatever product is being produced. If L_0 is the quantity of labor available in the economy, then the amount paid to labor is $w_0(L_0)$. The triangle below the marginal-product-of-labor curve, and above the wage rate, w_0, is the amount paid to landowners: $MP_T \times T$. The entire area under the MP_L curve up to the point L_0 measures the total product of the economy, Q, simply because the combined marginal products of the first through the last units of labor in the economy, ΣMP_L, equal the total output. Thus, what is left over will be paid to landowners, where land is also paid its marginal product. Constant returns to scale guarantee that what is left over after paying for labor is exactly equal to the rental paid for land when the rent equals the marginal product of land. (See Example 13-3.)

The marginal-productivity theory of distribution was interpreted by John Bates Clark, one of its originators, as justifying whatever distribution of income emerged in a capitalist society. However, this viewpoint is a normative interpretation of a positive theory. There is no reason why the distribution of income resulting from paying factors their marginal products should be considered ethically correct. One can argue that according to the marginal-productivity theory, people are paid "what they contribute," but such an argument equates the term *contribution* with *marginal product*. Calling a marginal product a factor's "contribution" appears to lend moral support to the marginal-productivity theory, but the temptation should probably be avoided.

SUMMARY

1. The Marshall-Hicks laws of derived demand relate the elasticity of demand for an input to the elasticity of product demand, the share of the input in costs, the elasticity of substitution, the time period, and the supply of cooperating factors.

2. Profits are maximized if for each input $MRP_i = r_i$. These conditions are the reverse side of the coin of the $MR = MC$ condition. In the case of monopoly, the value of the marginal product, VMP, is greater than MRP; in the case of perfect competition, $VMP = MRP$.

3. In the one-input case, the demand curve for the input is just the MRP curve below the ARP curve.

4. With more than one input, the short-run elasticity of demand for labor (or any input) is less than the long-run elasticity.

5. For the industry, the elasticity of demand for an input is less than the individual firm's elasticity of demand.

6. The supply curve of labor is determined by consumer utility maximization between consumption and work. An increase in wages increases labor supplied by the substitution effect and, if leisure is a normal good, reduces labor supplied by the income effect. If wages are high enough, the labor-supply curve can begin to bend backwards. Economic rent is that portion of any factor's return that exceeds what is required to coax the factor into service. All factors in less than perfectly elastic supply earn economic rents.

7. According to the marginal productivity theorem of distribution, the product is completely distributed when factors are paid their marginal product.

QUESTIONS AND PROBLEMS

1. Suppose labor makes up 20 percent of the cost of producing strawberries. Suppose wages rise by 10 percent.
   a. How much will the average cost of producing strawberries increase?
   b. If labor and other inputs are used in fixed proportions, and the price elasticity of demand for strawberries is -0.5, what will be the wage elasticity of demand for strawberry workers? (*Hint:* the increase in the average cost equals the increase in the price of strawberries in the long run.)

2. A hypothetical labor-union leader was heard to remark, "I believe that firms maximize profits, but the marginal-productivity theory of distribution is ridiculous." Evaluate the union leader's remark.

3. What are the five rules of derived demand?

4. Which is more elastic, the demand curve for lettuce workers or the demand curve for California lettuce workers? Which rule of derived demand did you use?

5. Australia has a lot of available land; Japan has very little. Everything else being equal, which country would you expect to have the highest elasticity of demand for labor and why?

6. Which is more elastic, Farmer Smith's demand curve for labor or the total-farm demand curve for labor?

7. The ABC Company can sell widgets for $2 each in a competitive market and can hire workers at $11 per day. It faces the production function given in Table C. Draw the *ARP* and *VMP* (or *MRP*) curves. How many days of labor will the firm hire? What will the firm's profit be?

8. The XYZ Company can sell plastic oranges for $3 each. It can produce plastic oranges by the production function given in Table D. Draw the *MRP* and *ARP* curves. What is the firm's demand curve for labor? At what wage rate would the firm go out of business?

Table C

Days of Labor	Output (unit)
0	0
1	10
2	18
3	24
4	28
5	30

Table D

Days of Labor	Output (units)
0	0
1	5
2	15
3	20
4	24
5	27
6	29
7	30

9. Under what conditions will *MRP* be less than *VMP*?

10. Is it possible for *MRP* to be greater than *VMP*?

11. Suppose the *w/r* ratio rises by 10 percent, and the *K/L* ratio rises by 5 percent. What is the elasticity of substitution? What should happen to the relative share of labor to capital, *wL/rK*?

12. Draw the indifference curves for a "workaholic" who considers the first 8 hours of work to have a positive marginal utility, while the last 16 hours of work have a negative marginal utility. In equilibrium, is work still a "good"?

13. Consider a consumer for whom leisure is inferior. Could he or she have a backward-bending supply curve of labor?

SUGGESTED READINGS

Ferguson, C. E. *The Neoclassical Theory of Production and Distribution*. London: Cambridge University Press, 1969.

Hicks, J. R. *The Theory of Wages*. London: Macmillan, 1932.

Reder, M. "Alternative Theories of Labor's Share." In M. Abramovitz et al., eds. *The Allocation of Economic Resources*. Stanford, Calif.: Stanford University Press, 1959, pp. 180–206.

Robinson, J. "Euler's Theorem and the Problem of Distribution." *Economic Journal* 44 (1934): 398–414.

APPENDIX 13A

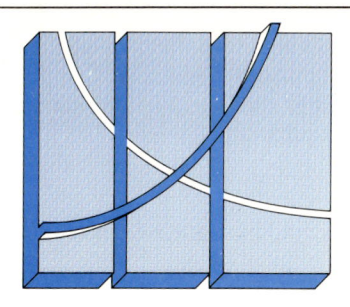

THE LAWS OF DERIVED DEMAND

This appendix shows how the elasticity of demand for an input is related to (1) the product elasticity of demand, (2) the elasticity of substitution, and (3) the importance of the input. We assume there are constant returns to scale.

Assume output is produced by labor and capital, according to the constant-returns-to-scale production function $Q = F(L, K)$. If the labor and capital inputs change, then

$$\Delta Q = MP_L \Delta L + MP_K \Delta K \\ = (MP_K)[(MP_L/MP_K)\Delta L + \Delta K]. \tag{A-1}$$

But cost minimization implies $w/r = MP_L/MP_K$; substitution into (A-1) implies

$$\Delta Q = (MP_K)[(w/r)\Delta L + \Delta K] \text{ or} \\ = (MP_K/r)[w\Delta L + r\Delta K]. \tag{A-2}$$

Now, consider the case in which output is constant, or $\Delta Q = 0$. It follows from (A-2), then, that

$$w\Delta L + r\Delta K = 0. \tag{A-3}$$

Now define the term $\%\Delta x$ to mean $\Delta x/x$, the percentage or proportion change in the variable x. By the definitions of $\%\Delta L$ and $\%\Delta K$ and $\%\Delta L$, we can write (A-3) as

$$wL(\%\Delta L) + rK(\%\Delta K) = 0. \tag{A-4}$$

Since total costs $C = wL + rK$, the shares of labor and capital in total costs add to unity, that is,

$$1 = wL/C + rK/C. \tag{A-5}$$

Divide both sides of (A-4) by C and use (A-5) to eliminate wL/C; thus:

$$(rK/C)(\%\Delta K - \%\Delta L) + \%\Delta L = 0. \tag{A-6}$$

But from the definition of the elasticity of substitution, $\sigma = (\%\Delta K - \%\Delta L)/(\%\Delta w - \%\Delta r)$. It follows from substitution into (A-6) and some rearranging that

$$\%\Delta L = -(rK/C)\sigma(\%\Delta W - \%\Delta R). \tag{A-7}$$

If the rental rate is constant, $\%\Delta R = 0$, as would be the case if the industry in question were a constant-cost industry,

$$\%\Delta L = -(rK/C)\sigma\%(\Delta W). \tag{A-8}$$

Equations (A-7) or (A-8) are fundamental. They can be used to derive the laws of derived demand. Equation (A-8) tells us the percentage change in the demand for labor *holding output constant*. What is $\%\Delta L$ when output is not constant? Since there are constant returns to scale, $L = aQ$, where a is the amount of labor per unit of output for any given wage/rent ratio. Equation (A-8) gives us the percentage change in labor demand holding output constant at some arbitrary level; thus, Equation (A-8) can be taken to be the percentage change in the coefficient a. The total percentage change in the demand for labor is then simply the sum of the percentage changes, that is,

$$\%\Delta L = \%\Delta a + \%\Delta Q = -(rK/C)\sigma\%\Delta w + \%\Delta Q. \tag{A-9}$$

Now the elasticities of demand for labor and output are simply

$$\eta_L \equiv -\%\Delta L/\%\Delta w \text{ and } \eta_Q = -\%\Delta Q/\%\Delta P. \tag{A-10}$$

Substituting (A-10) into (A-9) yields

$$\eta_L = (rK/C)\sigma + \eta_Q(\%\Delta P/\%\Delta w).$$

It was shown in the discussion of Shepherd's lemma that $\%\Delta AC = \theta(\%\Delta w)$, where θ is the share of labor in total costs. In the long run, $P = AC$ so that $\%\Delta P$ is simply the percentage increase in average costs. Thus, $\%\Delta P/\%\Delta w$ is simply the share of labor costs in total costs (for example, if labor is 50 percent of total costs, a 2 percent increase in wages will increase average costs and price (in the long run) by 1 percent. Thus, we obtain

$$\eta_L = (rK/C)\sigma + (wL/C)\eta_Q. \tag{A-11}$$

It follows that a higher η_Q or a higher σ will increase the elasticity of demand for labor, η_L. An increase in wL/C, the share of labor costs in total costs, has an ambiguous impact because a rising (wL/C) implies a falling (rK/C). Rewriting (A-11) to take into account the fact that $rK/C = 1 - wL/C$ yields the equivalent expression,

$$\eta_L = \sigma + (wL/C)(\eta_Q - \sigma). \tag{A-12}$$

Thus, a higher wL/C will increase η_L if and only if the elasticity of demand for output, η_Q, exceeds the elasticity of substitution, σ.

CHAPTER 14

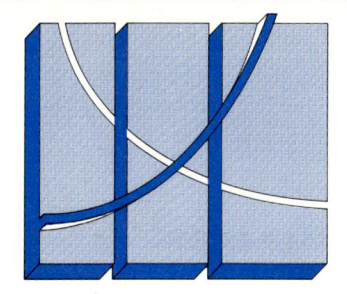

IMPERFECTLY COMPETITIVE RESOURCE MARKETS

Chapter 13 examined resource markets that were perfectly competitive in the sense that firms were price takers in the markets for their inputs, or factors of production. We now turn to the case in which firms possess some price-making power in their output and factor markets. We will first study the case where a firm has a monopoly on the product market but no price-making power on the factor side. We will then study the monopsony case, where the firm's decisions do affect factor prices. The effects of minimum-wage laws and unions on the labor market will be analyzed under conditions of competition and monopsony. Finally, we will consider how factor markets might operate when information is imperfect—when firms cannot determine, in advance, which employees will be most productive and must, therefore, use screening techniques.

MONOPOLY ON THE PRODUCT SIDE OF THE MARKET

A **monopsony** is a single firm that buys or hires all the units available at a given price of a particular input and must therefore pay a higher price per unit to hire or buy more of the input.

Chapter 13 argued that if a firm faces perfect competition on the input side, the firm hires inputs up to the point where the marginal revenue product (MRP) of each input equals its price. If the firm has a monopoly on the product market, the firm's MRP is less than the value of each input's marginal product (VMP) because $MRP = MR \cdot MP$ and $VMP = P \cdot MP$—but with a monopoly, $MR < P$. Having monopoly power on the product-market side does not necessarily make a firm a **monopsony** on the factor-market side. For example, the local telephone company must still compete with all other industries for secretarial labor, land, capital, and electricians.

TABLE 14-1 A Firm with Monopoly Power on the Product Side of the Market

Quantity of Labor Input (workers), L (1)	Quantity of Output (units), Q (2)	Product Price (dollars per unit), P (3)	Marginal Product of Labor (units), MP (4) = Δ(2)/Δ(1)	Total Revenue (dollars), TR (5) = (2)×(3)	Marginal Revenue (dollars), MR (6) = Δ(5)/Δ(2)	Marginal Revenue Product of Labor (units), MRP (7) = (6)×(4)	Value of Labor's Marginal Product (dollars), VMP (8) = (3)×(4)
0	0	0		0			
			10		40	400	400
1	10	40		400			
			9		21	189	279
2	19	31		589			
			8		4	32	184
3	27	23		621			

Profit Maximization

Table 14-1 describes a simple firm with monopoly power on the product side of the market. Columns (1) and (2) give the production function. The table is based on the inverse demand curve $P = 50 - Q$. Column (3) shows how the product price falls as output is increased. Thus, when output is 10 units (and labor input is 1 worker), the price of the product is $40 per unit; when the output is 27 units and labor input in 3 workers, however, the price of the product falls to $23 per unit. The marginal product (MP) of labor is given in column (4), while column (5) shows the total revenue of the firm. Column (6) calculates the marginal revenue as $\Delta TR/\Delta Q$. Finally, columns (7) and (8) calculate the marginal revenue product of labor, MRP as $MR \cdot MP$ and the value of the marginal product of labor, VMP, as $P \cdot MP$.

As the table shows, the MRP schedule falls faster than the VMP schedule. Each schedule falls in part because of the law of diminishing marginal product, but for most demand curves, marginal revenue falls faster than price, so that MRP must fall faster than VMP.

How much output the firm produces and the price it charges depend on the price of labor. If the firm is competitive in the input market, the firm can hire all the labor it wants. Suppose the monopolist in Table 14-1 can hire as many workers as it wants at the wage rate of $w = \$180$ per worker. The first worker will be hired because MRP = $400, and hiring the first worker adds $220 (MRP - w) to profit. The second worker will also be hired, because he or she adds $189 - $180 = $9 to profit. At the point where 2 workers are hired, profit is maximized. Hiring the third worker adds only $32 to revenue but costs $180; thus, the third worker will be turned away.

FIGURE 14-1 Monopoly Profit Maximization

Profit is maximized where $W = MRP$, when the labor input is L_0. The existence of a monopoly on the product side of the market implies social inefficiency, because at L_0 units of labor, VMP is greater than the wage. The social loss is the shaded area abc.

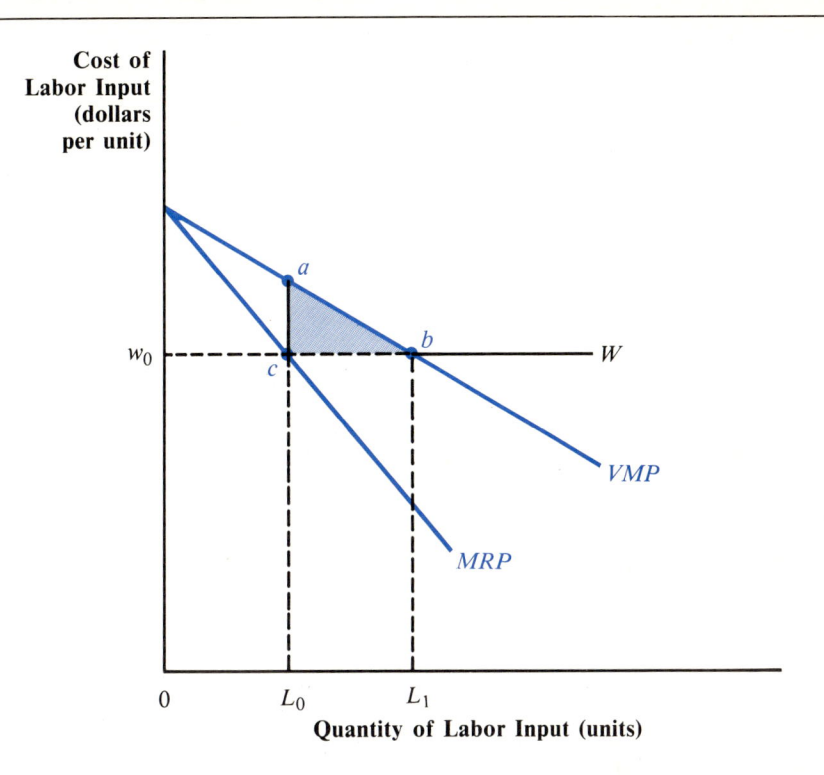

Figure 14-1 shows the general case. The *MRP* curve lies below the *VMP* curve and falls faster. When the wage rate is w_0, the firm maximizes its profit at the input level L_0 where labor's *VMP* is a. For input levels less than L_0, $MRP > W$, and it pays to hire more inputs; for input levels greater than L_0, $MRP < W$, and it pays to cut back on the use of inputs.

The Social Costs of Monopoly

A firm that operates as a monopoly on the product market is socially inefficient, as we learned in earlier chapters. In Figure 14-1, when L_0 units of labor are employed, profits are maximized for the firm but it still remains true that $VMP > W$. Because *VMP* is calculated as the price of the product multiplied by the marginal product, and because the product price signifies the marginal benefit of the good to society, *VMP* can be thought of as the marginal social benefit of the input to society. If the wage rate is the marginal social cost of the input to society, the social bonus from hiring one more unit of the input is $VMP - W$. By hiring up to the point where $VMP = W$, society would gain the shaded triangle abc, which is another way of measuring the social cost of monopoly. (See Chapter 11 for a corresponding discussion of the output market.)

PRACTICE EXERCISE 14-1

Q. Suppose that $P = 15 - Q$ is the inverse demand curve facing a monopoly and that the production function is given in Table A. If the wage rate is $3, what price will the firm charge and how many workers will be hired?

Table A

Quantity of Labor Input, L	Quantity of Output, Q
1	5
2	9
3	12
4	14

Table B

Quantity of Labor Input, L	Total Revenue (dollars), $P \times Q$
1	50
2	54
3	36
4	14

A. The revenue for each level of input may be determined by multiplying the price by the output quantity, where $P = 15 - Q$. Using Table A we can obtain the data in Table B. With a wage rate of $3, it pays the firm to hire the second worker because $MRP_L = \$4$ for the second worker. The third worker has a negative marginal product. If two workers are hired, the firm's output is 9 units and the price must be $6.

The same conclusion can be reached using Table 14–1. If the wage rate is $180 per worker, the monopolist maximizes profit when 2 workers are hired. While it is not profitable *to the firm* to hire the third worker, society would benefit. The third worker's *VMP* is $23 × 8 = $184. Because the worker's wage is $180, the opportunity cost to society of another worker is also $180.

Because the worker's *VMP* is more than $180, society would receive net benefits if the monopolist hired the third worker.

Market Equilibrium

How is the price of the input determined when the hiring firm has monopoly power on the output side of the market? The answer is the same as in Chapter 13. By considering all the industries that use the input, we must somehow arrive at the market-demand curve for the input. If all the firms hiring the input are monopolists, the market-demand curve is the simple horizontal summation of all the monopolists' input-demand curves. There is no need to take into account the external effect on product price of all firms expanding output because each firm has a monopoly and has already taken falling product prices into account. Chapter 13 explained that when the firm faces competition in the product market, these external effects must be considered because the firm does not take falling product prices into account. If the input is used by both competitive industries and monopolies, the market-demand curve is simply the sum of the various industry-demand curves. The price of the input is then found where the quantity demanded equals the quantity supplied. In equilibrium, the price of an input equals the marginal revenue product of the input in all the industries and the value of the input's marginal product in the competitive subset of industries.

MONOPSONY IN THE RESOURCE MARKET

When a firm must pay a higher price per unit in order to hire more of an input, the firm is a *monopsony*. Strictly speaking, a pure monopsony is a single firm hiring all the available units of a particular input. The suppliers of the input are themselves price takers, and their collective behavior may be represented by an upward-sloping supply curve. A concrete example of a monopsony might be an isolated town in which everyone works for the local textile factory. To keep the analysis simple, we will assume that there is only one firm; but an industry may be an *oligopsony*, a market in which a few firms hire a single input.

Marginal Factor Cost

The **marginal factor cost** (*MFC*) of an input is the increase in the cost of the input due to hiring one more unit.

For a monopsony, the additional cost of hiring another unit of an input—its **marginal factor cost** (*MFC*)—is higher than the price of the input, except for the first unit purchased. When another unit of an input is hired, the monopsonist must pay higher prices to all the previous units that would have been hired at a lower price. If the price of the input is rising, so is the average cost of the input; thus, the marginal factor cost must exceed the average factor cost (or wage) because of the average/marginal rule ($M = A + Q\Delta A/\Delta Q$).

TABLE 14-2 A Firm with Monopsony Power in Its Input Market

Quantity of Labor Input (workers), L (1)	Wage Rate (dollars per worker), W (2)	Total Cost of Labor Input (dollars), TC (3) = (1) × (2)	Labor's Marginal Factor Cost (dollars), MFC (4) = Δ(3)/Δ(1)
0	0	0	
			1
1	1	1	
			3
2	2	4	
			5
3	3	9	

Table 14-2 provides a simple example. The quantity of labor supplied to a firm is determined by the wage rate. When the wage is $1, total factor costs are $1. When the wage is $2, 2 workers are supplied, and total factor costs equal $4; thus, $MFC = \$3$. Notice in Table 14-2 that MFC rises by $2 for each added worker, while the wage rate rises by only $1 for each added worker.

In the general linear case, the supply curve of labor can be described as $w = a + bL$. It follows that $\Delta w/\Delta L = b$; that is, when one more unit of labor is hired, the wage rate is pushed up by $b. According to the average/marginal rule,

$$MFC = w + L\Delta w/\Delta w = w + Lb = a + bL + bL = a + 2bL. \quad (1)$$

This relationship means that if the supply curve of labor is linear, the MFC curve will be twice as steep as the supply curve. Figure 14-2 shows the general case of a linear supply curve; the MFC curve rises twice as fast and, thus, is horizontally halfway between the supply curve and the vertical axis.

If the supply curve for an input is upward-sloping, the marginal factor cost of the input exceeds its price. If the supply curve is linear, then the MFC curve is twice as steep as the inverse supply curve because $W = a + bL$ and $MFC = a + 2bL$.

Monopsonistic Equilibrium

The monopsonist follows the same rules of profit maximization as any other firm: it hires an input until marginal benefit equals marginal cost. The appropriate measure of marginal benefits in this case is the input's marginal

FIGURE 14-2 Labor Supply and Marginal Factor Cost

The *MFC* exceeds the cost of the input if the supply curve is upward-sloping. If $W = a + bL$, the $MFC = a + 2bL$, and the *MFC* curve is twice as steep.

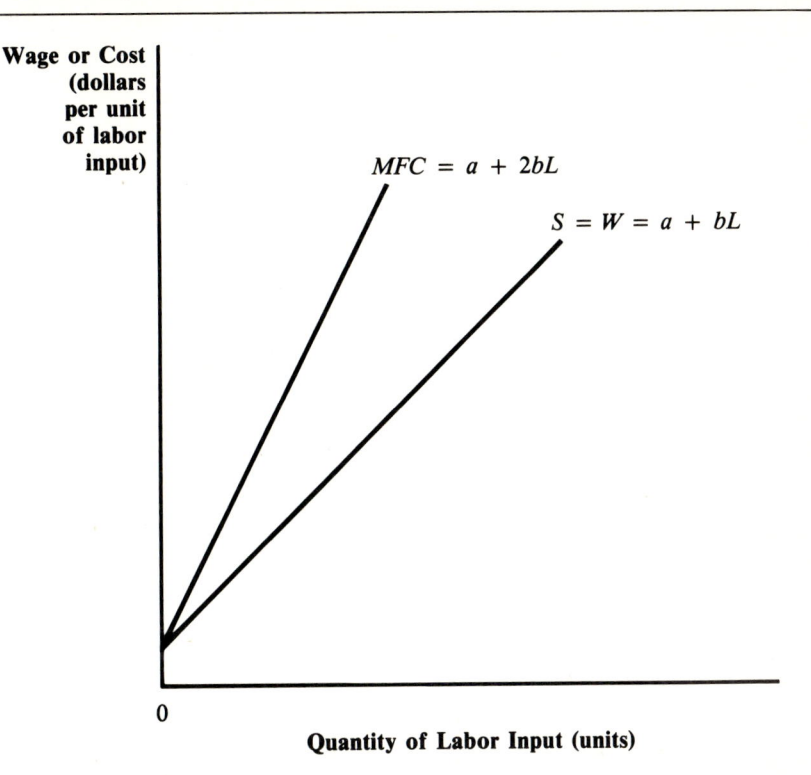

Wage or Cost (dollars per unit of labor input)

$MFC = a + 2bL$

$S = W = a + bL$

Quantity of Labor Input (units)

revenue product (*MRP*); the appropriate cost measure is the input's marginal factor cost (*MFC*). As long as *MRP* > *MFC*, the addition of one more unit of the input adds more to revenue than it does to cost. Thus, the firm will hire more inputs until *MRP* = *MFC*.

PRACTICE EXERCISE 14-2

Q. Suppose a firm is a monopsony in the market for the labor it hires. The firm can hire some quantity of labor, L, at the wage rate $w = 10 + 4L$. If the $MRP = 100 - L$, what is the optimal quantity of labor and what is the wage rate?

A. The firm hires until $MFC = MRP$. The *MFC* curve rises twice as fast as the supply curve, $w = 10 + 4L$, so $MFC = 10 + 8L$. Thus, when the firm is maximizing profit, $10 + 8L = 100 - L$, or $9L = 90$ and $L = 10$. The wage rate is $w = 10 + 4L = 10 + 4(10) = \$50$.

FIGURE 14-3 Monopsonistic Equilibrium

Profit maximization for a monopsony in the input market occurs at point e, where $MFC = MRP$. Because the MRP ($= w^*$) exceeds the wages paid to labor, w_0, it is said that the monopsony firm exploits its workers.

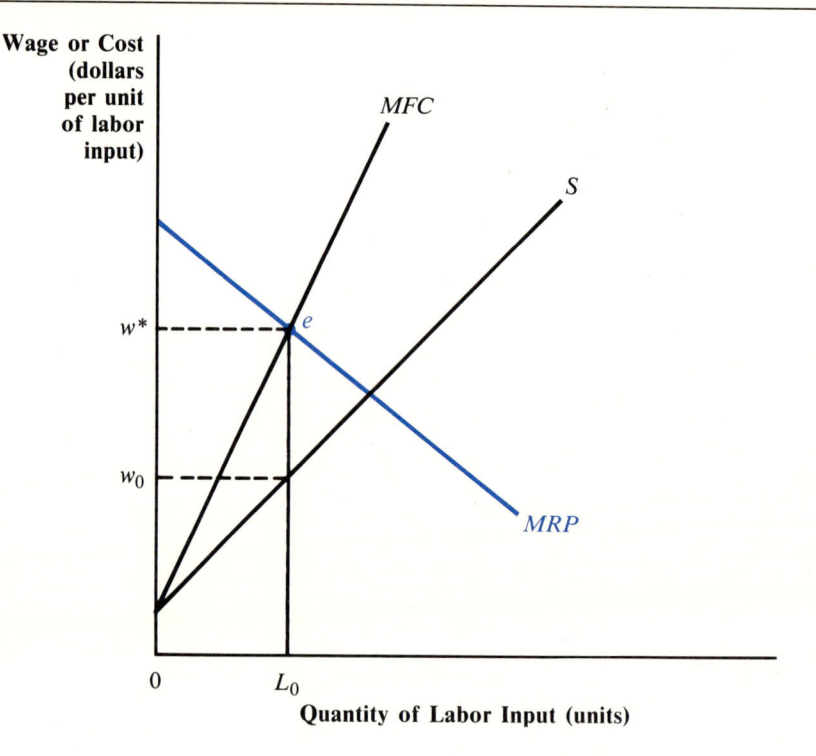

Wage or Cost (dollars per unit of labor input) vs. Quantity of Labor Input (units). Curves shown: MFC, S, MRP. Equilibrium at point e with wage w^* on MFC curve and w_0 on S curve at quantity L_0.

Figure 14-3 shows the equilibrium for a monopsonist. The firm hires L_0 units of labor and pays the input w_0 per unit because L_0 is that quantity of labor at which $MRP = MFC$—where the firm maximizes profit. In monopsony, inputs are paid less than their MRP because while $MRP = MFC$ at a wage of w^*, the monopsonist needs to pay only w_0 to obtain the desired labor quantity L_0. The English economist Joan Robinson has interpreted this result to mean that the monopsonistic employer exploits his or her employees.[1]

A monopsonistic firm pays an input less than its marginal revenue product. The excess of *MRP* over the input cost is the degree of exploitation of the input.

MINIMUM-WAGE LAWS AND UNIONS

Minimum-wage laws were first established in the United States in the late 1930s. A *minimum-wage law* requires firms to pay no less than a specified

---

1. See Joan Robinson, *The Economics of Imperfect Competition* (London: Macmillan, 1933), chap. 26.

MINIMUM-WAGE LAWS AND UNIONS

FIGURE 14-4 **Minimum Wage Under Perfect Competition**

A minimum wage, m, higher than the competitive equilibrium wage rate w_0 results in a smaller quantity of labor demanded, L_1, and a higher quantity supplied, L_2. The difference, the excess supply of labor, may represent increased unemployment.

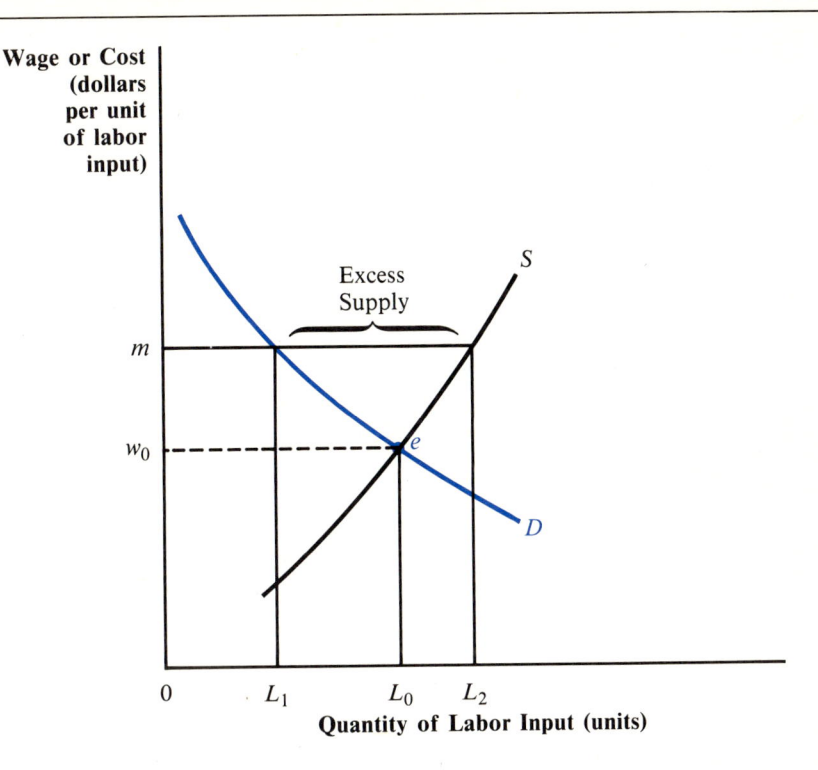

amount per hour for labor. What is the impact of a minimum-wage law on an industry? A union wage may be regarded as a privately negotiated minimum wage for an industry.

The Competitive Case

Figure 14-4 shows the impact of a minimum-wage law on a competitive labor market. Without the minimum-wage law, the equilibrium wage rate is determined at the intersection of the curves representing demand and supply for labor, at point e. Because each firm can hire all the workers it wants at the going wage, the equilibrium wage rate equals labor's marginal revenue product for each firm in the marketplace. The equilibrium wage/quantity pair is (w_0, L_0).

Suppose a minimum wage of m is established at a level higher than w_0, the free-market wage rate. Assuming that business firms abide by the law, the quantity of labor hired will now be only L_1 units—the quantity demanded at wage rate m. The amount of employment, therefore, falls from L_0 to L_1. The quantity of labor *supplied* at a wage rate of m is L_2. The difference between the quantity of labor supplied, L_2, and the quantity of labor demanded, L_1, is the potential unemployment created by the minimum-wage law.

FIGURE 14-5 Minimum Wage Under Monopsony

If a minimum wage of m is imposed on a monopsony, employment increases from L_0 to L_1 because the effective MFC curve becomes the horizontal line at m, up to point t plus that part of the MFC curve above point n.

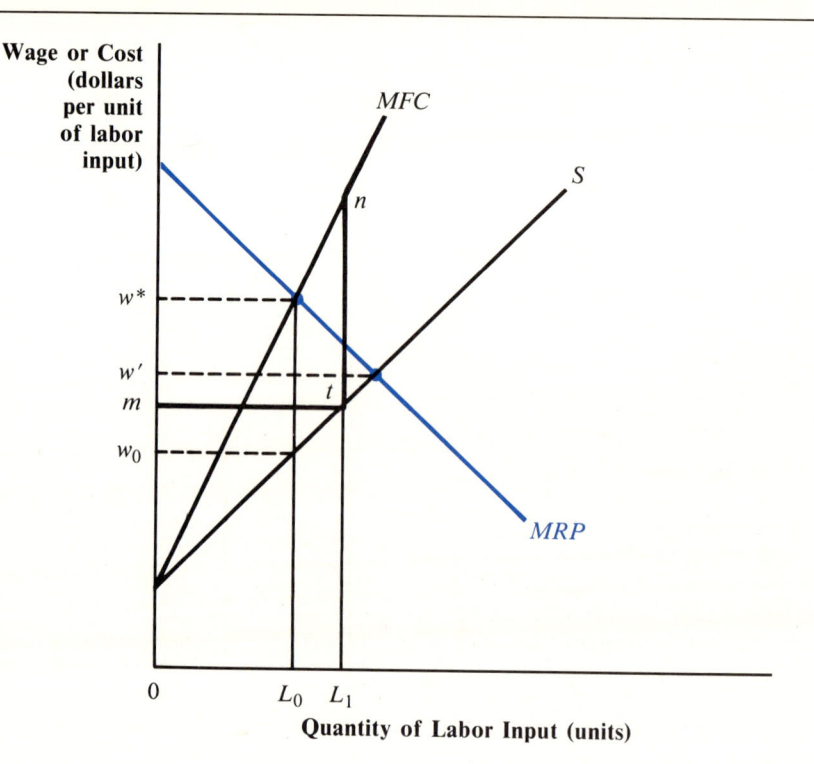

According to this analysis, minimum-wage laws will result in lower employment and an excess supply of labor in the sector of the economy paying the minimum wage. In this view, a minimum-wage law creates a legally recognized cartel. When the minimum-wage law is obeyed, the immediate beneficiaries would be the workers who continue employment at the new, higher wage rate; the losers are those who lose their jobs in the covered sector and must find work in less valued alternatives. Without the enforcement mechanism of the minimum-wage law, business firms would have an incentive to pay less than m. Deviant firms and unemployed workers would always find it in their interest to strike an agreement to pay a wage less than the minimum wage; there is empirical evidence that such agreements occur frequently in the American economy.[2]

The Monopsony Case

In the competitive case, minimum-wage laws appear to interfere with the workings of the market and contribute to economic inefficiency. Exactly the

---

2. See Orley Ashenfelter and Robert S. Smith, "Compliance with the Minimum Wage," *Journal of Political Economy*, April 1979, pp. 335–50.

EXAMPLE 14-1   The Two Faces of Unionism

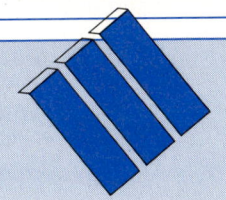

The traditional view of unions is that they interfere with efficient resource allocation by restricting the use of labor in the production process. For example, Albert Rees estimated that from the 1930s to the 1960s unions lowered U.S. real GNP by approximately 0.8 percent.

Richard Freeman and James Medoff have questioned the traditional view. They argue that unions improve productivity by allowing workers to improve working conditions through the collective voice of their union rather than through the traditional mechanism of finding employment elsewhere. There are three possible sources of productivity improvement: (1) worker turnover is reduced, (2) the union helps the firm train new employees through their association with senior workers, and (3) enterprise efficiency is enhanced through the improved communications between worker and firm.

If unions raise productivity, they should raise the profits of unionized firms versus nonunionized firms. By controlling for all the other variables affecting profits, Kim B. Clark has shown that nonunion firms earned about 19 percent lower profits than union firms in the 1970–80 period. Thus, the Freeman-Medoff hypothesis may hold only for particular industries.

Sources: Richard Freeman and James Medoff, "The Two Faces of Unionism," *The Public Interest* (Fall 1979); Albert Rees, "The Effects of Unions on Resource Allocation," *Journal of Law and Economics,* 1963; Kim B. Clark, "Unionization and Firm Performance: The Impact on Profits, Growth, and Productivity," *American Economic Review,* December 1984, p. 911.

---

opposite conclusion is reached when workers are employed by a monopsonistic employer. When a worker is hired by a monopsony, the worker's marginal revenue product exceeds the wage rate. If the firm is forced to pay a higher wage rate (as long as it is lower than the initial *MRP*), then the firm will try to hire more workers at the established minimum wage.

In Figure 14-5, without a minimum-wage law the firm would hire L_0 units at the wage rate w_0. As in Figure 14-3, the *MRP* for L_0 units (represented by w^*) is greater than the wage paid of w_0. If the state passes a minimum-wage law, the monopsony firm will be required to pay the wage m, which is less than w^* but greater than w_0. The minimum-wage law alters the effective *MFC* curve faced by the firm. Because the firm must pay at least m, the new *MFC* curve will be the horizontal line segment mt plus the old *MFC* curve northeast of point n. The firm will now hire the quantity L_1 units of labor at the wage rate m. Thus, *employment increases*, and workers are better off. At employment level L_1 there is still some monopsonistic exploitation. If the

FIGURE 14-6 Union Wage Under Competition

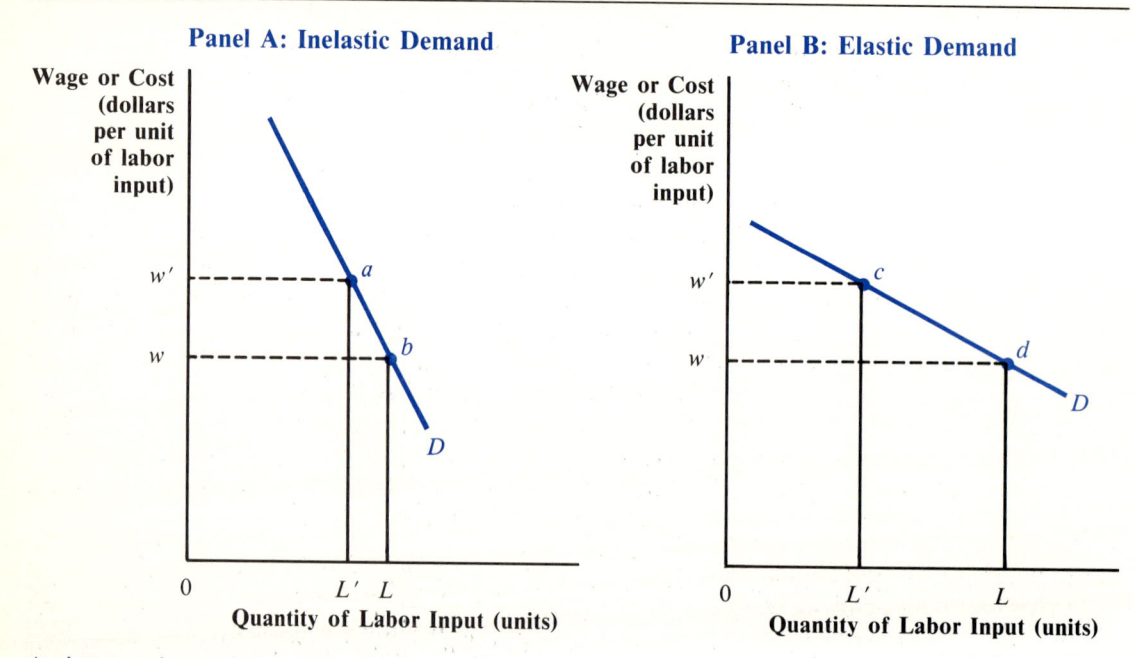

Panel A: Inelastic Demand

Panel B: Elastic Demand

An increase in wages, to w', brought about by collective bargaining decreases employment (from L to L') in a competitive market. The decrease is smaller when demand for labor is relatively inelastic in the industry, as in Panel A. Relatively elastic demand, as in Panel B, causes a greater drop in employment.

minimum wage were set at w', the rate at which the *MRP* curve intersects the supply curve, S, the minimum-wage law would achieve the same results as the competitive case without a minimum-wage law.

Unions

The minimum-wage analysis can also be applied to unions. In a simplified sense, unions can be regarded as an instrument for achieving a minimum wage for a particular unionized industry. (This view may be simplistic; for an alternative view, see Example 14-1.) Instead of a minimum wage being achieved by state action, the union wage is determined by collective bargaining between the firm and the representatives of the labor force.

The effect of unions on employment depends very much on whether the industry in question bids for labor competitively or behaves as a monopsony.

In the case of competition, the traditional view is that unions are like a legally recognized cartel selling labor services. The incentive to form such a cartel will be greater when the elasticity of demand for a particular type of labor is smaller. For example, in Panel A of Figure 14–6, the demand curve for labor is relatively inelastic; a union-induced increase in wages, from w to w', causes a slight reduction in employment, from L to L'. In Panel B, the demand curve is relatively elastic, and the same increase in wages causes a larger reduction in employment. Thus, one would expect unions to be more popular in industries where the demand for labor is somewhat inelastic.

Union membership has declined in the United States. In 1970, 31 percent of nonagricultural employment was unionized; in 1980, only 25 percent of nonagricultural employment was unionized. There has also been a steady decline in the estimated percentage of working time lost through work stoppages or strikes designed to boost wages partly because the demand for labor has become more elastic. Two of the central propositions of the theory of derived demand (Chapter 13) are (1) that the elasticity of demand for an input is higher the higher is the elasticity of substitution and (2) that the elasticity of demand for an input is higher the higher is the price elasticity of demand for the product. Presumably, the increased use of mechanical robots in such industries as the automobile industry has provided firms with more substitutes for labor. It can also be argued that the national industrial composition, in terms of output, has shifted from industries like manufacturing and mining to industries like trade, finance, and services. This latter set of industries may be more competitive and may face higher elasticities of demand. (See Example 13–1 in Chapter 13.) Thus, changes in technology may have helped reduce the power of unions.

In the case of monopsony, a union has considerable scope to improve the lot of workers because the union can not only raise wages, it can also raise employment. When workers are employed by a monopsony, their incentive to form a union is enormous. While monopsonies are seldom encountered, an excellent example would be major-league baseball. Before the increase in the union activities of baseball players (the first strike was in 1972), players were tied to their team by the "reserve clause," which restricted the freedom of players to negotiate with other teams during the period of their contract. The reserve clause gave teams cartel control over their players, and major-league baseball acted as an effective monopsony. G. W. Scully studied the monopsonistic exploitation of baseball players in 1969 and found that most players were paid far less than their marginal revenue products. For example, a player with a slugging average of 0.525 had an estimated *MRP* of $384,000 but was paid only $68,000 in 1969. In this context, the rise of player unions is understandable.[3]

---

3. See G. W. Scully, "Pay and Performance in Major League Baseball," *American Economic Review*, December 1974, pp. 915–30. Nursing provides another example: see Richard Hurd, "Equilibrium Vacancies in a Labor Market Dominated by Nonprofit Firms: The 'Shortage' of Nurses," *Review of Economics and Statistics*, May 1973, pp. 234–40; C. R. Link and J. H. Landon, "Monopsony and Union Power in the Market for Nurses," *Southern Economic Journal*, April 1975, pp. 649–59. Isolated coal-mining and sugar plantations might also be noted.

FIGURE 14-7 Screening Cost and Worker Productivity

The screening cost in Panel A is less than the difference in wages between high-productivity workers, MRP_H, and the average wage level, MRP_A. The MRP_H worker benefits from screening in this case because the firm can pay such workers $MRP_H - C$. In Panel B, both high- and low-productivity workers would be better off receiving the average wage, MRP_A.

Panel A: Lower Screening Cost

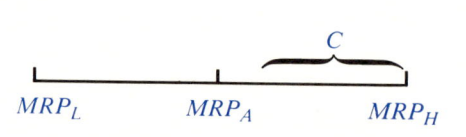

MRP_L MRP_A C MRP_H

Panel B: Higher Screening Cost

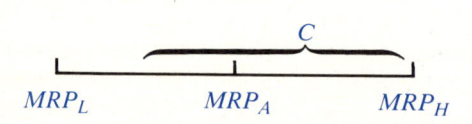

MRP_L MRP_A C MRP_H

SCREENING

Screening occurs when a buyer uses observable characteristics that are correlated with performance in order to rank prospective workers, goods, or services.

Although we have assumed so far that the firm knows the marginal revenue product of the labor input being hired, this is not necessarily the case. Firms hire many workers, and it is difficult for the firm to determine at the time of hiring the productivity of any particular worker. This information may not be known for some time, especially if considerable on-the-job training is required. In such circumstances, the employer must spend resources on the **screening** of potential employees.

Employers can reduce screening costs by relying on worker **signals**—the credentials or qualifications workers present that employers believe to be indicators of productivity. For example, firms may learn from experience that college graduates with math and business degrees are, on the average, more productive in certain occupations than high-school graduates or college graduates from other disciplines. Some employers may require particular academic majors; other employers may require degrees from particular schools; still others may require particular grades; some employers may even require a combination of many educational signals.

The No-Signaling Case

What does an employer do in the absence of effective signals? Let's assume that there are many risk-neutral firms and two types of workers. Type 1

SCREENING

Signals are messages sent from one agent to another (such as a résumé).

workers have a marginal revenue product of $1 and Type 2 workers have an *MRP* of $2, but the employer does not know which is which. In this state of ignorance, firms could simply offer a wage somewhere between $1 and $2. Suppose, for simplicity, that half of the potential employees are Type 1 and half are Type 2. The average *MRP* of any worker hired would then be $1.50. Competition among firms would presumably lead them to offer a wage of $1.50.

Clearly, when firms must put all workers into the same pool, the low-productivity worker benefits from the existence of high-productivity workers, but the high-productivity worker loses. There is, therefore, an incentive for the high-productivity worker to distinguish himself or herself from the low-productivity worker. Moreover, any firm that could distinguish one type of worker from the other could raise its profits as long as the costs of screening applicants were not too high.

Screening Devices

There are many ways to try to distinguish between high-productivity types of workers and low-productivity types before hiring. First, a firm might offer long-term contracts that give little incentive for the low-productivity employees to apply. Firms might find that, over time, they can determine worker quality. Such firms might offer the following contract: "We will pay you a low wage in the beginning and, if you work out, we will give you a high wage." The low wage will not attract low-quality workers, because they may know they will eventually be fired. High-quality workers, however, may jump at the chance to prove themselves. Thus, it makes some sense to offer long-term wage contracts that pay workers less than their marginal revenue product at the beginning of their careers and more at the end (see Example 11-3).

Second, firms may engage in such screening procedures as extensive testing and interviewing of prospective employees. Suppose the productivity of high-quality workers is MRP_H, that of low-productivity workers is MRP_L, and average productivity is MRP_A. To be realistic these *MRP*s should be regarded as present values of lifetime productivities. It costs $C to screen the high-productivity types from the low-productivity types. Figure 14-7 shows the role of screening costs. Panel A of Figure 14-7 assumes that screening costs are less than the difference between the marginal revenue product of the average workers and that of the high-productivity workers. In this case, it pays the high-productivity workers to submit to screening. The firm can pay them $MRP_H - C$, which exceeds the average, equilibrium wage MRP_A. Alternatively, we could think of the high-quality worker as paying the screening cost C and receiving the wage MRP_H, which amounts to the same thing. Notice that the low-productivity worker is worse off than in the no-screening case.

Panel B assumes that the cost of screening is greater than the difference $MRP_H - MRP_A$. If the high-quality worker's net wage is $MRP_H - C$, it is clear that the worker would be better off with the pooled equilibrium wage. In this case, screening costs are too high and both the low-productivity and the high-productivity types are better off without screening.

Paradoxically, in this example, the economy's average net product is higher in the case illustrated in Panel B. In the Panel A case, where workers are screened, the average net product for society is the average of $MRP_H - C$ and MRP_L. For example, if $MRP_H = \$2$, $MRP_L = \$1$, and $C = \$0.25$, the average net product MRP is (assuming exactly half of the workers are of each type) $0.5(\$1) + 0.5(\$2 - \$0.25) = \$1.375$. In Panel B, no screening costs are paid, and the average net product for society is the average of MRP_H and MRP_L, or \$1.50.

It is tempting to conclude that screening is not good for the economy, but this conclusion should be avoided. The Figure 14–7 model assumes that the only benefit of screening is to allow firms to distinguish one type of worker from another. The firm's ability to discriminate may also raise the productivity of high-productivity workers; the inability to discriminate may lower the productivity of high-productivity workers. The model supposes that a worker's productivity is independent of his or her pay.[4]

A third type of screening is the use of educational signals. If firms rely exclusively on educational signals, people with more education are paid high wages and people with less education are paid low wages. Can this work? The answer is yes, under some circumstances. If potential high-quality workers can purchase education more cheaply than those with less potential, the net gains for each kind of worker may be maximized by low-quality workers' obtaining less education and high-quality workers' obtaining college degrees.[5] High-quality workers may not have to study as hard as low-quality workers; thus, even if dollar costs are the same, the personal-effort costs of going to school may be lower for the former than for the latter.

SUMMARY

1. When there is monopoly on the product side of the market and perfect competition on the input side, the firm hires any input up to the point where its marginal revenue product (*MRP*) equals its cost. From a social viewpoint, too few inputs are hired because the value of the marginal product is greater than the *MRP*.

2. When a firm is a monopsony in the input market, the marginal factor cost (*MFC*) of the input exceeds its price because hiring an additional unit of the input drives up the cost of previous units of the input hired. Firm

---

4. The model is based on Joseph E. Stiglitz, "The Theory of 'Screening,' Education, and the Distribution of Income," *American Economic Review*, June 1975, pp. 283–300.
5. See Michael Spence, "Job Market Signaling," *Quarterly Journal of Economics*, August 1973, pp. 355–74.

profits are maximized when the *MFC* equals the *MRP*. Because *MFC* exceeds the price of the input, the input is said to be exploited.

3. In competitive markets, minimum-wage laws or union attempts to raise wages drive up wages but reduce employment. In monopsonistic markets, minimum-wage laws or union wage-raising efforts increase both wages and employment.

4. Firms can distinguish between low-productivity workers and high-productivity workers by (1) offering long-term contracts that benefit high-productivity workers, (2) screening prospective employees, and (3) requiring educational signals, or qualifications. Without screening, high-productivity workers must be pooled with low-productivity workers in an unsatisfactory equilibrium for the former group of workers.

QUESTIONS AND PROBLEMS

1. A monopoly can hire all the labor it wants at $4 an hour. The *VMP* of labor is $20 - L$ and the *MRP* of labor is $20 - 2L$, where L = hours worked. What is the profit-maximizing quantity of labor, L? What is the social cost of the monopoly?

2. The firm's production function is given in Table C. The firm's demand curve for its product is $P = 30 - Q$. What price, P, will the firm charge if the wage rate is $15? How many units of labor will be hired?

3. The XYX Corporation does not face diminishing returns, but it has a monopoly in the product market. Its production function is $Q = 2L$, and the demand curve is $P = 40 - Q$.
   a. What are the *MRP* and *VMP* curves?
   b. If the wage rate is $32, calculate the profit-maximizing levels of price, labor input, and output and the level of profit.

4. Carter's peanut farm has a monopsony over labor. Its *MRP* is $14 - L$ and the wage rate is $w = 2 + L$. What are the profit-maximizing levels of

Table C

Quantity of Labor Input, L	Quantity of Output, Q
1	10
2	18
3	24
4	28

labor input and wages? What would the level of labor input be if a minimum wage of $8 were imposed?

5. Compare and contrast the effects of minimum-wage laws in a competitive labor market and under monopsony.

6. Assume that half of the population has an *MRP* of $10 and the other half an *MRP* of $2. Firms cannot distinguish between workers unless they pay a screening cost of $3.
   a. Will workers be screened?
   b. What would happen if screening costs increased to $5?

7. How might high-productivity workers be distinguished from low-productivity workers at the time they are hired?

SUGGESTED READINGS

Rees, A. "The Effect of Unions on Resource Allocation." *Journal of Law and Economics*, October 1963, pp. 69–78.

Robinson, Joan. *The Economics of Imperfect Competition*. (London: Macmillan, 1933), chaps. 25, 26.

Spence, M. "Job Market Signaling." *Quarterly Journal of Economics*, August 1973, pp. 355–74.

Stiglitz, Joseph E. "The Theory of 'Screening,' Education, and the Distribution of Income." *American Economic Review*, June 1975, pp. 283–300.

Tregarthen, Timothy. "Players Head for the Courts." *The Margin*, November 1987, pp. 9–11.

CHAPTER 15

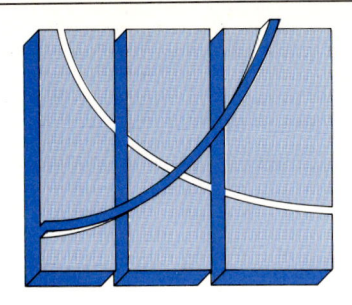

CAPITAL AND INTEREST

Capital is the set of tangible, physical goods in existence at any given time.

Capital as a factor of production is on a different footing from labor and land as factors of production. While labor and land are natural factors, capital is a product of economic decisions to save and invest. **Capital** consists of the tangible physical goods in existence at any given time: plants, trucks, lathes, industrial robots, inventories, machines, and assembly lines are all means of production that have themselves been produced. Capital is the stock of useful goods that firms use, in combination with labor and land, to produce all the various goods and services in the economy. The services of a piece of the economy's capital stock flow into the indefinite future. The act of production serves to use up only part of the capital stock—namely, the economic **depreciation** of the capital good.

Depreciation is the loss in the value of a capital good as it is used up over time.

Capital is not used up at one point in time but is used up over time. Production processes are time-consuming: they take time to get started (for example, building a plant); and the production of physical goods may take time (wheat, wine, housing, and space satellites are not produced overnight).

Historically, capital theory has always been the subject of much controversy. For centuries the governments of the world have regulated interest rates. To medieval religious philosophers the payment of interest was wrong because capital was considered to be unnatural and barren. Today, many states in the United States still have *usury laws* that prohibit the payment of interest above a certain rate.

This chapter is devoted to an explanation of the theory of capital and interest as developed by the great American economist Irving Fisher. We use the theory to explain intertemporal consumption (or saving), intertemporal production (or investment), and the fundamental determinants of interest rates. It should be pointed out that Fisher's work was stimulated by the earlier studies of John Rae and Eugen von Böhm-Bawerk.[1]

INTEREST RATES: NOMINAL AND REAL

An interest rate determines how many dollars you can get in one year by investing so many dollars now. If you invest $\$Y_0$ now in return for $\$Y_1$ in one year, the rate of interest, i, is:

$$i \equiv (Y_1 - Y_0)/Y_0. \tag{1}$$

For example, investing $100 at 5 percent for one year yields $105; thus, Equation (1) gives the interest rate in decimal form: $i \equiv (105 - 100)/100 = 0.05$, or 5 percent.

*A **nominal interest rate** is an interest rate expressed in current dollars, unadjusted for inflation.*

*A **real interest rate** is an interest rate expressed in constant, inflation-adjusted dollars.*

Interest rates may be either nominal or real rates. A **nominal interest rate** is expressed in terms of current dollars, unadjusted for inflation. A **real interest rate** is expressed in terms of inflation-adjusted constant dollars. For example, if the nominal interest rate is 6 percent per year and the inflation rate is 2 percent per year, then the real interest rate will be about 4 percent. A person who invested $100 on January 1 would have $106 by January 1 of the next year; however, with 2 percent inflation the $106 could buy goods and services that only $104 would have purchased a year earlier.

To give more precision to these ideas, suppose a bundle of goods costs $\$p_0$ today and $\$p_1$ in one year. If $\$p_0$ is invested today, next year the consumer will have $\$p_0 (1 + i)$, where i is the nominal interest rate. How many bundles can the consumer purchase with $\$p_0 (1 + i)$? The answer is obtained by dividing by the new price level, $\$p_1$. The consumer can now buy

$$p_0(1 + i)/p_1.$$

But by definition the inflation rate is

$$\pi = (p_1 - p_0)/p_0 = p_1/p_0 - 1.$$

Thus:

$$(1 + \pi) = p_1/p_0.$$

Substituting the above expression into $p_0(1 + i)p_1$, we can see that the consumer will be able to buy in one year $(1 + i)/(1 + \pi)$ units of the bundle. But the consumer sacrificed one bundle; therefore, the real rate of interest is

$$r = (1 + i)/(1 + \pi) - 1. \tag{2}$$

The real interest rate may be approximated by the simpler formula, $r \approx i -$

---

1. Irving Fisher, *The Theory of Interest* (New York: Macmillan, 1930); John Rae, *The Sociological Theory of Capital* (1905); and Eugen von Böhm-Bawerk, *The Positive Theory of Capital* (1891). Rae's work originally appeared in 1834.

EXAMPLE 15-1   Real and Nominal Interest Rates

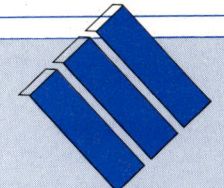

How high are real interest rates? The answer is: not that high. From 1955 to 1985, the average rate of interest on high-grade (Aaa) corporate bonds was 7.4 percent. The average rate of inflation, measured by the implicit gross-national-product deflator, was 4.7 percent. Thus, the approximate real interest rate on these bonds has averaged 2.7 percent over the past 31 years.

So if someone offers you a bond guaranteeing a *real* rate of interest of 4 percent a year, you should jump at the chance.

Source: *Economic Report of the President*, February 1986, pp. 256, 332.

π. By adding 1 to both sides of Equation (2) and multiplying by $(1 + \pi)$, we can write:

$$(1 + r)(1 + \pi) = (1 + i)$$

or

$$i = r + \pi + r\pi.$$

Because the expression $r\pi$ will be small if the inflation rate and the interest rate are small, it can be ignored. When $\pi = 0.02$ and $i = 0.06$, then $r = (1.06)/(1.02) - 1 = 0.0392$. In this example, using the approximation formula $r \approx i - \pi$, we would get a similar result: $0.06 - 0.02 = 0.04$. (See Example 15-1.)

INTERTEMPORAL CONSUMPTION AND SAVING

The theory of intertemporal consumption is a simplified account of the principles governing the allocation of a consumer's budget between present and future consumption. The consumer is assumed to estimate future income possibilities, to know the terms on which he or she can borrow and lend, and to have an idea about future tastes. The rational consumer is assumed to draw up a consumption plan that maximizes utility.

The Budget Constraint

To simplify the theory, we will assume that the consumer has a two-period horizon: a present year and a future year. He or she must decide on consumption for two years and put affairs in order by paying off all debts, or collecting all claims, before the end of the horizon.

The budget constraint shows the possible consumption plans that can be attained through borrowing or lending in capital markets. To keep the theory as simple as possible, we will assume that the capital market is perfectly competitive, meaning that anyone can borrow or lend freely at a single, fixed interest rate.

We will measure income, consumption, and interest rates in terms of an unchanging monetary standard. (A price index, like the one described in Chapter 4, can be used to compare income and consumption in different time periods.) Thus, we will focus exclusively on real interest rates, real consumption, and real income.

<u>An **income stream** shows how much a person earns in present and future years.</u>

A consumer's **income stream** is made up of his or her yearly income amounts in the current and future years. The person's **consumption stream** (or *plan*) is made up of yearly consumption amounts in the current and future years. We will assume, for simplicity, that all receipts and expenditures are recorded at the beginning of each year.

<u>A **consumption stream** shows how much a person consumes in present and future years.</u>

A consumer's income stream for the current year (year 0) and a future year (year 1) is the pair of income amounts (y_0, y_1). The person's consumption stream for the same two years would be the pair of consumption amounts (c_0, c_1). The real interest rate prevailing during both periods is r. (With only two periods, it is not necessary to introduce more interest rates.) In year 1 (the future year), no borrowing or lending takes place; there is only debt repayment.

As we reviewed in Chapter 2, the present value of a future sum of money is the amount that must be invested today to generate the future sum of money. For example, if the rate of interest is 0.10 or 10 percent, $100 invested today generates $110 in one year; that is, $100 is the present value of $110 to be received in one year. If $PV is invested for one year, it grows to $PV(1 + r)$. When $PV(1 + r)$ is invested for one year, it grows to $PV(1 + r)^2$. In general, the present value of y_t dollars in t years is

$$PV = \frac{(y_t)}{(1 + r)^t} \qquad (3)$$

where it is assumed that y_t is stated in constant, or real, dollars and r is the average real interest rate over the entire t years.[2] (See Example 15-2.)

The consumer's intertemporal budget constraint shows how borrowings are repaid or how savings are spent. Suppose the consumer saves in the present year; in other words, income in the present year exceeds consumption in the present year. Thus, saving (S) equals $y_0 - c_1$. When these savings are lent at the market interest rate, their future-year value is $S(1 + r)$. The

---

2. The present-value formula can also be used with nominal dollars and interest rates. The present value of y_t dollars in t years is $PV = y_t/(1 + i)^t$, where i is the nominal interest rate. Indeed, in most practical applications, this is the proper formula. For example, car payments and mortgage payments are stated in nominal terms. The present value of the stream of payments is equal to the value of the loan when the nominal interest rate is used to discount future payments.

FIGURE 15-1   The Intertemporal Budget Constraint

The budget constraint is made up of all the points, such as a, that represent consumption plans (c_0, c_1) consistent with the consumer's income over two years (y_0, y_1). The budget line intersects the horizontal axis at c_0^*, the present value of the income stream. It intersects the vertical axis at point c_1^* which equals $y_1 + y_0(1 + r)$, the future value of the income stream. The absolute value of the slope of the budget line is $1 + r$.

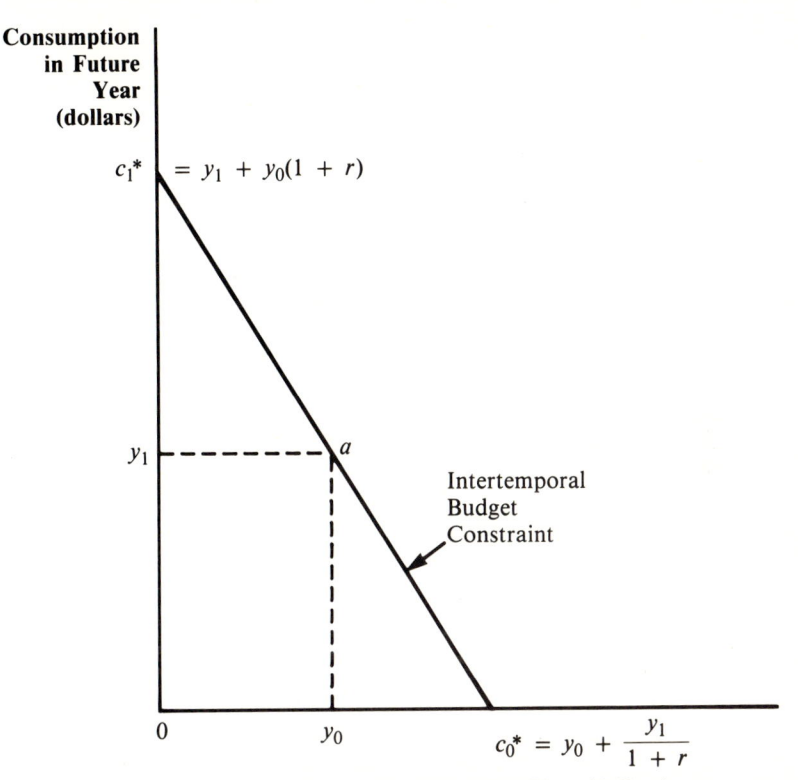

[Figure: Graph with "Consumption in Future Year (dollars)" on vertical axis and "Consumption in Present Year (dollars)" on horizontal axis. Vertical intercept at $c_1^* = y_1 + y_0(1 + r)$. Point a at (y_0, y_1). Horizontal intercept at $c_0^* = y_0 + \dfrac{y_1}{1 + r}$. Downward-sloping line labeled "Intertemporal Budget Constraint".]

consumer's consumption in year 1 (the future year) will equal his or her year 1 income plus the future-year value of his or her savings; that is,

$$c_1 = y_1 + (y_0 - c_0)(1 + r). \tag{4}$$

Equation (4) could also be used to calculate the future-year consumption of a consumer who borrows rather than saves. For the borrowing consumer, $c_0 > y_0$. The borrowing consumer would have to repay $(c_0 - y_0)(1 + r)$ out of the future year's income; thus, year 1 consumption could be only

$$c_1 = y_1 - [(c_0 - y_0)(1 + r)],$$

which is the same as Equation (4). If we divide Equation (4) by $(1 + r)$ and rearrange, Equation (4) can also be written as

$$c_0 + c_1/(1 + r) = y_0 + y_1/(1 + r). \tag{5}$$

As Equation (5) shows, the present value of the consumption stream must equal the present value of the income stream.

Figure 15-1 shows an intertemporal budget constraint. Future consumption or income is measured vertically; present consumption or income is

FIGURE 15-2   Intertemporal Indifference Curves

The indifference curves between present and future consumption are similar to ordinary indifference curves. Utility increases on higher curves such as U', where consumption bundles d and c are preferred to bundles a and b. A balanced bundle, such as e, is even better. The indifference curves are downward-sloping and convex to the origin.

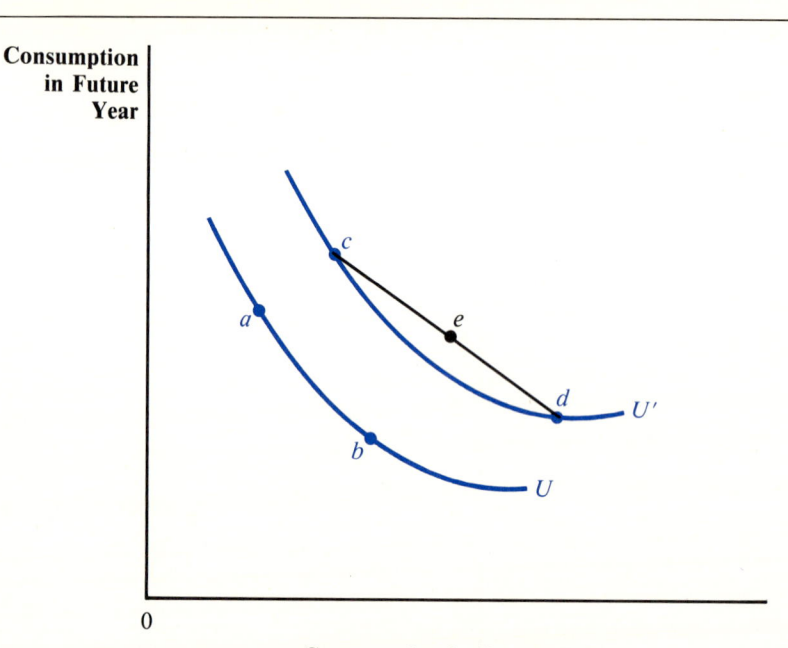

measured horizontally. Point a represents the income stream (y_0, y_1). The maximum present consumption, c_0^*, would occur when the consumer borrows the present value of his or her future income, or $y_0 + y_1/(1 + r)$. The maximum future consumption, c_1^*, would occur when the consumer loaned all current income to obtain a future amount of $y_1 + y_0(1 + r)$. The absolute value of the slope of the budget line is $1 + r$, because the sacrifice of $1 in the present yields $(1 + r)$ in the future.

The budget constraint shows all the combinations of present and future consumption consistent with the consumer's wealth. The budget constraint also shows the various income streams having the same present value or yielding the same wealth. Since the consumer can achieve all of the points on a given budget line, we reach a fundamental principle:

In a perfectly competitive capital market, the consumer will be indifferent between all income streams giving rise to the same present value or wealth because all such income streams place the same budget constraint on possible consumption plans.

Intertemporal Consumption

Assume now that the consumer ranks different intertemporal consumption streams according to the utility function

$$U = U(c_0, c_1).$$

FIGURE 15-3   The Optimal Consumption Plan: Saving

Utility is maximized at point e, where the rate of time preference, or the absolute slope of the indifference curve, RTP, equals the slope of the budget line, $1 + r$. Point a is the consumer's present income position. The consumer saves the amount $y_0 - c_0$ in year 0 because income is relatively higher in the present.

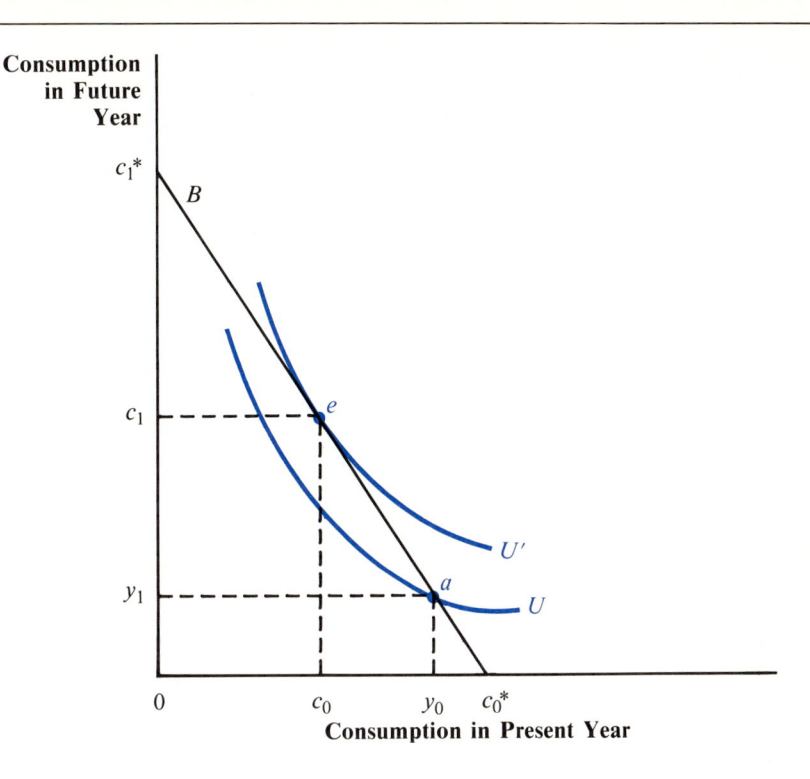

Just as in the ordinary theory of consumer behavior, there exist indifference curves between present and future consumption; consuming more is assumed to be better than consuming less. In Figure 15-2, indifference curves U and U' are alternative indifference curves between present-year and future-year consumption. The consumer is indifferent between points a and b along U or between c and d along U'. Since plan c contains more of both present and future consumption than plan a, indifference curve U' represents a higher level of utility than indifference curve U. The indifference curves are downward-sloping, indicating that the consumer is willing to sacrifice present consumption for enough future consumption, or vice versa. Finally, the indifference curves are convex to the origin, which indicates that balanced consumption bundles are preferred to unbalanced bundles (point e is better than c or d).

Optimal Consumption Plans

A rational consumer will arrange his or her intertemporal consumption until utility is maximized subject to the budget constraint. Figure 15-3 combines the intertemporal budget constraint of Figure 15-1 with the intertemporal

FIGURE 15-4   The Optimal Consumption Plan: Borrowing

In contrast to the case in Figure 15-3, when future income is relatively higher than current income, as at point b, the consumer may optimize consumption (at point e) by borrowing $c_0 - y_0$ and repaying this sum later.

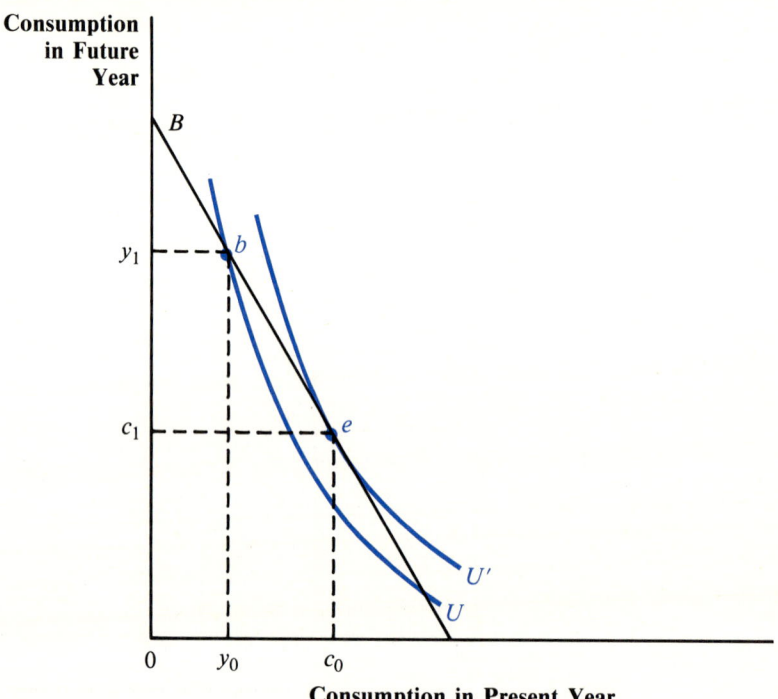

The **rate of time preference (RTP)** is the marginal rate of substitution of future consumption for current consumption.

indifference curves of Figure 15-2. The consumer's current income position is indicated by point a, where the absolute slope of the indifference curve U is less than the absolute slope of the budget line. The absolute slope of the indifference curve measures the **rate of time preference (RTP)**, which is the marginal rate of substitution of future for present consumption.

The rate of time preference is the *consumer's* personal valuation of another unit of present consumption; the slope of the budget line, $1 + r$, is the *market's* valuation of another unit of present consumption. As long as the RTP is less than $1 + r$, the consumer will sacrifice present consumption for future consumption. In Figure 15-3, the consumer maximizes utility at point e, where $RTP = 1 + r$.

The consumer's optimal intertemporal consumption plan is achieved 1) when the present value of the consumption plan equals the present value of the income stream and 2) when $RTP = 1 + r$.

The consumer in Figure 15-3 is saving because current income, y_0, is greater than optimal current consumption, c_0. Thus, optimal saving is the difference: $S = y_0 - c_0$. Why does the consumer save? The income stream (y_0, y_1) is biased sufficiently in favor of current income that RTP at point a is lower than $1 + r$. Income in the present is high; income in the future is

FIGURE 15-5 Increased Wealth

An increase in wealth increases both future and present consumption when consumption bundles are normal goods. If the income stream shifts from point *a* to point *c*, saving increases; if it shifts to point *d*, saving decreases.

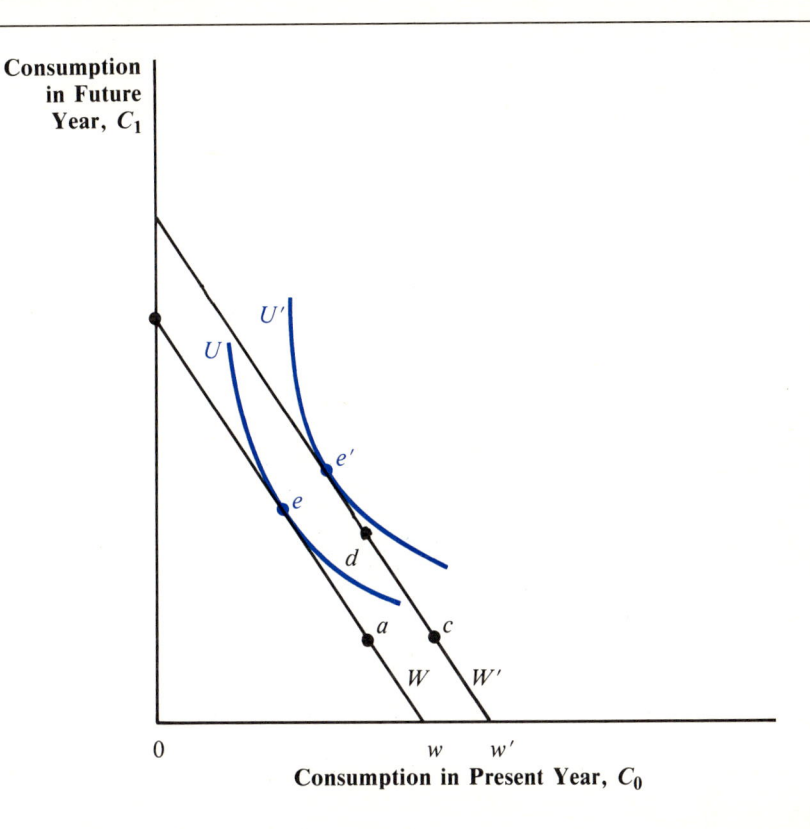

relatively low. Thus, the consumer balances present and future consumption by saving.

If the income stream were different, the consumer might be a borrower. For example, in Figure 15-4 the consumer's present income is low and future income is high. At point *b*, the *RTP* is greater than $1 + r$. Accordingly, the consumer would balance present and future consumption by borrowing the amount $(c_0 - y_0)$ and repaying the amount $(c_0 - y_0)(1 + r)$ in the future.

Wealth and Substitution Effects

Consider now the effects of an increase in wealth, *W*—defined as the present value of his or her income stream—on the consumer's consumption plan. Wealth is measured by the horizontal (current-year) intercept. In Figure 15-5, wealth increases from *W* to *W'*, but the interest rate remains constant. Thus, the slope of the budget line remains the same. If both current and future consumption are normal goods, an increase in wealth will increase consumption in both periods. Thus, point *e'* is northeast of point *e*.

The change in wealth considered in Figure 15-5 could have arisen from

FIGURE 15-6 Substitution and Income Effects

When the interest rate rises, the slope of the budget line (the absolute value of $1 + r$) changes. The new budget line, W', is steeper than the old line, W. Increased returns on savings increase the consumer's wealth and overall consumption level. The substitution effect on saving—the move from e to e'—is an increase in savings; the income effect on savings—the move from e' to e''—is a *reduction* in saving. Total saving may rise or fall (as shown).

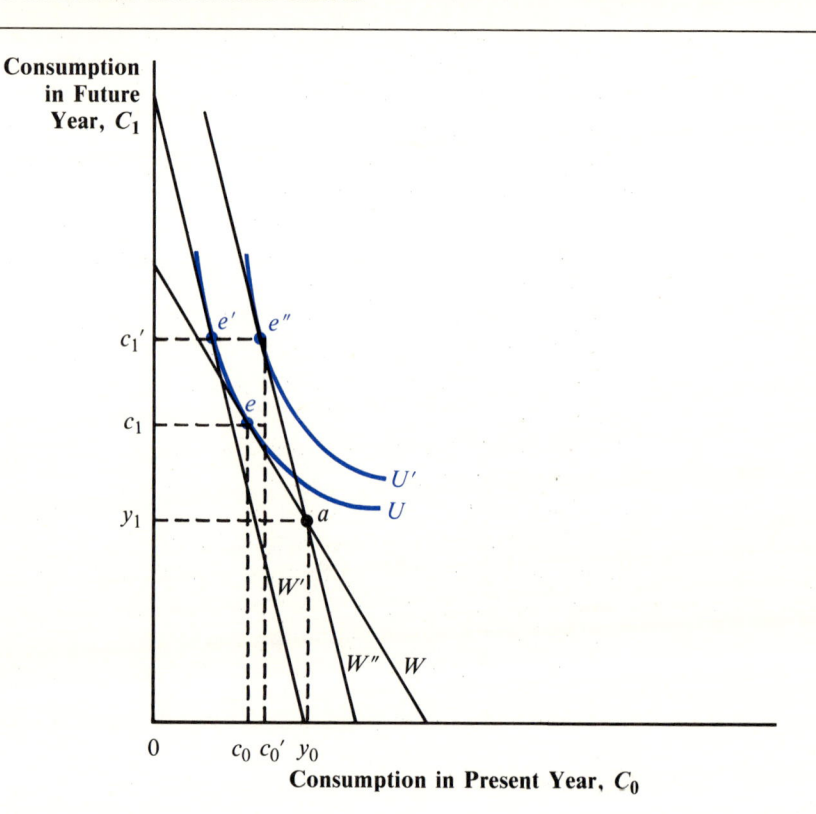

any combination of changes in current and future income. For example, the income stream could have shifted from point a to either point c or d; the effect on consumption (but not on saving) would be the same. What happens to saving depends on what happens to current income. If the new current-income level were represented by point c, saving (the difference between current income and current consumption) would increase; if the new current-income level were represented by point d, saving would decrease.

Does an increase in the rate of interest stimulate lending (saving out of current income) and discourage borrowing (*dissaving*)?

Figure 15-6 shows a consumer whose budget line is W before an increase in the interest rate. The consumer's income stream is a and the equilibrium consumption plan is e; therefore, the consumer is saving. When the interest rate increases, the budget lines become steeper. If the income stream remains the same when the interest rate changes, the new budget line, W''', must go through the initial income stream, a. Because the increase in the interest rate also allows the consumer's savings to earn a higher rate of return, the consumer's level of utility rises from U to U' as the consumption plan shifts from e to e''. The indifference curves have been drawn so that current consumption rises from c_0 to c_0'. Because income remains the same as consumption rises, saving falls even though the interest rate has risen.

FIGURE 15-7 Interest Rates and Saving

Interest rate r^* is whatever rate induces zero saving. From r^* to some rate r', the saving curve is upward-sloping, because the substitution effect of an increase in interest more than offsets the income effect. Above r', the opposite is true: the income effect dominates and induces the consumer to decrease savings and increase consumption.

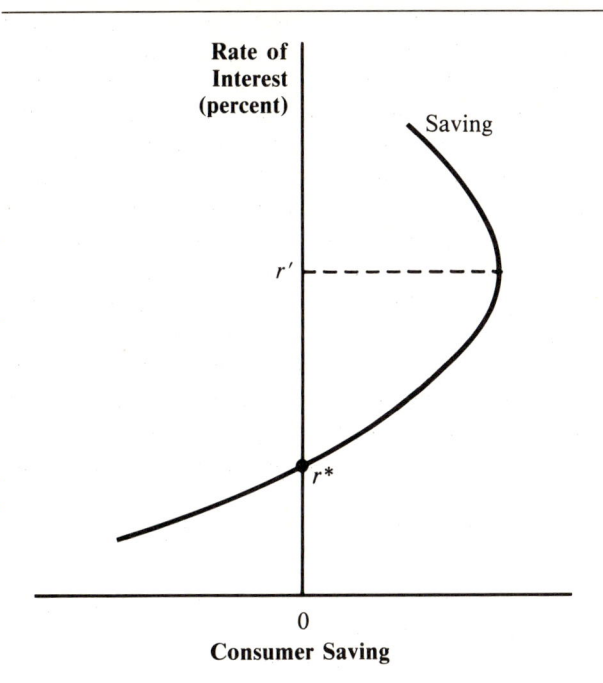

[Graph: Rate of Interest (percent) on vertical axis, Consumer Saving on horizontal axis. A backward-bending Saving curve is shown, with r^* marked at zero saving and r' marked at the point where the curve bends back.]

To see why in this particular instance saving decreases when the interest rate increases, we must break down the move from e to e'' into the customary income and substitution effects. The substitution effect shows the effect on saving of a change in interest rates, holding utility constant. Thus, the consumer's behavior is first examined in relation to the interim budget line, W'. The substitution effect is the move from point e to e' that reduces present consumption and increases saving. But wealth has increased. The income effect on saving of the increase in interest rates is the shift from e' on budget line W' to e'' on budget line W''. Greater wealth stimulates present and future consumption. If the income effect is large enough, as in the diagram, the increase in present consumption attributable to the income effect can exceed the reduction in present consumption attributable to the substitution effect. In this case, present consumption rises, and saving falls. Of course, the indifference curves could have been drawn so that the substitution effect exceeded the income effect. In that case, an increase in the interest rate would increase saving.

What would be the effect of an increase in interest rates on a borrower? In the case of a borrower, the income effect must reduce current consumption. Thus, both the substitution effect and the income effect would be a reduction in current consumption. Because borrowing equals present consumption minus income, an increase in the rate of interest will reduce borrowing.

Figure 15-7 shows the global relationship between the rate of interest and saving. The diagram assumes that there is a positive rate of interest, r^*, that will induce zero saving. It is possible that the consumer will want to save

FIGURE 15-8 Present Value of Income Streams

Income stream a has a lower present value than income stream a' when interest rates are the same. Given a choice, the consumer will prefer any point on budget line W' to any point on W because it provides a higher level of utility.

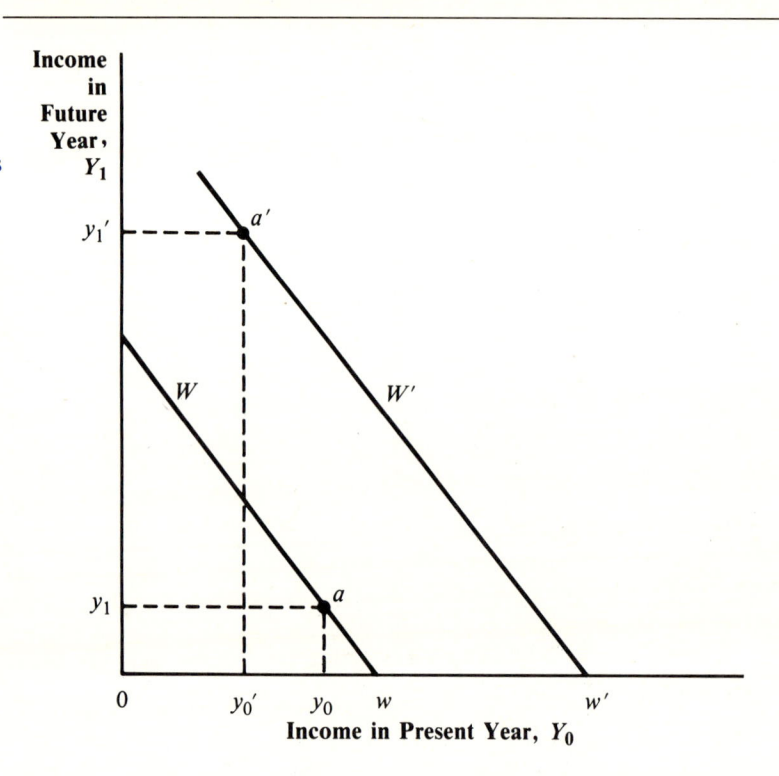

even at a zero interest rate. The saving curve is upward-sloping until the interest rate r' is reached. Because saving is positive above r^*, the substitution effect of an increase in interest rates discourages current consumption, and the income effect encourages current consumption. Between interest rates r^* and r', the substitution effect dominates the income effect, but as saving increases, the income effect becomes larger. Eventually, at r', the income effect begins to dominate the substitution effect. For any interest rate increase above r', saving actually declines (as in Figure 15-6).

INTERTEMPORAL PRODUCTION AND INVESTMENT

Investment, or intertemporal production, requires modifying the present and future income stream of the business firm. To study investment, we will again consider a simple two-period model.

The Present-Value Rule

We have seen that the consumer facing a perfectly competitive capital market is indifferent between income streams yielding the same present value, or wealth. Such income streams lie on the same budget line and, thus,

FIGURE 15-9 The Income-Possibilities Curve

With a cash flow of (y_0, y_1) at point b, the firm can invest bc of current income and increase future income by ce. The income-possibilities curve, *IPC*, is based on all similar possibilities for increasing future income through investment. The absolute value of the slope of *IPC* is the gross rate of return on investment, $1 + \rho$.

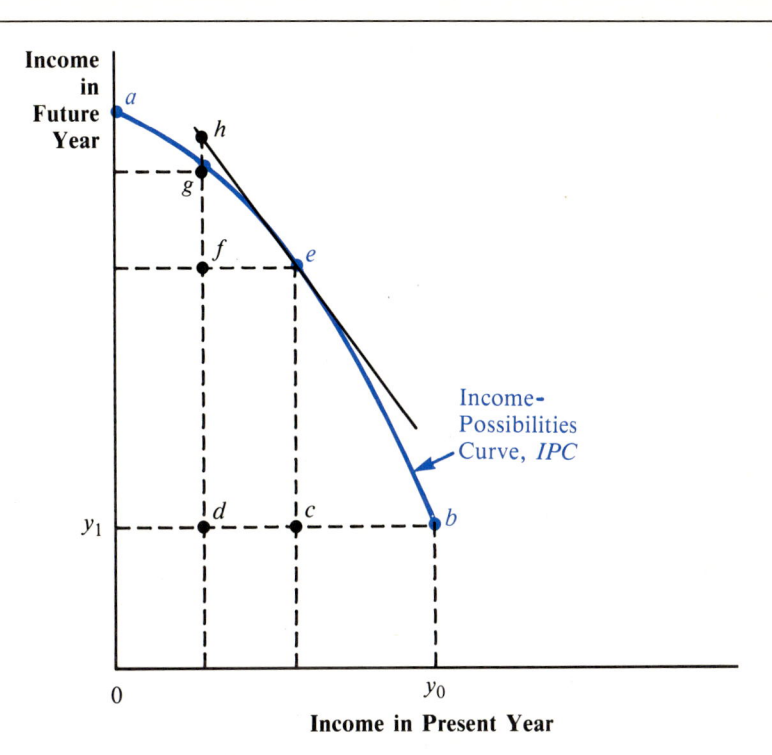

give rise to the same optimal consumption plan. Ruling out nonsatiation, between any two income streams, any economic agent will prefer the one with the highest present value. In Figure 15-8, the fact that income stream a', with a present value of w', is better than income stream a, with a smaller present value of w, illustrates the **present-value rule**.

Investment and the Rate of Return

The **present-value rule** is that the economic agent can achieve the highest intertemporal utility by choosing the income stream with the highest present value, regardless of the shape of the income stream or preferences.

The present-value rule is important to the theory of intertemporal production, or internal investment, because the choice between alternative investments is really a choice between alternative income streams.

A firm has an endowment of future and present income even before it undertakes any investment. A typical firm owns a particular stock of capital goods. If this stock is maintained, the firm can generate a profit stream by employing labor and other variable inputs. In a two-period context, the firm's initial income stream is the pair of numbers (y_0, y_1) representing net income in the present year and in the future year.

In Figure 15-9, the firm's current capital stock is assumed to generate the income stream (y_0, y_1), which is represented by point b. By devoting, say, bc of its current income to investment, the firm can increase its future income by the quantity ce. The further investment of cd will increase future income

FIGURE 15-10   Maximizing the Firm's Present Value

The present value of the firm is maximized by investing up to point e, where the rate of return equals the rate of interest. The value of the initial capital stock, before investing, is k.

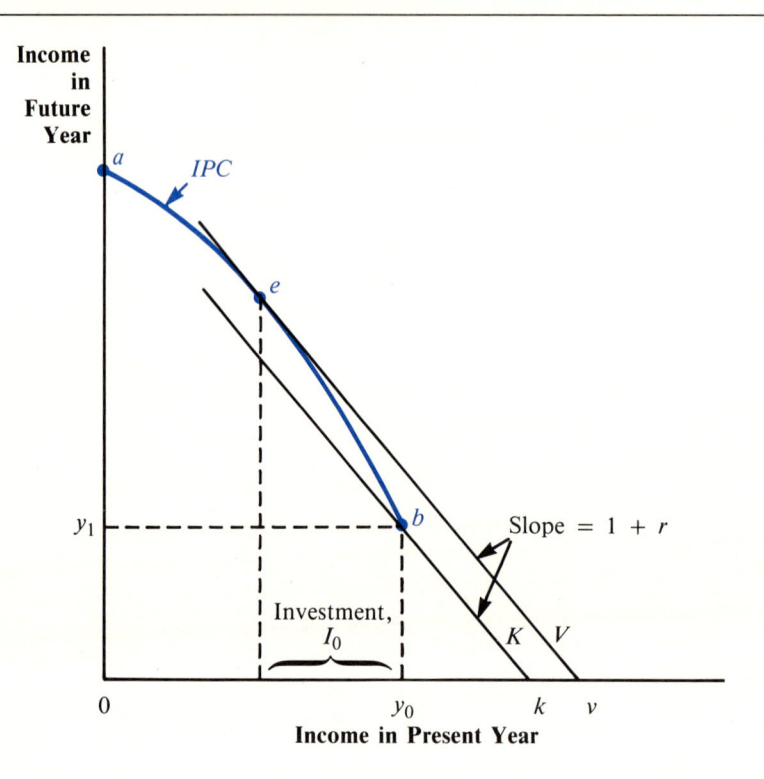

[Figure: IPC curve from point a through e to b, with tangent line of Slope = $1 + r$ touching at e; axes labeled "Income in Future Year" (vertical) and "Income in Present Year" (horizontal); y_1 marked on vertical axis, y_0, k, v on horizontal axis; Investment I_0 bracketed between y_0 and b's projection; K and V labeled along the tangent line.]

by fg. Various investments will then give rise to the **income-possibilities curve (IPC)**. The rate of return, ρ, on any investment, I, is

$$\rho = \frac{(\Delta Y - I)}{I} = \frac{\Delta Y}{I} - 1 . \tag{6}$$

Given the concavity of the *IPC* to the origin, the average rate of return on investment from b to e is higher than the average rate of return from e to g. To measure the rate of return at a given point, such as e, we can construct the tangent he; the rate of return is then

$$\rho = fh/cd - 1.$$

Income-possibilities curve (IPC) shows the intertemporal income streams available to the firm through different investment projects.

Hence, the absolute value of the slope of the *IPC* at any point, minus one, measures the rate of return on investment at that point. The absolute value of the slope itself measures the gross rate of return, $(1 + \rho)$.

The role of the law of diminishing returns to investment, reflected in the concavity of the *IPC*, is to limit the amount of external investment the firm will wish to make at any given interest rate. Should the firm invest externally in the capital market or invest in its own product? Further internal invest-

FIGURE 15–11   Effect of an Increase in Interest Rate

If the capital-market interest rate rises, the firm tends to decrease internal investment, as shown by the drop from I_0 to I_1. The higher interest rates available from external investments mean that fewer internal projects will yield higher rates of return.

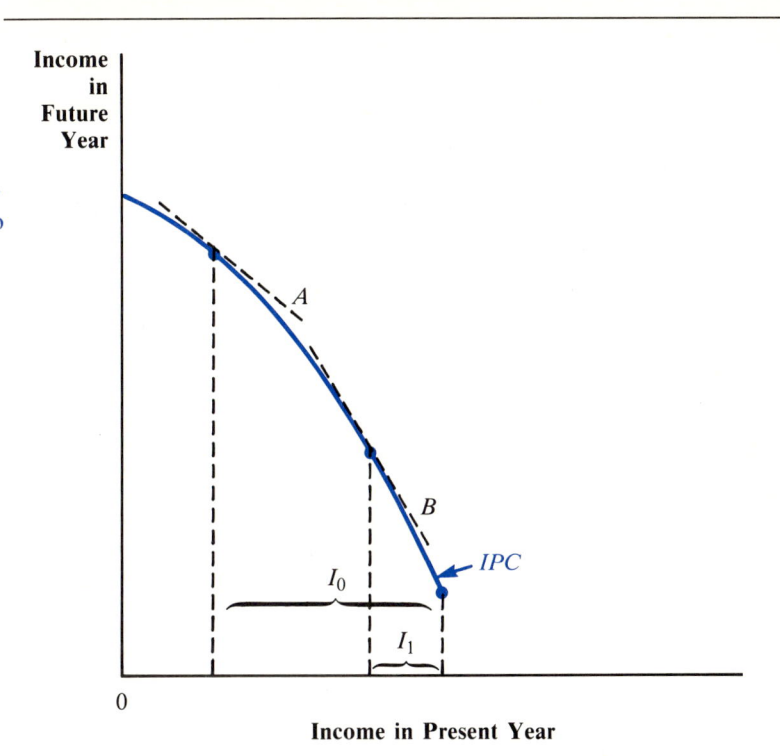

ments will be made provided the rate of return exceeds the rate of interest. The firm stops expanding investment at the point where the rate of return equals the rate of interest.

When the rate of return equals the rate of interest, the firm is selecting an income stream that maximizes the present value of the firm—as shown in Figure 15–10. The present value of any point on the income-possibilities curve *ab* is the horizontal (present-year) intercept of a straight line drawn through the point with an absolute slope of $1 + r$. Because the firm's initial capital stock generates the income represented by the initial income stream, *b*, the value of the initial capital stock is *k*, the intercept of line *K* through *b*. For investments falling short of I_0, the firm will move to an income stream between *e* and *b*. Such a point will have a present value higher than *k*. Clearly, the maximum present value, *v*, is attained at point *e*.

A higher rate of interest will discourage investment. The higher is the market interest rate, the higher is the opportunity cost of investing in real capital goods as opposed to putting funds to work in the capital market. At higher interest rates, the firm can find fewer internal investments that will pay more than the market. Figure 15–11 illustrates the effect of a higher

EXAMPLE 15–2 Short-Term and Long-Term Interest Rates

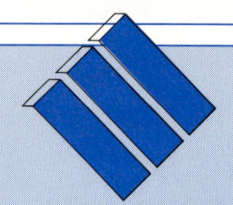

Some bonds have maturity dates of a few months; others have maturity dates of 30 or more years. Generally speaking, a bond with a maturity date more than one year from the present is considered long-term, while a bond with a maturity date of less than one year is considered short-term. How do interest rates compare on short-term and long-term instruments? Suppose bond A has a maturity date of one year, and bond B has a maturity date of two years. Let r_1 be the one-year interest rate in the first year, and let r_2 be the expected one-year interest rate in the second year. What would be the interest rate r^* on the two-year bond? To simplify, assume the two-year bond pays a fixed amount in two years.

If you invested $1 in a succession of one-year bonds, you would have, at the end of two years, the amount $(1 + r_1)(1 + r_2)$, because at the end of one year you would have the amount $(1 + r_1)$ to invest in another one-year bond at the interest rate r_2. On the other hand, if you invested $1 in the two-year bond, at the end of two years you would have $(1 + r^*)^2$. The dollar that is paid for the two-year bond must be the present value of the maturity value, M; that is,

$$\$1 = M/(1 + r^*)^2.$$

Clearly, an investor will be indifferent (ignoring risk and liquidity considerations) between the two bonds if at the end of two years the dollar grows to the same future value. Thus, indifference requires that

$$(1 + r_1)(1 + r_2) = (1 + r^*)^2.$$

Thus, it is clear that $r^* = r_1$ if and only if $r_1 = r_2$. In other words, the long-term interest rate will equal the short-term interest rate if short-term interest rates are expected to stay constant. Long-term rates will exceed short-term rates if short-term rates are expected to rise; that is, if $r_2 > r_1$, then $r^* > r_1$. Finally, long-term rates will fall short of short-term rates if short-term rates are expected to fall; that is, if $r_2 < r_1$, then $r^* < r_1$.

The accompanying figure shows that the interest rate on 3-month Treasury bills has generally been less than the interest rate on 10-year government bonds. Long-term government bonds must pay a premium rate because they are subject to somewhat greater price risk (because as interest rates change over time, their prices vary inversely). Short-term interest rates exceed long-term rates only when interest rates are expected to fall. Notice that the short-term rates exceed the long-term rates only on upswings.

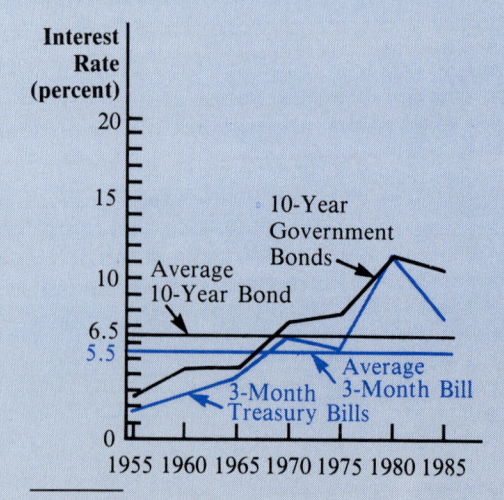

Source: *Economic Report of the President*, January 1987, p. 334.

FIGURE 15-12   The Interest Rate in an Equilibrium Market

The equilibrium real interest rate, r, is determined where the saving curve intersects the investment curve, or where the quantity of funds savers wish to save equals the quantity investors wish to invest.

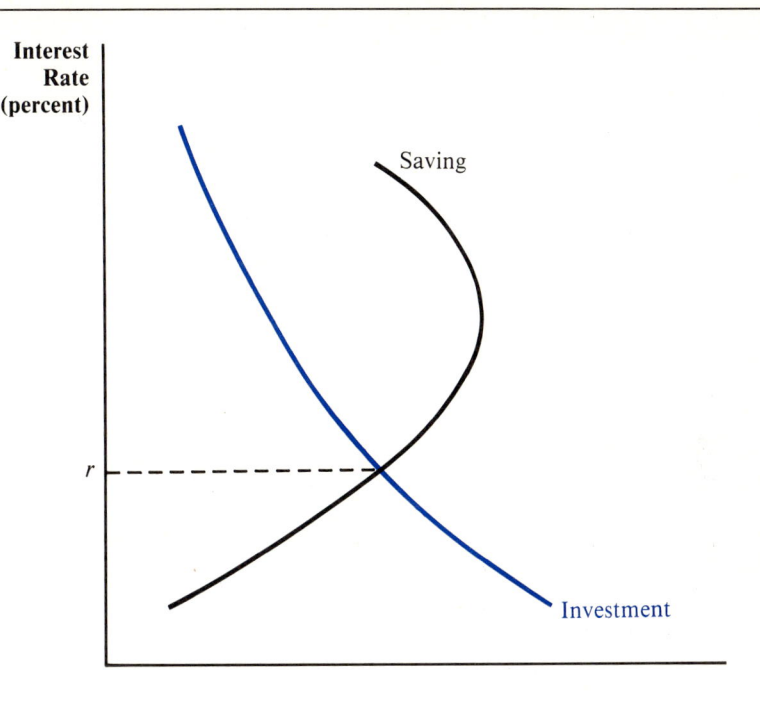

(Graph: Interest Rate (percent) on vertical axis versus Quantity of Saving or Investment (dollars) on horizontal axis. A backward-bending Saving curve intersects a downward-sloping Investment curve at interest rate r.)

interest rate. When the interest rate rises, the slope of the income-possibilities curve becomes steeper, shifting from the slope of A to the slope of B. Thus, the firm's optimal internal investment falls from I_0 to I_1 when the interest rate rises.

MARKET EQUILIBRIUM

The market for borrowing and lending is the capital market. Both firms and households will find themselves on both sides of the market. Some households are borrowing and some are lending; some firms are borrowing and some are lending. The capital market will be in equilibrium when the rate of interest is such that (1) each household is maximizing its utility, (2) each firm is maximizing its present value, and (3) the aggregate quantity of borrowing equals the aggregate quantity of lending.

Figure 15-12 shows the determination of the real interest in the simplified economy considered above. Where the investment curve intersects the saving curve determines the equilibrium real interest rate. The thriftiness of the population underlies the saving curve; the productivity of investments underlies the investment curve.

FIGURE 15-13   The Effect of a Deficit on Consumption

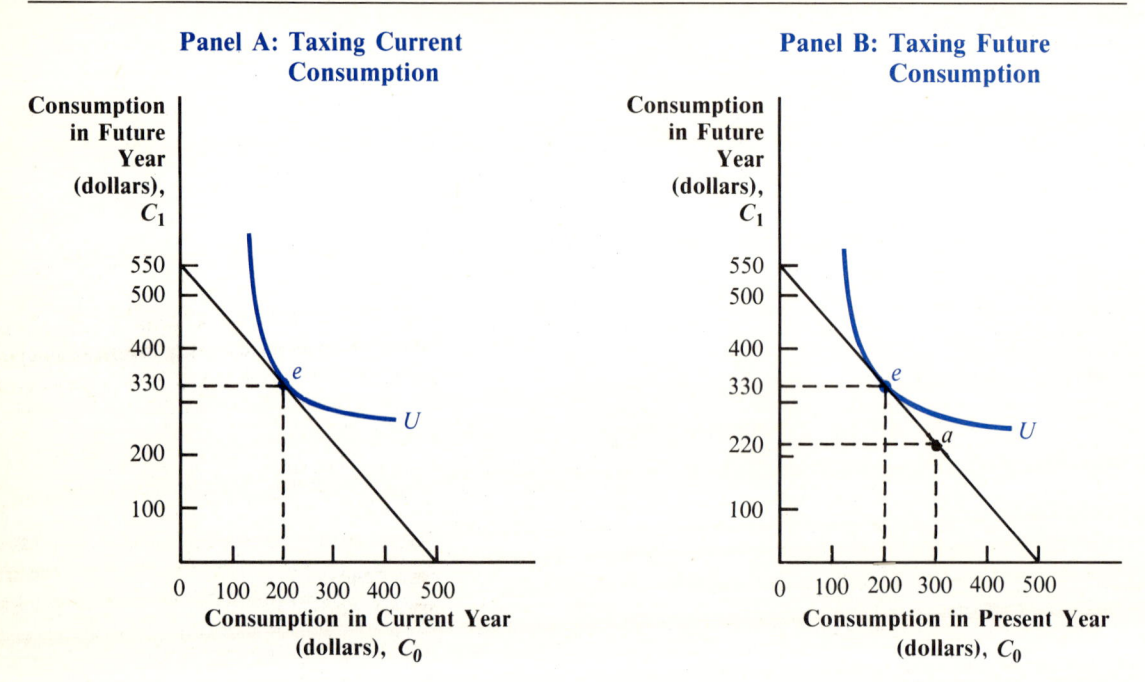

Panel A: Taxing Current Consumption

Panel B: Taxing Future Consumption

Suppose a consumer's income is $300 in the current year and $330 in a future year. In Panel A, taxes are $100 in the current year; in Panel B, taxes are $110 in the future year to finance a deficit. If the equilibrium interest rate is 10 percent, taxing current income has the same effect on consumption as taxing future income. Thus, saving is $100 larger in Panel B than in Panel A.

DO DEFICITS AFFECT REAL INTEREST RATES?

When the government spends more than it receives through current taxation, the government is said to *run a deficit*. In 1987, such a deficit was estimated to be about $170 billion. The U.S. government runs deficits year after year. Do such deficits raise real interest rates? According to the theory presented in this chapter, not necessarily.

If the deficit is viewed by the population as representing future taxation, the public must save to pay future taxes. For example, the consumer would consider $100 in taxes today the equivalent of $110 in taxes in one year if the interest rate were 10 percent. Imagine a consumer with an income of $300 today and $330 in one year. Panel A of Figure 15-13 shows the consumer facing $100 in taxes today; Panel B shows the same consumer facing $110 in taxes in one year. In both cases, the consumer spends the identical amount in each year. If government spending is $100, Panel A corresponds to no deficit and Panel B corresponds to a current-year deficit of $100. Notice that in Panel B, saving equals exactly $100 more than in Panel A, so that the additional saving just matches the current deficit.[3]

Commonsense business economists and politicians often hold that government deficits must increase real interest rates, because they force the government to compete for limited capital funds. Pure theory suggests, however, that anything is possible. If people do not anticipate future taxes, deficits will not attract matching savings as outlined by Figure 15-13. Just as theory presents an inconclusive analysis, the empirical evidence is also conflicting.[4] Until convincing empirical evidence is gathered, we cannot reach a conclusion about the effect of deficits on interest rates.

SUMMARY

1. Interest rates may be real or nominal. The nominal interest rate expresses the yield in terms of current dollars, unadjusted for inflation; the real interest rate expresses the yield in terms of constant, inflation-adjusted dollars.

2. In a perfectly competitive capital market, each economic agent can borrow or lend at a single, fixed interest rate. The intertemporal budget constraint shows that the present value of the consumption stream must equal the present value of the income stream; it implies that whatever is borrowed must be repaid (with interest) or whatever is saved must eventually be spent (with interest). The rate of time preference, *RTP*, is the marginal rate of substitution between future and present consumption. Utility is maximized when the *RTP* equals $1 + r$, where r is the real interest rate. Any income stream that yields the same present value generates the same maximum utility. Consumers are more likely to save when present income is high and future income is low; they are more likely to borrow when present income is low and future income is high. An increase in the rate of interest has a substitution effect tending to increase saving, and it also has an income effect that tends to reduce saving and increase consumption.

3. The optimal internal investment or production plan occurs when the present value of an investment project is maximized. In the two-period case, it occurs when the rate of return equals the rate of interest.

---

3. Robert Barro has extended the argument to the more realistic case in which the economy goes on forever, but generations are linked by the desire to leave the family's fortune to its children. The argument that deficits do not influence the real interest rate goes back to David Ricardo (1772–1823). See Robert Barro, "Are Government Bonds Net Wealth," *Journal of Political Economy*, November/December 1974.

4. The hypothesis that deficits do not influence real interest rates has been tested, but the evidence is mixed. See Willem Buiter and James Tobin, "Debt Neutrality: A Brief Review of Doctrine and Evidence," in George M. von Furstenburg, ed., *Social Security vs. Private Saving* (Cambridge, Mass.: Ballanger, 1979). Paul Evans, in "Do Large Deficits Produce High Interest Rates?" *American Economic Review*, March 1985, presents some evidence that deficits do not affect interest rates.

4. In market equilibrium, the rate of interest balances the saving of households and the investment of business firms.

5. The equilibrium real rate of interest may or may not be influenced by deficit financing.

QUESTIONS AND PROBLEMS

1. The nominal interest rate is 10 percent and the inflation rate is expected to be 4 percent over the next year. What is the expected real interest rate?

2. Calculate the exact real interest rates for the following two situations (annual rates):
   a. Nominal interest = 20 percent, inflation = 15 percent.
   b. Nominal interest = 6 percent, inflation = 1 percent.

3. A consumer has the two-period income stream ($200, $420). The interest rate is 0.05, or 5 percent.
   a. Draw the consumer's intertemporal budget line.
   b. What is the present value of the income stream?
   c. What is the future value of the income stream?
   d. Draw the intertemporal budget line for the interest rate $r = 0.20$ and the same income stream.

4. How is the rate of time preference (*RTP*) related to the rate of substitution of future for present consumption?

5. The interest rate is $r = 0.1$. Show the likely equilibrium configurations for the following consumers, assuming that both have the same indifference maps:
   a. John has the income stream ($100, $220).
   b. Betty has the income stream ($200, $110).

6. Two internal investment options are available to a business firm: option A, which costs $100 now and returns $290 in one year; and option B, which costs $200 now and returns $400 in one year. Using the present-value rule, which investment option would be preferred with the interest rates of 5 percent, 10 percent, and 2 percent?

7. Present an argument explaining why a government deficit may not affect real interest rates.

8. Present an argument explaining why a government deficit may raise real interest rates.

SUGGESTED READINGS

Barro, Robert J. *Macroeconomics*. New York: John Wiley and Sons, 1984, chap. 15.
Fisher, Irving. *The Theory of Interest*. New York: Macmillan, 1930, chaps. 1–3, 10–11.
Hirshleifer, J. "On the Theory of Optimal Investment Decision." *Journal of Political Economy*, August 1958.

CHAPTER 16

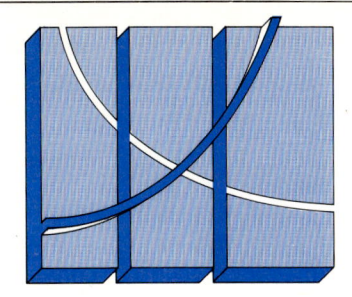

GENERAL EQUILIBRIUM

Partial-equilibrium economics studies equilibrium in a single market or for a single consumer or firm.

General-equilibrium economics studies the forces determining equilibrium in an entire economy.

In analyzing **partial-equilibrium economics**, we ignore the feedback effects between the individual firm, consumer, or market and the rest of the economy. For example, the individual consumer faces given prices; a particular market is studied on the assumption that all other market prices are given. In analyzing **general-equilibrium economics**, an entire economy is studied. No market exists in isolation; any market will be affected by prices in other markets. Studying general-equilibrium economics provides an insight into how the various elements of the economy are interrelated. The prices that we observe in the market place are not arbitrary; they are the outcome of a subtle system of general-equilibrium forces in which all parts are brought into mutual coordination.

This chapter studies two models of general equilibrium: the *pure-exchange model* (introduced in Chapter 6) and the *two-sector production model*. These models are used to show how the general equilibrium of a competitive economy is related to economic efficiency. The two-sector production model is also used to show how commodity prices are related to factor prices.

THE NATURE OF GENERAL EQUILIBRIUM

The economy consists of resources (land, labor, and capital), technology or knowledge of production processes, and the preferences of the population for different goods and services. The study of general-equilibrium economics was initiated by the great French economist, Leon Walras (1834–1910). The Walrasian economic system consists of a great many markets in which the supply and demand for each commodity or factor depends on what is

FIGURE 16–1 The Budget Constraint in a Pure-Exchange Economy

The budget constraint of a consumer in a pure-exchange economy passes through his or her endowment point, e; its absolute slope is p_b/p_a.

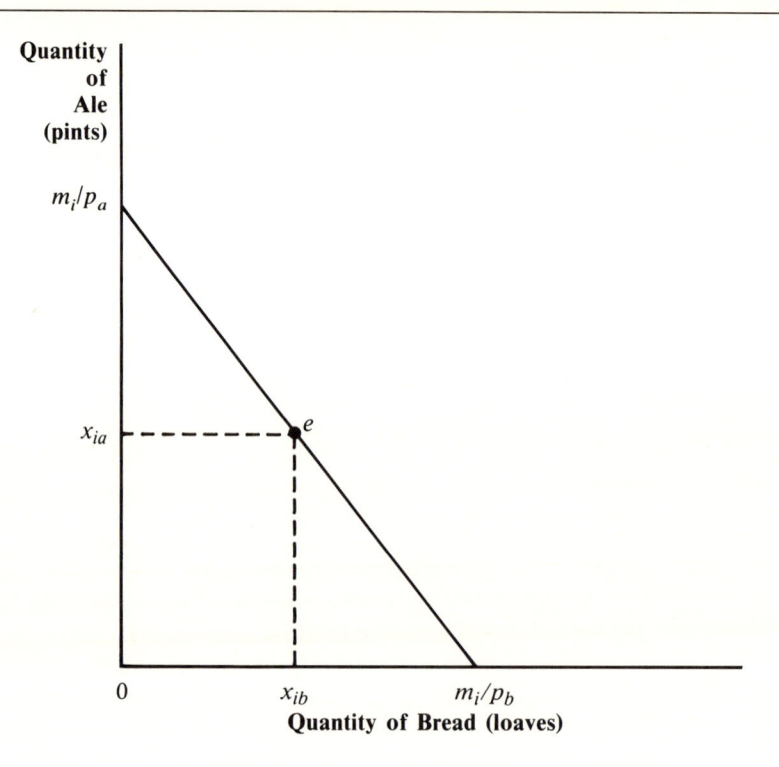

[Figure: Graph with vertical axis "Quantity of Ale (pints)" marked at m_i/p_a and x_{ia}; horizontal axis "Quantity of Bread (loaves)" marked at x_{ib} and m_i/p_b; budget line from m_i/p_a to m_i/p_b passing through endowment point e at (x_{ib}, x_{ia}).]

A **competitive equilibrium**, or a **Walrasian equilibrium**, has three characteristics: (1) each consumer maximizes utility subject to a budget constraint; (2) for the given set of prices, each business firm is maximizing the present value of profits and distributing those profits to the households owning the firm; (3) prices are such that the market quantities demanded for all goods and services equal their market quantities supplied.

going on in other markets. The economy is described by a system of *simultaneous* equations describing each person, each firm, and the supply and demand for each good or service. These equations are solved simultaneously, so that whatever happens to one person or industry can conceivably affect every person or industry. As an example, the price of tea cannot be known until the price of coffee is known because the demand for tea depends on the price of coffee; the price of coffee cannot be known until the price of tea is known because the demand for coffee depends on the price of tea. In other words, the price of tea is determined at the same time as the price of coffee.

A general equilibrium for a competitive economy is sometimes called a **competitive equilibrium**, or a **Walrasian equilibrium**, in honor of Walras.

Models of general equilibrium must completely specify every element of the economy: every consumer and his or her preferences; every production function; the quantity of each and every resource; who owns the resources; who owns the various business firms in the economy. Any model of general equilibrium containing a realistic number of consumers, firms, and commodities must be highly sophisticated.[1] Here, we shall examine very simple

---

1. See Gerard Debreu, *Theory of Value* (New York: Wiley, 1959); or Kenneth Arrow and Frank Hahn, *General Competitive Analysis* (New York: Holden-Day, 1971).

THE PURE-EXCHANGE MODEL

models. For example, we shall look at an economy with no more than two consumers, two goods, or two productive factors. Fortunately, most of the properties of the simple models generalize to the more complicated models.

THE PURE-EXCHANGE MODEL

The simplest general-equilibrium model is the two-agent, two-good pure-exchange economy. In a pure-exchange economy, there is no production; the people are simply endowed with a certain supply of each good. Such an economy was studied in Chapter 6 and will be reviewed here.

Walras's Law

Suppose there are two agents, 1 and 2, and two goods, ale and bread. Agent 1 owns quantity x_{1a} of ale and x_{1b} of bread. Agent 2 owns x_{2a} of ale and x_{2b} of bread. Each agent's income is determined by his or her supply of both goods. If p_a and p_b are the money prices of ale and bread, any agent i's income is

$$m_i = p_a x_{ia} + p_b x_{ib}.$$

Agent i consumes c_{ia} units of ale and c_{ib} units of bread. Each agent can only spend his or her income; that is,

$$p_a x_{ia} + p_b x_{ib} = p_a c_{ia} + p_b c_{ib}. \tag{1}$$

Figure 16–1 shows each agent's budget constraint. Point e describes the endowment (x_{ia}, x_{ib}) through which the budget constraint must pass (the consumer can always buy his or her original endowment). The slope of the budget constraint in absolute value is the relative price of bread, p_b/p_a, which is how many units (say, pints) of ale it takes to buy a unit (say, a loaf) of bread.

Suppose we now add up the budget constraints of both consumers. Let X_a be the aggregate or market supply of ale and X_b that of bread. Let C_a be the aggregate or market demand for ale and C_b that for bread. Because both consumers face the same prices, p_a and p_b, the aggregate budget constraint is simply:

$$p_a X_a + p_b X_b = p_a C_a + p_b C_b \tag{2}$$

The left-hand side of Equation (2) is this simple economy's gross national product, or GNP. Subtracting the left-hand side from the right-hand side yields an interesting equation:

$$p_a(C_a - X_a) + p_b(C_b - X_b) = 0. \tag{3}$$

Walras's law states that the sum of the values of all excess demands must be zero.

This equation is called **Walras's law**. Each term represents the dollar value of each good's excess demand (if the term is negative, the good is in actual excess supply). If we let the agents pick any point on their budget con-

FIGURE 16-2   The Edgeworth Box

The vertical height and horizontal width of the Edgeworth box measure the market supplies of ale and bread, respectively. Point e is the initial-endowment point for both agents. Point c is a general, competitive equilibrium because market demand equals market supply and both agents are maximizing utility.

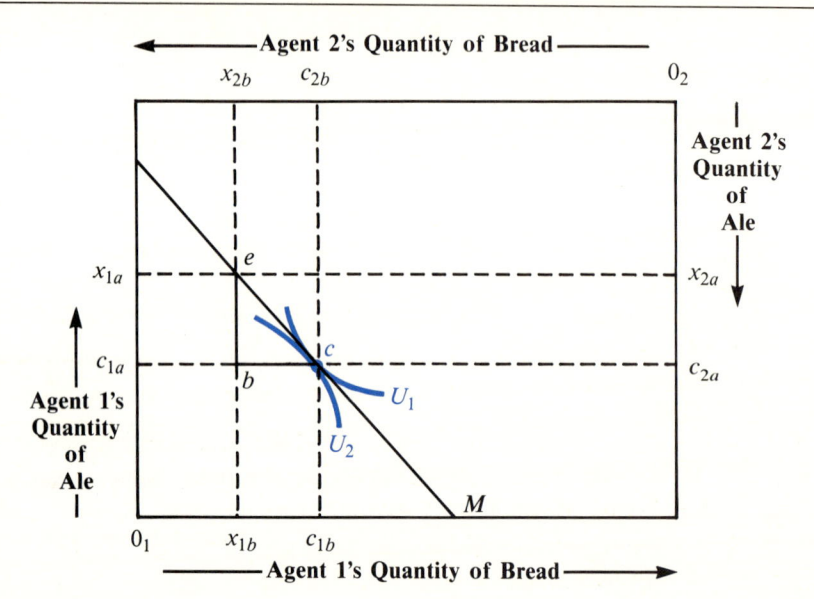

straints for any set of prices, Equation (3) says that the sum of the values of all excess demands (positive and negative) must be zero. If ale is in excess demand, then bread must be in excess supply and must be of equal value.

When a particular market is in equilibrium, its excess demand is zero. Walras's law implies that if the ale market is in equilibrium, the bread market must also be in equilibrium. When $X_a = C_a$ the first term in Equation (3) is zero; but then Equation (3) implies that the second term must also be zero, or X_b must equal C_b. Walras's law is interesting because it is a completely general proposition. If an economy contains n markets (for goods and factors), if $(n - 1)$ markets are in equilibrium, then the nth market must also be in equilibrium.

In the case of two goods, Walras's law states that it is necessary to examine the supply and demand for only one of the goods. For example, the economy will be in general equilibrium if $C_a = X_a$ or if $C_b = X_b$. If one of the equations holds, then the other holds. It follows that the second equation is not independent of the first. We really have only one independent equation to determine the unknown prices, p_a and p_b, but simple mathematics suggests that one equation can't determine two unknowns! Is this a problem? No! All that the equation $C_b = X_b$ needs to determine is the one *relative price*, p_b/p_a, rather than the two *money* prices. In a two-good model without money, there is only one market in which ale trades for bread at some relative price.

The Edgeworth Box

As in Chapter 6, we can determine the equilibrium price ratio by examining the Edgeworth box. In Figure 16-2, Agent 1's endowment or consumption is measured with respect to the origin 0_1 while Agent 2's endowment or consumption is measured with respect to origin 0_2. Agent 1's indifference curves are convex to 0_1, with utility increasing in the usual northeast direction; Agent 2's indifference curves are convex to origin 0_2, with utility increasing in the southwest direction. The horizontal width of the box measures the total amount of bread, X_b; the vertical height of the box measures the total amount of ale, X_a. Point e is the endowment point for both agents. A competitive equilibrium exists if each agent is maximizing utility and if supply equals demand. Point c represents a competitive equilibrium, because the budget line M is tangent to both indifference curves at that point and the market demand for each good equals the market supply. In equilibrium, Agent 2's excess supply of bread ($= cb$) matches Agent 1's excess demand for bread ($= cb$). The equilibrium price ratio is $p_b/p_a = eb/bc$.

To find the competitive equilibrium, we must determine the quantities consumed by Agents 1 and 2 and the equilibrium price ratio. With two agents, there are five unknown variables: c_{1a}, c_{1b}, c_{2a}, c_{2b}, and p_b/p_a. The five equations used to solve for the five unknowns are: the two budget constraints for the two consumers; the two individual equilibrium conditions at which the marginal rate of substitution equals the price ratio for each agent; and supply equals demand. If MRS_i is Agent i's marginal rate of substitution of ale for bread, the five equations are

$$p_a x_{ia} + p_b x_{ib} = p_a c_{ia} + p_b c_{ib} \tag{4}$$

$$p_a x_{2a} + p_b x_{2b} = p_a c_{2a} + p_b c_{2b} \tag{5}$$

$$MRS_1 = p_b/p_a \tag{6}$$

$$MRS_2 = p_b/p_a \tag{7}$$

PRACTICE EXERCISE 16-1

Q. Suppose Harry and Jerry have the utility function, $U = xy$, where the $MRS_{yx} = y/x$. Harry has an endowment of $20x$ and $30y$, and Jerry has an endowment of $30x$ and $70y$. Draw the Edgeworth box, and compute the equilibrium p_x/p_y ratio.

A. The Edgeworth box has the dimensions of $50x$ and $100y$. Because $MRS = y/x$ for both Harry and Jerry, and y/x for the economy equals $100/50 = 2$, it follows that for both Harry and Jerry $MRS = 2$. Because $p_x/p_y = MRS$, it must be that $p_x/p_y = 2$.

FIGURE 16-3   Excess Supply and Excess Demand

When there is a disequilibrium price ratio, the demands of each consumer are described by different points in the Edgeworth box. For the price ratio indicated by the budget line through point e, there is an excess demand for ale (df) and an excess supply of bread (gh).

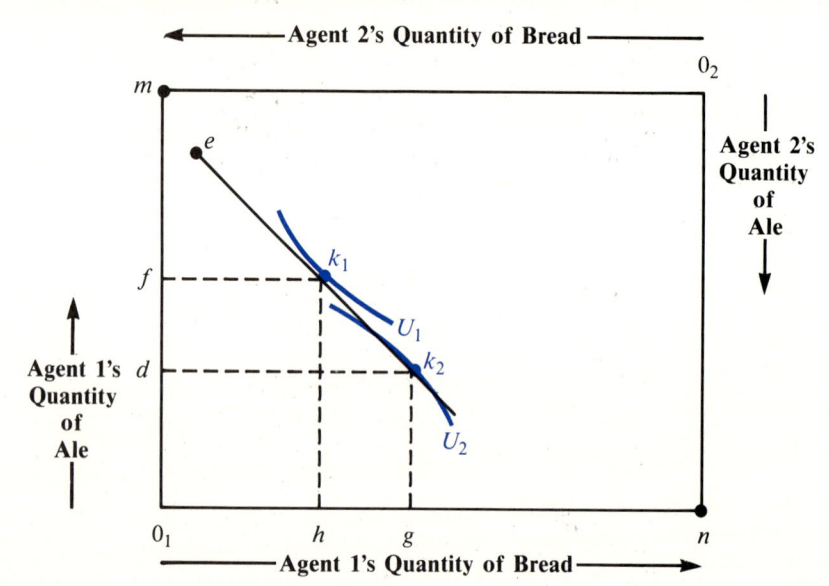

$$X_b = c_{1b} + c_{2b} \text{ or } X_a = c_{1a} + c_{2a} \tag{8}$$

In Figure 16-2, Equations (4) and (5) are represented by the fact that both consumers are on the budget line M; Equations (6) and (7) are represented by the fact that both consumer's indifference curves are tangent to the price budget line with slope eb/bc; Equation (8) corresponds to being able to describe the demands for both agents by a single point, c, in the Edgeworth box.

Figure 16-3 shows a disequilibrium price ratio—where Equations (4), (5), (6), and (7) are satisfied but where supply does not equal demand. Agent 1 chooses point k_1; Agent 2 chooses point k_2. In this case, there is an excess demand for ale or, equivalently (by Walras's law), there is an excess supply of bread. In particular, there is an excess demand of ale equal to df, because Agent 1 demands 0_1f pints and Agent 2 demands md pints with a total supply of only 0_1m pints; the excess supply of bread equals gh, because Agent 1 demands 0_1h loaves and Agent 2 demands ng loaves with a total supply of 0_1n loaves.

Figure 16-2 assumes that an equilibrium price ratio exists. Generally speaking, if the endowment point is inside the Edgeworth box (not on the edge), if the indifference curves are convex, and if the agents can survive with the initial endowments, a competitive equilibrium is known to exist. In Figure 16-4, the indifference curves U_1^0 and U_2^0 are the initial utility levels going through the original-endowment point e. As in Chapter 6, each agent

FIGURE 16-4 The Offer Curves

The offer, or price/consumption, curves PC_1 and PC_2 must intersect; there is at least one competitive equilibrium point, c.

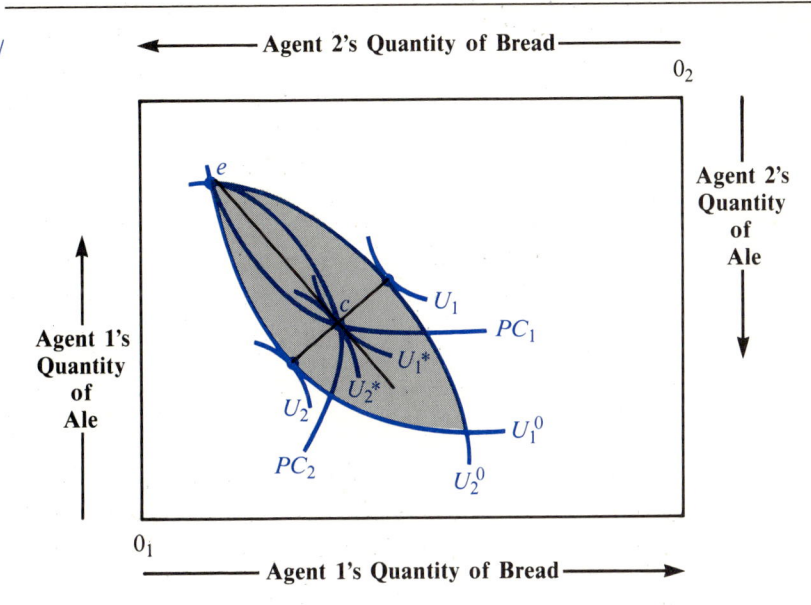

[Figure: Edgeworth box diagram with origins 0_1 (lower left) and 0_2 (upper right). Axes show Agent 1's Quantity of Bread (bottom), Agent 1's Quantity of Ale (left), Agent 2's Quantity of Bread (top), Agent 2's Quantity of Ale (right). Point e is the endowment in the upper left; offer curves PC_1 and PC_2 intersect at point c. Indifference curves U_1^0, U_2^0, U_1^*, U_2^*, U_1, U_2 are shown. The shaded lens-shaped region between U_1^0 and U_2^0 is the region of mutually beneficial trade.]

An **offer curve** shows the offer of one good for some other good at different price ratios.

has an **offer curve**, or price/consumption curve, starting at point e that shows the offer of one good for the other at different price ratios. To derive an offer curve, we can rotate the various budget lines through point e and plot the points of tangency with each agent's indifference curves. In the case of Agent 1's offer curve, PC_1, the vertical displacement from e to any point on PC_1 measures Agent 1's excess supply of ale, while the horizontal displacement measures Agent 1's excess demand for bread. The reverse holds for Agent 2. Because voluntary exchange must improve each agent's welfare, Agent 1's offer curve, PC_1, and Agent 2's offer curve, PC_2, must each lie above their initial indifference curves. Thus, PC_1 must be northeast of U_1^0 and PC_2 must be southwest of U_2^0. It follows that PC_1 must intersect PC_2 somewhere in the shaded region; point c is the competitive equilibrium.

Pareto Optimality

Pareto optimality is a resource allocation in which any reallocation that makes one person better off must make another person worse off.

Chapter 6 defined **Pareto optimality** as a resource allocation in which any reallocation that makes one person better off must make some other person worse off. With ordinary indifference curves, a sufficient condition for Pareto optimality in the pure-exchange economy is simply that Agent 1's *MRS* equals Agent 2's *MRS*. (But see Practice Exercise 16–2.) If both consumers place exactly the same marginal valuations on bread, a reallocation that makes one person better off must hurt the other.

PRACTICE EXERCISE 16-2

Q. Patti and Terri have the same utility function, $U = \min(x, y)$. Patti has an initial endowment of $20x$ and $80y$, and Terri has an initial endowment of $80x$ and $20y$. Draw the contract curve, and calculate the equilibrium p_x/p_y ratio. Is the competitive equilibrium a Pareto optimum?

A. Pareto optimality does not always require that each MRS equal the other. In this case, the MRS is not defined for the quantity $x = y$. The contract curve consists of the main diagonal of the Edgeworth box, as shown in Figure A. Note that the contract curve still exists even though the marginal rates of substitution are not equated. The endowment point is e, and the price ratio that maximizes both utilities is $p_x/p_y = 1$, where each consumes $50x$ and $50y$ (point b). Allocation b is a Pareto optimum because to make Terri better off in the shaded region must make Patti worse off.

Figure A

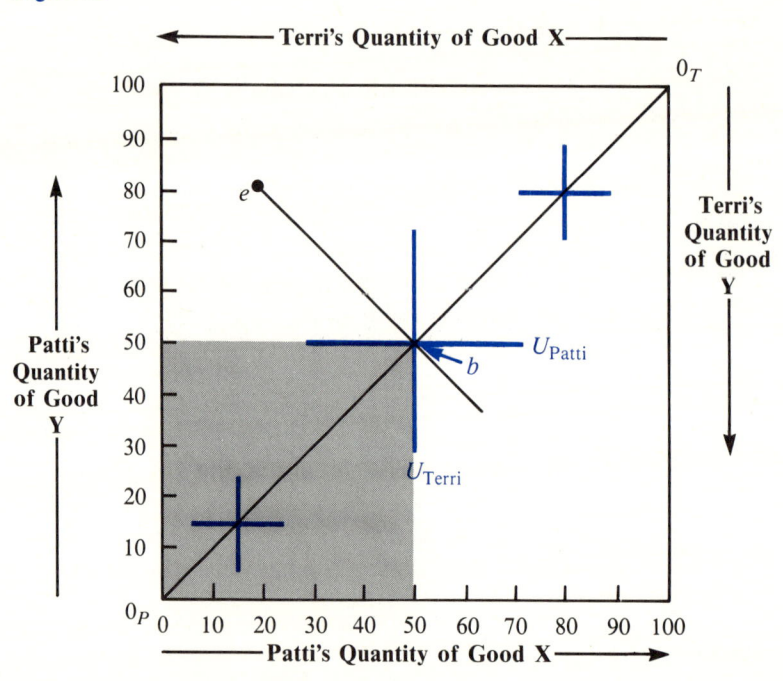

Figure 16-5 shows the entire set of Pareto-optimal solutions, which are defined by the mutual tangencies between the agents' indifference curves. The points p, p', and p'' are representative Pareto-optimal allocations. For example, to move into the shaded region northeast of point p must help Agent 1 and hurt Agent 2. If the agent's marginal rates of substitution were different, as at point d, both consumers could be made better off.

FIGURE 16-5 The Contract Curve

The set of Pareto-optimal allocations along the contract curve consists of all the points for which agent 1's *MRS* equals agent 2's *MRS*, such as allocations p, p', and p''. The allocation d is not a Pareto optimum.

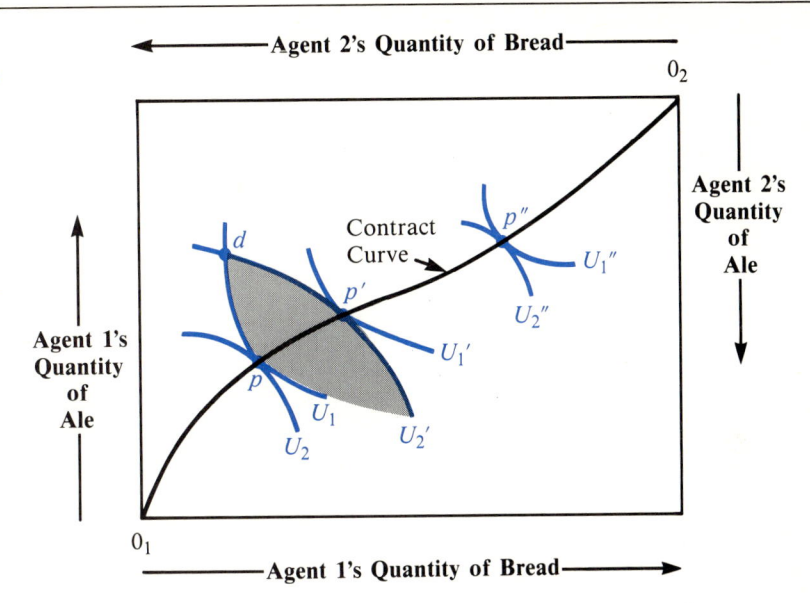

The curve connecting 0_1 to 0_2 is often called the **contract curve**, because at any point on the curve the contract would be considered final. Figure 16-6 shows the utility distribution for the curve in Figure 16-5. Any move from a point on the contract curve that helps one agent must hurt the other.

FIGURE 16-6 The Utility-Possibilities Curve

The utility-possibilities curve shows the Pareto-optimal allocations of utility between each agent and corresponds to the contract curve in the Edgeworth box.

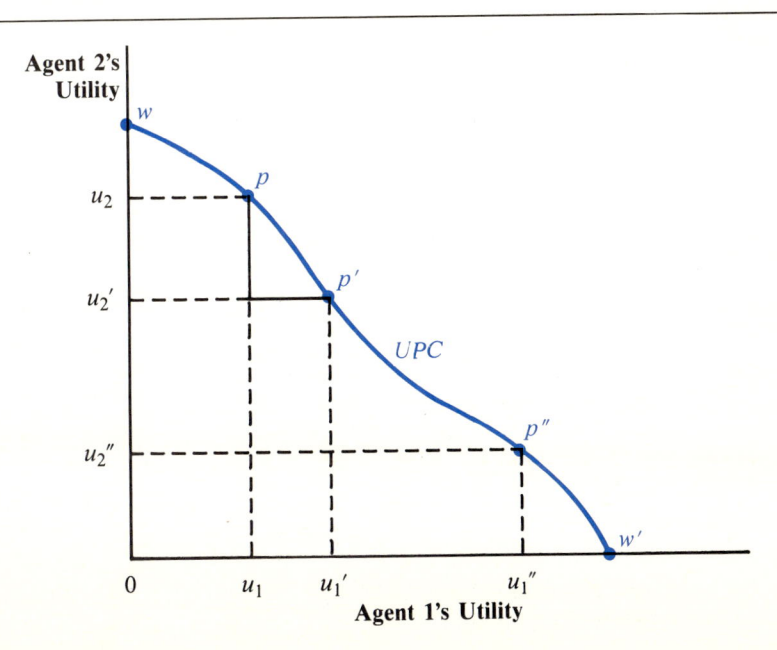

FIGURE 16-7 The First Welfare Theorem

Any competitive equilibrium (without externalities) is also a Pareto optimum, even if indifference curves have an unusual shape.

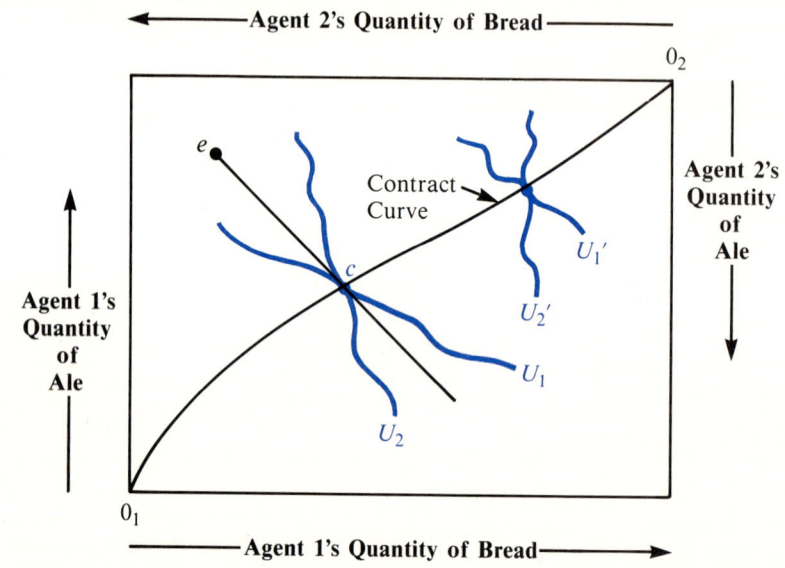

[Edgeworth box diagram: Agent 1's Quantity of Bread on horizontal axis (left to right from 0_1), Agent 1's Quantity of Ale on vertical axis. Agent 2's axes reversed from 0_2 in upper right. Contract Curve runs diagonally through box. Point e marked in upper left, point c near center. Indifference curves labeled U_1, U_1', U_2, U_2'.]

A **contract curve** is the set of Pareto-optimal allocations and, when indifference curves are smoothly convex, occurs when the marginal rates of substitution of one good for another are the same.

A **utility-possibilities curve** shows the Pareto-optimal allocations of utility corresponding to a fixed endowment of goods.

The contract curve shows the utility levels that are optimal for the two agents. As the economy moves along the contract curve, one agent's utility increases as the other agent's utility decreases. For example, from p to p' to p'' in Figure 16–5, Agent 1's utility increases and Agent 2's utility decreases. Every point on the contact curve is associated with a particular distribution of utilities between the two agents. Figure 16–6 shows the corresponding utility distribution for each point on the contract curve. The points p, p', and p'', for example, in Figure 16–5 correspond precisely to the points with the same labels in Figure 16–6. The downward-sloping curve, ww', in the utility space is called the **utility-possibilities curve**. The utility-possibilities curve describes the Pareto-optimal allocations of utilities corresponding to the Pareto-optimal allocations of goods.

It is clear from the utility-possibilities curve or from the contract curve that economic efficiency can be attained under many different states of the world. Because any point along ww' in Figure 16–6 is a Pareto-optimal contract, the distribution of real welfare may be skewed in favor of any consumer. Efficiency is compatible with any distribution of income in a community. Thus, the concept of Pareto optimality separates the concept of efficiency from any considerations of economic equity.

Economic efficiency characterizes the distribution or exchange of a given endowment of goods along the contract curve, where one agent's utility is maximized given the utility of the other. The corresponding utility-possibilities curve is downward-sloping and shows that efficiency need not be equitable.

The utility-possibilities curve in Figure 16-7 may be called a *point utility-possibilities curve*, because it corresponds to a particular point of supply of each good.

The Two Basic Theorems of Welfare Economics

Welfare economics describes the link between markets and welfare. There is a two-fold link between a general competitive equilibrium and a Pareto-optimal allocation of resources. The first theorem is that every competitive equilibrium is characterized by Pareto optimality; the second theorem is that any Pareto-optimal allocation may be the result of some competitive equilibrium. These theorems constitute the modern statement of Adam Smith's invisible hand:

> Every individual endeavors to employ his capital so that its produce may be of greatest value. He generally neither intends to promote the public interest, nor knows how much he is promoting it. He intends only his own security, only his own gain. And he is led by an *invisible hand* to promote an end which was no part of his intention. By pursuing his own interest he frequently promotes that of society more effectively than when he really intends to promote it.[2]

Modern economists no longer can speak of the welfare of "society," because the utilities of different individuals cannot be compared. The advantage of the concept of Pareto optimality is that we need not compare the utilities of different individuals. The concept of a welfare optimum means only that the economy achieves a point on the utility-possibilities curve.

The First Theorem of Welfare Economics. If the utility of each agent depends only on his or her own consumption (that is, if there are no externalities), every competitive equilibrium will also be a Pareto-optimal allocation.

The most important assumption of this first theorem is that there are no *externalities* (for example, there are no smokers bothering nonsmokers in a closed room), which are studied in the following chapter. This first welfare theorem is very easily proved. When each agent's utility depends only on his or her own consumption, Pareto optimality is achieved when the agents' marginal rates of substitution are equated. In competitive equilibrium, $MRS_i = p_b/p_a$ for each economic agent; thus, it must be that the agents' MRSs are also equated. Notice that the theorem does not even require that the indifference curves be everywhere convex. For example, Figure 16-7 shows a competitive equilibrium in which each agent's indifference curves have concave sections, but it is still true that where the equilibrium occurs there is a Pareto optimum.

---

2. Adam Smith, *An Inquiry Into the Nature and Causes of the Wealth of Nations*, ed. Edwin Cannon (New York: Modern Library, 1937), p. 423.

FIGURE 16–8 **A Pareto Optimum May Not Be Sustainable by Competition**

Point p is a Pareto optimum, but it cannot be the result of a competitive equilibrium because agent 1's indifference curves are concave to his or her origin. With budget line M, agent 1 desires point a and agent 2 desires point p.

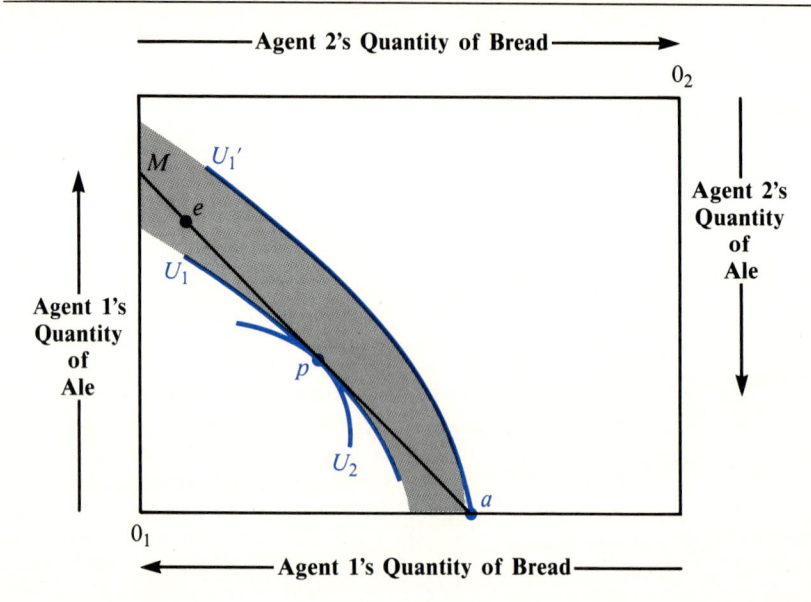

The second theorem of welfare economics is more complex and forms the basis for the normative prescriptions of many economists. Suppose an economist believes that a particular Pareto optimum is a desirable goal. The second theorem states that the Pareto optimum can be achieved in a competitive market, but the conditions for the theorem are far more stringent.

The Second Theorem of Welfare Economics. If each agent's utility depends only on his or her consumption, if all indifference curves are convex, and if the consumption of every agent is beyond the subsistence level, then any Pareto optimum can be achieved as the result of a competitive equilibrium by the proper assignment of the initial endowment of goods.

Figure 16–8 shows a Pareto-optimal allocation of resources, point p, that cannot be sustained as a competitive equilibrium. Agent 1's indifference curves are concave to their origin, instead of convex. Nevertheless, point p is still a Pareto-optimal allocation because any move into the shaded region makes Agent 1 better off and Agent 2 worse off. Point p is not a competitive equilibrium, however. Given the budget line M, Agent 2 would choose point p, but Agent 1 would choose point a. Thus, p cannot be a competitive equilibrium even though it is a full-fledged Pareto optimum.

Pareto-optimal allocations need not always be achievable by a competitive mechanism.

FIGURE 16-9 The Second Welfare Theorem

Point *p* is any Pareto optimum inside the Edgeworth box. Point *p* is also a competitive equilibrium for any endowment, *e*, on the budget line *M* tangent to both indifference curves at point *p*.

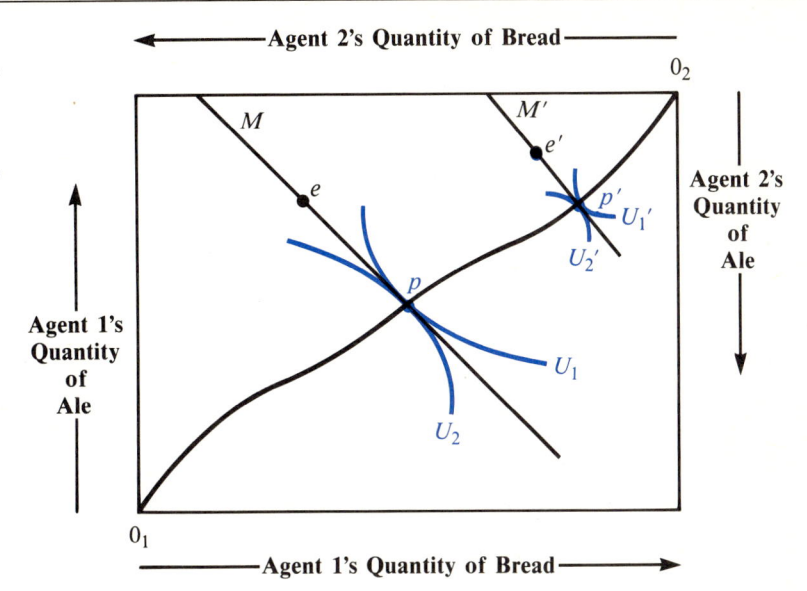

The second welfare theorem is illustrated in Figure 16–9. The indifference curves are convex to the origin of each agent. It is assumed that each agent can survive at any point inside the Edgeworth box or along one of the sides (where the consumption of one of the goods is zero). Point *p* is any Pareto optimum inside the box. The budget line *M* is just tangent to both U_1 and U_2 at point *p*. Any point *e* on the budget line will result in a competitive equilibrium at the point *p*, with the price ratio indicated by the slope of *M*. Point *p* is a competitive equilibrium because supply equals demand and because both agents are maximizing their utility.

The significance of the second theorem of welfare economics is that it provides some hope for achieving both equity and efficiency. For example, if point *p* in Figure 16–9 is considered to be equitable in terms of the distribution of income, then to achieve *p* it is necessary only to start from an endowment such as *e*. If the endowment were elsewhere—say, at point *e'*—then it would be necessary to impose a set of lump-sum taxes and subsidies that would move the endowment from *e'* to *e*. Such a system of lump-sum taxes and subsidies would lead the economy to both efficiency and equity.

In practice, lump-sum taxes and subsidies are difficult to impose. If such taxes are impossible or impractical, then there is a conflict between equity and efficiency. The original-endowment point *e'* in Figure 16–9 leads to the Pareto optimum at *p'*, where Agent 2's utility is relatively low. Thus, Adam Smith's invisible hand may lead to a satisfactory solution only if the starting position itself is equitable.

FIGURE 16-10   Constant-Returns Isoquants

With constant returns to scale, the technology may be completely represented by the unit isoquant. For example, the $X_j = 2$ isoquant is just a radial expansion of the $X_j = 1$ isoquant. The marginal products of labor and capital are the same along a given scale line R.

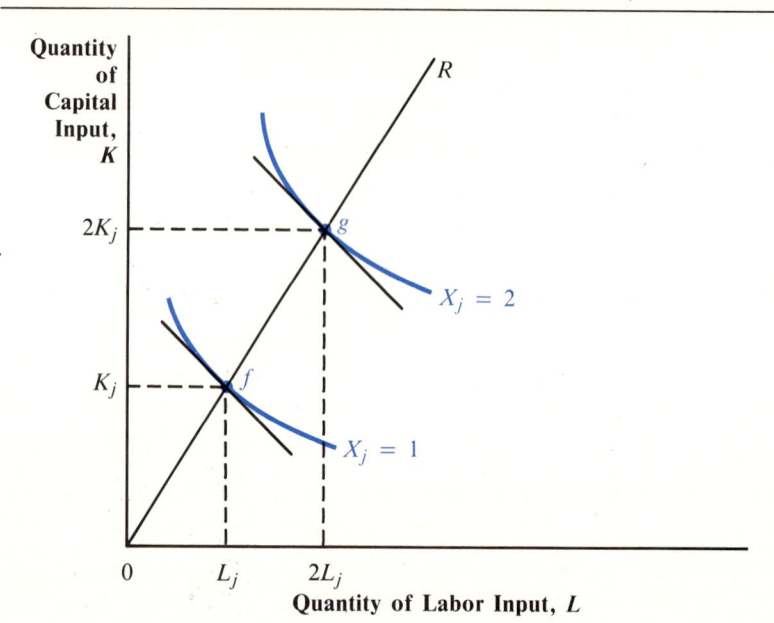

THE TWO-SECTOR PRODUCTION MODEL

Thus far we have assumed that the supply of each good is fixed, but goods are produced by profit-maximizing firms. It is necessary, therefore, to modify the pure-exchange model by adding the possibility of production. To keep the model simple, we will assume that the two goods are produced by only two factors, labor and capital, under constant returns to scale. This model is sometimes called the *two-sector production model* or the *two-by-two model* (two factors, two goods).

Constant-Returns-to-Scale Production

If X_j is the output of good j, and the inputs of labor and capital into good j production are L_j and K_j, the production function is

$$X_j = F_j(L_j, K_j). \tag{9}$$

Recall (from Chapter 7) that with constant returns to scale an equal-proportion increase in all inputs increases output by the same proportion. Thus, if each input is multiplied by the constant λ, so is the output level.

$$\lambda X_j = F_j(\lambda L_j, \lambda K_j). \tag{10}$$

But Equation (10) holds for any λ that is greater than 0. If we let $\lambda = 1/X_j$, then the production function can be written as:

$$1 = F_j(L_j/X_j, K_j/X_j). \tag{11}$$

FIGURE 16–11 The Optimal Input Ratio

A higher wage/rent ratio increases the optimal capital/labor ratio.

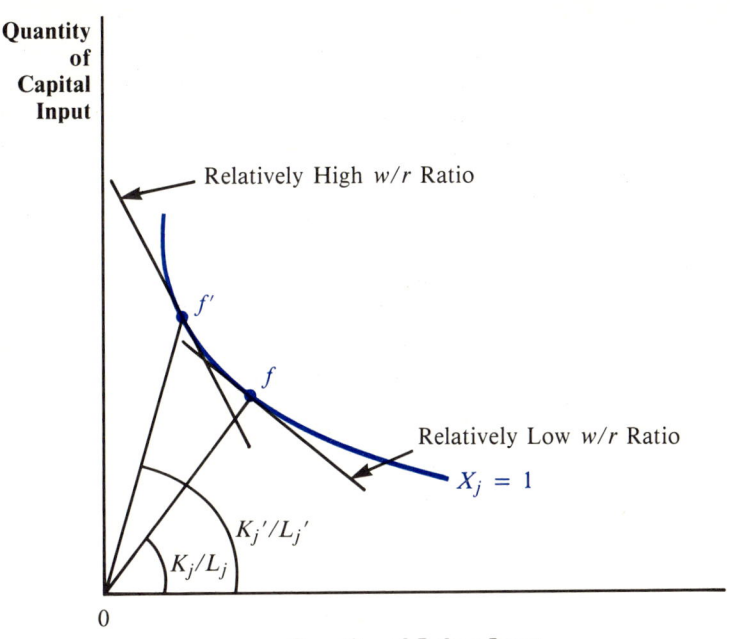

Figure: Isoquant diagram with Quantity of Capital Input on vertical axis and Quantity of Labor Input on horizontal axis. The unit isoquant $X_j = 1$ is shown with two tangent isocost lines: one at point f' (Relatively High w/r Ratio) corresponding to capital/labor ratio K_j'/L_j', and one at point f (Relatively Low w/r Ratio) corresponding to capital/labor ratio K_j/L_j.

A unit isoquant shows the levels of capital and labor inputs required to produce one unit of a good.

The curve labeled $X_j = 1$ in Figure 16–10, which shows the inputs of labor and capital required to produce one unit of good j, is called the **unit isoquant**.

The unit isoquant gives a complete representation of the technology of producing good j when there are constant returns to scale. Along the scale line R, the capital/labor ratio used in good j is constant. Because a large firm uses inputs in the same ratio as a number of small firms in a constant-returns industry, it does not matter whether the industry consists of many small firms or a few large firms. If the firm is producing at point f in Figure 16–10, one unit of the good is produced. If inputs are doubled from point f to point g, with constant returns to scale, the isoquant $X_j = 2$ is just a two-fold radial expansion of the unit isoquant. Because the firm at point g is the same as two firms at point f, the marginal products of labor and capital (MP_L and MP_K) will be the same at points f and g. Indeed, MP_L and MP_K will be constant all along the scale line, R. The marginal rate of technical substitution of capital for labor, $MRTS_{KL}$, which equals the ratio of the marginal products, also will be constant along a given scale line, R.

As shown in Chapter 8, the optimal ratio of capital to labor depends on the factor-price ratio of labor to capital, w/r. Recall that the firm minimizes costs by equating MRS_{KL} and MP_L/MP_K and w/r. As labor becomes relatively more expensive, the firm will economize by substituting capital for labor. Figure 16–11 shows that the higher is the wage/rent ratio, the higher is the K_j/L_j ratio.

FIGURE 16-12   The Two-Industry Contract Curve

The contract curve is the color line $0_a f 0_b$. Ale is capital-intensive and bread is labor-intensive if the contract curve is above the diagonal, $0_a 0_b$.

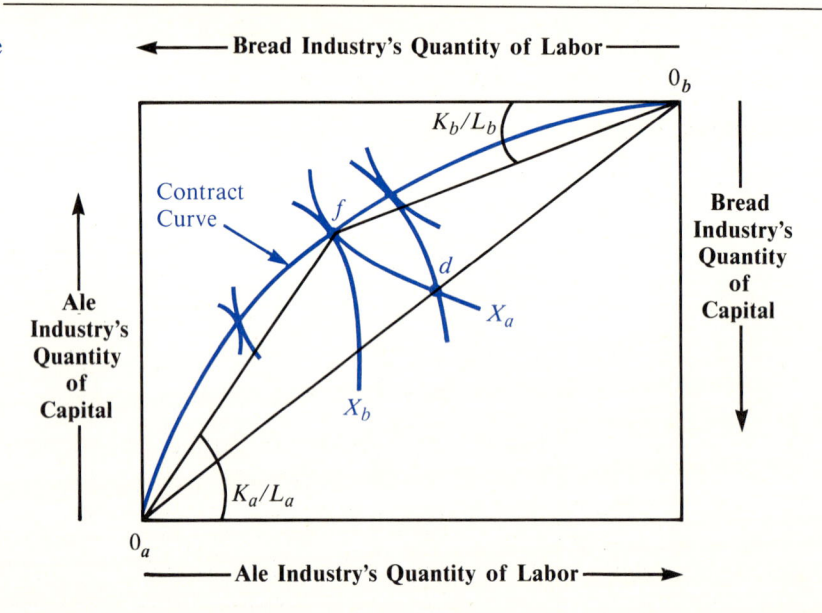

The Production-Possibilities Frontier

Now consider the amounts of ale and bread (X_a and X_b) that can be produced in the economy. The amounts of labor and capital used in both industries cannot exceed the total amounts available, L and K. It must be the case that

$$L = L_a + L_b \text{ and } K = K_a + K_b \tag{12}$$

Suppose the supplies of labor and capital are perfectly inelastic to the economy. Because L and K are given, we can construct an Edgeworth box describing the allocation of labor and capital between the two industries.

In Figure 16-12, the horizontal width measures the total supply of labor and the vertical height measures the total supply of capital. The allocation of labor and capital to the ale and bread industries is measured relative to the origins 0_a and 0_b. The ale industry's isoquants are convex to 0_a, and output increases in the northeast direction. The bread industry's isoquants are convex to 0_b, and output increases in the southwest direction. Point f is a typical tangency. Just as in the theory of pure exchange, the set of mutual tangencies along $0_a f 0_b$ represents the contract curve. Note that the contract curve is assumed to lie above the diagonal line, $0_a 0_b$. When capital is on the vertical axis, ale is capital-intensive and bread is labor-intensive. How do we know this? At point f, the ratio K_a/L_a equals the slope of the ray $0_a f$ and the ratio K_b/L_b equals the slope of the ray $0_b f$. The slope of the diagonal, $0_a 0_b$, is simply K/L. Because $0_a 0_b$ is flatter than $0_a f$ and steeper than $0_b f$, it follows that

THE TWO-SECTOR PRODUCTION MODEL

FIGURE 16–13 **The Production-Possibilities Frontier**

The production-possibilities frontier (*PPF*) shows the maximum output of one good given the output of the other. Its slope is the opportunity cost of the good on the horizontal axis—bread, in this case. The *PPF* is concave to the origin. The absolute slope at any point is the marginal rate of transformation of ale for bread (MRT_{ab}).

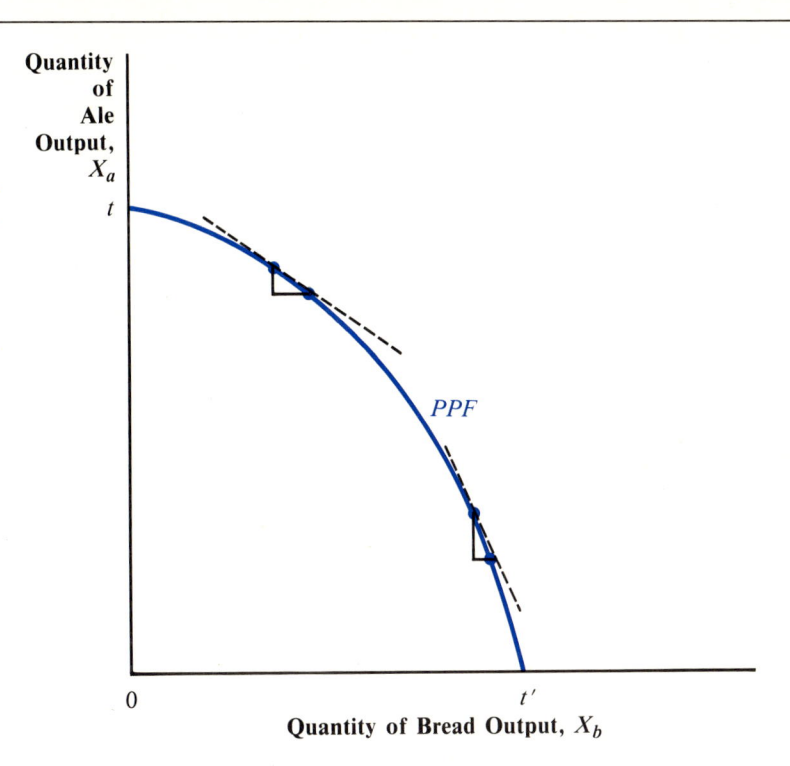

[Graph: Quantity of Ale Output, X_a on vertical axis from t; Quantity of Bread Output, X_b on horizontal axis from 0 to t'; concave PPF curve with tangent lines]

$$K_a/L_a > K/L > K_b/L_b. \tag{13}$$

Pareto optimality in production requires that resources be allocated in such a way that the output of one good is maximized given the outputs of the remaining goods. Any point on the contract curve corresponds to Pareto-optimal production. For example, if the allocation of labor and capital between the two industries is off the contract curve at point *d* in Figure 16–12, a move along ale's isoquant from *d* to *f* will maximize the output of bread for the given output of ale. Point *f* is a Pareto-optimal allocation. Because the isoquants are tangent along the contract curve, there is Pareto optimality in production when the $MRTS_{KL}$ for ale equals the $MRTS_{KL}$ for bread.

There is Pareto optimality in the production of ale and bread when the marginal rates of technical substitution of capital for labor ($MRTS_{KL}$) are the same.

Each point on the contract curve corresponds to a point on the *production-possibilities frontier (PPF)* in Figure 16–13. Moving from 0_b to 0_a along the contract curve in Figure 16–12 is equivalent to moving from *t* to *t'* along

FIGURE 16-14 Production and the Wage/Rent Ratio

When the output of the labor-intensive good (bread) expands, the capital/labor ratios increase in both industries. When the economy moves from f to f', for example, the capital/labor ratio increases because the ray $0_a f'$ is steeper than $0_a f$. The wage/rent ratio is higher at f' than at f.

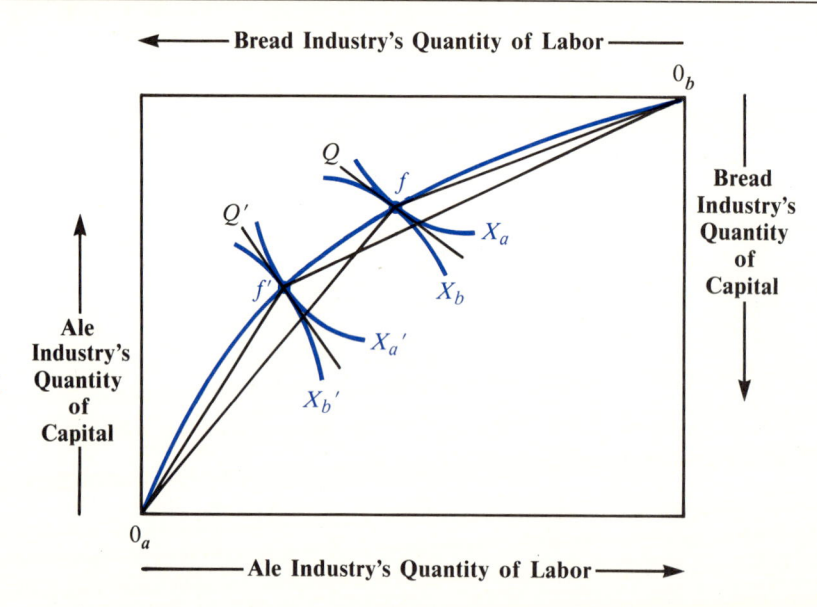

The **marginal rate of transformation (MRT)** of good A for good B is the amount of A that must be sacrificed for another unit of B.

the *PPF* in Figure 16-13. The absolute slope of the *PPF* is the relative cost of bread, or the **marginal rate of transformation (MRT)** of ale for bread.

As the economy moves from t to t' in Figure 16-13, the MRT_{ab} increases. In other words, the *PPF* is concave to the origin. The economy faces increasing costs when more of a good is produced. The next section will examine the economics behind the law of increasing costs. (See Example 16-1.)

Factor Prices and Costs

Suppose now that labor and capital resources are perfectly mobile between the industries producing ale and bread. As long as the wage (w) and the rent (r) are the same, the labor and the owners of capital are indifferent between employing their resources in one industry or the other. If, say, the ale industry paid higher wages than the bread industry, labor would be attracted to ale production until both industries paid the same wage. Thus, wages and rents will be equalized between the two industries because of the action of supply and demand.

When both industries pay the same w/r, cost minimization places industries on the contract curve. Because both industries equate their $MRTS_{KL}$ to the same w/r, it follows that the $MRTS_{KL}$ for ale equals the $MRTS_{KL}$ for bread. Thus, any point on the contract curve, or the equivalent *PPF*, is characterized by $w/r = MRTS_{KL}$ for either industry.

A central feature of the *PPF* is that it is concave to the origin. As more bread is produced, its opportunity cost increases as long as both industries use different capital/labor ratios. In Figures 16-12 and 16-14, bread is labor-

THE TWO-SECTOR PRODUCTION MODEL

FIGURE 16-15 Costs and the Wage/Rent Ratio

Assume that at the initial wage/rent ratio, indicated by the slope of line C, both goods cost the same amount. If the wage/rent ratio increases, the isocost line for a unit of bread (C_2) will be higher than the isocost line for a unit of ale (C_1). Because bread is labor-intensive, an increase in the w/r ratio increases the relative cost of producing bread.

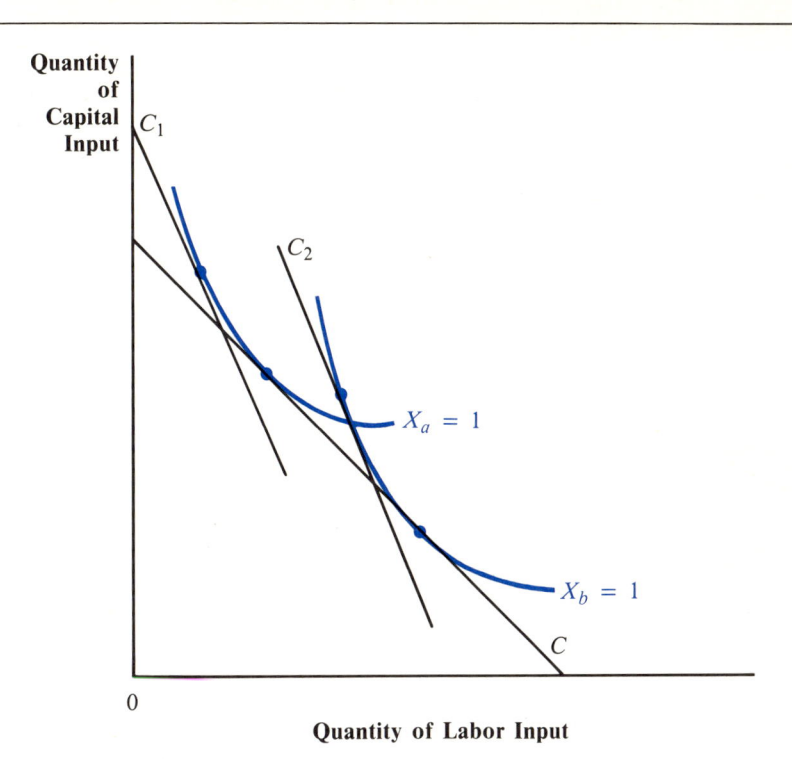

intensive and ale is capital-intensive. When the output of bread expands, the demand for labor increases relative to capital. To maintain equilibrium in the market for resources, the wage/rent ratio must rise. A higher wage/rent ratio drives up the cost of labor-intensive bread relative to capital-intensive ale. Thus, the *PPF* should be concave to the origin to reflect the increasing relative cost of bread. If both industries used the same capital/labor ratio, the *PPF* would be a straight line under the assumption of constant returns to scale because the expansion of any industry would not be associated with a change in relative factor prices.

Figure 16-14 shows the way factor prices change when the output of the labor-intensive good expands. The original allocation of resources is point f; the wage/rent ratio is indicated by the tangent line Q. The capital/labor ratios in the ale and bread industries are indicated by the slopes of $0_a f$ and $0_b f$. If we increase the output of bread by shifting to point f', the wage/rent ratio is indicated by the tangent line Q'. The slope of Q' is steeper than that of Q because the capital/labor ratios in each industry have increased. The capital/labor ratios in ale and bread are now $0_a f'$ and $0_b f'$, which are higher than before.

Thus, as the wage/rent ratio increases, the cost of producing the labor-intensive good will rise relative to the cost of the capital-intensive good. Figure 16-15 shows two unit isoquants—one for each industry—and shows

EXAMPLE 16–1 The Decline of Manufacturing

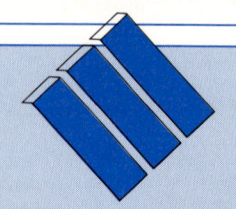

To illustrate the fundamental ideas of general equilibrium, let us consider the much discussed decline of the U.S. manufacturing industry. From 1969 to 1985, the share of U.S. employment in general manufacturing fell from 25 percent to 19 percent. This chapter suggests that such a change would take place if the relative price of manufactured goods fell relative to services. Indeed, over the 1969–85 period the average price of U.S. manufactured goods relative to all goods fell by some 26 percent. Viewed from the standpoint of general-equilibrium economics, there has been a massive change in relative prices and a move along the U.S. production-possibilities frontier.

PPF analysis shows that when one industry contracts, resources are released to other industries. Which industries benefited from the contraction of manufacturing? Since 1969, the sectors of the economy that have expanded have been trade, finance, insurance, real estate, and services. The service sector includes such industries as health services, business services, hotels, private education, and personnel services.

Many have worried that the decline of jobs in manufacturing would not be offset by growth elsewhere, but this has proved not to be the case over the long run. Even in the service sector, wages earned nearly replace the wages lost in manufacturing. For example, in 1984 the average manufacturing job paid $23,668 annually, while the average services job paid $21,731 annually. Thus, services earn about 96 percent of what manufacturing jobs earn.

In terms of total employment, from 1969 to 1984 the number of people with jobs increased from 81.5 million to 106.8 million. The number of manufacturing jobs declined from 20.5 million to 19.8 million. The economy's *PPF* has shifted outward by a considerable margin, and there has been a movement from manufacturing and agriculture to other sectors of the U.S. economy. This trend is no cause for alarm; relative prices have simply turned against traditional industries in favor of newer industries.

When relative prices of goods change, the prices of the factors of production that have comparative advantages in those goods also change. The decline in manufacturing has been associated with hardships imposed on those agents who have specialized in activities associated with heavy industry. This decline is viewed as socially undesirable by some economists. However, a broader view must take into account the reason those resources were in manufacturing in the first place. From 1909 to 1969—about 60 years—the share of manufacturing in the U.S. economy remained roughly constant. Those engaged in manufacturing benefited immensely over this period. When manufacturing expanded in the late 19th century, the flip side was *contraction* in other industries. During the 1909–69 period, it was easy to forget the hardships people must have faced in shifting to a manufacturing economy.

Perhaps the most important lesson of general-equilibrium economics is that hidden in every business success is a business failure.

Sources: Lynn E. Browne, "Taking in Each Other's Laundry—The Service Economy," *New England Economic Review* (July/August 1986, Federal Reserve Bank of Boston), pp. 20–31; *The Economic Report of the President, 1987*, pp. 256–57.

FIGURE 16-16   A Movement Along the PPF

The economy produces at point x if the price ratio, p_b/p_a, is represented by the (absolute) slope of M. If p_b/p_a increases to equal the slope of R, production shifts to x'.

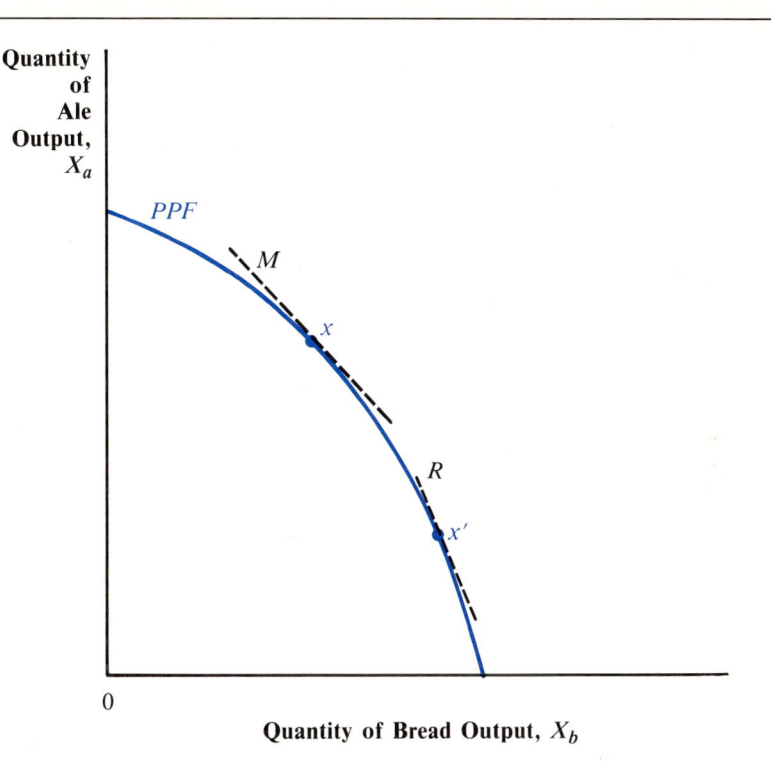

that ale is capital-intensive and bread is labor-intensive. Before the wage/rent ratio changes, a unit of each good costs the same (units can always be defined so that both goods initially have the same costs). If the slope of line C corresponds to the initial w/r ratio, then the tangency of C with both unit isoquants indicates that both goods cost the same amount. If the w/r ratio increases, so that the isocost curves are steeper, the isocost curve tangent to $X_a = 1$ (C_1) will be lower than the one tangent to $X_b = 1$ (C_2). It now costs more to produce bread than it does to produce ale.

The Stolper-Samuelson Theorem

The above two-sector model of production can be used to analyze the relationship between goods prices and factor prices. We have seen that factor prices change in a definite way as the economy moves along the PPF, but what causes a movement along the PPF? The answer is simple: a change in the relative price, p_b/p_a.

Figure 16-16 shows how the outputs of ale and bread are determined in a competitive economy. We learned in Chapter 10 that in the case of perfect competition, prices reflect costs in the long run. Because costs can be measured by the MRT_{ab} in the two-sector model, the competitive production of both goods is determined by the equation:

FIGURE 16–17   **An Inefficient Mix of Goods**

The allocation of resources shown here is not a general Pareto optimum because $MRT_{ab} > MRS^1_{ab} = MRS^2_{ab}$ when output is at point x and when point c describes the distribution of ale and bread.

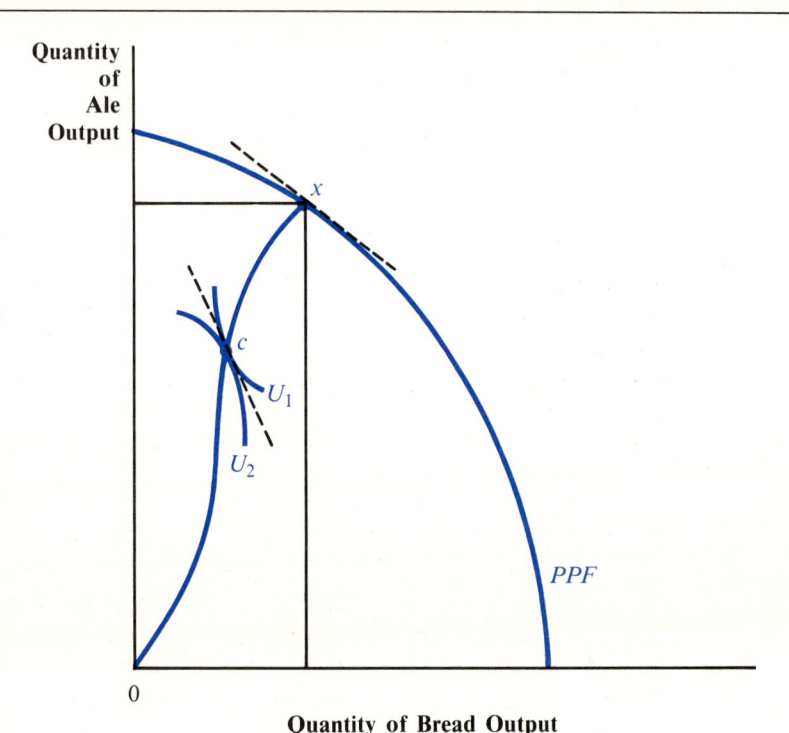

$$p_b/p_a = MRT_{ab}. \qquad (14)$$

In Figure 16–16, suppose the price ratio, p_b/p_a, is represented by the (absolute) slope of M. Accordingly, Equation (14) is satisfied at point x.

If there is a change in commodity prices, factor prices will change. Suppose the relative price of bread, p_b/p_a, rises. In Figure 16–16, the production point will shift from x to x', where the output of bread is increased. If bread is labor-intensive, an increase in its output will increase the wage/rent ratio.

In a pioneering contribution, Wolfgang Stolper and Paul Samuelson argued that an increase in the relative price of the labor-intensive good will increase real wages and lower real rents. This conclusion is called the *Stolper-Samuelson theorem*. If we know that the w/r rises, when will real wages rise? To say that real wages rise unambiguously requires that wages increase whether measured in terms of bread or ale. For example, if wages go up 10 percent, and both prices rise by less than 10 percent, then real wages must increase.

To see how the Stolper-Samuelson theorem works, recall that in a competitive industry,

$$w = p_i MP^i_L \text{ and } r = p_i MP^i_K; \qquad (15)$$

that is, factor prices equal the value of the factor's marginal product. Thus, the marginal product itself measures the factor price *in kind*. For example, $w/p_a = MP_L^a$ is the wage rate measured in terms of ale. To prove the Stolper-Samuelson theorem, we need only examine what happens to the marginal products of labor and capital in both industries.

If the w/r ratio rises, *both* industries will choose a higher K_i/L_i ratio—but as a result the MP_K^i in both industries will fall because of the law of diminishing returns. Because L_i/K_i falls, there is less labor per unit of capital; thus, the same law of diminishing returns requires that MP_L^i must rise in both industries. Because the marginal product of labor rises in both industries, it immediately follows that both w/p_a and w/p_b rise. Accordingly, workers are better off because their wages rise faster than any price. Likewise, the owners of capital are worse off because r/p_i falls for both goods.

The Stolper-Samuelson theorem states that an increase in the relative price of the labor-intensive good must increase real wages and lower real rents.

There are many applications of the Stolper-Samuelson result. Suppose a country taxes a particular class of goods that can be identified as labor-intensive or capital-intensive. Because a tax on a good lowers the price paid to producers (see Chapter 2), taxing labor-intensive goods will make workers worse off; likewise, subsidizing the production of labor-intensive goods will make workers better off. Stolper and Samuelson themselves applied the result to tariff protection. If a country imports labor-intensive goods (as does the United States), a tariff on imports will raise the price of such goods and increase real wages. Clearly, the Stolper-Samuelson theorem offers the following insight: factor owners have an enormous incentive to manipulate the relative prices of commodities in favor of the goods that intensively use the resources they own.

Pareto Optimality

We have considered Pareto optimality in exchange and Pareto optimality in production. Briefly, there is Pareto optimality in exchange when each agent has the same marginal rate of substitution of ale for bread; there is Pareto optimality in production when each industry has the same marginal rate of technical substitution of capital for labor. In summary,

$$MRS_{ab}^1 = MRS_{ab}^2 \tag{16}$$

$$MRTS_{KL}^1 = MRTS_{KL}^2 \tag{17}$$

There will be general Pareto optimality *for the entire economy* if it is impossible through any reallocation of resources to make one person better off without hurting someone else. Conditions (16) and (17) are not enough to guarantee that an efficient mix of goods is produced.

The best way to understand the conditions for Pareto optimality when there is production is to examine a situation in which there is an opportunity for making everyone better off through some resource reallocation. Figure 16-17 shows an allocation of resources that satisfies Pareto optimality in

FIGURE 16-18 General Pareto Optimality

There is general Pareto optimality if the slope of the *PPF* equals the slope of the individual indifference curves.

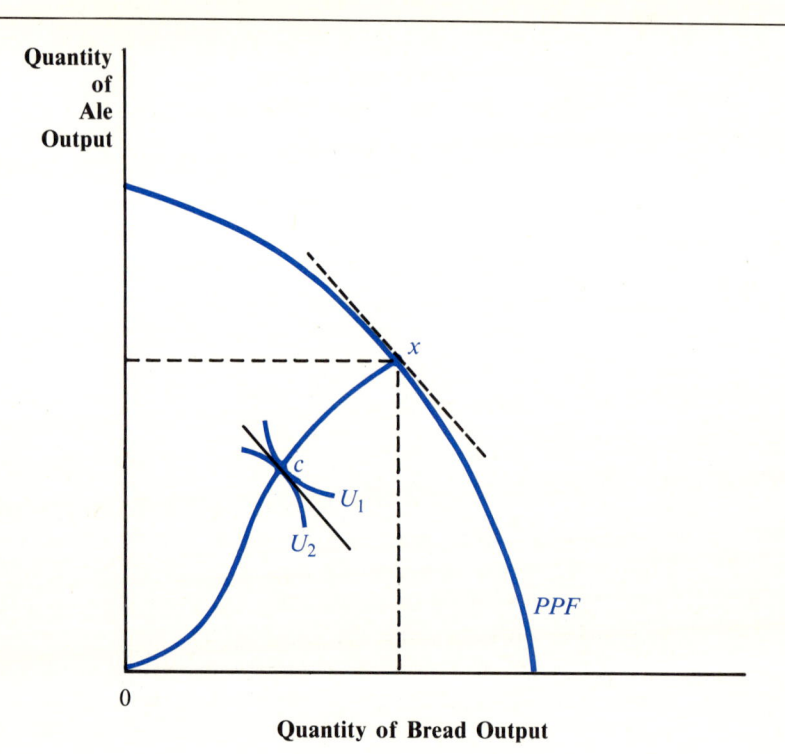

exchange—Equation (16)—and Pareto optimality in production—Equation (17). There is Pareto optimality in production because the economy is on the production-possibilities frontier at point x. We can now draw an Edgeworth box on the *PPF* diagram, corresponding to producing at point x, by letting points 0 and x be the origins for the two consumers. With the allocation of ale and bread indicated at point c, there is Pareto optimality in exchange. Assume, at point c, that $MRS^1_{ab} = MRS^2_{ab} = 2$, but that at point x, $MRT_{ab} = 4$. Thus, each consumer is willing to exchange two pints of ale for another loaf of bread, but the economy can produce four pints of ale by cutting back bread production by one unit. Therefore, if the economy cuts bread production by one unit, we could induce, say, Agent 1 to trade one loaf of bread for two pints of ale. This trade leaves Agent 1 on the same indifference curve, but we have two pints of ale left over without hurting Agent 2. If we give these two pints of ale to Agent 2, we improve Agent 2's welfare without hurting Agent 1's welfare. Thus, points like x and c are not consistent with general Pareto optimality for the entire economy. To eliminate the possibility of a Pareto improvement for everyone, it is necessary for each MRS^i_{ab} to equal MRT_{ab}.

Figure 16–18 describes a Pareto-optimal allocation of resources. Both

FIGURE 16-19 The Grand Utility-Possibilities Curve

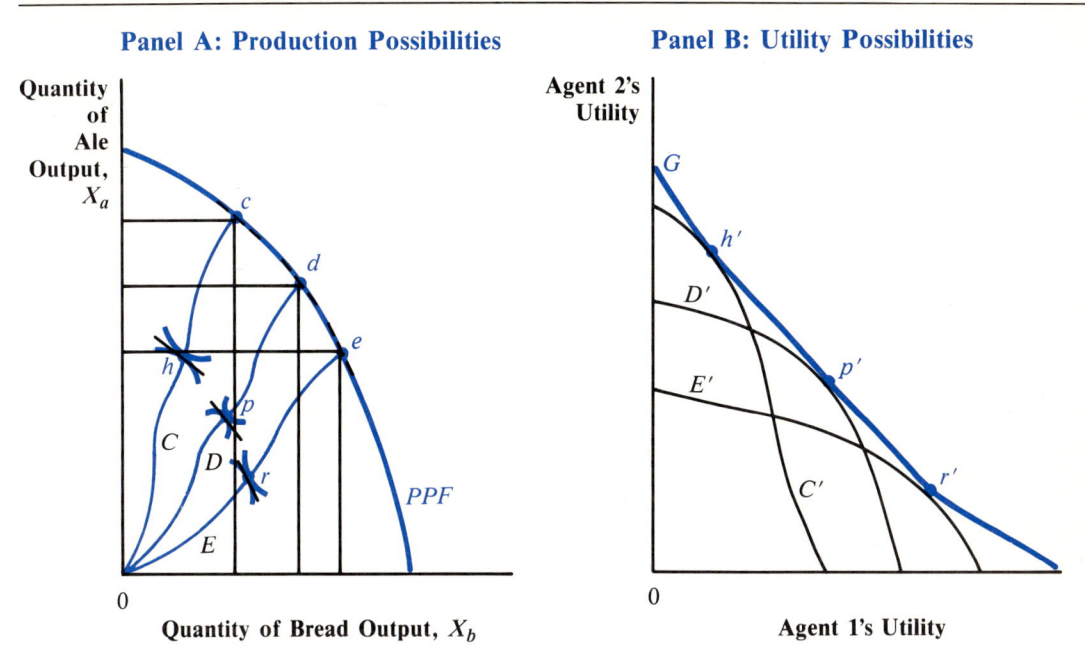

Panel A: Production Possibilities

Panel B: Utility Possibilities

Producing the quantities c, d, and e in Panel A leads to the point utility-possibilities curves C', D', and E' in Panel B. The grand utility-possibilities curve, labeled G in Panel B, is the envelope of all the utility-possibilities curves generated by each point along the *PPF*. It represents the Pareto-optimal distribution of utilities, because to make one person better off must make the other worse off.

consumers have the same MRS_{ab}; production is on the *PPF*; each MRS^i_{ab} = MRT_{ab}. There are three conditions for general Pareto optimality:

$$MRS^1_{ab} = MRS^2_{ab} \tag{18}$$

That is, there is *efficiency in distribution*.

$$MRTS^1_{KL} = MRTS^2_{KL} \tag{19}$$

That is, there is *efficiency in production*.

$$MRS^1_{ab} = MRS^2_{ab} = MRT_{ab} \tag{20}$$

That is, there is *efficiency in output composition*.

The Grand Utility-Possibilities Curve

Each point on the *PPF* is associated with a point utility-possibilities curve. For example, in Panel A of Figure 16-19, points c, d, and e on the *PPF* generate the contract curves C, D, and E. These contract curves are associated with the point utility-possibilities curves C', D', and E' in Panel B. If

Pareto optimality is possible at points c, d, and e, the utility-possibilities curves C', D', and E' must intersect each other. Consider the allocation of resources at point c in Panel A. If there is a point on the contract curve C—say, point h—where each MRS equals the MRT at point c, then Pareto optimality prevails and results in the distribution of utilities indicated by point h' in Panel B. Any other utility-possibilities curve must pass to the southwest of point h', because it is impossible to make everyone better off (by the definition of Pareto optimality).

If we consider all of the utility-possibilities curves generated by moving from point to point along the *PPF*, the envelope of all such curves is the **grand utility-possibilities curve**—labeled G in Figure 16–19. The grand utility-possibilities curve is downward-sloping and illustrates a Pareto-optimal allocation of resources, because it is impossible to make one person better off without hurting the other. Every point on G is associated with points like c, d, and e in Figure 16–19, where conditions in Equations (18), (19), and (20) are satisfied.

> The **grand utility-possibilities curve** is the envelope of all point utility-possibilities curves generated by moving from point to point along the production-possibilities frontier.

In the two-sector model of production, we can again show that the competitive equilibrium is a Pareto optimum by showing that Equations (18), (19), and (20) hold.

There is efficiency in exchange if each consumer faces the same price ratio. If $MRS^i_{ab} = p_b/p_a$, as required by utility maximization, Equation (18) will be satisfied.

There is efficiency in production because each industry minimizes costs by setting $MRTS^i_{KL} = w/r$, which implies that condition (19) will be satisfied.

Finally, we must show that $p_b/p_a = MRT_{ab}$. To demonstrate this point we need to show that $MRT_{ab} = MC_b/MC_a$ because competition implies $p_i = MC_i$. By definition,

$$MRT_{ab} = -\Delta X_a/\Delta X_b. \tag{21}$$

Now we know that

$$\begin{aligned}\Delta X_i &= MP^i_L \Delta L_i + MP^i_K \Delta K_i \\ &= MP^i_L[\Delta L_i + (MP^i_K/MP^i_L)\Delta K_i].\end{aligned} \tag{22}$$

Because $w/r = MP^i_L/MP^i_K$ (cost minimization), Equations (21) and (22) imply that

$$MRT_{ab} = -MP^a_L[\Delta L_a + (r/w)\Delta K_a]/MP^b_L[\Delta L_b + (r/w)\Delta K_b]. \tag{23}$$

The labor and capital released by one sector equals the labor and capital absorbed by the other; that is, $\Delta L_a = -\Delta L_b$ and $\Delta K_a = -\Delta K_b$. Thus, Equation (23) reduces to

$$MRT_{ab} = MP^a_L/MP^b_L. \tag{24}$$

But $MC_i = w/MP^i_L$; thus,

$$MRT_{ab} = MP^a_L/MP^b_L = (w/MP^b_L)/(w/MP^a_L) = MC_b/MC_a. \tag{25}$$

Because MRT_{ab} equals the ratio of marginal costs, perfect competition implies that $MRT_{ab} = p_b/p_a$, demonstrating (20).

Thus, a competitive equilibrium is a Pareto optimum (The First Welfare Theorem). What about the other way around? Can we again show that a Pareto optimum can be achieved by a competitive equilibrium (The Second Welfare Theorem)? Yes, but we must work backwards.

As an illustration of the Second Welfare Theorem, imagine we are on point h' of the grand utility-possibilities curve, G in Panel B of Figure 16–19. Imbedded in a Pareto optimum is a dual set of prices corresponding to a general competitive equilibrium (as long as certain conditions like convex indifference curves are satisfied). Point h' in Panel B corresponds to the production point c in Panel A. The price ratio that would achieve point c is p_b/p_a, which equals the MRT at point c and also each MRS at point h. In other words, prices must be such as to lead producers to maximize their profits at point c and such as to lead consumers to maximize their utilities at point h. As we learned in our discussion of the Stolper-Samuelson theorem, corresponding to a set of commodity prices (p_a, p_b) is a set of factor prices (w, r) for labor and capital. Finally, by assigning each agent the proper endowment of labor and capital, each agent will have just enough income to purchase the commodity bundle generating the Pareto-optimal solution.

SUMMARY

1. A competitive general equilibrium is a set of prices at which each consumer is maximizing utility, each firm is maximizing profit, and supply equals demand for every good or factor.

2. Walras's law states that the sum of the values of all excess demands equals zero. Thus, if $n - 1$ markets are in equilibrium, the nth market must also be in equilibrium. In the pure-exchange model, the competitive equilibrium results in a Pareto optimum (Welfare Theorem I). If indifference curves are convex and consumers are not living at a subsistence level, any Pareto optimum can be achieved as a general competitive equilibrium. The contract curve in the Edgeworth box corresponds to the utility-possibilities curve and describes all Pareto-optimal solutions.

3. In the two-sector model, the production-possibilities frontier corresponds to the contract curve in an Edgeworth box. The *PPF* will be concave to the origin even if both industries exhibit constant returns to scale provided different capital/labor ratios are used. An increase in the relative price of the labor-intensive good will stimulate its production, increase the wage/rent ratio, and increase real wages and lower real rents. The grand utility-possibilities frontier is the envelope of all the point utility-possibilities curves corresponding to each point on the production-possibilities frontier.

QUESTIONS AND PROBLEMS

1. Marie and Lucille share a total supply of 400 nuts and 100 apples. If Marie owns 100 nuts and 50 apples, describe the initial resource allocation using an Edgeworth box.

2. George has an endowment of 50 nuts (n) and 80 apples (a). Bob has an endowment of 200 nuts and 120 apples. Assume both have the same utility function, $U = X_n X_a$ so their $MRS_{na} = X_n X_a$.
   a. Is there room for beneficial exchange?
   b. What is the equilibrium price ratio, p_a/p_n?
   c. How many nuts and apples will George and Bob consume in the competitive equilibrium?
   d. Draw the contract curve.

3. Alice has the utility function, $U = \min(X_a, X_n/4)$ and Mary has the utility function $U = 4X_a + X_n$. Alice's endowment is $X_a, X_n = (50, 600)$, and Mary's endowment is $(X_a, X_n) = (150, 200)$.
   a. Draw the contract curve.
   b. What is the equilibrium p_a/p_n? How much will each consume?
   c. Draw the utility-possibilities curve.

4. Suppose Bill and Harry have the same utility function, $U = \min X_a, X_n$. Bill's endowment is $X_a, X_n = (50, 100)$ and Harry's is $X_a, X_n = (100, 50)$.
   a. Draw the contract curve.
   b. What is the equilibrium p_a/p_n? How much will each consume?
   c. Draw the utility-possibilities curve.

5. Suppose apples are produced by a labor-intensive, constant-returns-to-scale technology, and nuts are produced by a capital-intensive, constant-returns-to-scale technology. The only productive factors are land and labor. As long as wages are the same, workers are indifferent between jobs.
   a. How will the contract curve look?
   b. Sketch the production-possibilities frontier.
   c. If the price of nuts rises relative to the price of apples, what will happen to their production and to real wages and real land rents?

6. The textile industry is labor-intensive. Slobovians export textiles. According to the Stolper-Samuelson model, if Slobovians restrict the export of textiles (and thereby drive down their domestic price), what will happen to real wages and real rents?

SUGGESTED READINGS

Lerner, A. P. "Factor Prices and International Trade." *Economica*, February 1952.

Quirk, J., and R. Saposnik. *Introduction to General Equilibrium Economics and Welfare Economics*. New York: McGraw-Hill, 1968.

Stolper, W. F. and P. A. Samuelson. "Protection and Real Wages." *Review of Economic Studies* 1 (1941).

Walras, L. *Elements of Pure Economics*. Translated by W. Jaffé. London: George Allen and Unwin, 1954.

CHAPTER 17

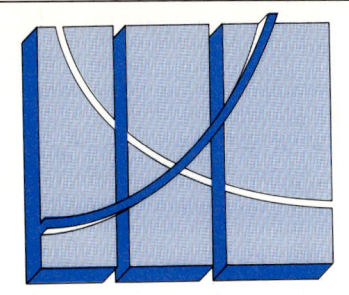

EXTERNALITIES, PUBLIC GOODS, AND PUBLIC CHOICE

Chapter 16 showed that the private provision of goods and services will be optimal under conditions of competition. The link between Pareto optimality and competition, however, is severed if *externalities* are present in the private deals struck by two parties to an exchange. In general, externalities are such problems as air and water pollution, problems of paying for the national defense, and the overexploitation or abuse of resources held in common by all members of society. This chapter is devoted to the question: how does society achieve an efficient allocation of resources in the presence of externalities?

WHAT ARE EXTERNALITIES?

An **externality** is an unpriced benefit or cost directly conferred or imposed on one agent by the actions of another agent.

An **externality** is an unpriced benefit or cost *directly* conferred or imposed on one agent by the actions of another agent. The most familiar examples would be exhaust fumes from automobiles, the pollution of air and water from industrial wastes, and the effects of secondhand smoke on nonsmokers. Externalities arise because it is impractical to appropriate *all* of the direct benefits or costs of some of the activities of any economic agent through a pricing system. In other words, externalities are public spillover effects from certain private acts of production and consumption.

It is important to distinguish between direct and indirect benefits or costs. If, for whatever reason, some people stop buying wheat, then other wheat buyers are made better off because of the income effect of the price reduction, and wheat sellers are made worse off. The welfare effects of price changes are *pecuniary externalities* but are not direct externalities.

FIGURE 17-1   External Costs in the Steel Industry

If the steel industry imposes external costs on other agents in the economy, the socially optimal level of steel production is Q^*. If the steel industry ignores external costs in making its output decision, it will produce Q units (where $MPB = MPC$)—which is too much output from society's viewpoint.

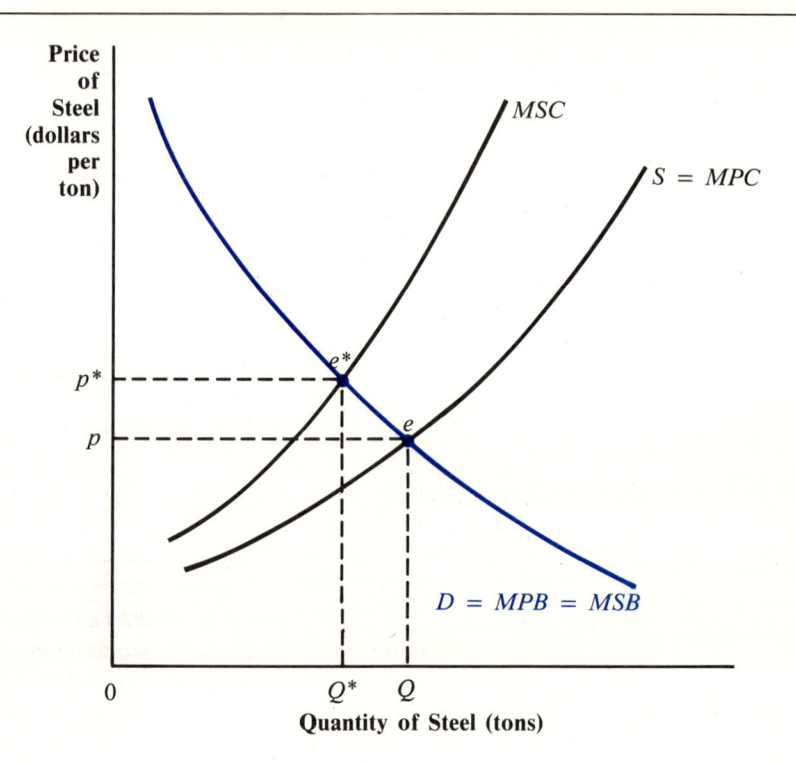

The simplest class of externalities are consumption externalities, in which case the consumption of a particular good by Jones affects the utility of Smith. For example, if Jones buys a new car and Smith buys a new car to "keep up with the Joneses," Jones's purchase makes Smith worse off. Externalities are received when you derive utility from a neighbor's flowers and when you experience disutility from your neighbor's barking dog or the smoke from your coworker's cigarette. Externalities may be positive or negative, depending upon whether they make other people better off or worse off.

The most important externalities, however, are air and water pollution, hazardous solid wastes, and noise pollution. For example, in 1983, the United States spent $29 billion on air-pollution abatement and control, $24 billion on water-pollution control, and $10 billion on solid-waste control. The total expenditures of $63 billion constituted about 2 percent of GNP.

Public goods are an extreme case of externalities. Public goods are characterized by (1) *nonrival consumption* and (2) high *exclusion costs*. If a dam is built that protects a particular geographic area from flooding, everyone who lives in the protected area benefits. Because the consumption of flood-

Public goods are characterized by nonrival consumption and high exclusion costs.

WHAT ARE EXTERNALITIES?

control services by one person does not reduce the consumption by others, consumption is nonrival. Moreover, anyone living in the area cannot be excluded from the benefits of flood control: exclusion costs are so high it is not practical (or possible) to exclude anyone from using the good. Goods such as clean air, clean lakes, or national defense are also examples of public goods.

Externalities drive a wedge between social and private costs or between social and private benefits. Economic efficiency requires that **marginal social benefits** (*MSB*) equal **marginal social costs** (*MSC*) for any economic activity. If there are no externalities, *MSB* = marginal private benefits (*MPB*) and *MSC* = marginal private costs (*MPC*). In the case of Adam Smith's invisible hand, *MPB* = *MSB* and *MPC* = *MSC*.

Marginal social costs are the sum of marginal external costs (*MEC*) and marginal private costs:

$$MSC = MEC + MPC. \quad (1)$$

For example, the production of an extra ton of steel may pollute the air and water resources of a community by dumping wastes into local lakes and smoke into the atmosphere. These externalities raise the costs of washing automobiles and clothes and interfere with recreational activities such as boating, fishing, and swimming. Marginal external costs can be positive or negative. For example, the production of honey may reduce the cost of growing apples in the neighboring orchard (because the bees help to pollinate the apple blossoms). There are, thus, external diseconomies (the steel example) or external economies (the honey example).

Marginal social benefits are the sum of marginal external benefits (*MEB*) and marginal private benefits:

$$MSB = MEB + MPB. \quad (2)$$

For example, the growing of flowers generates private benefits for both oneself and one's neighbor, and smoking imposes negative marginal external benefits on others. Growing flowers is an example of an external economy; smoking is an example of an external diseconomy.

Figure 17–1 shows how an external diseconomy arising from the cost side prevents the attainment of the socially optimal level of steel production. If we assume the steel industry is perfectly competitive, the demand curve, *D*, shows the marginal private benefits of producing an extra ton of steel. We are also assuming that *MPB* = *MSB* in the case of steel production. The supply curve, *S*, shows the marginal private costs of producing an extra ton of steel, but because there are external costs, *MSC* > *MPC*. The *MSC* curve lies to the left of the *MPC*, or competitive supply, curve. The optimal level of steel production from society's viewpoint is Q^*, because at that output *MSC* = *MSB*, but a competitive market produces *Q* units, because at that output *MPC* = *MPB*. When there are external diseconomies, the competitive market produces too much.

The **marginal social benefits** (*MSB*) of an economic activity are the sum of marginal private benefits (*MPB*) and marginal external benefits (*MEB*).

The **marginal social costs** (*MSC*) of an economic activity are the sum of marginal private costs (*MPC*) and marginal external costs (*MEC*).

FIGURE 17-2 Social Gains from Voluntary Agreements When Externalities Are Present

The *MB* curve shows the marginal benefit to the rancher from increasing the size of the herd; the *MC* curve shows the external marginal cost imposed on the neighboring farmer. Without negotiation or liability, the rancher would move to point *a*. With costless negotiation, the size of the herd would be *r*, and the rancher would operate at point *b*.

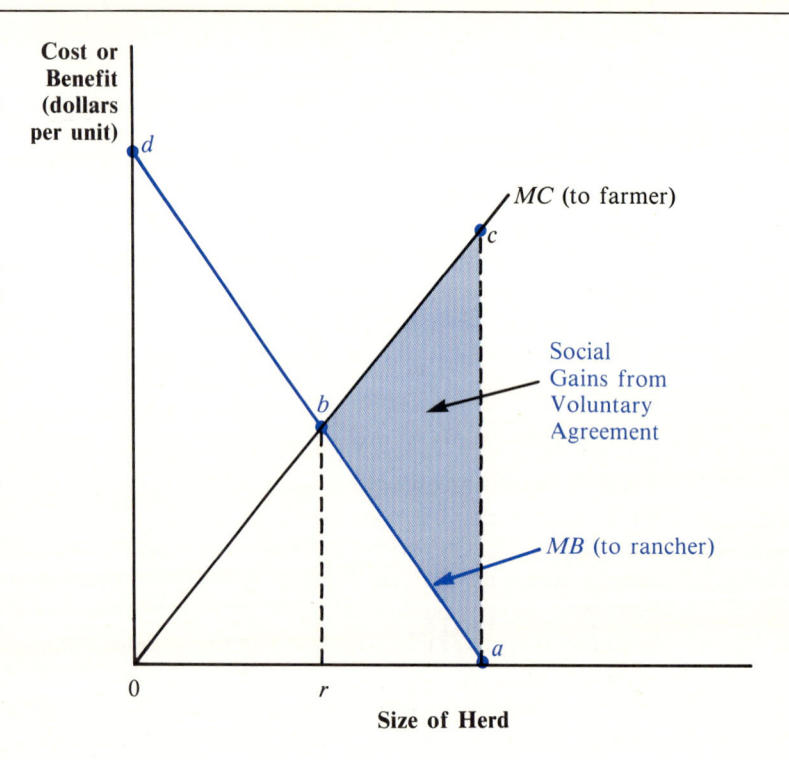

INTERNALIZING EXTERNALITIES

Internalization of a potential externality is the process of putting private price tags on external costs or benefits.

When externalities are present, private agents ignore the external costs their actions impose on others. In such cases, one solution is the **internalization** of those costs by somehow requiring the party that generates the externality to pay a price corresponding to the costs imposed on others.

Potential externalities may be internalized (1) by making voluntary agreements between those imposing and those incurring external costs, (2) by redefining property rights between the parties, (3) by setting up a system of marketable permits for generating the externality, or (4) by taxing or subsidizing the externality generator.

Voluntary Agreements

One method of internalizing potential externalities is to set up a market for the external cost or benefit. The proposition that voluntary agreements can internalize externalities is called the *Coase theorem,* after Ronald H. Coase. Coase gave an example of a rancher whose cattle occasionally stray onto a neighboring farm and damage the neighbor's crops. If the rancher were legally liable for the damage to the farmer, then private bargaining would result in a deal between the farmer and the rancher.

In Figure 17-2, the *MB* curve shows the net marginal benefit to the rancher of increasing the size of the herd. In accordance with the law of diminishing returns, marginal benefit declines as the size of the herd increases. The *MC* curve shows the marginal cost imposed on the farmer by a unit increase in the size of the herd; the larger is the herd, the higher are the marginal costs imposed on the neighboring farmer.

If the rancher did not have to take the farmer's extra costs into account and if the rancher could not negotiate with the farmer, the rancher would attempt to increase the size of the herd to the point where marginal benefit equals 0 (at point *a*). In this case, the rancher totally ignores the external costs imposed on the farmer when making a decision about herd size.

Suppose, however, that the rancher and the farmer could costlessly negotiate. If the rancher were liable to the farmer for any damages, the rancher would have to compensate the farmer by paying the marginal external costs imposed on the farmer. In this case, the rancher would increase herd size until marginal benefits equal marginal costs (at point *b*). Compared to the previous case, society would gain the area *abc*. Whenever the herd is pushed beyond the optimal size of *r* units, society loses the excess of marginal cost over marginal benefit. When the rancher is liable to the farmer, the rancher's net gains would be the area 0*bd* because the farmer must be compensated.

Coase pointed out that if the rancher were not liable to the farmer, the same allocation of resources would be achieved by costless negotiation. In this case, the farmer would bribe the rancher to keep the herd at the optimal level of *r* units. The farmer simply pays the rancher not to increase the herd. The marginal-cost schedule, thus, becomes the rancher's marginal-cost schedule. When the rancher is not liable, the rancher's net profits will be larger than in the rancher-liable case because 0*rbd* is larger than 0*bd*.

In our discussion of the Coase theorem, the wealth of the rancher or the farmer did not affect the positions of the *MC* and *MB* curves. Thus, the above example assumes there are no income effects on the marginal-valuation curves.

According to the Coase theorem, (1) if there is costless negotiation between the parties involved in a potential externality, the allocation of resources will be optimal; and (2) if there are no income effects on the marginal benefits or costs of the activity, the allocation will be the same under any system of liability.

Government Taxes and Subsidies

Government taxes or subsidies are another method of internalizing externalities when voluntary cooperation becomes impossible because of the number of parties involved. For example, in the case of automobile pollution, the transaction costs involved in negotiating among the many parties directly involved are prohibitive. Accordingly, the government can impose a

FIGURE 17-3 The Marginal Costs and Marginal Benefits of Clean Water

This diagram compares the costs and benefits of cleaning up the water in a lake. Levels of water quality are measured along the horizontal axis from 0 (lifeless water) to 100 percent clean. The marginal benefit of clean water to recreational users is the horizontal line MSB; the marginal cost of producing clean water by the firm utilizing water-treatment facilities is shown by the upward-sloping MSC curve.

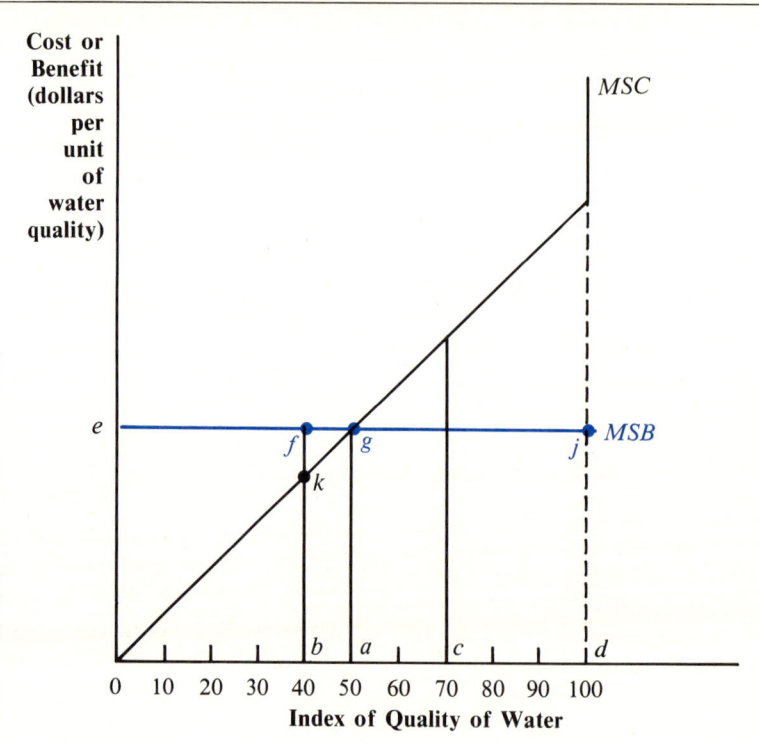

tax or subsidy on the externality generator in order to equate marginal social benefits with marginal social costs.

Figure 17-3 shows an example. Suppose that when a steel plant discharges industrial wastes into Lake Michigan, the wastes reduce recreational opportunities (fishing, boating, and swimming). Water quality has an economic value to fishers, swimmers, and boaters. The horizontal axis measures water quality using some index of water quality ranging from 0 to 100. Point 0 represents polluted, lifeless water and 100 represents the healthiest natural lake. To simplify, suppose the recreational users of the water would pay a constant amount per unit of water quality. Thus, the marginal and average benefit of clean water (MSB) is a horizontal line.

By installing filtering systems or even hauling away industry wastes, the firm can reduce wastes. If the firm makes no effort to reduce wastes, the lake will become completely lifeless (point 0). As the firm begins to treat its waste discharges, higher levels of water quality are achieved. Assume that the marginal cost of producing higher levels of water quality is upward-sloping, as shown by the MSC curve in Figure 17-3.

The efficient level of water quality would be 50 units because at that point marginal (social) costs equal marginal (social) benefits. If the water-quality level is only 40 units, the marginal cost of abatement is less than the marginal benefit to recreational users; thus, it pays to expand water-treatment facilities. If the water-quality level is 70 units, the marginal cost of abatement exceeds the marginal benefit; accordingly, by reducing abatement society can save in costs more than the forgone benefits. When the quality of clean water is at the optimal level, there is an optimal amount of water treatment as well as an optimal amount of polluted water.

If there are many users of the lake as a recreational facility, it would be very difficult for each fisher or swimmer to strike a bargain with the polluting firm. Two problems would arise. First, with many users, the transaction costs of negotiating with each person would be prohibitive. Second, water quality is a public good because providing water quality to one person must necessarily provide water quality to all. As a consequence, any individual fisher or swimmer might try to be a **free rider** on anyone else's bargaining efforts. Someone is a free rider if he or she can consume or use a scarce good or service without paying. If there were many users of the lake, each person might decide to let someone else do the negotiating. Everybody's job is frequently nobody's job.

> A **free rider** is a person who consumes a scarce good or service without paying for it.

Because the free market will not provide the efficient level of water quality in the above case, the government could impose a tax or grant a subsidy. In Figure 17–3, *e* is the marginal benefit of clean water. In order for the government to mimic the market, it must know the marginal-benefit curve. In this case, the government could tax the firm *e* dollars for each unit by which perfect water quality was reduced by discharge into the lake. Such an **effluent charge** would be treated like any other cost internal to the firm. Suppose the firm achieved a water-quality level of only 40 units. The firm would pay an effluent charge of 60 units × $*e*. By improving water quality by 10 additional units, the firm would incur extra treatment costs of *bkga* and save effluent charges equal to *bfga*. The firm, therefore, maximizes its profit by achieving a water-quality level of 50 units.

> An **effluent charge** is a tax imposed on a polluting agent for each unit of pollution generated.

Alternatively, the firm could be paid (subsidized) for each unit by which totally polluted water quality was improved instead of being taxed for each unit by which perfect water quality was reduced. The result would be exactly the same.

There are many problems that must be faced before a system of effluent charges can be imposed. First, it is difficult to estimate the marginal benefits of clean water (or air). Second, piecemeal solutions to environmental problems are difficult because solving one problem may create other problems as firms shift to other forms of waste disposal. Third, there is no agreed-upon standard for measuring environmental quality. For example, water quality is determined by measuring bacteria levels, biochemical oxygen demand, and levels of dissolved oxygen, turbidity, total suspended solids, nutrient levels, toxic pesticides and solvents, and even temperature. Fourth, there are enormous problems in the administration of effluent charges.[1]

---

1. This discussion of effluent charges is based on Joseph J. Seneca and Michael K. Taussig, *Environmental Economics*, 3rd ed. (Englewood Cliffs, N. J.: Prentice-Hall, 1984), pp. 63–73. For a report on many environmental issues and relevant statistics, see *Environmental Quality*, The Fifteenth Annual Report of the Council on Environmental Quality, 1984, Washington, D.C.

ALLOCATING A COMMON-PROPERTY RESOURCE

Redefinition of Property Rights

Property rights specify the way in which goods may be bought, sold, or used. Poorly defined property rights can result in externalities. Who owns the air, the water, or the fish in the sea? When resources are the community property of all, it is likely that many individuals will exploit the resource beyond socially optimal levels. For example, when fish are owned by all, the individual fisher will ignore the costs he or she imposes on others by depleting the resource.

Consider a lake stocked with fish. Assume the lake is common property and that everyone has free access to it. To be specific, let the production function for fish be the simple quadratic function, $Q = 10L - 0.1L^2$, where L is the number of hours spent fishing. Thus, the average product (AP) of an hour of fishing is

$$AP = 10 - 0.1L$$

As argued in Chapter 5, if the average curve is a straight line, the marginal curve falls twice as fast; thus, the marginal product of fishing is

$$MP = 10 - 0.2L$$

Figure 17-4 shows the marginal and average products of fishing. The amount of fishing activity depends on the opportunity costs of fishing and on the nature of property rights.

We can measure the opportunity cost of fishing in terms of sacrificed wages. Assume the wage (W) is $12 per hour in nonfishing occupations and that the price of fish (P) is $2 per pound. Thus, an hour's work is worth 6 pounds of fish. Thus, the opportunity cost of fishing is 6 pounds of fish per hour, or W/P. If the fishing industry is a small part of the economy, we may take the real wage—W/P—to be given to the fishing industry.

A **common-property resource** is a resource to which everyone has free access.

If the lake is a **common-property resource**—that is, if everyone has free access to the lake—then L hours of fishing will earn the average product of fishing, or $AP = 10 - 0.1L$. As long as $AP > W/P$, people will fish on the lake. People will be indifferent between fishing and working elsewhere when $W/P = AP$. In the present case,

$$AP = 10 - 0.1L = 6 = W/P,$$

so that $L = 40$ hours of labor. The total output of fish would be 240 pounds $= 40[10 - 0.1(40)]$. The rest of the economy sacrifices the equivalent of 240 pounds of fish because people sacrifice an income of $12 per hour $\times$ 40 hours, or $480, and the price of fish is $2 per pound. Figure 17-4 shows the solution when the lake is a common-property resource: $W/P = AP$ at point a.

The above example shows that common-property resources are overexploited because the individual fisher imposes an external cost on others. In

FIGURE 17-4   Gains from Converting a Common-Property Resource to a Private-Property Resource

The *AP* and *MP* curves show the average and marginal products of fishing in a particular lake. If the lake remains a common-property resource, the allocation solution is point *a*; as a private-property resource, the allocation solution is point *b*. Society gains *abc* when the lake is converted to private property.

Fisher's Product (pounds of fish per worker hour) vs *Fisher's Quantity of Labor (worker hours spent fishing)*. Curves: $AP = 10 - 0.1L$ and $MP = 10 - 0.2L$. Points *b* (20, 6), *a* (40, 6), *c* (40, 2). Shaded region labeled "Gains from Private-Property Solution."

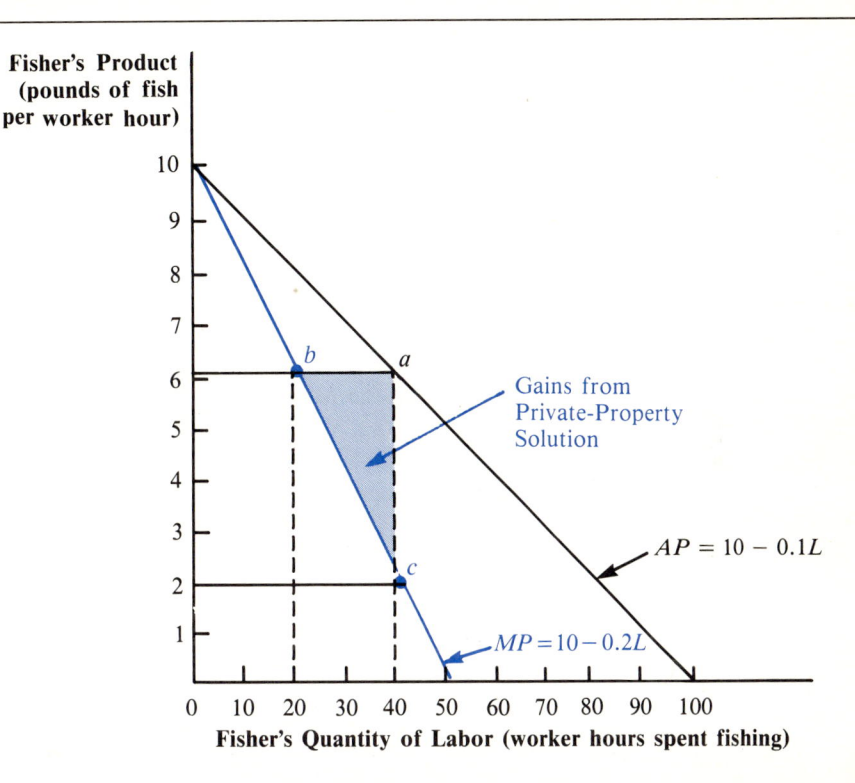

Figure 17-4, the private gain (*AP*) from the 40th hour of fishing is 6 pounds of fish, but the social gain (*MP*) from the 40th hour of fishing is only 2 pounds of fish. In effect, the 40th hour of fishing imposes an external cost of 4 pounds of fish on everybody else. Consider what happens to the average catch as the number of hours fished increases from 39 to 41. The average catch falls from 6.1 pounds [= 10 − 0.1(39)] to 5.9 pounds [= 10 − 0.1(41)]. The extra 2 hours of fishing reduces the average catch by 0.2 pounds of fish. Thus, when there are 40 hours of fishing (the average of 39 and 41), the extra two hours of fishing reduces the total catch of the others by 8 pounds (= 0.2 × 40), or by 4 pounds per extra hour of fishing.

To internalize the externality, we need only merge all the fishers into a firm that monitors or limits the fishing on the lake to the socially optimal amount.

Now imagine that the lake is private property and that the owner can costlessly prevent unauthorized access to the lake. The owner would then hire fishers up to the point where *W*/*P* = *MP*, because as long as *MP* > *W*/*P* there is a profit to be made from employing a fisher for another hour. In the case of private property,

$$MP = 10 - 0.2L = 6 = W/P,$$

so that $L = 20$ hours of fishing. The owner of the lake earns a rent (R) of $R = (P \times Q) - (W \times L)$. Because $Q = L(AP) = 20[10 - 0.1(20)] = 160$, $R = (\$2 \times 160) - (\$12 \times 20) = \$80$. In Figure 17–4, the private-property solution is $MP = W/P$, or point b.

In the common-property case, 240 pounds of fish are produced, and society sacrifices income elsewhere worth 240 pounds of fish. In other words, society does not gain anything from the common-property resource. In the private-property case, 160 pounds of fish are produced, but society sacrifices wages elsewhere of only $W(L)/P = \$12(20)/2 = \$240/2 = 120$ pounds of fish. Thus, society gains 40 pounds of fish. In Figure 17–4, the gain from converting the property to private property is the area abc.

Government Taxes or Subsidies and Government Permits

If converting the resource from common property to private property is not feasible, another solution would be to impose taxes (see Practice Exercise 17–1) or to set up a system of permits.

In the fishing example just discussed, the government could issue permits to fishers, where each permit allows one pound of fish. Because the socially optimal level of fishing is 20 hours and because $AP = 8$ pounds of fish at that point, the optimum quantity of fish would be 160 pounds. The market value of 160 pounds of fish = \$320. Because 20 labor hours have a market value of \$240, the permits are worth \$80, or \$0.50(= \$80 ÷ 160) per permit pound. If the permits were transferable, fishers would bid the price of each permit pound to \$0.50. At any price less than \$0.50, a permit would allow one to make more than could be made elsewhere. (See Example 17–1.)

PRACTICE EXERCISE 17–1

Q. In the example of fishers on a lake for whom $AP = 10 - 0.1L$ and $MP = 10 - 0.2L$, the price (P) of fish was \$2 per pound, the wage (W) was \$12 per hour, and the social optimum was 20 hours of fishing. Assuming the lake is a common-property resource, what is the optimal tax per hour of fishing?

A. At the optimum, 20 hours of labor are used. Thus, $MP = 6$ and $AP = 8$. An hour of fishing yields $\$2 \times 8 = \$16$ worth of fish, but wages are \$12 in alternative occupations. By imposing a tax of \$4 per hour on fishing, a fisher can earn only \$12 per hour, after paying the tax, for each hour of fishing. With such a tax, private incentives would lead to 20 hours of fishing—the social optimum. If $L > 20$ hours, the average product of fishing would fall to less than 8 pounds and the net wage, after paying the tax, would be less than \$12.

> EXAMPLE 17-1   The Depletion of the Ozone Layer

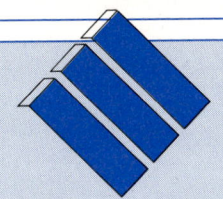

There is some evidence that chlorofluorocarbons, used in aerosol sprays such as deodorants and shaving creams, contribute to the depletion of the ozone layer that shields the earth from the sun's harmful ultraviolet rays.

The quantity of chlorine gases emitted can be controlled by (1) a system of emission standards that force the makers or users of these gases to use different technologies or (2) a permit system. Because the pollutant accumulates in the environment, the desired reduction in these gases should be stated over a long period of time. A group of Rand Corporation economists compared the compliance costs of a simple mandatory system with a permit system over a 10-year period. They assumed that the desired reductions were in the neighborhood of 800 million pounds over the 10-year period. The present value of the cumulative costs of the mandatory controls was $185.3 million (in 1976 dollars), and the present value of the costs of a permit system was only $94.7 million. In other words, the compliance costs of a mandatory system were double those of the permit system.

Source: Tom Tietenberg, *Environmental and Natural-Resource Economics* (Glenview, Ill.: Scott, Foresman, 1984), pp. 279–80.

Common-property resources are overexploited because each user ignores the costs his or her actions impose on others. The socially optimal allocation can be achieved by (1) establishing a market for permits, (2) imposing a tax on each user, or (3) converting the resource to private property (if possible).

GOVERNMENT REGULATION OF POLLUTION

While economic theory suggests that effluent charges are the best way to control pollution, the United States has relied on direct controls or prohibitions. The Environmental Protection Agency (EPA) has primary responsibility for regulating environmental quality. The EPA's regulations impose ceilings on the physical amount of some pollutant discharged into the atmosphere or into rivers and lakes. To comply, firms must install waste-disposal equipment or adopt a different technology that generates fewer wastes. The EPA can prohibit the use of certain inputs in the production process; for example, new cars must use unleaded gasoline and pesticides cannot contain DDT.

Direct regulations are not as economically efficient as effluent charges or

FIGURE 17-5 The Bubble Approach to Waste-Reduction Requirements

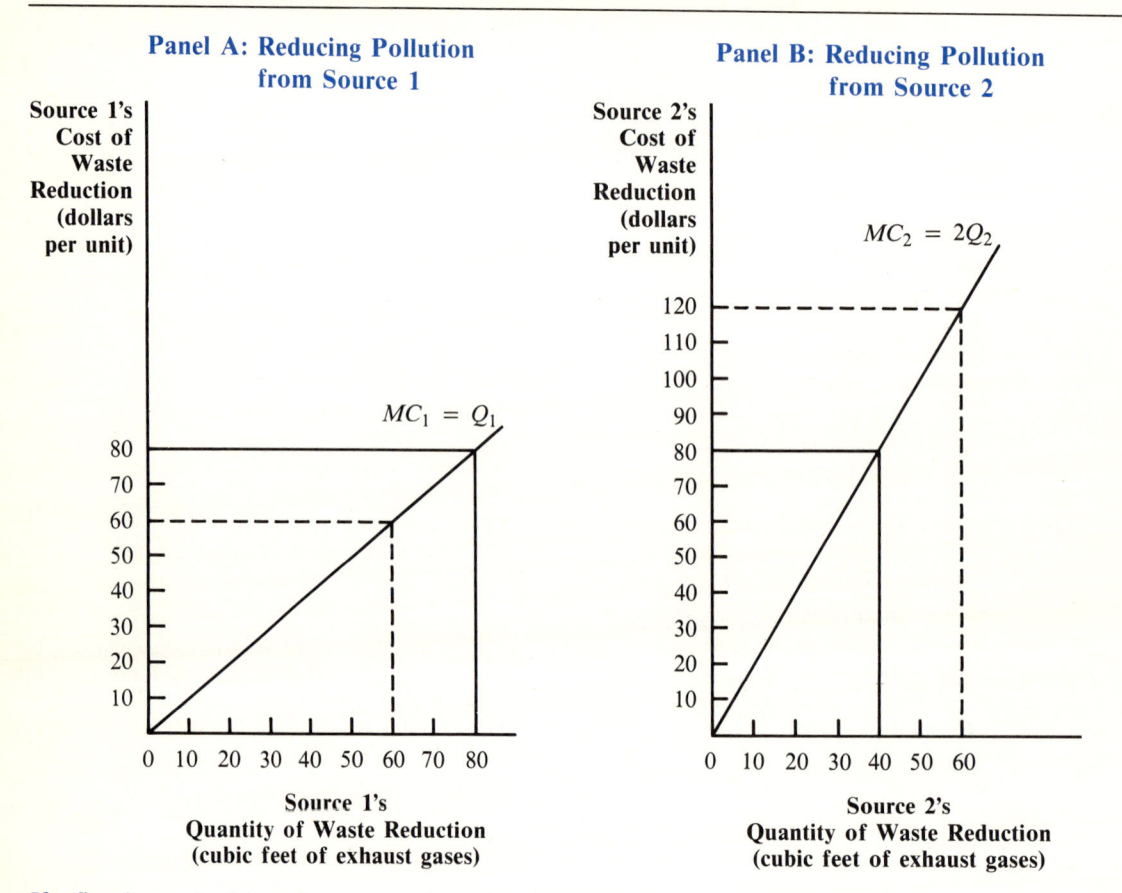

Panel A: Reducing Pollution from Source 1

Source 1's Cost of Waste Reduction (dollars per unit)

$MC_1 = Q_1$

Source 1's Quantity of Waste Reduction (cubic feet of exhaust gases)

Panel B: Reducing Pollution from Source 2

Source 2's Cost of Waste Reduction (dollars per unit)

$MC_2 = 2Q_2$

Source 2's Quantity of Waste Reduction (cubic feet of exhaust gases)

If a firm is required to reduce wastes in each of its two sources of pollution by 60 cubic feet of exhaust gases, the total costs of waste reduction will be higher than if the firm faces an overall limitation of 120 cubic feet. In the overall case—the bubble approach—wastes are reduced at the low-cost sources before they are reduced at the high-cost sources.

schemes based on cost minimization. For example, suppose a chemical plant contains different types of equipment devoted to different processes. These stationary sources of air pollution have been traditionally controlled on an equipment-by-equipment or stack-by-stack basis, but the cost of controlling pollutants depends on the process or the equipment being used. In Figure 17-5, the horizontal axis measures the quantity of wastes reduced, and the vertical axis measures the marginal cost of reducing wastes. In Panel A, the MC_1 curve shows the marginal cost of reducing pollution from Source 1; in Panel B, MC_2 shows the marginal cost of reducing pollution from Source 2. Assume that waste reduction is measured in terms of the volume of exhaust gases (Q). For simplicity, let $MC_1 = Q_1$ and $MC_2 = 2Q_2$. If the EPA required that each process reduce its exhaust gases by 60 cubic feet, the total costs to the plant would be $1,800 + $3,600 = $5,400$. Total costs of waste reduction equal the area under each marginal-cost curve up to 60 cubic feet. As a comparison of Panels A and B shows, waste reduction from Source 2 is more expensive. To minimize costs, the chemical plant should increase waste reduction from Source 1 and reduce waste reduction from Source 2. Costs will be minimized when $MC_1 = MC_2$. If the overall requirement for waste reduction is 120 cubic feet, costs will be minimized when Source 1 reduction is 80 cubic feet and Source 2 reduction is 40 cubic feet. In this case, the total costs of waste reduction would be reduced from $5,400 to $4,800, which is the sum of the areas under MC_1 and MC_2 up to 80 and 40 cubic feet, respectively. The overall requirement of reducing wastes by 120 cubic feet would be equivalent to an effluent charge of $80 per cubic foot (as discussed earlier).

The EPA, responding to criticisms of inefficiency, has begun to experiment with the overall method of waste reduction. The new policy is called the *bubble approach*, where a number of stacks or plants are grouped together and treated as if they were enclosed by a large bubble. By late 1984, the EPA had approved 37 bubbles. A study of 52 Du Pont plants estimated that the bubble approach would save 60 percent over using the traditional source-by-source emission standard.[2]

PUBLIC CHOICE

It is one thing to consider the optimal government action in the case of externalities; it is quite another matter for the government to actually determine and carry out the optimal decision. The question posed by *public-choice theory* is: how can the government choose actions that achieve Pareto optimality for society as a whole?

Unanimity: The Benefit Theory of Taxation

The most obvious difficulty with making public decisions is that people are different and, therefore, have different preferences for government action. For example, a flood-control project is a pure public good as far as the community is concerned. If all people were the same, and each received the same benefits, it would be necessary only to share the tax burden equally, but people are different. People who live on high ground will benefit less from a flood-control project than people who live on low ground. Rich people will benefit more than poor people. Fearless people benefit more than cautious people. It would be difficult to finance the project by soliciting

---

2. For a discussion of the bubble concept, see *Environmental Quality*, 1984, pp. 50–65; the Du Pont case is discussed in M. T. Maloney and B. Yandle, "Bubbles and Efficiency," *Regulation* (May/June 1980). For an excellent textbook discussion, see Tom Tietenberg, *Environmental and Natural-Resource Economics* (Glenview, Ill.: Scott, Foresman, 1984), pp. 305–307.

FIGURE 17-6 Determining Pareto Optimality in an Economy with Public Goods

Panel A shows the production-possibilities frontier between a private good and a public good. Panel B shows typical indifference curves for Agent B. Panel C shows Agent A's maximum utility for the given utility level of Agent B.

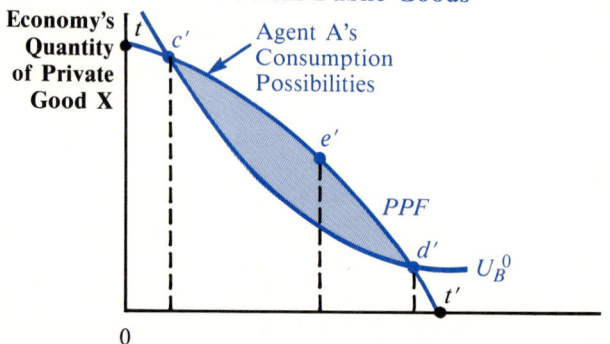

Panel A: Production Possibilities for Private Versus Public Goods

Economy's Quantity of Private Good X

t, c', Agent A's Consumption Possibilities, e', PPF, d', U_B^0, t'

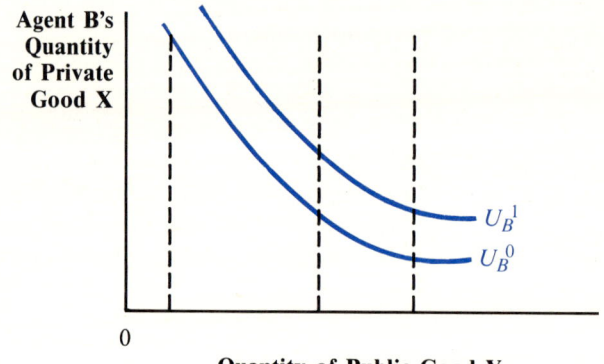

Quantity of Public Good Y

Panel B: Indifference Curves for Agent B

Agent B's Quantity of Private Good X

U_B^1, U_B^0

Quantity of Public Good Y

Panel C: Agent A's Utility-Maximizing Consumption

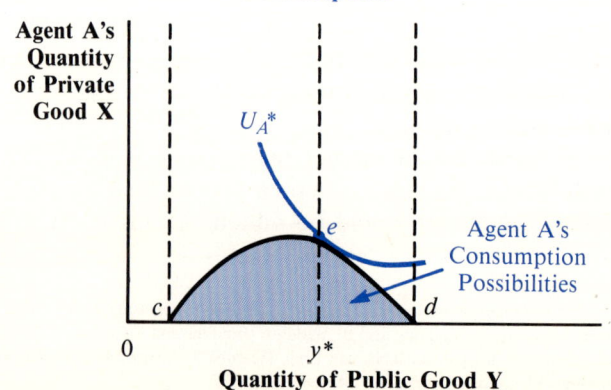

Agent A's Quantity of Private Good X

U_A^*, e, Agent A's Consumption Possibilities, c, d, y^*

Quantity of Public Good Y

voluntary contributions equal to each person's marginal benefits, because people would benefit whether they paid or not, so many people would attempt to be free riders. Unanimity could be achieved only if people were truthful or if the community had perfect information about the benefits each would receive from the flood-control project.

To keep matters simple, suppose a project costs $120 and that there are only three people in the community, persons A, B, and C. Assume the project is worth $60 to A, $50 to B, and $30 to C. It is clear that the project is worth building because it is possible to make everyone better off. For example, if A paid $50, B paid $45, and C paid $25, all three members of society would receive some net benefit. But if each were asked, "How much is the project worth to you?" they might each have the incentive to undervalue their true benefits because of the fear of being taxed according to their stated values. Why should Agent A identify himself as placing the highest value on the public good? With imperfect information, people may ride free.

What are the conditions for Pareto optimality in a world with public goods and perfect information? (Later, when information is not perfect, we shall show how it might be possible to elicit the truthful revelation of preferences by a clever system of penalties.)

To examine the conditions for Pareto optimality in this situation, we can use a model developed by Paul Samuelson.[3] Consider a world with two goods, X and Y. Assume that good X is a pure private good (such as bread), but that good Y is a pure public good (such as national defense). If x is the supply of the private good, and x_i is the amount received by the ith agent, then it must be the case that $x = \Sigma_i x_i$. However, in the case of a public good, the consumption by the ith agent $y_i = y$, because with a public good, no one can be excluded from the provision of some given amount of the good. Thus, if there are but two agents, A and B, the appropriate utility functions are:

$$U_A = U_A(x_A, y) \tag{3}$$

and

$$U_B = U_B(x_B, y). \tag{4}$$

Panel A of Figure 17–6 shows the production-possibilities frontier (*PPF*), or the economy's possible allocations between the private good and the public good. The quantity of the private good is measured vertically; the quantity of the public good is measured horizontally. At point t, only the private good is produced; at point t', only the public good is produced. The *PPF* is convex to the origin, which reflects the assumption that there are diminishing returns to variable factors.

Panel B of Figure 17–6 shows Agent B's indifference curves. The private good is again measured along the vertical axis, and the public good is measured along the horizontal axis. Panels A and B are vertically aligned so

---

3. Paul A. Samuelson, "A Diagrammatic Exposition of a Theory of Public Expenditure," *Review of Economics and Statistics* 37 (November 1955): 350–56.

that the public good's scale of measurement is the same along both horizontal axes. Whatever amount of the public good is produced in the economy (whatever point is chosen on the *PPF*) automatically provides the same level of public services to both Agent B and Agent A. Because more is better than less, the higher is the indifference curve, the higher is the agent's utility. The indifference curve U_B^0 represents a lower level of utility than indifference curve U_B^1.

A Pareto optimum can be defined as an allocation of resources that maximizes one person's utility given the other person's utility. Indifference curve U_B^0 represents a given level of utility for Agent B and appears in both Panel A and Panel B. Because good X is a private good, Agent A's consumption of X is obtained by subtracting B's consumption of the private good from its total production. Thus, by vertically subtracting B's indifference curve U_B^0 from the *PPF*, we obtain the maximum amounts of A's consumption of X for each output of Y and for the given utility level for Agent B. The shaded area in Panel A is A's feasible consumption set.

Panel C of Figure 17-6 shows Agent A's consumption possibilities of private and public goods. Only Agent A's quantity of the private good is measured along the vertical axis this time, but the economy's quantity of the public good is again measured along the horizontal axis (in exactly the same scale). The line *ced* in Panel C is the upper boundary of Agent A's feasible consumption set (for the given level of B's utility). To maximize Agent A's utility given B's utility, we need only move to point *e* on *ced* where U_A^* is tangent to *ced*.

Just as in the case of a competitive economy without public goods, there are many Pareto optima. Had we chosen another level of utility for Agent B, we would have had a different *ced* curve in Panel C and a different Pareto optimum.[4]

Pareto optimality in the case of public goods is achieved when Agent A's marginal rate of substitution, MRS^A, equals the slope of *ced*. Because *ced* is the difference between the *PPF* and B's indifference curve, the (absolute) slope of *ced* is the difference between the absolute slope of the *PPF*—the marginal rate of transformation, *MRT*—and Agent B's marginal rate of

---

[4]. A simple example would be the case where the production-possibilities frontier is $x + y = 1$ and $U_i = x_i y$ ($i = A, B$). The *MRS* is then $(\partial U_i/\partial y)/(\partial U_i/\partial x_i) = x_i/y$. The marginal utility of the public good divided by the marginal utility of the private good is the amount of the private good the agent is just willing to sacrifice for another unit of the public good. If $x + y = 1$, the *MRT* = 1. Condition (5) then becomes

$$x_A/y + x_B/y = 1.$$

It follows that

$$x_A + x_B = x = y.$$

Since $x + y = 1$, $x = y = 0.5$. In the case of identical individuals with the above utility function and constant costs of production, the optimum quantity of the public good is independent of the distribution of income. As far as the private good is concerned, any combination $x_A + x_B = 0.5$ will work. All these solutions are Pareto optimal.

substitution, MRS^B. Thus, Pareto optimality requires that $MRS^A = MRT - MRS^B$. Rearranging this equation yields the basic condition:

$$MRS^A + MRS^B = MRT, \qquad (5)$$

MRS^i is Agent i's marginal valuation of the public good, and MRT is the marginal cost of producing the public good. Because both agents benefit from an extra unit of the public good, they are in the aggregate willing to sacrifice $MRS^A + MRS^B$ of the private good for another unit of the public good. When the aggregate marginal benefit of the public good equals its marginal cost, optimality is achieved.

Voting Mechanisms

Achieving the Pareto optimum is difficult because people will not reveal their true valuations. Two mechanisms for allocating resources when there are public goods are: majority rule and demand-revealing taxes.

Majority Rule

Imagine again that a flood-control project is proposed to three voters. The flood-control project costs $90, and, if the proposal is passed, each voter will be taxed $30. The project will be built if two of the three voters approve the project—that is, if the majority rules. Suppose voter A considers the project worth $60, voter B considers it worth $40, and voter C believes it worth $20. The *average voter* considers the project worth $40 (60 + 40 + 20) ÷ 3 = $40; likewise, the **median voter** considers the project worth $40 (the median voter is the one for which half the remaining population likes the project more and the other half likes the project less). In this case, if the project is brought to a vote, the majority will vote in favor—only voter C will vote against the project.

> The **median voter** likes a project more than one half and less than the other half of the remaining voters.

Is majority rule efficient; that is, does majority rule bring about a Pareto-optimal result? In the simple case just considered, efficiency reigns. The median voter determines the outcome in a majority rule situation. Voter B is the median voter, but in the above case, the average and the median are exactly the same. Efficiency prevails when the average voter has the same preferences as the median voter. Whenever the average voter gets his or her way, the total benefits of the project will always exceed its costs. Thus, it is possible to make everyone better off.

Now consider a case where the average voter differs from the median voter. Suppose that we have the same flood-control project costing $90 and that the cost is shared equally among voters A, B, and C. Assume that voter A considers the project worth $21, that B considers the project worth $29, and that C considers it worth $100. Clearly, B is the median voter. The project will not be approved because $29 falls short of the $30 cost share. Both A and B will vote against the project. The average voter considers the project worth (100 + 29 + 21) ÷ 3 = $50. The 3-person community would benefit from the flood-control project because voter C could always compensate A and B for their losses, but with simple majority rule, the project would not pass.

Majority rule will be efficient if the average voter has the same preferences as the median voter; majority rule will be inefficient if the average and the median voter have different preferences.

The difficulty with majority rule is that the intensity of preferences do not matter. Only the preference of the median voter matters. Those who like the project more than the median voter may prefer the project only slightly, but those who like the project less than the median voter may have very strong dislikes. Thus, majority rule can result in projects being passed with benefits falling short of costs. If the median voter opposes a project, and those voting for the project have a strong preference, majority rule can result in a project being rejected even though its total benefits exceed total costs.

Demand-Revealing Mechanisms

The problem with majority rule could be solved if people would truthfully reveal their demand for public goods. Economists Edward Clarke, William Vickery, and Theodore Groves (working independently) have shown how to design mechanisms for the truthful revelation of preferences.

Imagine a group of people are planning to build a bridge and to share the cost equally. To each agent, the net value of the bridge is simply his or her benefit minus his or her cost share. Thus, let v_i denote the *net* value of the bridge to the *i*th agent. The bridge is worth building if $\Sigma_i v_i \geq 0$. The criterion for building the bridge will be that each person submits his or her bid, w_i (which would equal v_i in the case of complete truth telling), and the bridge will be built if $\Sigma_i w_i \geq 0$.

The claimed values, w_i, need not equal the true values, v_i. The above mechanism relies on truth telling. Misrepresentations can cause serious problems. Suppose agent *i* has a net value, $v_i < 0$. An agent with a negative value of −$10 might wish to submit a bid of, say, −$10 million, to prevent the bridge from being built. Moreover, an agent placing a positive value of $2 on the bridge might submit a bid of $20 million to guarantee that the bridge will be built. As long as there are no costs of misrepresentation, strategic maneuvering might result in bids that deviate dramatically from their true values.

To insure truth telling, we need only penalize voters for misrepresentation, but how can we know if people are lying if only they know their true values? The answer is to design a mechanism so that under all circumstances each voter's best strategy is to tell the truth. To accomplish this goal, we can impose a tax on a voter for the damages he or she inflicts on the rest of the community. A voter damages the rest of the community when his or her vote changes the social decision.

Suppose that George values a project at −$10 and that the rest of the community claims a net value of $100 on the project. Then without George's vote, the project would be carried out. If George votes and tells the truth, the community will still carry out the project because −$10 + $100 = $90, but if George misrepresents his preferences by stating that his value is −$110, the project would not be carried out. The rest of the community would be damaged by $100 (the net claimed value gained by the project). By taxing George $100 for changing the social decision, George would be better off telling the truth. Truth telling results in a loss of only $10; telling a lie results in a loss of $90—the $100 tax minus the $10 gain from not having the project.

When George votes his true value, he does not change the social decision. Consider now a case where a voter's true value changes the social decision. Assume Frank places a net value of $50 on the bridge, but the rest of the community places a value of −$40 on the bridge. Frank's vote results in the bridge being built. Even though he is charged a tax of $40 for casting a true vote, his net benefit is $10 ($50 benefit from the bridge minus the $40 tax). If he lied, and said the bridge was worth only $10, then the bridge would not be built. There would be no tax, but Frank would lose the bridge benefit worth $50 to him. Thus, he benefits most from telling the truth.

Now consider an example where the voter likes a project, but the rest of the community has a stronger dislike of the project. Suppose Betty places a net value of $10 on a project while the rest of the community claims a net value of −$50 on the project. If Betty tells the truth, the project will not be carried out: she will lose $10 from not having the project and everyone else will presumably gain the claimed costs of $50. If she lies by casting, say, a $60 vote, the project will be carried out, but she will then face a $50 damage tax because her vote changes the social decision. Betty is better off by $40 if she tells the truth.

By placing a tax on each agent equal to the damage imposed on the rest of the community when the agent's vote changes the social decision, each agent has an incentive to tell the truth.

A possible difficulty with the above taxing scheme is that it generates revenues for the government. These revenues must somehow be disposed of without affecting the decisions of any voter. Economists Nicolaus Tideman and Gordon Tullock have argued that the total amount of these revenues would be so small in practice that tax revenues can be neglected. According to Tideman and Tullock, the total taxes collected for the entire U.S. economy would be less than $10,000![5]

---

5. See T. Nicolaus Tideman and Gordon Tullock, "A New and Superior Process for Making Social Choices," *Journal of Political Economy* 84 (December 1976): 1145–60. For a simple textbook exposition based on algebra see Hal Varian, *Microeconomic Analysis* (New York: W. W. Norton, 1978), pp. 200–203.

So far there are still serious obstacles in the way of implementing mechanisms that insure the truthful revelation of preferences. One problem is not everybody votes because the private cost of voting appears to exceed the private benefits. Another problem with demand-revealing mechanisms is their complexity; instead of voting yes or no, people would have to vote dollar valuations. Politically, such a procedure might be very unpopular. A final problem is that the demand-revealing mechanism may have an unwanted impact on the distribution of real income in the community, simply because some gain while others lose.

SUMMARY

1. Externalities are unpriced benefits or costs directly received by or imposed on one agent by the actions of another agent. Pollution is the major example of an externality. Public goods are an extreme case of an externality; they are goods that are nonrival in consumption the benefits of which people cannot be excluded from enjoying.

2. Externalities may be internalized through voluntary agreements between parties or by taxing or subsidizing the externality generator. According to the Coase theorem, government action may not be required if negotiation costs are relatively small and if property rights are well defined.

3. The socially optimal allocation of a common-property resource can be achieved by establishing a market for permits, imposing a tax on each user, or converting the resource to private property.

4. When government action is desirable, effluent charges are a more efficient method of control than direct quantitative restrictions on pollution.

5. In the case of pure public goods, efficiency requires that the sum of everyone's marginal benefits (as measured by the marginal rate of substitution of private goods for public goods) equal the marginal cost of producing the public good. Without perfect information on the part of the government, efficiency is difficult to achieve because each voter has an incentive to misrepresent his or her preferences. Majority rule tends to be an inefficient mechanism for decision making because the median voter determines the outcome. If the median voter's preferences diverge from the average, which is likely, inefficiency will result. Economists have developed demand-revealing mechanisms that impose a tax on voters equal to the damage their vote inflicts on the rest of the community.

SUGGESTED READINGS

Coase, Ronald H. "The Problem of Social Costs." *Journal of Law and Economics*, October 1960.

Environmental Quality. The Fifteenth Annual Report of the Council on Environmental Quality. Washington, D.C., 1984.

Samuelson, P. A. "A Diagrammatic Exposition of a Theory of Public Expenditure." *Review of Economics and Statistics* 37 (November 1955): 350–56.

Seneca, J. J. and M. K. Taussig. *Environmental Economics*, 3rd ed. Englewood Cliffs, N. J.: Prentice-Hall, 1984.

Tideman, T. N. and G. Tullock. "A New and Superior Process for Making Social Choices." *Journal of Political Economy* 84 (December 1976): 1145–60.

Tietenberg, T. *Environmental and Natural-Resource Economics*. Glenview, Ill.: Scott, Foresman, 1984.

Varian, H. *Microeconomic Analysis*. New York: W. W. Norton, 1978, 200–203.

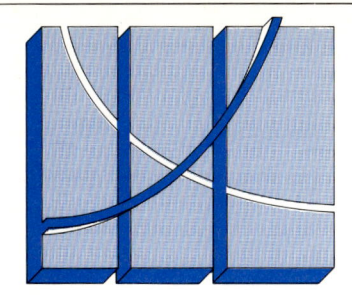

ANSWERS TO EVEN-NUMBERED QUESTIONS AND PROBLEMS

CHAPTER 1

2. A free good is one in which supply exceeds demand at a zero price. Examples include sand in the Sahara desert, tumbleweed in Texas, many wildflowers, a litter of certain types of puppies, and seats in a typical college baseball game.

4. The production-possibilities frontier shows the maximum output of one good given the output levels of all other goods in the economy. The curve is concave to the origin, which shows that as more of one good is produced more and more of other goods must be sacrificed.

6. Friedman's view about testing a theory by examining its assumptions has both good and bad points. It is insightful because it is more important for a theory to work than to have assumptions with which one agrees. Sometimes the assumptions are descriptively false but capture just enough of the real world to generate accurate predictions. On the other hand, scientific progress requires that "bad" assumptions be replaced by "better" assumptions.

CHAPTER 2

2. a. Present value = Y/i = $50/0.05 = $1,000.
   b. Present value = $210/(1.05) + $110.25/(1.05)^2 = $200 + $100 = $300.

4. To the extent that suppliers are prosecuted more than demanders, it is probably the case that legalizing an illegal product would probably lower its

FIGURE A-1

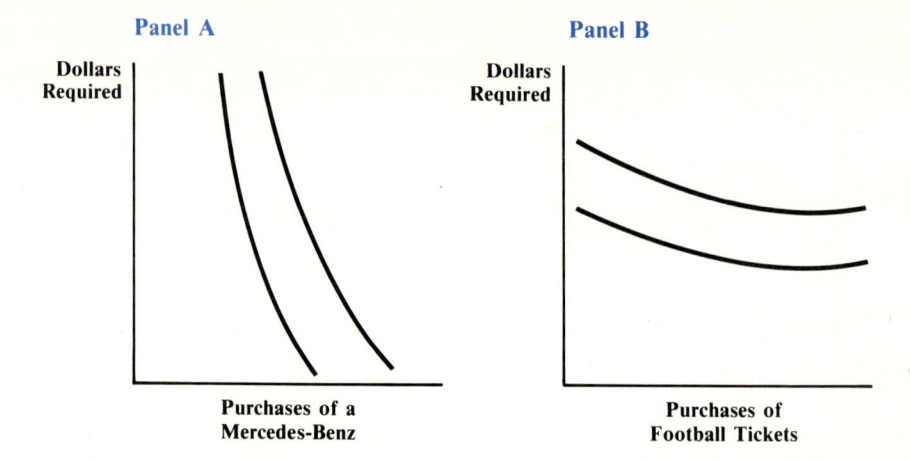

Panel A — Dollars Required vs. Purchases of a Mercedes-Benz

Panel B — Dollars Required vs. Purchases of Football Tickets

price. The reason is that the supply would presumably increase more than its demand.

6. a. $E(p) = 200 - 2p - (-40 + p) = 240 - 3p$.
   b. $E(p) = 0$ when $p = \$80$.
   c. $E(60) = 240 - 3(60) = 60$ units of shortage.
   d. $E(100) = 240 - 3(100) = -60$, or 60 units of surplus.

8. The total supply price for a restaurant meal is the sum of the supply prices for food and service, namely,

$$10 + Q + 30 + Q = 40 + 2Q.$$

Equilibrium occurs when the total demand price equals the total supply price, or

$$40 + 2Q = 100 - Q, \text{ or } 3Q = 60, \text{ or } Q = 20.$$

The equilibrium quantity of restaurant meals is 20, the price of a meal is $100 − $20, or $80. The implicit price of the food is $10 + $20, or $30; the implicit price of the service is $30 + $20, or $50. The answers, therefore, are:
   a. 20.
   b. $80.
   c. $30.
   d. $50.

CHAPTER 3

2. Suppose money is on the vertical axis. Assume that for George a Mercedes-Benz is highly desirable. His indifference curves are shown in Panel A of Figure A-1. He is willing to give up a lot of money for an extra hour of using a Mercedes-Benz. Thus, his indifference curves are steep. Assume that for George a ticket to a Houston Oilers football game is relatively undesirable. His indifference curve might appear as in Panel B,

CHAPTER 4 ANSWERS

TABLE A-1

	$u = x_1 x_2$	$u = nx_1 + nx_2$	$u = x_1^2 x_2$
u_1	x_2	$1/x_1$	$2x_1$
u_2	x_1	$1/x_2$	x_1^2

where it is relatively flat and shows that he is willing to give up very little money for time spent at such a football game.

4. They need not be parallel because they are not straight lines.

6. The indifference curve is a straight line; the marginal rate of substitution is constant at 2 units of clothing per unit of food. The two products may be regarded as perfect substitutes.

8. The indifference curve is downward-sloping and concave to the origin.

10. To derive the marginal utility x_i, u_i, we need only take the partial derivative of u with respect to x_i. See Table A-1.

12. The probability of drawing an ace is $1/13 = 4/52$. The expected value of $26 is $(1/13)($26) = 2.

14. a. $Eu = (1/2)u(10) + (1/2)u(50) = (1/2)(10) + (1/2)(30) = 20$.
    b. $Eu = (1/6)u(20) + (5/6)u(30) = (1/6)(18) + (5/6)(24) = 23$.
    c. $Eu = (1/3)u(20) + (2/3)u(40) = (1/3)(18) + (2/3)(28) = 24\ 2/3$.

CHAPTER 4

2. Panel A of Figure A-2 shows the equilibrium. The budget constraint must intersect the bread axis at $1,000/$2 = 500$ and the ale axis at $1,000/

FIGURE A-2

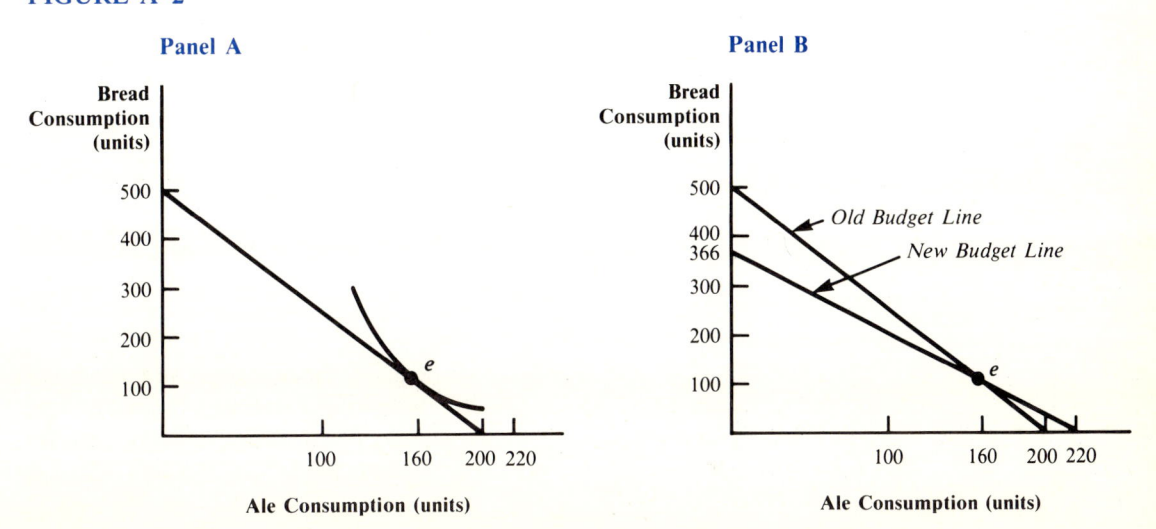

$5 = 200$. The slope of the budget constraint is 2.5 ($= 500/200$). If ale consumption is 160 units at equilibrium, bread consumption must be 100 units in order to just spend the $1,000 income ($1,000 = $5(160) + $2(100)). Panel B shows what happens when the price of bread increases by $1 and income increases by $100. Because the consumer was buying 100 units of bread, the increase in income just compensates the consumer for the increase in the price of bread in the sense that he or she can still buy the original bundle of 160 ale units and 100 bread units. Consequently, the new budget line goes through the original point, e. The new consumption point must be to the right of e. Thus, bread consumption must fall.

4. Equilibrium prevails when the marginal rate of substitution (MRS) equals the price ratio, and income is all spent on both goods X and Y. Thus, $MRS_{yx} = MU_x/MU_y = ay/bx = p_x/p_y$; and $p_x x + p_y y = M$. From the first, we see that $y = bxp_x/ap_y$. Substitution into the budget constraint yields:

$$p_x^x + p_y[bxp_x/ap_y] = p_x^x(1 + b/a) = M.$$

Thus, the demand function for x is $x = aM/p_x(b + a)$. By similar reasoning, the demand function for y is $y = bM/p_y(a + b)$.

a. Notice that p_x is not in the demand function for y (and vice-versa). Accordingly, regardless of p_x, the demand for y will be the same. The price/consumption curve derived by varying p_x will thus be a horizontal line at the equilibrium quantity of y for the given M and p_y.

b. The income/consumption curve will simply be $y/x = bp_x/ap_y$.

c. The price elasticity of demand for x (or y) is -1; the income elasticity of demand is 1. For example, because $x = aM/p_x(b + a)$, multiplying both sides by p_x yields:

$$p_x^x = aM/(b + a).$$

It follows that the expenditure on good X is constant. This fact implies that the price elasticity of demand must be -1. The income elasticity of demand is unity because from the demand function it is clear that as M rises, holding prices constant, x rises by the same percentage.

6. The income elasticity is:

$$(\Delta x/\Delta M)(M/x) = bM/(a + bM).$$

a. The income elasticity > 1 if $a < 0$ because the numerator exceeds the denominator.

b. The income elasticity < 1 if $a > 0$ because the numerator falls short of the denominator.

c. The income elasticity $= 1$ if $a = 0$ because the numerator equals the denominator.

8. The consumer would economize on gas consumption. The budget line with the new price of gas and the $100 rebate would intersect the old budget line at the equilibrium point. Because the new budget line reflects a higher relative price of gas, less gas must be consumed.

TABLE A-2

Price	Quantity Demanded
$100	1
$50	2
$25	4
$10	10
$5	20

10. The year 1 bundle would cost 50($4) + 50($2) = $300 at year 2 prices. In year 2, the consumer is spending 40($4) + 70($2) = $300. Thus, the consumer could have purchased the year 1 bundle in period 2. It follows that the consumer must be better off in year 2.

CHAPTER 5

2. a. Market-demand curve, or $Q = 100q = 100(10 - 2P) = 1{,}000 - 200P$.
   b. $400 = 1{,}000 - 200P$, or $P = \$3$.
   c. Price elasticity $= -(200)(3/400) = -1.5$.
   d. The market-demand curve is a straight line with a P-intercept of $5 and a Q-intercept of 1,000.

4. The coordinates of the demand curve are as shown in Table A-2. Total revenue is always $100, so the price elasticity of demand is -1. The elasticity does not depend on price.

6. The textbook explanation is that goods with a high income elasticity tend to be small proportions of the budget when incomes are small. Thus, the compensated price elasticity will tend to be relatively high because the base for computing the elasticity is small. On the other hand, necessities are a large proportion of the budget when income is small and causes the compensated price elasticities to appear small.

8. The formula is $MR = P(1 + 1/\eta)$. Knowing MR and P, we can deduce the price elasticity. When $MR = \$5$ and $P = \$15$, it follows that $\eta = -1.5$.

10. The compensated price elasticity of demand for food would be $-0.34 + (0.23)(0.26) = -0.28$.

12. The price elasticity is

$$\eta P_p = (\partial Q/\partial P)(P/Q) = aAP^{(a-1)}M^b(P/Q)$$
$$= aP^{-1}Q(P/Q) = a.$$

The income elasticity is

$$\eta_M = (\partial Q/\partial M)(M/Q) = bAP^aM^{(b-1)}(M/Q)$$
$$= bM^{-1}Q(M/Q) = b.$$

TABLE A-3

Quantity of Labor Input (worker hours), L	Output, Q	Labor's Average Product, AP_L	Labor's Marginal Product, MP_L
1	17	17	
			13
2	30	15	
			12
3	42	14	
			11
4	53	13.25	

CHAPTER 6

2. There can be trade between Sally and George if their endowments are dissimilar in the sense that their MRSs between the two goods are different. If preferences are identical, trade can occur only when endowments are different.

4. Two points are needed. If Paul's origin is toward the southwest corner, then Paul's allocation is southwest of Marie's, and the total of X and Y allocated to each does not exhaust the total supply.

6. The contract curve will be a straight line from the southwest corner to the northeast corner. Along the diagonal the marginal rate of substitution (MRS) for each person is simply the ratio of total amount of good Y to total amount of X, or $y/x = 40/20 = 2$. Because in competitive equilibrium each person is maximizing utility, the ratio of the price of X to the price of Y must be equal to the common MRS, or 2. The initial endowments are irrelevant. Thus, $p_x/p_y = 2$.

8. Since both consumers have the same preferences and the same endowment, their marginal rates of substitution are the same. Thus, the endowment point is on the contract curve. The core of the economy is just a point. The core allocation is the competitive equilibrium, with the price ratio being equal to the MRS at that point.

CHAPTER 7

2. a. The (K, L) combinations are (4, 1), (2, 2), and (1, 4).
   b. Yes, the law of diminishing returns applies. For example, for $K = 3$, increasing the labor input from 1 to 2 increases output by 18 units, and increasing the labor input from 2 to 3 increases output by only 16 units.
   c. There are increasing returns to scale because doubling inputs more than doubles output; for example, when (K, L) doubles from (2, 2) to (4, 4), output more than doubles from 30 to 92.

CHAPTER 8 ANSWERS

TABLE A-4

Quantity of Labor Input (worker hours), L	Labor's Average Product, AP_L	Labor's Marginal Product, MP_L
0		
		10
1	10	
		15
2	12.5	
		20
3	15	
		15
4	15	
		10
5	14	
		8
6	13	
		6
7	12	
		4
8	11	

    d. The curves are drawn by plotting the points shown in Table A-3.

    4. The isoquant for $Q = 2L + K$ is a straight line that intersects the K-axis at $K = Q$ and the L-axis at $L = Q/2$; thus, the slope (with L on the horizontal axis) is -2. The isoquant for $Q = \text{Min}(2L, K)$ is a right-angled isoquant at the point $K/L = 2$.

    6. a. See Table A-4.

    b. Labor's average-price curve reaches its maximum at $L = 3$ or 4.

    8. The isoquant map is in the region $K \geq L$. In other words, if K is on the vertical axis, it is above the 45-degree line from the origin. Where each isoquant touches the $K = L$ line, its slope is zero.

CHAPTER 8

    2. Assume, for example, that $MP_L/MP_K > w/r$. In this case, the isoquant is steeper than the isocost line. This situation means that substituting capital for labor at the rate, $MP_L/MP_{K'}$, that holds output constant must lower costs because that rate exceeds the rate, w/r, at which substituting capital for labor holds costs constant. Alternatively, it can be seen that $w/MP_L < r/MP_K$ means that an extra unit of output using L costs less than an extra unit of output using K; so more L and less K can lower costs while keeping output the same.

TABLE A-5

Quantity of Output (units), Q	Total Cost (dollars), TC	Average Variable Cost (dollars), AVC	Average Total Cost (dollars), ATC	Marginal Cost (dollars), MC
1	25	10	25	
				15
2	40	12.5	20	
				10
3	50	11.33	16.67	
				15
4	65	12.5	16.25	
				20
5	85	14	17	
				25
6	110	15.83	18.33	

4. The reason is that $MC = w/MP_L$, so when MP_L goes up (down) MC goes down (up).

6. The AVC, ATC, and MC curves are drawn by plotting the data shown in Table A-5.

8. Substitute for $A = AVC = aQ$; and $\Delta A/\Delta Q = a$. Thus,

$$MC = aQ + Qa = aQ + aQ = 2aQ.$$

CHAPTER 9

2. The minimum average total cost (ATC) occurs when ATC = marginal cost (MC); thus, $5q + 45/q = 10q$, or $q = 3$. When $q = 3$, $ATC = \$3$. For any other q, $ATC > \$3$. For example, if $q = 4$, $ATC = \$31.25$.

a. The individual firm's supply curve is $q = (1/10)p$; the market-supply curve is $Q = 6p$. Thus, $6p = 180 - p$ in equilibrium so that $p = \$(180/7) = \$25 5/7$. $Q = 6p = 154 2/7$. This point is not the long-run equilibrium, because p is less than ATC.

b. The long-run equilibrium number of firms is 50, price is $30, and output is 150.

c. The long-run supply curve is a horizontal line at $p = \$30$.

4. The main difference is that the horizontal sum of each firm's supply curve is the market-supply curve for a constant-cost industry, but that for an increasing-cost industry the horizontal sum is more elastic than the market-supply curve.

6. Since the long-run supply curve is perfectly horizontal, the amount of producers' surplus is zero.

8. New firms would enter, the product price would drop until profits returned to normal.

10. Yes, perfect competition can exist. The superior resource would command a Ricardian differential rent.

CHAPTER 10

2. The inverse demand curve is $p = 10 - 0.2Q$. Thus, the marginal-revenue curve is $MR = 10 - 0.4Q$.

4. Using the halfway rule, $MR = 50 - 10Q$. Thus, $50 - 10Q = 10$ when profit is maximized, or $Q = 4$. Thus, the monopoly price is $p = \$30$. The elasticity of demand is $-(0.2)(30/4) = -1.5$. Check: $\$10 = \$30(1 - 1/1.5) = \$10$.

6. By the marginal-average rule, $MR = p + Q(\Delta p/\Delta Q)$. But η is defined as $(\Delta Q/\Delta p)(p/Q)$. Substituting gives the formula.

8. Under perfect competition, the firm would produce $Q = 8$ units at a price of $p = \$10$. The deadweight loss is $(\$30 - 10)(4)(0.5) = \$40$.

10. $MR_1 = 10 - 2Q_1$; and $MR_2 = 20 - 2Q_2$. Setting these equal to MC $(= \$2)$, we find $Q_1 = 4$ and $Q_2 = 9$. Thus, $p_1 = \$6$ and $p_2 = \$11$. Total profit is $(6 - 2)(4) + (11 - 2)(9) = \$97$.

12. For the ordinary monopoly, $MR = 1,000 - 2Q = \$10$; so $Q = 495$ and $p = \$505$; profit is $(\$495)(495) = \$245,025$. For the two-part pricing case, the firm should charge a price of $\$10$ with an output of 990 units. The total consumers' surplus is the area under the demand curve and above $\$10$. This surplus is $\$990(990)(0.5) = \$490,050$. Each demander is charged $\$4,900.50$ as an entry fee, yielding a profit of $\$490,050$.

CHAPTER 11

2. Prices are not uniform because of information and transaction costs.

4. It is the maximum price he or she is willing to pay and is that sampled price for which the marginal benefit of search equals the marginal cost of search.

6. No, the marginal benefit of search would decrease. For example, if the possible wages were $w = \$1, \$2$, or $\$3$, each with an equal 1/3 probability, the marginal benefits of search would be $M_1 = \$1$, $M_2 = \$0.33$, and $M_3 = 0$.

8. With perfect speculation, 70 units are sold in each period at $p = \$30$. Without speculation, $p = \$20$ the first period and $p = \$40$ the second period. The net gain from perfect speculation would be $\$100 = \$10(10)/2 + \$10(10)/2$, area $b + f$ in Figure 11-4 of the textbook.

10. You have sold at $\$3$, and can buy at $\$3.20$, losing $\$0.20$ a bushel. Therefore, you have lost $\$0.20(5,000) = \$1,000$.

12. If the insured person's insurance coverage is not monitored and the veracity of claims cannot be verified, people would buy several insurance policies and then proceed to collect on each claim. There could be no private insurance.

FIGURE A-3

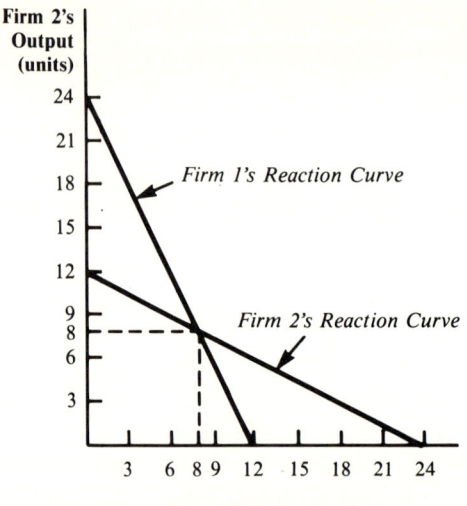

Figure shows Firm 2's Output (units) on vertical axis with values 3, 6, 8, 9, 12, 15, 18, 21, 24 and Firm 1's Output (units) on horizontal axis with values 3, 6, 8, 9, 12, 15, 18, 21, 24. Firm 1's Reaction Curve and Firm 2's Reaction Curve intersect at approximately (8, 8).

14. The high-risk people would buy a multiple number of low-risk policies, causing such policies to lose money. A separating equilibrium would not be possible.

16. In the case of a separating equilibrium, high-risk people would not be hurt because with the perfect information provided by the screening cost the insurance companies could offer complete insurance coverage to both classes of customers. Recall that in a separating equilibrium, with imperfect information, the high-risk people buy complete insurance. But in the case of a pooling equilibrium, a screening cost that enabled low-risk people to be identified would make high-risk people worse off because they would be classed with people of their own high risks.

CHAPTER 12

2. The 4-firm concentration ratio is obtained by just adding the shares of the top 4 firms; thus, it is just 0.85. The Herfindahl index is $H = 0.3084$, which is obtained by squaring the market shares and adding.

4. The change in the Herfindahl index is $2S_1 S_2$. Thus, the change in the Herfindahl index is 0.08.

6. In monopolistic competition, $P > LRMC$. Strictly speaking, monopolistic competition is inefficient because if each firm increased output until $p = LRMC$, efficiency would prevail. However, because every firm may face different marginal costs, it would not seem possible for the government to bring about such a solution. The government just does not have enough information.

8. The marginal revenue for firm 1 is

$$MR_1 = P - x_1 = [26 - (x_1 + x_2)] - x_1 = 26 - 2x_1 - x_2.$$

Setting $MR_1 = MC = 2$, we obtain the reaction curve for firm 1: $24 - 2x_1 - x_2 = 0$. The reaction curve for firm 2 is symmetrical. Thus, $x_1 = x_2 = x = 8$. $Q = 2x = 16$ and $p = 26 - Q = \$10$. The reaction curves are shown in Figure A–3.

10. The marginal-revenue curve has a break or horizontal portion so that numerous marginal-cost curves could pass through that part. The firm that cuts price finds demand relatively inelastic; the firm that raises price finds demand relatively elastic.

12. A cartel is not a Nash equilibrium because if any firm increases output, or cuts price, in the face of other firms maintaining their cartel outputs or prices, the defecting firm gains.

14. Such a game is zero sum because firm 1's profits plus firm 2's profits equal a constant (zero). The Nash equilibrium is when firm 1 follows strategy II and firm 2 follows strategy B. It is Nash equilibrium because if firm 2 is following strategy B, firm 1 maximizes its profits following strategy II; if firm 1 is following strategy II, firm 2 minimizes its losses following strategy B.

CHAPTER 13

2. The remark is a bit too strong. If firms maximize profits, it must be true that factors are paid their marginal-revenue products. To the extent that firms have monopoly power, factors would not be paid the value of their marginal products. The statement ignores the logical links between profit maximization and the theory of factor payments.

4. The demand curve for California lettuce workers is more elastic because the demand for California lettuce must be more elastic than the demand for all lettuce workers throughout the United States. This conclusion is reached using the first rule of derived demand—the more elastic is the demand for the product, the more elastic is the demand for the factor.

6. Farmer Smith's demand curve for labor must be more elastic because her demand curve will assume the price of the product is fixed, whereas the total farm demand for labor must take into account the fact that additional (say) wheat production must lower the price of wheat.

8. The marginal-revenue-product (MRP) and average-revenue-product (ARP) schedules are as shown in Table A–6. The firm's demand curve for labor is that portion of the MRP schedule below \$22.50. At any wage above \$22.50, the firm would go out of business.

10. No, it is not possible. $MRP < VMP$ because as long as the demand curve is downward-sloping, $MR < p$. If $MRP > VMP$, the law of demand is violated.

TABLE A-6

Days of Labor, L	Marginal Revenue Product (dollars), MRP	Average Revenue Product (dollars), ARP
0		—
	15	
1		15
	30	
2		22.5
	15	
3		20
	12	
4		18
	9	
5		17.4
	6	
6		14.5
	3	
7		12.9

12. In Figure A-4 the indifference curve between consumption and work is downward-sloping up to 8 hours of work. After that the indifference curve between consumption and work is upward-sloping. Notice, however, that in equilibrium the budget line is still tangent to that portion of the indifference curve where work is a "bad."

CHAPTER 14

2. The revenue schedule is shown in Table A-7. If the wage rate is $15, two workers will be hired. The price of the product will be $p = 30 - 18 = \$12$.

4. Because marginal factor cost (MFC) is twice as steep as the inverse

TABLE A-7

Labor (units), L	Revenue (dollars), R
0	0
1	200
2	216
3	144
4	56

CHAPTER 15 ANSWERS

FIGURE A-4

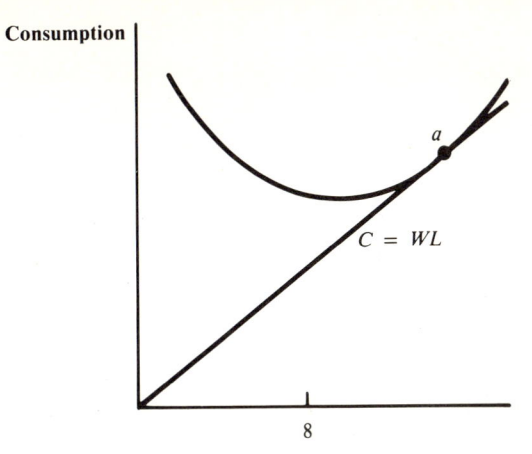

Consumption

a

C = WL

8

Quantity of Labor Input (hours of work)

supply curve of labor, $MFC = 2 + 2L$. Equilibrium is reached when $2 + 2L = 14 - L$, or $L = 4$. Thus, the wage rate would be $w = 2 + L = 2 + 4 = \$6$. If a minimum wage of \$8 were imposed, the firm would hire six units of labor because $\$8 = 14 - L$ when $L = 6$ and when the wage is \$8 exactly 6 units of labor are available.

6. a. The average MRP is \$6. With a screening cost of \$3, it pays the high-productivity workers to have themselves screened and earn a net of \$7 = \$10 − \$3.

b. If screening costs increased to \$5, high-productivity workers are better off not being screened because the no-screening wage of \$6 exceeds the net wage of \$5 (= \$10 − \$5).

CHAPTER 15

2. a. Real interest = $1.2/1.15 - 1 = 4.348$ percent.
   b. Real interest = $1.06/1.01 - 1 = 4.95$ percent.

4. The consumer maximizes by moving along his or her intertemporal budget line until its slope equals the slope of an indifference curve.

6. The present values of the investment options are shown in Table A–8.

TABLE A-8

	Present Values at Various Interest Rates		
	0.05	0.1	0.2
Option A	$176.19	$163.64	$141.67
Option B	180.95	163.64	133.33

FIGURE A-5

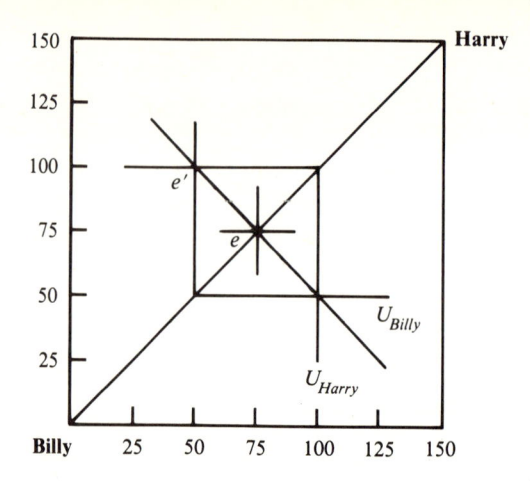

Option B is preferred when the interest rate (r) = 0.05, options A and B have the same present value when r = 0.1, and option A is preferred when r = 0.2. As interest rates rise, investment option A becomes more preferred because it has a smaller outlay in the present.

CHAPTER 16

2. a. George's initial marginal rate of substitution (MRS) of nuts for apples is = 50/80 = 5/8; Bob's initial MRS is 200/120 = 5/3. Thus, George places a lower value on apples than Bob. George will trade apples for nuts.

   b. Because MRS_{NA} = N/A must be the same for both George and Bob, the common ratio must be the total nut supply divided by the total apple supply, that is, N/A = 250/200 = 5/4. Thus, MRS_{NA} = p_A/p_N = 1.25.

   c. George's income (measured in nuts) is 50 + (1.25)(80) = 150. Because in equilibrium $p_A A = p_N N$, George will buy 75 nuts and 60 apples [(60)(1.25) = 75]. Bob's income is 200 + (1.25)(120) = 350. Bob will buy 175 nuts and 140 apples [(140)(1.25) = 175].

   d. The contract curve is the main diagonal, because preferences are identical and homothetic.

4. a. Figure A-5 shows the Edgeworth box and the initial endowment. The contract curve is simply the main diagonal.

   b. The equilibrium is p_A/p_N = 1. To arrive at this result, we calculate Bill's income as (in nuts) 100 + (1)(50) = 150 and Harry's income as 150 also. With the price of apples equal to the price of nuts, both Bill and Harry will consume 75 nuts and 75 apples at their utility-maximizing solution (point e in Figure A-5). Because the market clears, we have found an equilibrium price ratio.

   c. Each person's maximum utility is 150; the utility-possibilities curve is just a straight line intersecting each axis at 150.

6. Because the relative price of textiles falls, and textiles are labor intensive, it must be that real wages must fall and real rents rise by the Stolper-Samuelson theorem. The mechanism works so that as resources move out of labor-intensive textiles, the wage/rent ratio must fall to induce the rest of the community to absorb all the labor from the declining textile industry. Thus, every industry chooses more labor-intensive techniques, causing the marginal product of labor to fall and that of capital to rise.

CHAPTER 17

2. This statement is false because pecuniary externalities are not inefficient. An externality is involved when there are direct consumption or production effects of one agent's actions on another agent. When rich people cause poor people to pay more for their homes, it may be unjust but it is not inefficient.

4. All of these would be rival when congested but nonrival when not congested. If you drive across a bridge at 5 P.M., it may be congested; if you drive across the same bridge at 2 A.M., there may not be another car in sight.

6. Taxes or subsidies might be the best means of controlling externalities when voluntary negotiations fail because of transaction costs, when property rights cannot be redefined or enforced, or when a free market in pollution certificates is too costly to organize.

8. a. Under majority rule, the program would not be established because only Charlie would vote for it.

b. Under costless negotiation, Art might agree to pay $0.50, Bob $18.50, and Charlie $81. All would benefit and the program would be established.

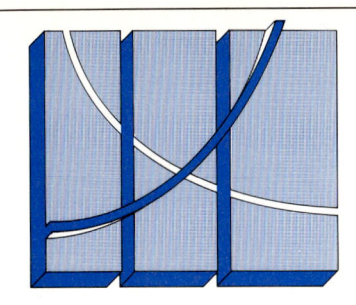

GLOSSARY

adding-up rule states that the sum of all income elasticities, weighted by the relative importance of each good in the budget, must be unity **(4)**.

adverse-selection problem occurs when one party engages in precontractual opportunistic behavior to lure the party at an information disadvantage into a disadvantageous contract **(11)**.

AFC see **average fixed costs (*AFC*)**.

agent is one who acts for, on behalf of, or as a representative for a principal **(11)**.

AP see **average product (*AP*)**.

ARP see **average revenue product (*ARP*)**.

ATC see **average total costs (*ATC*)**.

AVC see **average variable costs (*AVC*)**.

average fixed costs (*AFC*) equal fixed costs divided by output: $AFC = FC \div Q$ **(8)**.

average product (*AP*) is the quantity of output divided by the quantity of input—that is, $AP_A = Q/A$ **(7)**.

average revenue product (*ARP*) is total revenue divided by the total level of factor input **(13)**.

average total costs (*ATC*) equal average fixed costs plus average variable costs: $ATC = FC/Q + VC/Q = AFC + AVC$, or total cost divided by output **(8)**.

average variable costs (*AVC*) equal variable costs divided by output: $AVC = VC \div Q$ **(8)**.

barrier to entry exists if new entrants incur any disadvantages not facing the firms already in the market **(10)**.

benefit see **marginal benefit of search, marginal social benefits (*MSB*)**.

benefit of search see **marginal benefit of search**.

budget line   consists of all the commodity bundles that cost the same as the consumer's income, m. For two goods, X and Y, the slope is p_x/p_y in absolute value and is interpreted as the price of good X in terms of good Y **(4)**.

capital   is a stock giving rise to a flow of income **(15)**.
cartel   is an explicit collusive agreement among firms producing a particular product to share the market or to set a common price **(12)**.
cash market   see **spot, or cash, market.**
common-property resource   is a resource to which everyone has free access **(17)**.
comparative advantage   see **law of comparative advantage.**
comparative statics   is the study of changes in equilibrium **(2)**.
compensated-demand curve   is a demand curve for a given level of real income **(4)**.
compensated price elasticity of demand (η_p^c)   is the price elasticity measured along a compensated demand curve (that is, holding real income constant) **(5)**.
competition   see **monopolistic competition, perfect competition.**
competitive equilibrium, or Walrasian equilibrium,   is a set of prices and an allocation of resources such that 1) each consumer maximizes utility subject to a budget constraint, where income is determined by the sale of labor services and the consumer's share of business profits (prices taken as given), 2) each business firm is maximizing the present value of profits and distributing those profits to the households owning the firm, and 3) prices are such that the market quantities demanded for all goods and services equal the market quantities supplied **(6, 16)**.
complements   are two goods, X and Y, related in such a way that raising the price of good Y lowers the demand for good X **(5)**; see also **gross complement, net complements.**
concentration ratio   see *n*-**firm concentration ratio.**
constant-cost industry   is an industry in which an increase in industry output does not affect factor prices **(9)**.
constant returns to scale   characterize a production function for which a given percentage increase in all inputs increases output by the same percentage **(7)**.
consumer surplus   is the excess of the total consumer benefit that a good provides over what the consumer—or consumers in a market—actually have to pay **(4)**.
consumption   see **consumption stream, income/consumption (*IC*) curve, price/consumption (*PC*) curve.**
consumption stream   shows how much a person consumes in present and future years **(15)**.
contestable market   is a market in which 1) entry and exit by new firms is completely free, 2) new firms can produce with the same costs as the incumbent firms, 3) firms can easily escape their fixed costs by selling

their fixed inputs elsewhere (in other words, fixed costs are not sunk costs and can be recovered), and 4) customers buy from the firm (or firms) that first posts the lowest price (**12**).

contract curve is the set of Pareto-optimal allocations and, when indifference curves are convex, occurs when the marginal rates of substitution of one good for another good are the same (**6, 16**).

contrived scarcity is the restriction of output to the level where marginal cost equals marginal revenue but where price exceeds marginal cost (**10**).

core is an allocation of resources such that no person, or coalition of persons, acting on his or her own (that is, trading with no other person or coalition) can do any better (**6**).

cost see **average fixed costs** (*AFC*), **average total costs** (*ATC*), **constant-cost industry, decreasing-cost industry, fixed costs** (*FC*), **increasing-cost industry, information costs, least-cost rule, long-run cost function, marginal cost** (*MC*), **marginal factor cost** (*MFC*), **marginal social costs** (*MSC*), **opportunity cost, sunk cost, total costs** (*TC*), **transaction costs, variable costs** (*VC*).

Cournot equilibrium is a set of outputs for which each firm is maximizing profit given the outputs of the remaining firms (**12**).

covariance is a statistical measure of the relationship between the random variables X and Y (**5A**).

cross-price elasticity of demand (η_{xy}) measures the percentage change in the demand for one good in response to a 1 percent change in the price of another good (**5**).

curve see **compensated-demand curve, contract curve, demand curve, Engel curve, excess-demand curve, grand utility-possibilities curve, income/consumption** (*IC*) **curve, income-possibilities curve, indifference curve, kinked-demand curve, market-demand curve, offer curve, price/consumption** (*PC*) **curve, reaction curve, supply curve.**

deadweight loss is a loss of consumers' or producers' surplus that is not offset by a gain on anyone's part (**10**).

decreasing-cost industry is an industry in which factor prices decline as output rises (**9**).

decreasing returns to scale, or **diseconomies of scale**, characterize a situation in which increasing all inputs by a certain percentage increases output by a smaller percentage (**7**).

demand see **compensated-demand curve, compensated price elasticity of demand** (η_p^c), **cross-price elasticity of demand** (η_{xy}), **demand curve, demand price, excess-demand curve, income elasticity of demand** (η_m), **kinked-demand curve, law of demand, market-demand curve, price elasticity of demand.**

demand curve, or **demand schedule**, shows how quantity demanded for a good or service varies with the price of the product, holding other factors constant (**2, 4**); see also **market-demand curve.**

demand price, or **demand reservation price,** is the maximum price buyers are willing to pay for an extra unit of a good **(2)**.

demand schedule see **demand curve.**

depreciation is the loss in the value of a capital good as it is used up over time **(15)**.

diminishing marginal rate of substitution see **law of diminishing marginal rate of substitution, marginal rate of technical substitution ($MRTS_{KL}$).**

discrimination see **price discrimination.**

diseconomies of scale see **decreasing returns to scale.**

economic profit is revenue minus opportunity cost **(8)**.

economic region of production is that range of input combinations for a given level of output where the marginal products of the inputs are positive **(7)**.

economic rent is the payment made for a resource over and above what is required to keep the resource in its current use **(9)**.

economics see **general-equilibrium economics, normative economics, partial-equilibrium economics, positive economics.**

economies of scale see **increasing returns to scale.**

effect see **income effect, substitution effect.**

efficient see **minimum efficient scale (*MES*).**

effluent charge is a tax imposed on a polluting agent for each unit of pollution generated **(17)**.

elasticity see **compensated price elasticity of demand (η_p^c), cross-price elasticity of demand (η_{xy}), elasticity of substitution (ϵ), income elasticity of demand (η_m), price elasticity of demand, price elasticity of supply.**

elasticity of substitution (ϵ) is the percentage change in the capital/output ratio divided by the percentage change in the marginal rate of technical substitution along a given isoquant **(7, 13)**.

Engel curve shows the relationship between the demand for a good and the consumer's income level, *ceteris paribus* **(4)**.

Engel's law is that the income elasticity of demand for food is less than 1 **(5)**.

entry see **barrier to entry.**

EP see **expansion path (*EP*).**

equilibrium see **competitive equilibrium, Cournot equilibrium, equilibrium price, exchange equilibrium, general-equilibrium economics, Nash equilibrium, partial-equilibrium economics.**

equilibrium price is that price for which quantity demanded equals quantity supplied in a free, competitive market **(2)**.

excess-demand curve shows the algebraic difference between quantity demanded and quantity supplied at each price, or $E(p) = D(p) - S(p)$ **(2)**.

exchange see **pure-exchange economy.**

exchange equilibrium is a situation in which there is no further incentive for both parties to trade—that is, when all mutual benefits from trade are exhausted **(6)**.

expansion path (*EP*)   shows the optimal combinations of labor and capital as output expands for any given wage/rent pair (*w, r*) **(8)**.

expected-utility hypothesis   is that consumers rank uncertain prospects, such as (*a, b*; π), on the basis of their expected utility, $Eu = \pi u(a) + (1 - \pi)u(b)$ **(3)**.

expected value   is the weighted sum of the possible values of a random variable, with each value multiplied by its probability of occurrence **(3)**.

externality   is an unpriced benefit or cost directly conferred or imposed on one agent by the actions of another agent **(17)**.

factor   see **marginal factor cost** (*MFC*).

FC   see **fixed costs** (*FC*).

feasible trade   is a mutually beneficial exchange **(6)**.

fixed costs (*FC*)   are costs that do not vary with the level of output **(8)**; see also **average fixed costs** (*AFC*).

fixed inputs   cannot be varied in the short run **(7)**.

flow variable   is the change in the value of a variable per unit of time **(2)**.

free goods   are goods or services for which supply exceeds demand even at a zero price **(1)**.

free rider   is a person who consumes a scarce good or service without paying for it **(17)**.

futures market   is an arrangement in which a buyer and seller agree now on the future price and quantity of a commodity to be delivered at a specified date in the future **(11)**.

game   see **prisoners' dilemma game**.

general-equilibrium economics   studies the forces determining equilibrium in an entire economy **(16)**.

Giffen good   is a good for which the quantity demanded falls when the price falls **(4)**.

good   see **free goods, Giffen good, independent goods, inferior good, normal good, public goods, scarce goods**.

grand utility-possibilities curve   is the envelope of all point utility-possibilities curves generated by moving from point to point along the production-possibilities frontier **(16)**.

gross complement   is the relationship between good Y and good X if their cross-price elasticity is less than zero **(5)**.

gross substitute   is the relationship between good Y and good X if their uncompensated cross-price elasticity is greater than zero **(5)**.

halfway rule   states that if the demand curve is a straight line, the *MR* curve is twice as steep or lies halfway between the vertical axis and the demand curve **(5)**.

hazard   see **moral-hazard problem**.

hedging   is the temporary substitution of a futures-market transaction for an expected spot-market transaction **(11)**.

Herfindahl index   is the total of the squared values of the market shares of all the firms in the industry **(12)**.

homothetic production function is a technology for which the marginal rate of technical substitution depends only on the ratio of capital to labor **(7)**.

IC see **income/consumption (*IC*) curve.**

illusion see **money illusion.**

income see **income/consumption (*IC*) curve, income effect, income elasticity of demand (η_m), income-possibilities curve, income stream.**

income/consumption (*IC*) curve shows the locus of equilibrium commodity bundles as income changes, holding commodity prices constant **(4)**.

income effect is the change in quantity demanded that is attributable to the real income change that accompanies the price change **(4)**.

income elasticity of demand (η_m) is the proportional (or percentage) change in demand for a product divided by the proportional (or percentage) change in income, holding all prices fixed **(4, 5)**.

income-possibilities curve shows the intertemporal income stream available to the firm through different investment projects **(15)**.

income stream shows how much a person earns in present and future years **(15)**.

increasing-cost industry is one in which an increase in industry output raises the critical factor prices paid by individual firms **(9)**.

increasing returns to scale, or **economies of scale,** characterize a situation in which increasing all inputs by a certain percentage increases output by a larger percentage **(7)**.

independent goods are goods unrelated by price such that raising the price of one does not affect the demand for the other **(5)**.

index see **Herfindahl index, price index.**

indifference curve shows all the combinations of bundles of two commodities among which a particular consumer is indifferent **(3)**.

industry see **constant-cost industry, decreasing-cost industry, increasing-cost industry.**

inefficiency see **X-inefficiency.**

inferior good is one for which demand decreases as income increases, holding prices constant **(4)**.

information costs are the costs agents face in finding out about markets **(11)**.

inputs see **fixed inputs, variable inputs.**

interest rate see **nominal interest rate, real interest rate.**

internalization is the process of putting private price tags on external costs or benefits **(17)**.

internal rate of return is the interest rate that just equates the present value of the future stream of profits to the cost of an investment **(10)**.

isocost line represents all the combinations of inputs that cost the same amount **(8)**.

isoquant see **production isoquant, unit isoquant.**

kinked-demand curve is the demand curve of a firm whose rivals match price cuts but not price increases **(12)**.

GLOSSARY

law see **Engel's law, law of comparative advantage, law of demand, law of diminishing marginal rate of substitution, law of diminishing marginal rate of technical substitution, Walras's law.**

law of comparative advantage states that people (or countries) specialize in those goods in which they have the greatest advantage or the least disadvantage compared to other people (or countries) **(6)**.

law of demand states that the price of a good and the quantity demanded are inversely related—that is, the demand curve is downward-sloping **(4)**.

law of diminishing marginal rate of substitution states that the marginal rate of substitution of good Y for good X declines as more X is consumed, holding the level of satisfaction constant **(3)**.

law of diminishing marginal rate of technical substitution states that the marginal rate of technical substitution of capital for labor diminishes as more labor is used, holding output constant **(7)**.

least-cost rule states that to maximize output for a given cost outlay or to minimize total cost for a given output, the marginal product per wage dollar (MP_L/w) must equal the marginal product per capital-rent dollar (MP_K/r) **(8)**.

limit pricing is the setting of a monopolist's price at or slightly below the marginal-cost level of potential entrants to the market **(12)**.

line see **budget line, isocost line.**

linear regression gives the best linear unbiased equation that fits a set of observations **(5A)**.

long run is a period of time long enough to vary all inputs **(7, 9)**.

long-run cost function is the minimum cost of production for a given level of output and a given wage/rent pair **(8)**.

luxuries are goods whose income elasticity of demand is greater than 1 **(4)**.

marginal see **law of diminishing marginal rate of substitution, law of diminishing marginal rate of technical substitution, marginal benefit of search, marginal cost (*MC*), marginal factor cost (*MFC*), marginal product (*MP*), marginal rate of substitution (*MRS*), marginal rate of technical substitution ($MRTS_{KL}$), marginal revenue (*MR*), marginal revenue product (*MRP*), marginal utility (*MU*), marginal social costs (*MSC*), value of the firm's marginal product (*VMP*).**

marginal benefit of search is the expected gain from sampling one more store **(11)**.

marginal cost (*MC*) is the extra variable cost or total cost per unit of a change in output: $MC = \Delta TC/\Delta Q = \Delta VC/\Delta Q$ **(8)**.

marginal factor cost (*MFC*) is the increase in costs per unit change in an input or factor **(14)**.

marginal product (*MP*) of input A for the production function $Q = F(A, B, C, \ldots)$ is the extra output generated per unit of change in input A, or $MP_A = \Delta Q/\Delta A$, when all other inputs are held constant **(7)**; is the change in output divided by the change in the number of units of the input (holding other inputs constant) **(13)**; see also **value of the firm's marginal product (VMP).**

marginal rate of substitution (MRS) is the rate at which a consumer is just willing to substitute good Y for another unit of good X, holding the level of satisfaction constant **(3)**.

marginal rate of technical substitution ($MRTS_{KL}$) is the rate at which a unit of capital can be substituted for a unit of labor and still keep output constant **(7)**.

marginal rate of transformation (MRT) is the rate at which an amount of one good must be sacrificed for a unit of another good; it is the absolute slope of the production-possibilities frontier **(16)**.

marginal revenue (MR) is the increase in revenue (R) per unit increase in the quantity of a good sold (Q) per unit of time—that is, $MR = \Delta R/\Delta Q$ **(5)**.

marginal revenue product (MRP) is the marginal revenue for a product multiplied by the marginal product of the input **(13)**.

marginal social benefits (MSB) are the sum of marginal private benefits (MPB) and marginal external benefits (MEB) **(17)**.

marginal social costs (MSC) are the sum of marginal private costs (MPC) and marginal external costs (MEC) **(17)**.

marginal utility (MU) is the increase in total utility brought about by increasing the consumption of a good by one unit, holding consumption of all other goods constant **(3)**.

market is an established arrangement that buyers and sellers use to regularly exchange goods and services **(2)**; see also **contestable market, futures market, market-demand curve, market period.**

market-demand curve shows the total quantities demanded by all consumers in the market at each price; it is the horizontal summation of all individual demand curves in the market **(4)**.

market period is a period of time so short that the supply of a good cannot be changed **(9)**.

maximin see **minimax (maximin) principle of rational behavior.**

MC see **marginal cost (MC).**

median voter likes a project more than one half and less than the other half of the remaining voters **(17)**.

MES see **minimum efficient scale (MES).**

MFC see **marginal factor cost (MFC).**

microeconomics, or *price theory,* is the study of the economic decision making of firms, individuals, and governmental units in a market setting **(1)**.

minimax (or maximin) principle of rational behavior is that players in a game should maximize their minimum payoff or minimize their maximum loss **(12)**.

minimum efficient scale (MES) is the lowest level of output at which long-run average costs are minimized **(8)**.

money illusion occurs when an equal or proportionate change in all money prices and money income causes a change in demand **(4)**.

monopolistic competition is characteristic of an industry in which 1) there are many small firms, 2) the product is differentiated, 3) there is free entry and exit, and 4) each firm has some control over the price it charges **(12)**.

monopoly see **monopolistic competition, monopoly-rent-seeking behavior, natural monopoly, pure monopoly.**

monopoly-rent-seeking behavior is the effort made (through lobbying, persuasion, and advertising) to obtain a monopoly in order to gain the extra profit, or rent, a monopoly can achieve **(10)**.

monopsony is a single firm that buys or hires all the units available at a given price of a particular input and must, therefore, pay a higher price per unit to hire or buy more of the input **(14)**.

moral-hazard problem arises when one or more parties to a contract engage in post-contractual opportunistic behavior because of an information imbalance between parties **(11)**.

MP see **marginal product** (*MP*).
MR see **marginal revenue** (*MR*).
MRP see **marginal revenue product** (*MRP*).
MRS see **marginal rate of substitution** (*MRS*).
MRT see **marginal rate of transformation** (*MRT*).
$MRTS_{KL}$ see **law of diminishing marginal rate of technical substitution, marginal rate of technical substitution** ($MRTS_{KL}$).
MSB see **marginal social benefits** (*MSB*).
MSC see **marginal social costs** (*MSC*).
MU see **marginal utility** (*MU*).

Nash equilibrium occurs when every player is maximizing his or her payoff given the strategies followed by all the opposing players **(12)**.

natural monopoly exists when it is cheaper for one firm to produce a product at the output level that meets demand than for two or more firms to do so **(10)**.

necessities are goods whose income elasticity of demand is less than 1 **(4)**.

net complements are goods X and Y related such that the compensated cross-price elasticity of demand is less than zero **(5)**.

net substitutes are goods X and Y related such that the compensated cross-price elasticity is greater than zero **(5)**.

***n*-firm concentration ratio** measures the percentage of the top *n* firms responsible for domestic shipments in the industry **(12)**.

nominal interest rate is an interest rate expressed in current dollars, unadjusted for inflation **(15)**.

normal good is one for which demand increases when income increases, holding prices constant **(4)**.

normative economics involves making judgments as to the worth of existing economic policies and proposing changes in conditions and policies designed to improve existing situations **(1)**.

offer curve shows the utility-maximizing consumption bundles at different price ratios for a competitive price-taking consumer whose only income is a fixed endowment of goods; it is the price/consumption curve for a consumer in a pure-exchange economy (6); shows the offer of one good for some other good at different price ratios (16).

oligopoly is an industry with 1) a few relatively large firms, 2) modest or high entry barriers, 3) mutual interdependence of firms, and 4) similar or identical products (12).

opportunity cost is the value of the best opportunity that must be sacrificed in order to expand an activity by one unit (1, 8).

optimality see **Pareto optimality.**

Pareto optimality exists whenever any resource reallocation that makes one person better off must make some other person worse off. In other words, in a Pareto-optimal allocation of resources, it is impossible to make everyone better off. Without externalities and with smoothly shaped indifference curves, a condition for Pareto optimality is $MRS^A = MRS^B$ for every pair of consumers and every pair of goods (6, 16).

partial-equilibrium economics studies equilibrium in a single market or for a single consumer or firm in isolation (16).

PC see **price/consumption (*PC*) curve.**

perfect competition characterizes a market in which there is 1) a large number of buyers and sellers, 2) perfect information about product price and quality, 3) a homogeneous product, and 4) freedom of entry into and exit from the industry (9).

positive economics is the analysis of existing economic conditions and policies and their effects in the real world (1).

possibilities see **grand utility-possibilities curve, income-possibilities curve, production-possibilities frontier (*PPF*), utility-possibilities curve.**

PPF see **production-possibilities frontier (*PPF*).**

present value is the amount that must be invested at today's interest rates to generate a future sum of money (2); see also **present-value rule.**

present-value rule is that the economic agent can achieve the highest intertemporal utility by choosing the income stream with the highest present value, regardless of the shape of the income stream or preferences (15); see also **present value.**

price see **compensated price elasticity of demand (η_p^c), cross-price elasticity of demand (η_{xy}), equilibrium price, limit pricing, price/consumption (*PC*) curve, price discrimination, price elasticity of demand, price elasticity of supply, price index, price maker, price taker, reservation price.**

price/consumption (*PC*) curve shows the locus of equilibrium commodity bundles for two goods as the price of one of the goods changes, holding the price of the other good and money income constant (4).

price discrimination exists when a seller charges different buyers different prices for the same good although the seller's costs for that good do not vary (10).

price elasticity see **compensated price elasticity of demand (η_p^c), cross-price elasticity of demand (η_{xy}), price elasticity of demand, price elasticity of supply.**

GLOSSARY

price elasticity of demand (η_p)   is the proportional (or percentage) change in quantity demanded for a product divided by the proportional (or percentage) change in the price of the good itself, holding other prices, income, and taste constant (**4, 5**).

price elasticity of supply (η_s)   is the percentage change in quantity supplied divided by the percentage change in the price of the product (**9**).

price index   is a measure of the general level of prices in relation to the price level in some base year (**4**).

price maker   is a seller (or buyer) that is able to control the price of the good it sells (or buys) (**10**).

price taker   is a buyer whose purchases are not large enough to affect the price or a seller who is unable to control the price of the goods sold (**2**); is a seller with so little control over price that the market price must be taken as given (**9**).

price theory   see **microeconomics**.

principal   is one who has controlling authority when engaging services of an agent (**11**).

principle of rational behavior   see **minimax (or maximin) principle of rational behavior**.

prisoners' dilemma game   is a game between two players in which the Nash equilibrium involves a smaller total payoff to the players than the cooperative solution (**12**).

probability   is the chance that an event will occur, expressed as a fraction of 1 (**3**).

producers' surplus   is the excess of the amount suppliers receive over the minimum amount the suppliers would be willing to accept (**9**).

product   see **average product** (*AP*), **average revenue product** (*ARP*), **marginal product** (*MP*), **value of the firm's marginal product** (*VMP*).

production   see **economic region of production, homothetic production function, production function, production isoquant, production-possibilities frontier** (*PPF*).

production function   shows the maximum output that can be achieved from any prescribed set of inputs as well as the minimum amount needed of one particular input, given the level of output and prescribed levels of the remaining inputs (**7**); see also **homothetic production function**.

production isoquant   is the combination of two inputs that will produce a particular level of output (**7**).

production-possibilities frontier (*PPF*)   shows the combinations of goods that can be produced when the factors of production are utilized to their full potential (**11**).

profit   see **economic profit**.

property   see **common-property resource**.

public goods   are goods whose use is characterized by nonrival consumption and high exclusion costs (**17**).

pure-exchange economy   is an economy in which participants enter with fixed endowments of goods and then trade with others to achieve a more desirable consumption pattern (**6**).

pure monopoly is a type of market structure in which 1) there is only one seller of a product that has no close substitutes, so that the seller has the power to be a price maker; 2) the seller is free of external constraints; and 3) the seller is protected from competitors by barriers to entry into the market **(10)**.

quasi rent is the short-run rent earned by the firm's *fixed* productive factors—that is, it is the excess of revenue over variable cost **(9)**.

r see **reservation price (*r*)**.

random variable is a variable that may take on different values, each with a definite probability, as the result of statistical experiments **(3)**.

rate of return see **internal rate of return**.

rate of substitution see **law of diminishing marginal rate of substitution, law of diminishing marginal rate of technical substitution, marginal rate of substitution (*MRS*), marginal rate of technical substitution ($MRTS_{KL}$)**.

rate of technical substitution see **law of diminishing marginal rate of technical substitution, marginal rate of technical substitution ($MRTS_{KL}$)**.

rate of time preference (*RTP*) is the marginal rate of substitution of future consumption for current consumption **(15)**.

rate of transformation see **marginal rate of transformation (*MRT*)**.

ratio see **concentration ratio**.

rational behavior see **minimax (or maximin) principle of rational behavior**.

rational-expectations hypothesis is the assumption that individual firms utilize all the information available to them to predict the future price of a product **(9)**.

reaction curve shows, for a duopoly, the profit-maximizing output of one firm as a function of the other firm's output. It is downward-sloping, because the higher is the output of the other firm, the lower is the firm's optimal output **(12)**.

real interest rate is an interest rate expressed in constant, inflation-adjusted dollars **(15)**.

regression see **linear regression**.

rent see **economic rent, monopoly-rent-seeking behavior, quasi rent**.

reservation price (*r*) is the highest price a buyer is willing to pay or the lowest price a seller is willing to accept **(11)**.

resource see **common-property resource**.

returns to scale see **constant returns to scale, decreasing returns to scale, increasing returns to scale**.

revenue see **average revenue product (*ARP*), marginal revenue (*MR*), marginal revenue product (*MRP*)**.

RTP see **rate of time preference (*RTP*)**.

rule see **adding-up rule, halfway rule, least-cost rule, present-value rule, shutdown rule**.

scarce goods are goods or services for which demand exceeds supply at a zero price **(1)**.

scarcity see **contrived scarcity**.

GLOSSARY 513

screening occurs when a buyer uses observable characteristics that are correlated with performance in order to rank prospective workers, goods, or services **(14)**.
search see **marginal benefit of search.**
Shepherd's lemma is the equation that states that each dollar increase in wages (or rents) increases the cost of producing any given volume of output by the quantity of labor (or capital) used to produce that volume of output **(8)**.
short run is a period of time so short that existing plant and equipment cannot be varied—additional output can be produced only by expanding the variable inputs of labor and raw materials **(7)**; is a period of time so short that at least one input is fixed in supply **(9)**.
shutdown rule is that the firm should produce no output if price is less than average variable cost. By shutting down, the firm loses only its fixed costs **(9)**.
signals are messages sent from one agent to another (such as a résumé) **(14)**.
social benefits see **marginal social benefits (*MSB*).**
social costs see **marginal social costs (*MSC*).**
spot, or cash, market is an arrangement in which a buyer and seller agree now on price and quantity of a commodity to be paid for and delivered now **(11)**.
statics is the study of the relationships between forces that produce equilibrium **(2)**; see also **comparative statics.**
stock variable is a quantity of a good or commodity existing at a given point in time **(2)**.
stream see **consumption stream, income stream.**
substitutes are goods X and Y that are related such that raising the price of good Y raises the demand for good X **(5)**; see also **gross substitutes, net substitutes.**
substitution see **elasticity of substitution (ϵ), law of diminishing marginal rate of substitution, law of diminishing marginal rate of technical substitution, marginal rate of substitution (*MRS*), marginal rate of technical substitution ($MRTS_{KL}$), substitution effect.**
substitution effect is the change in the quantity of good X demanded that occurs when the price of good X changes and the consumer is compensated to keep utility constant **(4)**.
sunk cost is a fixed cost that cannot be recovered, even in the long run **(10)**.
supply see **price elasticity of supply, supply curve, supply price.**
supply curve shows how quantity supplied varies with the price of a product, holding other factors constant **(2)**.
supply price—sometimes called the *supply reservation price*—is the minimum price sellers are willing to accept for an extra unit of a good **(2)**.
surplus see **consumer surplus, producers' surplus.**

TC see **total costs (*TC*).**
theory is a set of careful assumptions offered to explain a certain phenomenon **(1)**.

time preference see **rate of time preference (*RTP*)**.

total costs (*TC*) are the sum of fixed and variable costs: $TC = VC + FC$ **(8)**; see also **average total costs (*ATC*)**.

trade see **feasible trade**.

transaction costs are the costs of operating markets—the costs of bringing together buyer and seller **(11)**.

transformation see **marginal rate of transformation (*MRT*)**.

uncertain prospect ($x, y; \pi$) is a situation in which x occurs with probability π and y occurs with probability $1 - \pi$ **(3)**.

unit isoquant shows the levels of capital and labor inputs required to produce one unit of a good **(16)**.

utility see **expected-utility hypothesis, grand utility-possibilities curve, marginal utility (*MU*), utility function**.

utility function is a numerical representation of the way an individual agent ranks different bundles of goods and services **(3)**.

utility-possibilities curve shows the Pareto-optimal allocations of utility corresponding to the Pareto-optimal allocations of a fixed endowment of goods **(16)**; see also **grand utility-possibilities curve**.

value see **expected value, present value, present-value rule, value of the firm's marginal product (*VMP*)**.

value of the firm's marginal product (*VMP*) is the price of the product multiplied by the marginal product of the factor input **(13)**.

variable see **average variable costs (*AVC*), flow variable, random variable, stock variable, variable costs (*VC*), variable inputs**.

variable costs (*VC*) are costs that do vary with the level of output **(8)**; see also **average variable costs (*AVC*)**.

variable inputs are factors that can be varied in the short run **(7)**.

variance is a measure of the dispersion of a random variable **(5A)**.

VC see **variable costs (*VC*)**.

VMP see **value of the firm's marginal product (*VMP*)**.

voter see **median voter**.

Walrasian equilibrium see **competitive equilibrium**.

Walras's law states that the sum of the values of all excess demands must be zero **(16)**.

X-inefficiency is the organizational slack that results from the absence of competitive pressures **(10)**.

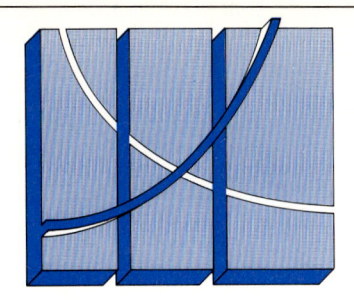

NAME INDEX

Alchian, Armen A., 59n
Allen, R. G. D., 87
Arrow, Kenneth, 66, 436n

Bain, Joe S., 285, 330, 354, 355n
Baltagi, Badi A., 139n
Barro, Robert, 433n
Baumol, William J., 263n, 354, 355
Becker, Gary, 36
Benston, George J., 284
Bernoulli, Daniel, 56, 57
Bernoulli, Nicholas, 56
Bohm-Bawerk, Eugen von, 416n
Boulding, K. E., 133n
Braithwait, Steven, 99
Brandow, George E., 134n, 135n, 136n
Brinner, R. E., 66n
Brown, Charles, 162n
Browne, Lynn E., 454n
Browning, Edgar, 79n
Browning, Jacqueline, 79n
Buiter, Willem, 433n

Cassady, Ralph Jr., 231n
Chamberlain, Edward, 335
Clark, John Bates, 392
Clarke, Edward, 480
Clarkson, Kenneth, 79n
Clotfeler, C. T., 66n
Coase, Ronald, 165, 466
Cobb, Charles W., 173
Commons, John R., 11n
Cooley, Thomas F., 258n
Cournot, Augustin A., 344, 345
Cox, Charles, 310

Deaton, Angus, 86
Debreu, Gerald, 51n, 436n
DeCanio, Stephen J., 258n
Demsetz, Harold, 332
Dillon, John L., 167n, 179
DiLorenzo, Thomas J., 283n
Diocletian, 29
Douglas, Paul H., 173
Durant, Will, 30

Edgeworth, Francis, 145, 156
Eisner, Robert, 66
Engel, Ernst, 81, 133
Euler, Leonhard, 390
Evans, David S., 165, 165n, 263n

Fellner, William, 55, 348n
Fisher, Franklin M., 281n, 284
Fisher, Irving, 416
Freeman, Richard, 407
Friedman, James W., 350n
Friedman, Milton, 5, 64, 244n, 253n, 296n
Friedman, Rose, 296n

Galbraith, John Kenneth, 36, 340
Gale, David, 227n
Gaskins, D. W., Jr., 355n
Gelhorn, Walter, 244n
Giffen, Sir Robert, 89, 90, 91
Gilroy, Curtis, 162n
Ginsberg, Ralph, 66n
Greene, Karen, 245n
Greenwood, Joen E., 284
Grether, David, 63n
Grossman, Sanford J., 165, 165n

Groves, Theodore, 480

Hahn, Frank, 436n
Harberger, Arnold C., 282n
Hayek, F. A., 294, 295
Heady, Earl O., 167n, 179
Henderson, James M., 153n
Herfindahl, Orris, 332
Herskovits, Melville J., 150n
Hicks, Sir John R., 87, 283, 366, 367n
Houthakker, H. S. L., 135n
Houthakker, Hendrik, 131

Irwin, Richard D., 214n

Jevons, William S., 44, 45n
Johnson, Lyndon B., 30
Johnson, Ronald N., 160, 160n

Kagel, John, 94
Kamerschen, David R., 282
Katz, David A., 133n
Kelejian, Harry, 139n
Knoeber, Charles R., 320n
Koohen, Andrew, 162n
Koopmans, Tjalling, 148n
Krueger, Anne, 280, 280n
Kuenne, Robert E., 153n
Kunreuther, Howard, 66

Lancaster, Kelvin, 36, 40n
Landon, J. H., 409
Laspeyres, Etienne, 98n
Leibenstein, Harvey, 278, 283
Leontief, Wassily, 185

515

NAME INDEX

Lerner, Abba, 283
Libecap, Gard D., 160
Lichtenstein, Sarah, 63n
Link, C. R., 409
Lustgarten, Steven H., 353

Maloney, M. T., 475
Marshall, Alfred, 44, 61, 101, 104, 366
McGowan, John J., 284
Medoff, James, 407
Miller, Edward M., 275n
Miller, Louis, 66n
Moore, Frederick T., 177n
Morgenstern, Oskar, 58, 357, 360
Muellbauer, John, 86
Muth, John, 258n

Nash, John, 358
Nelson, Randy, 290
Neumann, John von, 58, 357, 360
Newman, Peter, 156n
Nixon, Richard M., 29

Oates, Wallace, 139n

Paasche, Hermann, 98n
Panzer, John, 263n, 354, 355
Pareto, Vilfredo, 149
Parsons, Donald O., 319n
Philips, Louis, 108n, 130n, 135n
Plott, Charles, 63n
Posner, Richard A., 281n, 282n
Powell, A. Alan, 130n
Primeaux, Walter, 283, 290

Quandt, Richard E., 153n

Rees, Albert, 407
Ricardo, David, 157, 161, 433n
Robinson, Joan, 335, 404
Rothschilds, Michael, 324
Ruffin, Roy J., 350n
Rydenfelt, S., 253n
Salop, Steven, 297n
Samuelson, Paul, 477
Samuelson, Paul A., 96, 97, 120
Savage, Leonard, 64
Savage, Leonard J., 55n
Scherer, F. M., 330n, 355
Scherer, Frederick M., 282, 330n, 355
Schultze, Charles, 30
Scitovsky, Tibor, 297n, 302
Scully, G. W., 409n
Seneca, Joseph J., 469n
Shakespeare, William, 161
Shepherd, William G., 207n, 357n
Shmenner, Roger W., 165n
Siegried, John, 282
Silk, Leonard, 320n
Slovic, Paul, 63n
Slutsky, E. E., 87, 90n
Smith, Adam, 165, 340, 445, 447, 465
Smith, Richard Austin, 344n
Smith, Vernon L., 231n
Stackelberg, Heinrich von, 348n
Stigler, George J., 36, 91, 133n, 253n, 263n, 283, 294, 302, 335, 352n

Stiglitz, Joseph, 297n, 324
Strassmann, Diana, 357n
Strotz, Robert, 66
Sweezy, Paul, 351n, 352n
Sylos-Labini, Paolo, 355n

Taussig, Michael K., 469n
Taylor, Lester D., 131, 135n
Tideman, Nicholas, 481
Tiemann, Thomas, 282
Tietenberg, Tom, 473n, 475n
Tobin, James, 433n
Tregarthen, Timothy, 162n
Tullock, Gordon, 280, 481

Veblen, Thorstein, 36
Vernon, Raymond, 335
Vickery, William, 480
Viner, Jacob, 214n

Walras, Leon, 44, 435
Waugh, Frederick V., 142n
Weinstein, Arnold A., 39n
Weiserbs, D., 130n, 135n
Weston, J. Fred, 353
Wicksteed, Phillip, 390
Wiley, John, 66n
Willig, Robert, 263n, 354, 355
Wold, Herman, 115
Worcester, Dean A., 282
Working, E. J., 133n
Working, Holdbrook, 309n

Yandle, B., 475n

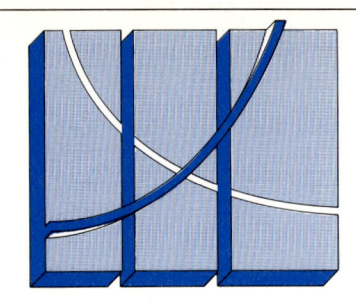

SUBJECT INDEX

Absence of entry, 252–53
Accounting costs, 191
　differences between opportunity costs and, 191
Accounting profit, 192
Adding-up rule, 81
Adverse selection, 310–11, 318–26
Agent, definition of, 311
American Cyanamid, 342
Arab oil embargo, 30
Arbitrage, 303
Arc elasticity, 109–11
Assumptions, 5
Auction market, 231
Autarky, 155
Average fixed costs, 208
Average/marginal rule, 126–28
Average product, 166
Average revenue product, 370
Average total costs, 209
Average variable costs, 208, 209

Barriers to entry, 248–49, 261–62
Baseball contracts, use of reserve clauses in, 409
Benefit theory of taxation, 475–79
Boeing, 340
Bristol-Meyers, 342
Bubble approach, 475
Budget constraints, 417–20
　effect of, on consumer demand, 70–73
Budget line, 73
Budget set, 72

Capital
　definition of, 415
　relative factor shares of, 375–76
　substitutability of, 187
Capitalism, 11
Capital/labor ratio, 373
Capital market, 431
Capital theory, 415
Capital-to-labor ratio, 185
Cardinal utility, 45
Cartel
　definition of, 341
　legality of, 344
　stability of, 343, 359
Cartel theory, 340–44
Cash market, 307
Centralized markets, 297
Certainty, consumer behavior in the case of, 37–53
Certainty equivalents, axiom of, 58–59
Ceteris-paribus conditions, 16, 17, 134
Change in demand, 84
Change in quantity demanded, 84
Chicago Board of Trade, 10
Circular flow, 14–15
Coase theorem, 466–67
Cobb-Douglas production function, 173, 187
　long-run cost function for, 201*n*
Commodity exchange, 10
Commodity Futures Trading Corporation, 310

Common-property resource
　allocation of, 470–73
　definition of, 470
Comparative advantage
　irrelevance of, 161–62
　law of, 157–62
　Ricardian model of, 158–61
Comparative statistics
　definition of, 18
　use of, in economics, 17
Comparison, axiom of, 38
Compensated-demand curve, 91–92
Competitive equilibrium, 151–57, 436
　definition of, 152
　illustration of, in an Edgeworth box, 153
Competitive labor market, impact of minimum-wage laws on, 405–406
Competitive resource markets, 365
　and characteristics of input supply, 379–88
　and industry demand for an input, 378–79
　laws of derived demand, 366–67
　and marginal-productivity theory of distribution, 389–92
　one-input case, 369–73
　and profit maximization on the input side, 367–69
　two-input case, 373–78
Competitive stability, 156–57

517

SUBJECT INDEX

Complements
  definition of, 106
  examples of, 107
Concentration
  increases in, 333–35
  measuring industrial, 330–35
Concentration ratio
  limits of, 330, 332
  selected, in manufacturing, 331
Conflict curve, 148–49
  definition of, 148
Constant-cost industry, 239
  definition of, 238
  freedom of entry for, 249
  and price elasticity, 243
Constant elasticity, versus constant slope, 113
Constant returns to scale, 168–69, 172–74, 212–13
  definition of, 168
Constant-returns-to-scale production, 448–49
Constant slope, versus constant elasticity, 113
Consumer behavior
  in the case of certainty, 37–44
  in the case of uncertainty, 53–61
  rationality of, 35–36
  theory of, 46
Consumer demand theory, 70–102
  applications of, 93–100
Consumer equilibrium, 73–77
  under budget constraint, 72
Consumer preferences
  effect of, on demand, 107–108
  and modern utility theory, 37–38
  and revealed-preference theory, 38
Consumer surplus, 101–102
Consumer tastes, stability of, 36
Consumption possibilities, 72
Consumption stream, 418
Consumption/work choice, 380–83
Contestable-market model, 354, 355–57
Contract curve, 443
Contrived scarcity, 278–79
Convexity, 171
  axiom of, 42–44
Cooperative oligopoly, 340–44
Core, 155
Corporations, 164
Cost/benefit analysis, 4
Costs
  maximizing output from a given outlay, 197
  minimizing, of a given output, 195–96
Cournot equilibrium, 348
Cournot oligopoly, 344–48
Covariance, 140

Cross-price elasticities, 135
  for coal and oil, 116
Cross-price elasticity of demand, 114–15
Customer utility, maximizing, 381–82

Data problems, 131
Deadweight loss, 281
Decentralized markets, 297
Decreasing-cost industry, freedom of entry for, 250–52
Deficits, effect of, on real interest rates, 432–33
Demand. *See also* Supply
  algebra of, 21–23
  conditions of, 16–17
  cross-price elasticity of, 114–15
  effect of consumer preferences on, 107–108
  equilibrium of, 15–17
  income as determinant of, 108
  income elasticity of, 80–81, 114
  for labor, 383–84
  laws of, 15–23, 85, 86–87, 94
  long-run, for labor, 376–78
  market elasticities of, 115–17
  price as determinant of, 106
  price elasticity of, 92–93, 108–13
Demand curve
  definition of, 16, 84
  downward slope of, 16
Demand price, 26
Demand reservation price, 26
Demand-revealing mechanisms, 480–82
Demand schedule, definition of, 84
Depreciation, definition of, 415
Derived demand
  laws of, 366–67, 395–96
  theory of, 365
Differential rents, 254–55
Diminishing marginal rate of substitution, law of, 44
Diminishing marginal rate of technical substitution (*MRTS*), law of, 171
Diminishing returns, law of, 5, 167
Disability insurance, case of, 311–18, 321–22
Disability payments, effect of, on labor-force participation, 319
Diseconomies of scale, 175
Dissaving, 424
Distribution, marginal-productivity theory of, 389–92
Duopoly, 346
Durable goods, 37

Econometrics, 131
Economic efficiency, 166

Economic profit, 192, 285
Economic region of production, 182–83
Economic rent, 254
Economics
  definition of, 2
  estimation problems in, 131–33
  problem of scarcity in, 1
Economic system
  definition of, 1
  property rights in, 11
Economic theory, 4–5
Economies of scale, 174–75, 262–63
  definition of, 174, 262
Economy, supply of goods in, 9–11
Edgeworth box, 145–46, 439–41
  illustration of competitive equilibrium in, 153
Edict of Diocletian, 30
Effluent charges, 469, 473–74
Elasticities, aggregation of, 115–17
Elasticity estimates, 133–35
Elasticity of substitution, 184–87, 373–75
  definition of, 187
  and long-run demand for labor, 376–78
  and relative factor shares, 375–76
Empirical demand analysis
  and elasticity estimates, 133–36
  estimation problems, 131–33
  regression analysis, 128–29, 131
Engel curves, 81
Engel's law, 134
Engineering efficiency, 166
Engineering estimates, 207
Environmental Protection Agency (EPA), 473
Equalization-of-profit rates, 335
Equilibria, types of, 322
Equilibrium price, 295
  definition of, 17
  solving for, 21–23
  stability of, 23, 24
Equilibrium-price stability, 23–24
Equilibrium quantity, solving for, 21–23
Euler's equation, 172, 182*n*
Euler's theorem, 390
Excess-demand curve, 23
Exchange, theory of, 144–45
  Edgeworth box, 145–46
  voluntary exchange, 146–47
Exchange economy, feasible state of, 146
Exchange equilibrium, 148
Excise taxes, effects of, on goods and services, 25–26

SUBJECT INDEX

Expansion path
  effect of changes in factor prices on, 215–16
  role of, 217–18
Expected utility, 57
Expected-utility hypothesis, 61–65
  definition of, 64
  in the real world, 66
Expected values, 55–56
Explicit costs, 191
Externalities, 463–65
  and allocation of common-property resources, 470–73
  definition of, 463
  and government regulation of pollution, 473–75
  internalizing, 466–69
  and public choice, 475–82
  and welfare economics, 445

Factor prices, 452, 455
  changes in, and optimal output level, 218–19
  effect of changes in, on expansion path, 215–16
Feasible trade, 147
Fixed costs, 205, 236
Fixed inputs, 167
Flight insurance, purchase of, 66
Flood insurance, purchase of, 66
Flow variable
  definition of, 11
  supply and demand as, 15
Food-stamps program, 79
Ford Motors, 340
Freedom of entry, 245, 247–48
  for the constant-cost industry, 249n
  for the decreasing-cost industry, 250–52
  for the increasing-cost industry, 249–50
Free goods, 2, 9
Free rider, 469
Free trade, case for, 256–58
Fundamental duality theorem, 227
Futures contract, 10
Futures market, 295, 306–308
  definition of, 307
Futures trading, effects of, 309–10

Game strategy, 358
Game theory, 357–61
  Nash equilibrium, 358–59
  nonzero-sum game, 361
  zero-sum game, 357, 359–61
General equilibrium
  definition of, 435
  nature of, 435–37
  and the pure-exchange model, 437–47

and the two-sector production model, 448–61
General-equilibrium economics, 15, 144
General Motors, 340
Giffen good
  definition of, 89–91
  and the law of demand, 106
Golden parachutes, 320
Government franchises, 264–65, 280–81
Government regulation, of pollution, 473–75
Government subsidies, as method of internalizing externalities, 467–69
Grand utility-possibilities curve, 459–61

Halfway rule, 125, 126
Hedging, 308–309
Herfindahl index, 330, 332–33
  as determinant of price/cost margin, 357n
Homothetic production functions, 175–76
Hostile takeovers, 320

IBM, 340
Identification problems, 131–33
Immigration, of labor, 391
Imperfectly competitive resource markets, 397
  minimum-wage laws and unions, 404–409
  monopoly on the product side of the market, 397–401
  monopsony in the resource market, 401–404
  screening, 410–12
Implicit costs, 191
Income
  as determinant of demand, 108
  determination of, 70
Income changes
  and the absence of money illusion, 82–83
  and Engel curves, 81
  and the income/consumption curve, 78, 80
  and income elasticity, 80–81
  for inferior and normal goods, 77–78
  inferior goods and the income/consumption curve, 81–82
Income/consumption curve, 78, 80
  definition of, 80
  inferior goods and, 81–82
Income determination of, 70
Income effect, 87, 89
  for Giffen goods, 90

Income effects, measurement of, 130
Income elasticity of demand, 80–81, 114
Income-possibilities curve, 428
Income stream, 418
Increasing-cost industry, 241–42
  definition of, 238
  freedom of entry for, 249–50
  and price elasticity, 243–44
Increasing returns to scale, 174–75
Independence, axiom of, 59
Independent goods, definition of, 106
Indifference curve
  definition of, 41
  properties of, 51–53
  when commodities are "bads," 48–50
Industry, 329
  demand of, for input, 378–79
  measuring concentration in, 330–35
Inefficiency, sources of, 278–81, 283
Inferior goods
  definition of, 78
  and the income/consumption curve, 81–82
Information, as scarce commodity, 2
Information costs, 294–96
  and adverse selection, 318–26
  definition of, 295
  and the economics of search, 296–302
  importance of, 290–91
  and moral hazards, 310–18
  and speculation, 303–10
Input, industry demand for an, 378–79
Input markets, differences between output markets and, 365
Inputs, optimal combination of, 195–97
Input supply, characteristics of, 379–89
Interest discounting, 13
Interest rates
  long-term, 430
  nominal, 416
  real, 416–17, 432–33
  short-term, 430
Internal rate of return, 285
Intertemporal consumption and savings, 417
  budget constraint in, 417–20
  optimal consumption plans, 421–23
  wealth and substitution effects,

423-26
Intertemporal production and investment, 426
  investment and the rate of return, 427-29, 431
  present-value rule, 426-27
Investment, and the rate of return, 427-29, 431
Invisible hand, 445, 447, 465
Irrelevance of the probability mechanism, axiom of, 59-61
Isocost curves, 192-94
Isocost line, 193
Isoquant map, 170

Joint demand, 26, 27-28
Joint profit maximization, 342-43
Joint supply, 28-29
Justice Department, U.S., use of Herfindahl index, 332-33

Kinked-demand-curve model, 351-53

Labor
  demand for, 383-84
  effect of minimum-wage laws on, 31
  immigration of, 391
  long-run demand for, 376-78
  relative factor shares of, 375-76
  substitutability of, 187
  wage elasticity of demand for, 377
Labor-force participation, effect of disability payments on, 319
Labor-market equilibrium wage rate, 386-87
Labor services, supply of, 380-87
Labor-supply curve, shape of, 384-86
Lagrangian function, 76n
Land resources, supply of, 387-89
Laspeyres price index, 98, 99, 100
Least-cost rule, definition of, 197
Least-squares property, 141
Lemons, detecting, 321
Leontief production function, 184-85
Lerner index, 283, 285
Lexicographic preferences, 50-51
Lexicography, 50
Limit pricing, 354-55
Linear programming, 222-27
Linear regression, 140-41
  definition of, 139
Long run, 167
  definition of, 204
  monopoly pricing and output in, 275-76
  pricing in the, 244, 246-55

profit maximization in the, 269-70, 275
Long-run average cost, 201-202
Long-run competitive equilibrium, 244, 246
Long-run cost curves, 198-99
  and minimum efficient scale, 207
Long-run cost function, 199-200
Long-run equilibrium, under monopolistic competition, 337
Long-run marginal cost, 202-203
Long-term interest rates, 430
Lottery tickets, purchase of, 66
Lump-sum subsidy, 94
  effect on utility of, 95-96
Luxuries, definition of, 81

Majority rule, 479-80
Manufacturing, decline of, 454
Marginal benefits, 4
  of search, 298-99
Marginal costs, 4, 209, 368
Marginal factor cost (MFC), 401
Marginal product, 166-67
  value of, 368
Marginal-productivity theory of distribution, 389-92
Marginal product (MP), 368
Marginal rate of substitution, 40
  link between marginal utility and, 47-48
Marginal rate of technical substitution ($MRTS$), 170-71, 185, 187
Marginal rate of transformation, 452
Marginal revenue
  definition of, 121
  link between price elasticity and, 121-26
  relationship between price and, 265-67
  relationship between price elasticity of demand and, 267-69
Marginal revenue (MR), 368
Marginal revenue product, 368
Marginal social benefits, 465
Marginal social costs, 465
Marginal utility, 45
  link between marginal rate of substitution and, 47-48
Market, definition of, 10-11
Market coordination, 164
Market demand, 101
  definition of, 101
  function of, 106-108
Market-demand curve, 101
Market economy, resource allocation in, 1
Market equilibrium, 401, 431
Market period

definition of, 229
pricing in the, 229-30
Market price dispersion, 301-302
Maximin principle of rational behavior, 360
McDonnell-Douglas, 340
Median voter, 479
Merger
  and Cournot oligopoly, 350-51
  effect of, on concentration, 332-33
Microeconomics, definition of, 1
Microeconomic theory, nature of, 4-6
Midpoints formula, 110-11
Minimax principle of rational behavior, 360
Minimum efficient scale, 202
  and long-run cost curves, 207
Minimum-wage laws, 31, 404-405
  impact of, on competitive labor market, 405-406
  and the law of comparative advantage, 162
  in a monopsony, 406-407
  and unions, 408-409
Modern utility theory
  and consumer behavior in the case of certainty, 37-44
  and consumer behavior in the case of uncertainty, 53-61
  and consumer preferences, 37-38
  and the expected-utility hypothesis, 61-62, 64-65
  and the rational consumer, 35-36
  and the utility function, 44-53
Monetary economics, supply and demand in, 15
Money illusion
  absence of, 82-83
  definition of, 82
  in statistical studies, 86
Monopolistic competition, 329, 335-37
  definition of, 335
  long-run equilibrium under, 337
  in the short run, 336-37
  welfare aspects of, 337, 339-40
Monopoly
  comparison of perfect competition and, 278-85
  correlation of profits with power, 332
  definition of, 261, 397
  demand curve in, 265
  and entry barriers, 261-65
  importance of, 282
  inefficiency of, 279
  pricing and output in the long

run, 275–76
pricing and output in the short run, 269–75
on the product side of the market, 397–401
profit maximization for, 398–99
relationship between marginal revenue and elasticity in, 267–69
relationship between price and marginal revenue in, 265–67
social costs of, 399–401
Monopoly equilibrium, characteristics of, 276–78
Monopoly power, measurement of, 283, 285
Monopoly profits, studies of, 284
Monopoly-rent-seeking behavior, 280
Monopsonistic equilibrium, 402–403, 404
Monopsony, in the resource market, 401–404
Moral-hazard problem, 310–18
strategies for, 318
Multinational corporations, and competition, 334–35
Multiplant monopolies, 275–76
Multiple-pricing schemes
conditions for price discrimination, 285–87
importance of information costs, 290–91
and perfect price discrimination, 287–88
reasons for price discrimination, 287
two-part pricing, 289–90
Multivariate regression, 128, 129

Nash equilibrium, 358–59
Natural monopoly, 262–63
Necessities, definition of, 81
n-firm concentration ratio, 330
N-firm Cournot oligopoly, 348–50
Nominal interest rates, 416
Nondurable goods, 37
Nonsatiation, axiom of, 39
Nonzero-sum game, 361
Normal goods, definition of, 72–77
Normative economics, 4

Offer curve, 152, 441
Oligopoly, 329
characteristics of industry, 340
cooperative, 340–44
definition of, 340
and game theory, 357–61
kinked-demand-curve model, 351–53

noncooperative, 344–51
persistence of profits in, 338
potential entrants, 354–57
Oligopsony, 401
OPEC (Organization of Petroleum Exporting Countries), 341, 343
Opportunity costs, 189–90
definition of, 3, 190
differences between accounting costs and, 191
Optimal consumption plans, 421–23
Optimal-search rule, 298–302
Ordinal utility, 44–45
Output
changes in factor prices and optimal levels of, 218–19
maximizing, from given cost outlay, 197
minimizing costs of given, 195–96
Output expansion path, 197–98
Output markets, differences between input markets and, 365
Overtime pay, 386
Ownership of goods or commodities, 9–10
Own-price elasticity of demand, 109n
Ozone layer, depletion of, 473

Paasche price index, 98, 99, 100
Pareto-optimal allocations, 155–56
Pareto optimality, 441–45, 457–59
definition of, 149
determining, in economy with public goods, 476–77
in production, 451
Partial-equilibrium economics, 15, 144
Patents, 263–64
Pecuniary externalities, 463
Perfect competition
achievement of, 335–36
and the case for free trade, 256–58
comparison of monopoly and, 278–85
definition of, 228
freedom-of-entry assumption for, 245, 247–48
meaning of, 228–29
minimum wages under, 405
and pricing in the long run, 244–55
and pricing in the market period, 229–30
and pricing in the short run, 230–36, 238–39, 240–44
Perfect price discrimination,

287–88
Per-unit subsidy, 94
Pfizer, 342
Point elasticity, 111–12
Pollution, government regulation of, 473–75
Pooling equilibrium, 322, 323–25
Positive economics, definition of, 4
Potential-entry models, 354
contestable markets, 355–57
limit pricing, 354–55
Preference reversal, explanation of, 63
Preferences, experimental studies of, 63
Present value, 12–14
Present-value formula, use of, with nominal dollars and interest rates, 418n
Present-value rule, 426–27
Price
as determinant of demand, 106
judging quality by, 46
pattern of, over time, 305–306
relationship between marginal revenue and, 265–67
Price ceiling, 29, 253
Price-ceiling analysis, 31
Price changes, 84
and compensated-demand curve, 91–92
and Giffen goods, 89–91
and the price/consumption curve, 84–85
and price elasticity of demand, 92–93
and substitution and income effects, 86–89
Price/consumption curve, 84–85, 385–86, 441
Price controls, 29–30, 253
Price discrimination
conditions for, 285–87
by electric utilities, 290
perfect, 287–88
reasons for, 287
Price elasticity, link between marginal revenue and, 121–26
Price elasticity of demand, 92–93, 108–13
compensated, 117–20
definition of, 108
relationship between marginal revenue and, 267–69
and total revenue, 120–28
Price elasticity of supply, 242–44
Price floor, 29
effects of, 31
Price indexes, 97–100
Price maker, definition of, 261

SUBJECT INDEX

Price setting, 342
Price taker, 71, 151
  consumer as, 71
  definition of, 16, 228
Price theory, 1
  supply and demand in, 15
Pricing
  in the long run, 244, 246–55
  in the market period, 229–30
  in the short run, 230–44
Principal, definition of, 311
Principal/agent problem, 311
Prisoners' dilemma game, 358–59
Probabilities
  conflicting views about nature of, 54–55
  definition of, 53–54
Producers' surplus, 256–58
Product information, and adverse selection, 325–26
Production
  determining least-cost method of, 223–27
  economic region of, 182–83
  organization of, in business firms, 164–65
  stages of, 181–82
Production costs
  and changes in factor prices, 215–19
  in the long run, 192–203
  and long-run and short-run cost curves, 211–15
  and opportunity costs, 190–92
  in the short run, 204–11
Production function, 166
  definition of, 166
  homothetic, 175–76
  and law of diminishing returns, 167
  in the long run, 167, 168–76
  marginal and average products, 166–67
  in the short run, 167, 176–83
  short-run costs and, 204–205
Production isoquants, 169–70
Production model, two-sector, 435, 448–61
Production-possibilities frontier, 450–52
  definition of, 2
  guns versus butter example of, 3
Production-possibilities frontier (*PPF*), 454
Profit, 231–32
Profitable speculation, 303–304
Profit maximization, 233–35
  for a monopoly, 398–99
  joint, 342–43
  in the long run, 275
  and long-run demand for labor, 376

and price discrimination, 286
second-order condition for, 270–72
in the short run, 267–68
on the input side, 367–69
Property rights
  in an economic system, 11
  creation of, 10–11
  redefining, 470–72
Public choice, 475–82
Public goods, 464–65
Pure exchange, theory of, 450
Pure-exchange economy, 144–45
Pure-exchange model, 435, 437–38
  Edgeworth box, 439–41
  Pareto optimality, 441–45
  and welfare economics, 445–47
Pure monopoly, 261

Quality, judging by price, 46
Quasi rent, 254, 255

Random variable, definition of, 54
Rate of time preference (*RTP*), 422
Rational economic agents, 4
Rationality, assumption of, 4
Reaction curve, 346–48
Real interest rates, 416–17
  effect of deficits in, 432–33
Regression analysis, 128–29, 131
Rent controls, 253
Rents, 254–55
Reservation price
  calculation of, 298
  definition of, 298
Reserve clause, 409
Resource allocation, in a market economy, 1
Resource market, monopsony in the, 401–404
Return rate, and investments, 427–29, 431
Returns to scale, 172
  constant, 172–74, 212–13
  decreasing, 213–15
  increasing, 174–75, 213–15
Revealed preferences, 96–97
Revealed-preference theory, and consumer preferences, 38
Revenue, total, and price elasticity of demand, 120–28
Ricardian differential-rent theory, 254–55
Ricardian model of comparative advantage, 158–61
Risk-averse behavior, 58
Risk aversion, 62
Risk groups, separating, 322–23

Saddle point, 360–61
St. Petersburg paradox, 56–58

Scarce goods, 2, 9
Scarcity
  contrived, 278–79
  law of, 2–3
  as mismatch between consumer wants and resources, 35
  problem of, in economics, 1
Screening, 410
  devices in, 411–12
  no-signaling case, 410–11
Second-order condition, for profit maximization, 270–72
Separating equilibrium, 322
Service flows, 37
Shepherd's lemma, 216–17, 366
Sherman Act, 344
Short run, 167
  definition of, 204, 230
  monopolistic competition in, 336–37
  monopoly pricing and output in, 269–75
  pricing in the, 230–36, 238–39, 240–44
  profit maximization in the, 267–68, 275
Short-run cost curves, economics behind, 209–11
Short-run costs, and the production function, 204–205
Short-run market equilibrium, 238
Short-term interest rates, 430
Shutdown rule, 236
Signals, 410, 411
Simplex method, 222
Socialist economies
  application of price theory to, 1
  disadvantages of, 11
Speculation, 303
  and the futures market, 306–10
  pattern of prices over time, 305–306
  profitable, 303–304
  unprofitable, 304–305
Spot market, 307
Statistical cost studies, 207
Statistics, 139
  basic concepts in, 139–40
  definition of, 17
  and least-square property, 141
  and linear regression, 140–41
Stock variable, 11
Stolper-Samuelson theorem, 455–57
Subsidies, costs of, 94–96
Substitutes
  definition of, 106
  examples of, 107
Substitution
  axiom of, 40–42
  elasticity of, 184–87, 373–75
Substitution effect, 86–87, 88–89

for Giffen goods, 90
  measurement of, 130
  wealth and, 423–26
Summation notation, 141
Sum of the squared deviations/ errors (*SSE*), 141
Sunk costs, 265
Supply
  algebra of, 21–23
  conditions of, 17
  equilibrium of, 15–17
  of labor services, 380–87
  of land resources, 387–89
  laws of, 15–23
  price elasticity of, 242–44
Supply curve
  definition of, 17
  of firm, 235–38
Supply price, 26

Taxes
  benefit theory of, 475–79
  as method of internalizing externalities, 467–69
Theory
  definition of, 5
  determination of good, 6
Total cost, 205, 207
Total-product curve, 178–81
Transaction costs, 296–97

Transitivity, axiom of, 39–40, 58
Two-part pricing, 289–90
Two-sector production model, 435, 448–61

Uncertain prospect, definition of, 58
Uncertainty, consumer behavior in the case of, 53–61
Unions, and minimum-wage laws, 408–409
Unit isoquant, 449
Unprofitable speculation, 304–305
Unskilled labor, effect of minimum-wage laws on, 31
Usury laws, 415
Utility function
  definition of, 44
  indifferences curves for "bads," 48–50
  lexicographic rankings, 50–51
  link between marginal utility and marginal rate of substitution, 47–48
  ordinal utility versus cardinal utility, 44–47
  properties of indifference curves, 51–52
  usefulness of, as concept, 47
Utility maximization, principle of, 106
Utility-possibilities curve, 443, 444

Variable costs, 205, 236
Variable inputs, definition of, 167
Variance, definition of, 139
Voluntary agreements, 466–67
Voluntary exchange, 146–47
Voting mechanisms, 479
  and demand-revealing mechanisms, 480–82
  and majority rule, 479–80

Wage elasticity of demand for labor, 377
Wage rate, labor-market equilibrium, 386–87
Wage/rent ratio, 373
Wages, and overtime pay, 386
Walrasian equilibrium, 436
Walras's law, 437–38
Wealth, and substitution effects, 423–26
Welfare aspects, of monopolistic competition, 337, 339–40
Welfare economics, basic theorems of, 445–47

Xerox, 340
X-inefficiency, 283